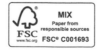

For Gus.

First published in 2019 by Nobrow Ltd.
27 Westgate Street, London E8 3RL.

1 3 5 7 9 10 8 6 4 2

Published in the US by Nobrow (US) Inc.
Printed in Poland on FSC® certified paper.

MIX
Paper from responsible sources
FSC® C001693

ISBN: 978-1-910620-61-8

www.nobrow.net

LUKE HEALY

AMERICANA

(AND THE ACT OF GETTING OVER IT.)

NOBROW

LONDON | NEW YORK

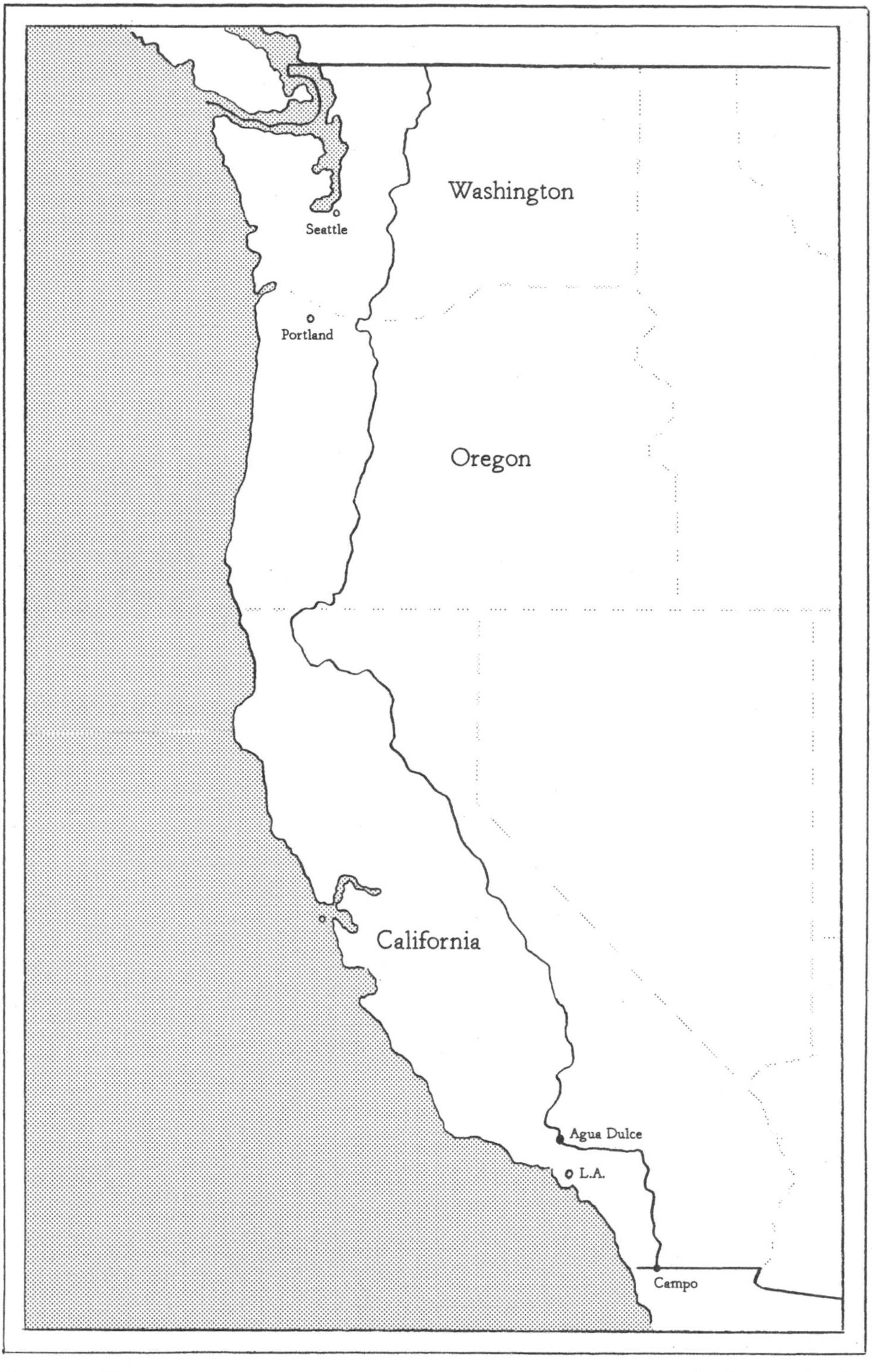
Washington
Seattle
Portland
Oregon
California
Agua Dulce
L.A.
Campo

Chapter 1: The Desert (Part I)

"Laughter is America's most important export."
—Walt Disney

I was born in Ireland, in 1991. On the day I was born, the IRA fired a mortar at the British Prime Minister's residence. This was a coincidence. An ersatz civil war was raging in the North, the economy was a disaster, there was massive unemployment, and mass emigration. To put it plainly, Ireland was a mess.

But over the course of the 1990s, Ireland transformed from one of the most conservative, poverty-stricken countries in Europe, to a country with a booming economy, and a highly educated, liberal workforce. This was, in part, the result of massive investment by American companies. They called it the "Celtic Tiger".

For the children of the '90s, this meant the mass importation of American pop culture. We wore T-shirts proudly emblazoned with Adidas and Nike logos. We watched Hollywood films at the cinema. We consumed incalculable hours of American TV. I never knew an Ireland that wasn't totally obsessed with America.

During my childhood, my family made four trips to the USA. This was unusually frequent for any Irish family, even in the newly booming economy. We were facilitated by a network of distant relatives

up and down the US East Coast, all strangers to us. Each time, calls
were made to see which of them had a free bed or stretch of floor and
a desire to show their Irish "cousins" a good time.

The first time we went to the United States was the first time
either of my parents had left Europe.

My earliest memory is of that first trip. A warm curb, on a
humid Florida evening. I was five years old. My hands rested on the
curb's edge as my head spun, following the joyous music and flashing
lights of the Disney World Fourth of July parade.

I cheered gleefully as the parade rolled past, bedecked in red,
white and blue, and threw my eyes upwards to catch the whops and
cracks of the fireworks display above. Even now, more than two decades
later, I can scarcely imagine a more iconically American experience.

From that moment, I was in love.

My other memories are scattered and scrappy. I vividly remember
sitting on a bus, listening to a woman say that her favourite food was
"Kentucky Fried Chicken".

It was Hollywood, for the most part, that told me what to think
of the USA. It was where all the greatest people in the world lived.
The funniest people, the bravest people, the smartest people. If you
wanted to be saved from terrible disaster, you'd better have some
Americans on your side.

My obsession with the USA did not fade as I aged. It only grew
more acute. As a teenager, when my parents let me move a tiny old
television into my bedroom, I would play DVDs of American comedies
on a loop as I went to sleep. And whether through conscious imitation,
or post-hypnotic suggestion, I started to speak with an American accent,

for which my brother teased me mercilessly.

My early twenties became a carousel of emigration and repatriation, as I tried again and again to live in the USA. I first moved there to attend college, though my residence was short lived. It was less than a year before I was asked to return to Ireland, at the mercy of an expiring visa. I returned to America again only six months later, but the pattern was set. Over and over, my American bliss was neatly traded for equivalent heartbreak when I was forced to vacate the country. The USA's stubbornness simply outclassed my own.

I sit in a car as it powers down a Southern California highway. The air inside is stuffy, even in the weak morning sunlight. I gaze out of the window, watching the dusty hills as another hiker listens to our driver, Susan.

"Well, my daughter hiked the trail a couple of years ago and ever since then my husband and I have been helping out however we can," Susan says to the hiker, a quiet German man who nods along placidly. "Her name's Rocket. Maybe you've heard of her. She wrote a blog."

I'm an uncomfortable combination of exhausted and exhilarated. I flew to Los Angeles from Dublin only four days ago, and the jet lag is still muddling my brain. I've moved unceasingly since I stepped off of the aeroplane, meeting friends in L.A. before catching a ride to San Diego only a few hours later, to get as close as possible to the Mexican border. My time in San Diego was a blur, filled with anxious last-minute preparations: buying food, mailing boxes, securing an American phone; I've barely had time to breathe, let alone attune to my new time zone.

"We should get to Campo in maybe another thirty minutes," Susan says from the front.

We are the third in a caravan of four cars, making our way to Campo, California, a small town on the USA's border with Mexico. This is where I will begin my attempt to walk the Pacific Crest Trail – a 2660-mile-long wilderness trail that winds its way through the American landscape from Mexico to Canada, border to border.

I watch the yellow sun climb in the pale California sky.

Susan pulls off the highway, and we snake our way along a series of smaller, paved roads. Outside, I see fewer and fewer buildings until the last we pass, a roadside taqueria, swings out of sight behind a corner and we are surrounded by nothing but undulating desert hills. The paved roads give way to dirt roads, and the car kicks up dust and sand as we navigate through corridors of yucca and chaparral.

I am excited and nervous. I have been planning this hike for two years. Dreaming of it.

Despite my better sense and ample experience in post-American heartbreak. Here I am. Again. The American allure built deep into my soul pulls me along for another ride.

Pacific Crest Trail.
Southern Terminus 16/04/16. Mile 0.

I've seen it a million times in pictures.

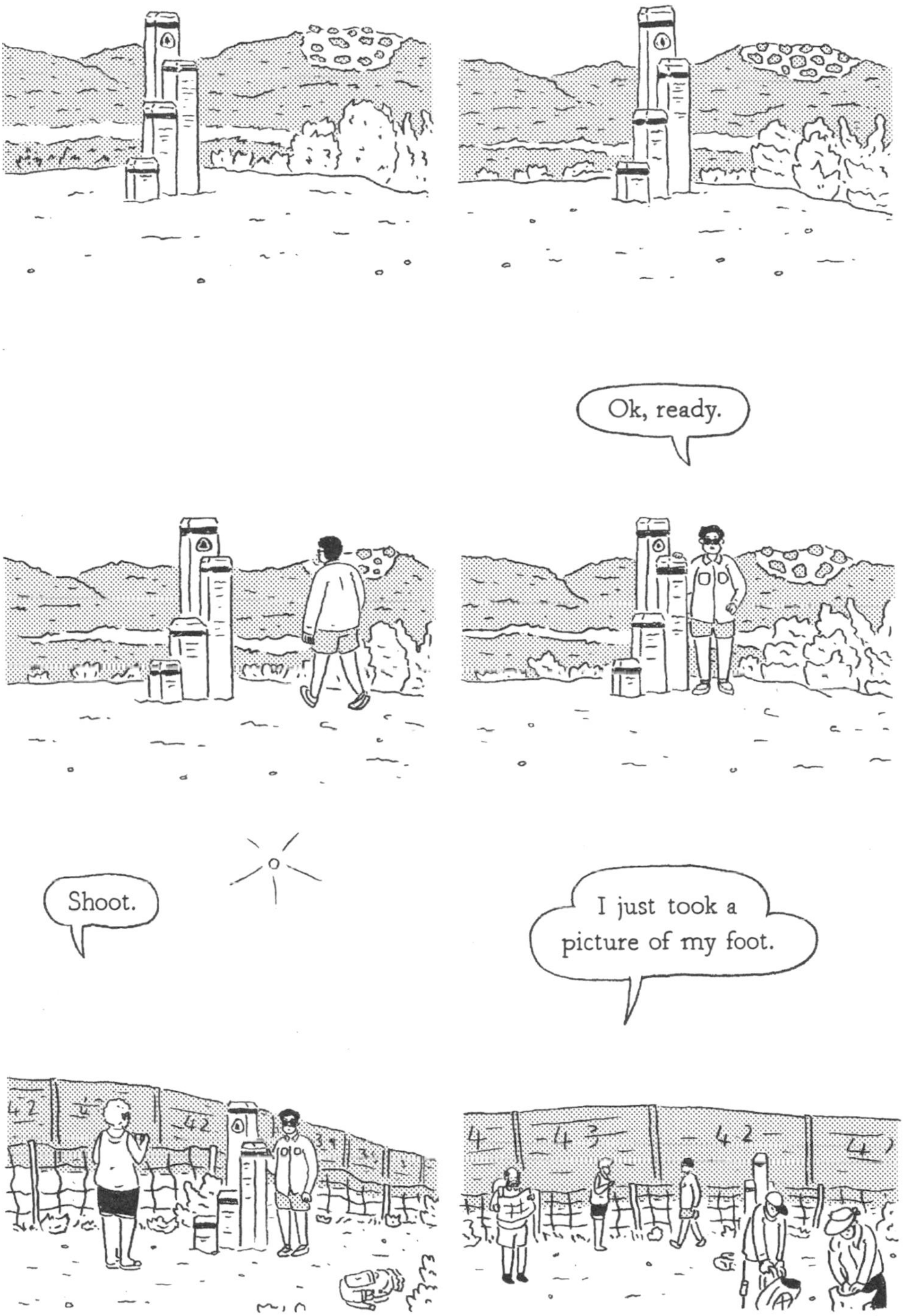
Ok, ready.
Shoot.
I just took a picture of my foot.

There are 2660 miles between here and Canada.

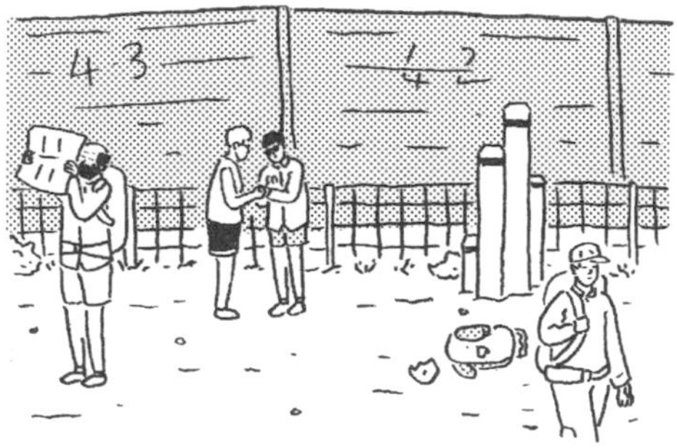

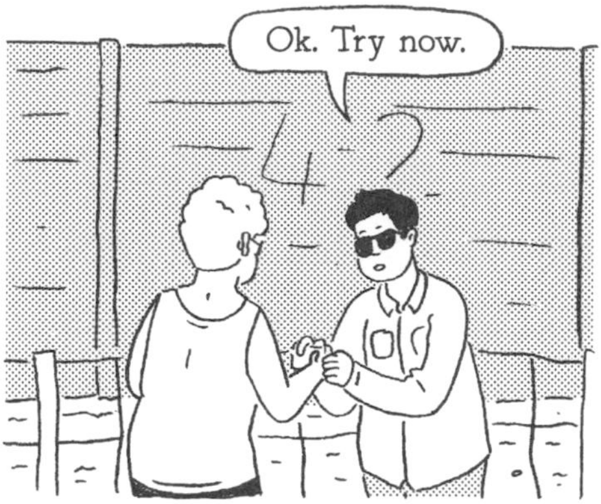
Ok. Try now.

Most of us won't make it.

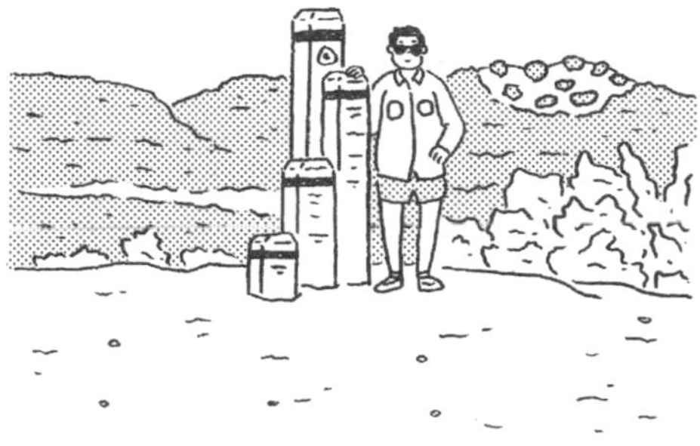

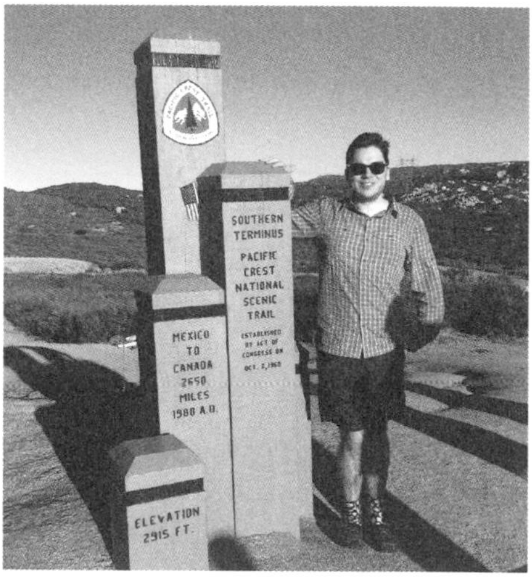
SOUTHERN TERMINUS
PACIFIC CREST NATIONAL SCENIC TRAIL
MEXICO TO CANADA 2650 MILES
ELEVATION 2915 FT.

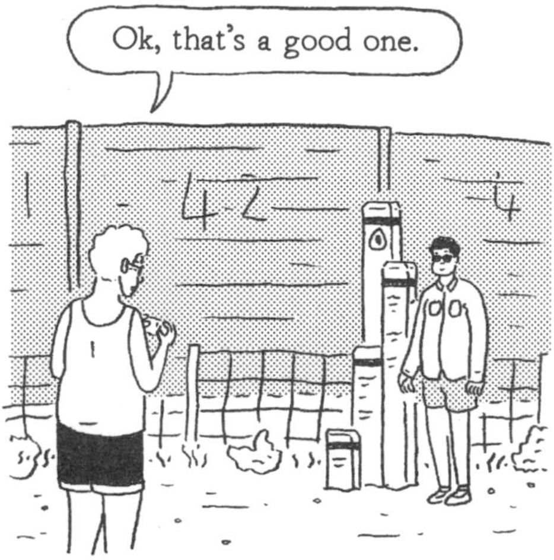
Ok, that's a good one.

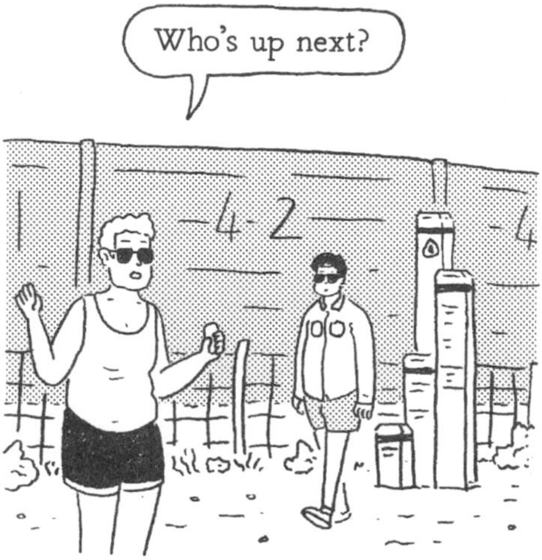
Who's up next?

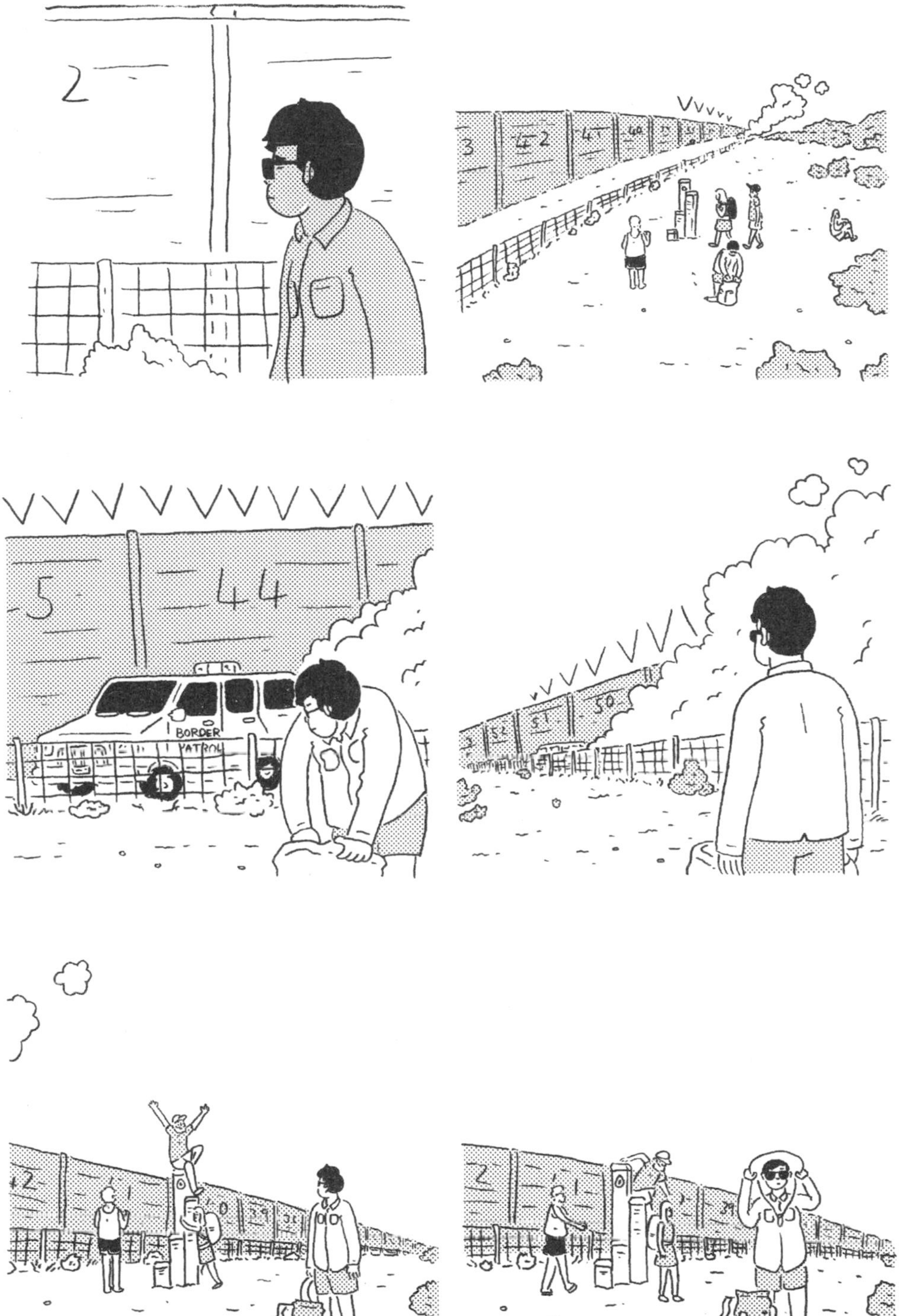
2
3
42
5
44
BORDER
PATROL
50
51
52

The Pacific Crest Trail passes through arid deserts, snowy mountains and damp rainforests as it winds its way from the Mexican border, up through the states of California, Oregon and Washington, to Canada.

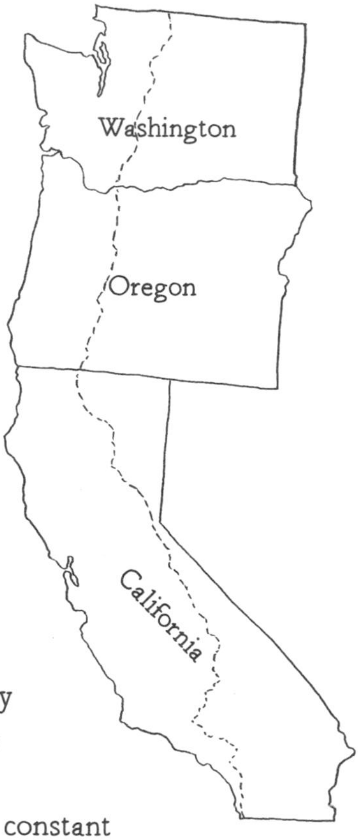
Washington
Oregon
California

Approximately three thousand hikers will pass through here this month.

I, like most of the others, am attempting to "thruhike" the trail, traversing its entire length in one hiking season, creating an unbroken footpath across one of the largest countries in the world.

I try not to think about what lies ahead in such grand terms.

Only a few hundred people successfully complete a thruhike each year. The extreme length of the trail, combined with a limited weather window, is unforgiving. It demands constant motion. Once I start, there will be no stopping – only quitting.

Like most hikers, I am travelling northbound, beginning from the Mexican border before summer arrives and dries up the desert springs. And I'll need to finish in Canada by late September, before the snowstorms roll in.

I fiddle with my own pack, as though I haven't spent the last two days checking and rechecking its contents. To the north, the desert's vastness hides behind the nearby hills.

For the next five months, this little ribbon of America will be my home. The clock is already ticking.

I try not to think about that either.

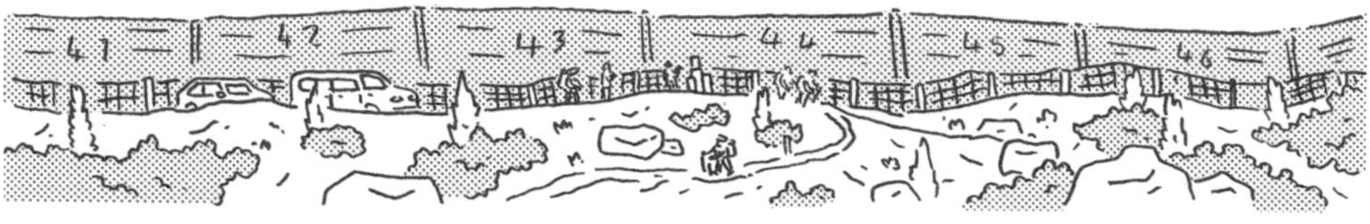
41
42
43
44
45
46

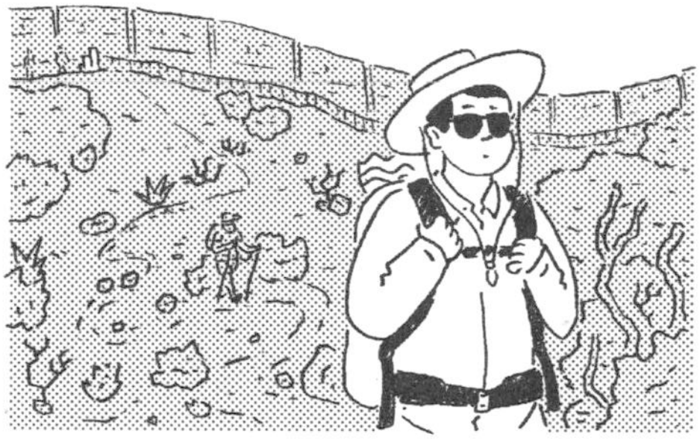

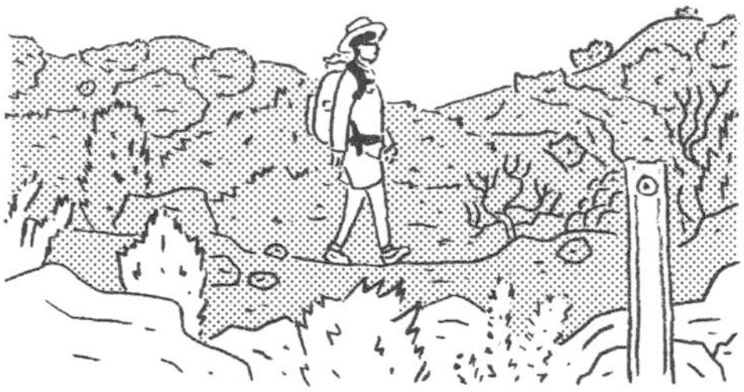

I've never seen landscape like this before in my life.

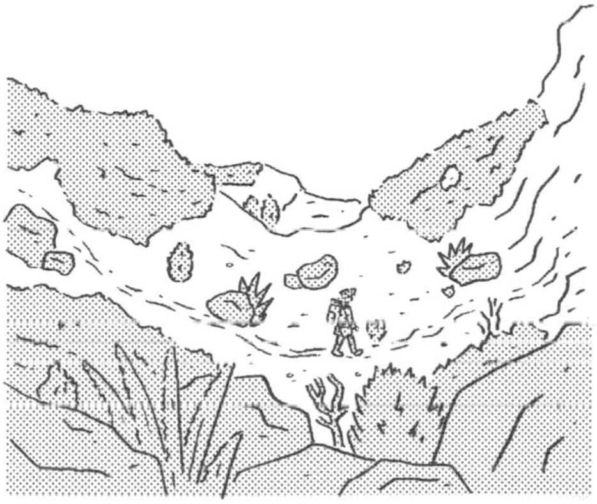

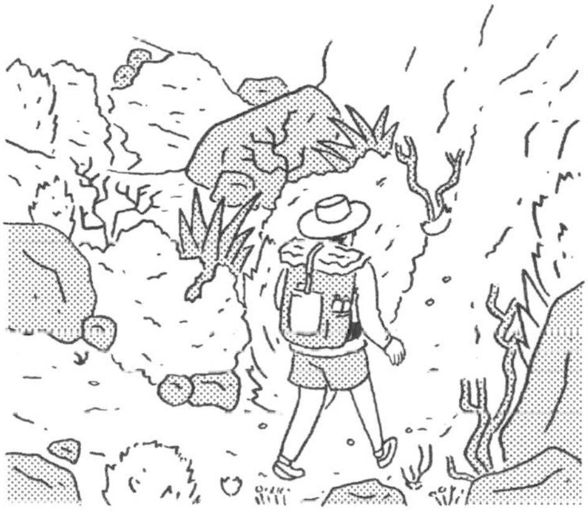

There are no deserts in Ireland.

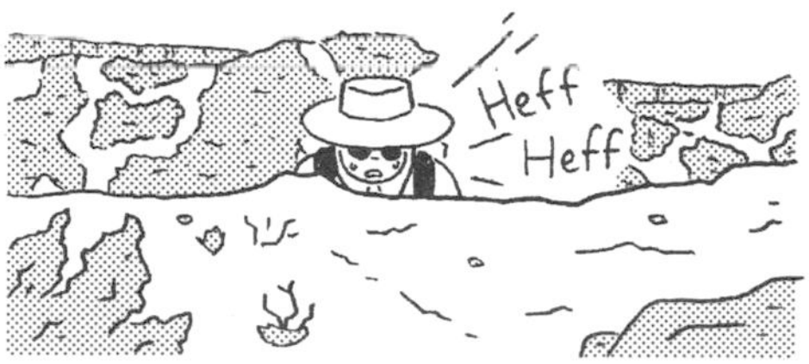
Heff
Heff

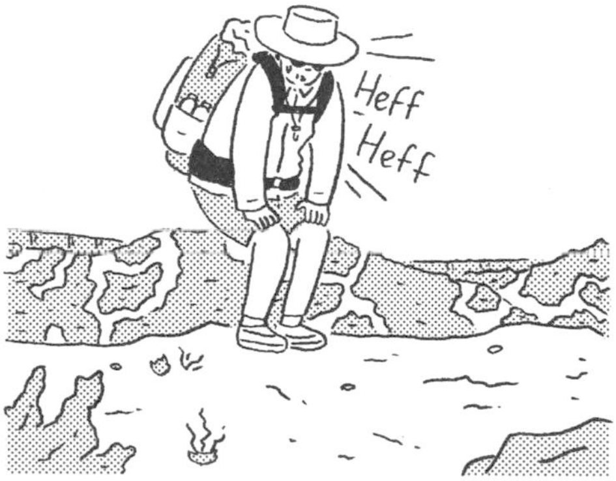
Heff
Heff

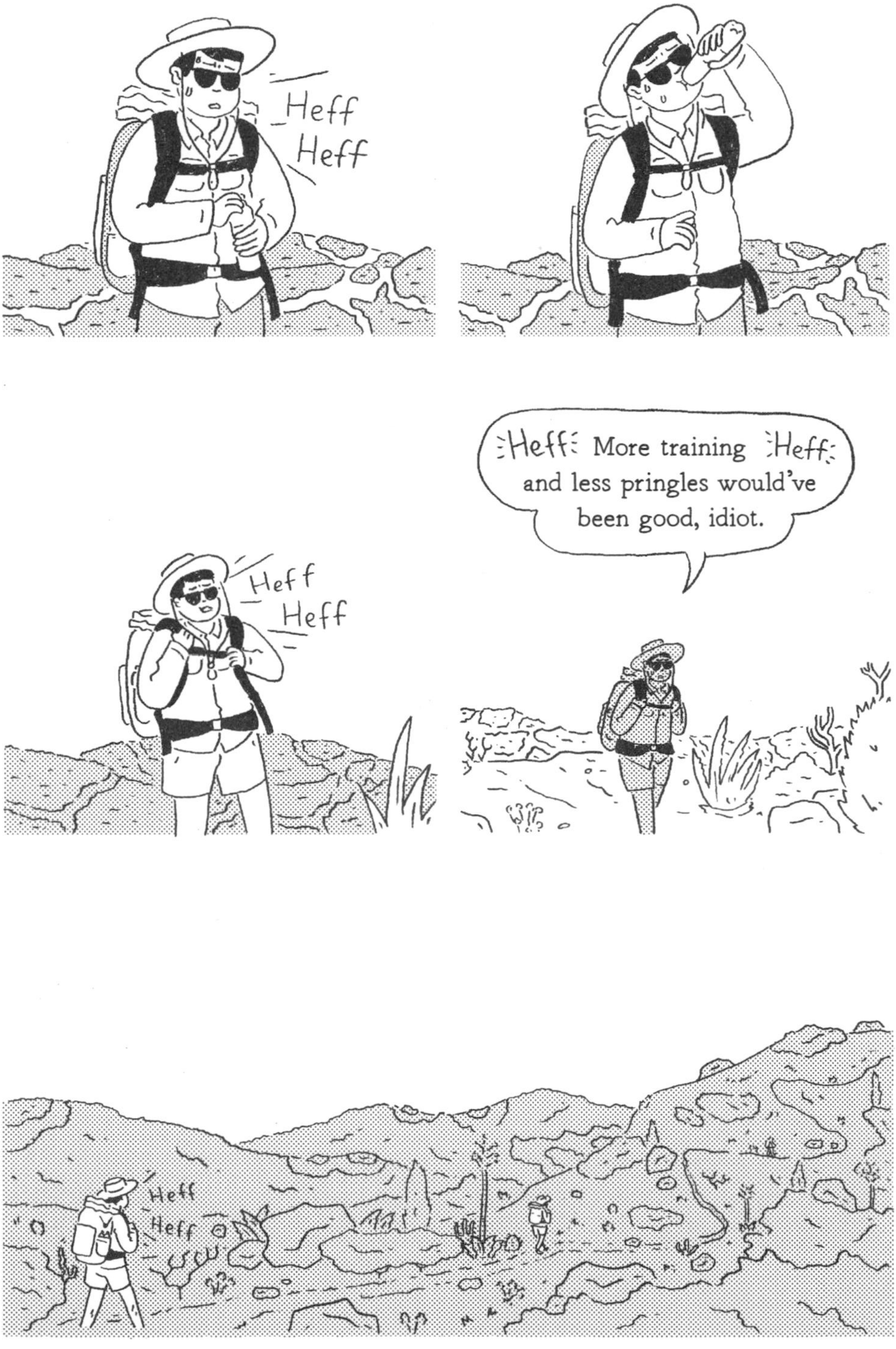
Heff
Heff
Heff
Heff
Heff More training Heff and less pringles would've been good, idiot.
Heff
Heff

Rough, scrubby bushes flank the trail on either side. The dry, rocky ground is firm under foot. Southern California is far from the sandy, cactus-covered cartoon I'd imagined.

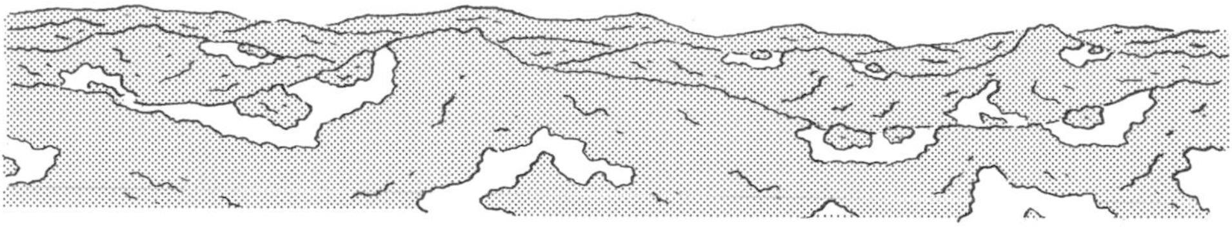

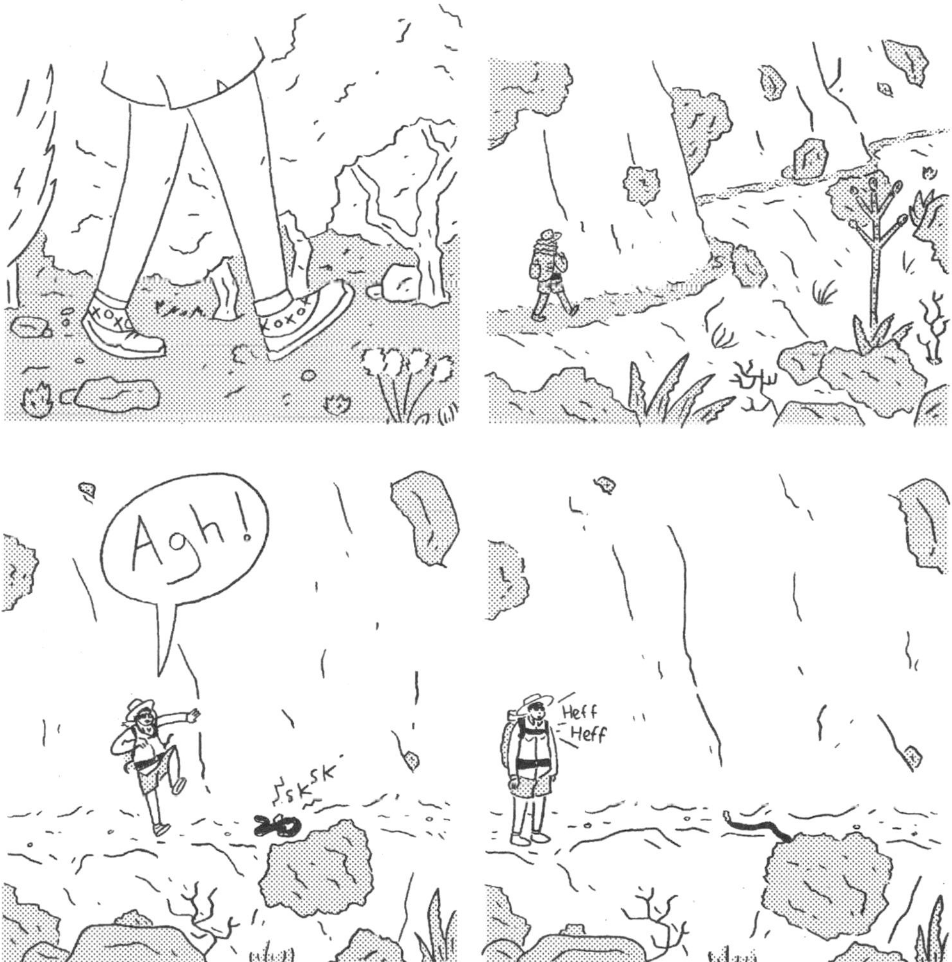
Agh!
SKSK
Heff
Heff

From higher up, I can see into Mexico for miles.

Heff
Heff

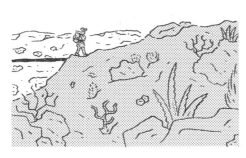

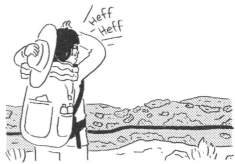

Donald Trump is running for president, promising to build a wall.

Heff
Heff

In Ireland, most people don't know that there already is a wall, along some stretches of the border at least.

Heff
Heff

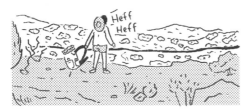

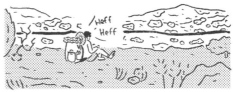

I didn't.

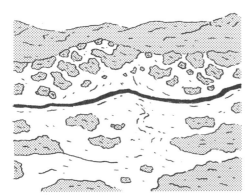

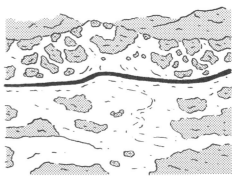

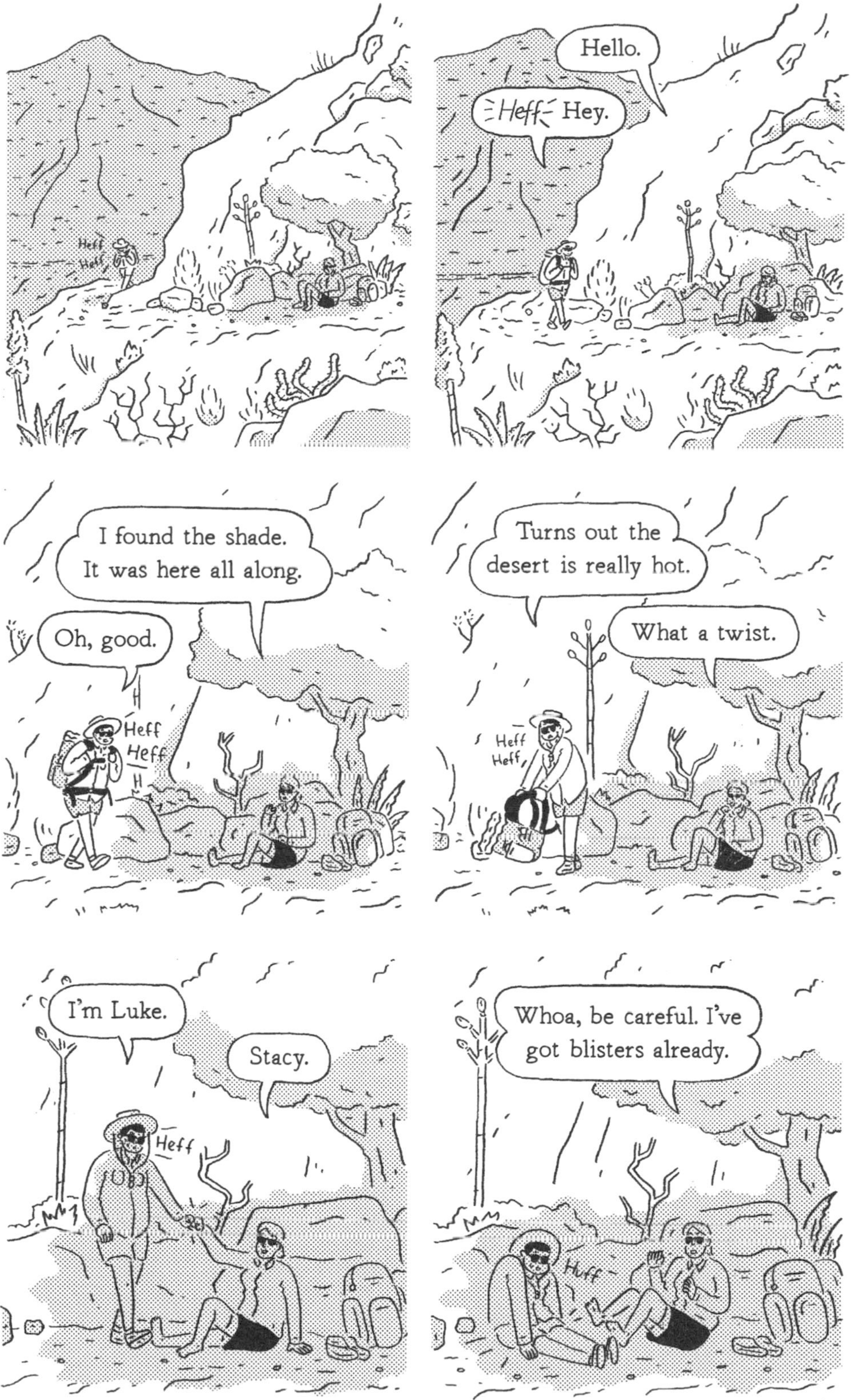
Heff
Heff
Hello.
Heff Hey.
I found the shade. It was here all along.
Oh, good.
Heff
Heff
Turns out the desert is really hot.
What a twist.
Heff
Heff
I'm Luke.
Stacy.
Heff
Whoa, be careful. I've got blisters already.
Huff

I sit in the shade with Stacy for a while and eat lunch. I packed the standard hiker fare that my guidebooks recommended and I'm already regretting it. The dehydrated noodles in my food bag don't exactly fill me with inspiration. I eat granola and sweet American peanut butter.

Stacy's from Alaska, and rattles off her extensive hiking credentials with ease. We hike together, and I struggle to match her confident pace. It's only been a few hours, and already I feel like somebody's been beating me up. When we pass another hiker, who is having trouble with his knee, I sheepishly produce a ziplock bag filled with ibuprofen and offer it up, resisting the urge to take one myself.

"Vitamin I," Stacy jokes, as we hike on.

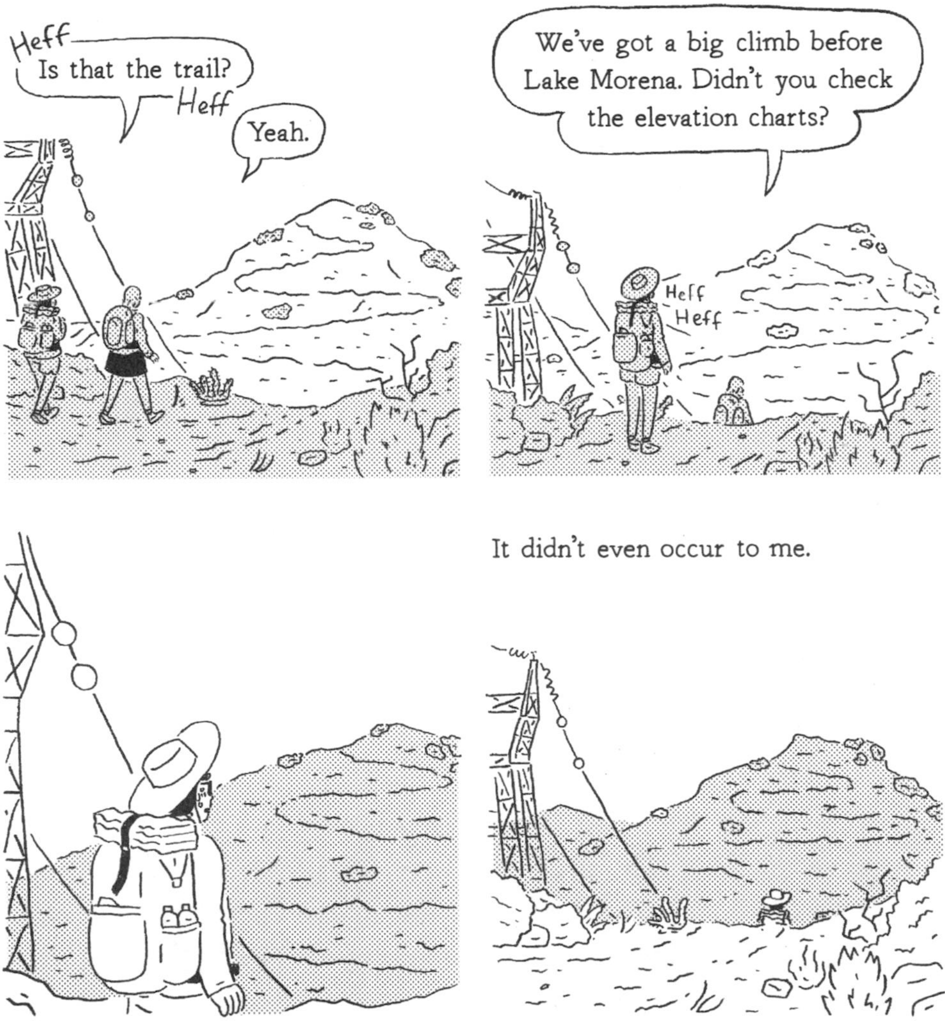

Heff
Is that the trail?
Heff
Yeah.
We've got a big climb before Lake Morena. Didn't you check the elevation charts?
Heff
Heff
It didn't even occur to me.

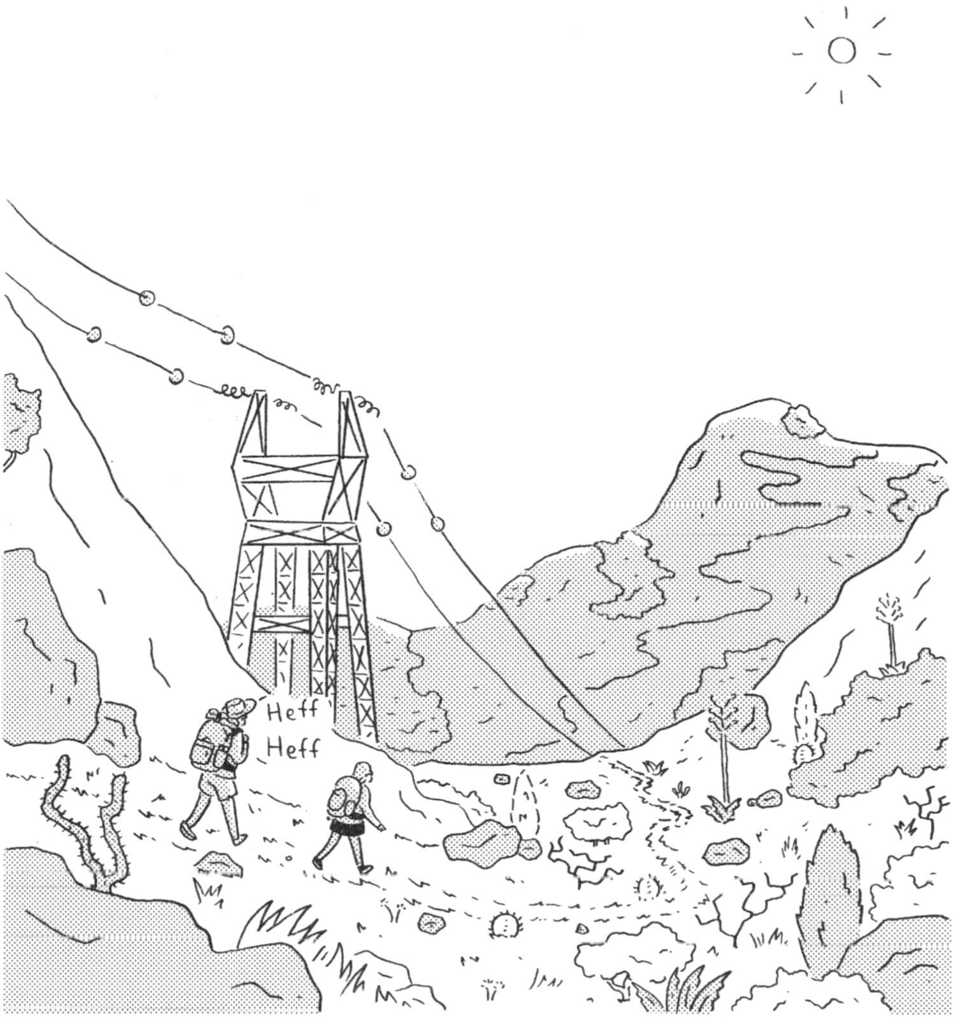
Heff
Heff

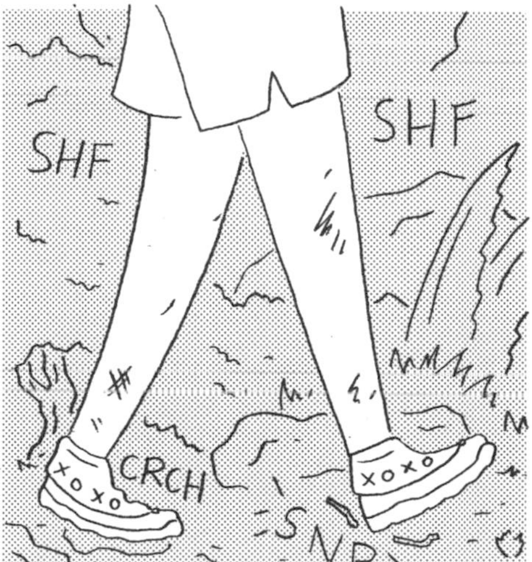
SHF
SHF
xoxo
CRCH
xoxo
SNP

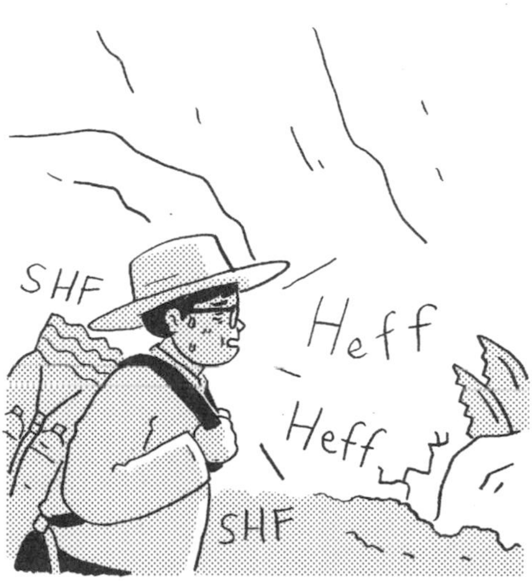
SHF
Heff
Heff
SHF

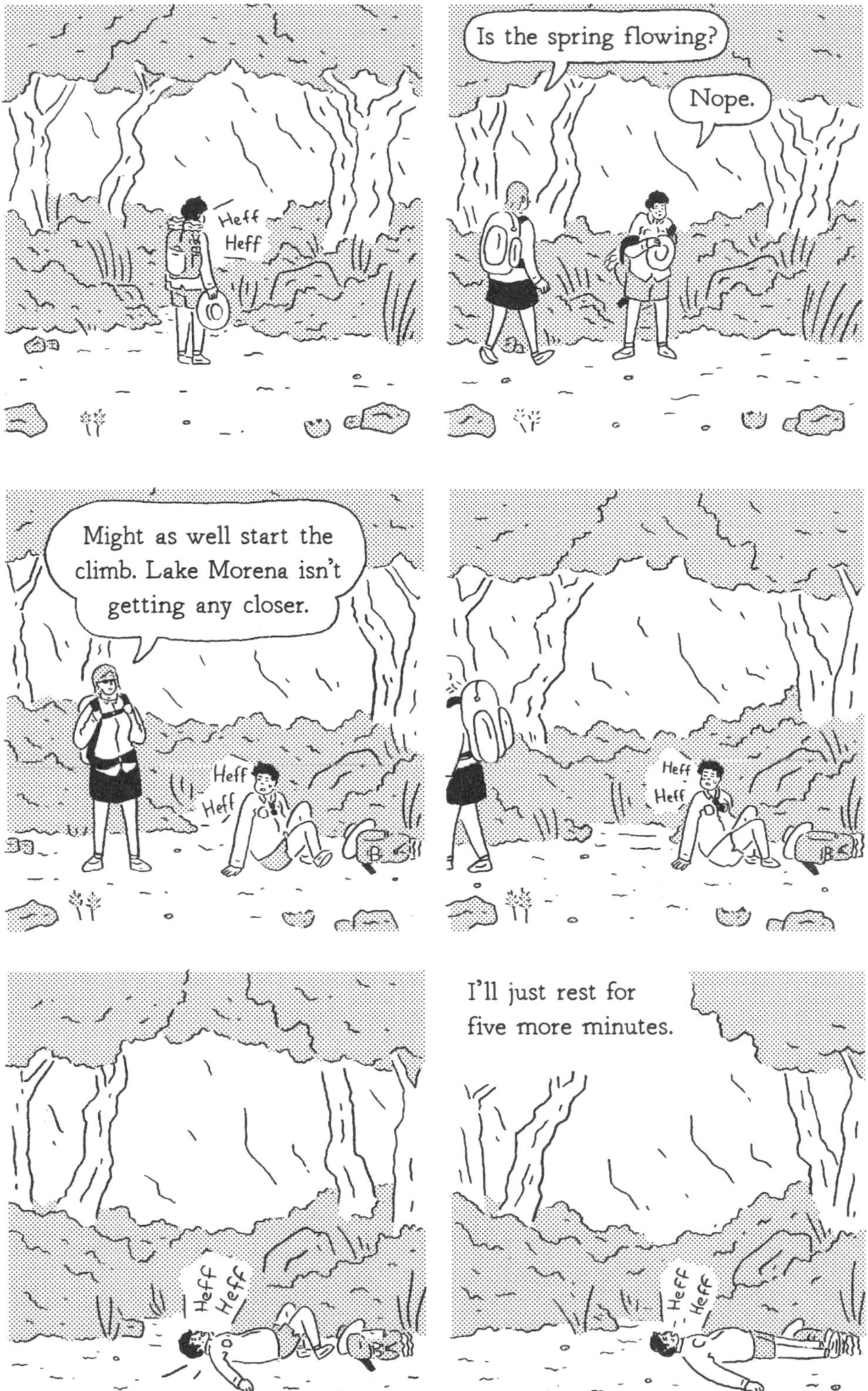
Heff
Heff
Is the spring flowing?
Nope.
Might as well start the climb. Lake Morena isn't getting any closer.
Heff
Heff
Heff
Heff
Heff
Heff
I'll just rest for five more minutes.
Heff
Heff

Slowly, other hikers trickle down to the dry spring and one-by-one, set up little lightweight tents in the clearing. I follow suit. I can tackle the climb tomorrow, in the cooler morning temperatures.

I check the state of my water supply, and think hard before pouring some into my cookpot to rehydrate a packet of powdered mashed potato. As I eat the disgusting mush, my muscles cramp up past the point of uselessness.

The hikers make for a surprisingly international group. David and Lisa, an excitable English couple, read facts from a pocket PCT guidebook aloud to us, and look very traditional in their hiking boots and long khaki trousers. Everyone else wears the standard thruhiker uniform of a long-sleeved shirt and running shorts.

There is a Dutchman, and an Australian. And me. There are only three Americans. Danny and Camy are a Mexican American father-daughter hiking team; Camy is only sixteen years old.

Spreadsheet, true to his name, spends most of the evening checking and double-checking his gear list and water report.

He's the only one of us who started his hike with a trail name, a tradition in the long-distance hiking community. Within a few weeks, most of us will be going by our own trail names, given to us by other hikers or self-selected to reflect our thruhiking alter egos.

21

I unpack my own meticulously packed bag. Until a few months ago, these things had all just been items on a spreadsheet, too.

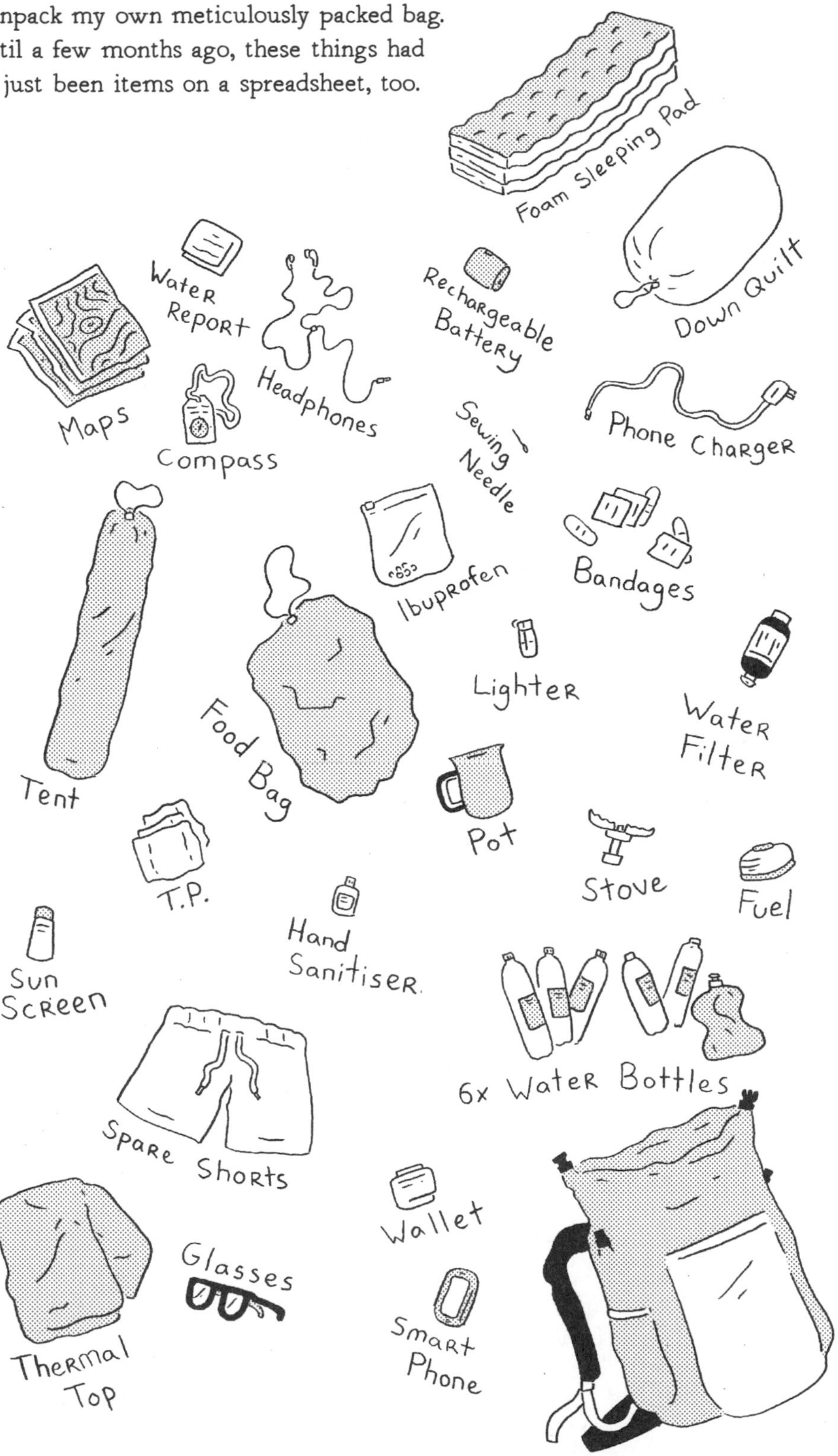
Foam Sleeping Pad
Down Quilt
Water Report
Maps
Headphones
Rechargeable Battery
Compass
Sewing Needle
Phone Charger
Ibuprofen
Bandages
Tent
Food Bag
Lighter
Water Filter
Pot
T.P.
Stove
Fuel
Hand Sanitiser
Sun Screen
6x Water Bottles
Spare Shorts
Wallet
Glasses
Thermal Top
Smart Phone

"So, why are you hiking the PCT?" is the question around camp.

"It just sounded like fun," I answer when my turn comes. It's mostly the truth. The fullness of its appeal is too complex to describe. I'm driven by my hunger for the American experience. But also by the hope that if I gorge myself on it, I'll become sick of the taste.

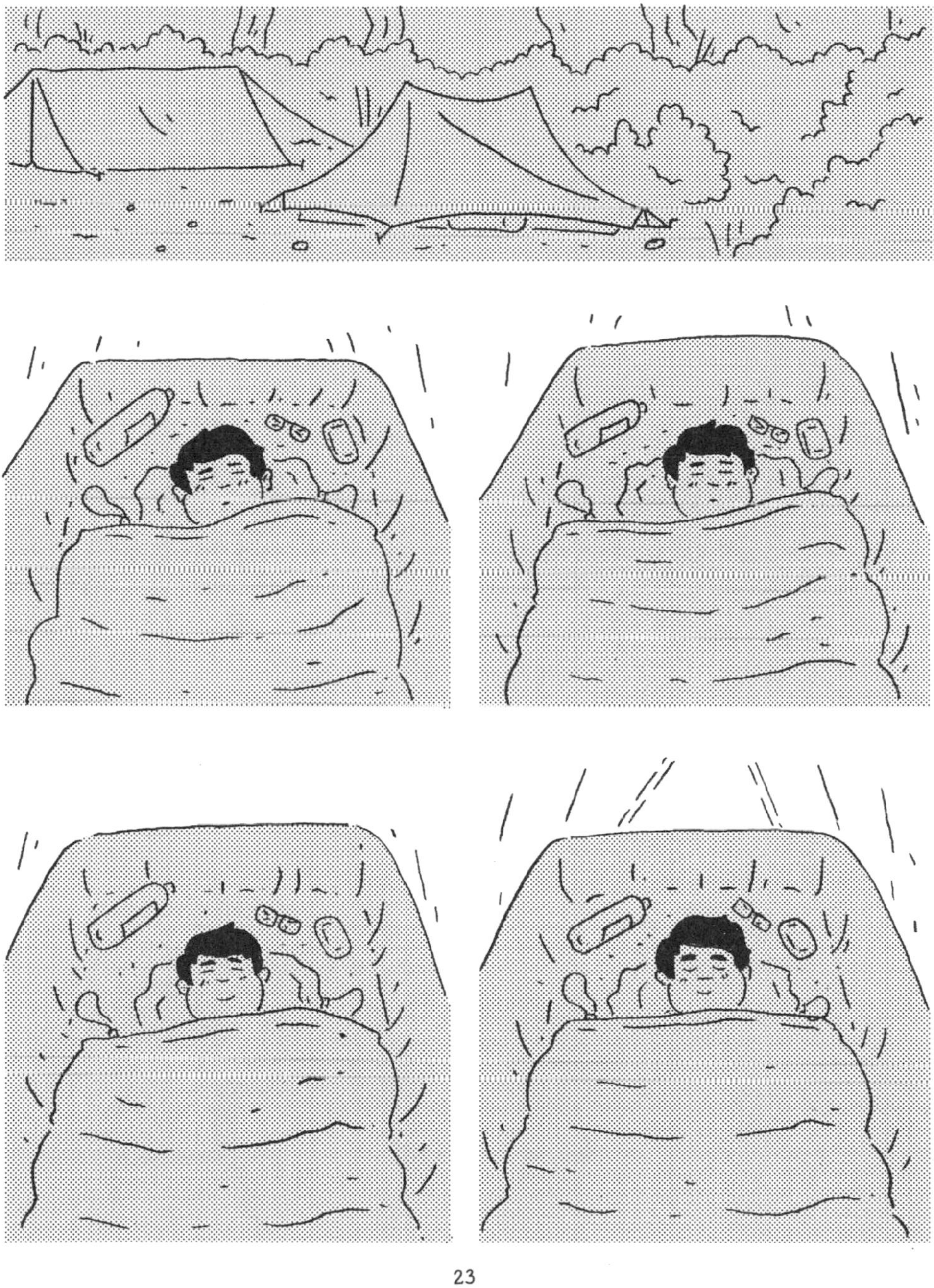

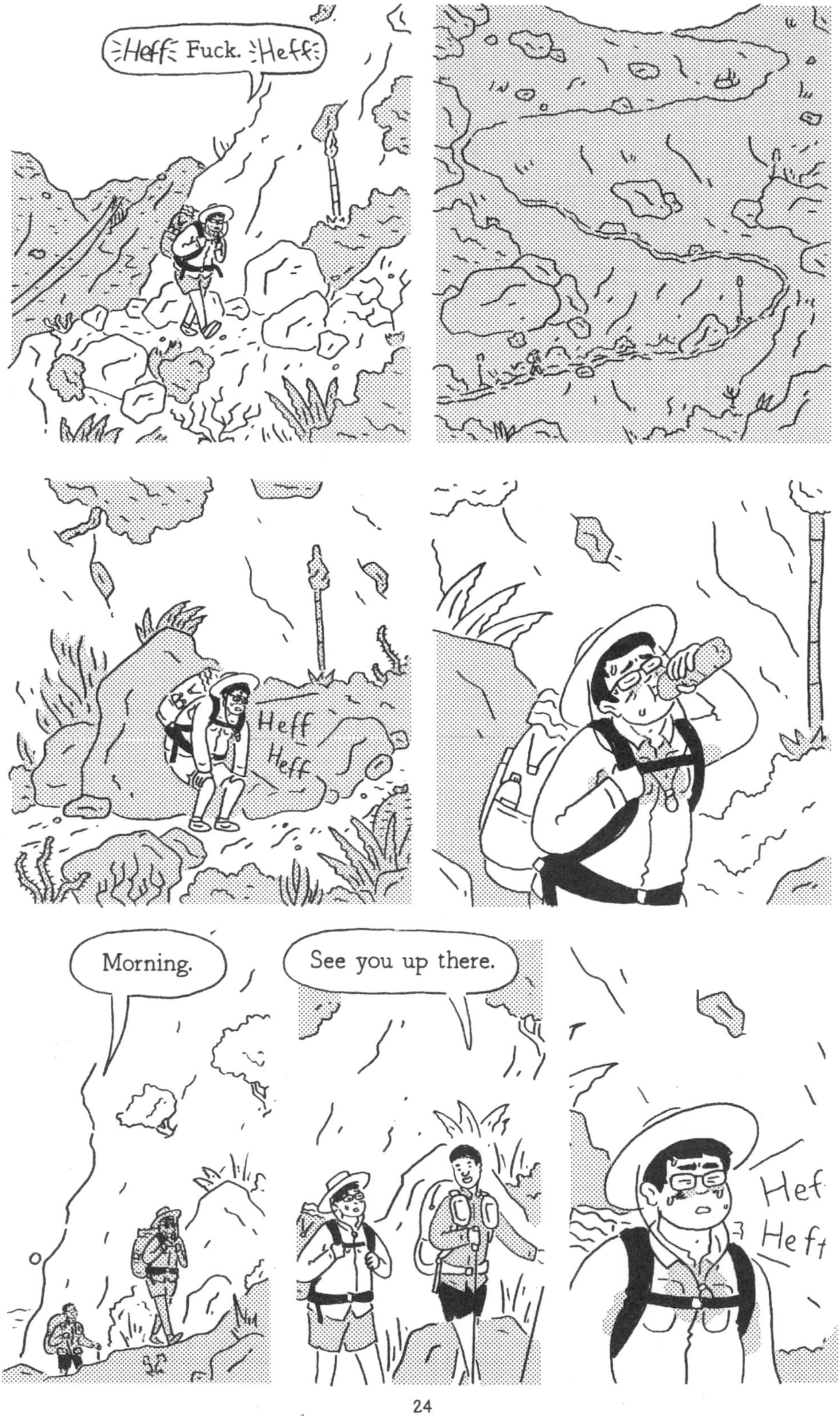

Heff Fuck. Heff
Heff Heff
Morning.
See you up there.
Hef
Hef

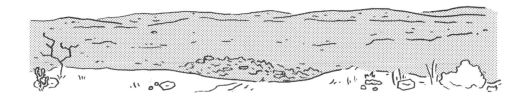

Even in the cooler morning light, I guzzle the last of my water stores dry and fiddle nervously with my empty bottles as I crest the hill to Lake Morena. From the hilltop, I catch no glimpse of the lake, only more miles of crackling desert.

Lake Morena is the first "town" on the PCT. Though really, it's not much more than a campsite and a general store, which I hike to with David and Lisa to buy cold Gatorade. Inside, the store owner produces a trail register and we write in our names. I see that Stacy passed through yesterday evening.

We find the campsite's bathroom, a squat, cube-shaped building. There is a water fountain by the entrance and we stand awkwardly, refilling our bottles as families come and go.

This is a convenient water source, I realise that. Over the next five months I will need to acquire water from a gaggle of odd sources, not least intimidating of which are the creeks, streams and springs that are listed somewhat vaguely on our water reports.

4 litres will probably get us to the next source, right?
...right.
SHF
SHF

I fall into a slow rhythm.

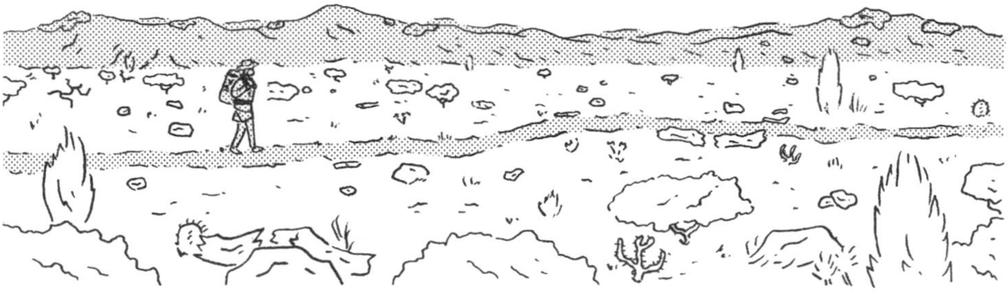

Up.

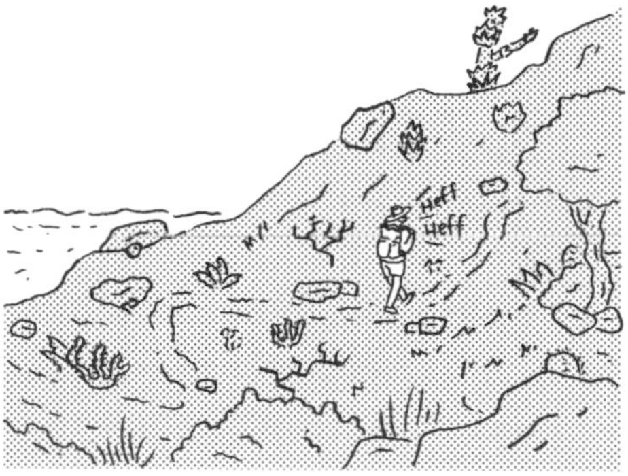
Heff
Heff

And down.

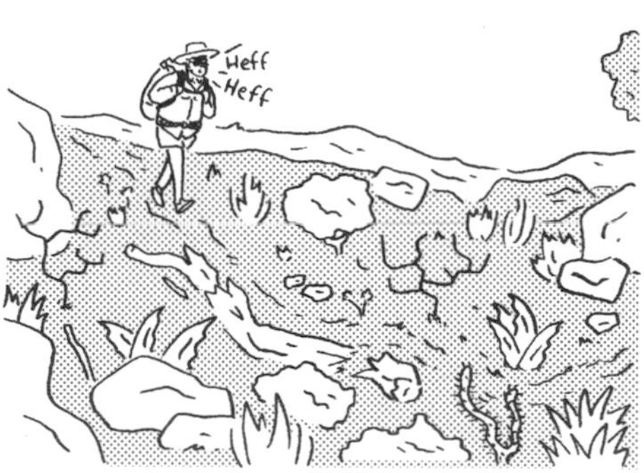
Heff
Heff

Up.

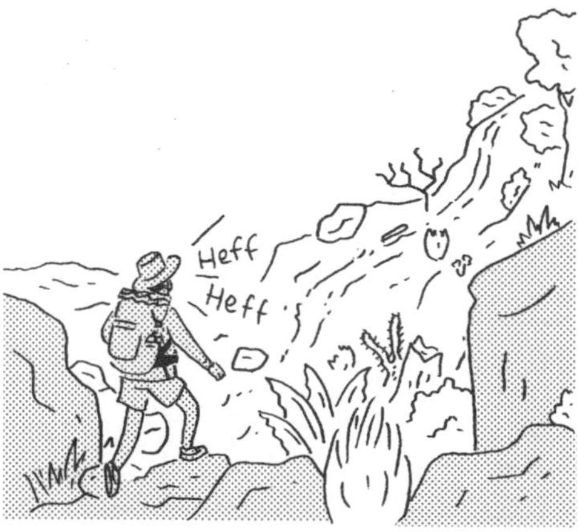
Heff
Heff

And down.

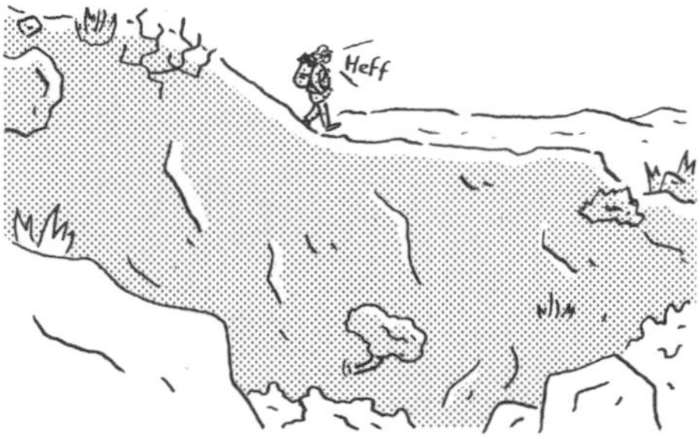
Heff

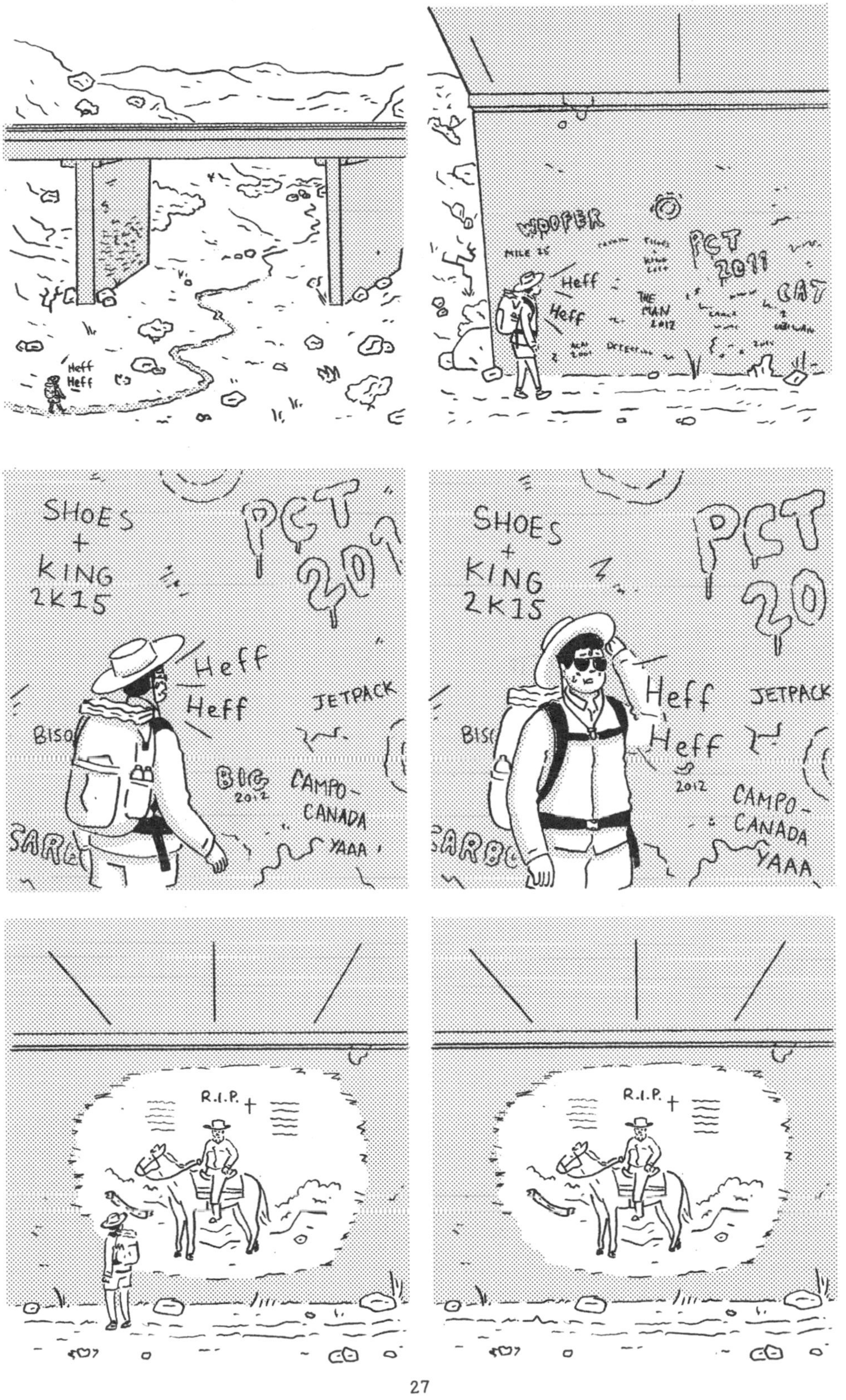
Heff
Heff
WOOFER
MILE 26
PCT 2011
Heff
Heff
THE MAN 2012
CAT
SHOES + KING 2K15
PCT 201
Heff
Heff
JETPACK
BISO
BIG 2012
CAMPO-CANADA
YAAA
SARB
SHOES + KING 2K15
PCT 20
Heff
Heff
JETPACK
BIS
2012
CAMPO-CANADA
YAAA
SARB
R.I.P.
R.I.P.

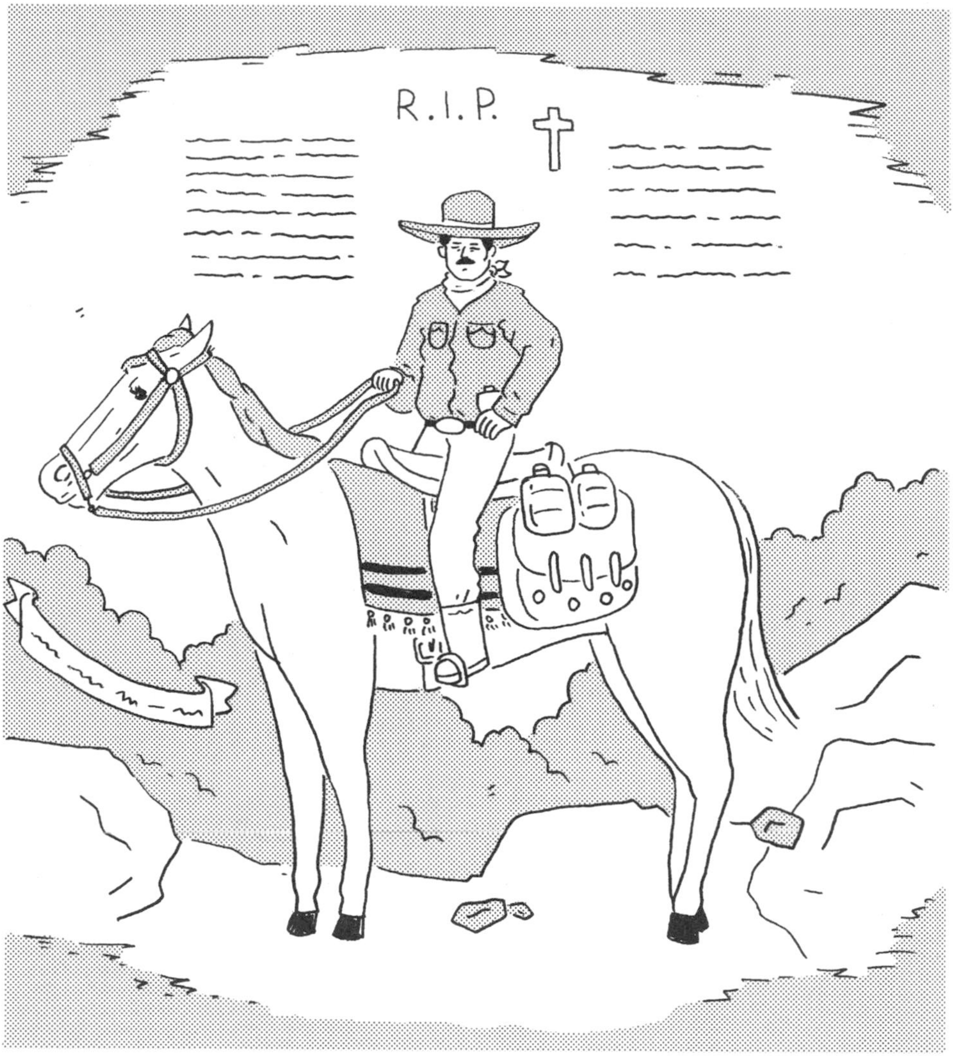
R.I.P.

I think about the mural as I hike on through the scrubby wasteland. It clings in my mind. I can't read Spanish, but can tell it commemorates the dead. The list of names, I suspect, recording those who died crossing the US-Mexican border, though I can't be sure.

I feel guilty, given access to this place for recreation, when others are dying to get here.

I've heard stories of people leaving caches of water, hidden in the desert, for those making the crossing. I've heard stories of border agents destroying those caches.

The border agents never destroy the PCT water caches.

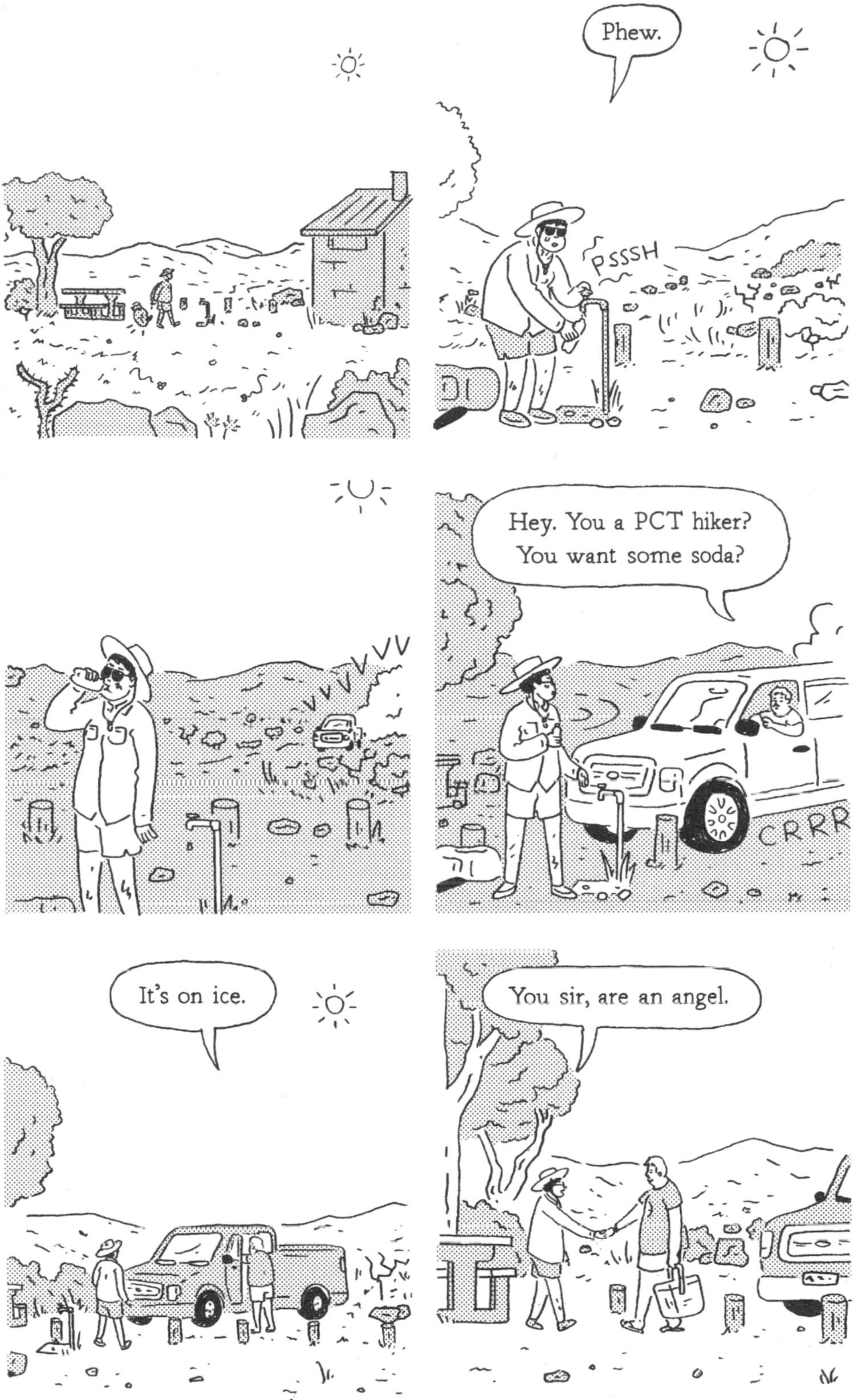
Phew.
PSSSH
Hey. You a PCT hiker?
You want some soda?
CRRR
It's on ice.
You sir, are an angel.

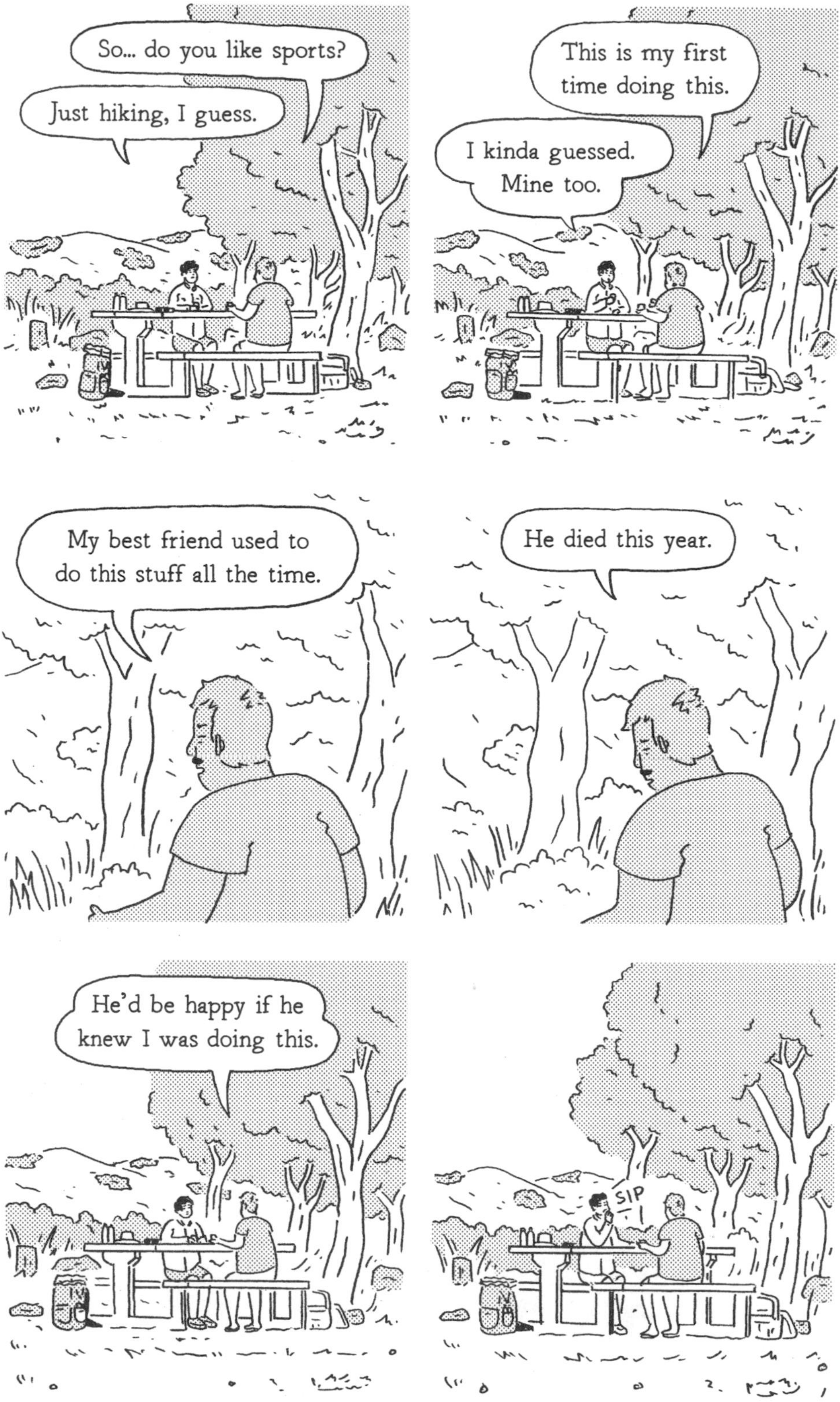
So... do you like sports?
Just hiking, I guess.
This is my first time doing this.
I kinda guessed. Mine too.
My best friend used to do this stuff all the time.
He died this year.
He'd be happy if he knew I was doing this.
SIP

Before yesterday, I'd never gone backpacking in my life.

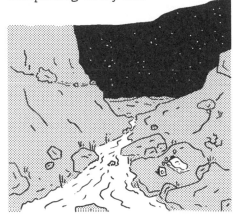

The desert is so cold at night.

In the sky, the stars unfurl so cleanly.

Interspersed only by the occasional border patrol chopper.

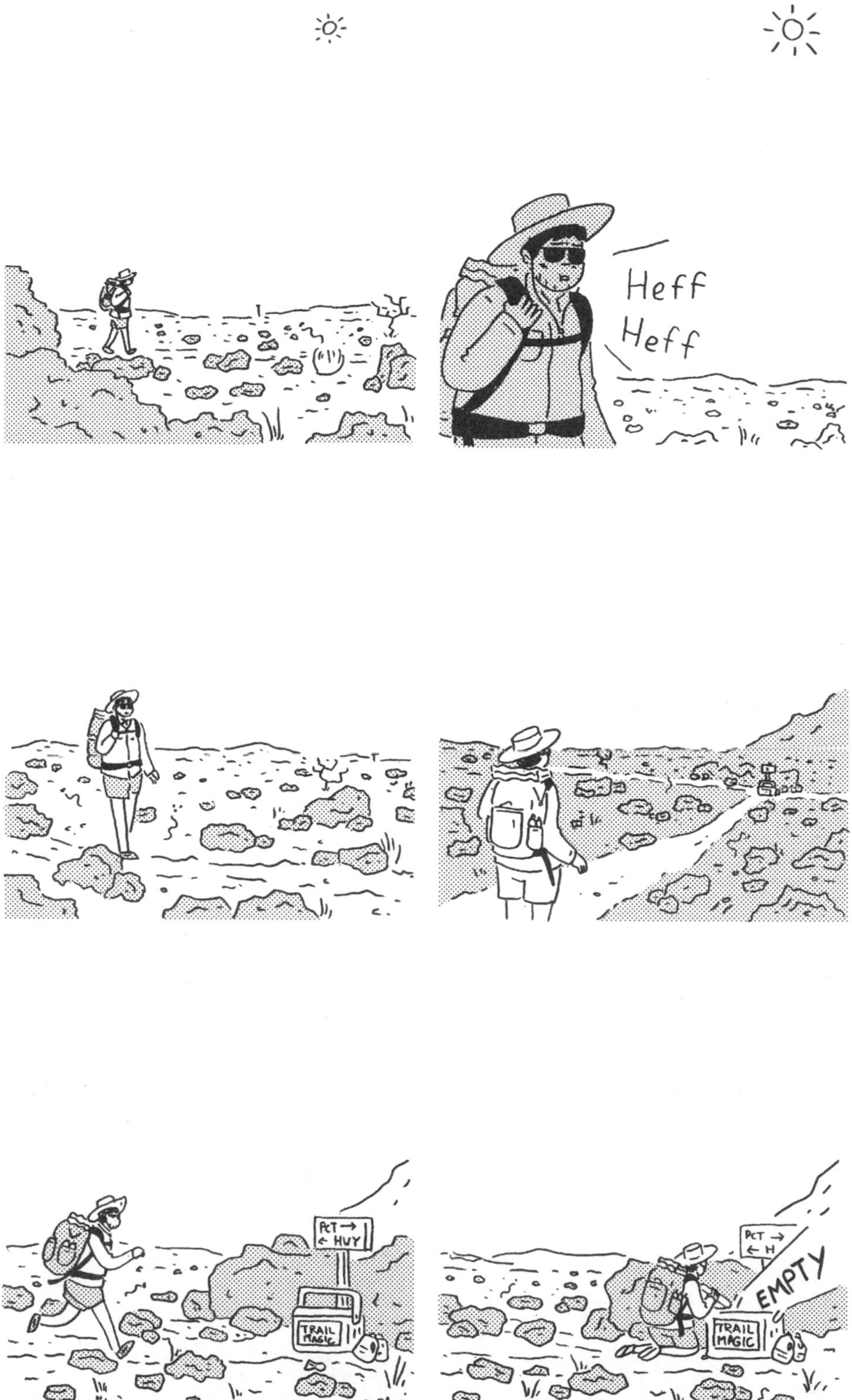
Heff
Heff
PCT →
← HWY
TRAIL MAGIC
PCT →
← H
EMPTY
TRAIL MAGIC

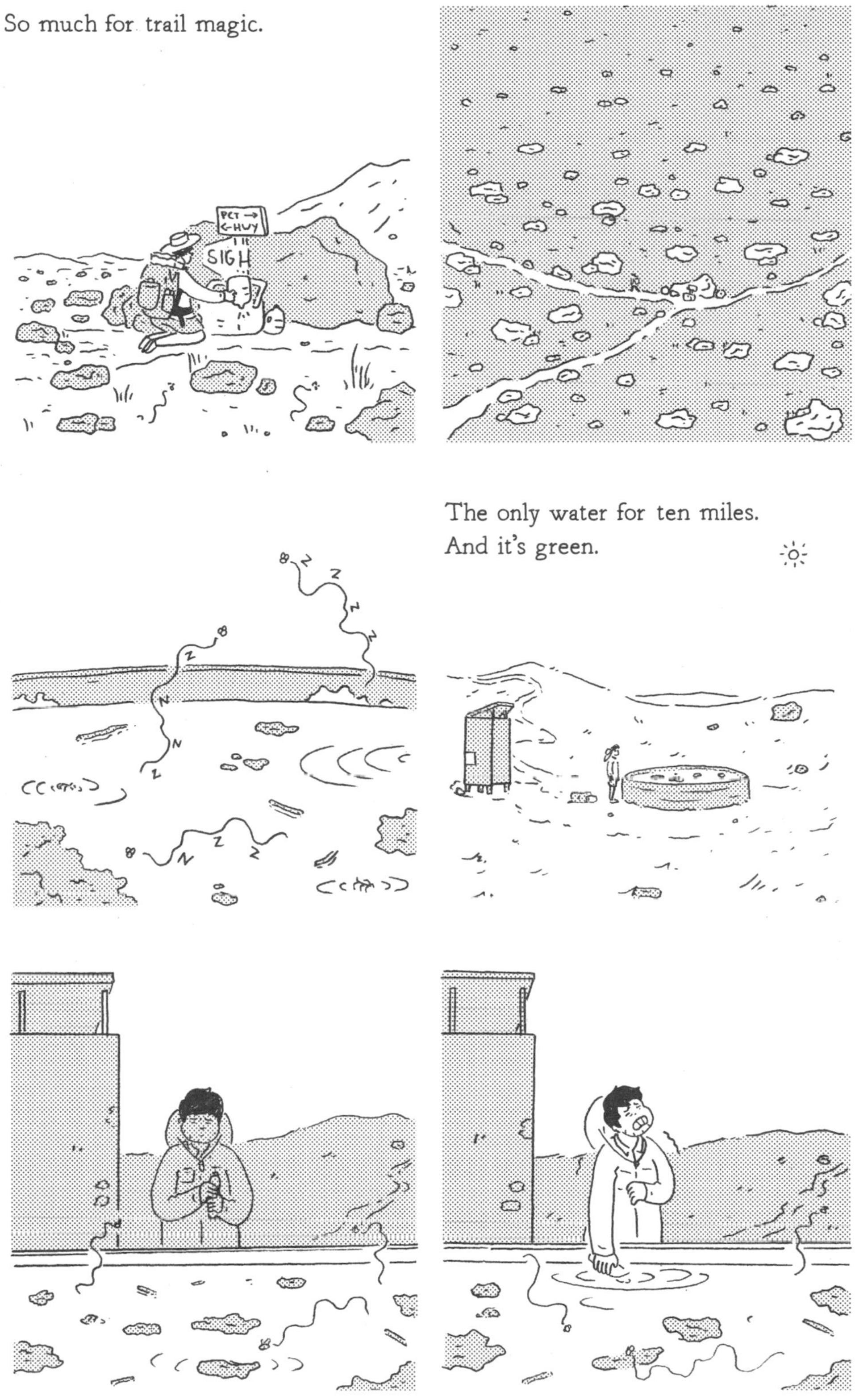
So much for trail magic.
PCT →
←HWY
SIGH
The only water for ten miles.
And it's green.

I drink every drop.

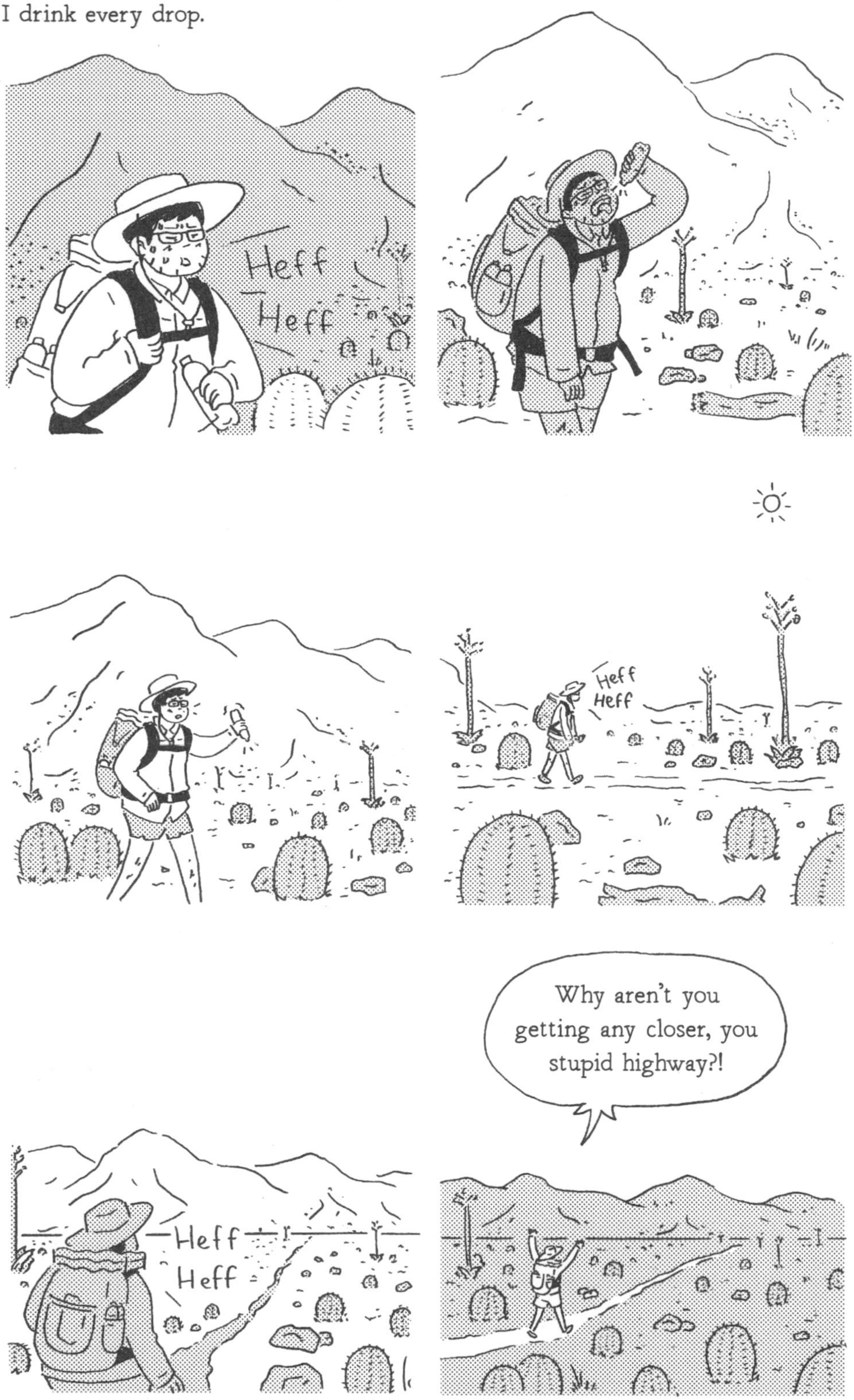
Heff
Heff
Heff
Heff
Heff
Heff
Why aren't you getting any closer, you stupid highway?!

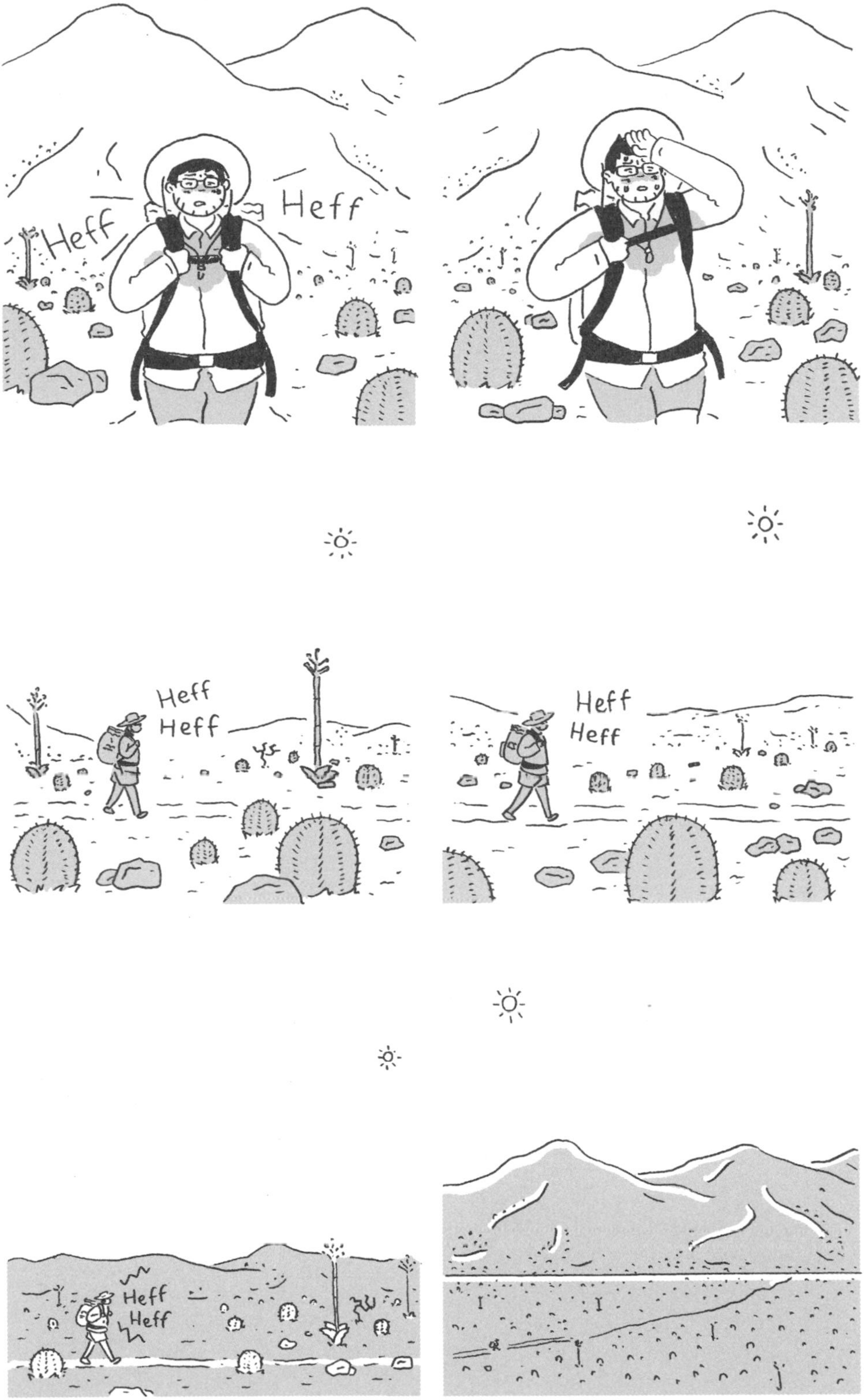
Heff
Heff
Heff
Heff
Heff
Heff
Heff
Heff

I count the steps. "Only one hundred more," I think.

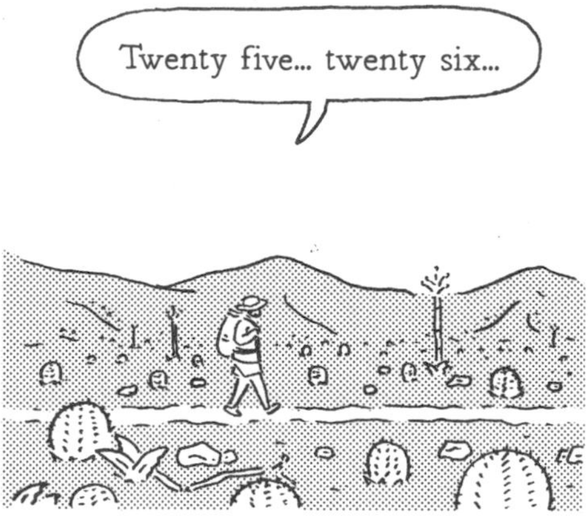
Twenty five... twenty six...

When I reach one hundred, I start again. And again. And again.

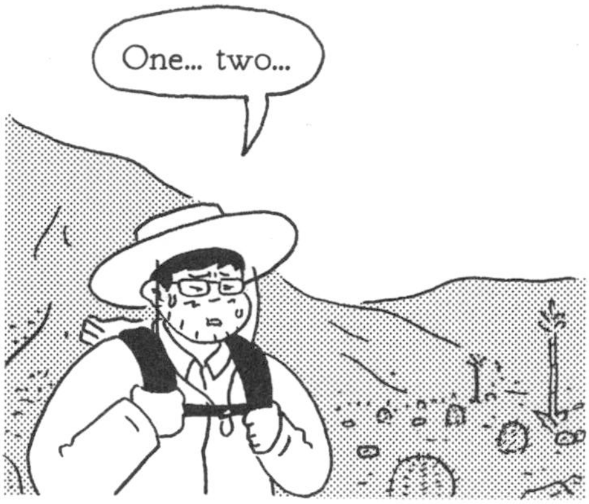
One... two...

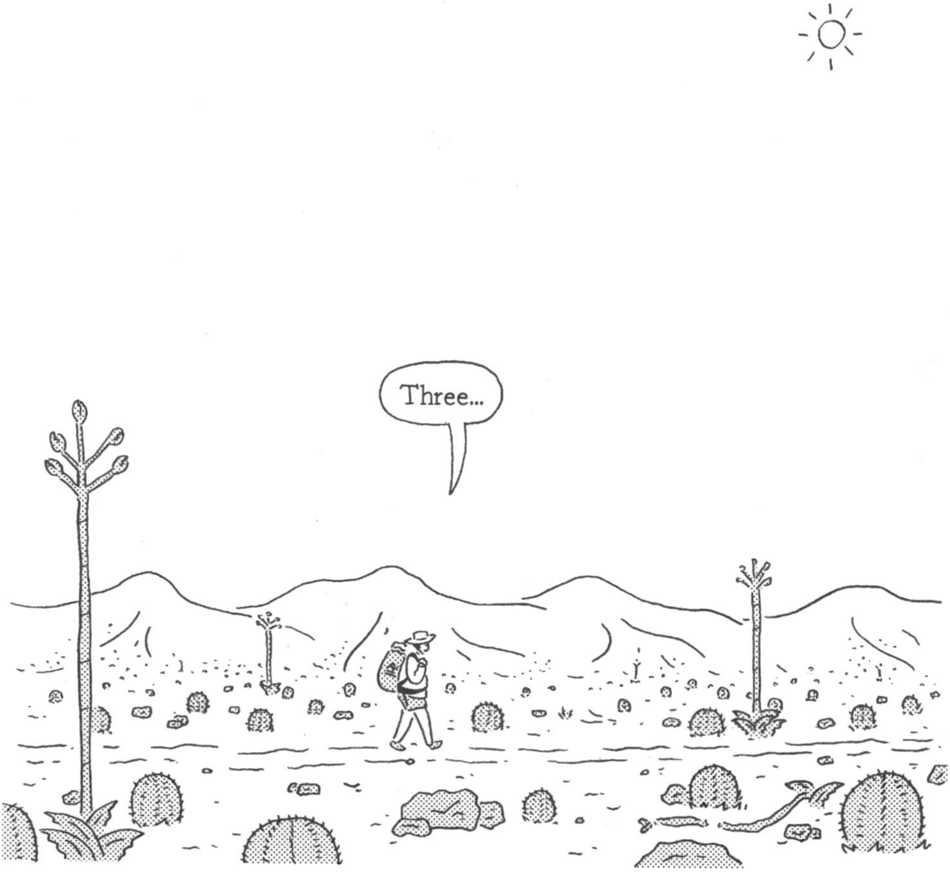
Three...

And then I'm at the road.

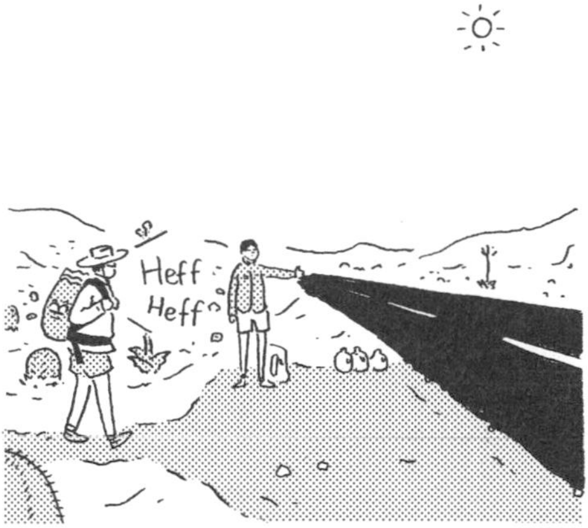
Heff
Heff

I've never hitch-hiked before, but I'm too thirsty to be nervous.

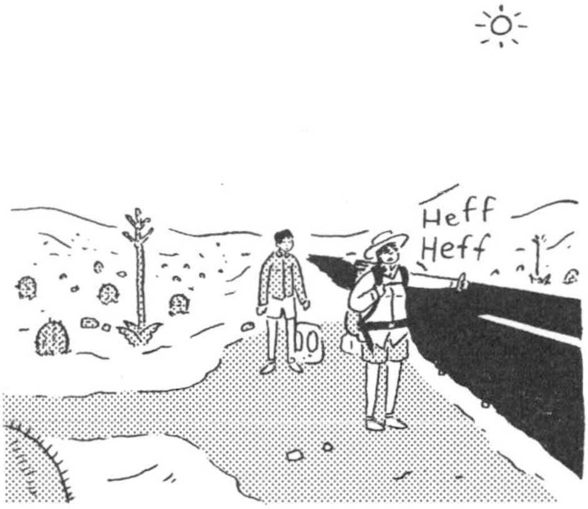
Heff
Heff

I ride to an RV park near the town of Julian. It's Wild West themed.

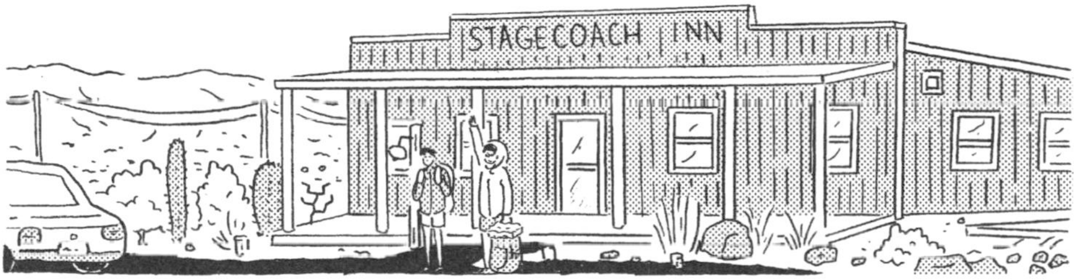
STAGECOACH INN

I get a thirty-two ounce cola and drink the entire thing in my tent.

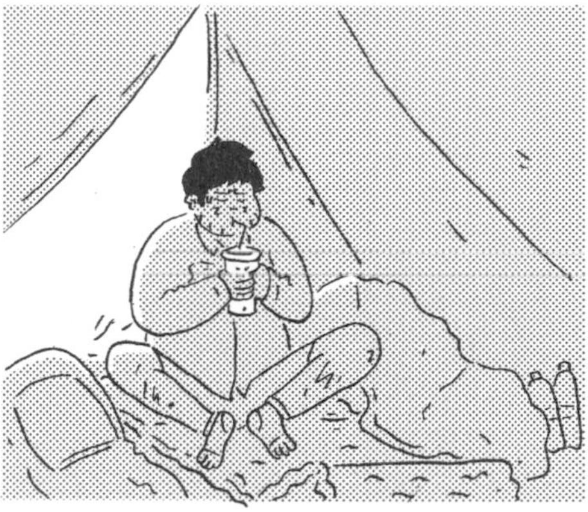

My hands shake on the dewy cardboard cup.

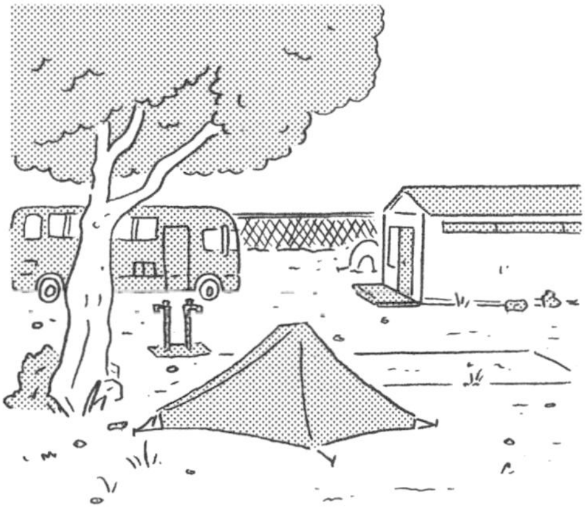

I shower.

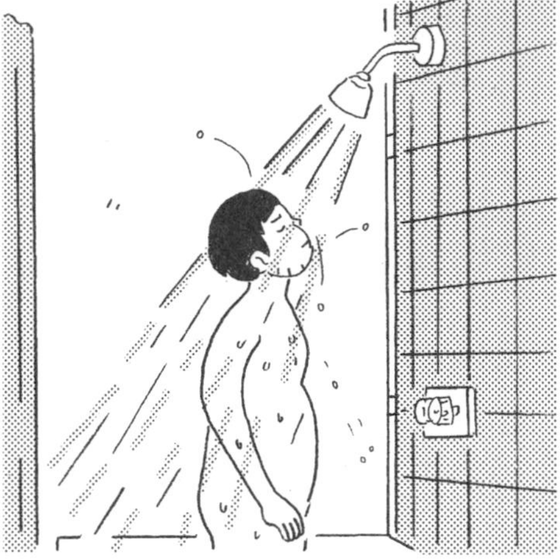

I do laundry, dressed in my rain gear.

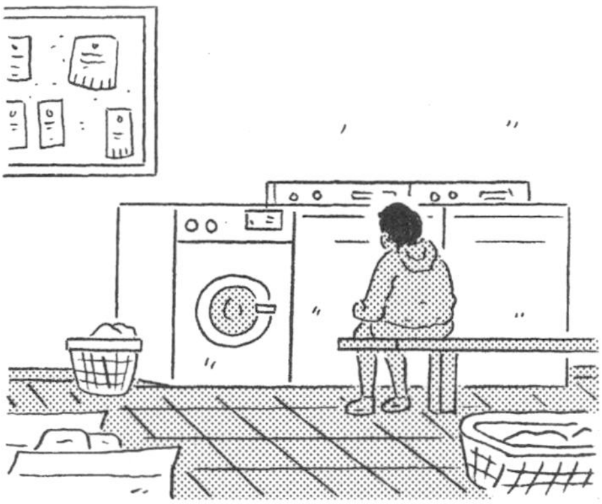

I soak my feet in the pool.

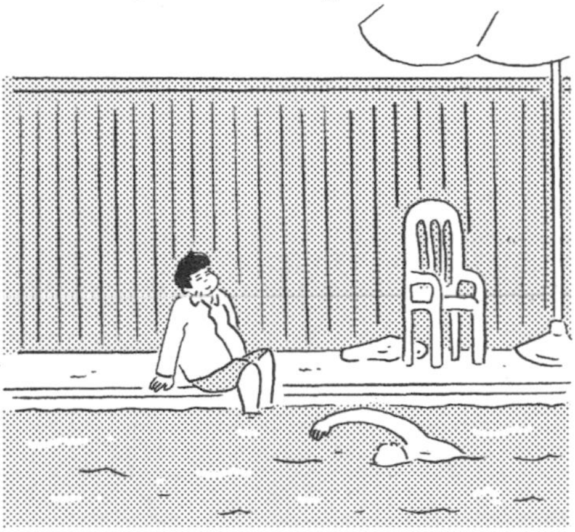

I drink more soda.

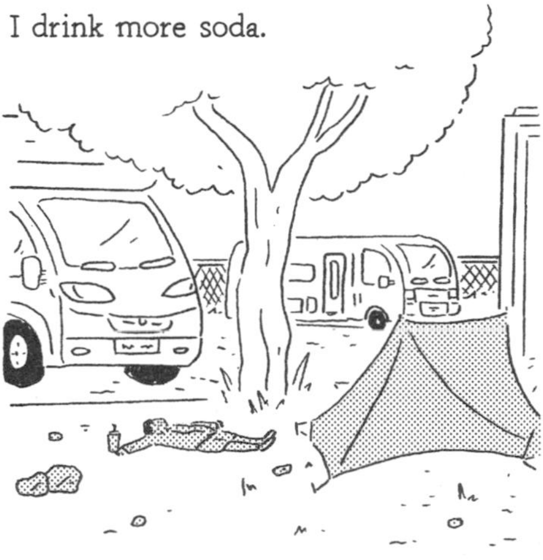

I fill every one of my bottles.

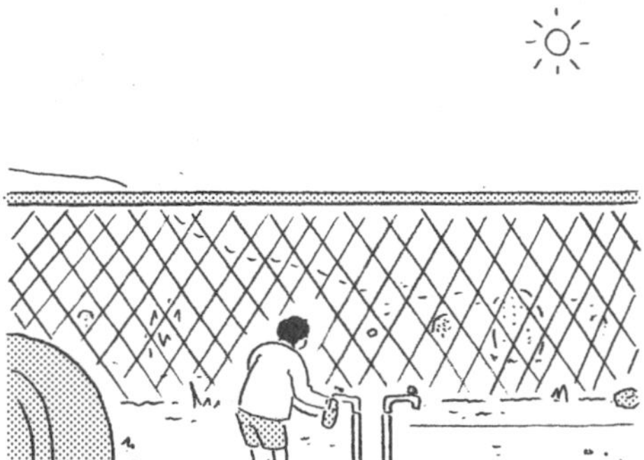

I sleep, surrounded by the generator hum of colossal RVs.

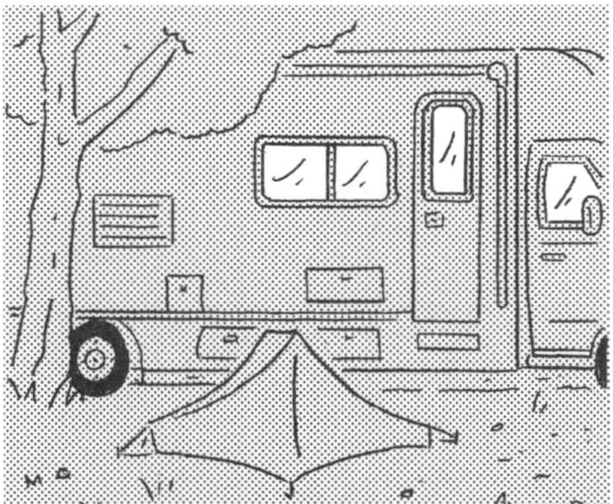

The pack of thruhikers moving north from Mexico is an ever diminishing crowd, as people run out of time, or money, or willpower, or become injured, or simply realise that they had no idea what they were getting themselves into. Thirty per cent of all thruhikers quit in their first week, many of those on the first day.

I wake in my sweaty little tent to a text from David and Lisa. They will take their first zero day in Julian, hiking zero miles, and allowing themselves to recover. I hurt all over; legs, back, shoulders, and particularly feet, but nothing feels truly injured, so I keep moving. I'm too restless to stop yet.

Amongst the thruhikers, distinct groups are starting to form. A lot of the hikers I pass are veterans of the Appalachian Trail, a long-distance trail on the USA's East Coast, which covers 2100 miles of extremely rugged terrain. Already, the AT hikers are grouping together, their experience and relative fitness allowing them to cover big miles and pull ahead of the slower newbies.

As I hitch-hike back to the trail, I tumble the numbers over in my head. Thirty per cent of thruhikers quit in their first week.

Scissors Crossing 21/04/16. Day 6.

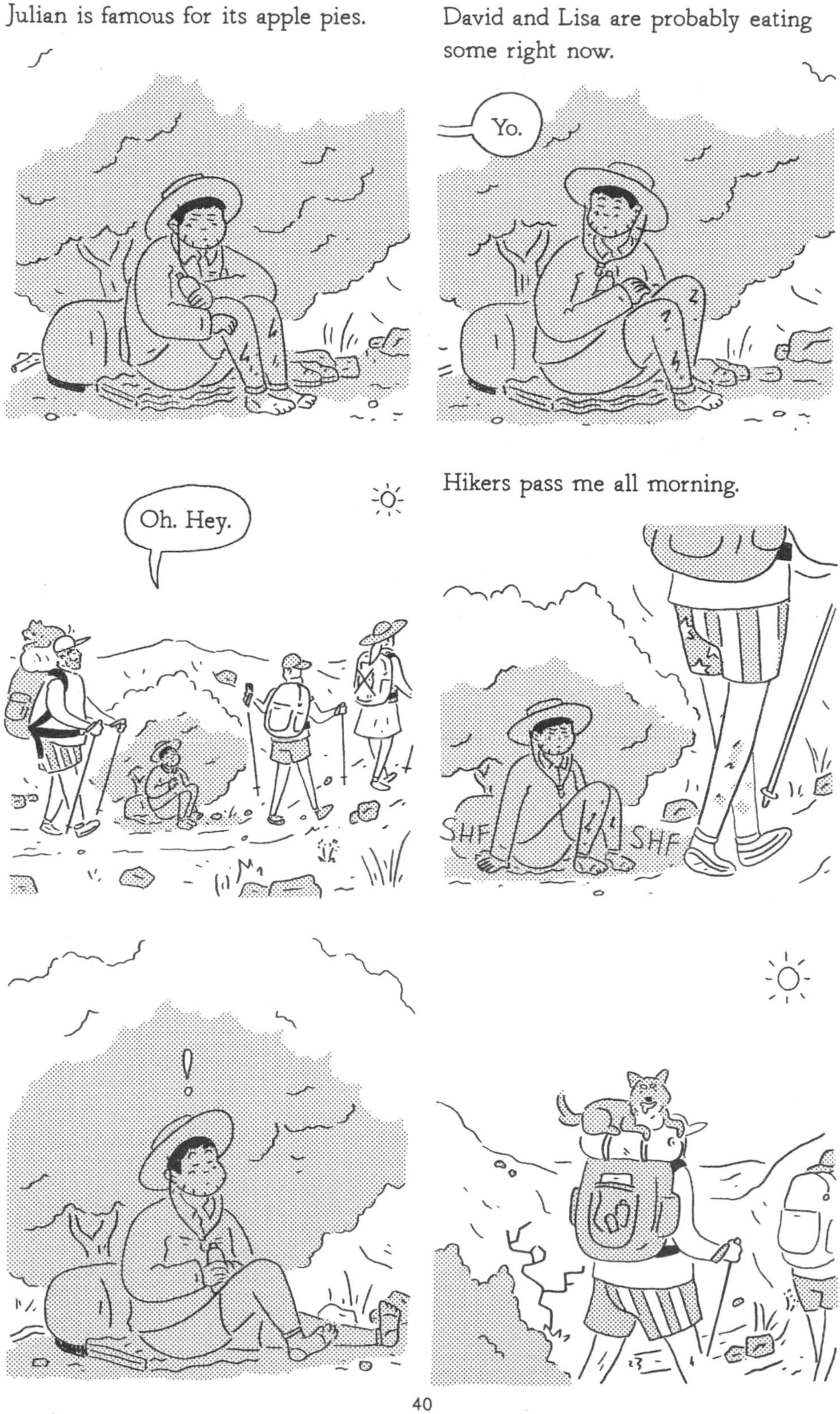
Julian is famous for its apple pies.
David and Lisa are probably eating some right now.
Yo.
Oh. Hey.
Hikers pass me all morning.
SHF
SHF
!

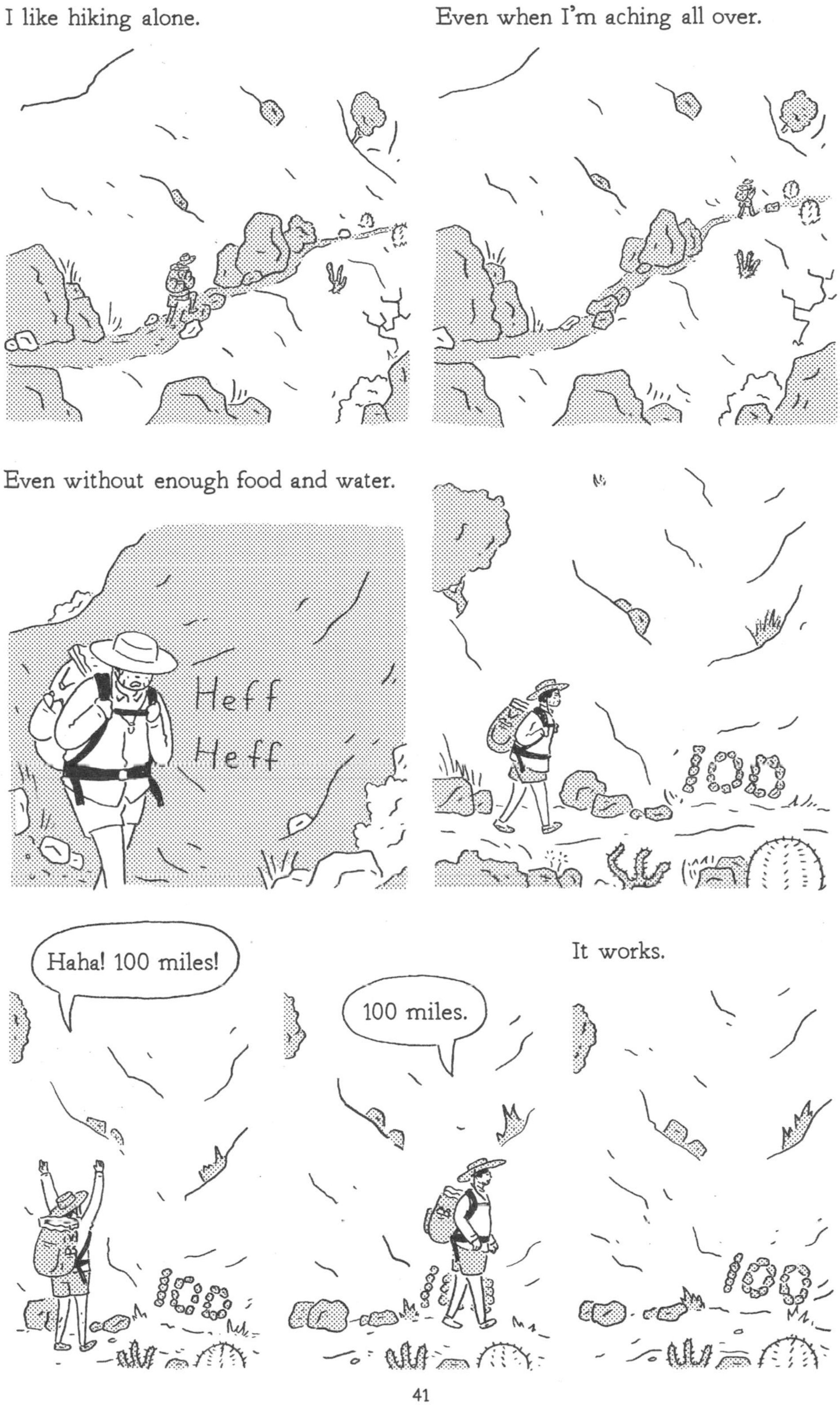
I like hiking alone.
Even when I'm aching all over.
Even without enough food and water.
Heff
Heff
100
Haha! 100 miles!
100 miles.
It works.

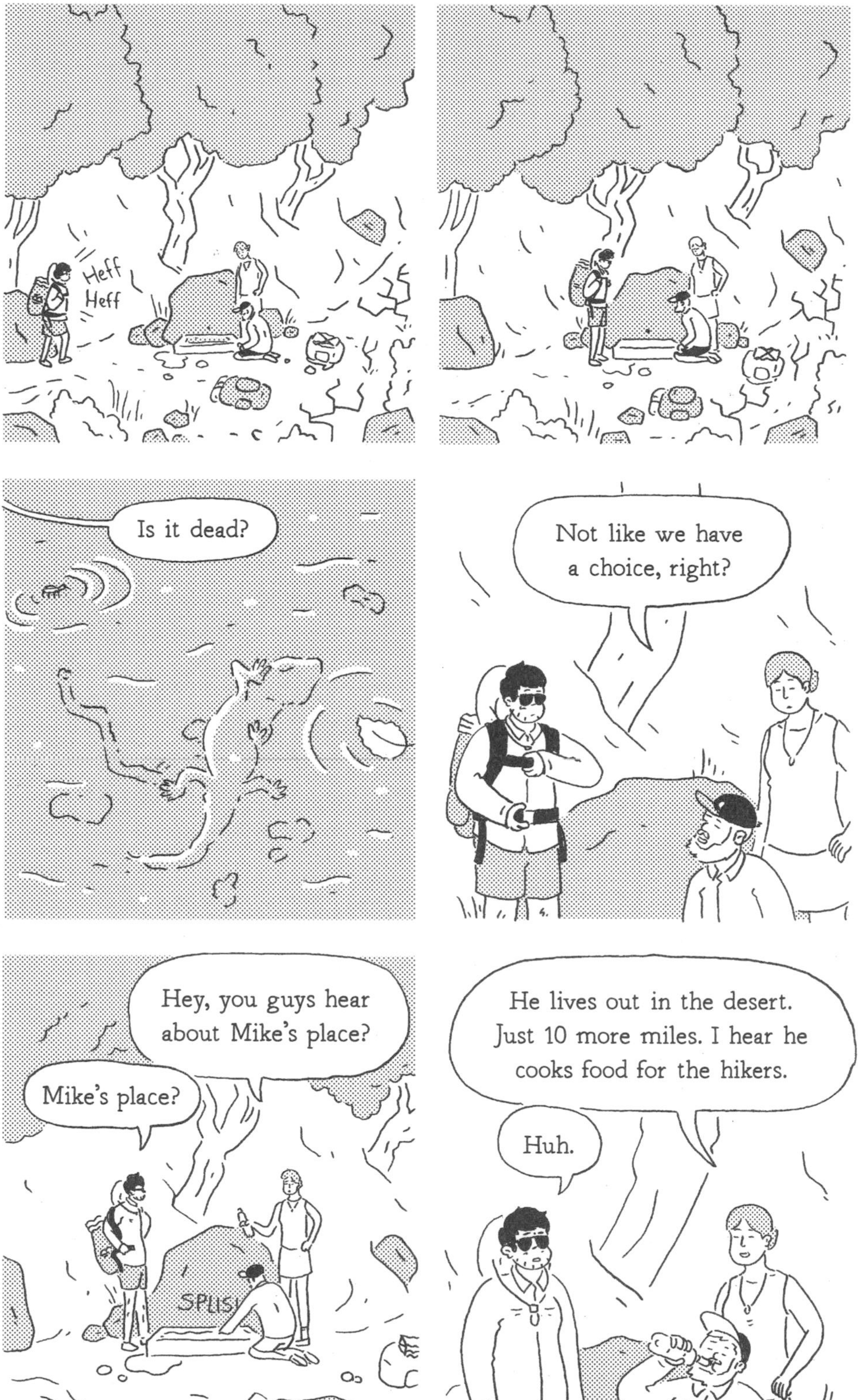
Heff
Heff
Is it dead?
Not like we have a choice, right?
Hey, you guys hear about Mike's place?
Mike's place?
SPLISH
He lives out in the desert. Just 10 more miles. I hear he cooks food for the hikers.
Huh.

Some combination of fatigue and dead lizard water slows me down. Getting to Mike's place would mean an eighteen-mile day, my longest so far. But the thought of my paltry food bag keeps me moving.

I also feel competitive. Every few hours some other fit-looking cluster of thruhikers pass me by. It makes me feel inept. My feet feel like they're going to burst.

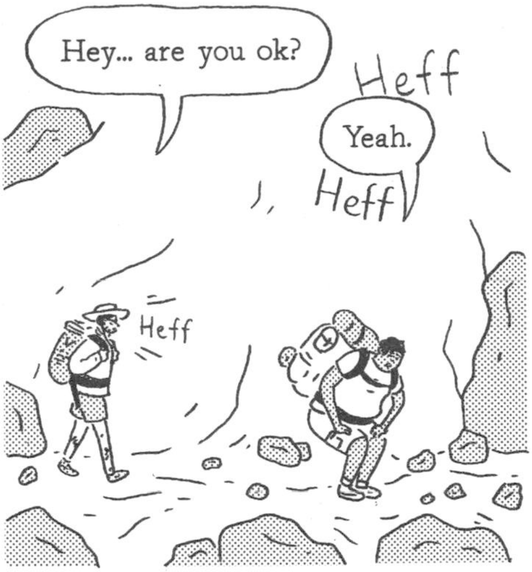
Hey... are you ok?
Heff
Yeah.
Heff
Heff

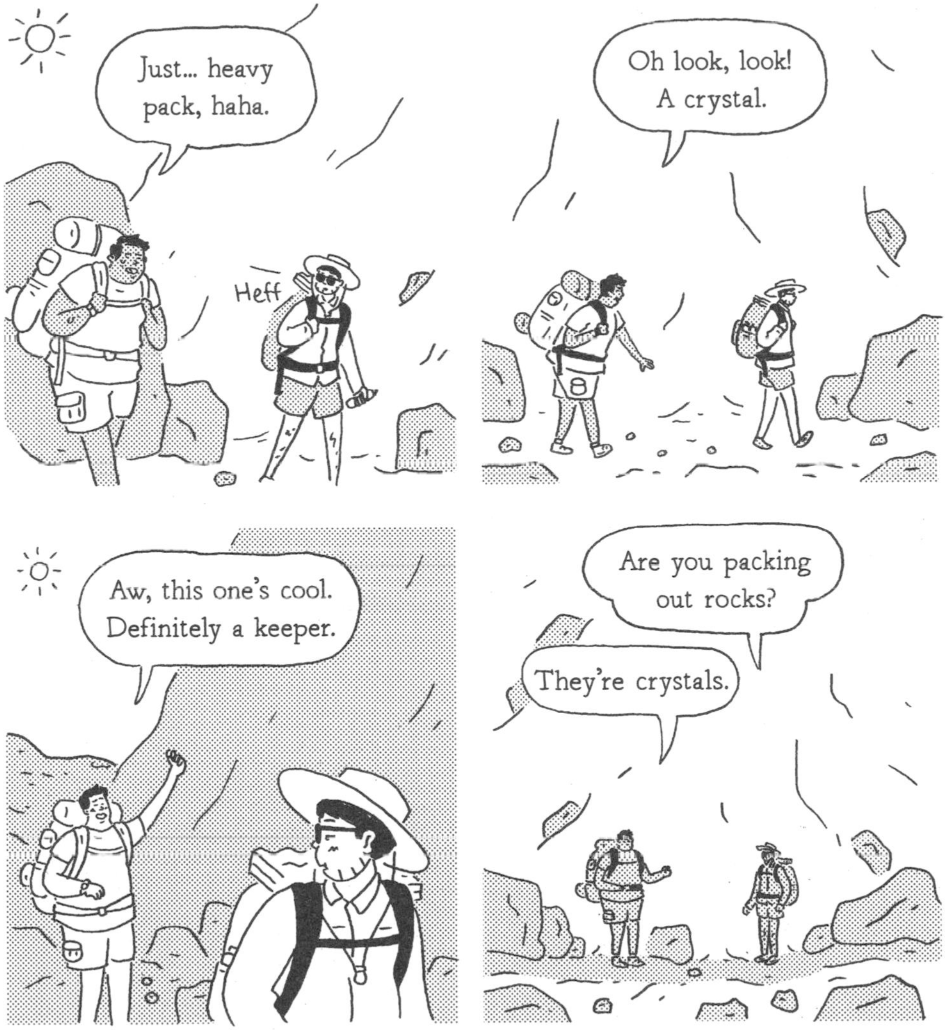
Just... heavy pack, haha.
Heff
Oh look, look! A crystal.
Aw, this one's cool. Definitely a keeper.
Are you packing out rocks?
They're crystals.

Even without crystals, my pack weighs a hundred tonnes.

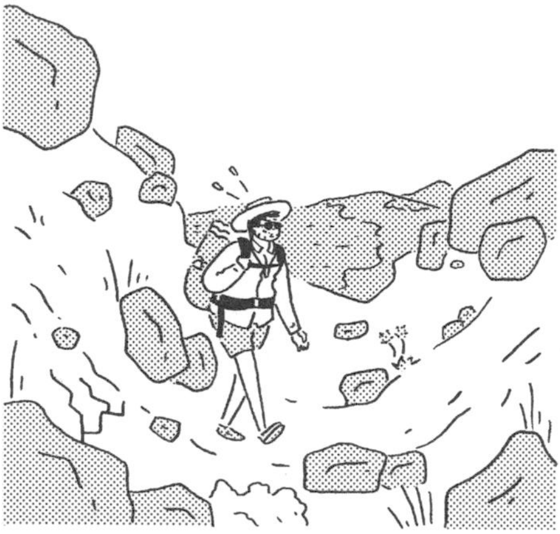

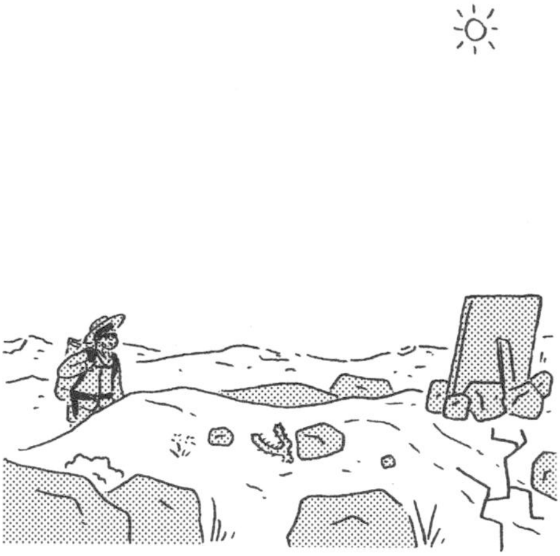

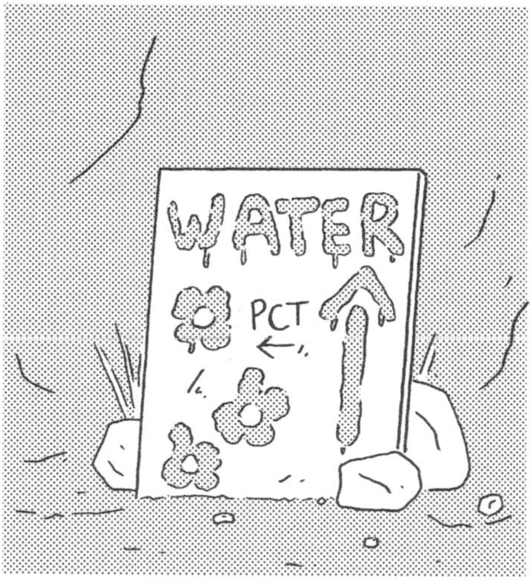
WATER
PCT

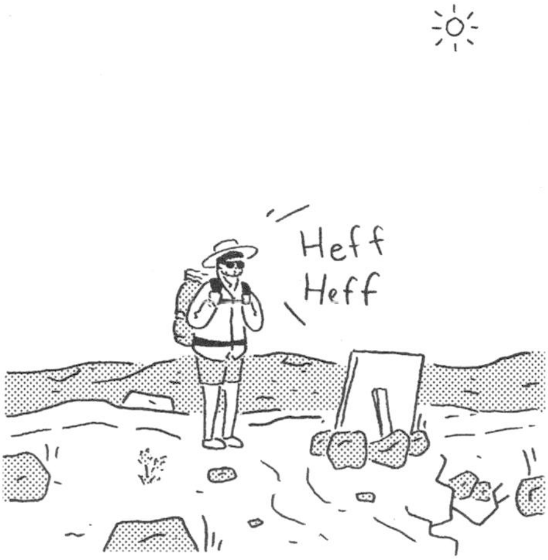
Heff
Heff

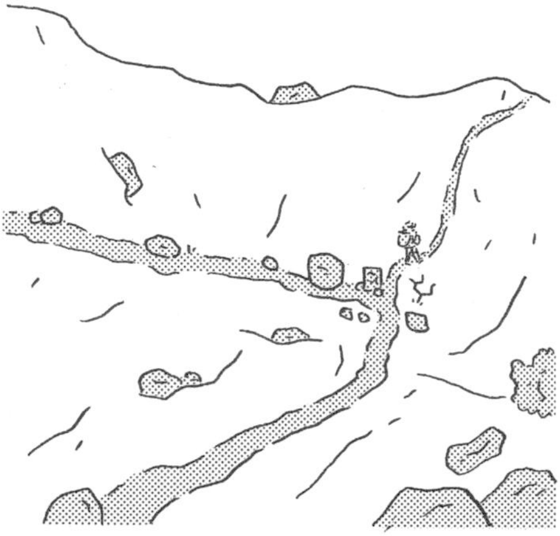

Taking soda from strangers.
Following tempting signs off trail.
My parents would be so proud.

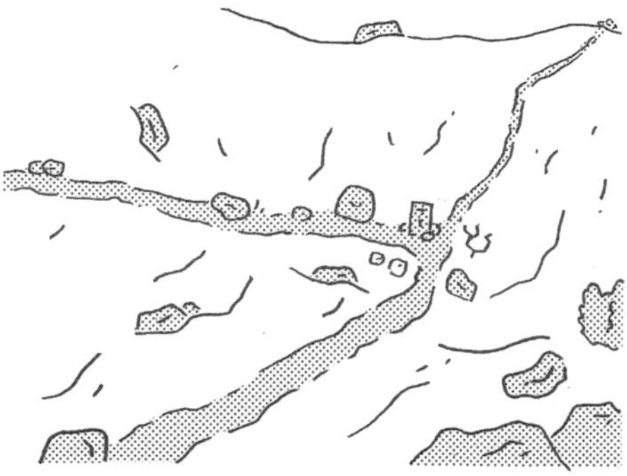

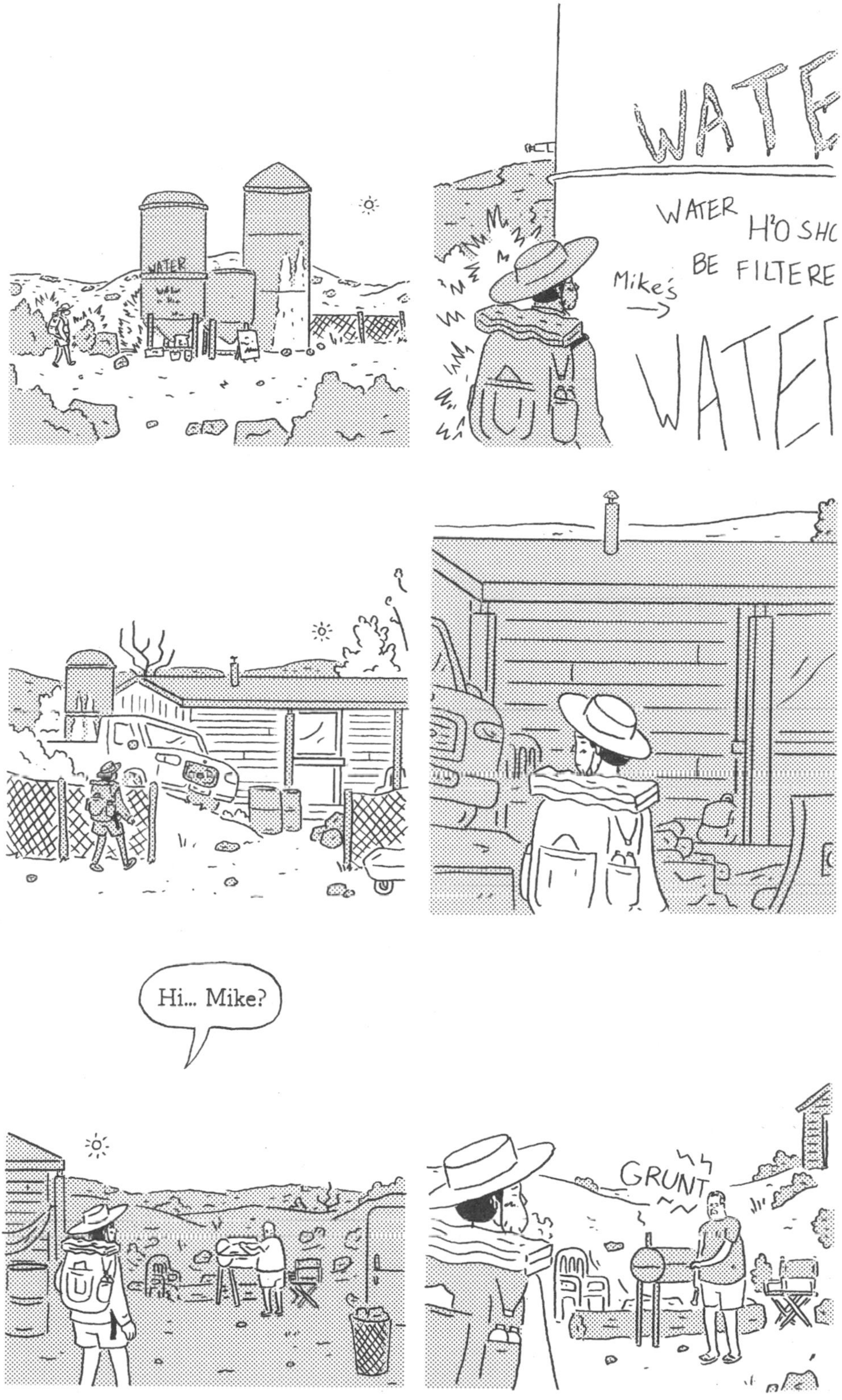
WATER
WATE
WATER
H2O SHC
BE FILTERE
Mike's →
WATE
Hi... Mike?
GRUNT

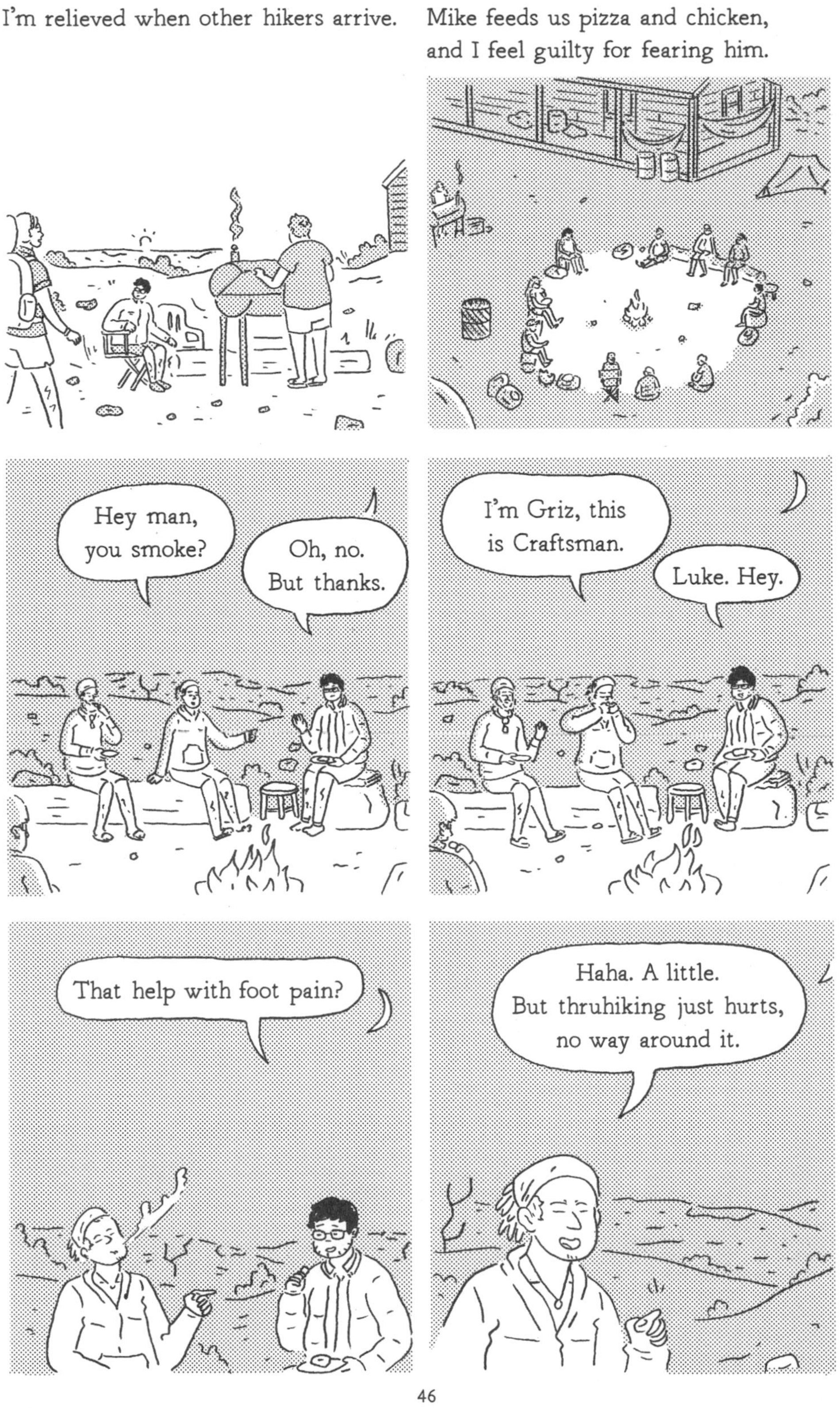
I'm relieved when other hikers arrive.
Mike feeds us pizza and chicken, and I feel guilty for fearing him.
Hey man, you smoke?
Oh, no. But thanks.
I'm Griz, this is Craftsman.
Luke. Hey.
That help with foot pain?
Haha. A little. But thruhiking just hurts, no way around it.

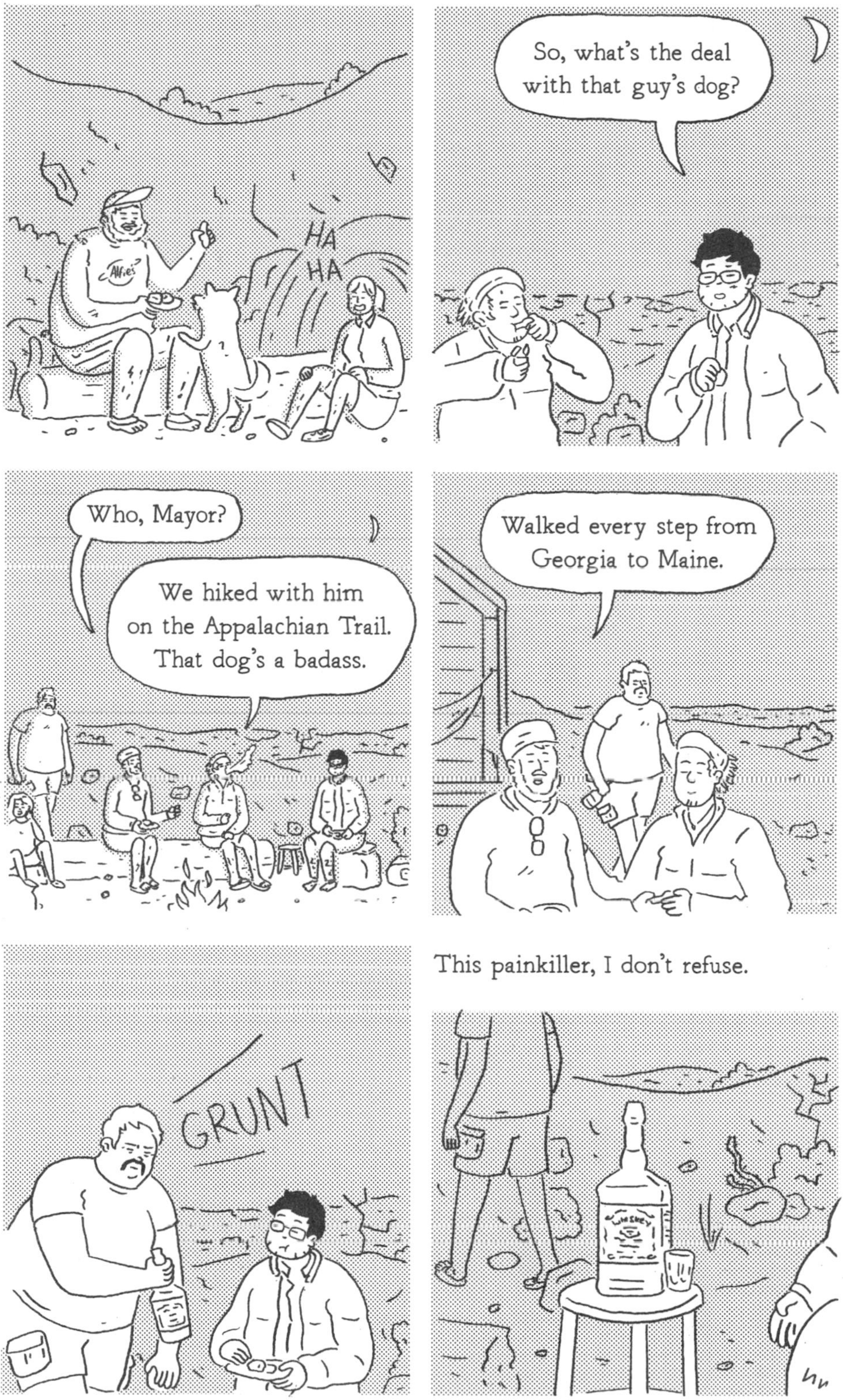
HA
HA
So, what's the deal with that guy's dog?
Who, Mayor?
We hiked with him on the Appalachian Trail. That dog's a badass.
Walked every step from Georgia to Maine.
GRUNT
This painkiller, I don't refuse.

I get a cot in a broken down shack on Mike's property.

Even though I'm a little drunk, and dead tired, it's still too cold to sleep.

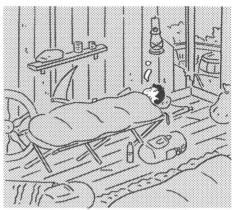

I can see the stars through a hole in the ceiling.

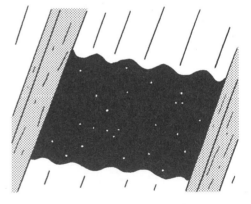

It's so, so quiet here.

I mingle a little with the hiking groups as we congregate around water sources, and lie in the shade of the weird-looking Joshua trees.

Griz and Craftsman both hike in sandals, with bare toes open to the dust and rocks and blazing sun.

Three hikers who look like models from an adventure magazine criss-cross with me, and we exchange greetings but not much more. I'm in a crappy mood. Pushing for Mike's place was a mistake. My body wasn't ready. My right knee throbs with bright, hot pain.

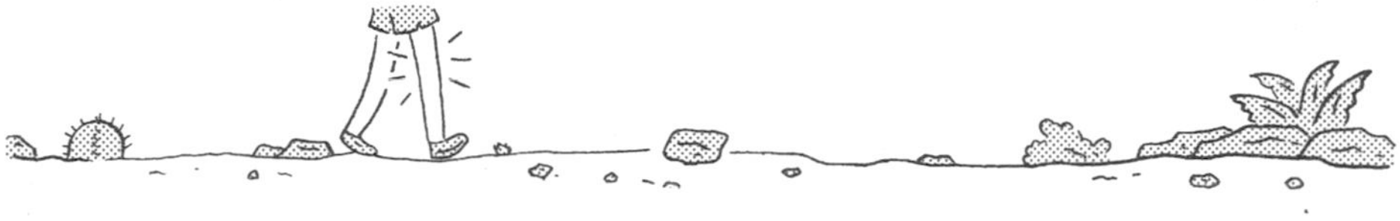

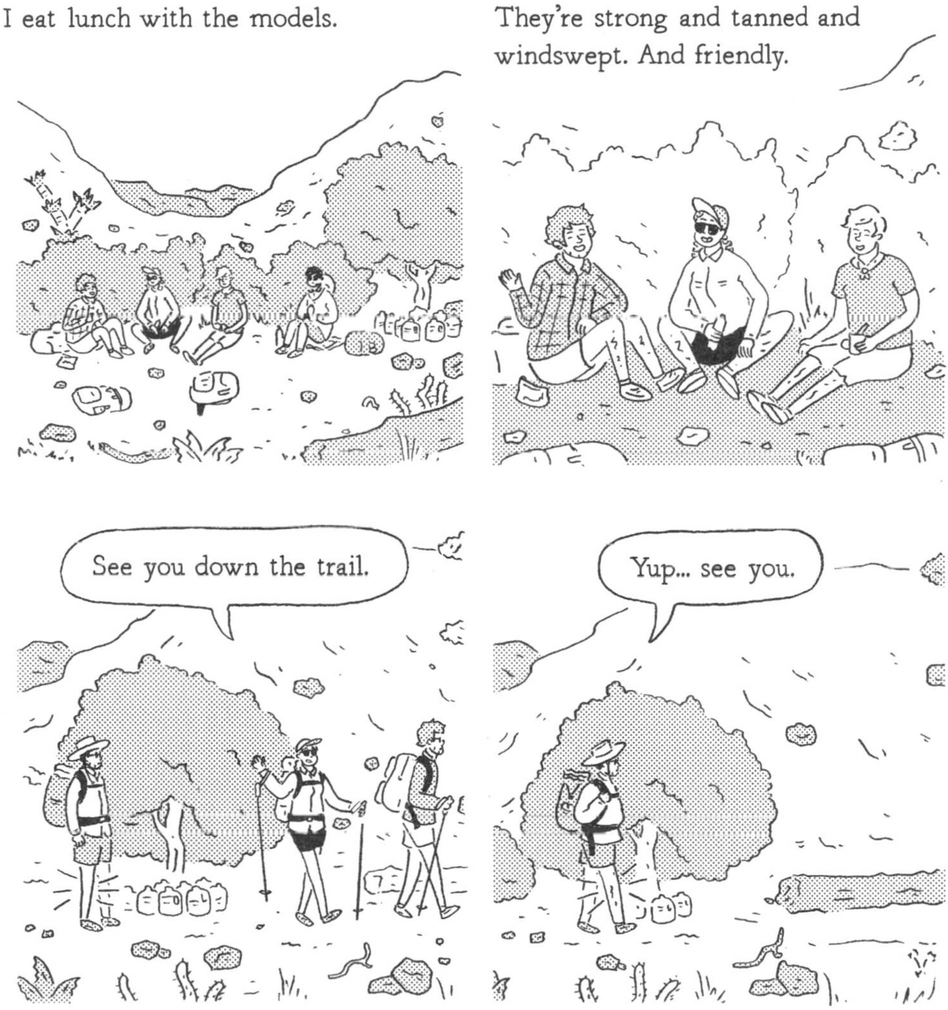
I eat lunch with the models.
They're strong and tanned and windswept. And friendly.
See you down the trail.
Yup... see you.

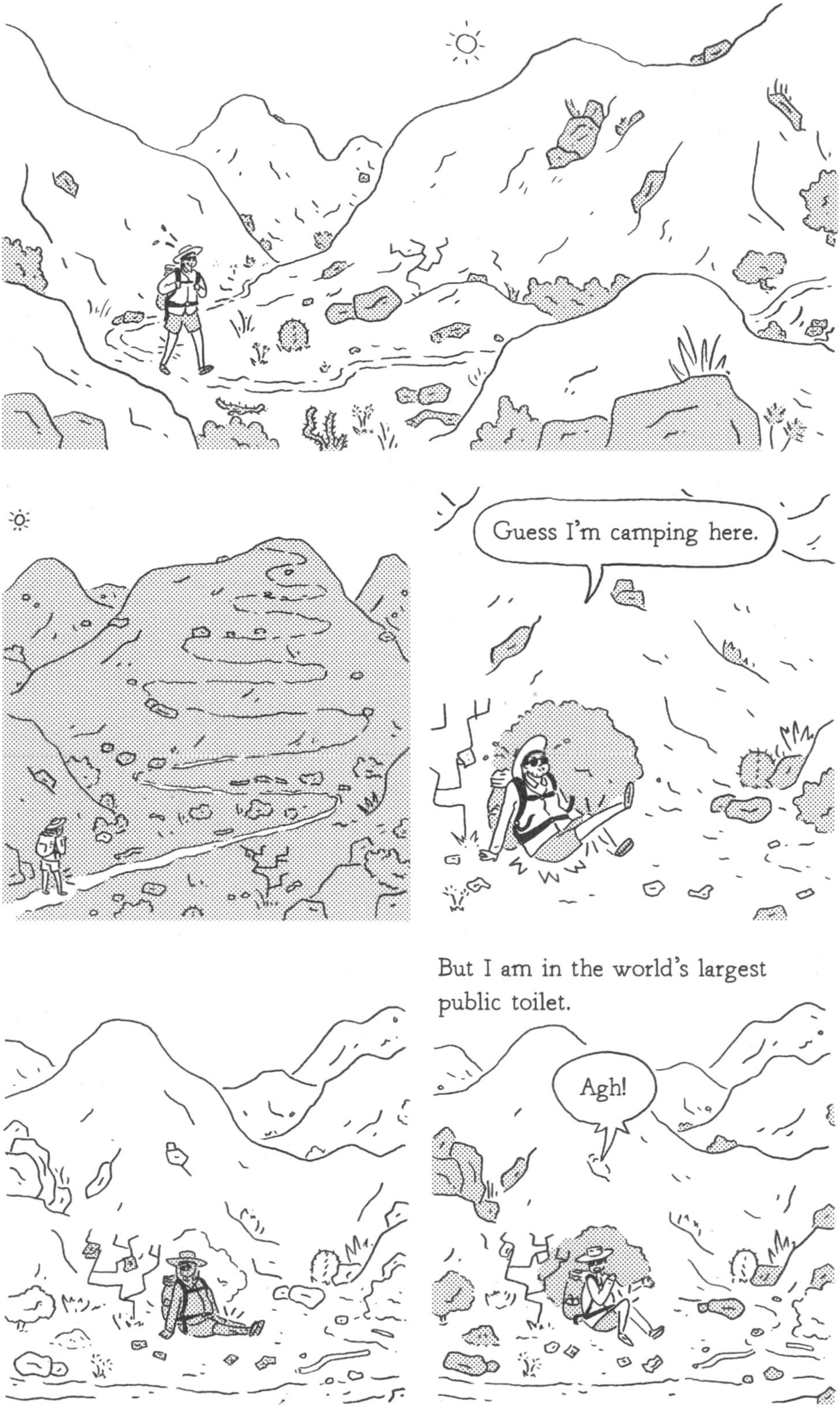
Guess I'm camping here.
But I am in the world's largest public toilet.
Agh!

Fuck people who don't bury their shit.

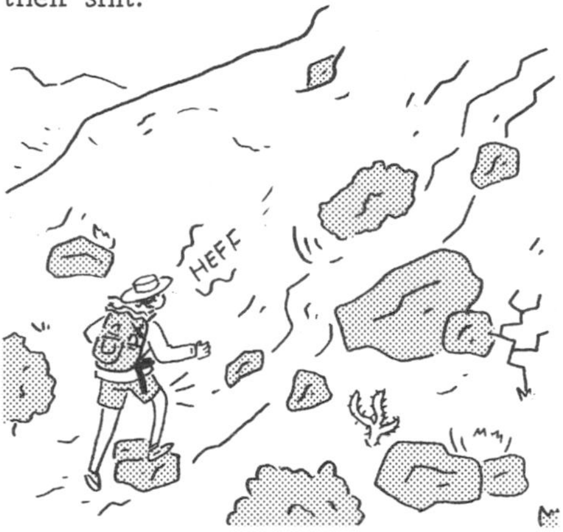
HEFF

Fuck people who don't pack out their toilet paper.

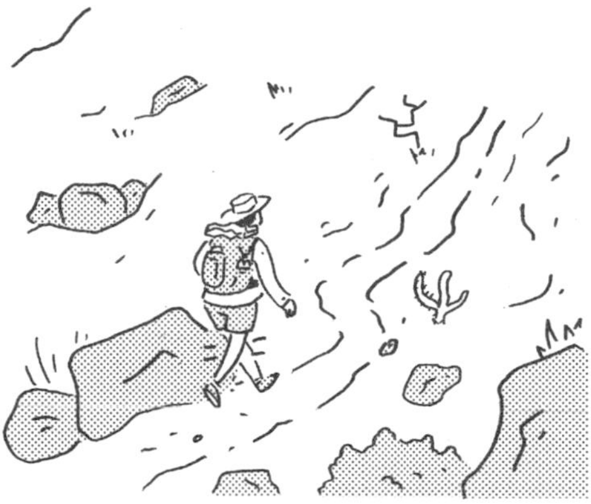

Fuck this hill.

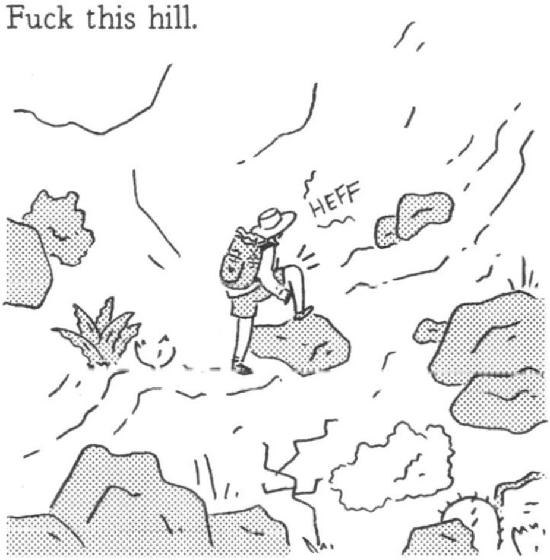
HEFF

Fuck this trail.

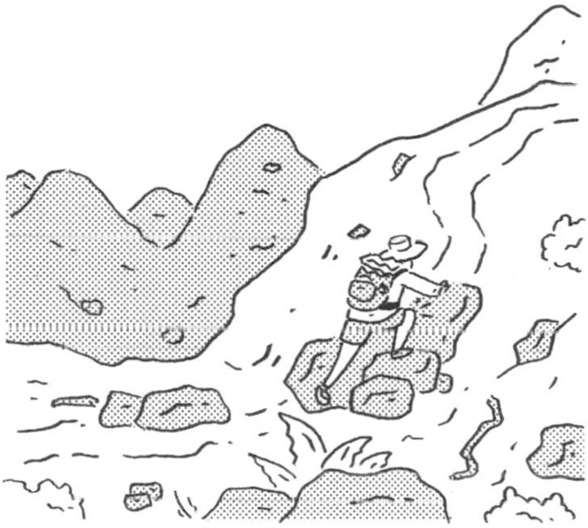

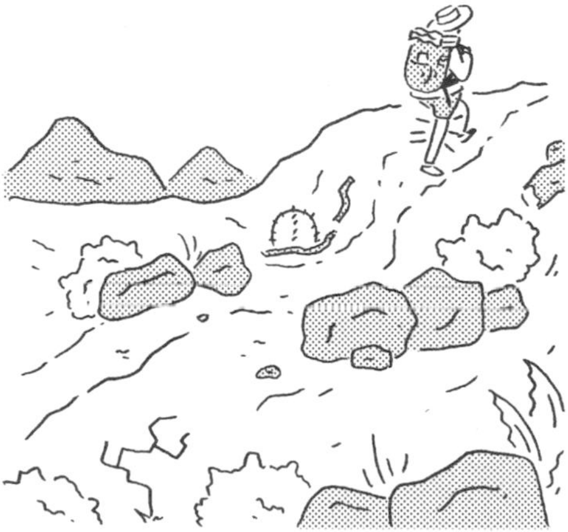

Fuck my big idiot self.

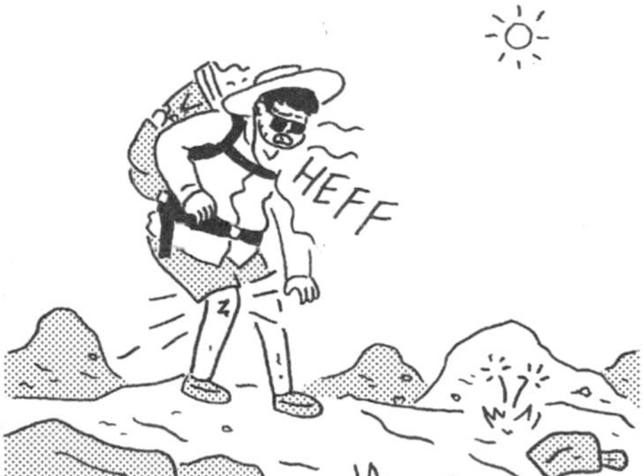
HEFF

I limp pathetically to the next water cache, hoping to camp there.

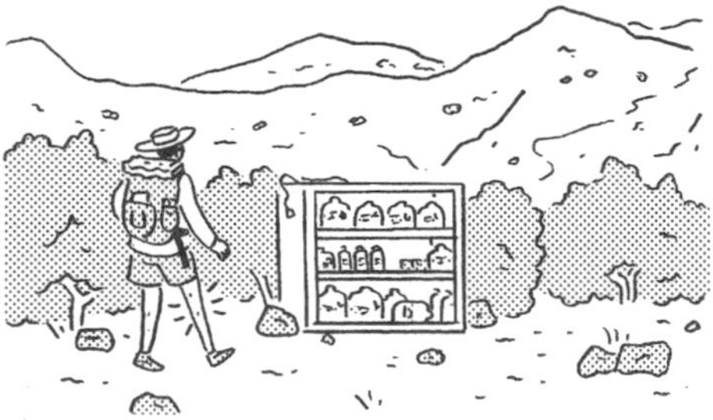

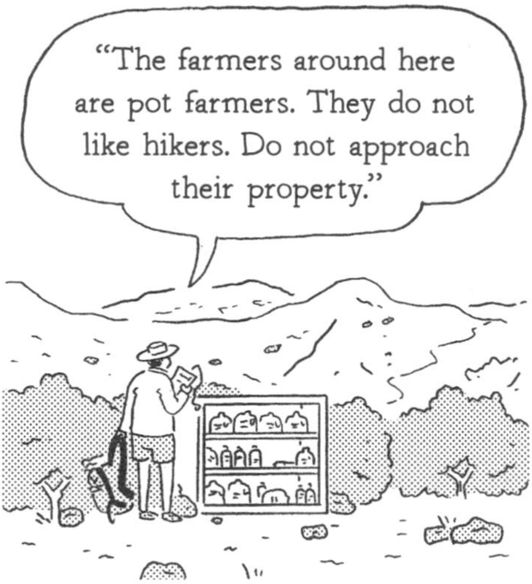
"The farmers around here are pot farmers. They do not like hikers. Do not approach their property."

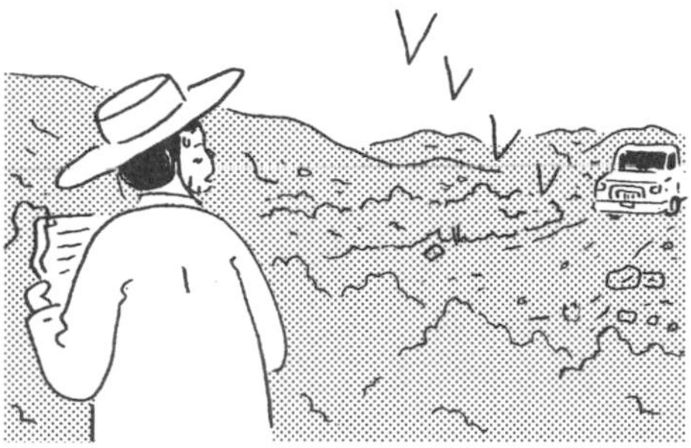
VVVV

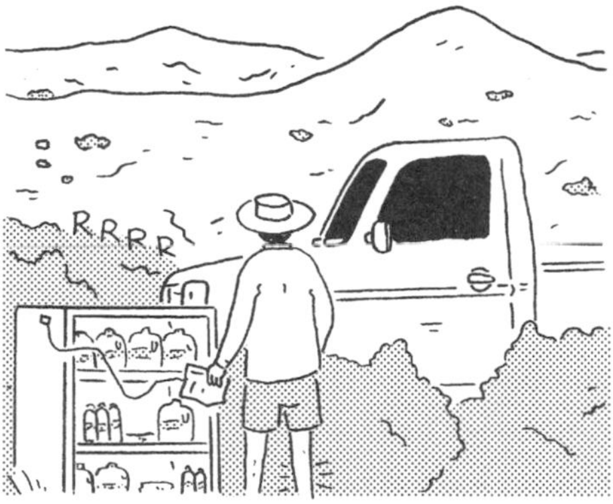
RRRR

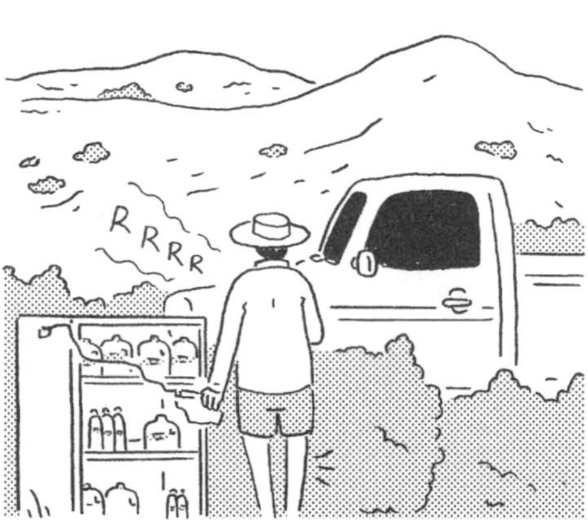
RRRR

I limp on.

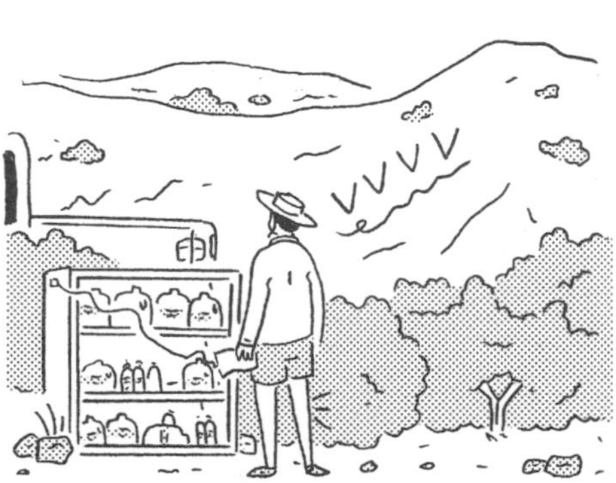
VVVV

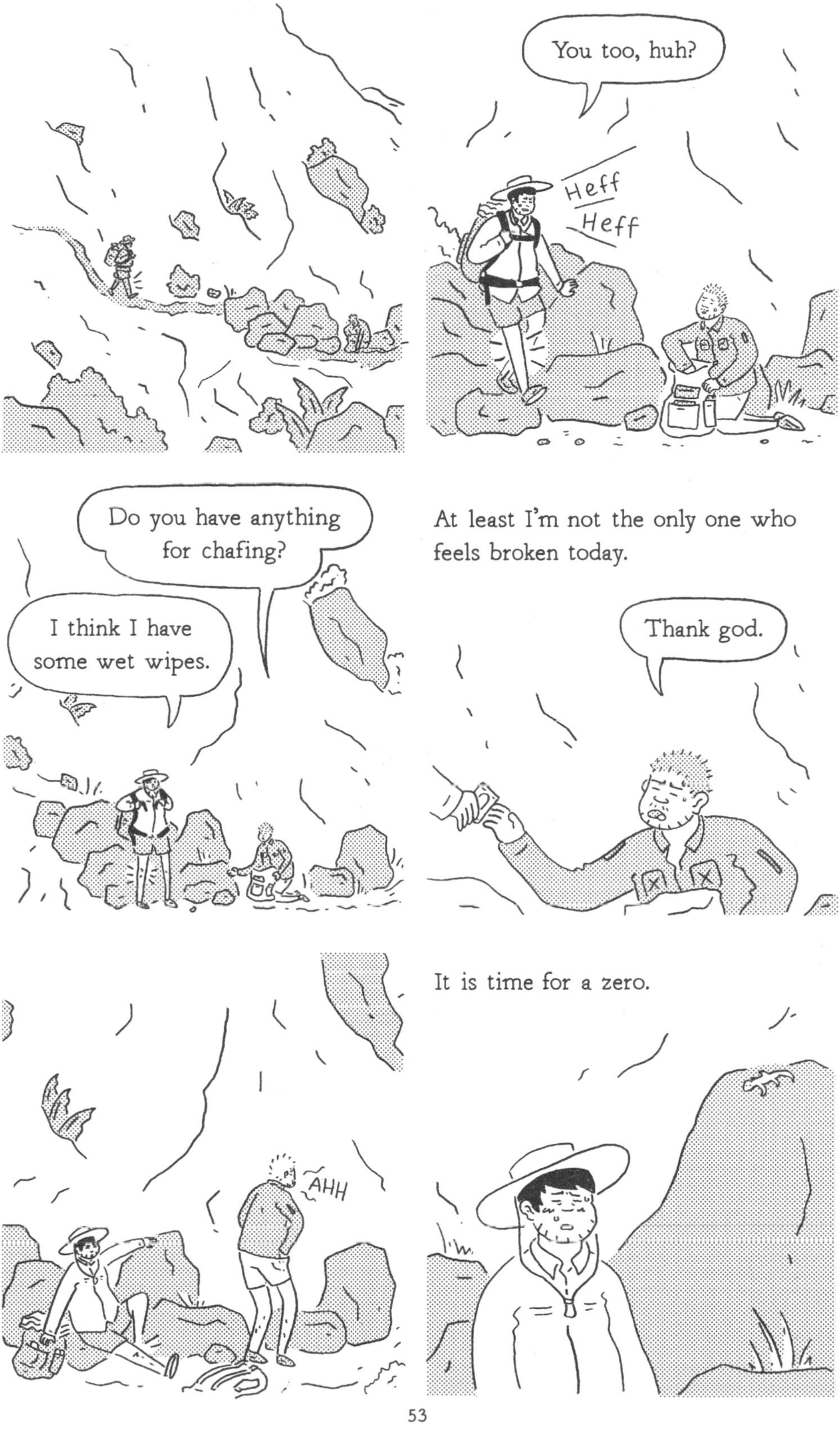
You too, huh?
Heff
Heff
Do you have anything for chafing?
I think I have some wet wipes.
At least I'm not the only one who feels broken today.
Thank god.
AHH
It is time for a zero.

Idyllwild 24/04/16. Day 9.

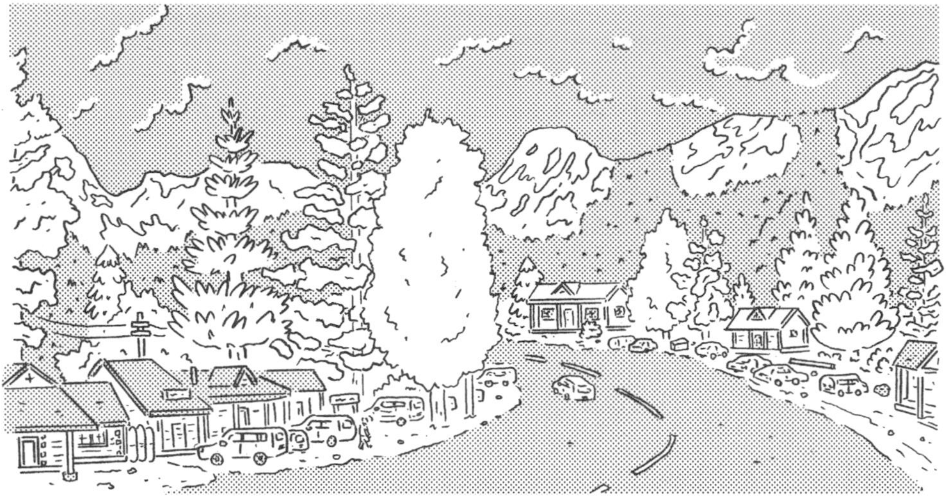

I hitch-hike to Idyllwild, a small town perched on the side of Mt. San Jacinto. Even in Southern California, increased altitude means dropping temperatures. From town, looking higher up the mountain, I can see little snowfields, unmelted by the springtime sun.

Hikers are easy to spot.

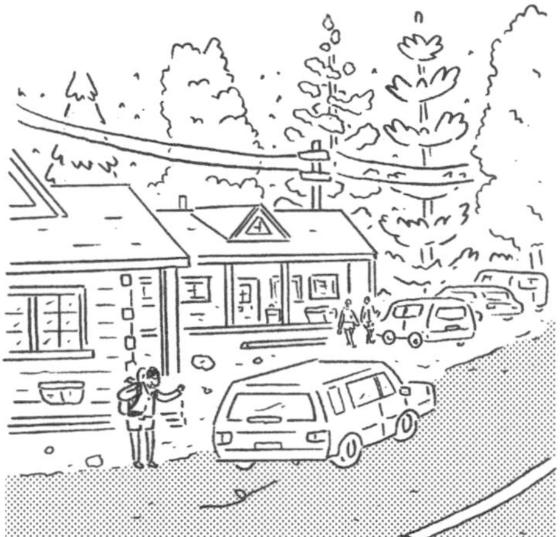

Clumped together in their desert shirts and running shorts.

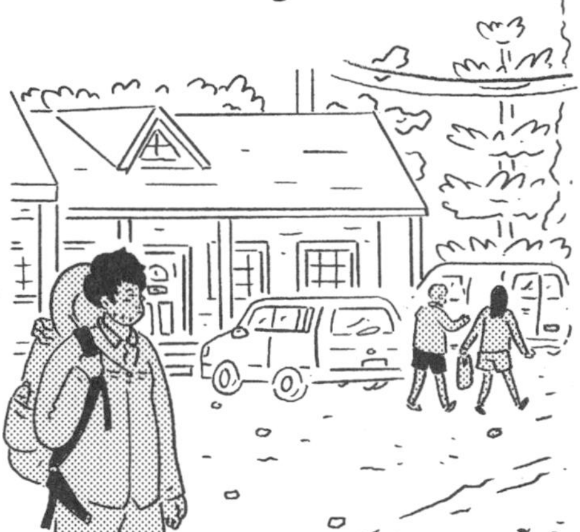

There's a little complex of cabins, tucked away into the woods. They've just rented out their last room to another hiker, who's willing to share.

Eli is twenty-one, only a few years younger than I am, but he seems younger than that. He enthusiastically invites me to stay, eager to split the cost of the room.

Outside, it begins to snow.

"Worst desert ever," we joke. We're asleep by 10 pm; "hiker midnight" to everyone waking with the sunrise and walking themselves to the point of exhaustion.

Eli and the others leave early in the morning, heading back to trail. I'm left alone in the cabin. It's the first time since Campo that I've had any real privacy. I expected to relish the feeling but instead I just feel lonely. And jealous of hikers who have already found their groups.

I try to take advantage of my zero day, though I know I should be resting my knee. After twenty-four hours off trail, I am walking with "hiker hobble" - an uneven gait that indicates the inevitable combination of joint, muscle and foot pain. At the local gear store, I buy some trekking poles, hoping they will help.

While I'm there, I ask the owner if he has anything to keep my quilt warmer at night. He recommends a neon orange emergency bivvy – basically a rain jacket for my sleeping bag, just big enough to fit inside of. I'm unsure if it will help, but it's small and light, so I take it.

As my zero wears on, more hikers I know arrive into town and I scrape together enough of them to fill the cabin once again. I split the cabin's bed with Stacy, and the others scatter themselves around the floor, surrounded by bright nylon gear and grubby ziplock bags.

I wake early and head back to the trail alone. The other hikers here are friendly, and invite me to spend more time with them. They'd be a good group to hike with. But I leave, still too restless to stop.

Mt. San Jacinto 26/04/16. Day 11.

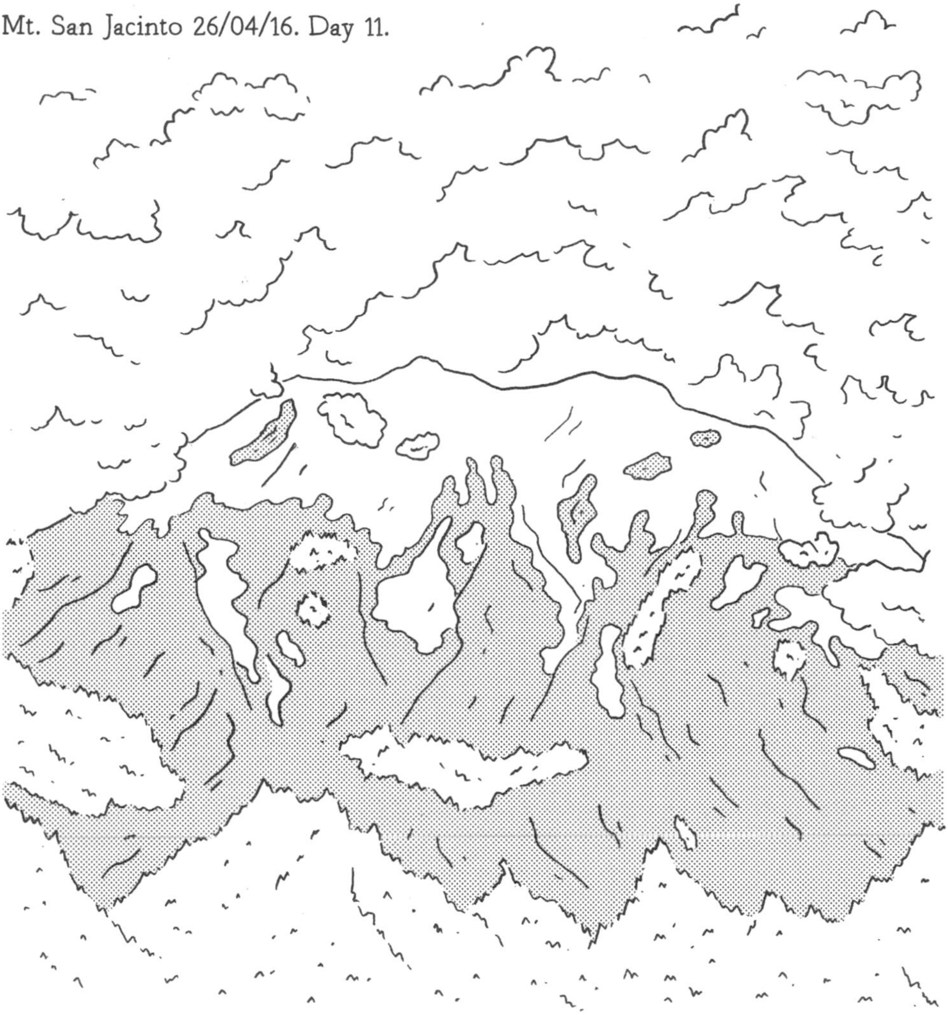

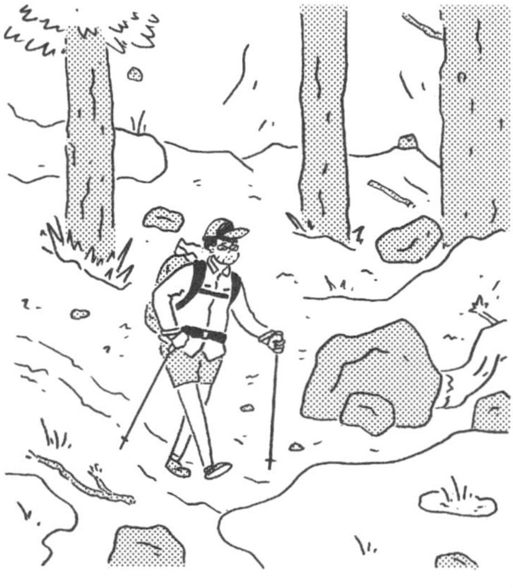

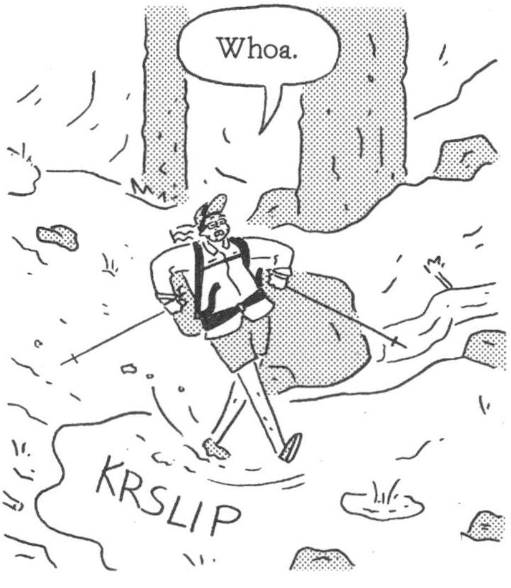
Whoa.
KRSLIP

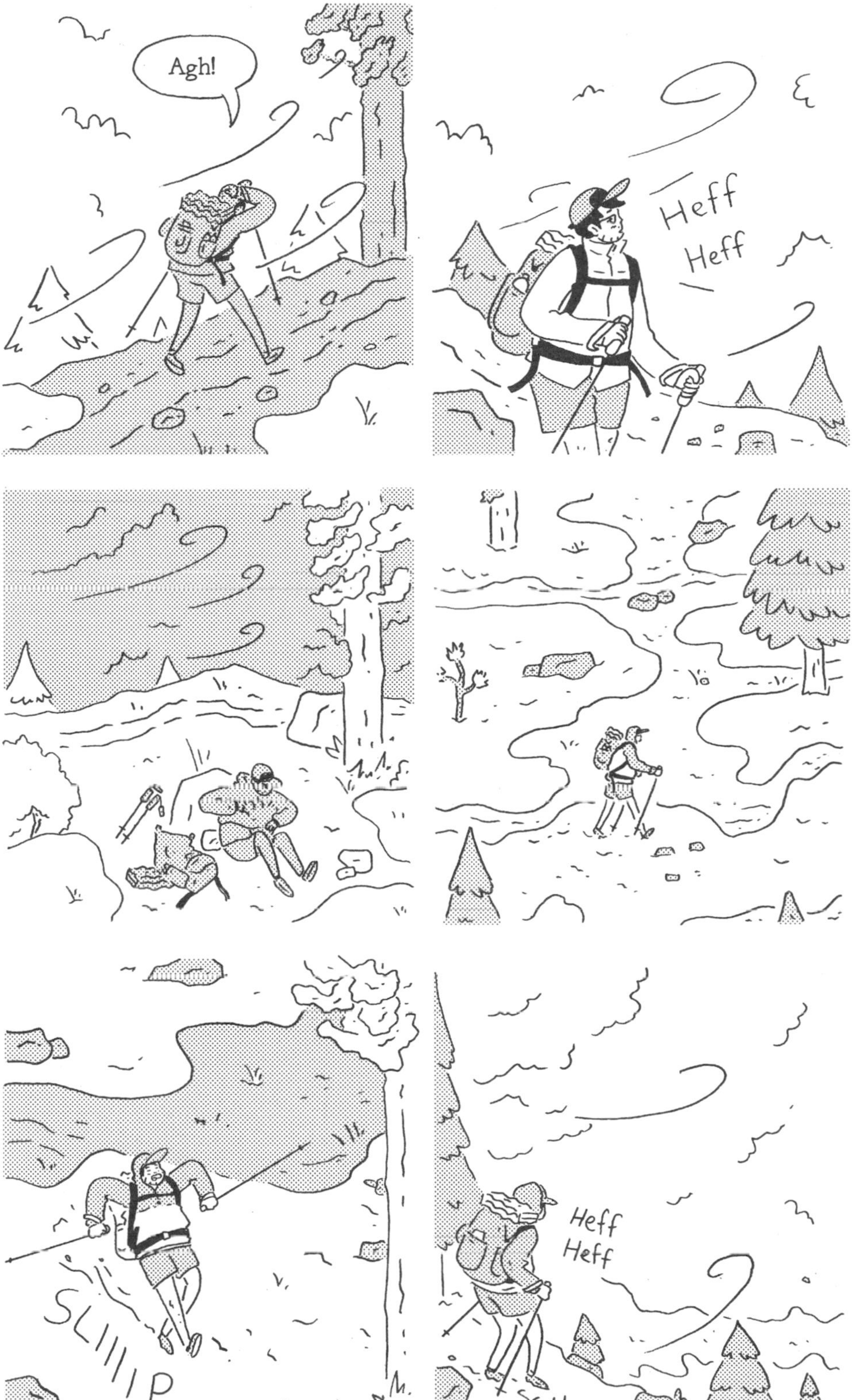
Agh!
Heff
Heff
SLIIIIP
Heff
Heff
SSH

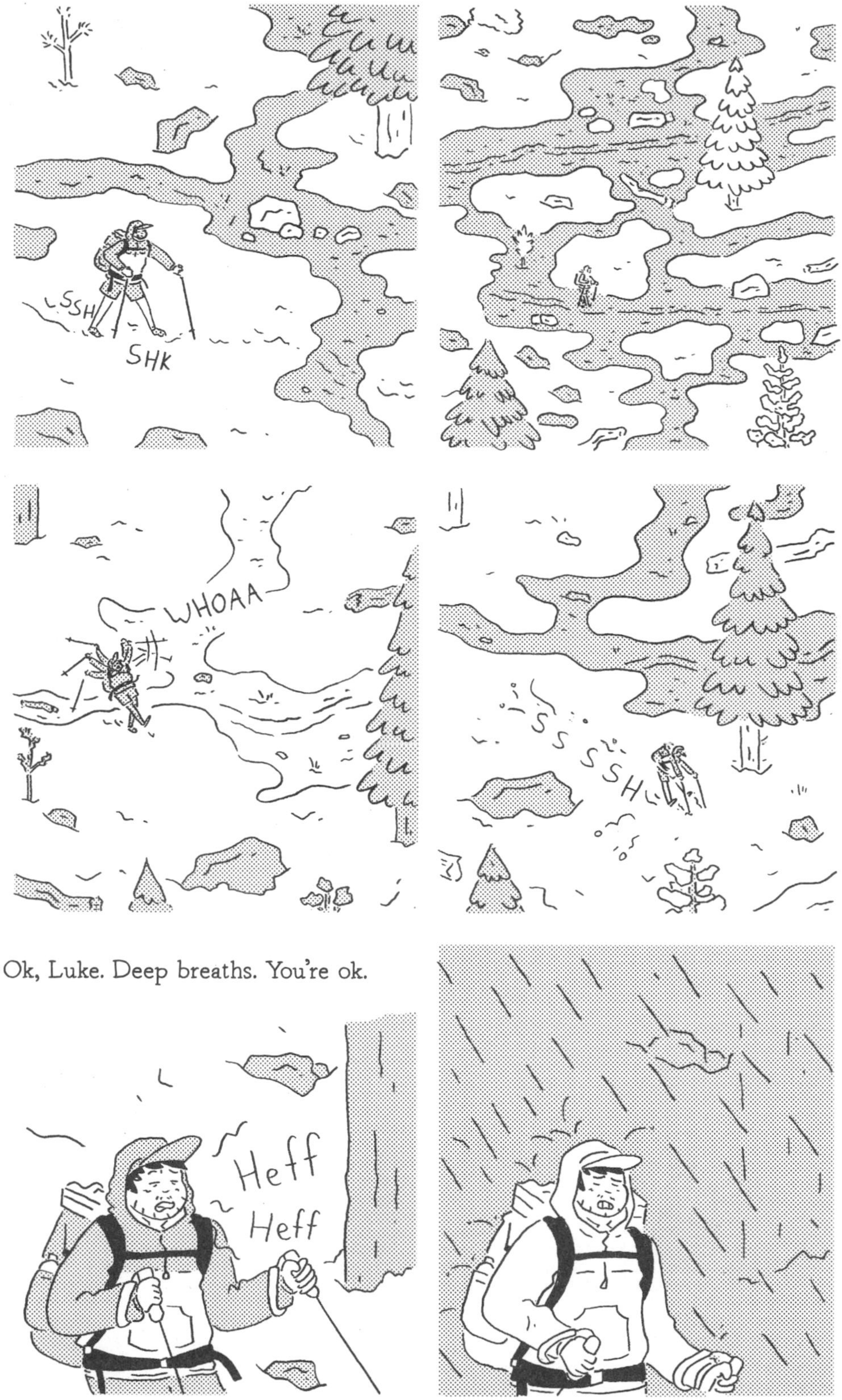
LSSH
SHK
WHOAA
SSSSH
Ok, Luke. Deep breaths. You're ok.
Heff
Heff

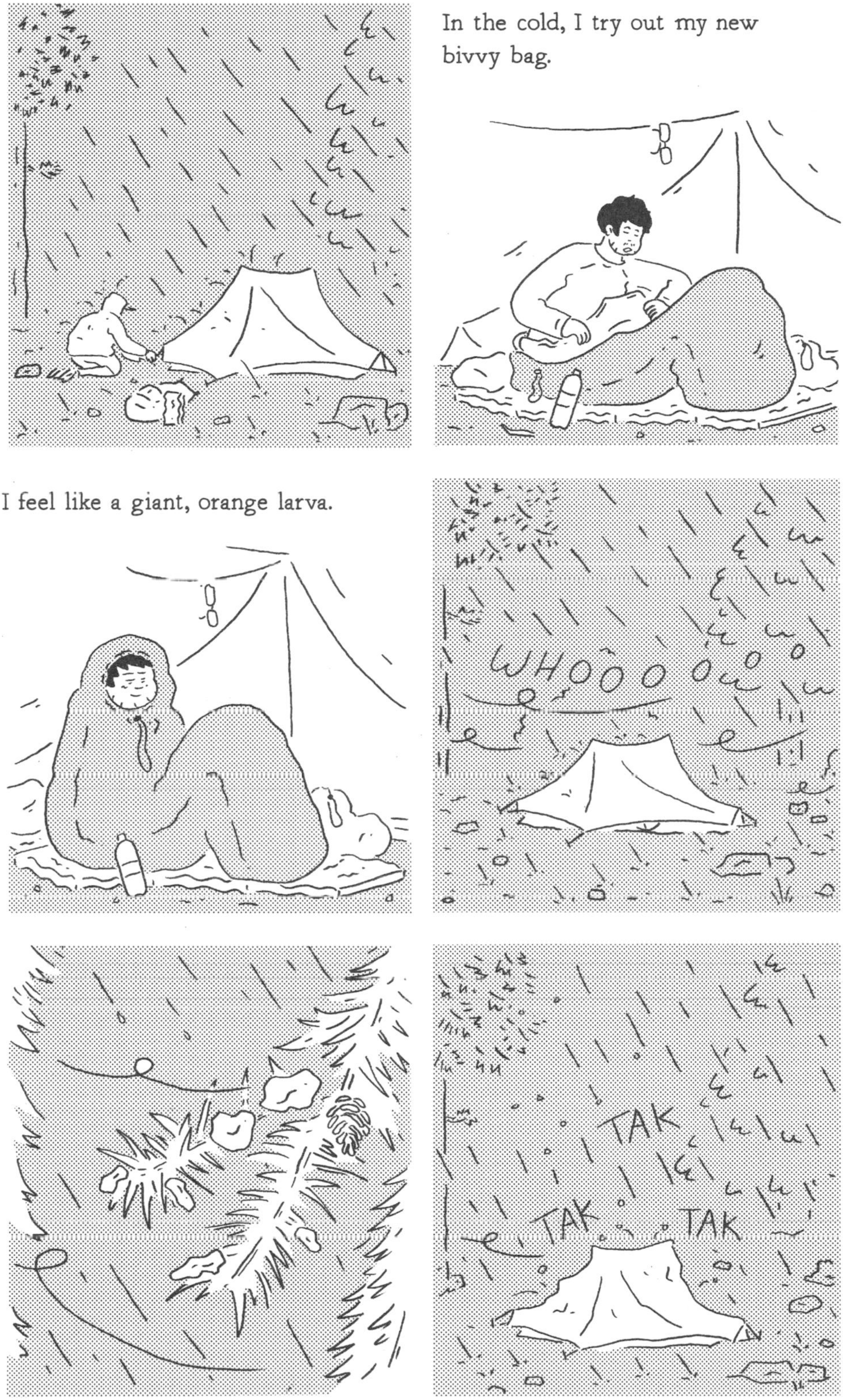
In the cold, I try out my new bivvy bag.
I feel like a giant, orange larva.
WHOOOOOO
TAK
TAK
TAK

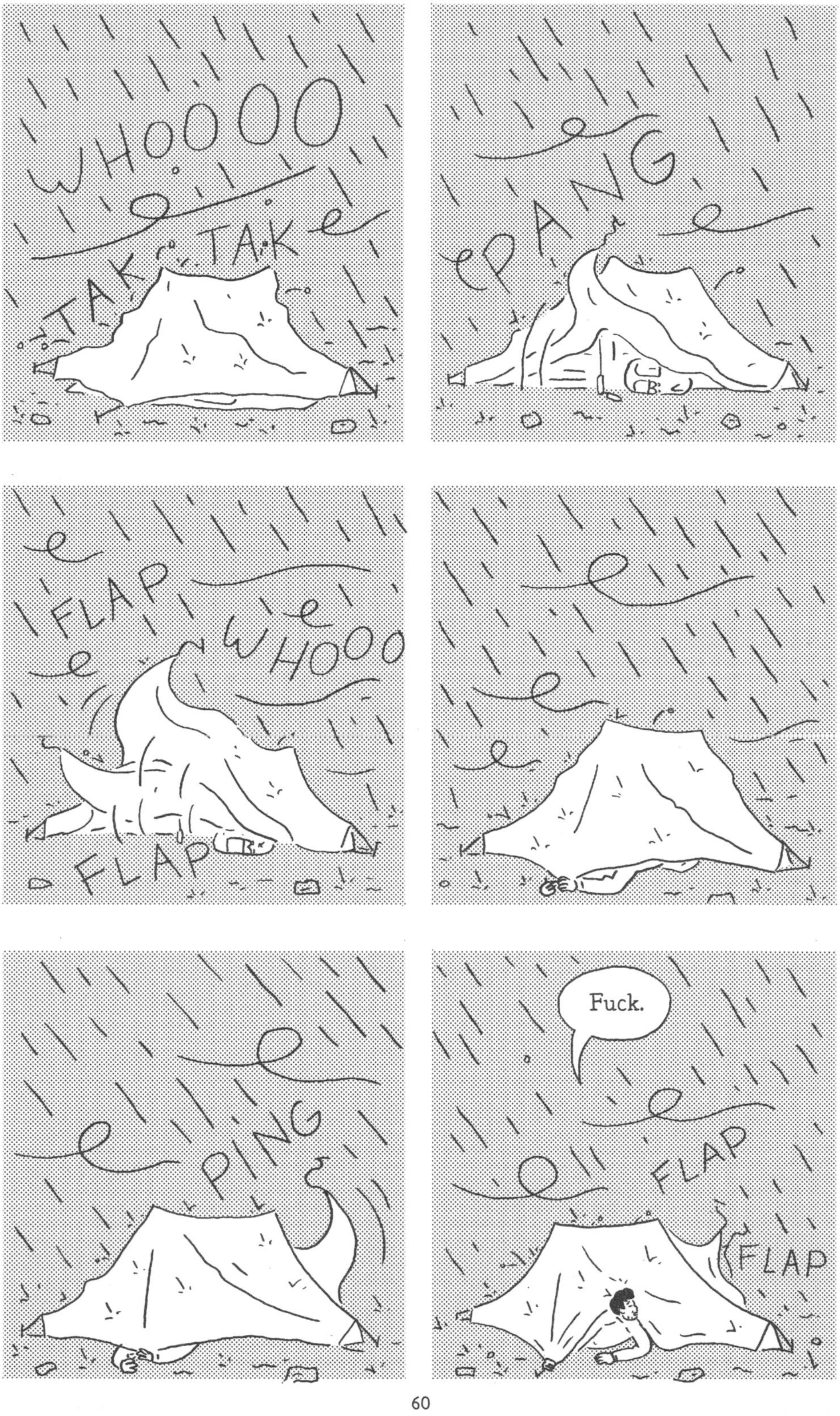
WHOOOO
TAK
TAK
PANG
FLAP
WHOOO
FLAP
PING
Fuck.
FLAP
FLAP

By morning, I am wet, frozen and exhausted. When the sun rises
and I finally crawl my way out of the sodden, half-collapsed tent,
I am surprised to see a group of hikers gathered around a fire just
a few dozen feet away.

Griz and Craftsman, the laidback hikers from Mike's place, warm their
hands with the rest of their crew.

They are hikertrash in the best sense; a term for people who fully
assimilate to life on trail. Filthy, gutsy, ready to grab a nap anywhere,
accept any hitch and eat even the most revolting of snack food.

"I reckon we'll just hitch around," Griz says as I approach the fire.
"Sounds good to me."

"How come you're hitching?" I ask. "Sick of the PCT already?"

"There's a fire closure," Griz responds. "A big one too. Recent."

"From 2014 I think," Craftsman adds.

"Yeah, it's like a fifty-mile burn. Unless you want to hike on the
highway's hard shoulder you'll need to hitch."

As I roll this over in my head, more hikers emerge from their tents. The adventure magazine models. They reintroduce themselves; Bojangles, the woman, and Ethan and Tumnus, brothers who look so similar, I have a hard time telling them apart.

"Are you all hitching around the fire closure too?" I ask.

"No, we're catching a ride with our Uncle Canyon. He lives in Palm Springs, only a few miles from San Jacinto," the brothers answer. Canyon has a shower, they say. And a pool. Canyon has it made.

"We're gonna stay the night at his place. Take a shower, swim a little. Then tomorrow he'll drive us past the closure."

I feel a surge of bravery rise in my gut. The models seem friendly and have a way around the fire closure. What would real hikertrash do?

"Hey, you guys mind if I tag along?" I ask.

"The more the merrier."

We wind our way down the snaking switchbacks.

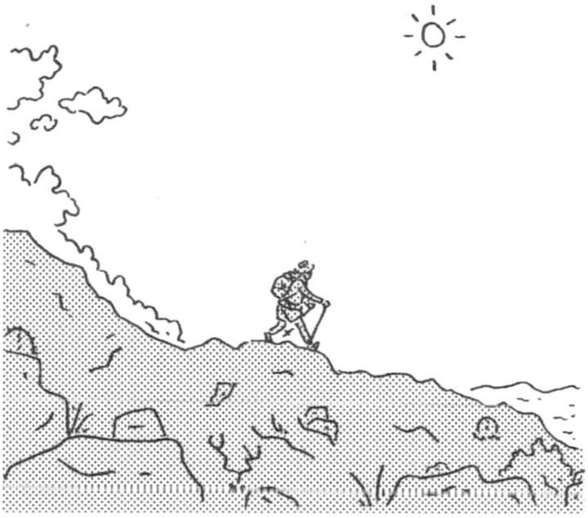

Across the valley, the hills are covered with enormous wind turbines.

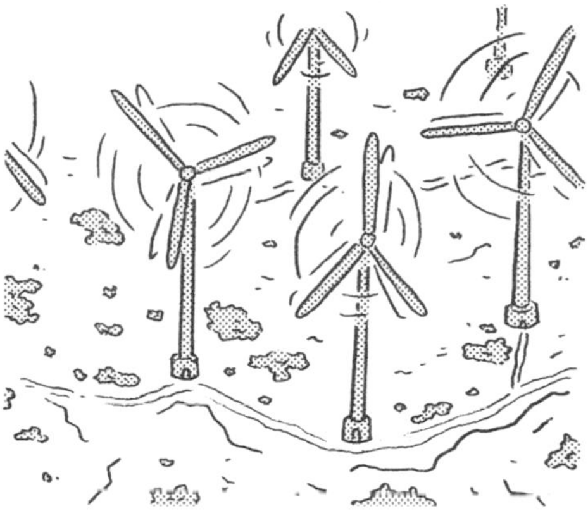

A highway runs through the valley below. We can hear the cars, even from thousands of feet up.

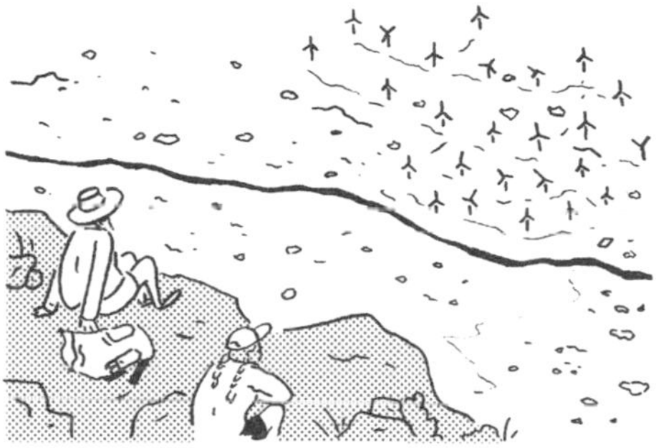

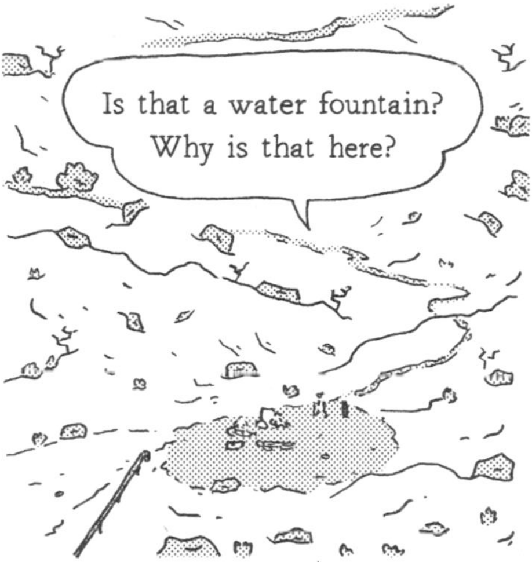
Is that a water fountain? Why is that here?

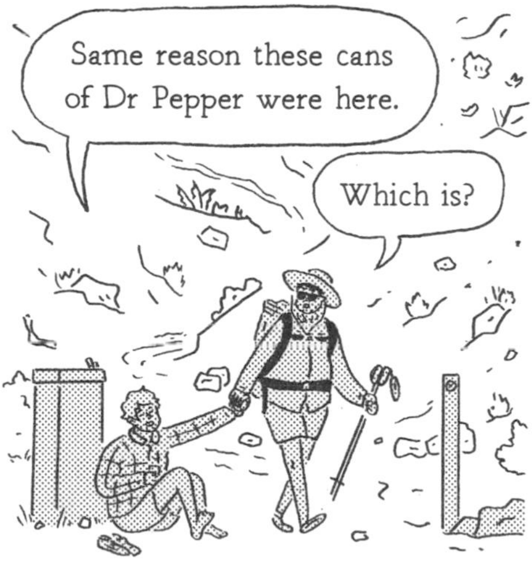
Same reason these cans of Dr Pepper were here.
Which is?

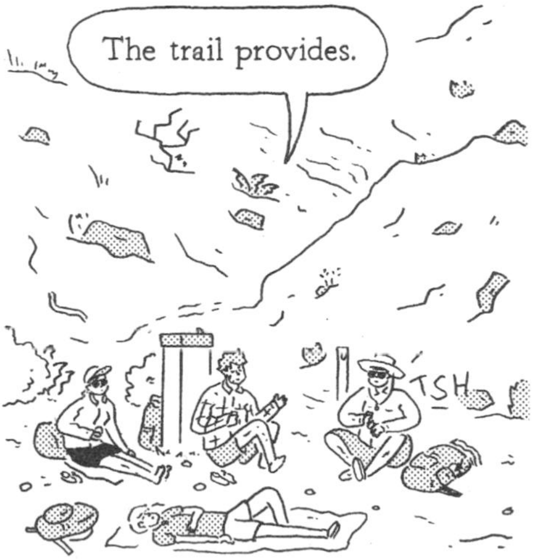
The trail provides.
TSH

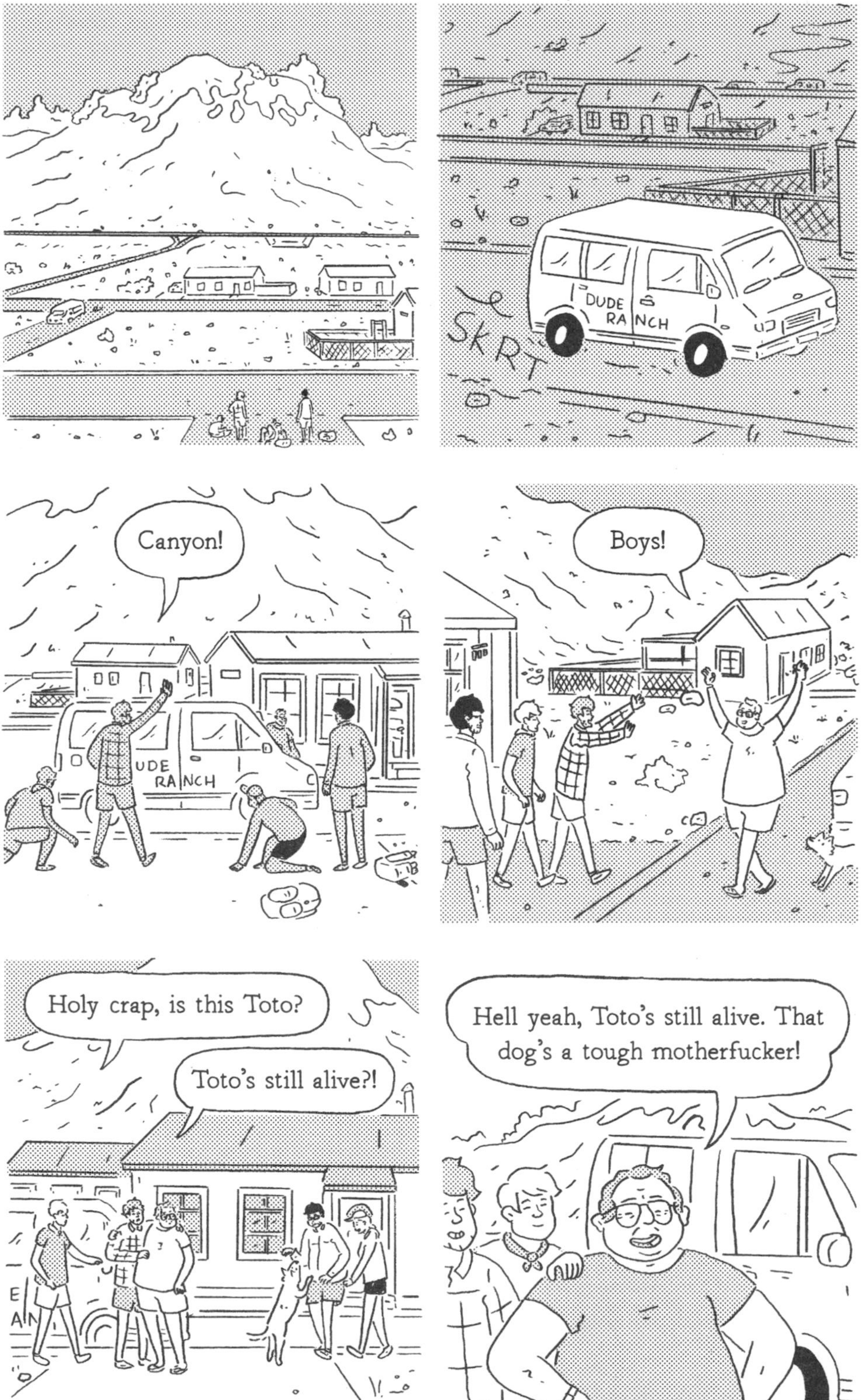
DUDE RANCH
SKRT
Canyon!
UDE RANCH
Boys!
Holy crap, is this Toto?
Toto's still alive?!
Hell yeah, Toto's still alive. That dog's a tough motherfucker!

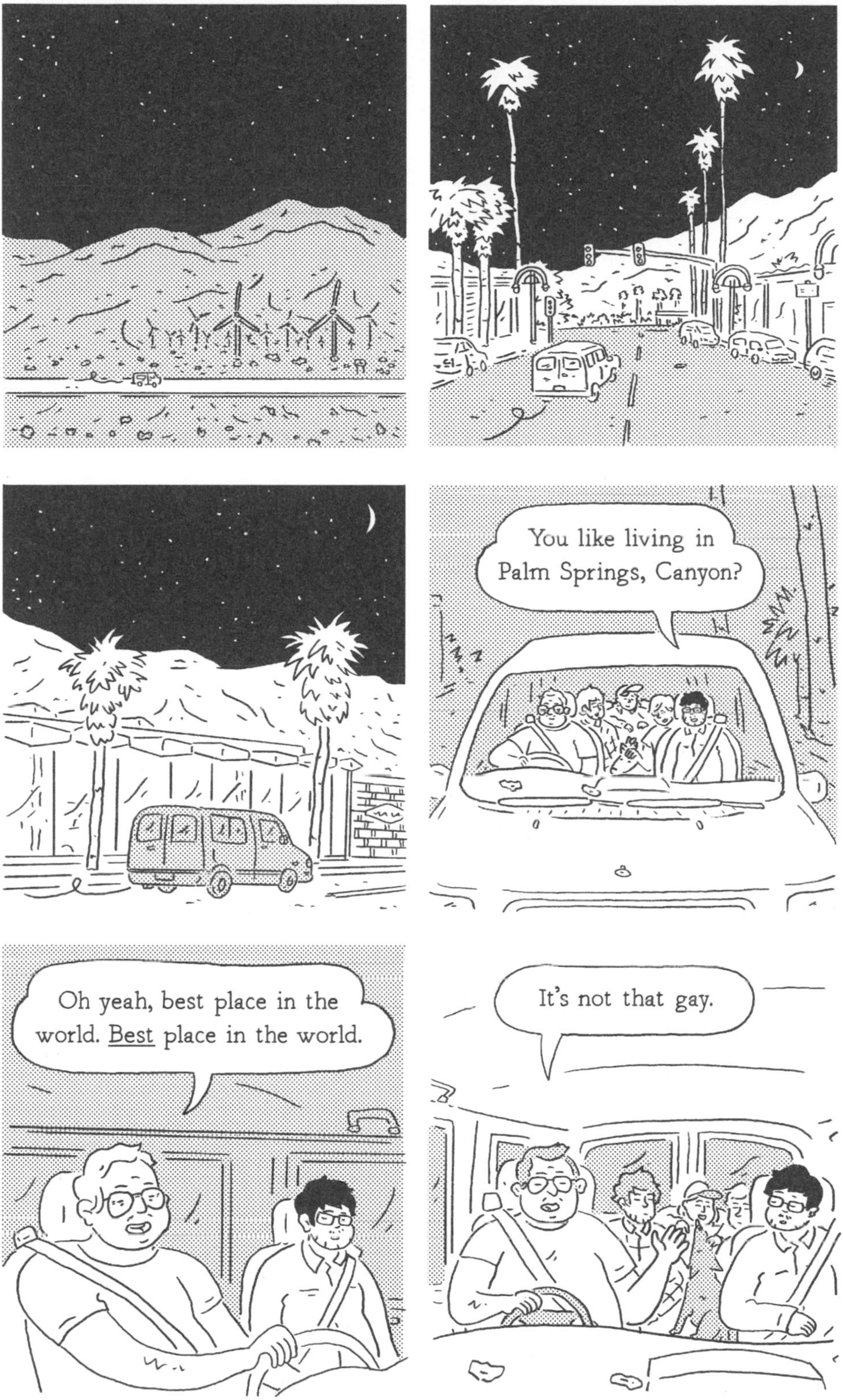

You like living in Palm Springs, Canyon?
Oh yeah, best place in the world. Best place in the world.
It's not that gay.

Canyon drives us on a tour of Palm Springs, stopping to show us the restaurant he parks outside of to bum free wifi, and to point out various tourist attractions. I suspect that he is homeless. I'm not sure whether Ethan and Tumnus know this.

I find Canyon hard to read. On first impression, he seems like a harmless stoner, who maybe read one too many Abbie Hoffman books in his youth. But the homophobic comments stress me out. As we drive around, he points out things that are "not that gay". He shouts "Move along ladies!" to a pair of men who cross the street holding hands.

Ethan can sense my discomfort, and tries to move Canyon off the topic. I appreciate that. Canyon talks at length about a get-rich-quick scheme that has something to do with selling palm trees.

We drive back out of Palm Springs for a few miles, and then, without warning, pull off the highway and on to the flat, roadless desert.

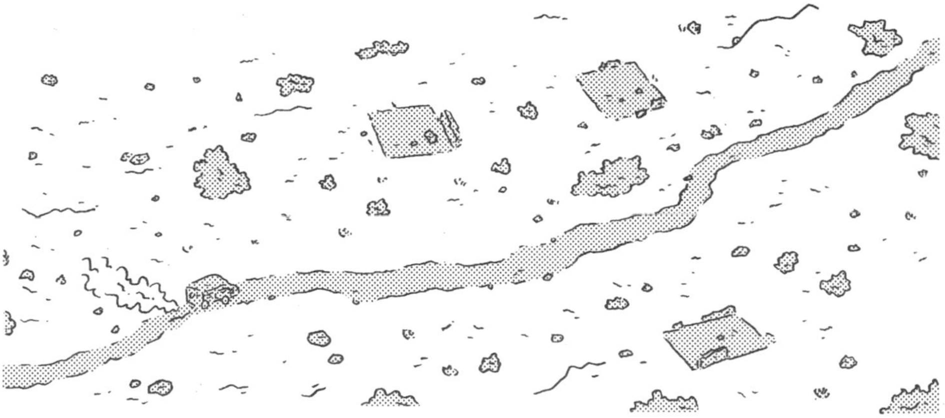

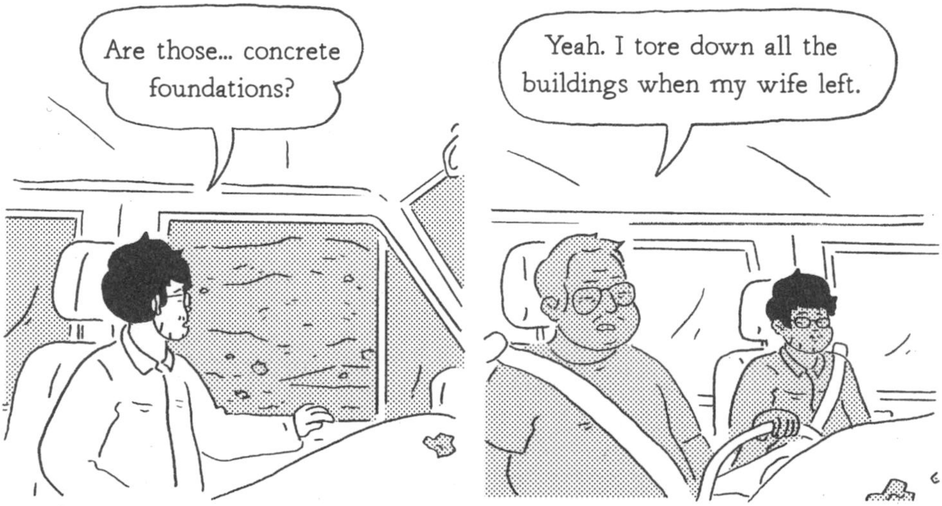
Are those... concrete foundations?
Yeah. I tore down all the buildings when my wife left.

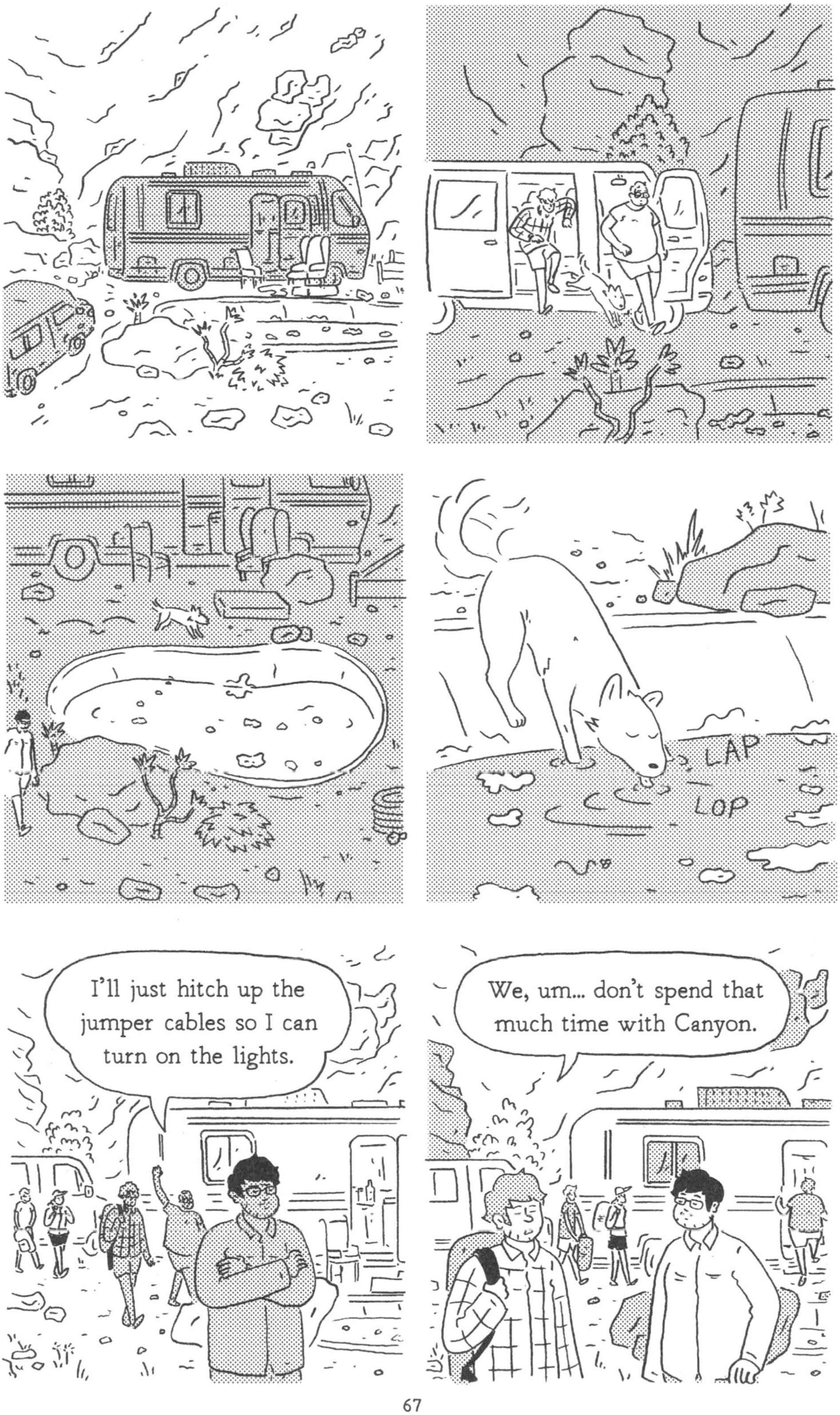

LAP
LOP
I'll just hitch up the jumper cables so I can turn on the lights.
We, um... don't spend that much time with Canyon.

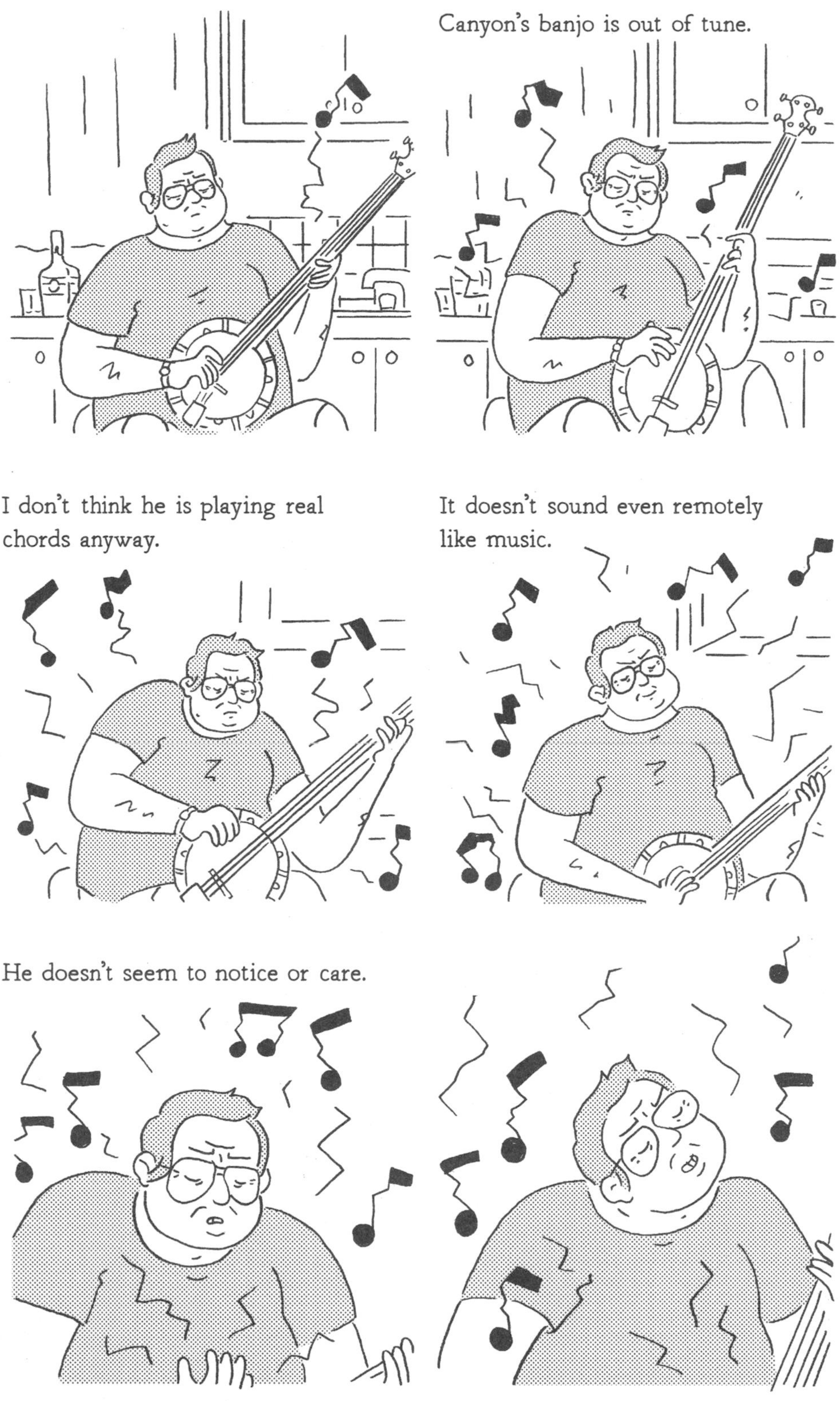
Canyon's banjo is out of tune.
I don't think he is playing real chords anyway.
It doesn't sound even remotely like music.
He doesn't seem to notice or care.

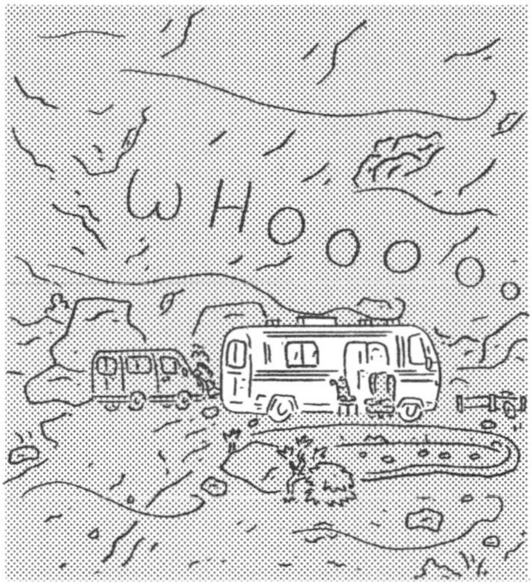
WHOOOOO

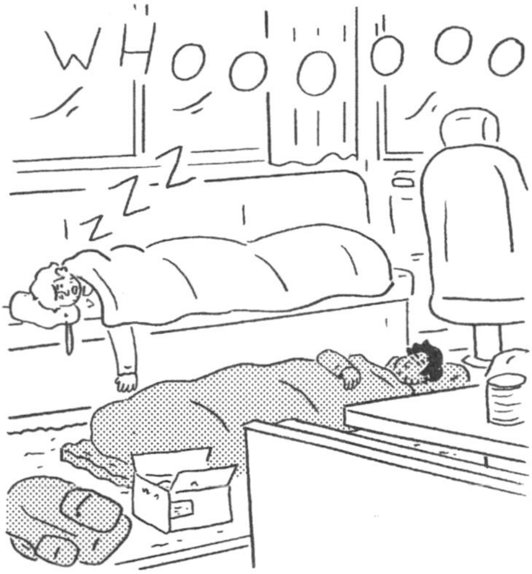
WHOOOOOO
Z Z Z

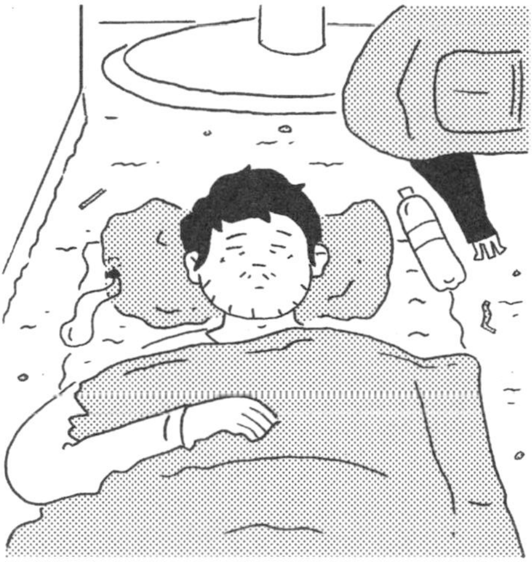

Across the plain from Canyon's RV, the wind turbines blink their red lights in rhythm. Mt. San Jacinto towers above us, an enormous monolith dividing the lush, well-watered coast from the arid inland desert. We climbed it. We hiked twenty miles in one day. Ethan sleeps on the couch. Canyon shifts and mumbles in his little bedroom.

Part of me feels like I should hate Canyon. Or fear him, maybe. But I don't. Mostly, I just feel guilt. And gratitude. Canyon, a person with so little, has been nothing but generous. A handful of worrying comments don't change that. Even though it feels like they should.

The clear, round sun rises over the field of wind turbines, vaporising any scrap of cloud that had crested San Jacinto in the night.

Canyon drives us to Big Bear, swerving violently, overtaking into oncoming traffic.

"You see that there? That's the world's first wind turbine. They built it here because it's always breezy," he tells us as we rocket by.

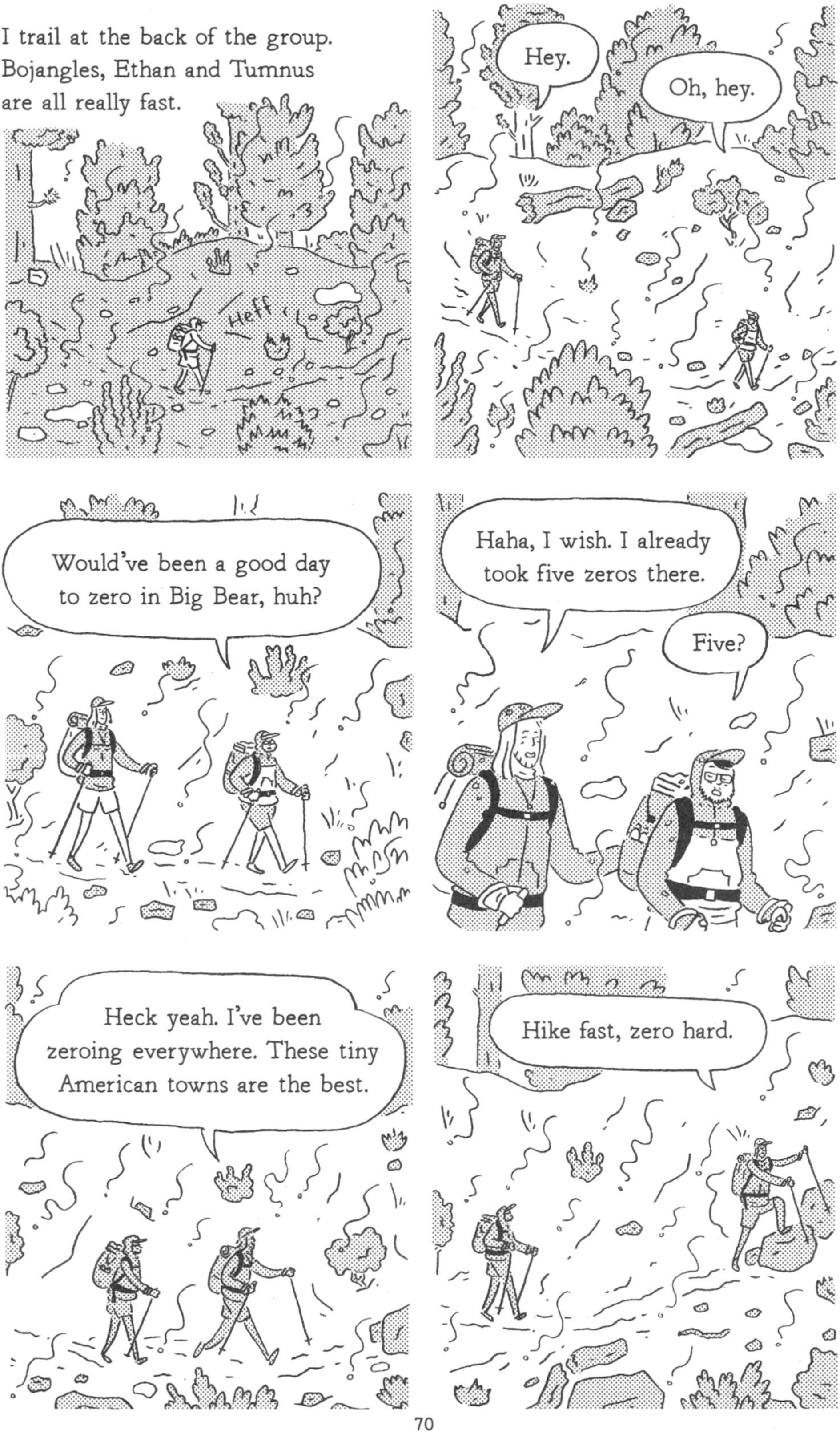
I trail at the back of the group. Bojangles, Ethan and Tumnus are all really fast.
Heff
Hey.
Oh, hey.
Would've been a good day to zero in Big Bear, huh?
Haha, I wish. I already took five zeros there.
Five?
Heck yeah. I've been zeroing everywhere. These tiny American towns are the best.
Hike fast, zero hard.

For a couple of days, I push myself to catch them, exhausted. Other hikers get competitive, too.

Ha! I finally caught up to you guys. I've been chasing you all day.

I'm Cheerleader, nice to meet ya.

Good trail name.

You always cheering people on? I could use it today, heh.

Heff
Heff

It's short for "Ugliest Cheerleader". I'm ugly, but I'm still prettier than someone who isn't on the team.

Ugh.

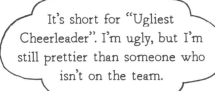

Hey, it's not like you'd have any trouble getting on the team.

71

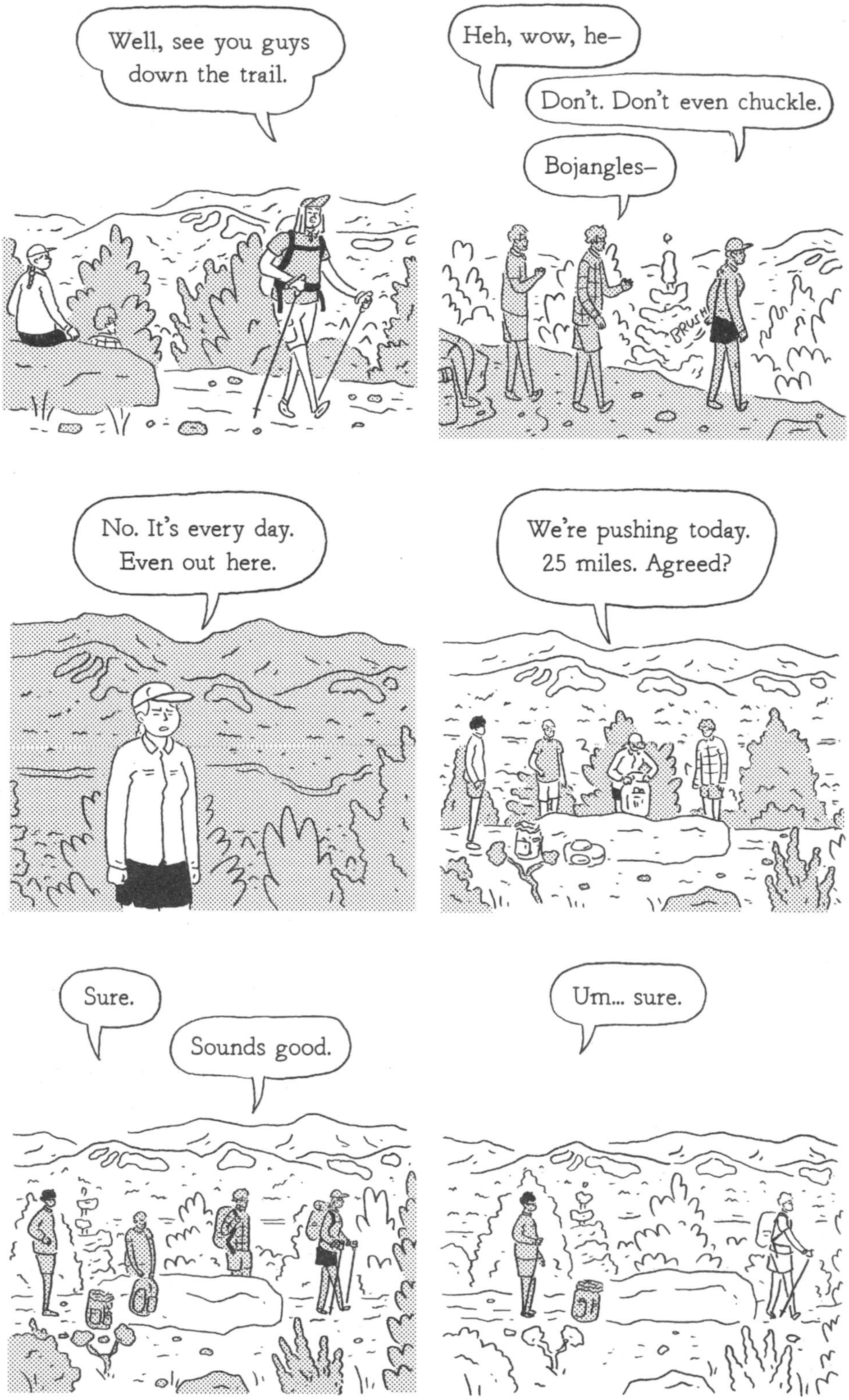
Well, see you guys down the trail.
Heh, wow, he–
Don't. Don't even chuckle.
Bojangles–
BRUSH
No. It's every day. Even out here.
We're pushing today. 25 miles. Agreed?
Sure.
Sounds good.
Um... sure.

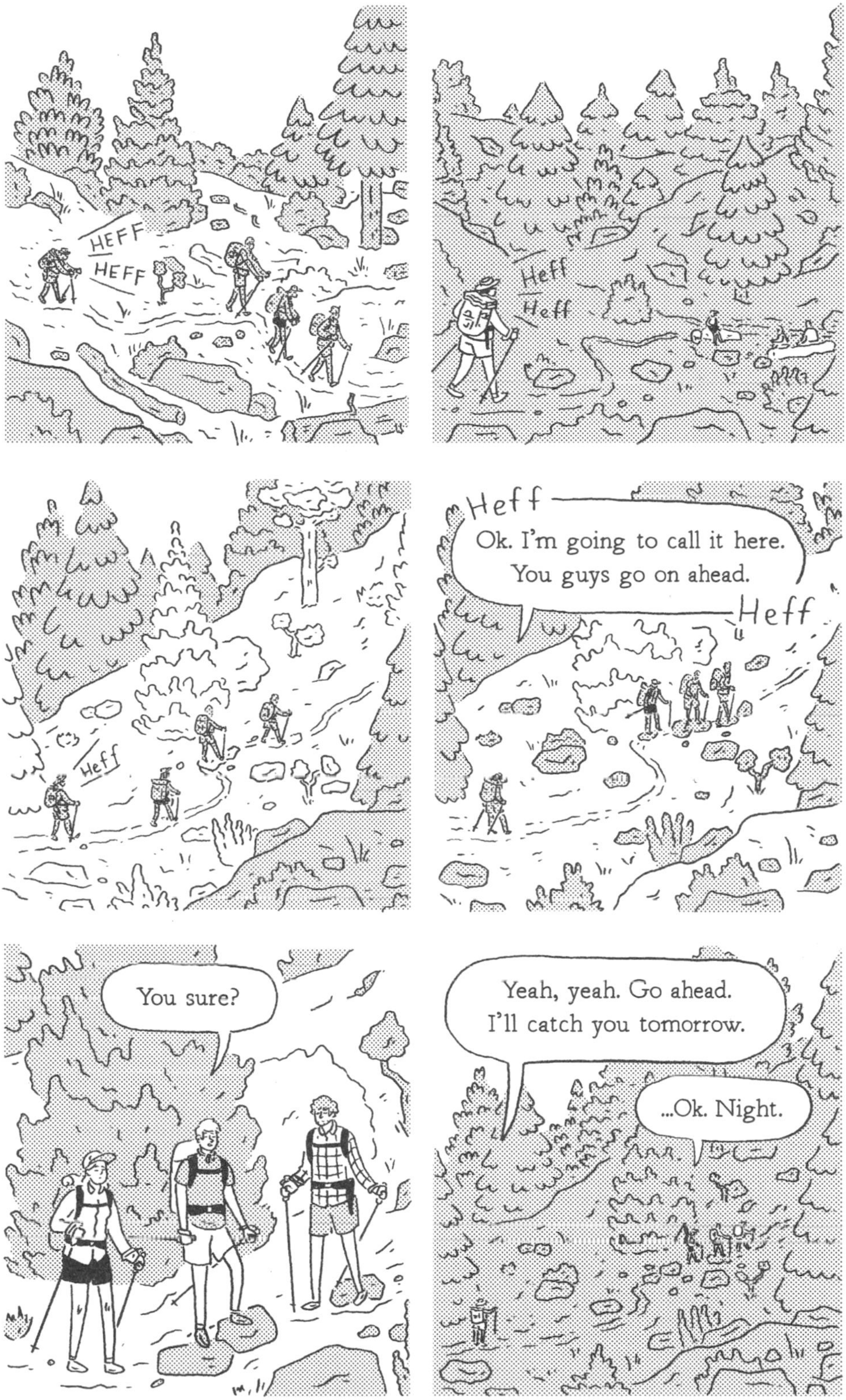
HEFF
HEFF
Heff
Heff
Heff
Heff
Ok. I'm going to call it here. You guys go on ahead.
Heff
You sure?
Yeah, yeah. Go ahead. I'll catch you tomorrow.
...Ok. Night.

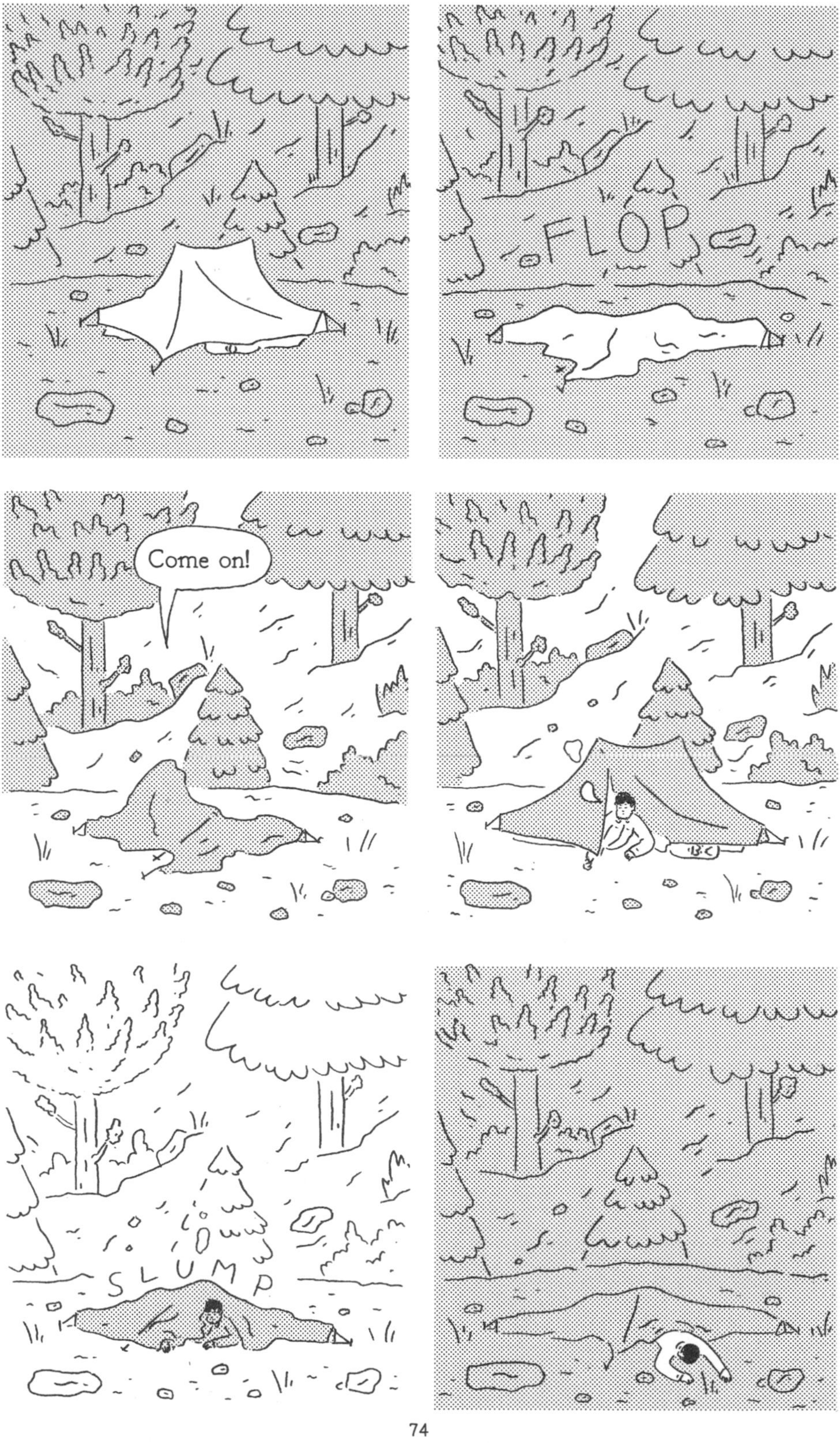
FLOP
Come on!
SLUMP

"The PCT is never easy. The PCT will beat you down. You will want to quit. Don't quit. Not on a bad day. Take a beat. Think it through. Stop moving." The trail angels I stayed with in San Diego told me that, on the night before I rode to the Mexican border.

The PCT is beating me down. I am exhausted. I haven't slept in days, first kept awake by the storm on San Jacinto, then by the howling winds in Canyon's RV, then by my own tent-pitching ineptitude.

I like Bojangles, Ethan and Tumnus. But even hiking flat out, I just can't seem to keep up. I am bad at this. My one virtue has always been my pigheaded stubbornness, but even that is failing me now.

Still, I get up and I hike. As if I have a choice.

Three hundred miles. That's almost the entire length of Ireland.

I could go home right now and it wouldn't be embarassing.

I ignore everyone and hike alone.

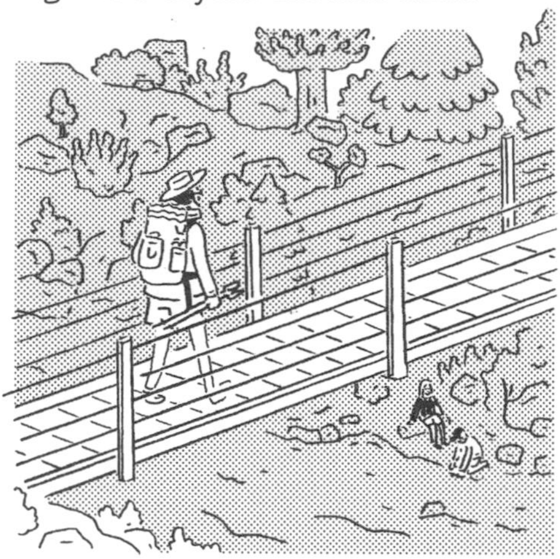

I collect water quickly and take breaks away from sources.

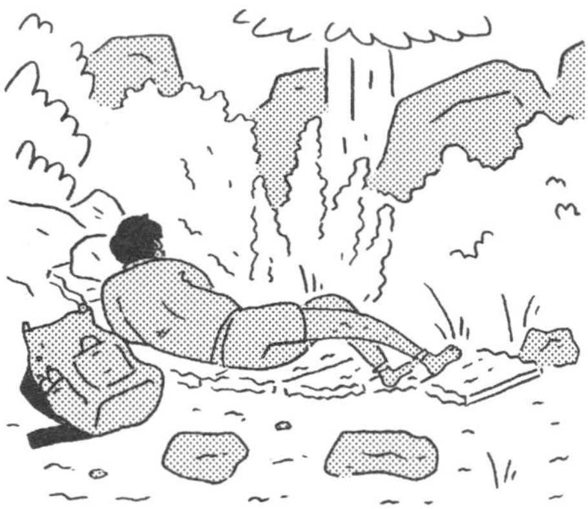

I want to be alone.

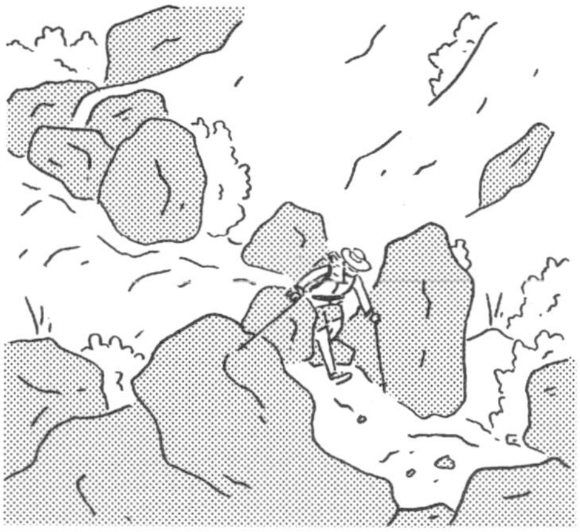

I want to catch Bojangles, Ethan and Tumnus.

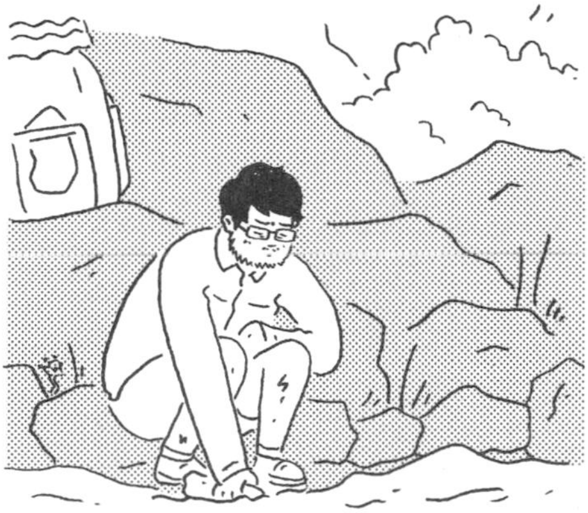

The trail hugs a ridge above Deep Creek, the first real flowing water I've seen.

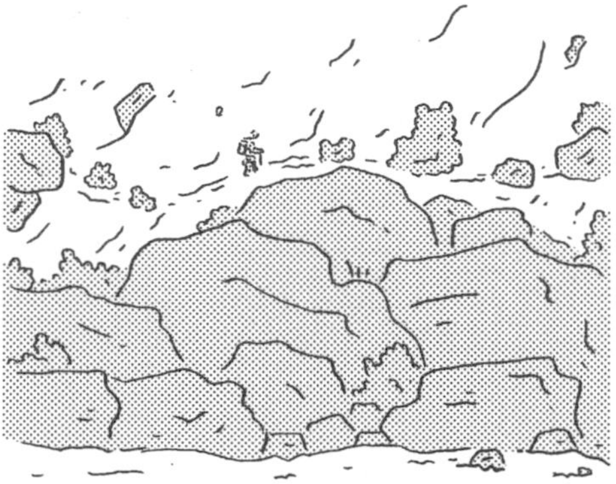

It's loud and alive, and I hate it.

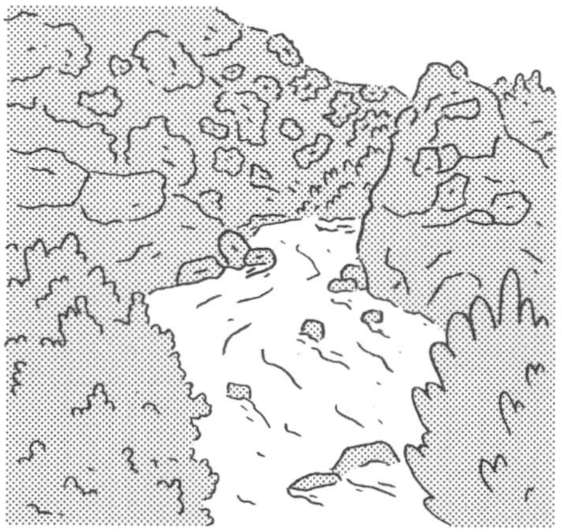

I hear people enjoying Deep Creek Hot Springs, long before I see them. Griz, Craftsman and the rest of their crew lounge on the sandy shore. Tall, willowy Ramon, the hiker who took five zeros in Big Bear, sits in a little basin of rock, soaking in the spring water.

"We call it the Johnny Cash Trail," Griz says, as I arrive, plopping myself down on the sand. "It's the hardest thruhike ever imagined. Forget the PCT, the AT, the CDT. The JCT is the ultimate challenge."

"Alright, enlighten me," says Waterboy, another hiker, who busies himself clearing a patch of sand to sleep on.

"I've been everywhere, man," Griz sings.

"I've been everywhere," Craftsman joins.

"I've been to Reno, Chicago, Fargo, Minnesota..."

"Buffalo, Toronto, Winslow, Sarasota..." Craftsman contributes, before the group bursts into laughter, cutting them both off.

"We're gonna drive around to all those cities and nail up trail markers. Blaze the dang thing. The hardest thruhike in the world."

They go on, joking about optimum routes for hiking the fictional JCT. I turn to Ramon, who is now dressed and drying his hair.

"Have you seen two guys and a girl come through here?" I ask.

"Who, Bojangles and the brothers? Yeah, they just left."

I stand up. I can still catch them, but before I can say my goodbyes, Ramon jumps in. "What, you're leaving without getting in?"

"Yeah, I just think I can catch them."

"Luke, how far away is Ireland? Eight thousand kilometres? You're never gonna be here again. You're in the middle of the desert. You've been sweating all day. Your muscles are aching. You just stumbled on to some natural hot springs. Don't be an idiot."

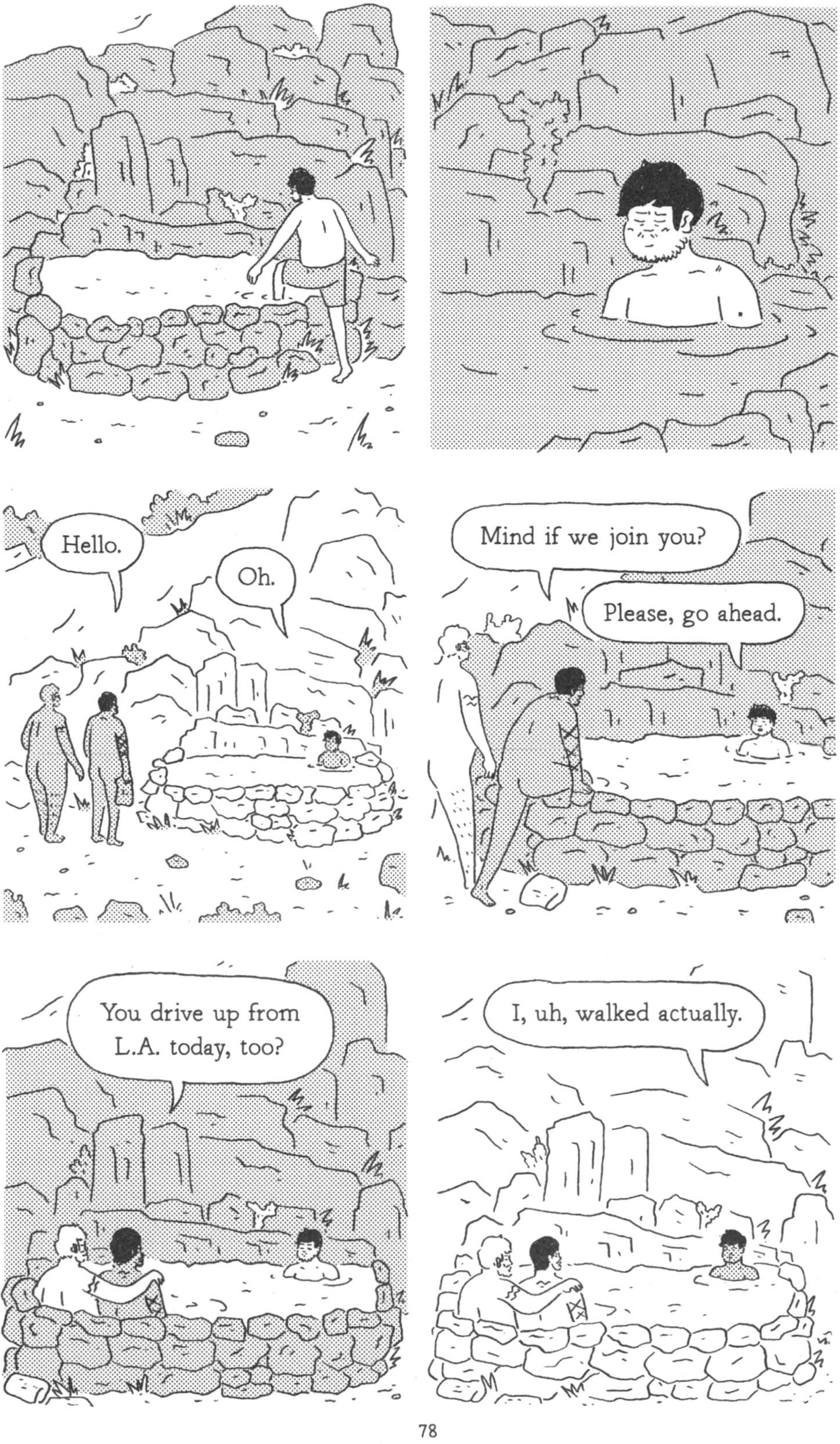
Hello.
Oh.
Mind if we join you?
Please, go ahead.
You drive up from L.A. today, too?
I, uh, walked actually.

Cajon Pass 29/04/16. Day 14.

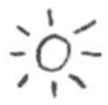

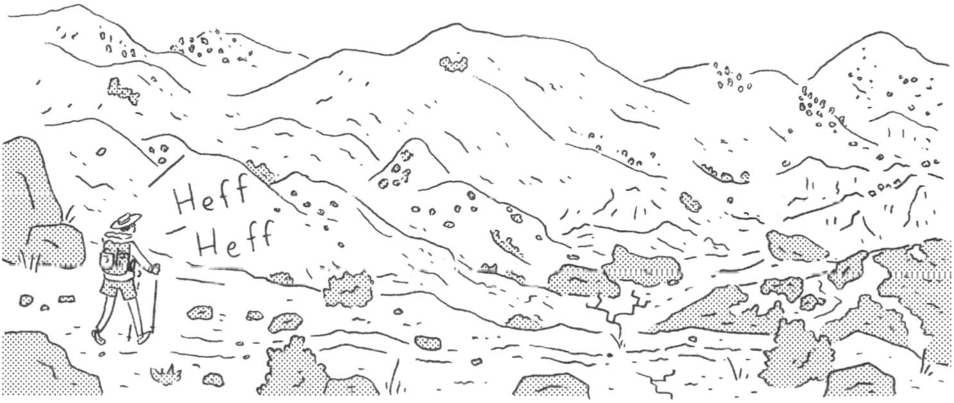
Heff
Heff

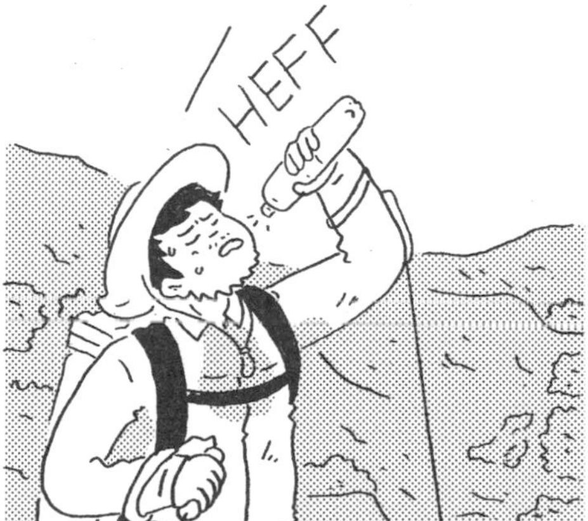
HEFF

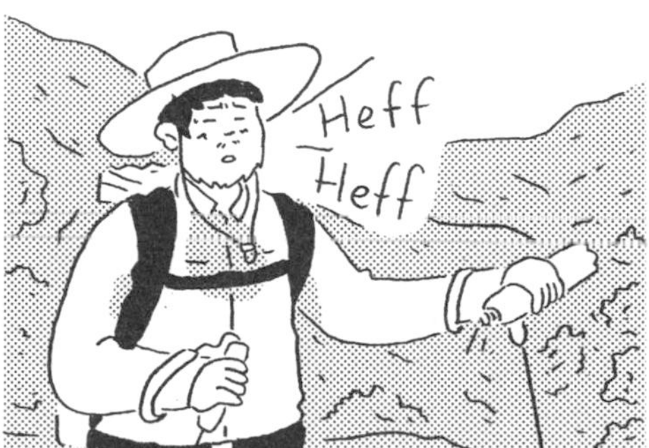
Heff
Heff

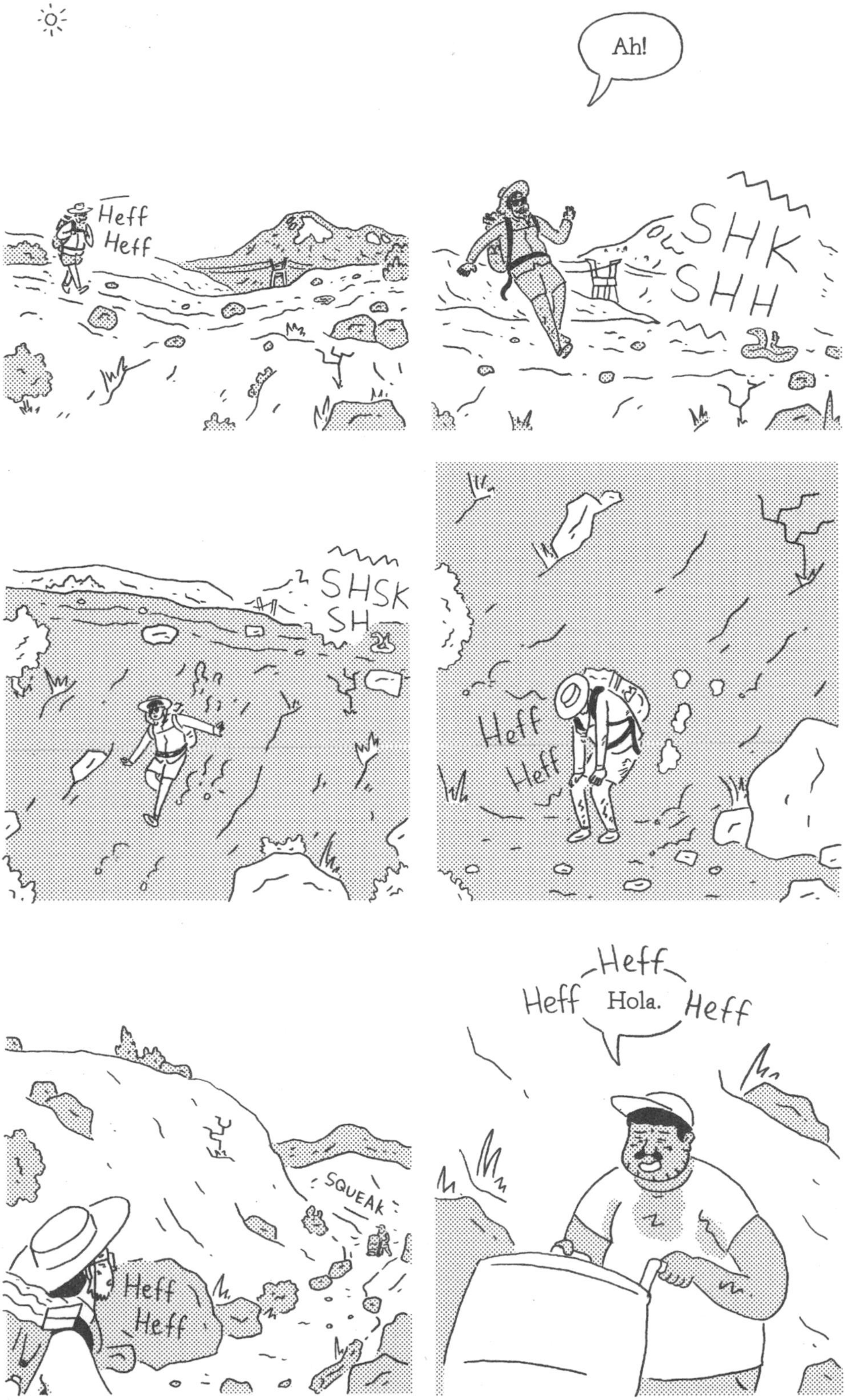

Heff
Heff
Ah!
SHK
SHH
SHSK
SH
Heff
Heff
Heff
Heff
SQUEAK
Heff
Heff
Heff
Hola.
Heff

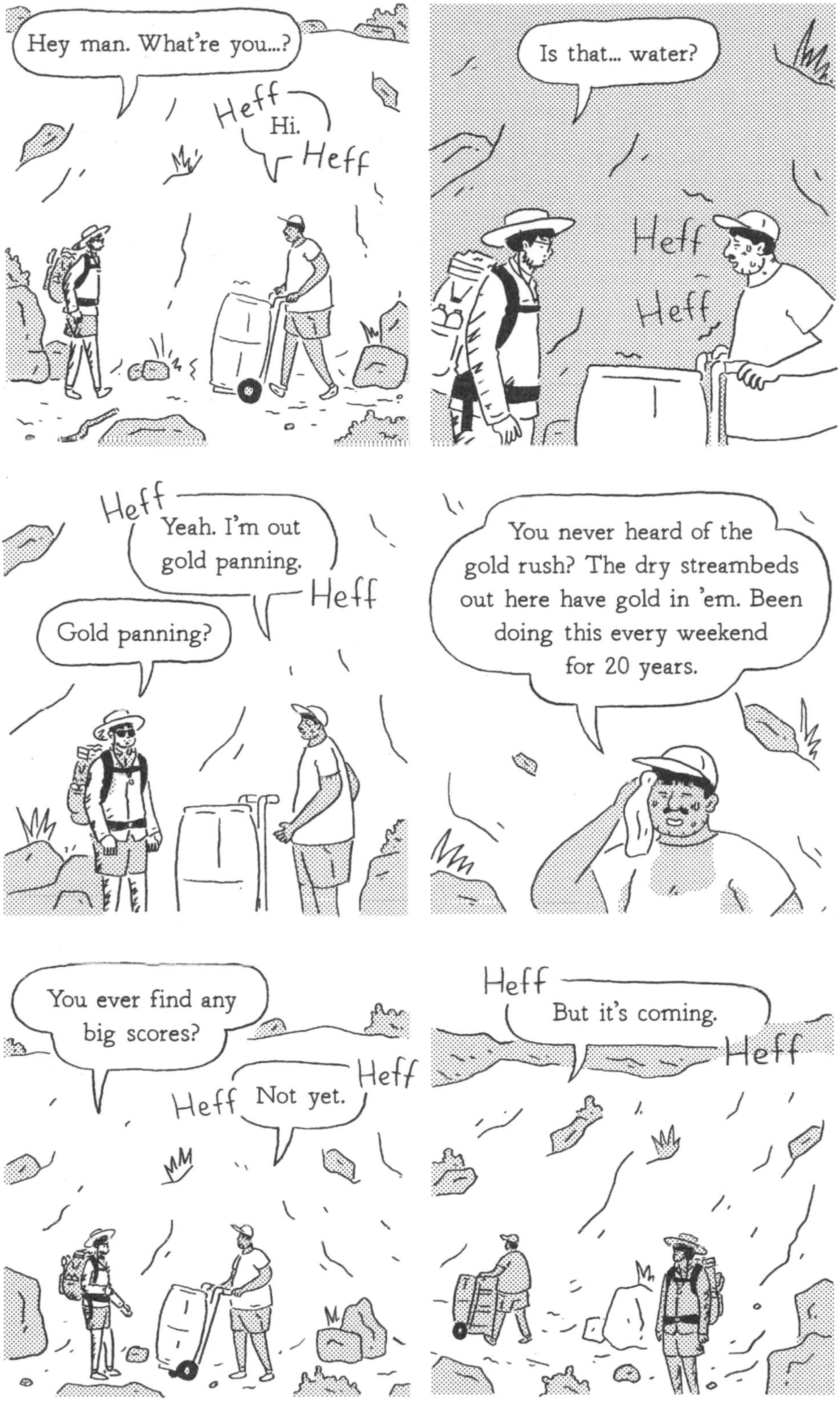
Hey man. What're you...?
Heff
Hi.
Heff
Is that... water?
Heff
Heff
Heff
Yeah. I'm out gold panning.
Heff
Gold panning?
You never heard of the gold rush? The dry streambeds out here have gold in 'em. Been doing this every weekend for 20 years.
You ever find any big scores?
Heff
Not yet.
Heff
Heff
But it's coming.
Heff

I should have asked for some of his gold panning water.

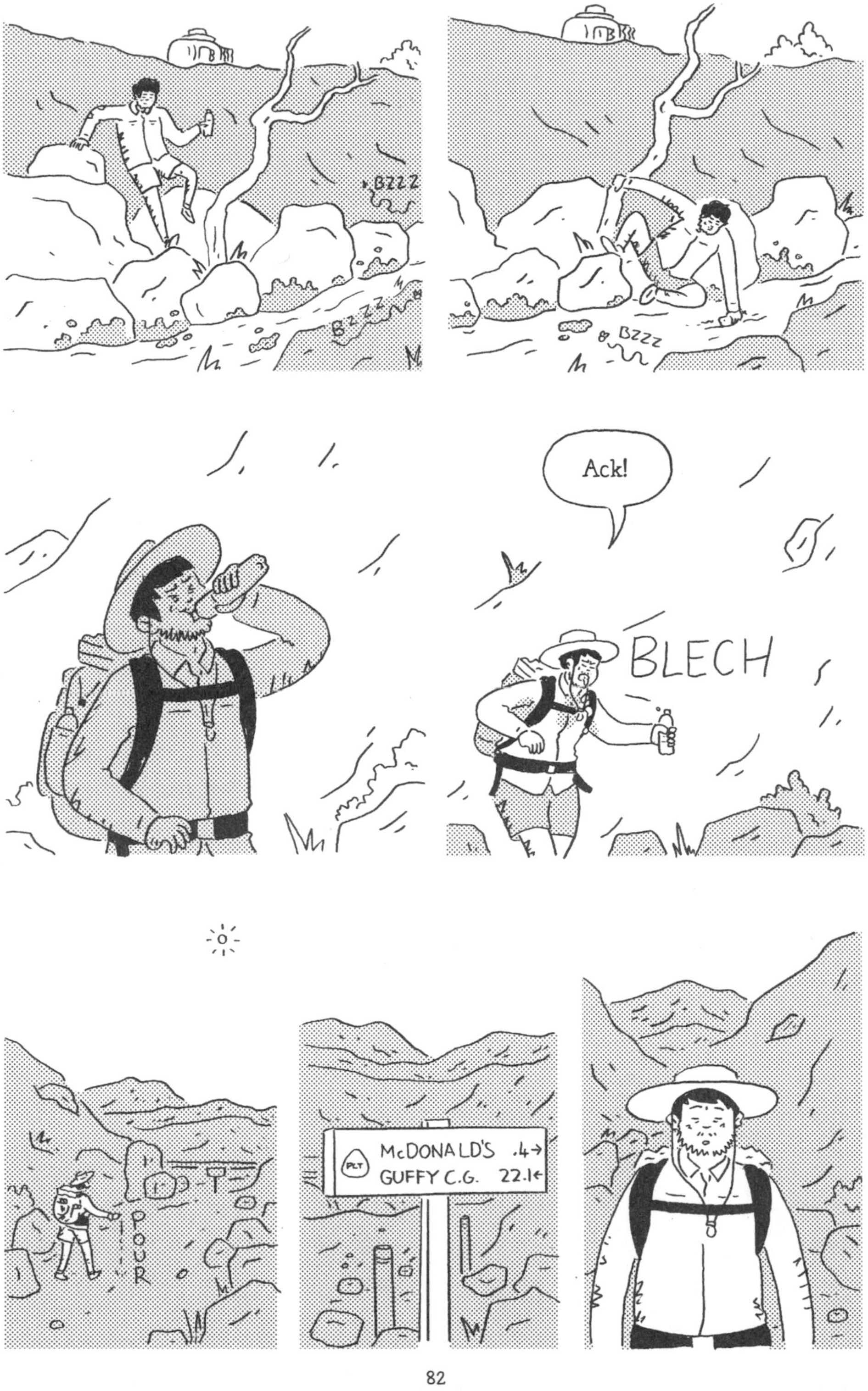
BZZZ
BZZZ
BZZZ
Ack!
BLECH
POUR
McDONALD'S .4→
GUFFY C.G. 22.1←

At Cajon Pass, the PCT crosses beneath Interstate 15.

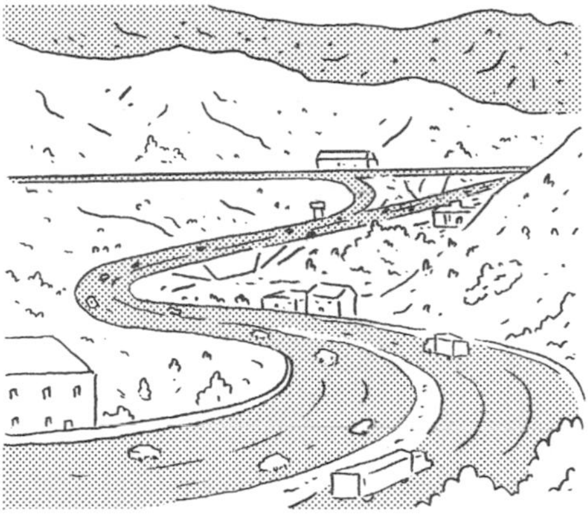

Just a few minutes east of the crossing, there is a small rest stop complete with gas stations, a motel and a McDonald's.

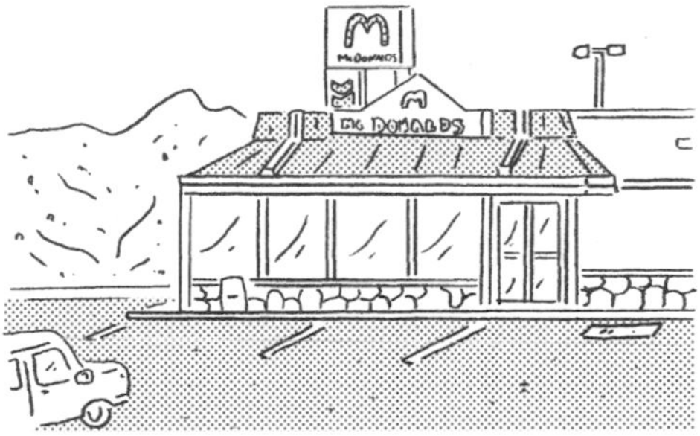

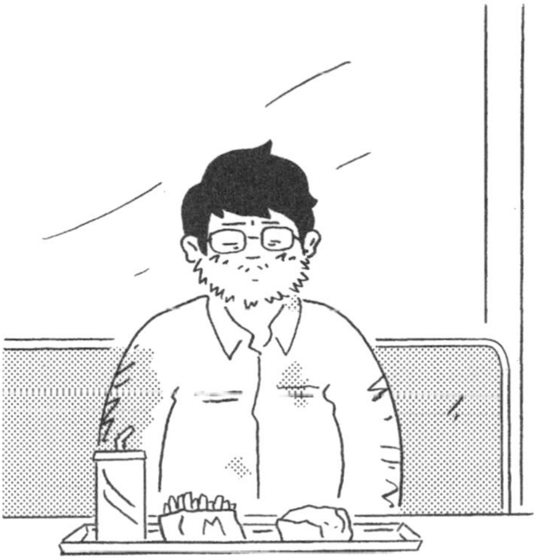

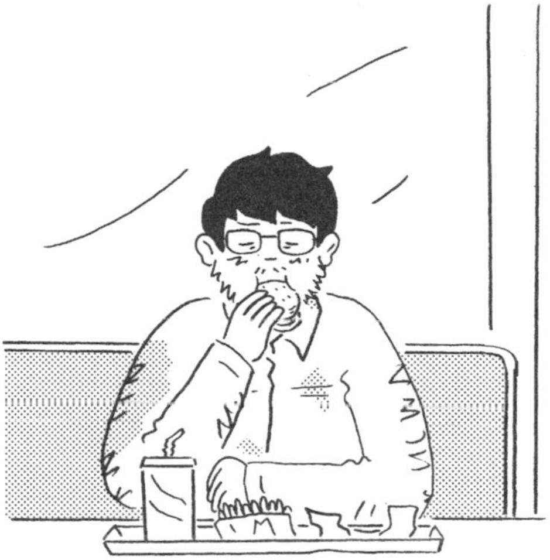

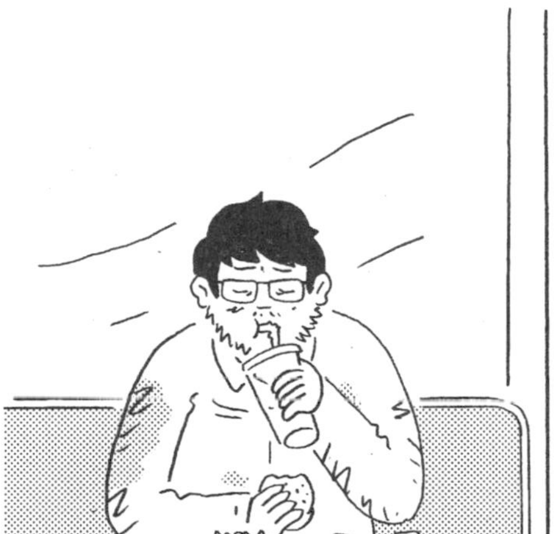

I am done.

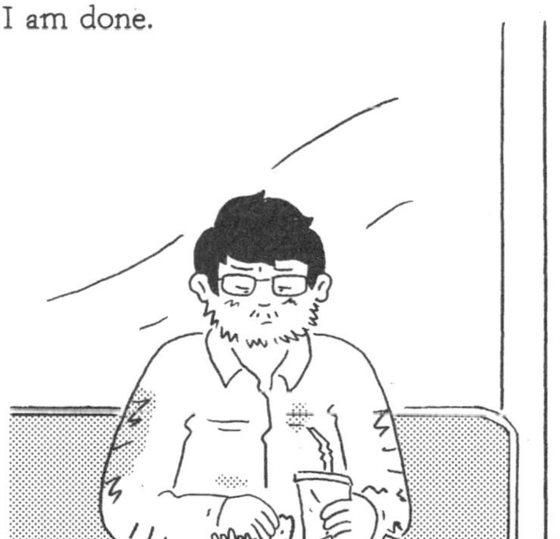

I look around at the other hikers. They laugh and joke in between bites of their first, or fourth, Big Mac. I sip my soda and think how funny it is, how American, to be saved from dehydration by an icy Coca-Cola.

I finish eating and walk along the highway overpass to the motel. I need to stop. I need to take the trail angels' advice before I cash in all my chips and quit. I rent a room to myself.

I ask the clerk if there's any way to get to L.A. from here.

"Not really," he says. "But if you pay for their gas, I'd let one of the employees here drive you out there during work hours."

I thank him, and tell him I'll think about it.

I run a bath and sink into it. I leave a clear dirt ring around the rim once the water drains. I fill the tub again to wash my clothes and rinse them until the water runs clear, which takes ten minutes, at least.

Finally, I collapse on to the bed. I check my emails and messages and to my surprise, see one from Luanne, the aunt of a friend. She saw online that I was hiking in California, and offers me a room at her place in L.A., should I need to take a break. I send her a thank you, and fight the urge to accept her offer immediately. I message my friends, Rachel and Mike, also L.A. residents, asking if I could crash at their place should I need to quit. They say yes. It's comforting to have options.

I call my parents. I'm not sure what else to do. When I tell them I think I'm going to quit, my mam offers support, my dad resistance.

"You'll never get a second chance at this. If you stop now, you'll never start again." I know he's right, but I disagree feebly anyway and tell them that I have to go.

I am getting thin for the first time in my life.

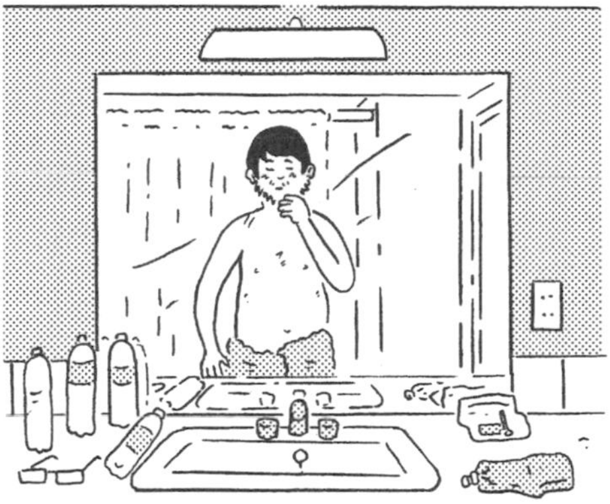

I can see muscle and bone that was never visible before.

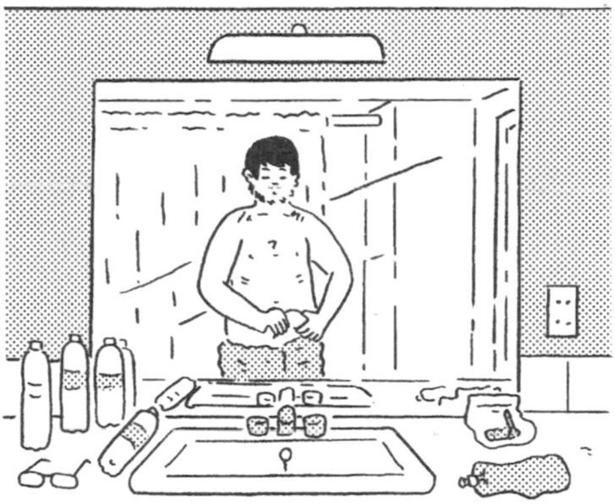

I am sunburned and wind burned.

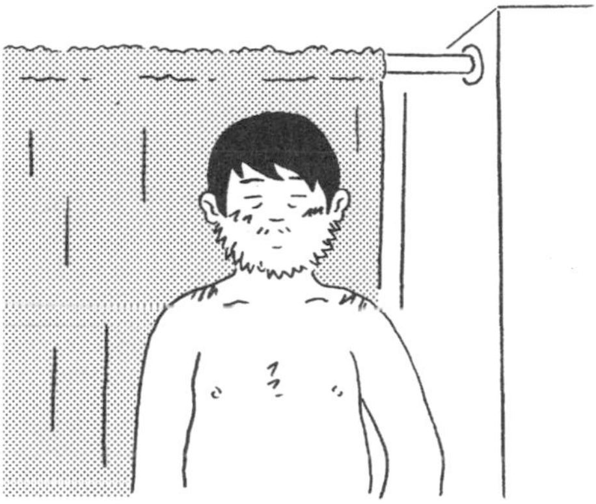

Every pore is clogged with dust and my skin is scuffed and chafed at every point of contact with my pack, my clothes and myself.

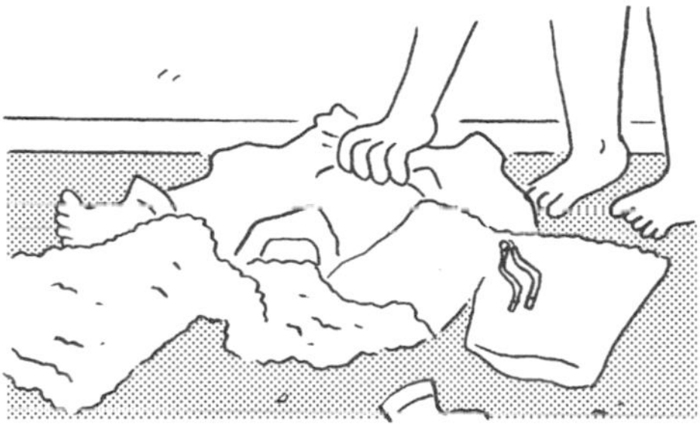

Every joint, muscle and bone aches and stiffens.

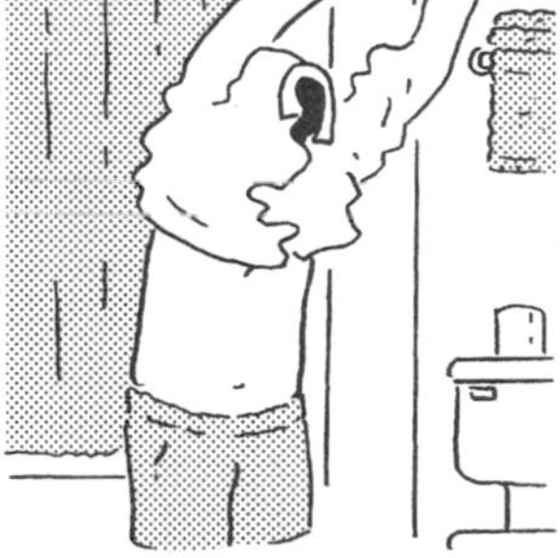

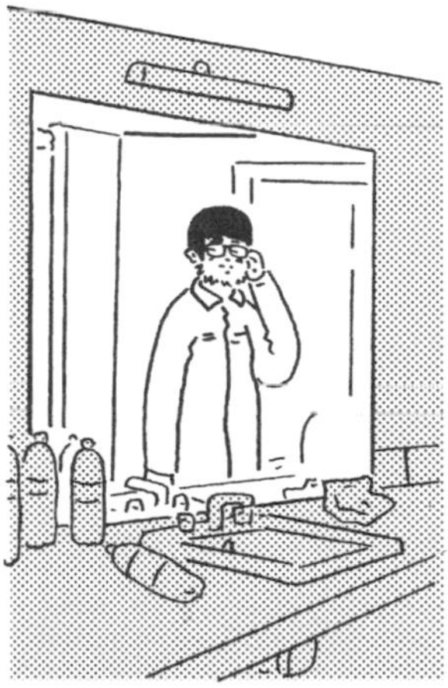

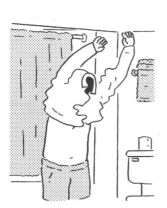

And I hike on.

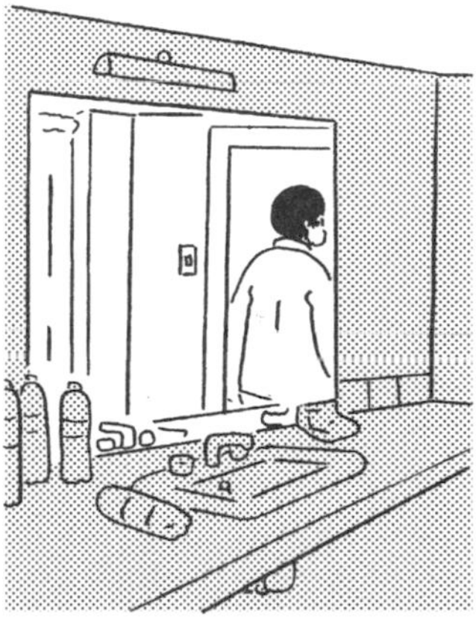

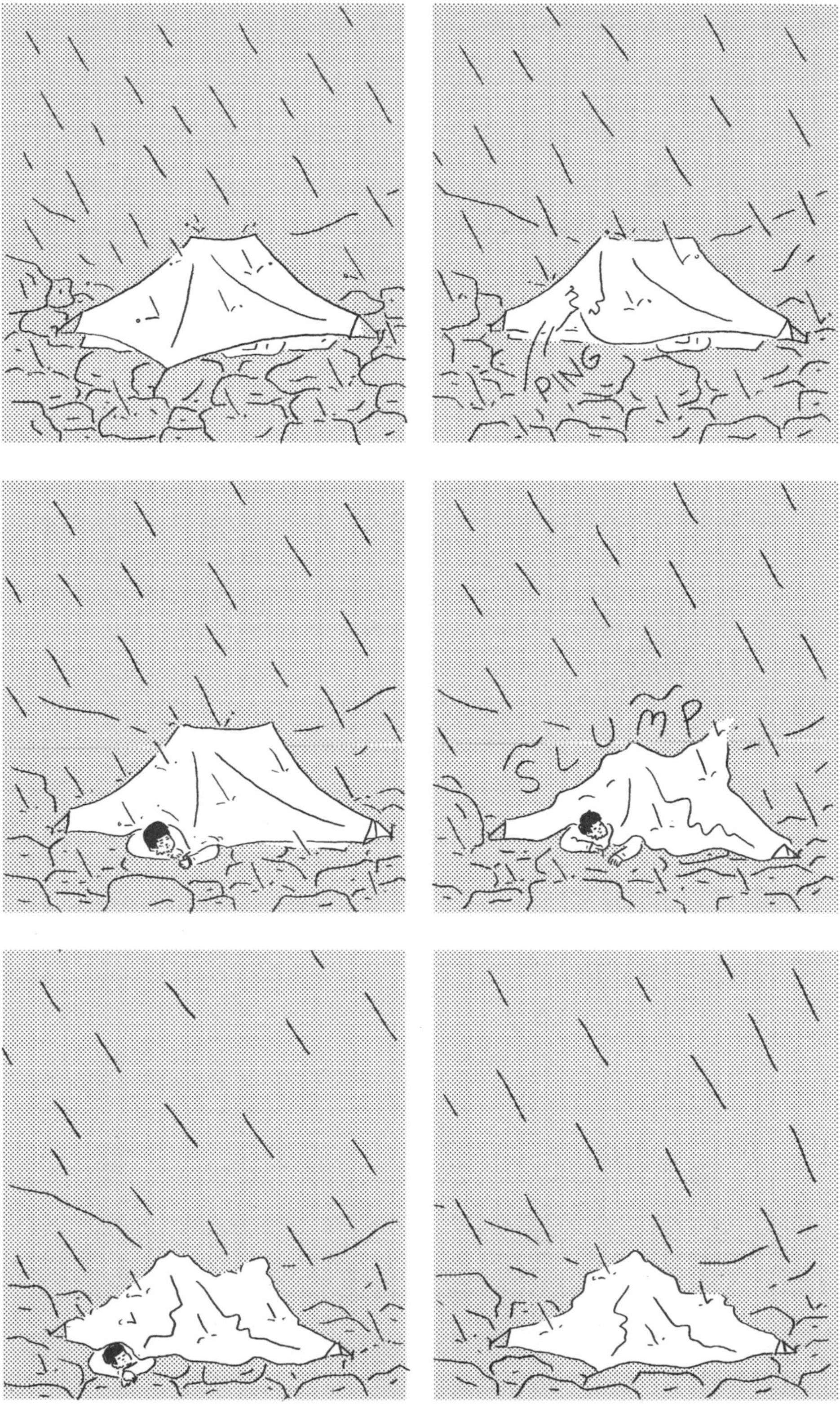
PING
SLUMP

I give up trying to sleep at 5 am.

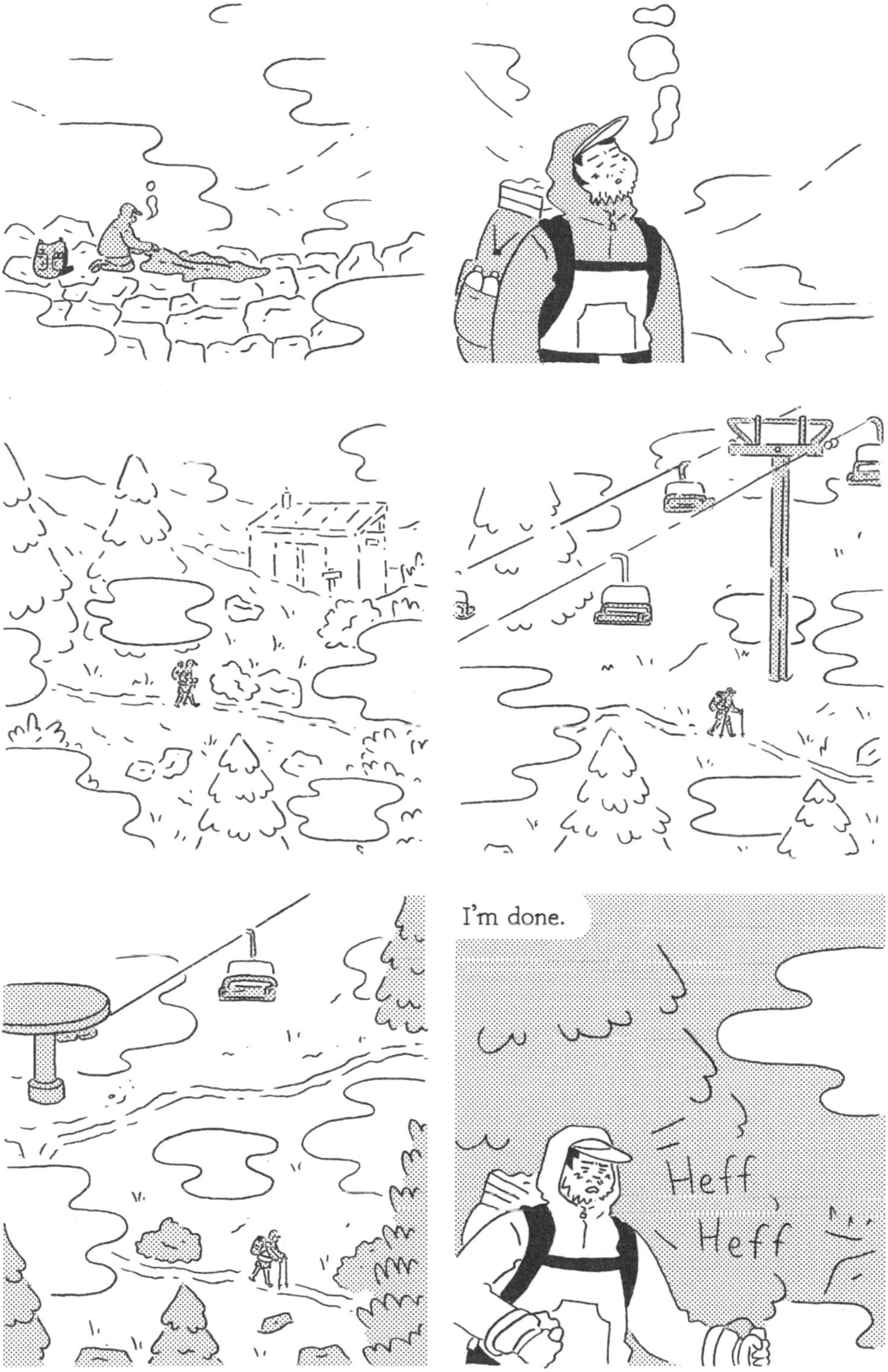
I'm done.
Heff
Heff

I feel so profoundly defeated.

I stumble through the mist until I reach a trailhead. I don't want to hitch, I'm not in the mood, but the trail provides, and as the road comes into view, a man with a truck calls me over. We wait for more hikers to arrive and I chat and joke and put on a smile. A tall, strong looking woman arrives down the trail and I motion her over. Her name is Toe Touch, and she also woke up at the crack of dawn. We all need town today. We load our packs into the truck and take off.

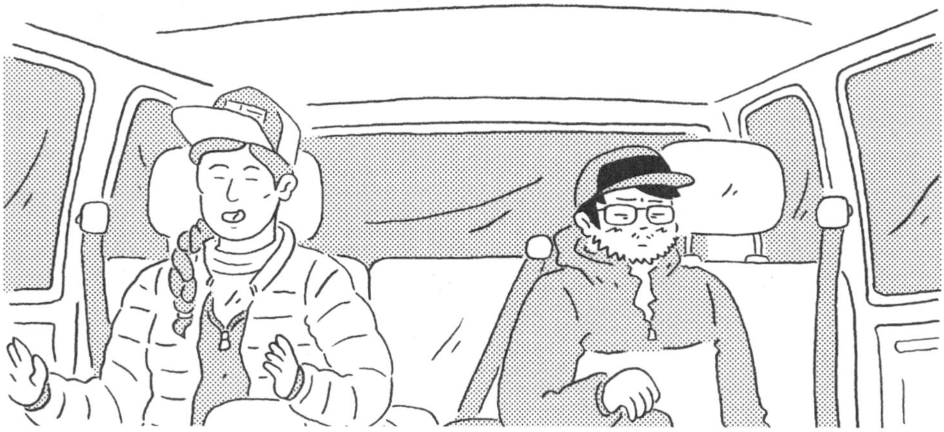

The hitch drops me and Toe Touch off at a little coffee shop, where I immediately order a big mug and settle in to return my bones to a more human temperature. Toe Touch leaves to find her friends, and to my surprise Bojangles, Ethan and Tumnus arrive. I thought I was further behind.

I unwind as I talk with them, drinking cup after cup of hot liquid.

"I didn't even bother to set up my tent again last night, after it collapsed. I just weighed it down at each corner with some rocks, and sleept inside it like a sodden sack of garbage."

"You really slept in a collapsed tent all night?" Bojangles asks, incredulously. The look on my face must be pretty pathetic, because a moment after I confirm my story, she cracks into laughter and despite myself, I follow.

"That's hilarious. It's like a giant, accidental bivvy. There's a trail name for you. Bivvy."

I laugh it off, embarrassed.

That night, I join Bojangles, Ethan and Tumnus for pizza. I know it will be the last time I see them. A barbershop quartet sings "Don't Stop Me Now" at the next table. I say goodbye.

I search online for buses to L.A., but the highway out of town is closed and nothing is running.

I don't want to hike again. I walk to a small motel on the other side of town and get a room. The desk is manned by an eight-year-old girl whose mother runs around trying to clean out the day's rooms before check-in time. I catch the owner's attention and ask her if she knows any way to get to L.A. Her cousin is driving there tonight, she says, and will let me ride with her for $100. I tell her I'll think about it.

I draft texts to both Rachel and Luanne, asking for a place to stay.

But I don't hit send.

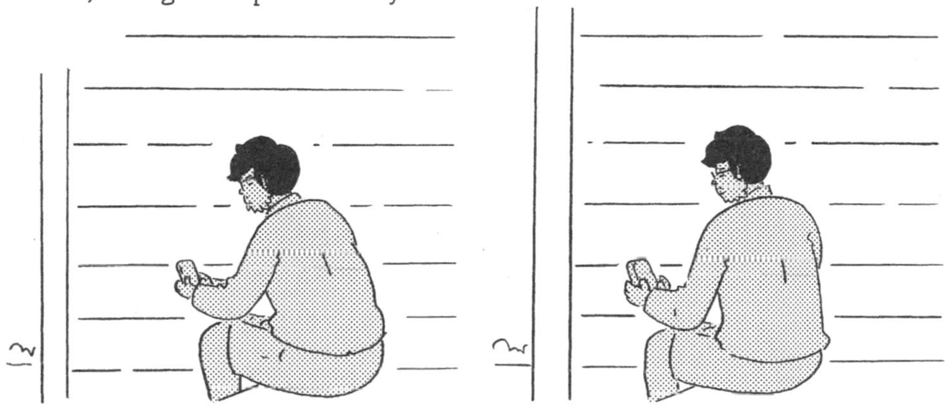

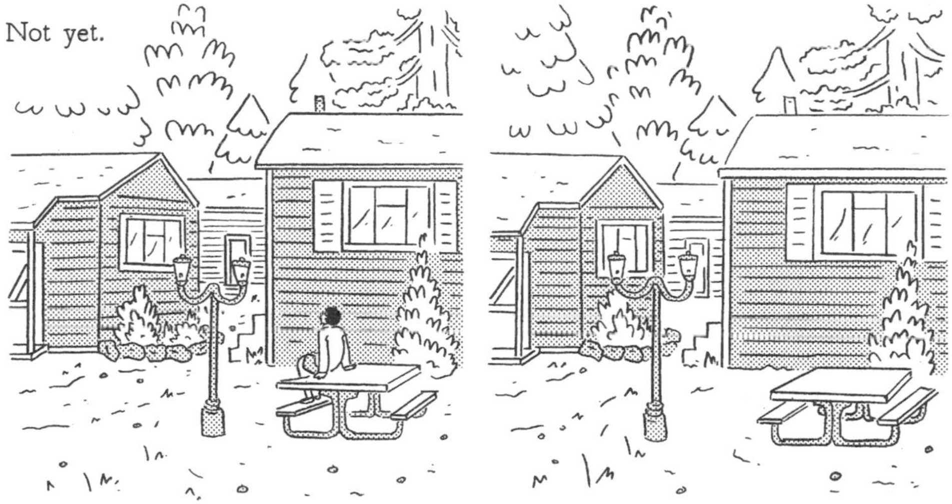
Not yet.

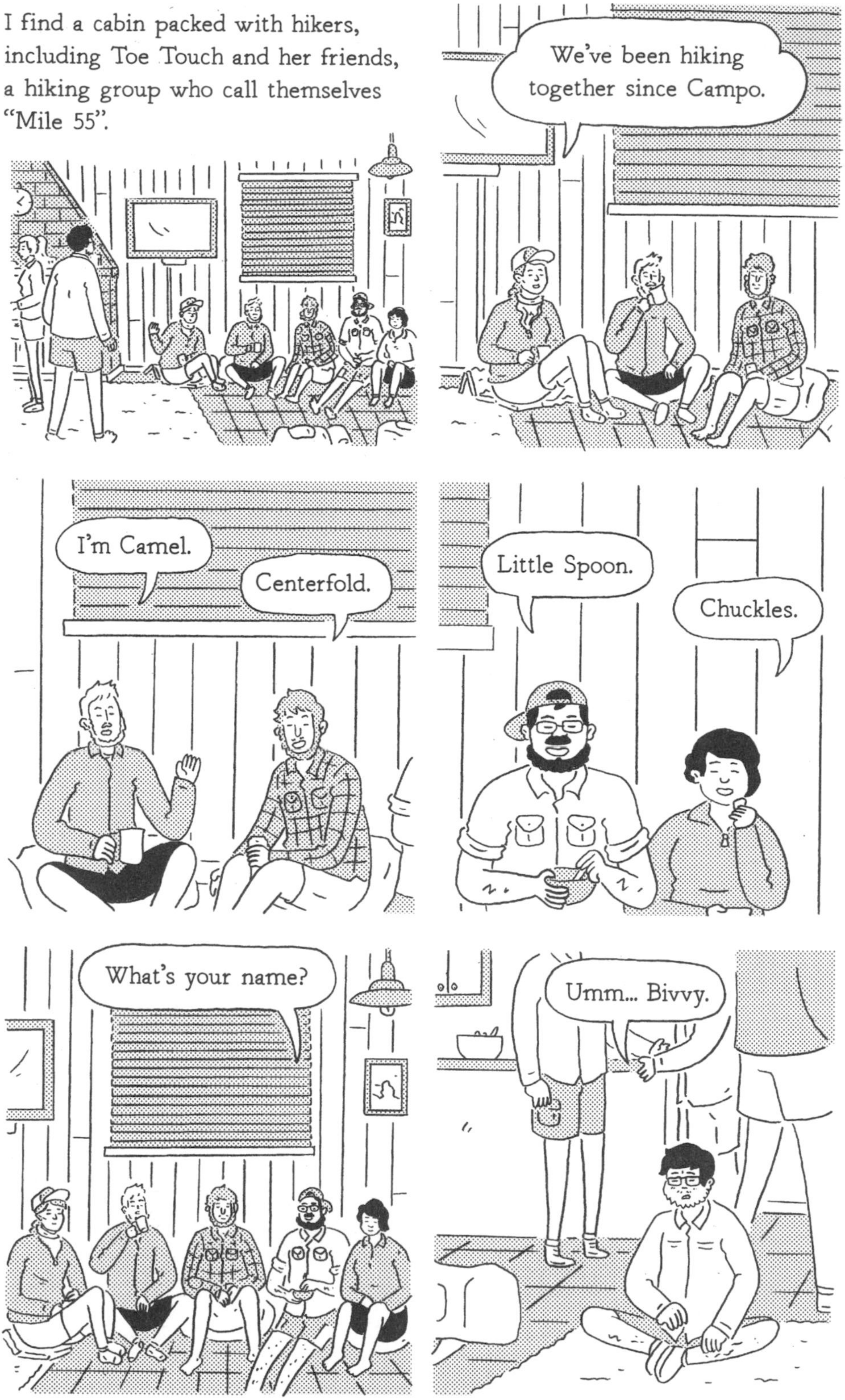
I find a cabin packed with hikers, including Toe Touch and her friends, a hiking group who call themselves "Mile 55".
We've been hiking together since Campo.
I'm Camel.
Centerfold.
Little Spoon.
Chuckles.
What's your name?
Umm... Bivvy.

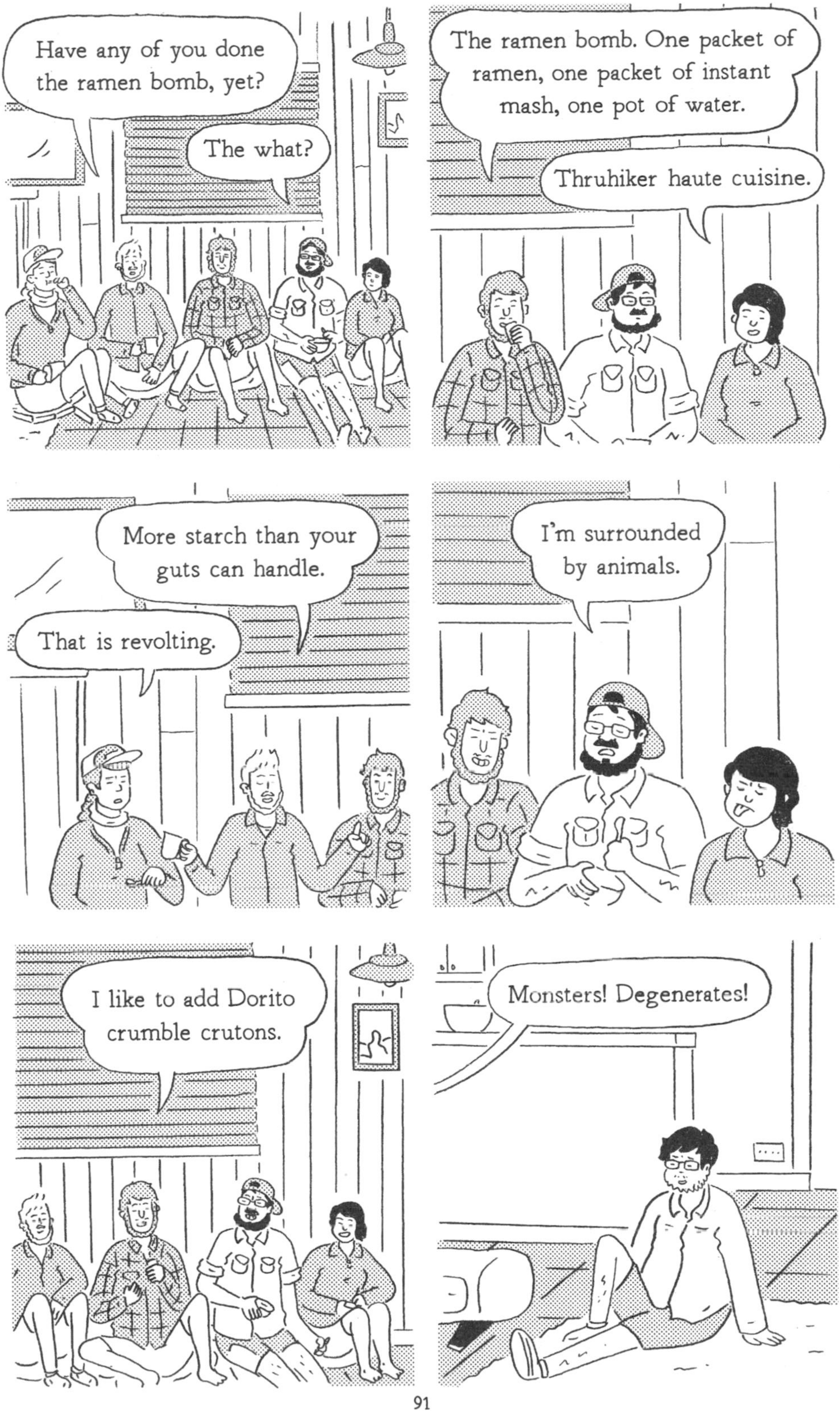
Have any of you done the ramen bomb, yet?
The what?
The ramen bomb. One packet of ramen, one packet of instant mash, one pot of water.
Thruhiker haute cuisine.
More starch than your guts can handle.
That is revolting.
I'm surrounded by animals.
I like to add Dorito crumble crutons.
Monsters! Degenerates!

Mt. Baden Powell 04/05/16. Day 19.

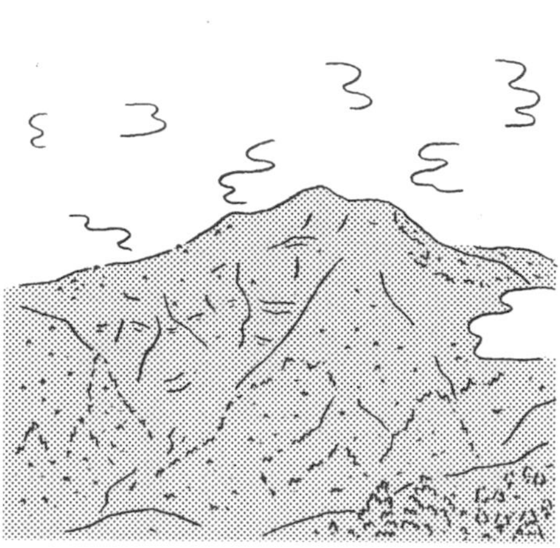

More fog.

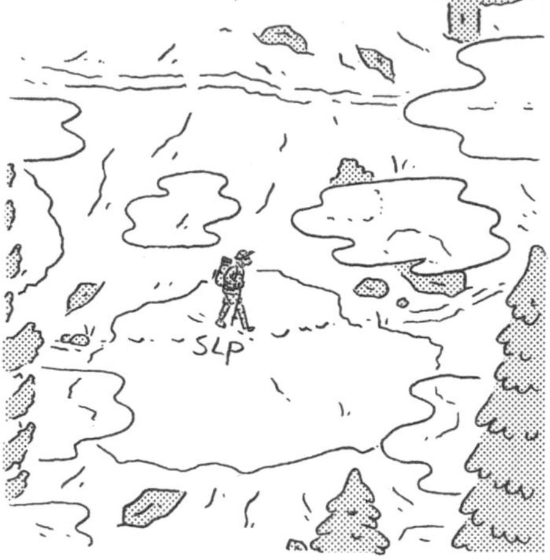
SLP

More cold.

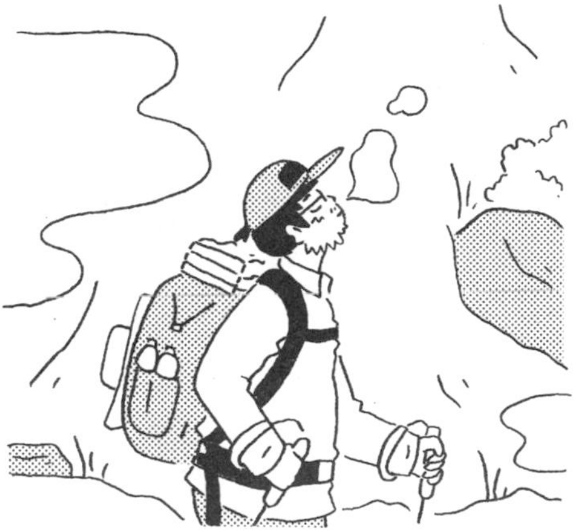

Southern California likes to keep you guessing.

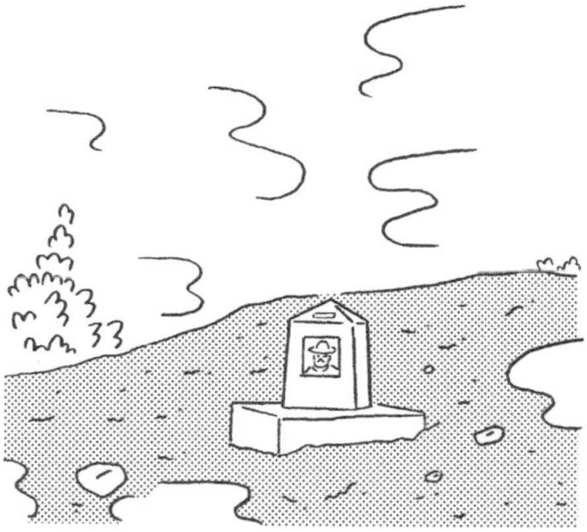

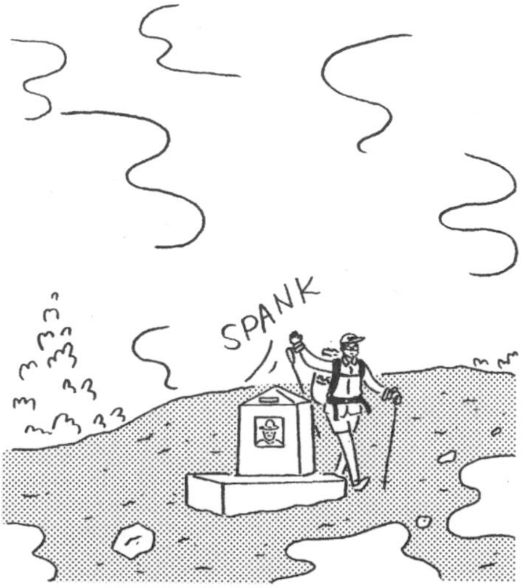
SPANK

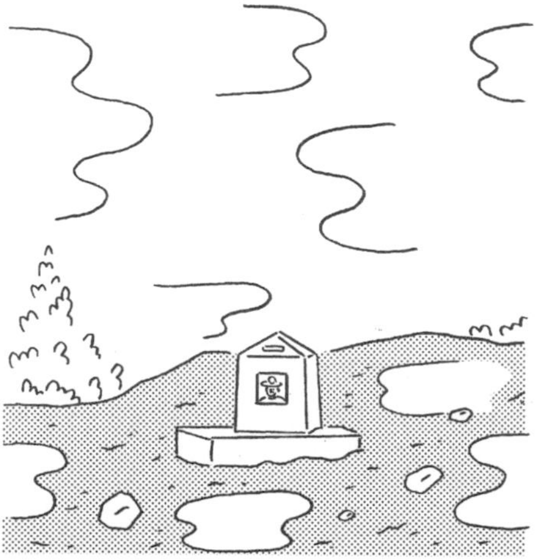

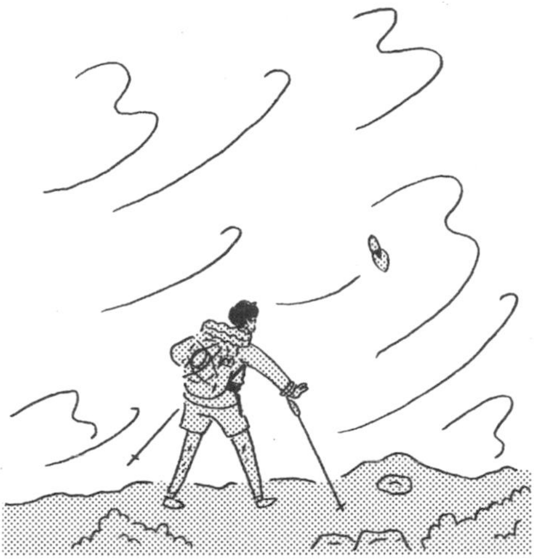

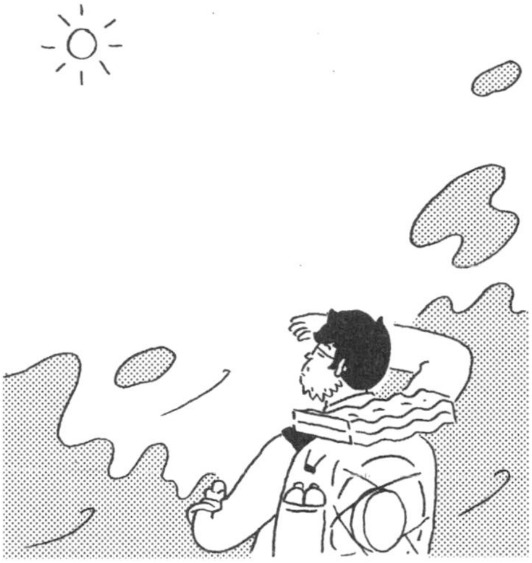

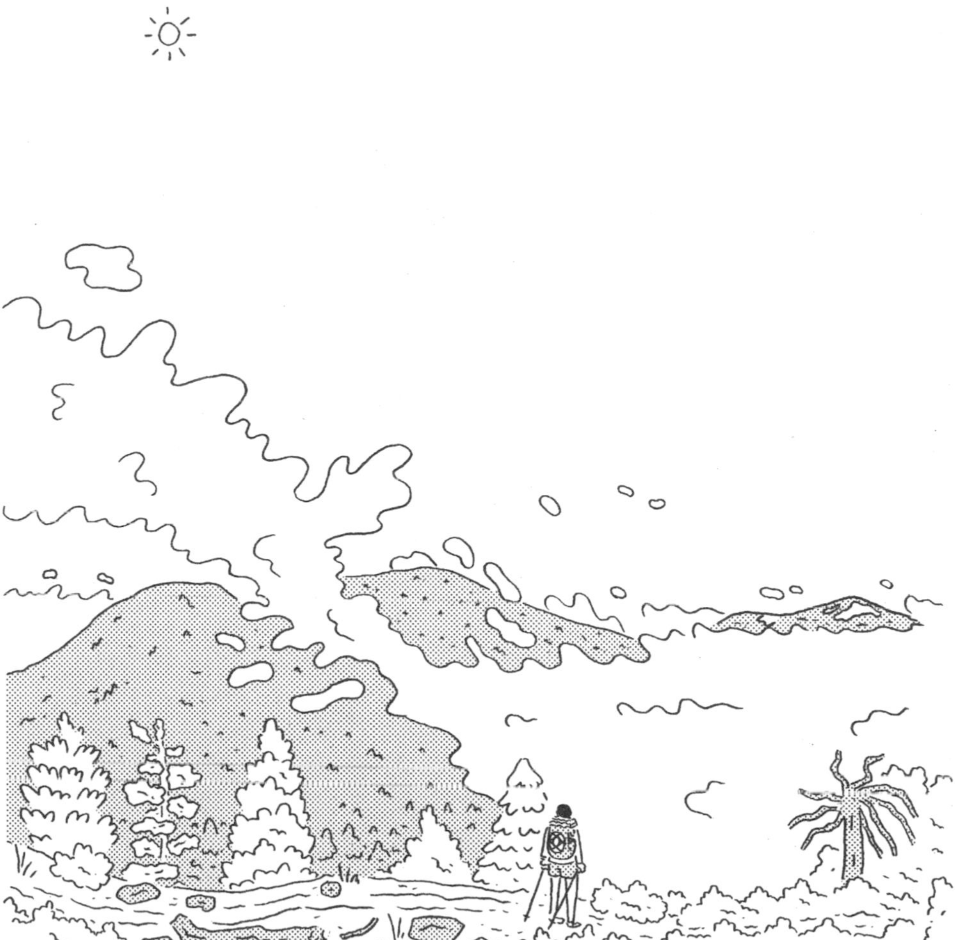

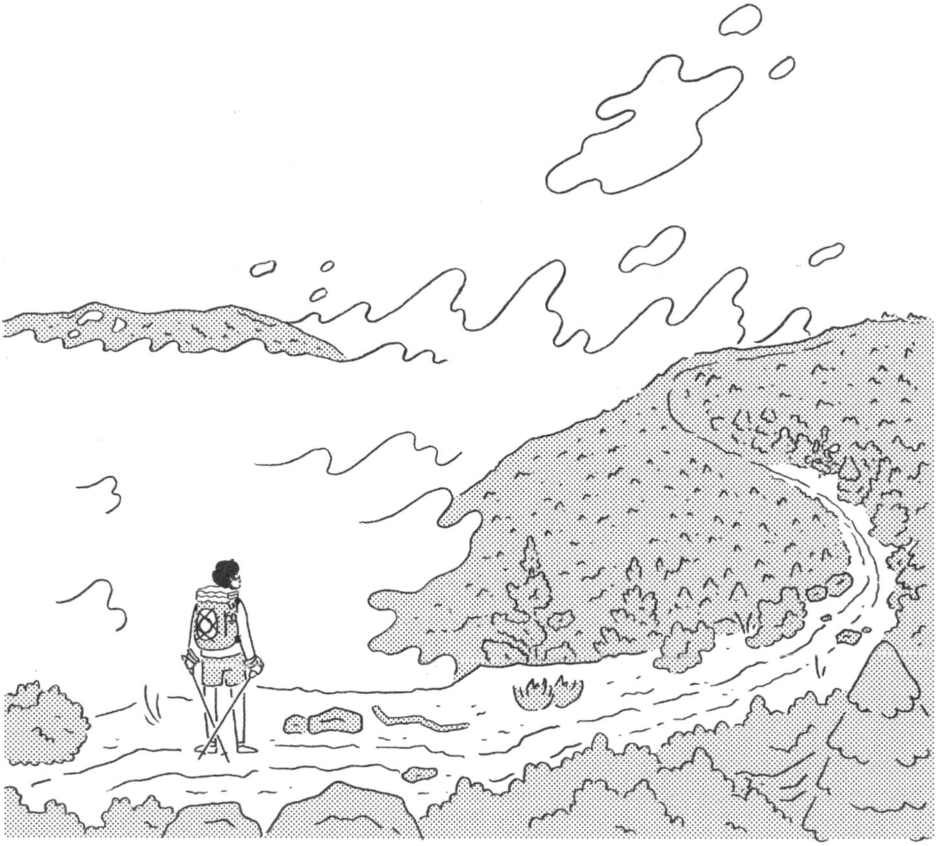

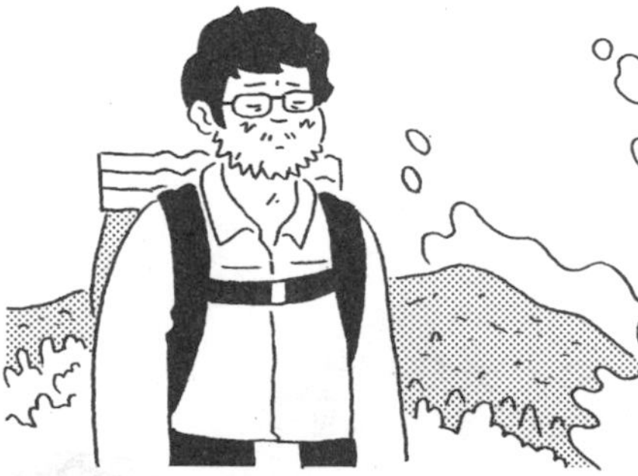

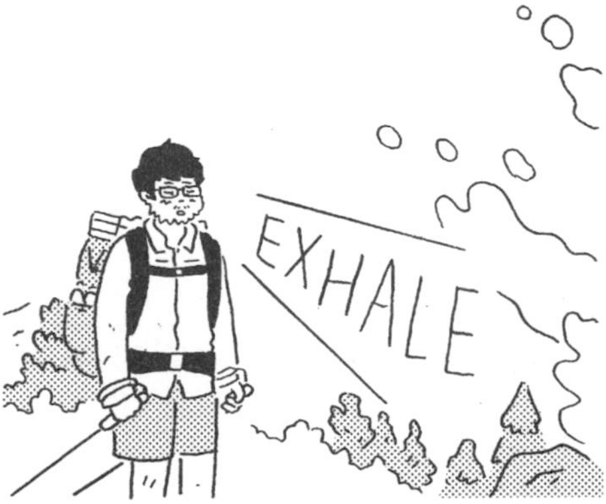
EXHALE

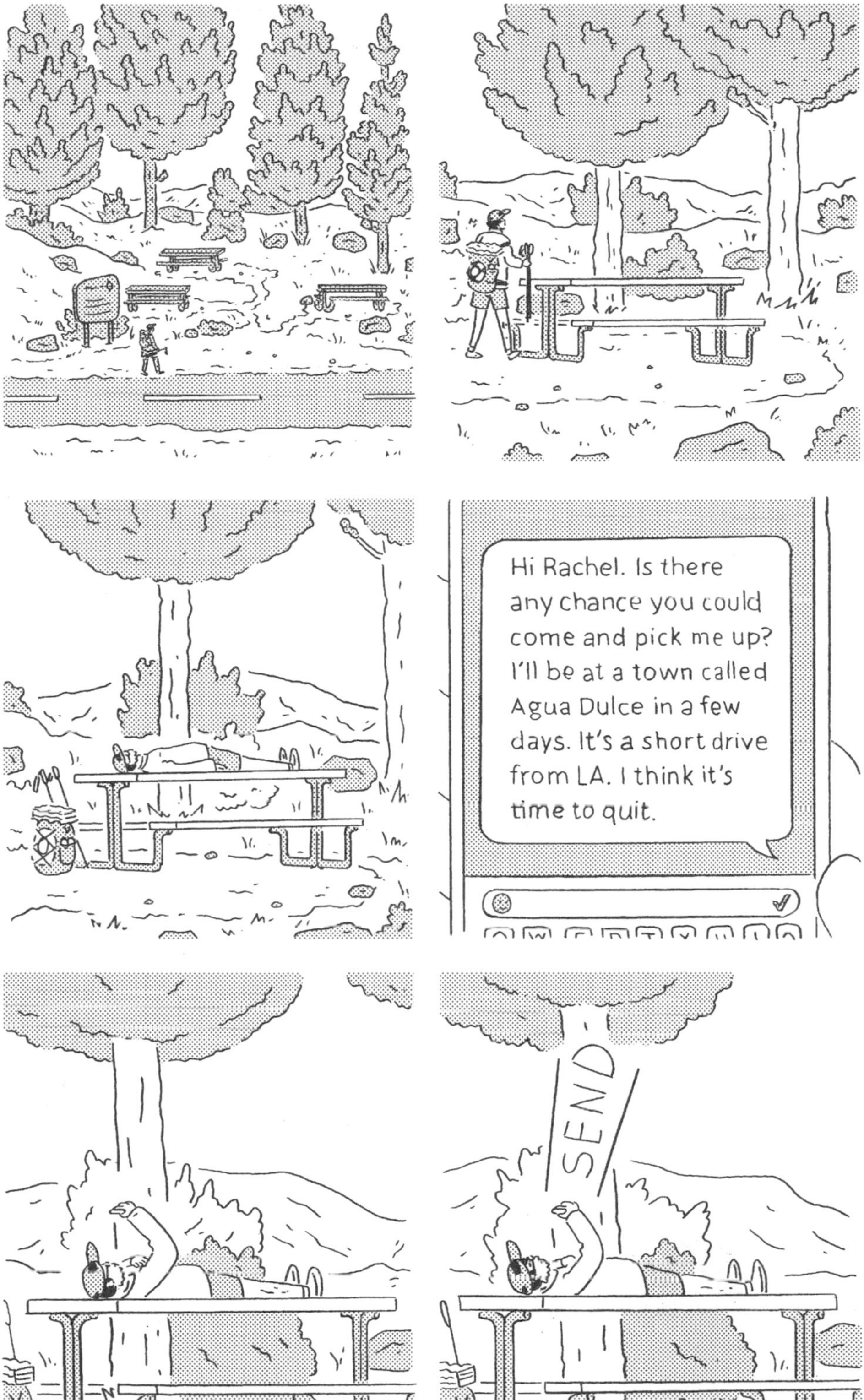
Hi Rachel. Is there any chance you could come and pick me up? I'll be at a town called Agua Dulce in a few days. It's a short drive from LA. I think it's time to quit.
SEND

Danny, Camy and Spreadsheet, who I'd camped with on my first night on the PCT, find me at the little rest stop alongside the Pacific Crest highway. They greet me with cheers and whoops. I feel as though a weight has been lifted already. I am a quitter, and it feels right. I only need to hike for five more days. Everything else can come after that.

I group up with them, but the hiking isn't easy. Between here and Agua Dulce, the trail is a mess of detours. The first pushes us off on to the remote mountain highway. Road walking in the heat is a killer. Our feet swell and throb, unused to the punishing concrete surface.

We talk about politics. The primaries for the presidential race are happening soon and it's a hot topic on trail. Most of the hikertrash are firmly in the left wing camp, but walking through small California towns, we constantly rub elbows with deep conservatives. I think about the hitches, townies and trail angels who have helped me along the way. I wonder how many of them would vote for Donald Trump.

"You'd never know," I say.

"I'd know," responds Danny, a dark skinned Mexican-American, and I feel like an asshole.

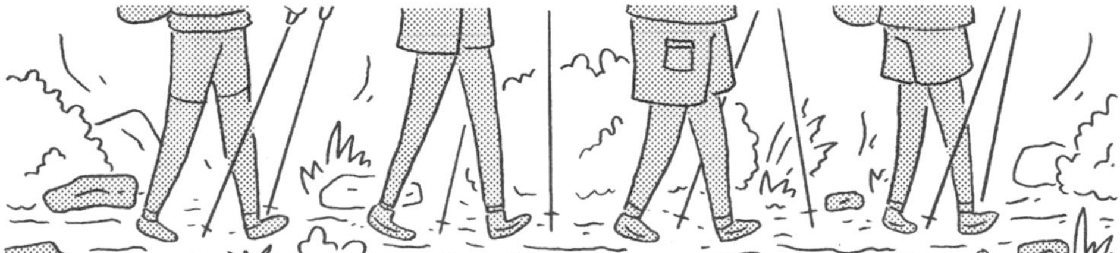

We pass the milestones.

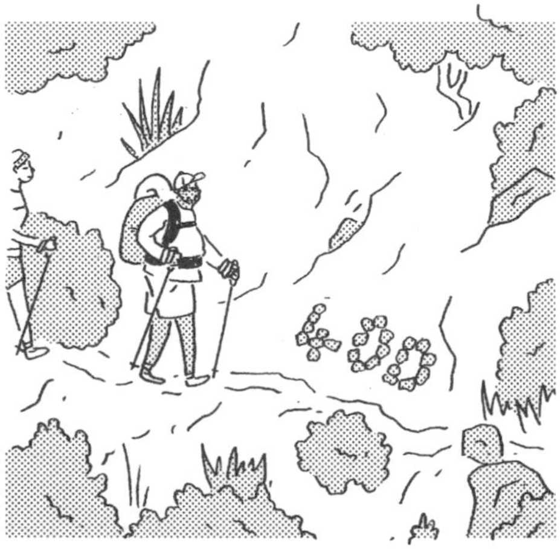
400

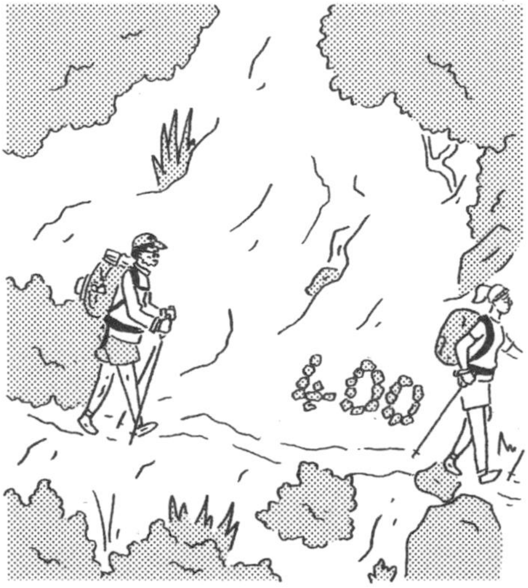
400

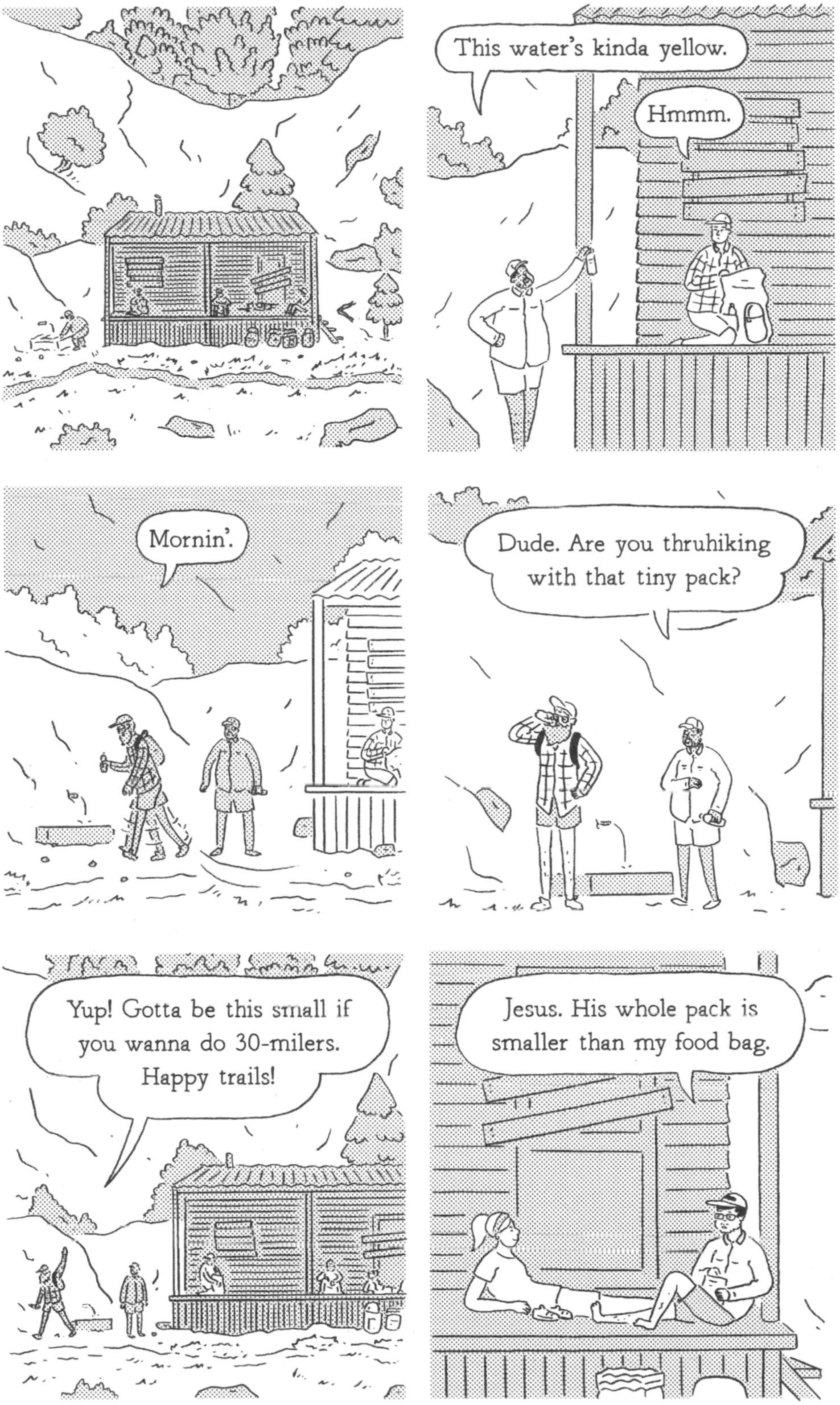
This water's kinda yellow.
Hmmm.
Mornin'.
Dude. Are you thruhiking with that tiny pack?
Yup! Gotta be this small if you wanna do 30-milers. Happy trails!
Jesus. His whole pack is smaller than my food bag.

We hike through a burned section of trail. The charred trees curl eerily from the earth, surrounded by energetic green shoots of new growth.

We all keep an eye out for poodle-dog bush, which if touched, causes a severe allergic reaction that can land a hiker in hospital. It grows quickly after a fire, thriving in the competition-free environment. We keep our noses trained for its distinct, marijuana-like odour.

Ahead, a section of trail is closed, detoured along an abandoned mountain road to avoid a stretch of trail completely consumed by poodle-dog bush. It's the site of one of the worst fires to hit the PCT in recent history. Huge sections of the park it runs through are still closed to everyone but passing thruhikers. We pass a memorial for two firefighters who lost their lives.

At the base of a valley, we join some other hikers, crouched in the shade behind a remote fire station. We pour water from the station's faucets and drink litre after litre. We wait until evening to tackle the abandoned road. It's too hot in the sun. Griz and Craftsman arrive and rope up their tarps to provide some shade.

The sun hangs high, well into the evening. I tell the others that I've decided to quit. They all protest, except for Griz, who congratulates me.

Hey man, you hiked 400 miles.

I'll hydrate to that.

The poodle-dog detour is brutal, even without the midday sun.

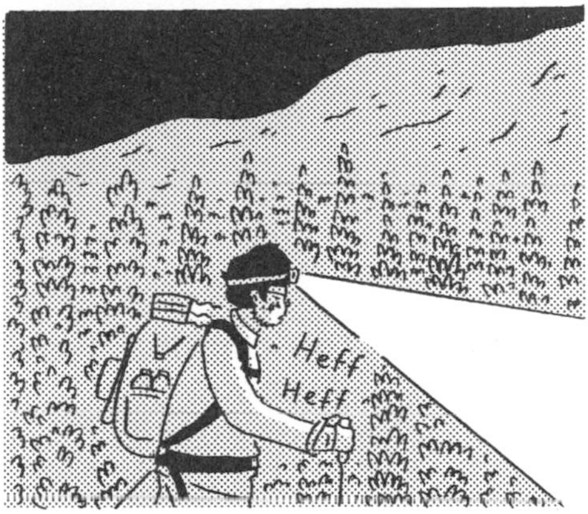
Heff
Heff

The entire detour is on a road.

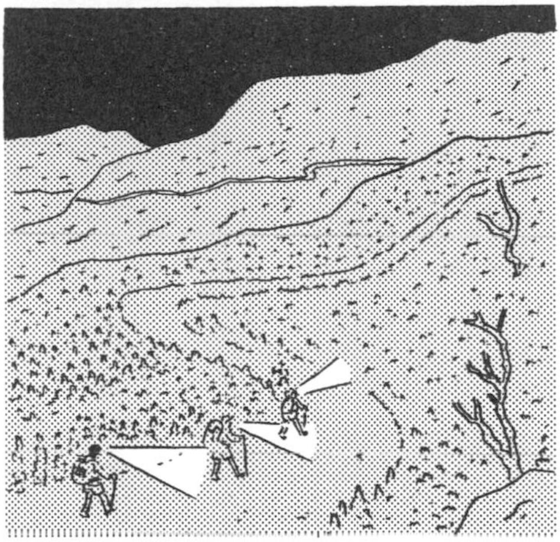

And uphill.

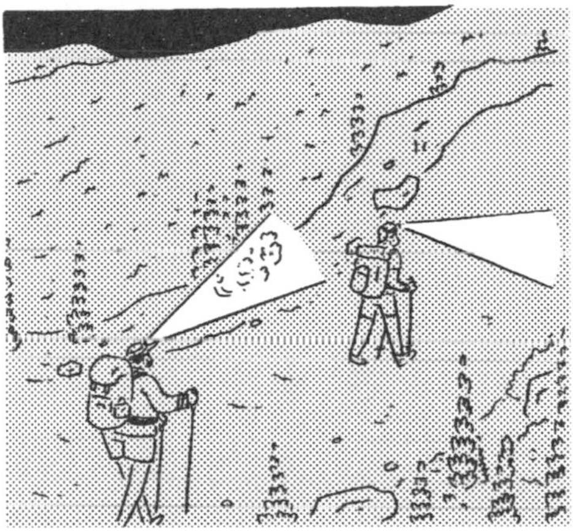

Our feet are screaming.

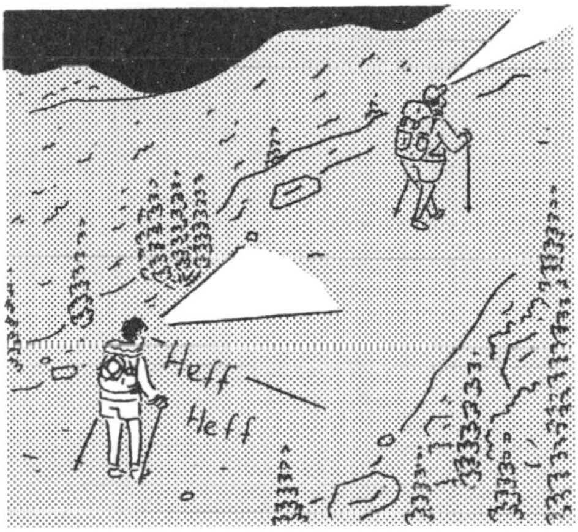
Heff
Heff

Poodle-dog bush curtains both sides of the road. Nowhere to sit, nowhere to rest, nowhere to pee.

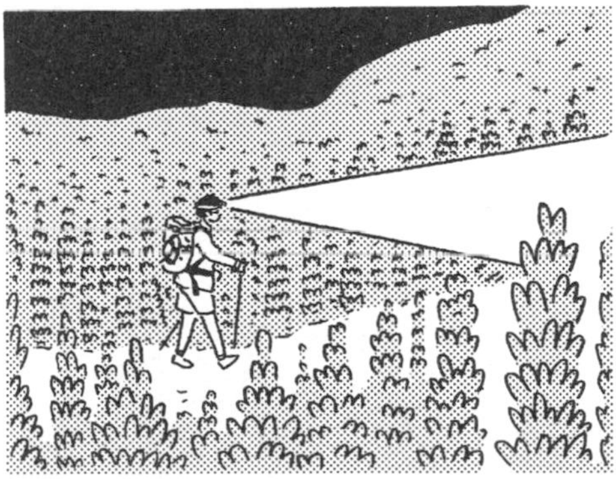

We bunch together, a band of headlamps bobbing through the night.

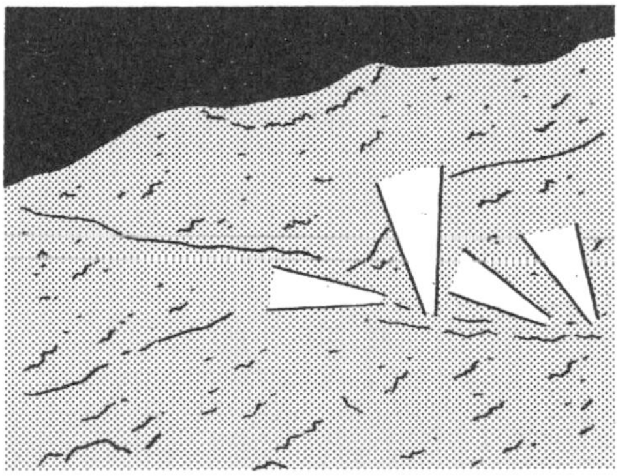

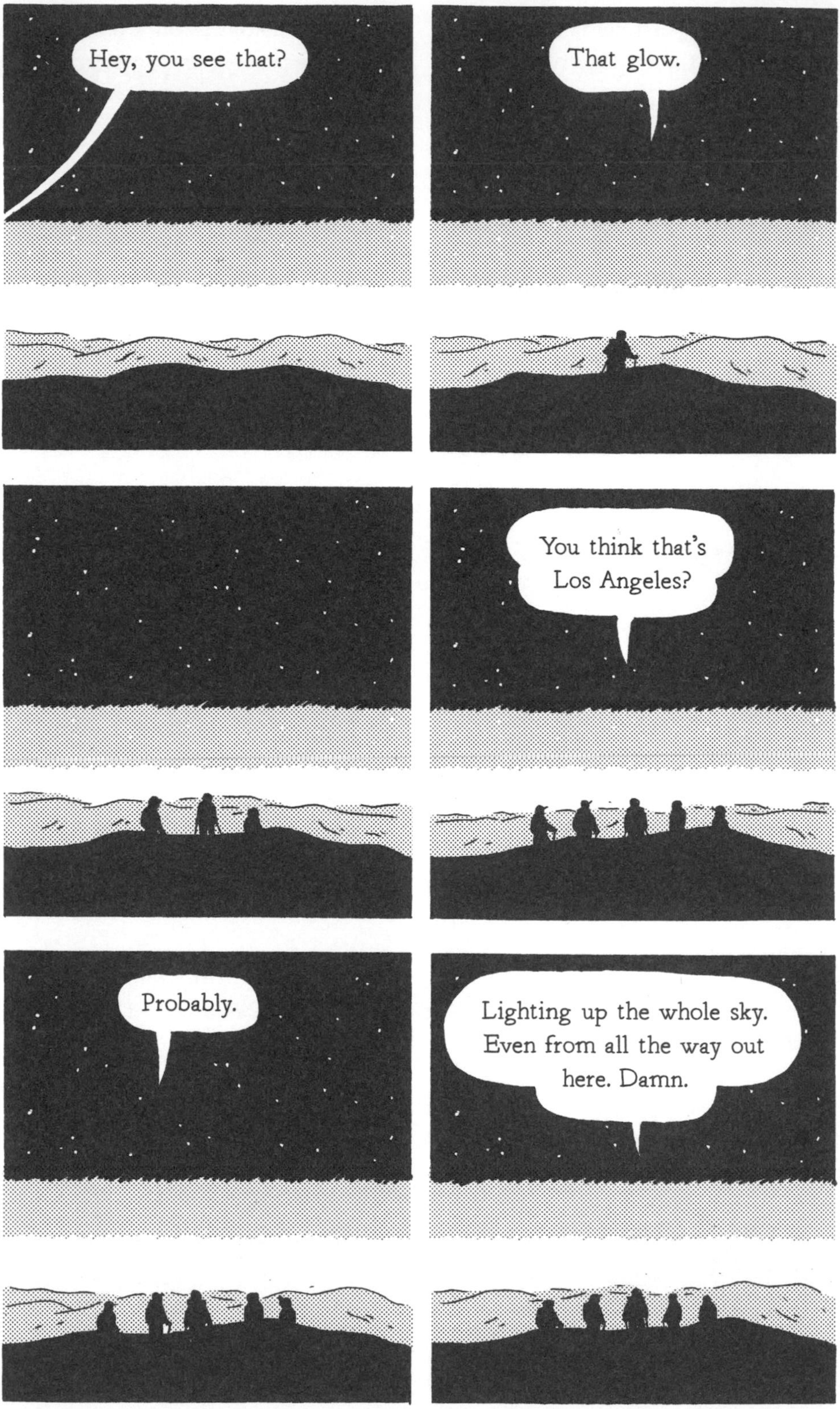
Hey, you see that?
That glow.
You think that's Los Angeles?
Probably.
Lighting up the whole sky. Even from all the way out here. Damn.

We reach the campsite just as it starts to rain, and set up in the dark.

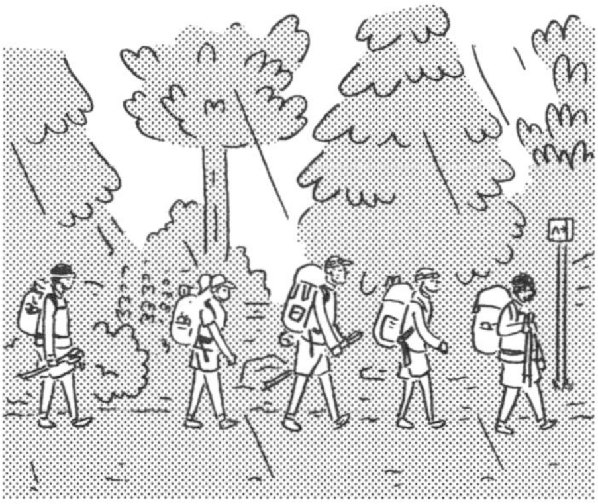

Our movements are automatic by now. Unpacking packs, looping knots, driving stakes.

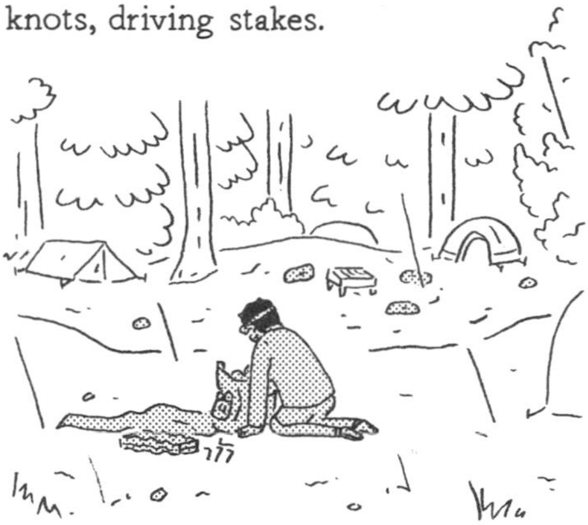

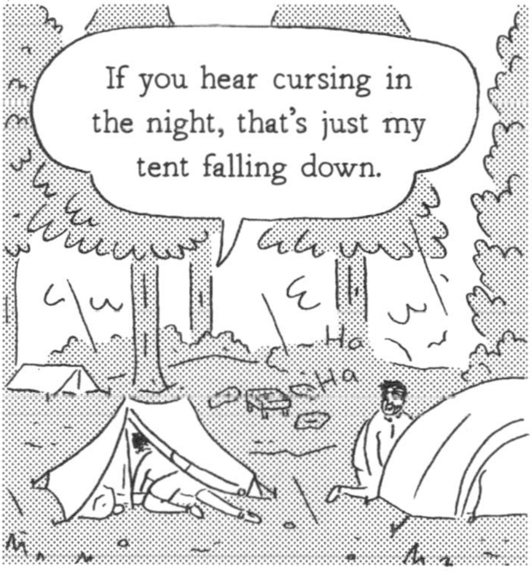
If you hear cursing in the night, that's just my tent falling down.
Ha
Ha

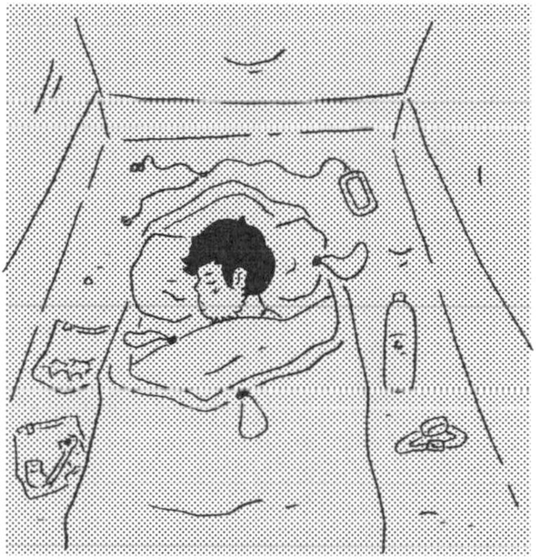

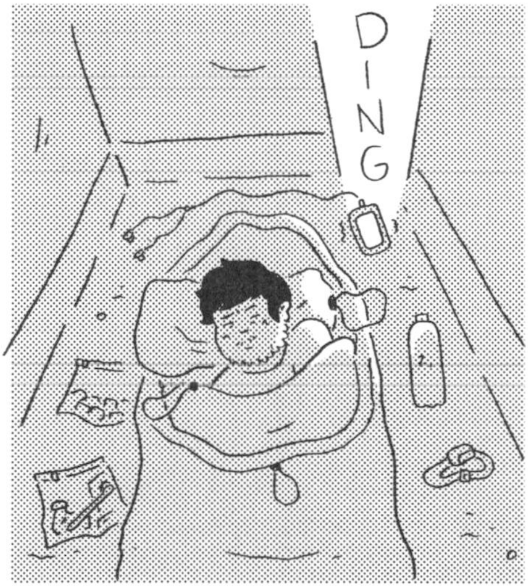
DING

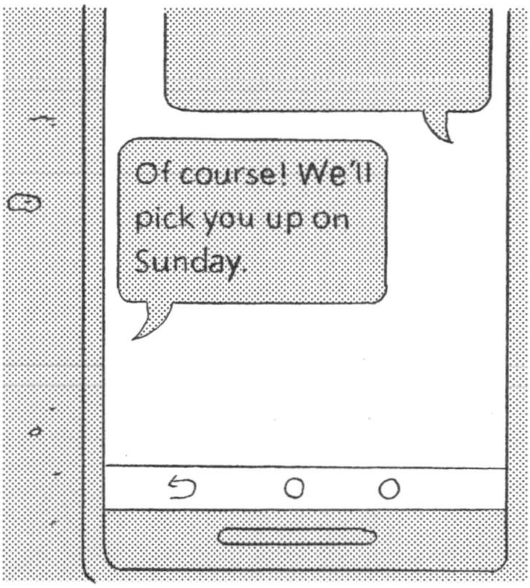
Of course! We'll pick you up on Sunday.

Some days it feels like the whole PCT is some big optical illusion.

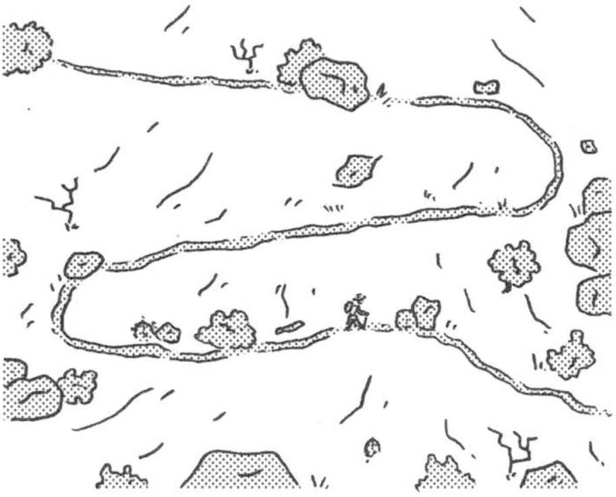

Just when you think you're going downhill, it switches back to climbing.

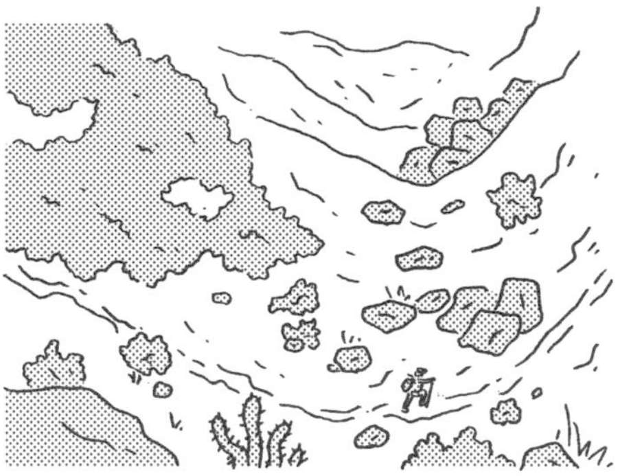

The top of a mountain is always a false summit.

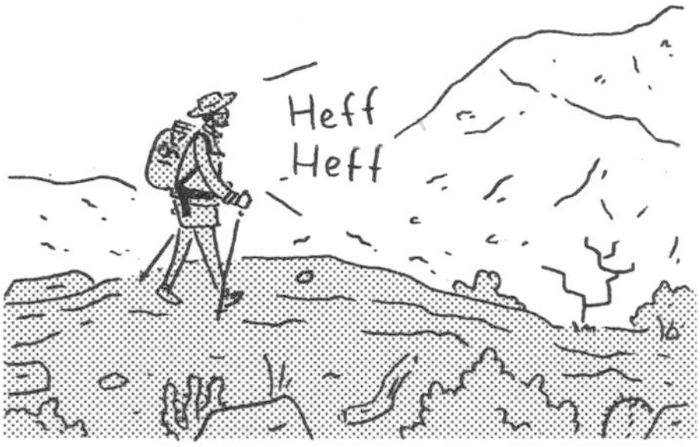
Heff
Heff

The trails you see in the distance are never the ones you'll have to hike.

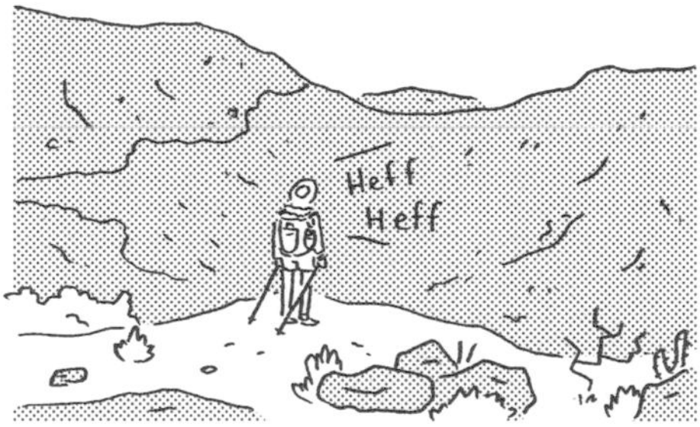
Heff
Heff

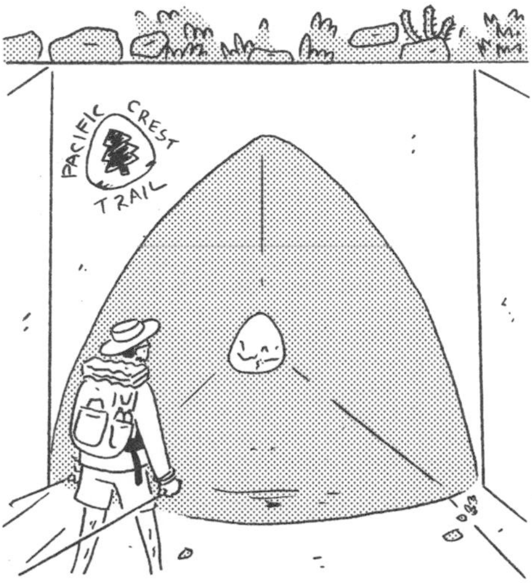
PACIFIC CREST TRAIL

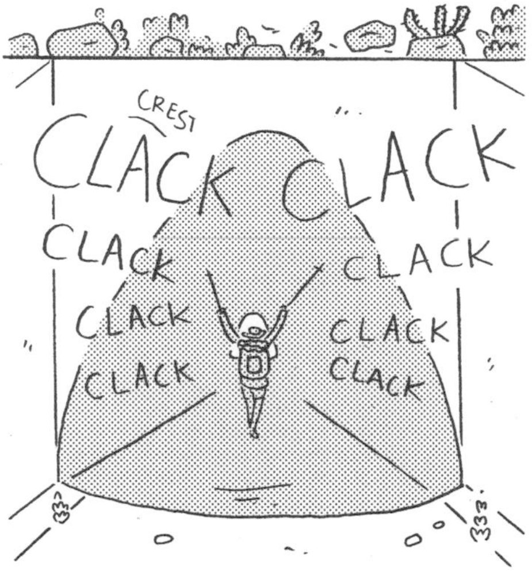
CREST
CLACK CLACK
CLACK
CLACK
CLACK
CLACK
CLACK
CLACK

I criss-cross with Mile 55 on my final stretch.

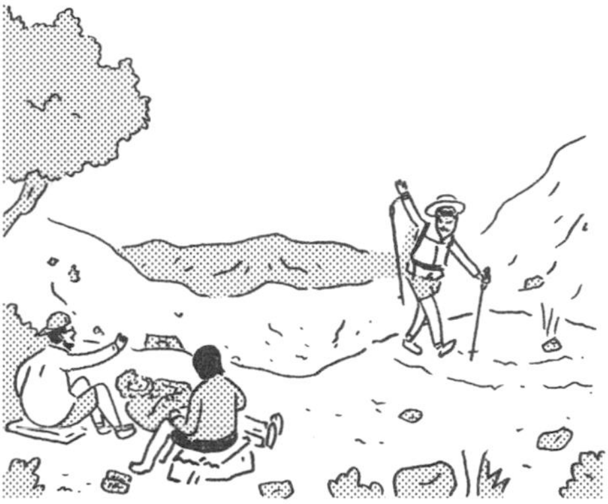

They always look like they're having a great time.

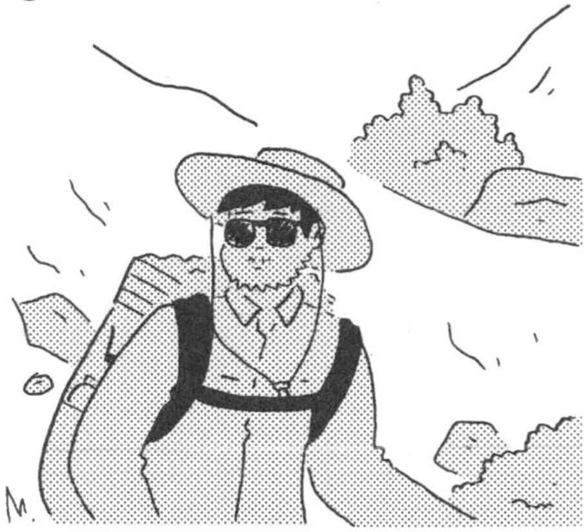

I hike with Toe Touch through the alien-looking Vasquez Rocks.

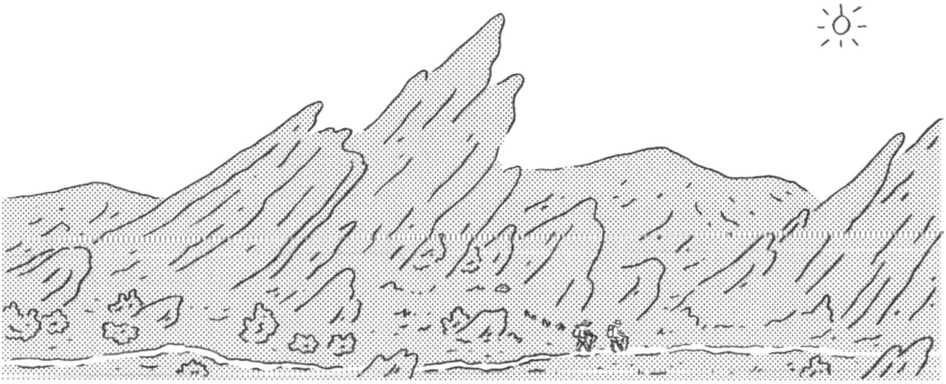

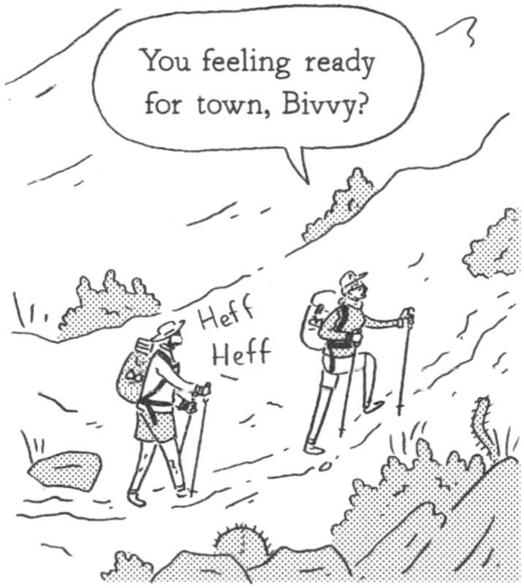
You feeling ready for town, Bivvy?
Heff Heff

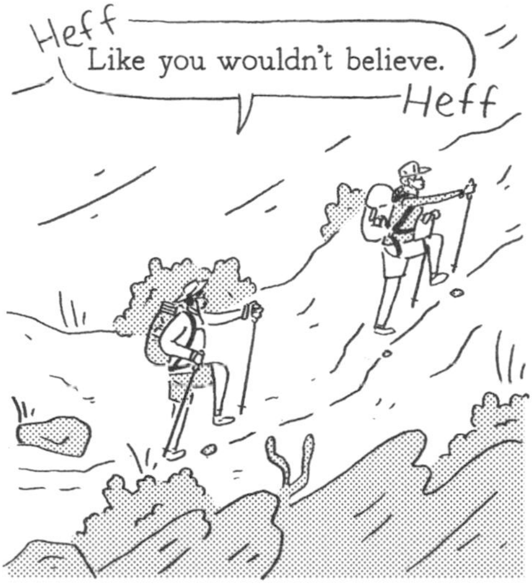
Heff
Like you wouldn't believe.
Heff

Agua Dulce 14/05/16. Day 29.

I set up my tent in a trail angel's yard.

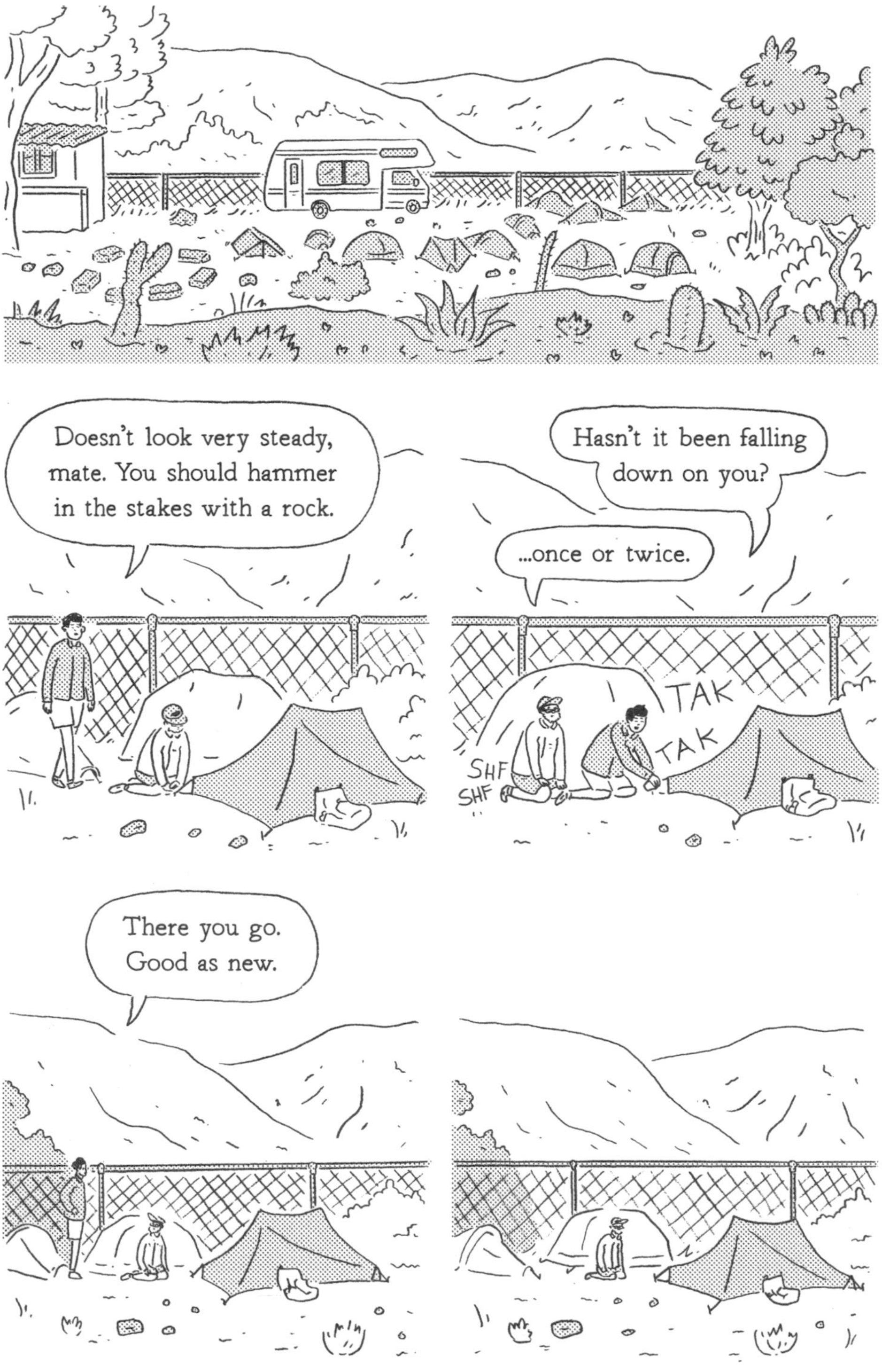
Doesn't look very steady, mate. You should hammer in the stakes with a rock.
Hasn't it been falling down on you?
...once or twice.
SHF SHF
TAK TAK
There you go. Good as new.

In the evening, I sit down for pizza with Mile 55.

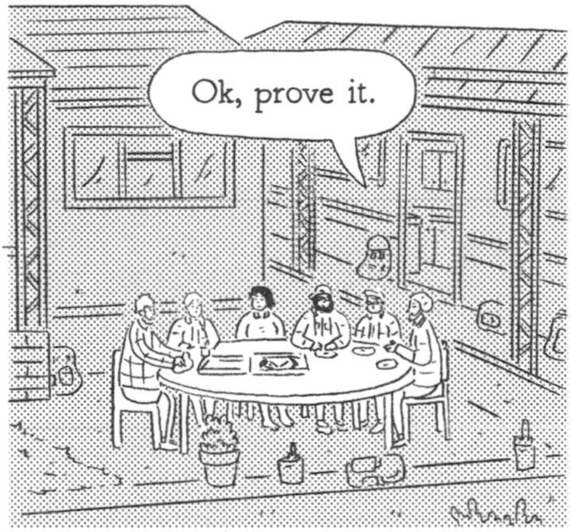
Ok, prove it.

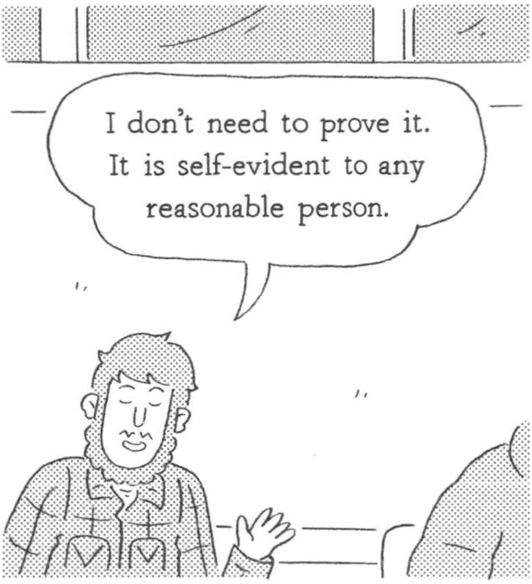
I don't need to prove it. It is self-evident to any reasonable person.

Centerfold and Toe Touch.

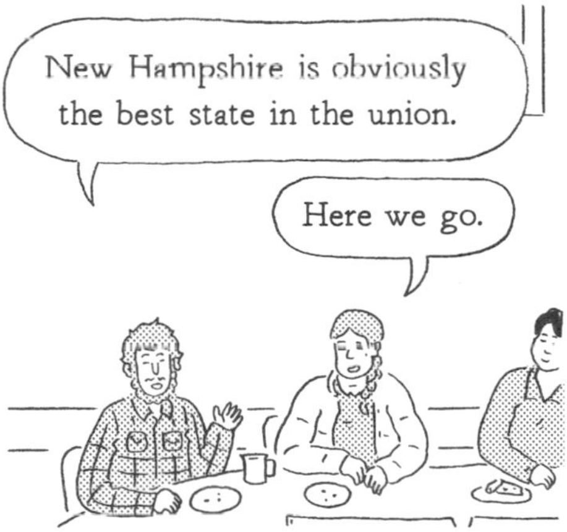
New Hampshire is obviously the best state in the union.
Here we go.

Chuckles and Little Spoon.

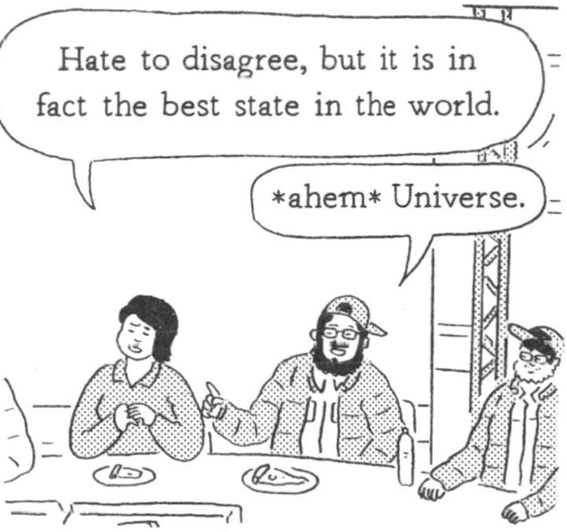
Hate to disagree, but it is in fact the best state in the world.
ahem Universe.

Camel.

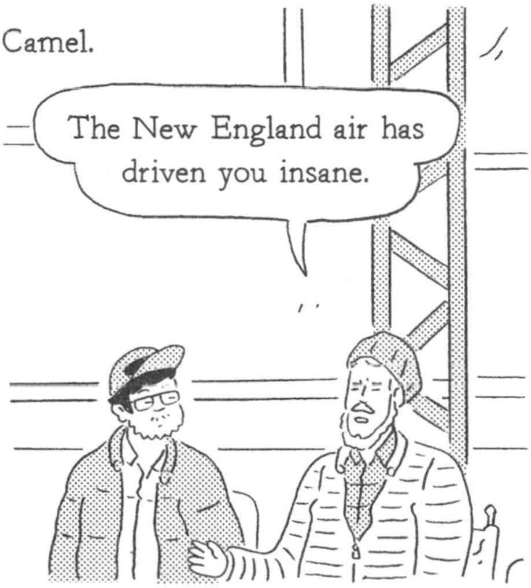
The New England air has driven you insane.

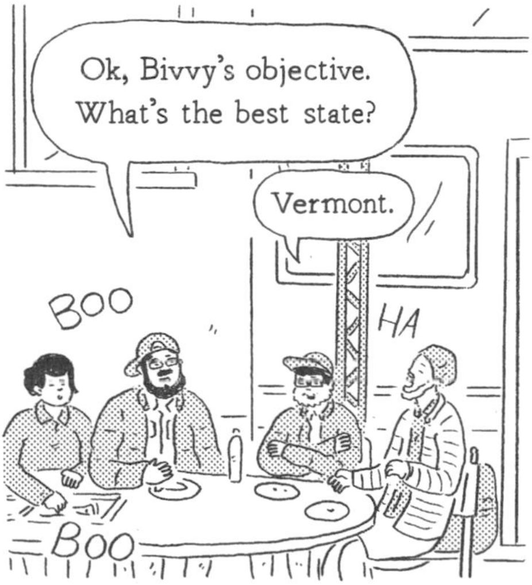
Ok, Bivvy's objective. What's the best state?
Vermont.
BOO
HA
BOO

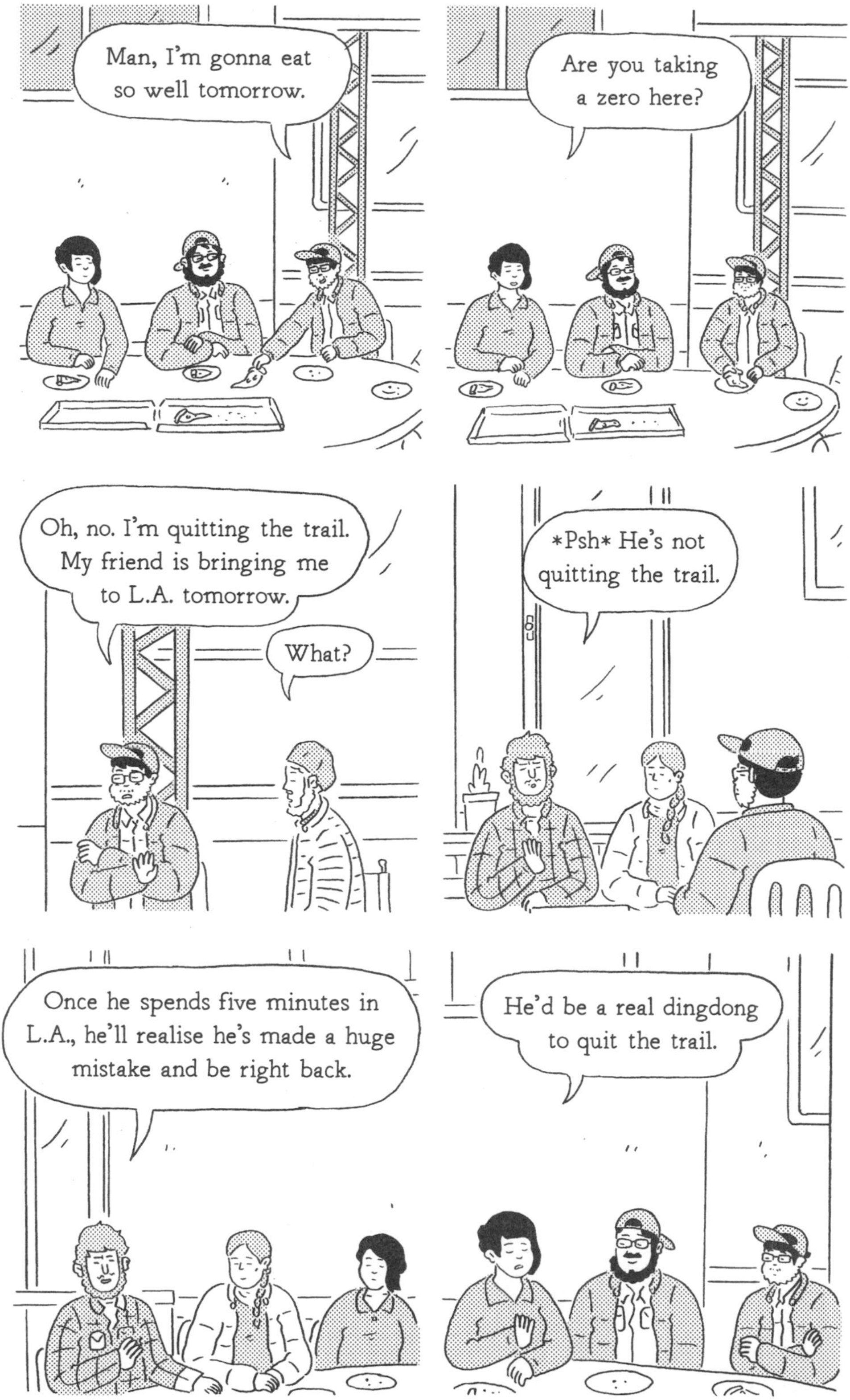
Man, I'm gonna eat so well tomorrow.
Are you taking a zero here?
Oh, no. I'm quitting the trail. My friend is bringing me to L.A. tomorrow.
What?
Psh He's not quitting the trail.
Once he spends five minutes in L.A., he'll realise he's made a huge mistake and be right back.
He'd be a real dingdong to quit the trail.

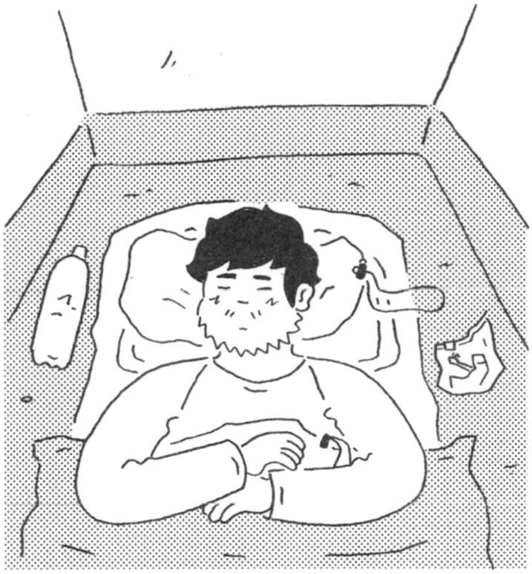

I've been hiking for 29 days.

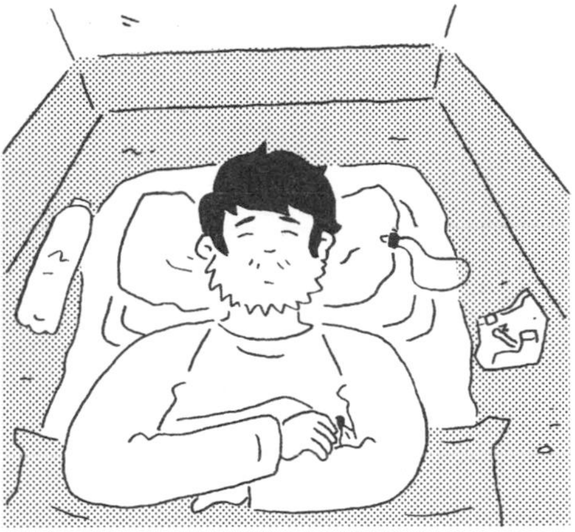

I have walked 450 miles.

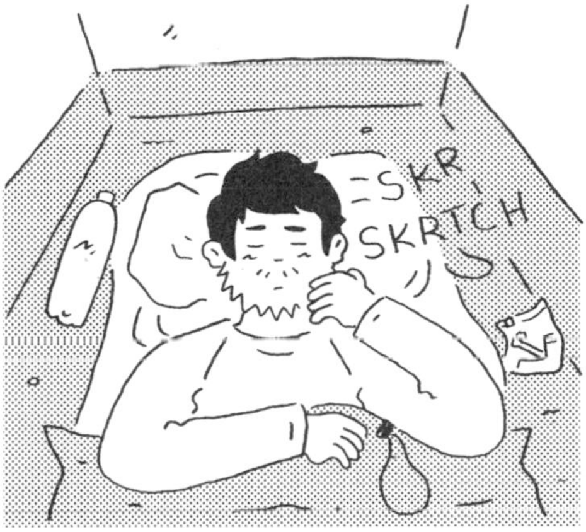
SKR
SKRTCH

I have showered 8 times.

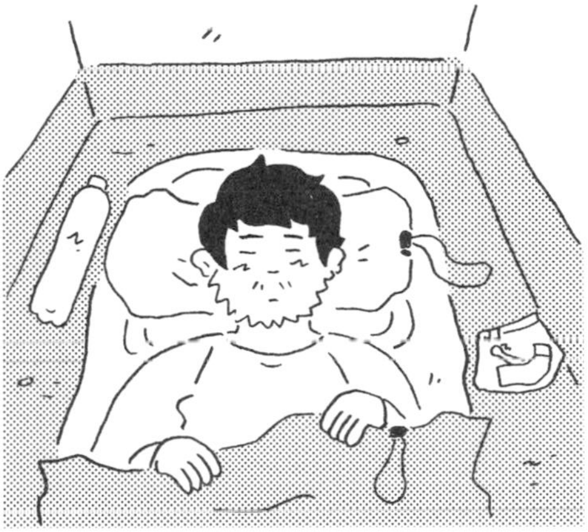

I have aches in every inch
of my body.

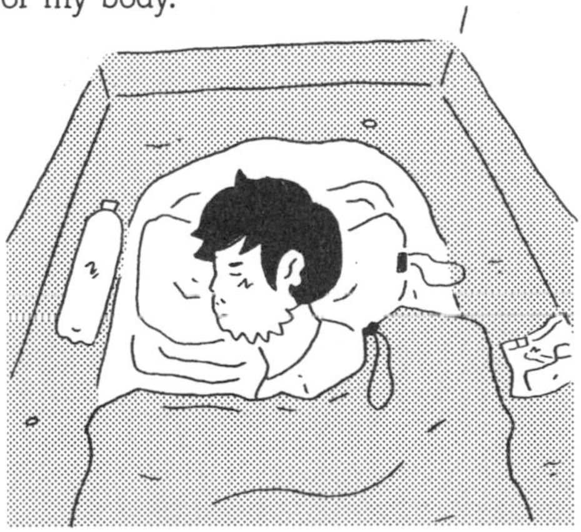

I am going home.

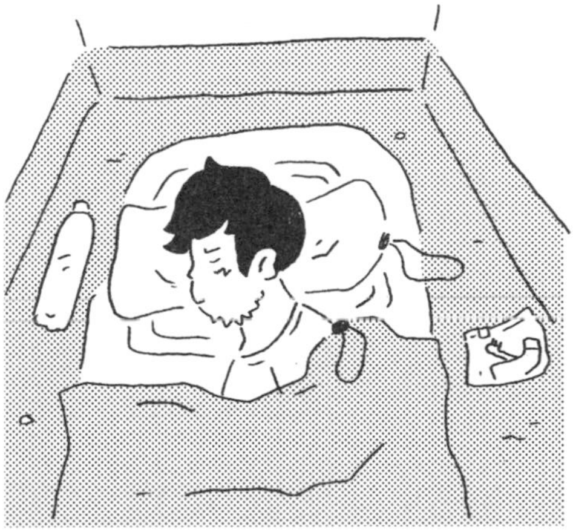

New York City, 2012.

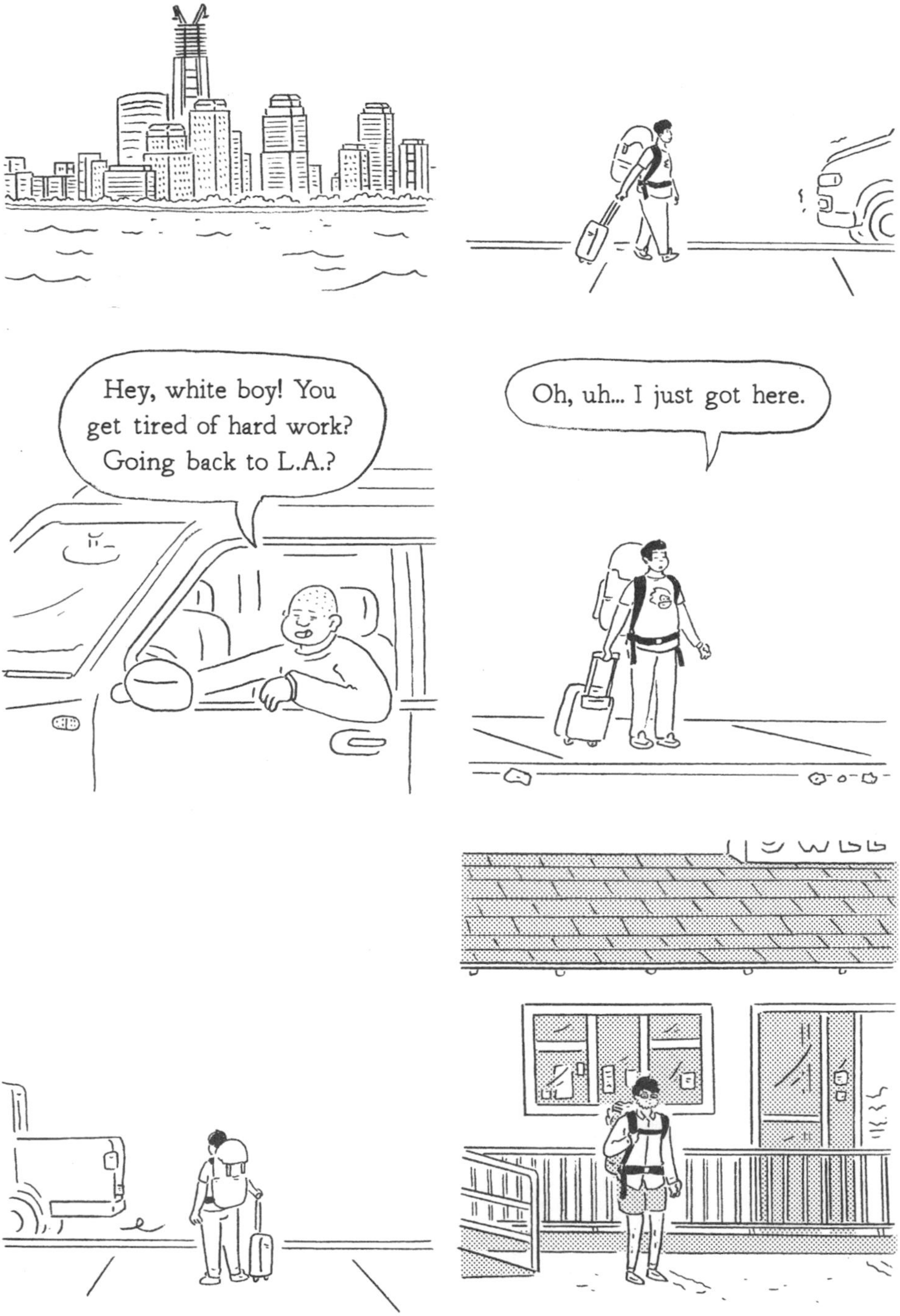

Hey, white boy! You get tired of hard work? Going back to L.A.?
Oh, uh... I just got here.

Rachel and Mike drive me back to Los Angeles.

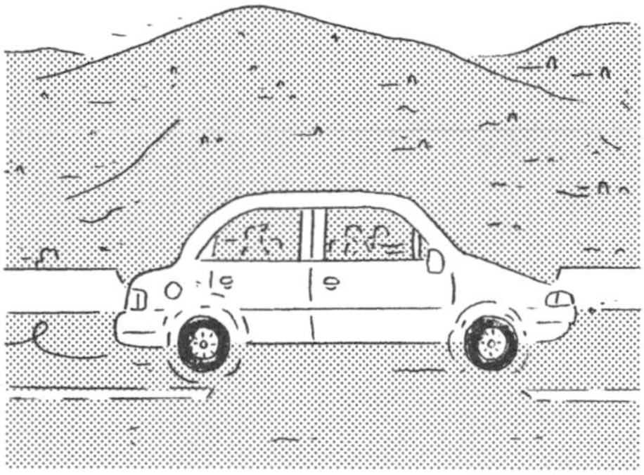

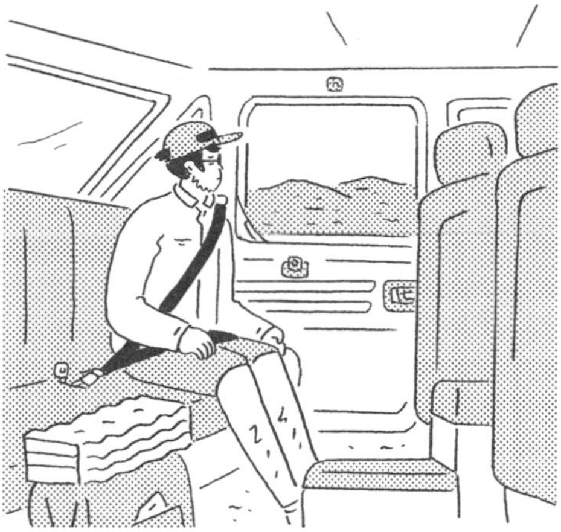

Even at this speed, my brain picks out the trails.

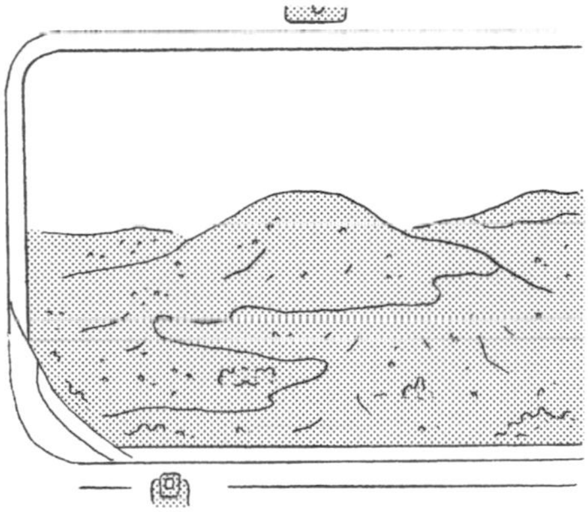

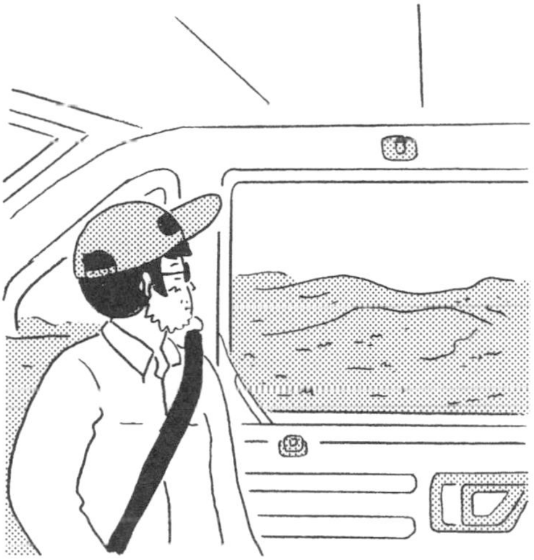

Aw, nuts.

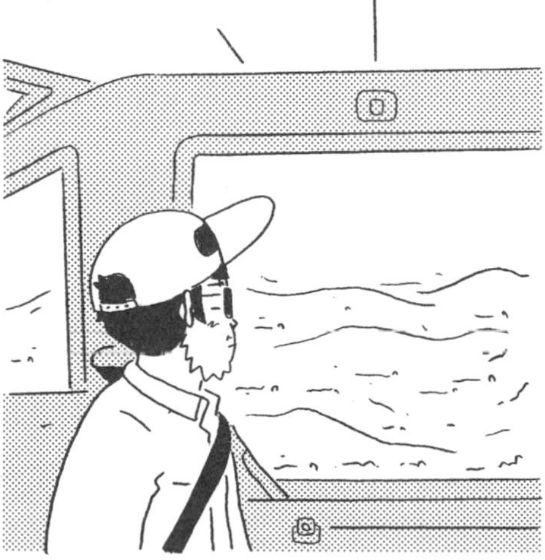

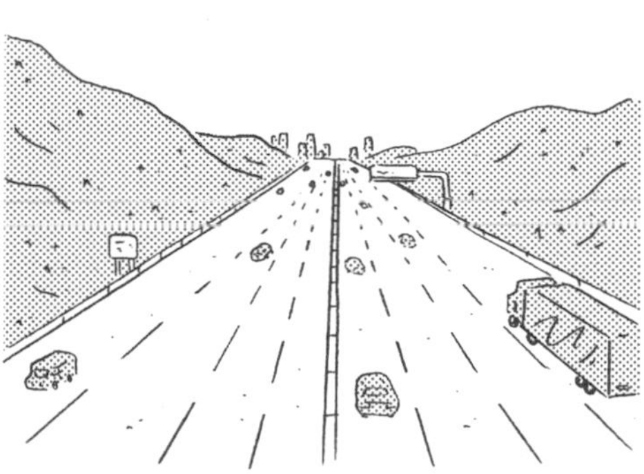

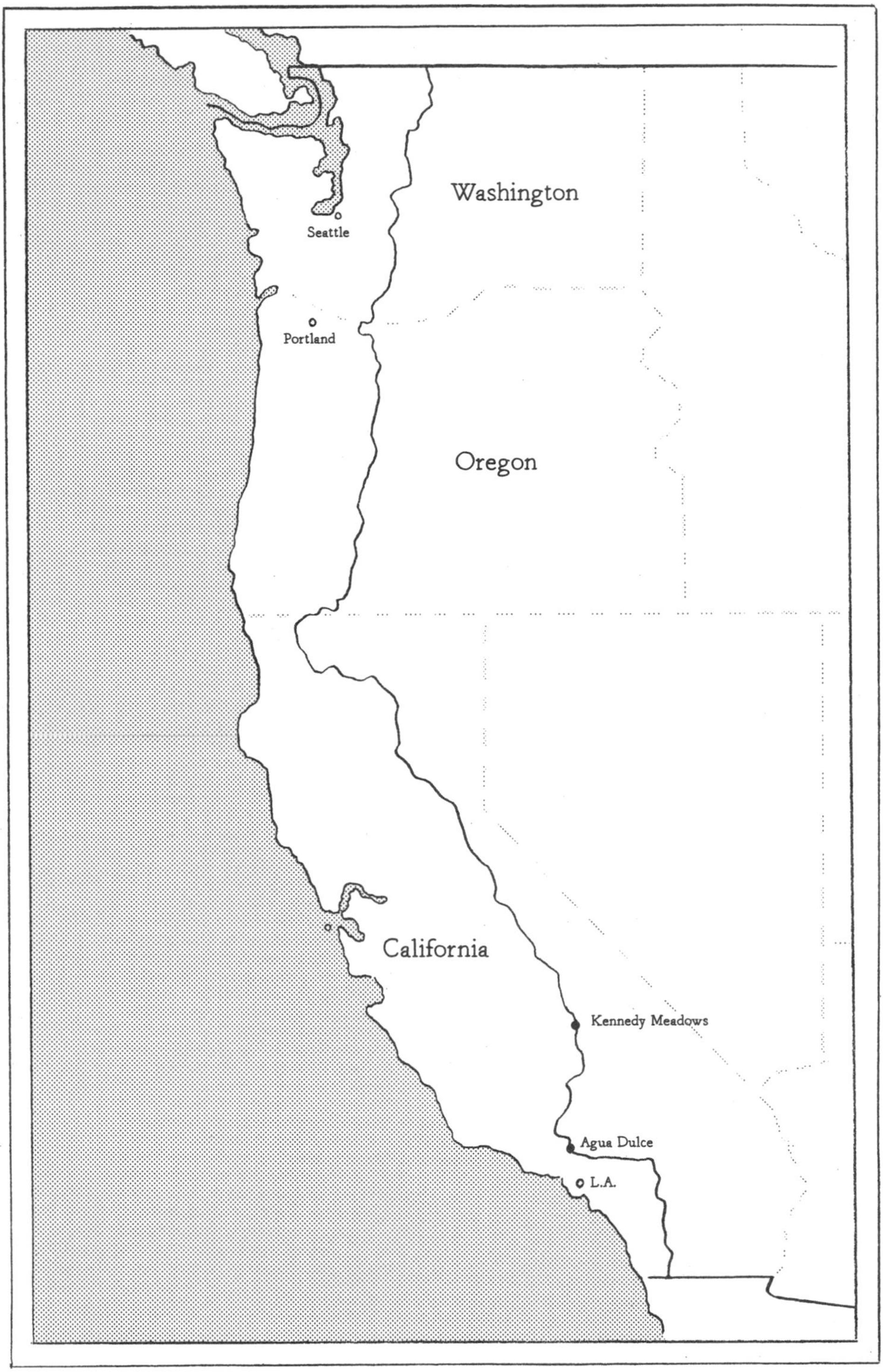
Washington
Seattle
Portland
Oregon
California
Kennedy Meadows
Agua Dulce
L.A.

Chapter 2: The Desert (Part II)

"Everybody has their own America... you've pieced
them together from scenes in movies and music and
lines from books. And you live in your dream America
that you've custom-made from art and schmaltz and
emotions just as much as you live in your real one."
–Andy Warhol

I first moved to the USA at the age of twenty-one, four years before
setting foot on the PCT. I relocated to study Cartooning at a tiny grad
school in the wilds of Vermont – a quiet, East Coast state.

Stepping off the train at White River Junction was like stepping
straight into a Hollywood movie. A Halloween movie perhaps, with
its spooky New England architecture and rapidly browning maple
leaves, but a movie, still. I'd spent months investigating the town from
my vantage point in Ireland, watching videos and clicking through
street photos, trying and failing to get a sense of the place. The sheer
3D-ness of Vermont was somehow a surprise to me. I was mesmerised
by the buildings and the bridges, and the fog that clung to the distant
Green Mountains. The same way I'd feel when taking my first steps
into the California desert, four years later.

White River Junction had about two thousand residents and one
real street, Main Street. Once, it had been a busy destination, a fact
made evident by the monochrome "glory days" photos that hung in

so many of the town's historic buildings. It was a railway town, though only one passenger train actually stopped there each day in 2012, now near-obsolete in the age of super highways.

I moved into an illegal apartment in a sectioned-off row house near the edge of town, and paid my landlord in cash. White River Junction had a stained glass store, and a store that sold lampshades painted with landscapes named "Lampscapes". I had to walk across the river to do my laundry and get groceries, crossing out of Vermont and into the neighbouring state of New Hampshire.

There were only three non-Americans attending the school in White River Junction: myself, Eleri from Australia and Iris from Brazil. Eleri and I got on well, and often presented a united front when protesting against certain quirks of US comics-making. Contending with imperial measurements, for example, or the impractical US paper sizes, with which we became intimately acquainted during hours in the school's book-making lab, folding minicomics and zines.

The comics scene at the time had a DIY attitude that I found exhilarating. The school was filled with punks, zinesters and dorks of all descriptions. Three or four times a year, this meant long road trips to comics festivals around the USA. In my first week, five of us piled into a car, with a trunk full of photocopied comics, and drove ten hours to Washington DC to sell our work.

I got to see a lot of the East Coast this way, from the back seat of a friend's car, pulling into indistinguishable rest stops and weirdo roadside attractions. I saw the USA, not only through a windshield, but also through the rose-tinted glasses of a young person pursuing their creative ambitions.

In the summer, between the first and second years of my degree, I received the email I'd been dreading. "Please provide us with details of your flight number. You must depart the United States of America on or before the date of October 1st 2013." My visa had expired.

My ejection at the end of that first year served as an unambiguous reminder of my place in the USA: "Non-resident", written plain across my visa.

My time in White River Junction was undeniably transformative. The self-consciousness and cynicism that had plagued me in Ireland began to fall away. It felt so liberating, I was practically intoxicated. My love for the USA was, quite simply, unrequited. And an unrequited love can only be sustained for so long.

I know very little about Luanne. We've met only once before, two years ago in New York City, and even then we spent only a couple of hours together. I text her from Rachel and Mike's car as we move with disorienting speed across the highway, back to Los Angeles.

"Meet me for lunch tomorrow. Then you can come back and stay at my place to rest up for a few nights. I have a spare room."

"Keep in mind, I'll be dressed like a hiker."

"Hmm. Somewhere casual then. How about... Chateau Marmont?"

Chateau Marmont is not casual. I stick out like a filthy, sweaty, incredibly sore thumb. I wear the same grimy brown shirt I've been wearing every day for a month, carrying my unwieldy hiking pack as we climb the immaculate driveway. Rachel fits in a little better, but is in full punk-zinester mode with a patch adorned jacket and a half-shaved head. The valet lets me check my pack so I don't have to carry it into the hotel, and I thank him with widened eyes.

We wait in the foyer, nervously eyeing each other, as people in expensive clothes, and the occasional movie actor, pass us by.

Luanne steps out of the elevator just as the receptionist's gaze turns from one of curiosity to one of suspicion. We hug and she leads us through to a table, where she treats us to an expensive lunch.

The only other time I'd met Luanne was at a New York comics festival. She was introduced to me as a fabulously successful writer, but at the time I failed to grasp what that meant. Seeing her now, amongst the glamorous Hollywood elite, I grasp the meaning quite clearly.

Luanne is like a whirlwind. She talks about her career as we ride back to her house in a private car, and she gossips a little about some famous actors she's friendly with. Her house is suitably gorgeous, a cliff top villa in Malibu, and she spares no effort in making me feel at home. I have my own bathroom with a tub, and I immediately excuse myself and fill it up. On the counter, there is a big bag of Epsom salt, and I tip a few handfuls into the bathwater before sinking in.

I feel funny. Relaxed, in one sense. I know that I won't have to get up and hike all day tomorrow or struggle with my collapsing tent before I can go to sleep tonight. But I also feel restless, a little guilty maybe. On my night in Agua Dulce, I'd bonded with Mile 55. Now, I think about them moving up the trail while I'm just lying still.

An impulse tells me to return to the trail immediately. Rejoin the hike before my window closes. After all, on the PCT, there is no stopping – only quitting. But with a swift reversal, I could possibly rejoin the trail without falling too far behind the other hikers I know...

I halt that train of thought. Through the bathwater, I can see my thinning, mistreated body. The salts sting the cuts on my feet and legs.

I've done this before. Again and again. So, I return to the trail and then what? Chase down Mile 55 like I chased down Bojangles and the brothers? People I barely know, but have convinced myself will be great friends. It's naïve, and thinking about it makes me embarrassed, so I push it out of mind as I plunge my head into the salty water.

I sit on Luanne's deck. On the beach below her cliff, surfers ride late into the warm L.A. evening. I can't hear them from up here, only the gentle swish and crash of the ocean waves. I tell her that I'd like to go back to the trail. I say it all at once, as though the decision was living inside my throat, waiting to burst out.

"I need to catch my friends," I say.

We drive to the Santa Monica Pier and watch the Ferris wheel and merry-go-round. We eat Caribbean food, which tastes amazing compared to my sad collection of instant ramen. We catch a movie and then at dinner afterwards, sit only a few tables away from its director.

At a gear store, I buy new socks and then in an awkward moment, Luanne buys me the ice axe and bear canister I'll need should I make it to the High Sierra mountains. I try to stop her, but she insists, and I sheepishly express my gratitude.

The next morning, we pack up my new mountaineering gear and mail it ahead to Kennedy Meadows, the last stop before the PCT climbs up into the High Sierras. Luanne drives me back up the highway to Agua Dulce. We follow the PCT, spotting its markers as it winds its way through the town, and pull up next to one final trail marker, nailed to a post.

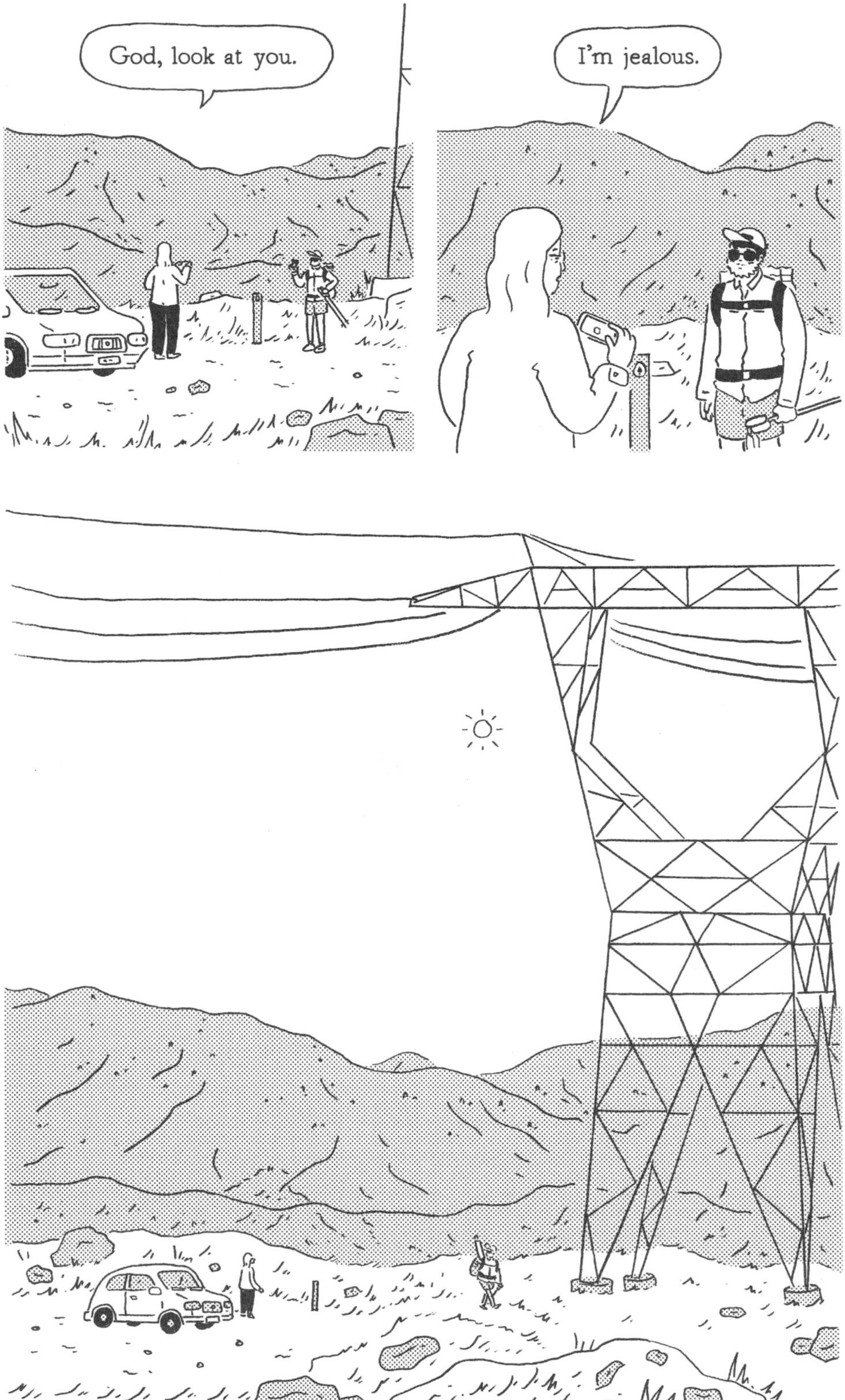
God, look at you.
I'm jealous.

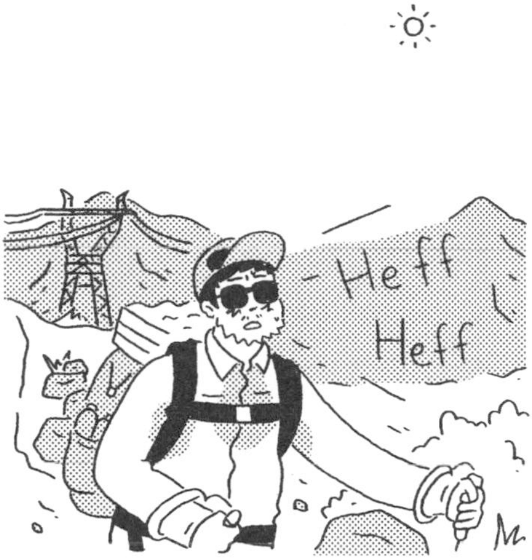
Heff
Heff

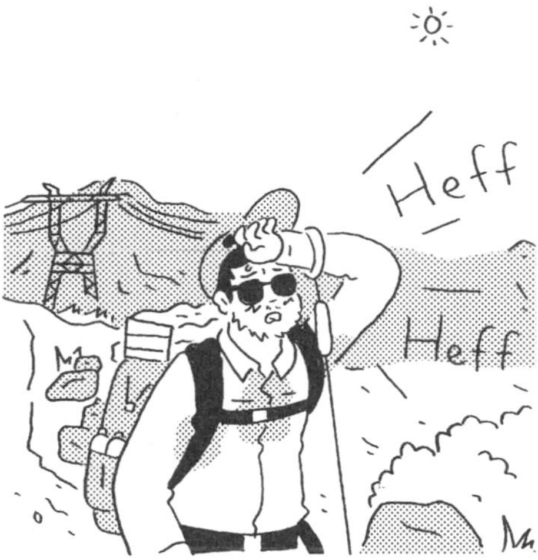
Heff
Heff

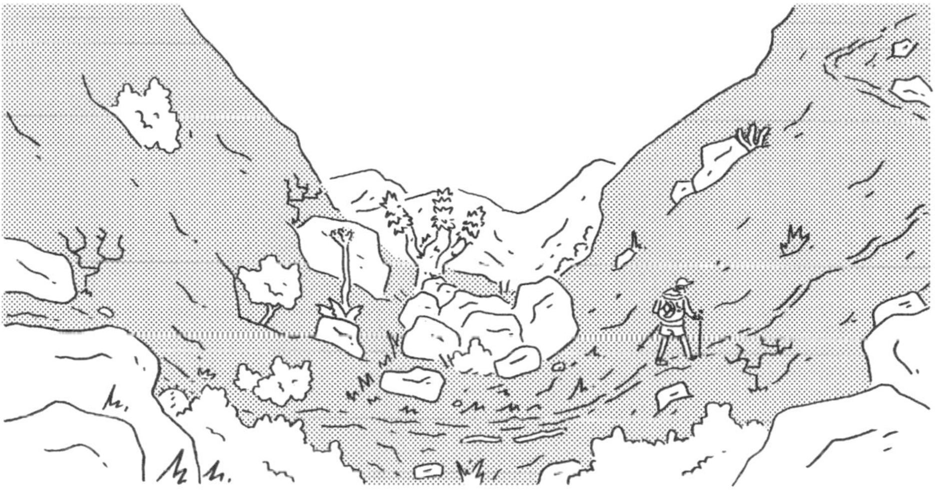

Is it possible to fall out of shape in three days?

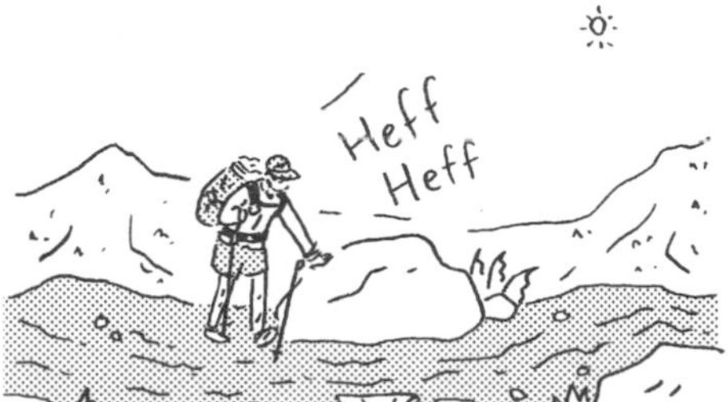
Heff
Heff

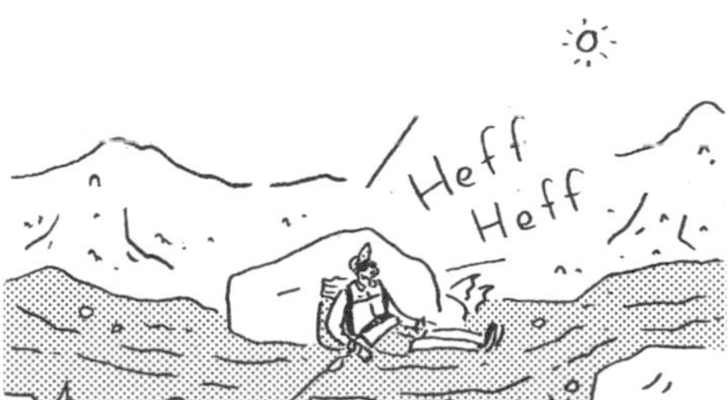
Heff
Heff

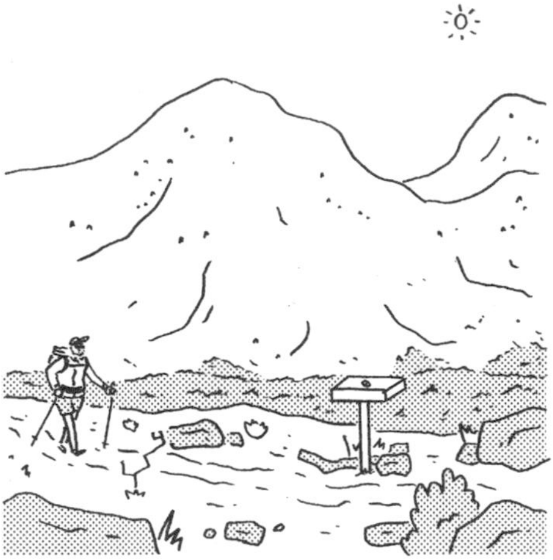

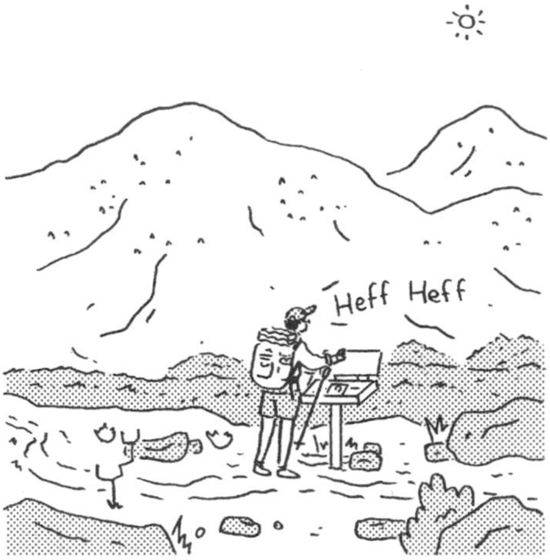
Heff Heff

Mile 55 are in the register.

Only three days ahead.

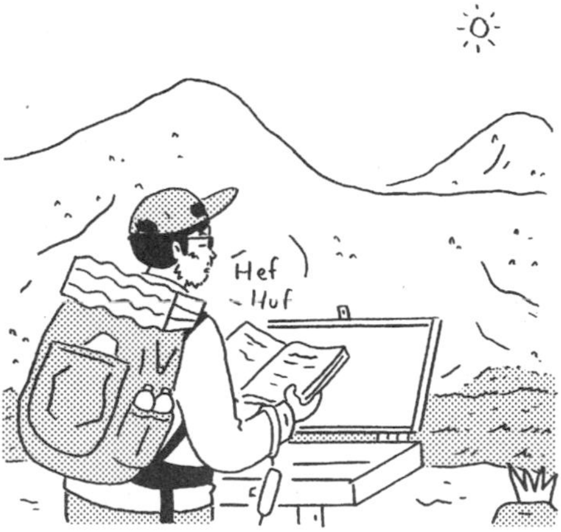
Hef
Huf

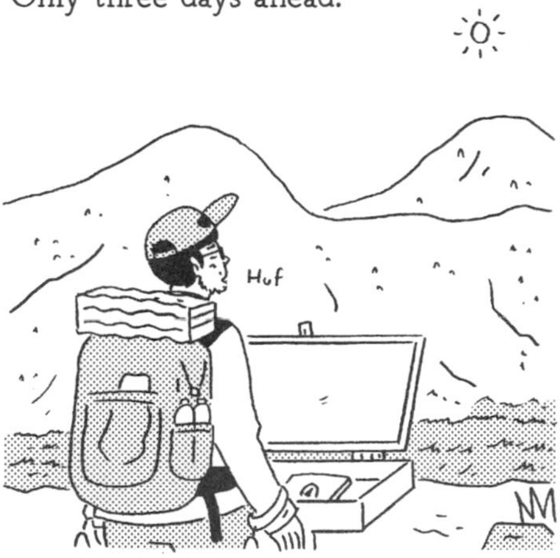
Huf

I never learn.

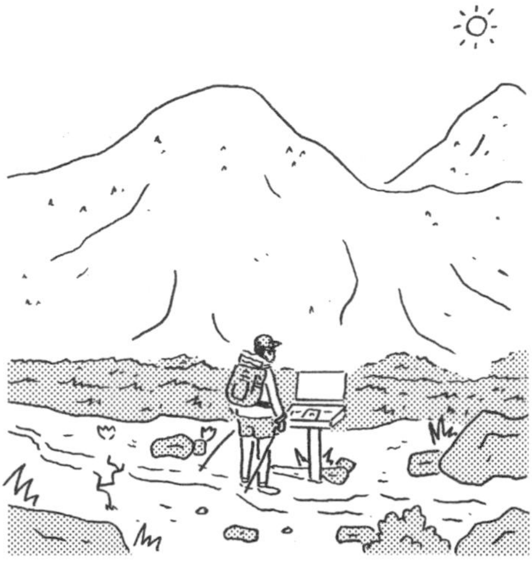

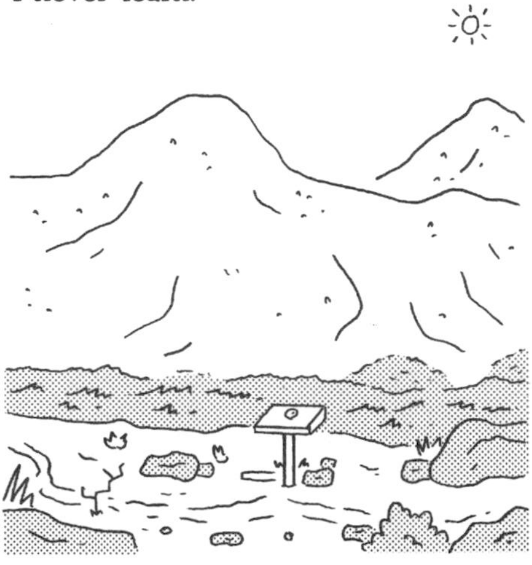

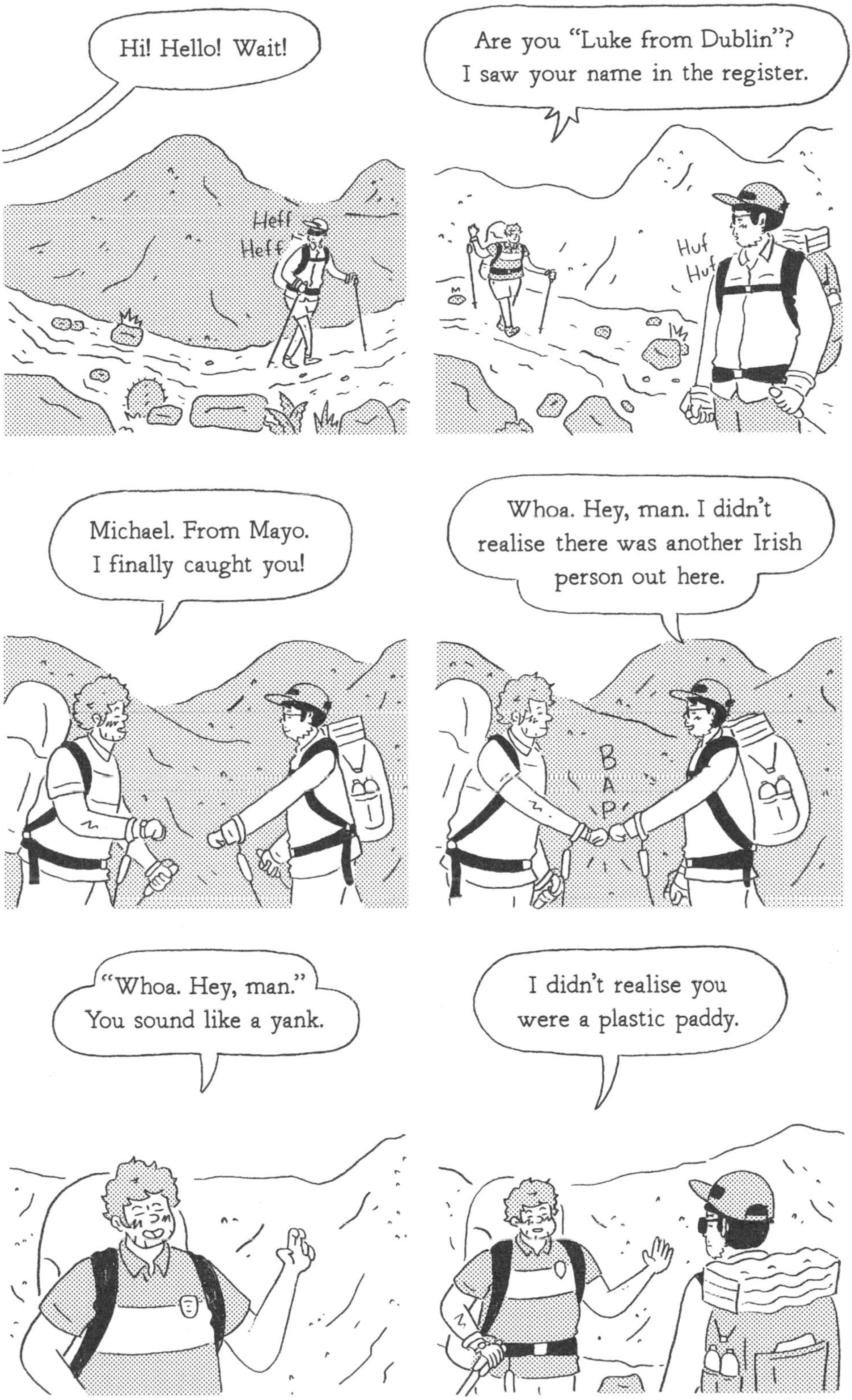
Hi! Hello! Wait!
Heff Heff
Are you "Luke from Dublin"? I saw your name in the register.
Huf Huf
Michael. From Mayo. I finally caught you!
Whoa. Hey, man. I didn't realise there was another Irish person out here.
BAP
"Whoa. Hey, man." You sound like a yank.
I didn't realise you were a plastic paddy.

Michael's pack looks heavy, and he huffs and puffs along in his Mayo county jersey. His skin is bacon red.

"Hey, do you need some sunscreen, or...?" I offer.

"Ah, sure I'm grand. I've been travelling for months now. Australia, South East Asia, and now here. My skin's built up a tan. I don't get burned any more really."

"Wow. Lucky man."

"Hey, Luke from Dublin. Can you do me a favour?" he asks, dropping his pack. "I'm hiking the PCT for charity, and anyone who donates gets a photo of me holding up their name on the trail." He pulls his tent's ground cloth and a marker from his pack, and scrawls "Mary, Mile 462" across a clear patch before folding it up, obscuring the dozens of other names already written on there.
He hands me his phone, and I take position to be his photographer.

"That's amazing you're doing it for charity," I offer.

"Yeah, but all these people want is to see their name on the PCT. So stupid," he mumbles back before throwing on a big smile. I take his picture and hike on.

120

At Casa De Luna, a trail angel house, hikers fill the garden. Terrie, the host, coerces me into wearing a hawaiian shirt, like all the other hikers. I don't recognise any of them. I have lost my bubble.

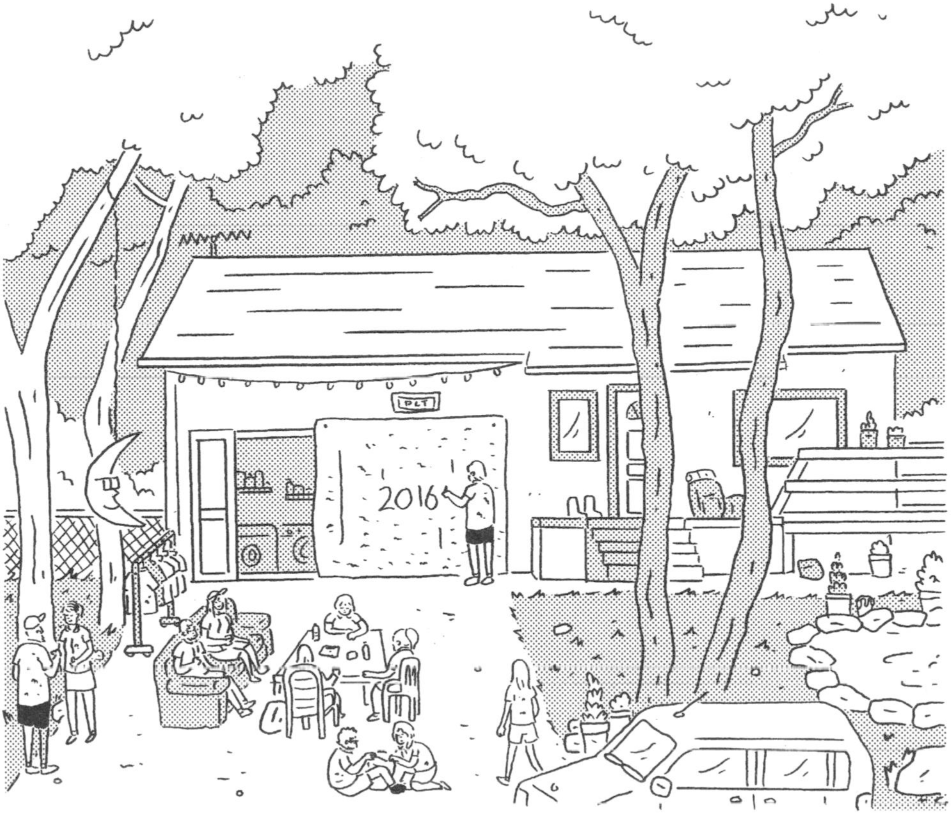
PLT
2016

I mill around shyly, introducing myself.

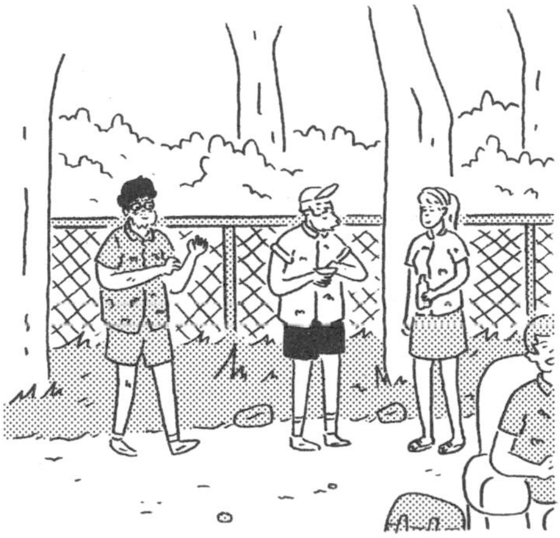

I walk alone to the nearby gas station for a snack-based dinner.

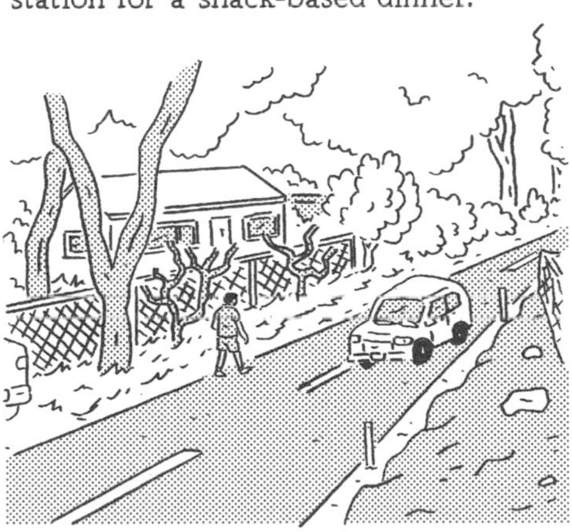

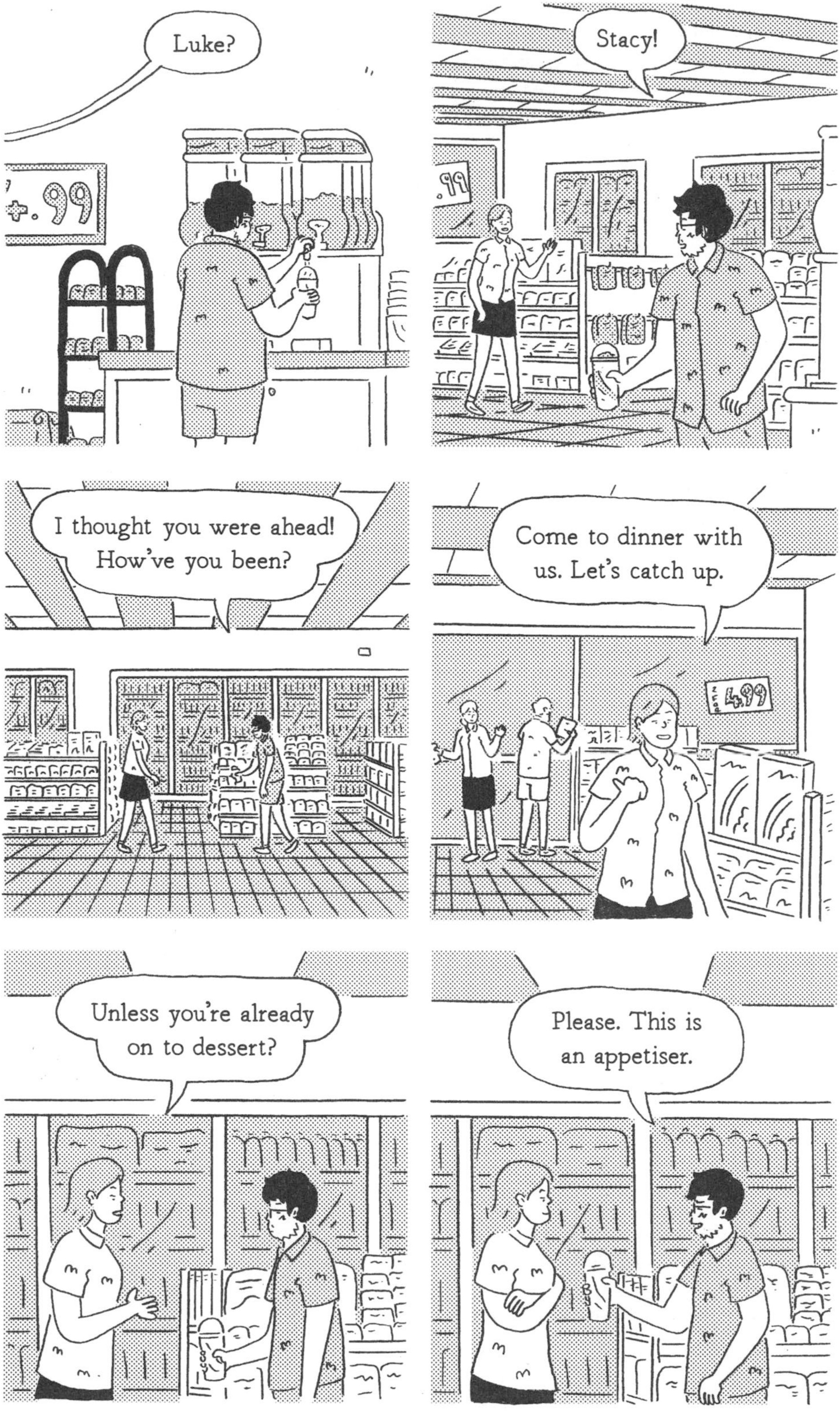
Luke?
Stacy!
I thought you were ahead! How've you been?
Come to dinner with us. Let's catch up.
Unless you're already on to dessert?
Please. This is an appetiser.

Dinner evolves into the local karaoke night.

Flashdance, yet another Irish hiker, gets up first. He, like me, sounds American. Though he has justification for it, having moved here as a child.

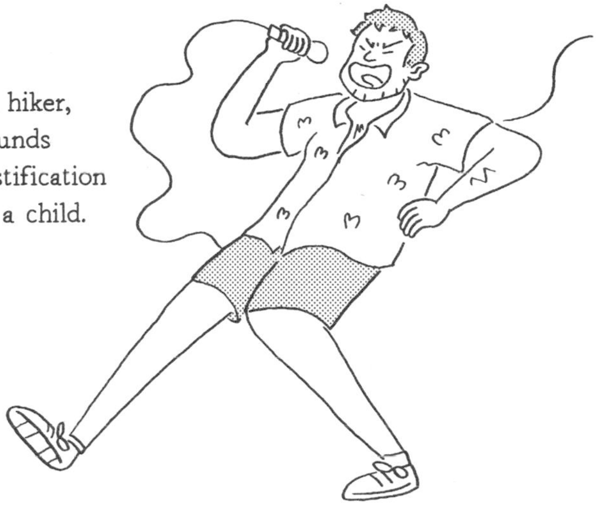

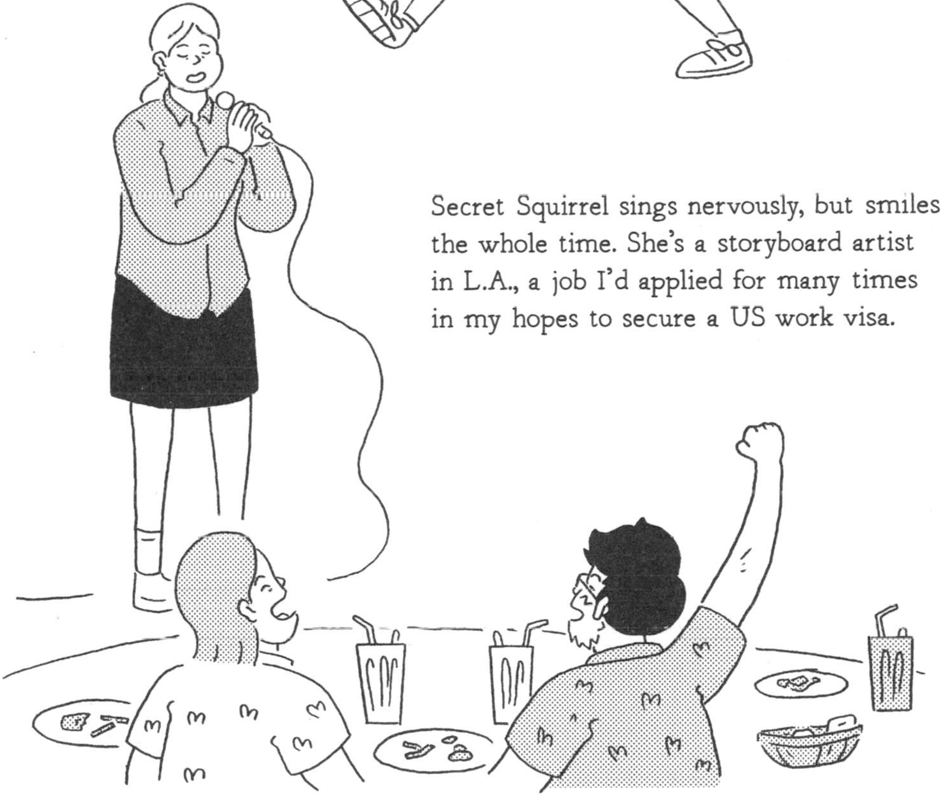

Secret Squirrel sings nervously, but smiles the whole time. She's a storyboard artist in L.A., a job I'd applied for many times in my hopes to secure a US work visa.

I'd imagined myself living both of their lives. Flashdance's as a kid, homesick for an America I'd only seen in movies. Squirrel's as a desperate college student, fighting hard to stay in an America that was trying to eject me. How funny it is, I think, to find them both here together. Or how narcissistic of me to notice.

Stacy invites me to hike out with them in the morning. I accept.

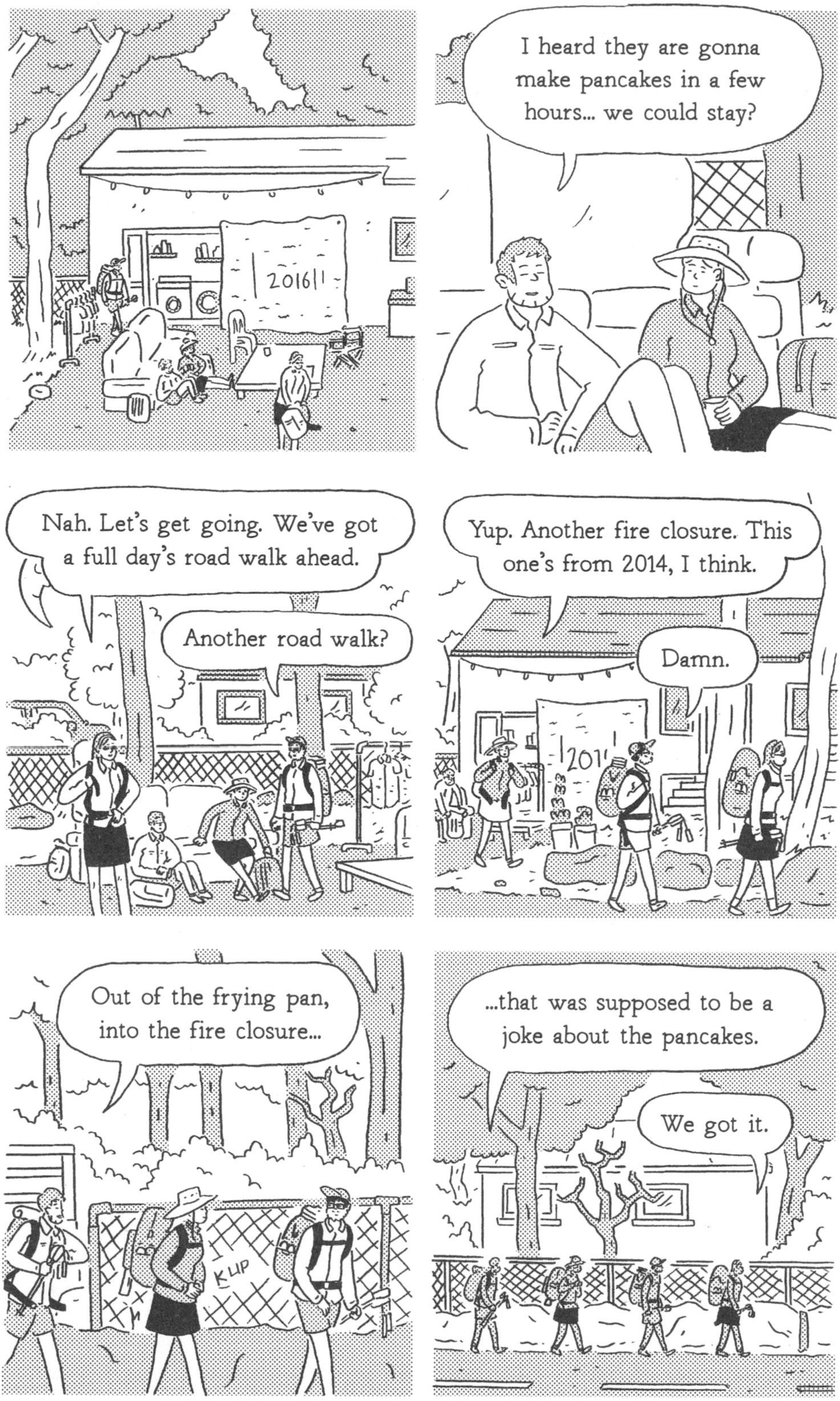
I heard they are gonna make pancakes in a few hours... we could stay?
Nah. Let's get going. We've got a full day's road walk ahead.
Another road walk?
Yup. Another fire closure. This one's from 2014, I think.
Damn.
Out of the frying pan, into the fire closure...
...that was supposed to be a joke about the pancakes.
We got it.

Expensive-looking McMansions dot the rim of a dried-out lake.

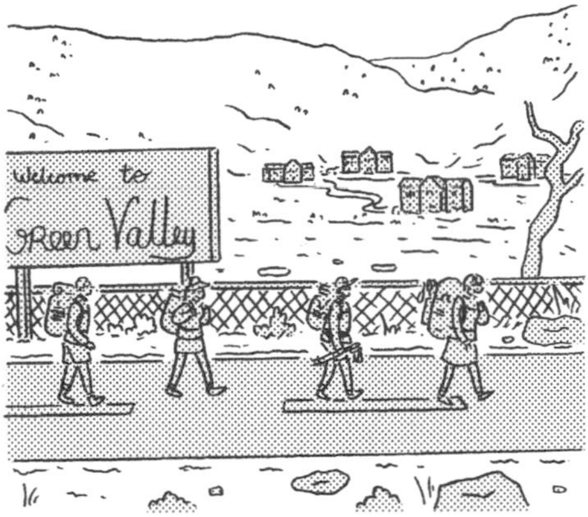
welcome to

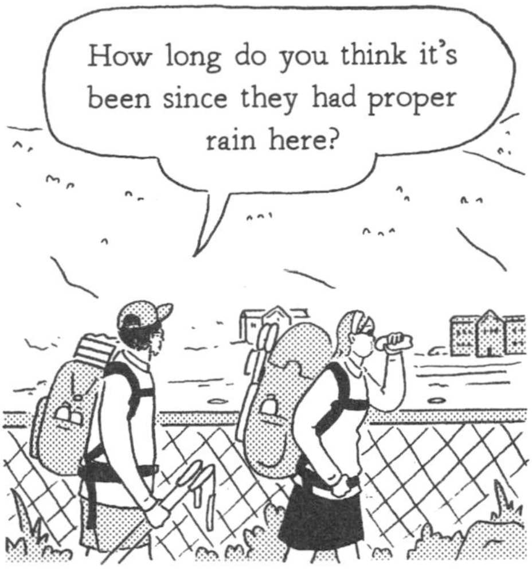
How long do you think it's been since they had proper rain here?

Miles down the road, we pass an incongruously-located ostrich farm.

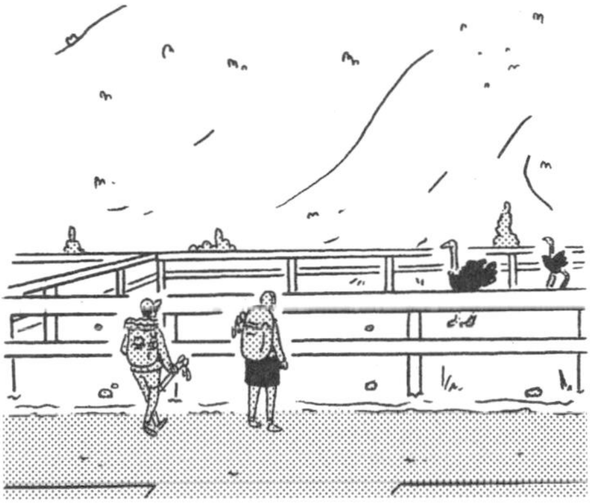

We spend a few minutes trying to coax them over to the fence.

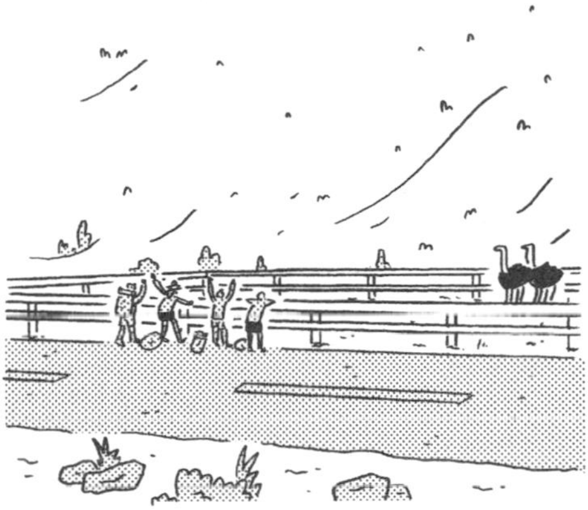

Their owner drives by, and tells us about the area. How firefighting helicopters had drained the lake in 2014.

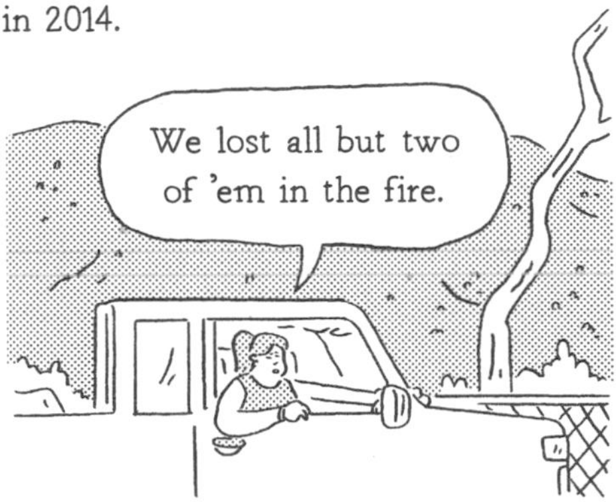
We lost all but two of 'em in the fire.

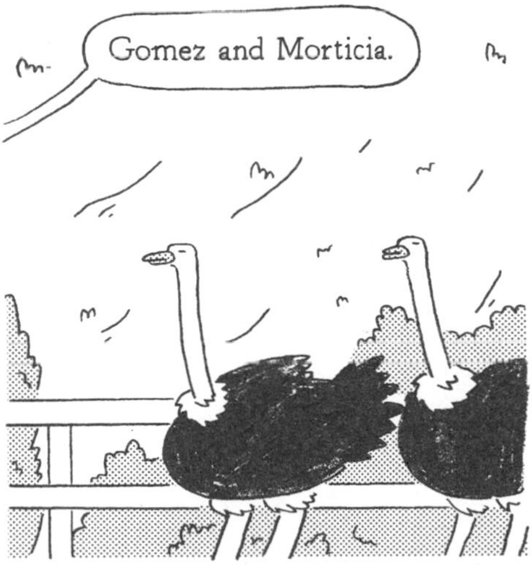
Gomez and Morticia.

We all hike in a line, dressed in thruhiker uniform.
Indistinguishable to the passing cars.

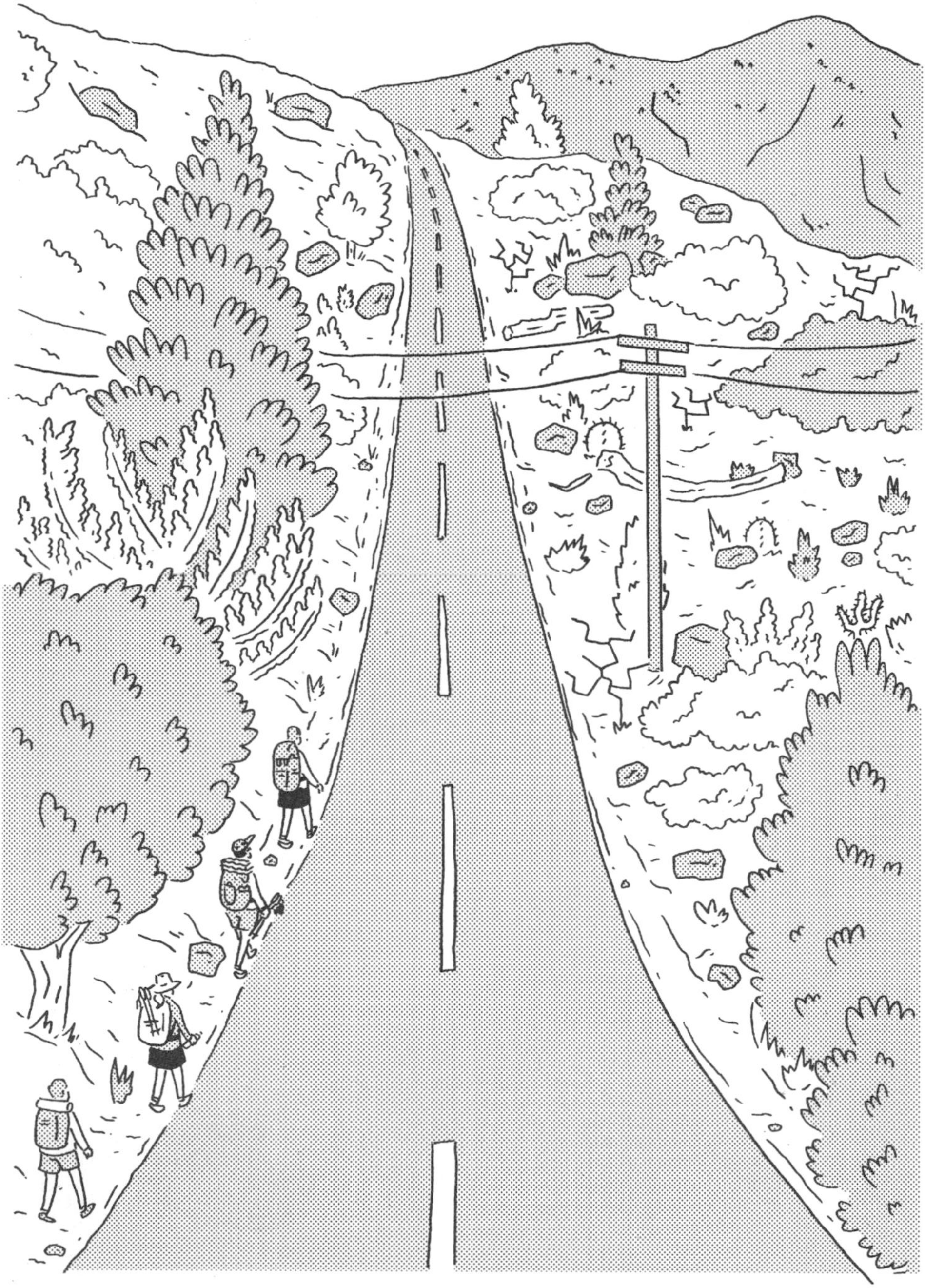

From a distance, Hikertown looks like a loose collection of beat up trailers and sheds clustered together in the otherwise blank section of desert. As I get closer, I discover that it's styled to look like a miniature Wild West town. "Doctor's Office" says the sign above one building. "Saloon" proclaims another.

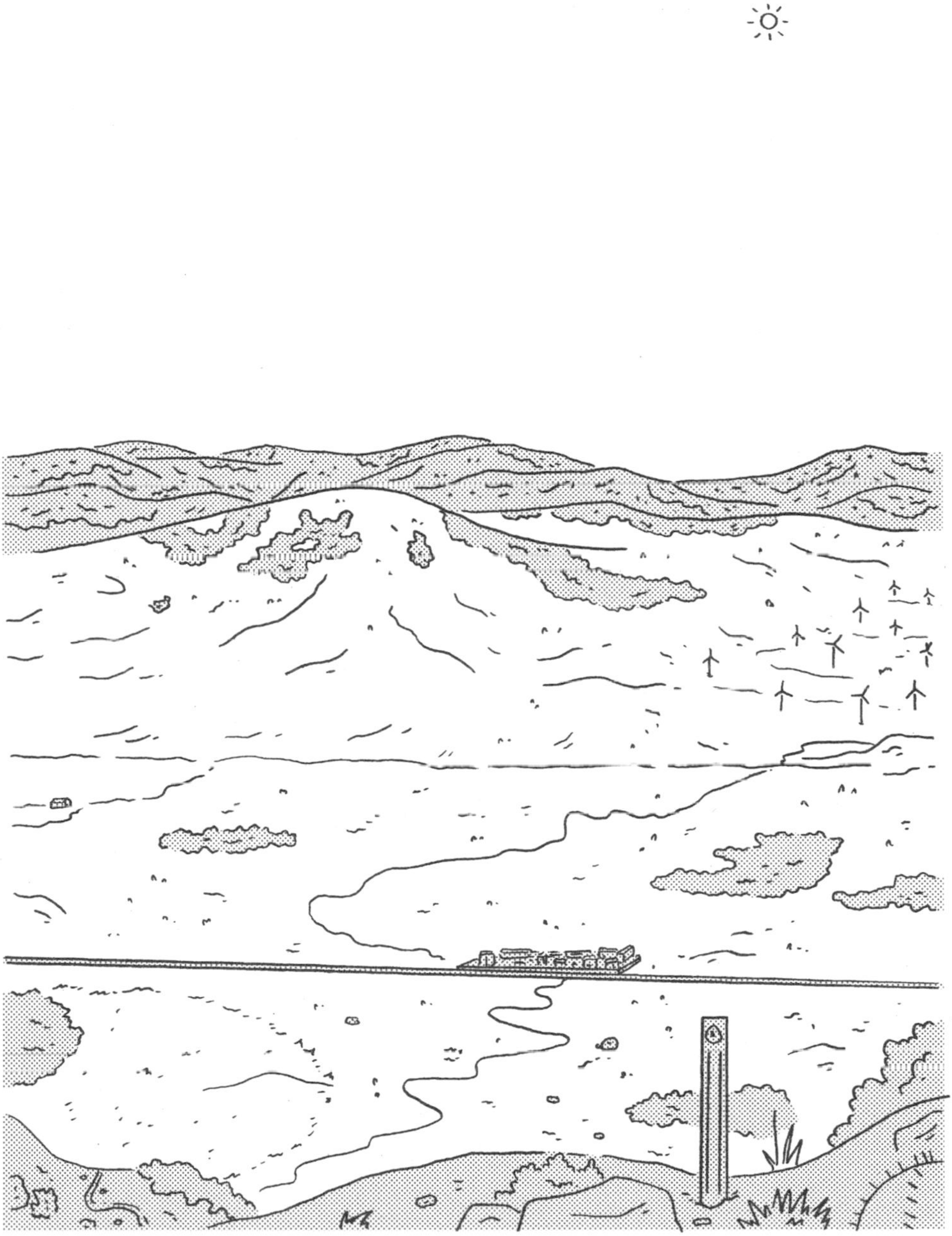

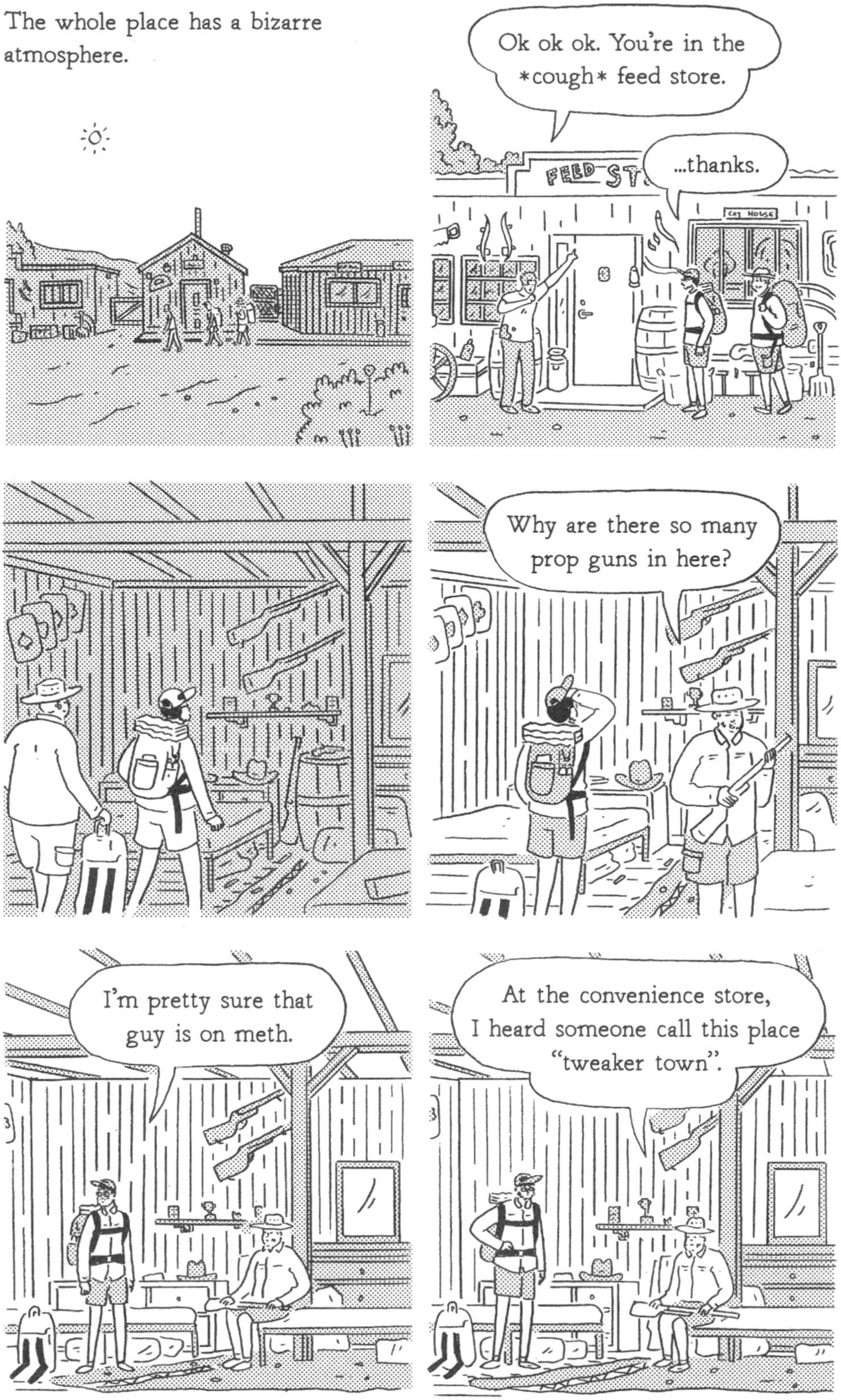
The whole place has a bizarre atmosphere.
Ok ok ok. You're in the *cough* feed store.
...thanks.
Why are there so many prop guns in here?
I'm pretty sure that guy is on meth.
At the convenience store, I heard someone call this place "tweaker town".

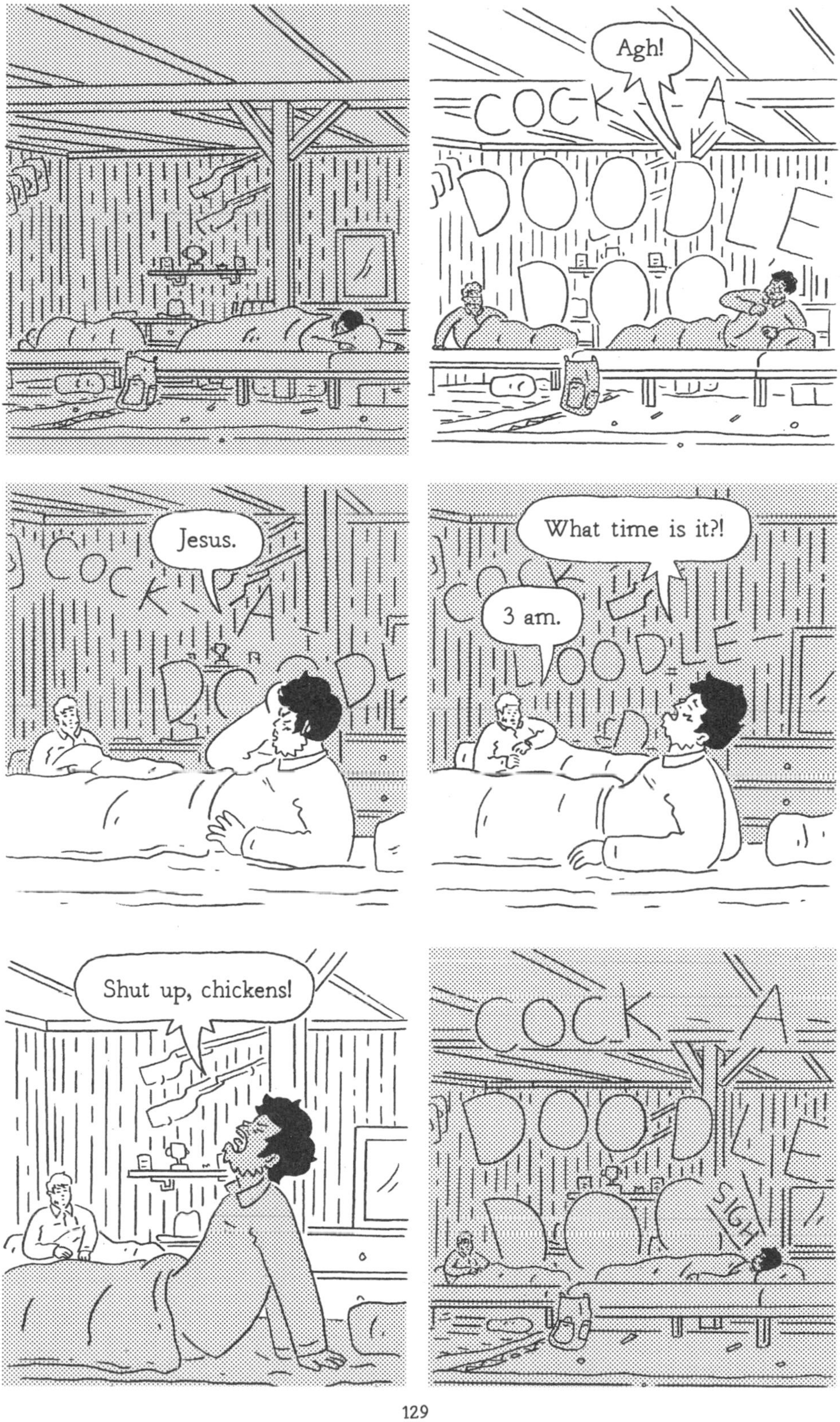
Agh!
COCK-A
DOODLE
Jesus.
What time is it?!
3 am.
Shut up, chickens!
COCK-A
DOODLE
SIGH

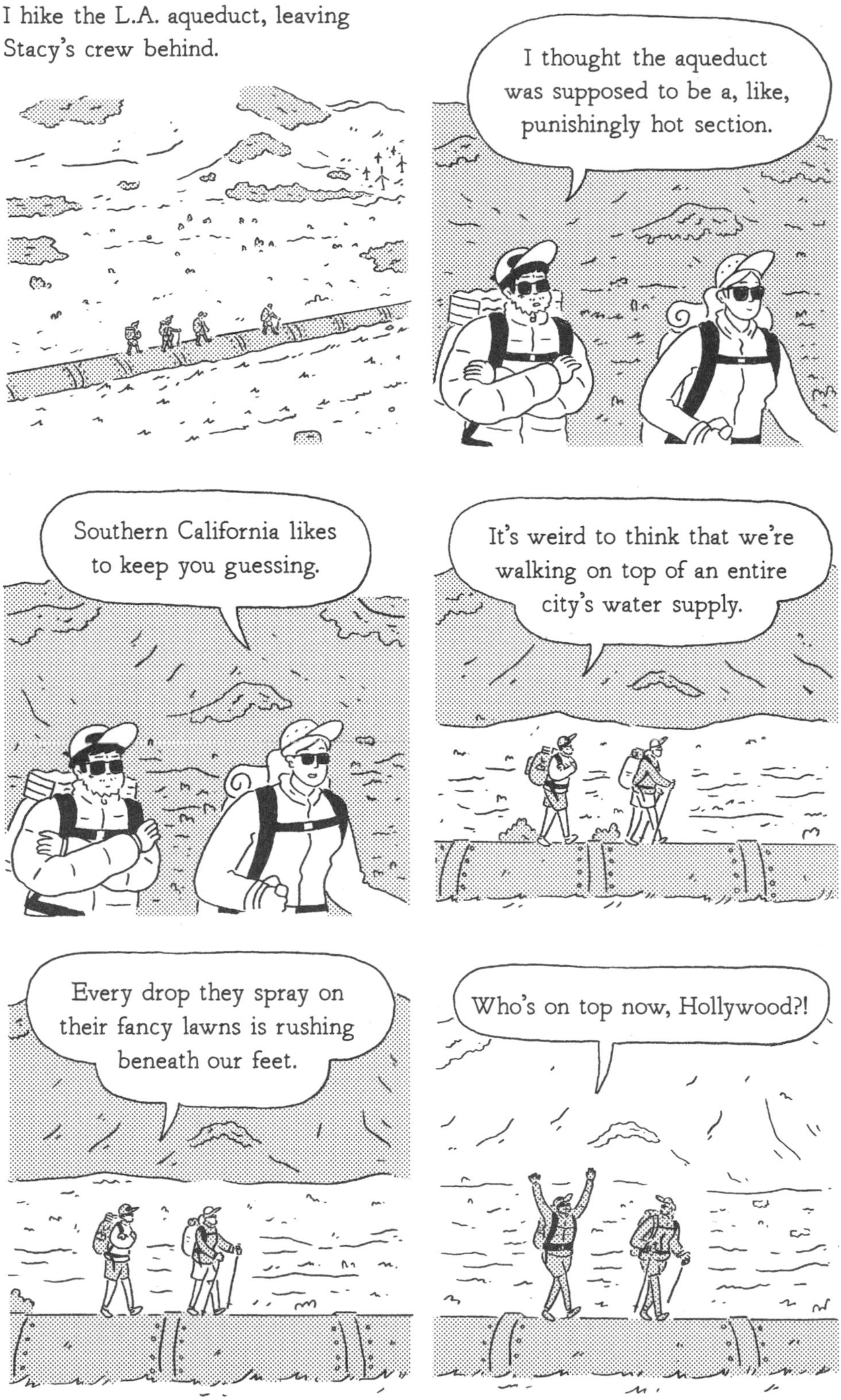
I hike the L.A. aqueduct, leaving Stacy's crew behind.
I thought the aqueduct was supposed to be a, like, punishingly hot section.
Southern California likes to keep you guessing.
It's weird to think that we're walking on top of an entire city's water supply.
Every drop they spray on their fancy lawns is rushing beneath our feet.
Who's on top now, Hollywood?!

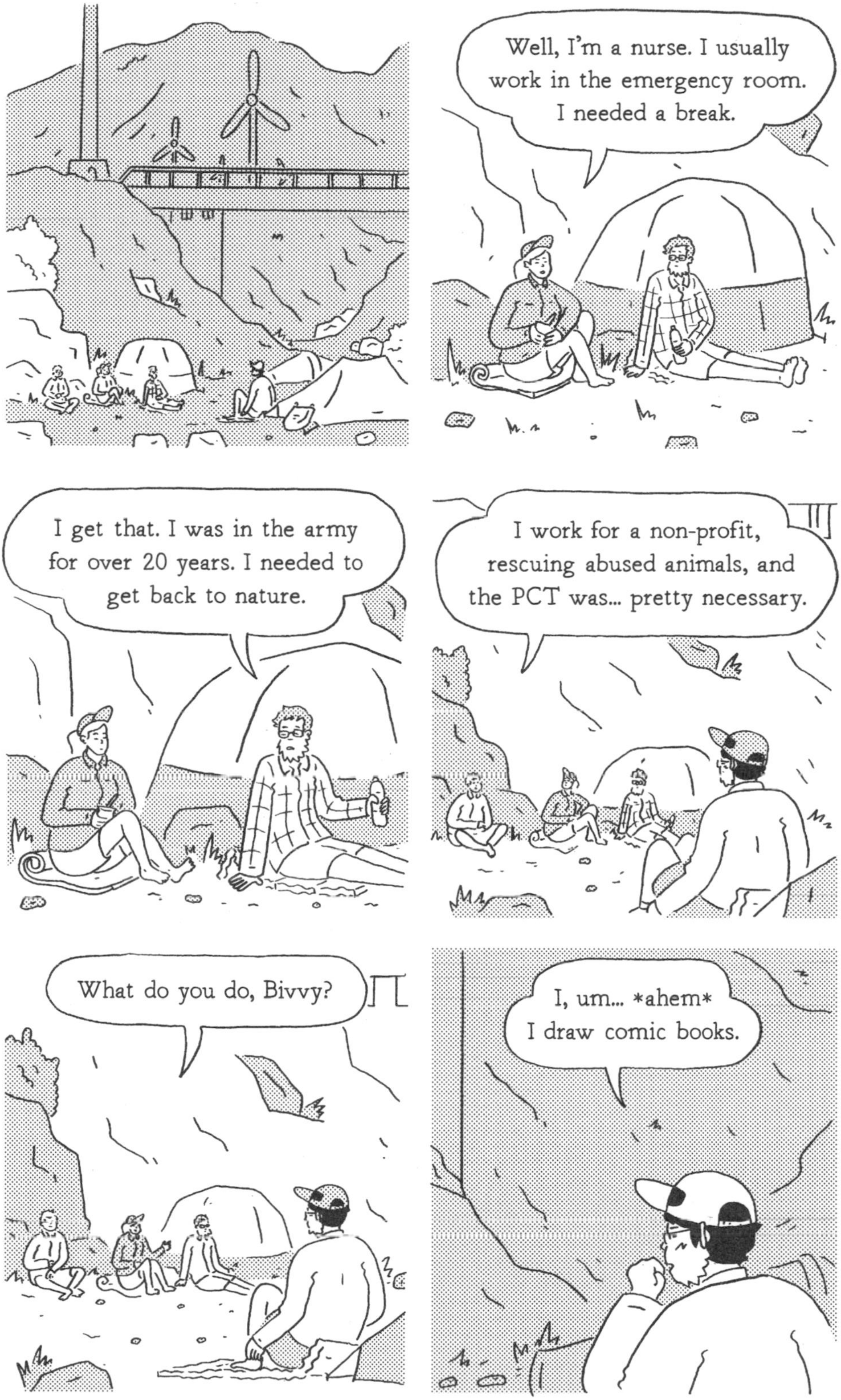
Well, I'm a nurse. I usually work in the emergency room. I needed a break.
I get that. I was in the army for over 20 years. I needed to get back to nature.
I work for a non-profit, rescuing abused animals, and the PCT was... pretty necessary.
What do you do, Bivvy?
I, um... *ahem* I draw comic books.

The miles peel away a little easier now, though we all look on with dread at the weather reports on our phones. There is a heatwave on the way, so we try to take advantage of our current cold weather and put in the miles, crossing the aqueduct in only two days.

I catch a ride into the town of Tehachapi. The driver gives me funny looks the whole way there.

"You really stink," he tells me, as I exit the car.

At the town's grocery store, I meet two other hikers who invite me to join them for food. At dinner, they talk about staying in the town's fancy hotel, in a room with an extra bed. I try to act nonchalant, but the opportunism clearly shows on my face, and they offer me a place to shower and sleep, free of charge. On one condition. I come with them to get a foot massage.

I protest, shuddering at the thought of asking anyone to massage my blistered, filthy hiker feet but I really want to stay in the fancy hotel, so I reluctantly go along.

The massage place sits nondescriptly alongside the other strip mall stores. Once we're inside however, it is immediately clear to me. This is a brothel. Women lounge around, wearing robes, and as soon as I enter, looks of absolute panic cross their faces.

The other hikers are oblivious.

"I really really need to get a shower," I say as I grab their key and leave.

The next night, I stay at the town's little airfield, where hikers have gathered on the grassy lawns.

Flashdance, hey.

Bivvy, good to see you.

What's up there?

You see that plane?

Yeah.

Squirrel just stuck out her thumb and hitched a ride on it.

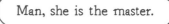

Man, she is the master.

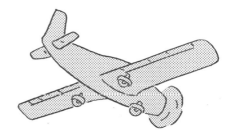

I stay in Tehachapi for a few days, sticking around so I can leave with Squirrel and Flashdance. I like them both, though when they're together, they get pretty goofy in a way that makes me bristle a little.

We go see movies, and hang around the town's amazing German bakery, abusing the free refills policy and public wifi. I download music on to my phone, sick of my own thoughts as I hike in silence day after day. We see the heatwave get closer and closer in the weather report.

I buy groceries and divide everything into ziplock bags, and then cardboard boxes to mail ahead to remote stops in the Sierra.

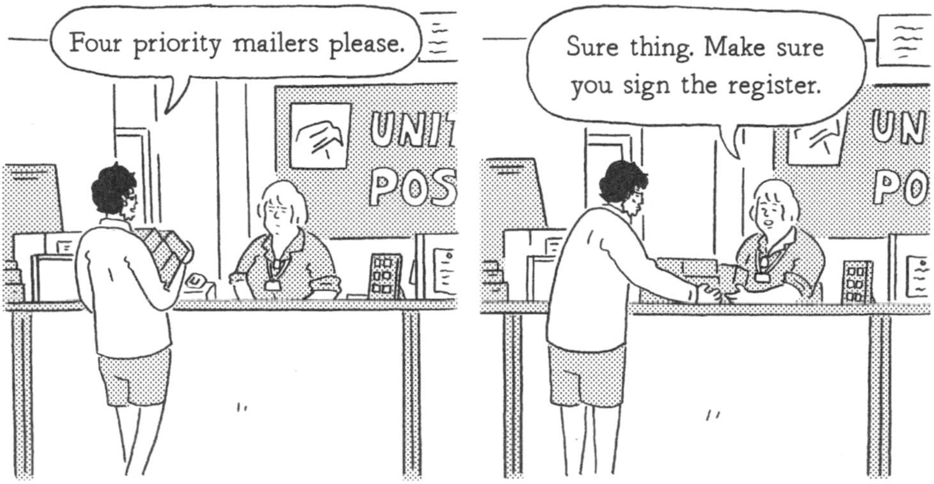
Four priority mailers please.
Sure thing. Make sure you sign the register.

I read the signatures. Mile 55 are only two days ahead.

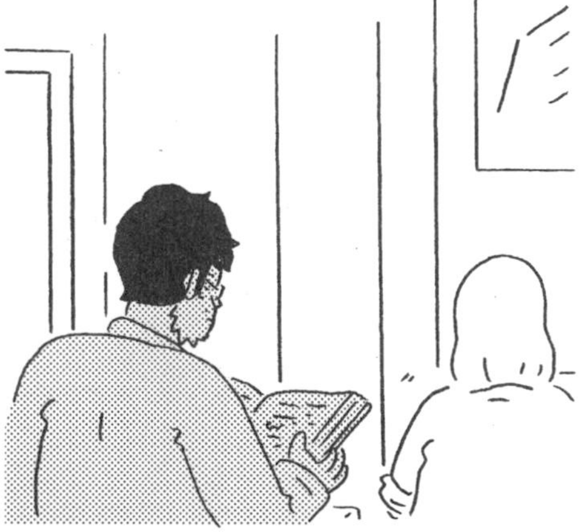

I'm catching up.

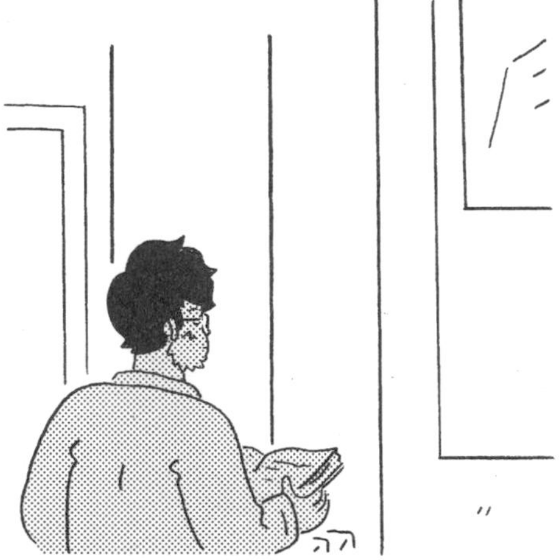

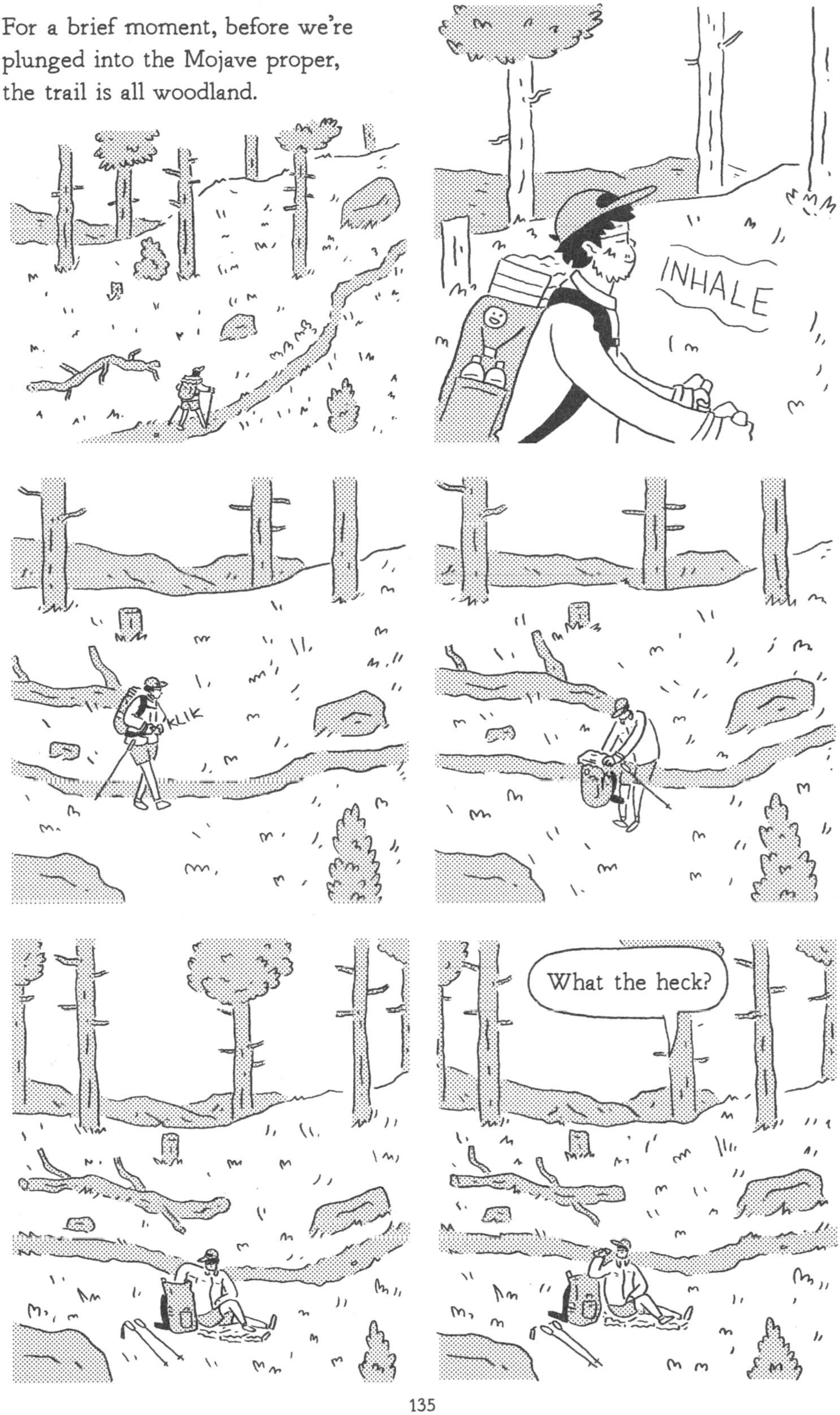
For a brief moment, before we're plunged into the Mojave proper, the trail is all woodland.
INHALE
KLIK
What the heck?

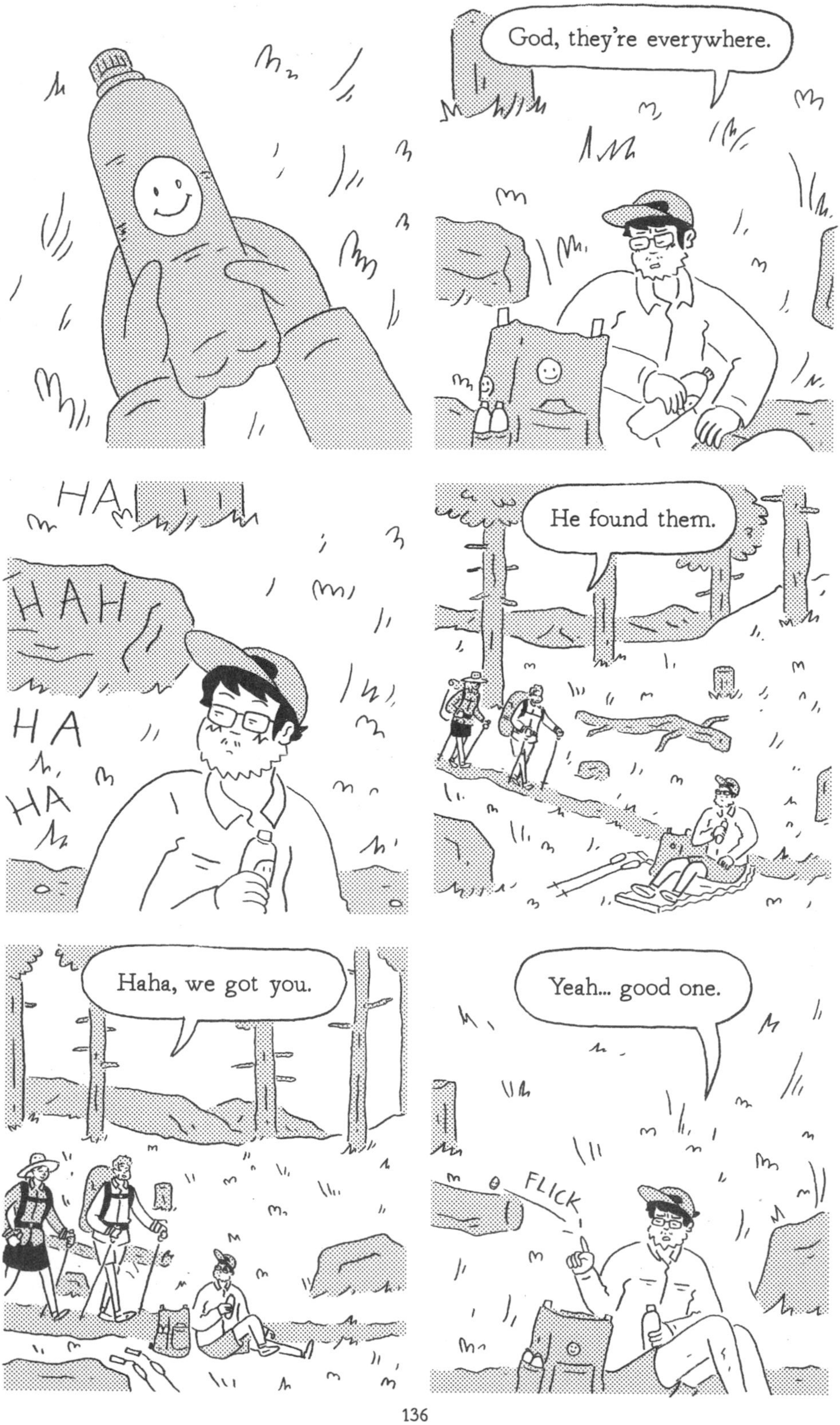
God, they're everywhere.
HA
HAH
HA
HA
He found them.
Haha, we got you.
Yeah... good one.
FLICK

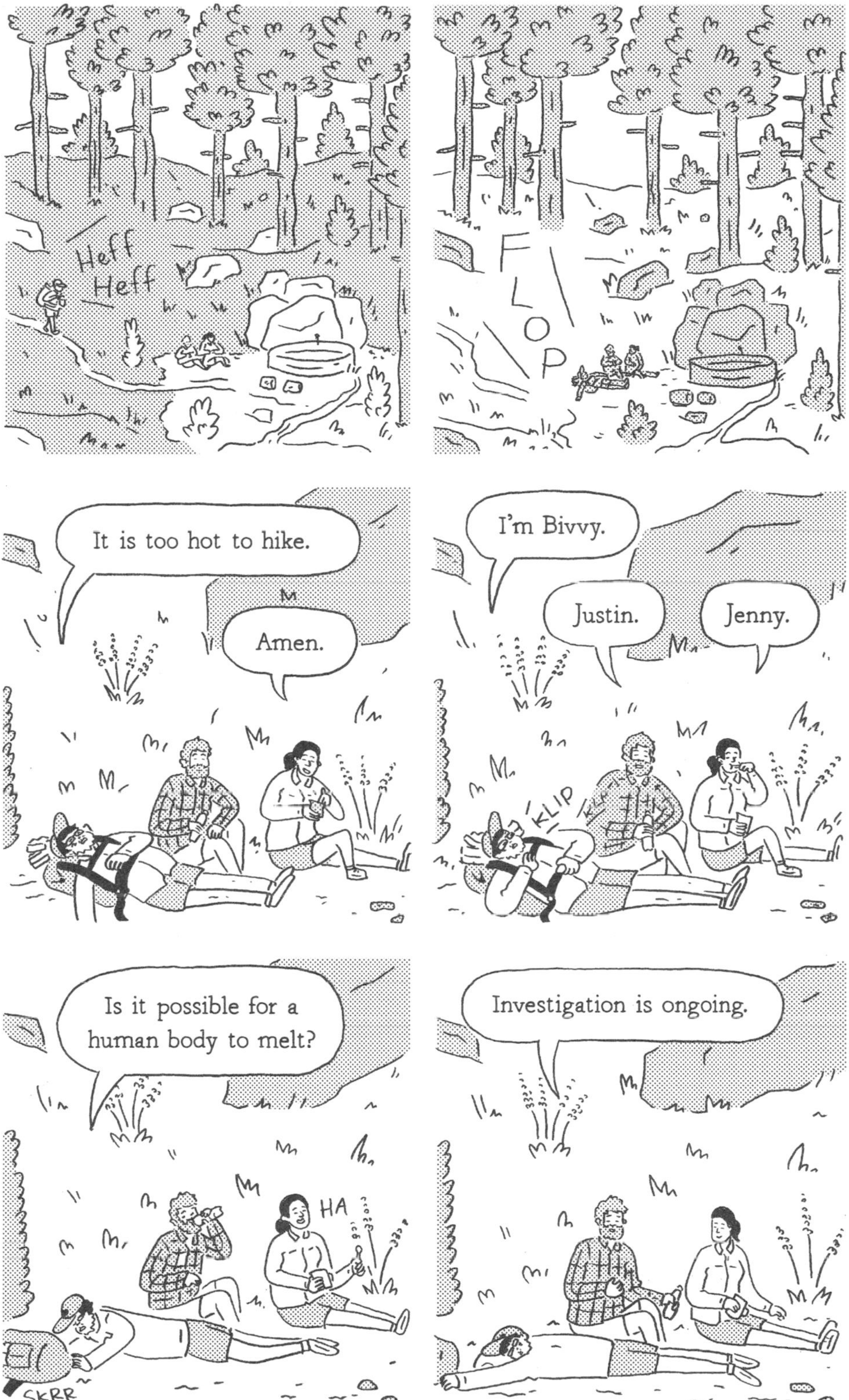
Heff
Heff
FLOP
It is too hot to hike.
Amen.
I'm Bivvy.
Justin.
Jenny.
KLIP
Is it possible for a human body to melt?
HA
SKRR
Investigation is ongoing.

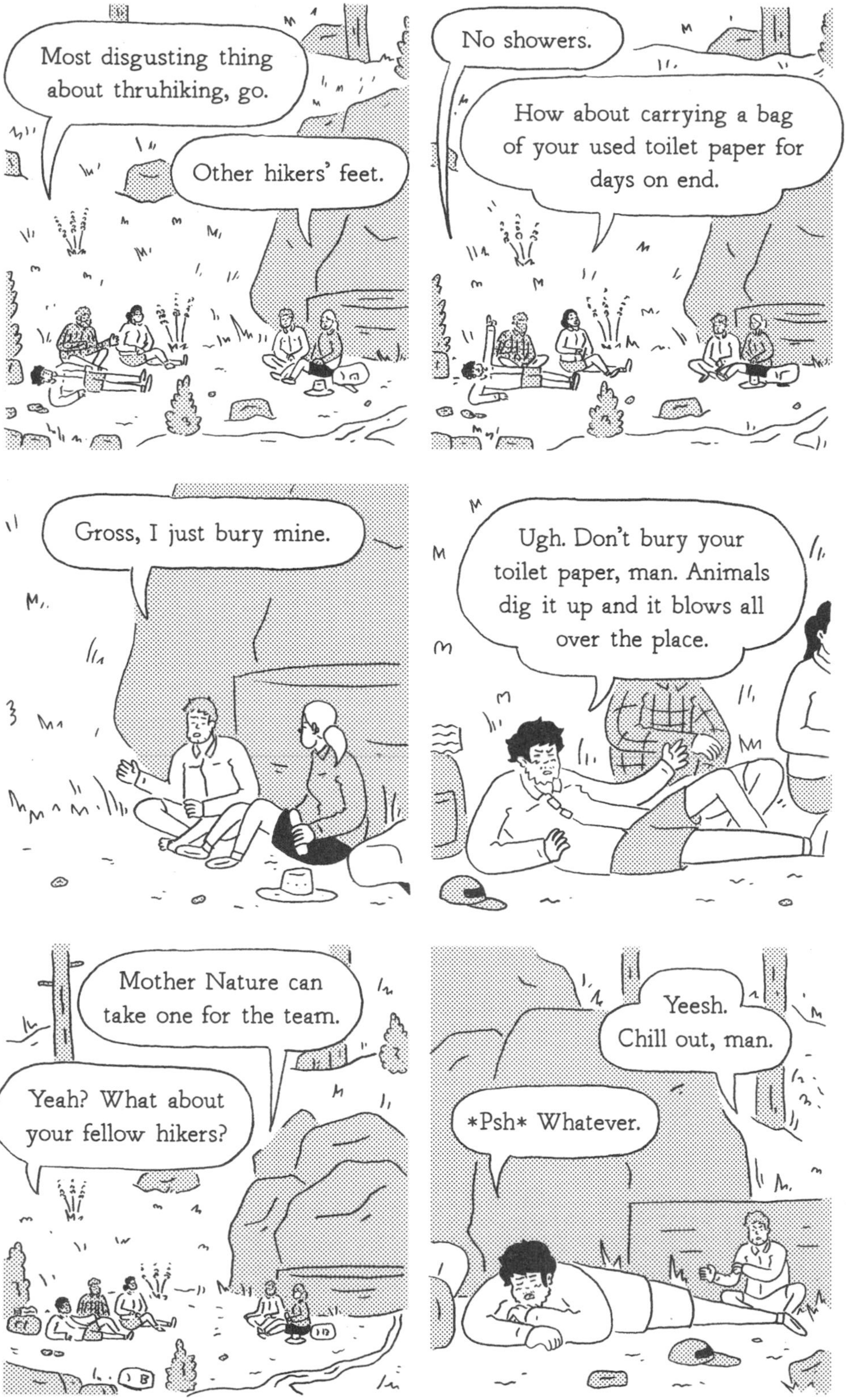
Most disgusting thing about thruhiking, go.
Other hikers' feet.
No showers.
How about carrying a bag of your used toilet paper for days on end.
Gross, I just bury mine.
Ugh. Don't bury your toilet paper, man. Animals dig it up and it blows all over the place.
Mother Nature can take one for the team.
Yeah? What about your fellow hikers?
Yeesh. Chill out, man.
Psh Whatever.

We enter the Mojave. In the distance, I see the monstrous peaks of the High Sierras, still more than one hundred miles away.

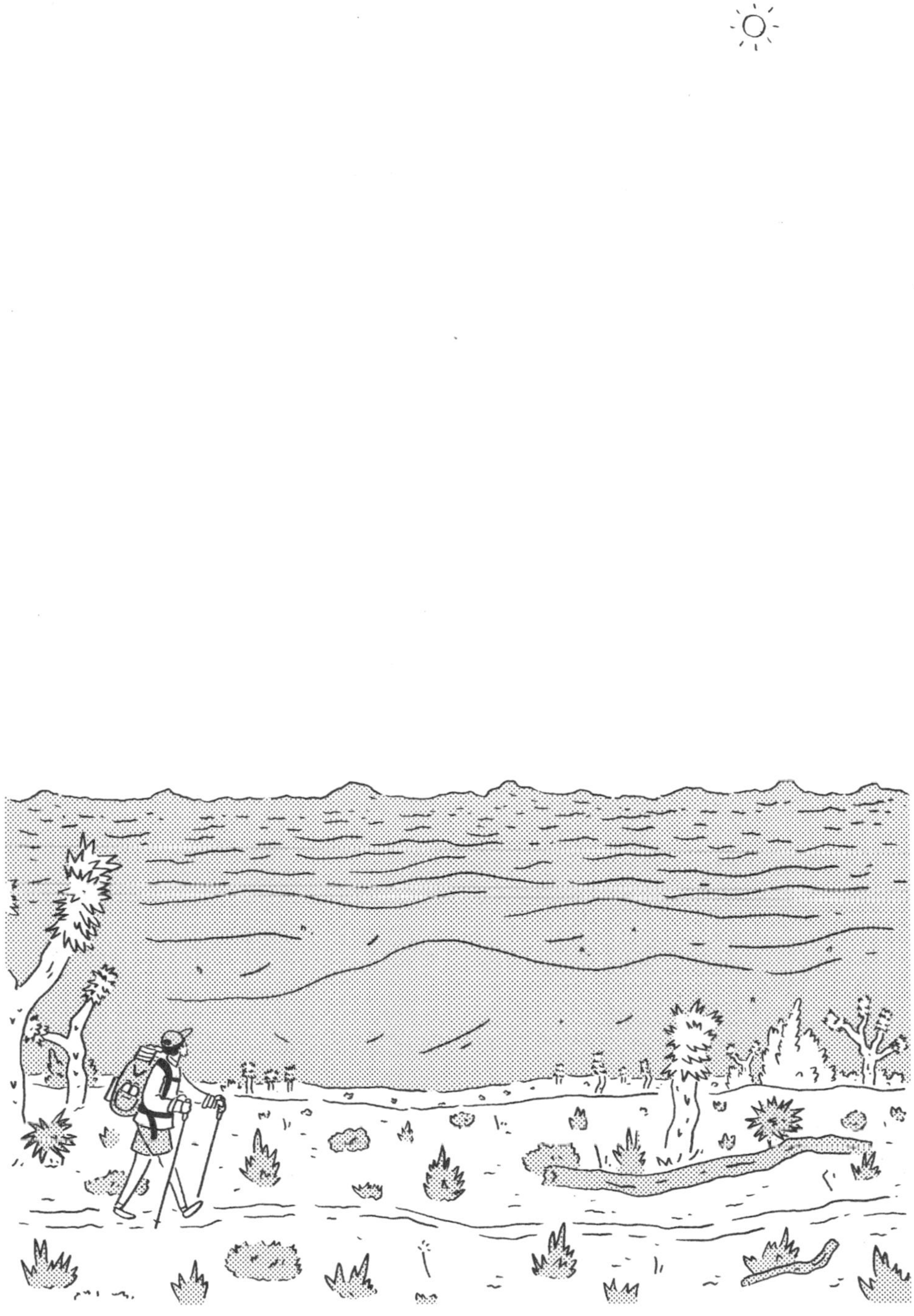

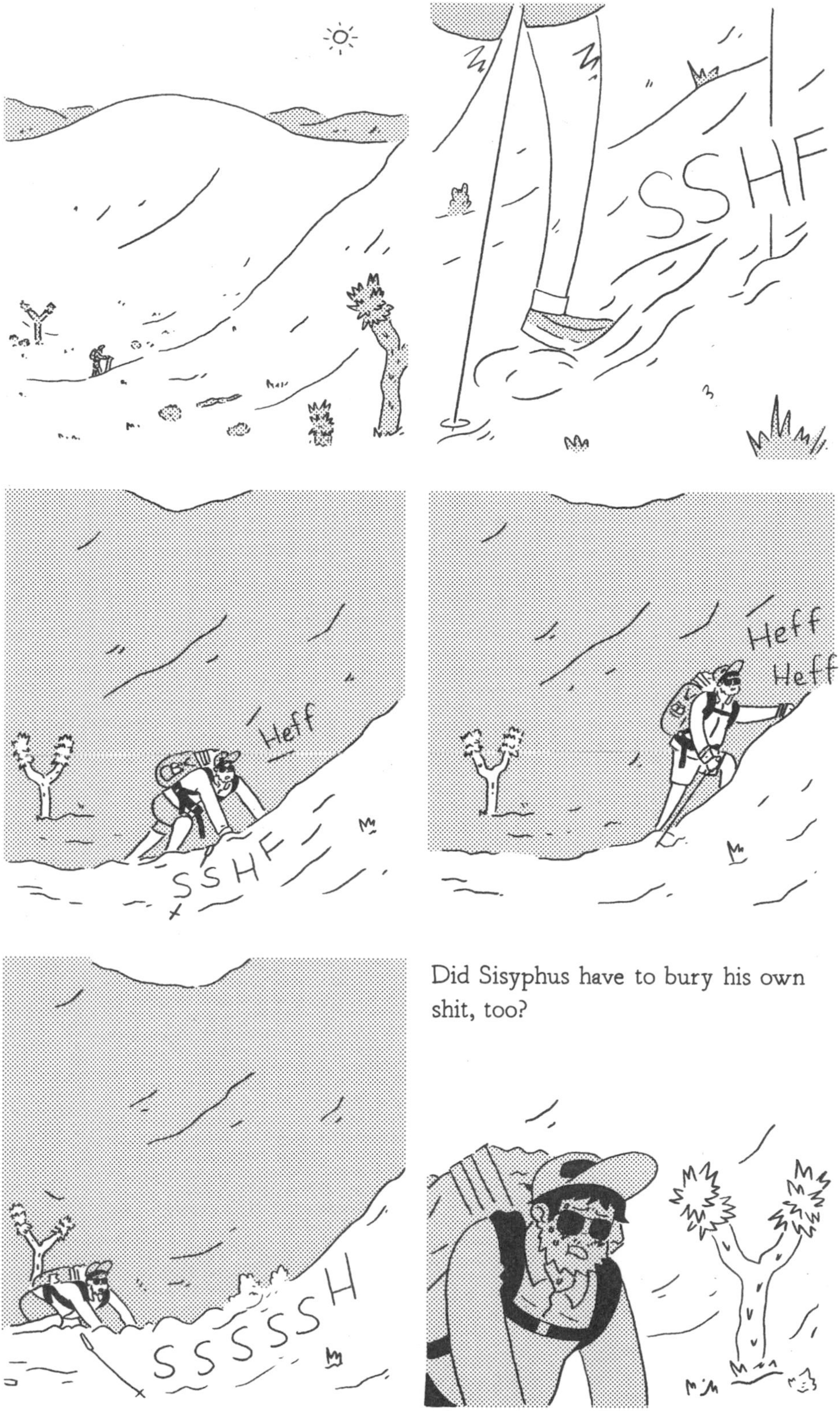
SSHF
Heff
SSHF
Heff
Heff
SSSSSH
Did Sisyphus have to bury his own shit, too?

We can't hike in the middle of the day now. The heatwave makes it too dangerous.

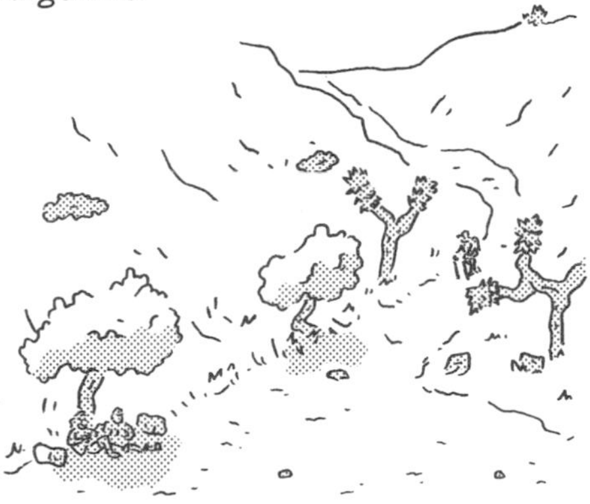

We congregate in shady spots at noon to wait out the heat. I make nice with Flashdance and Squirrel.

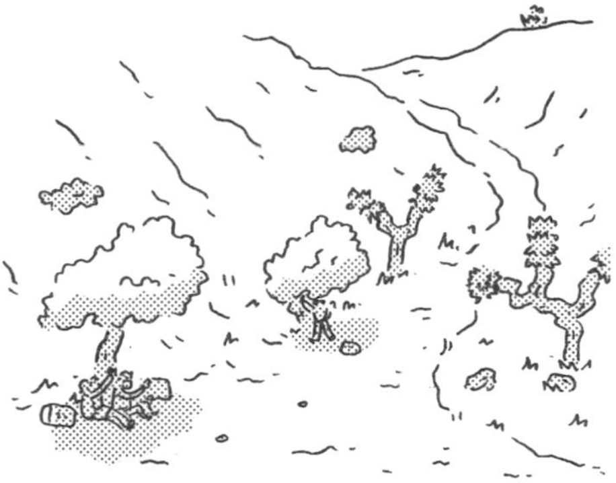

I'm not mad at them, really. We're just too different.

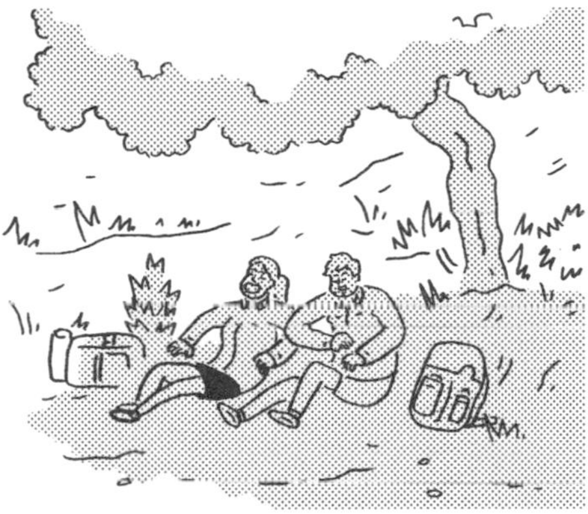

It feels like the opposite of Bojangles, Ethan and Tumnus. I wasn't a fit with them...

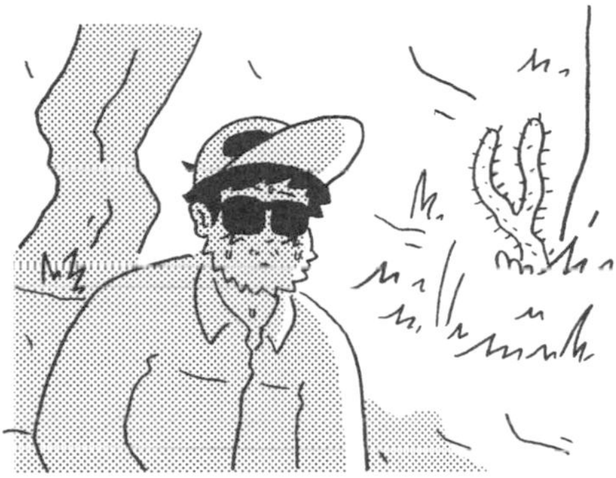

...but in the same way, Flashdance and Squirrel don't fit with me.

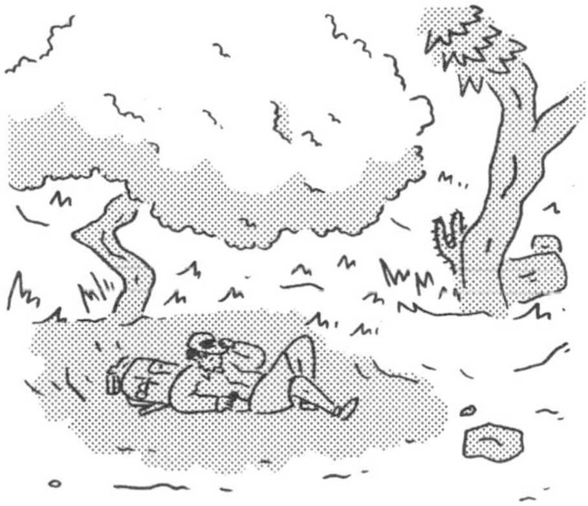

Whatever that distinction is worth.

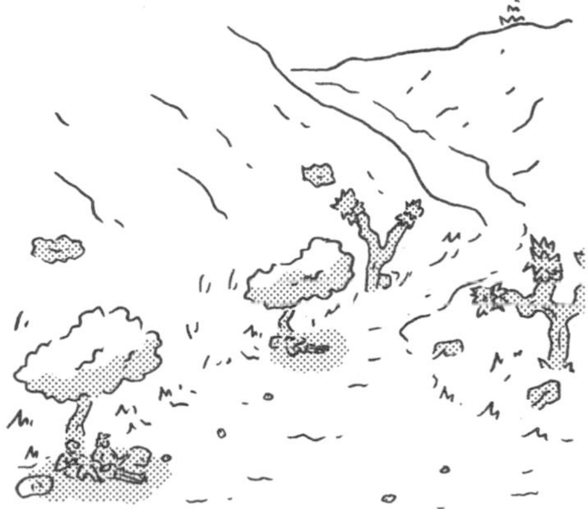

I decide to hike on alone. Again.

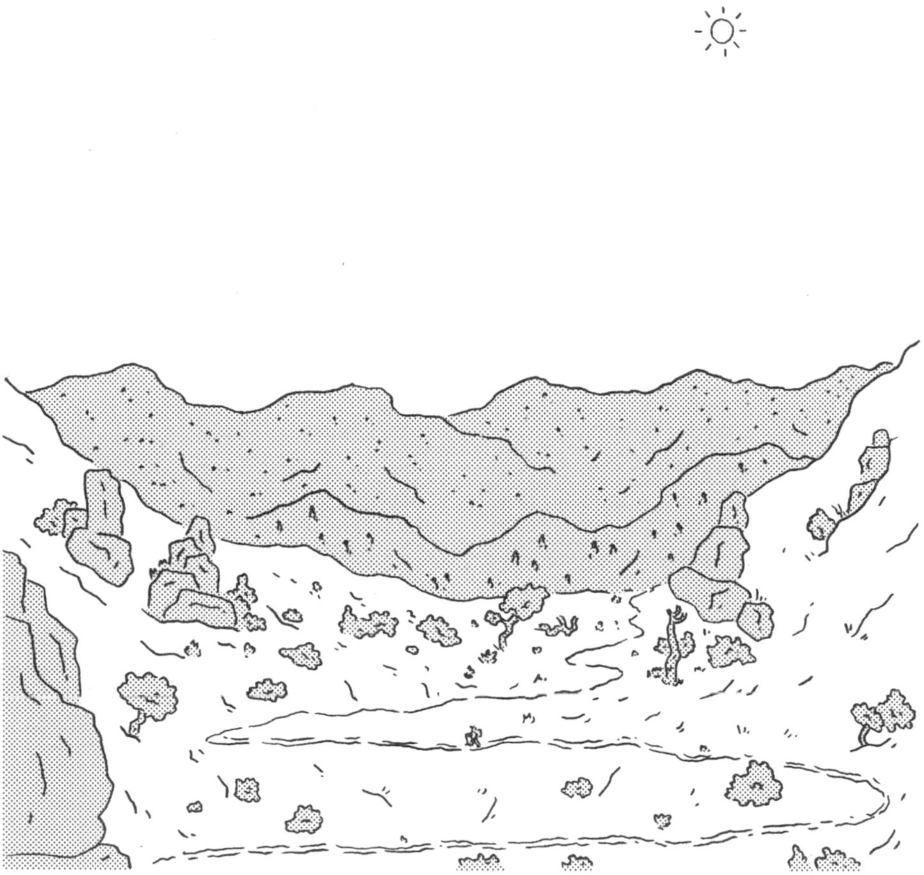

I can't tell if it's the right choice or just a defence mechanism.

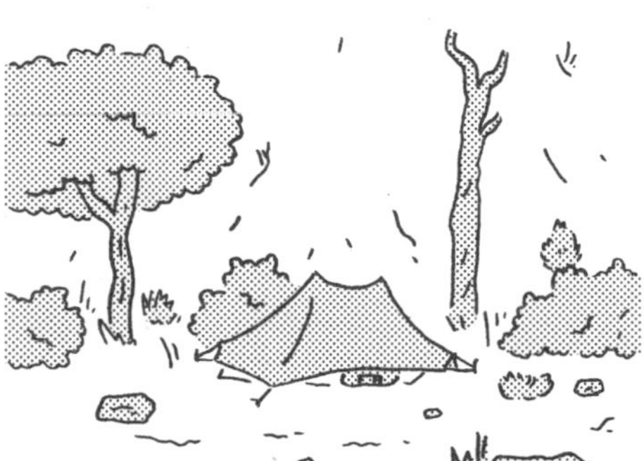

Either way, it works.

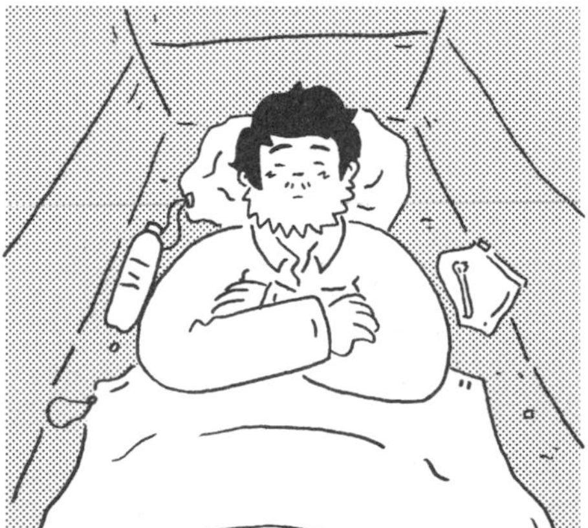

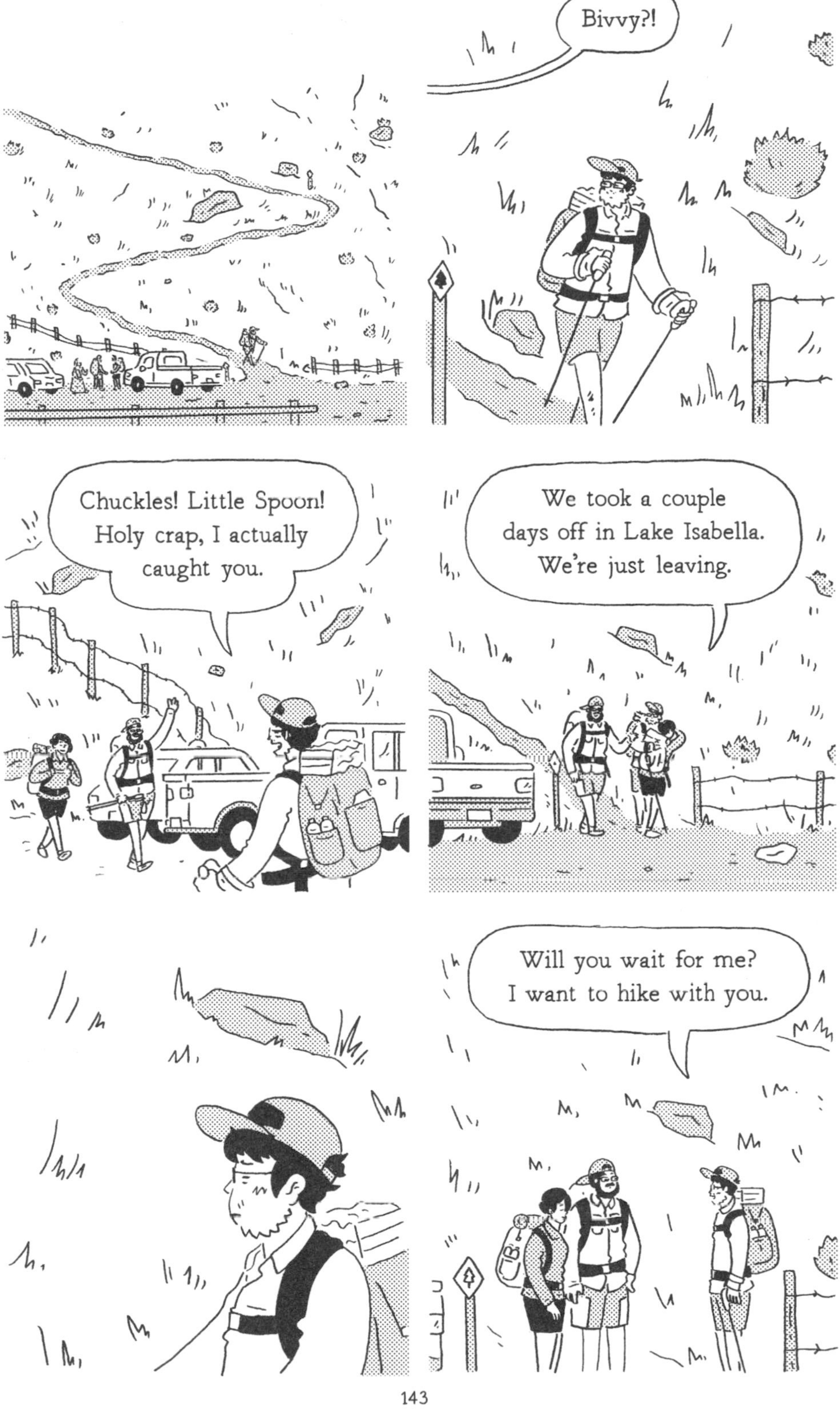
Bivvy?!
Chuckles! Little Spoon! Holy crap, I actually caught you.
We took a couple days off in Lake Isabella. We're just leaving.
Will you wait for me? I want to hike with you.

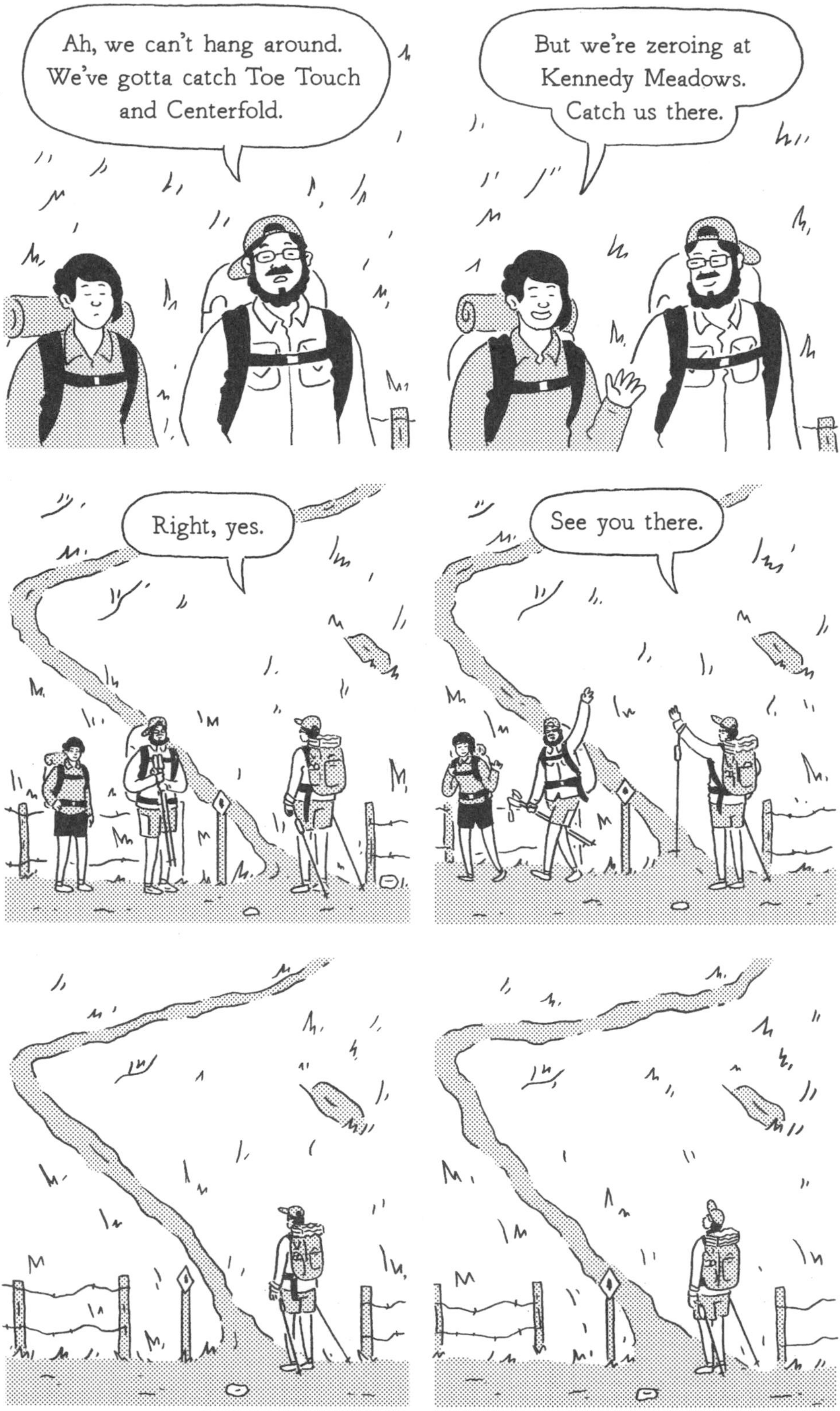
Ah, we can't hang around. We've gotta catch Toe Touch and Centerfold.
But we're zeroing at Kennedy Meadows. Catch us there.
Right, yes.
See you there.

The heatwave explodes, and hiking during the day becomes almost impossible. As I pick my way along the trail in Mile 55's wake, I do my best to focus on anything except the dry stickiness in my mouth.

Kennedy Meadows, the end of the PCT's desert section is only days away. I trudge along resolutely, ignoring my body's complaints.

There is a tradition on the PCT; As hikers find their way into Kennedy Meadows, they receive a round of applause.

I close my eyes and imagine it.

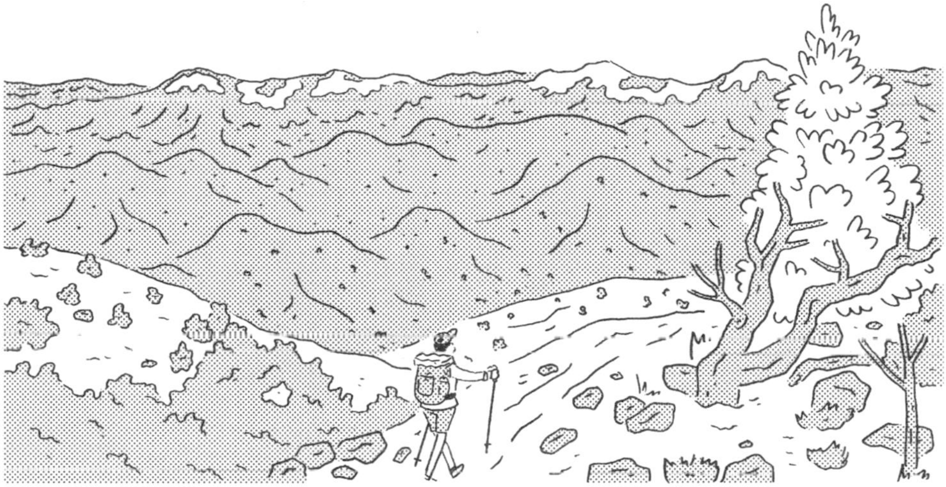

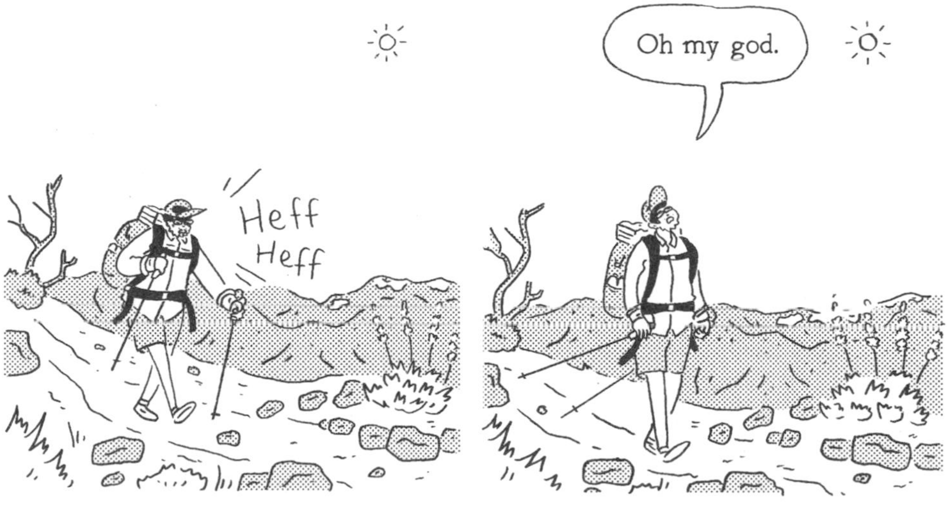
Heff
Heff
Oh my god.

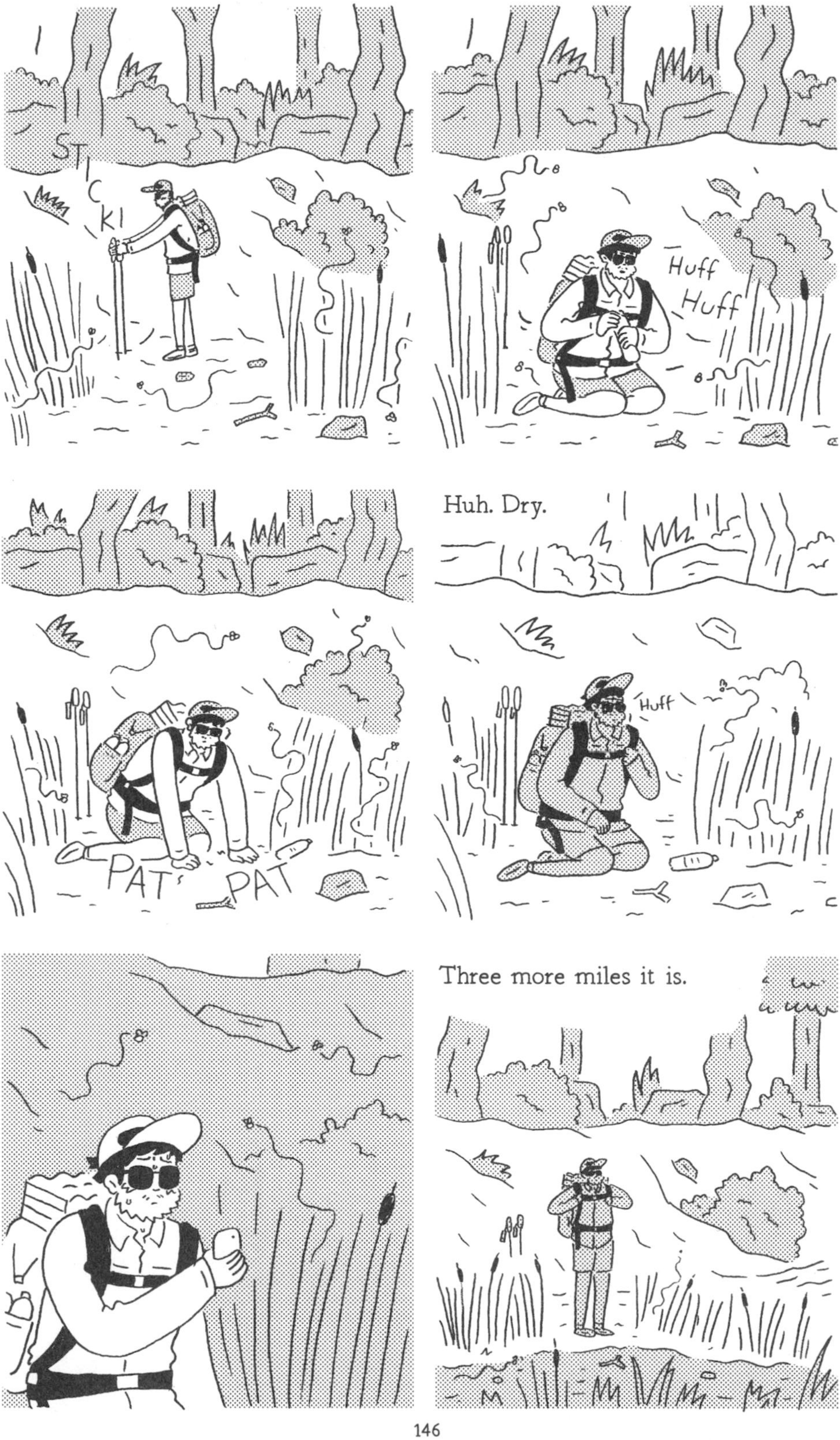
STICK
Huff
Huff
PAT PAT
Huh. Dry.
Huff
Three more miles it is.

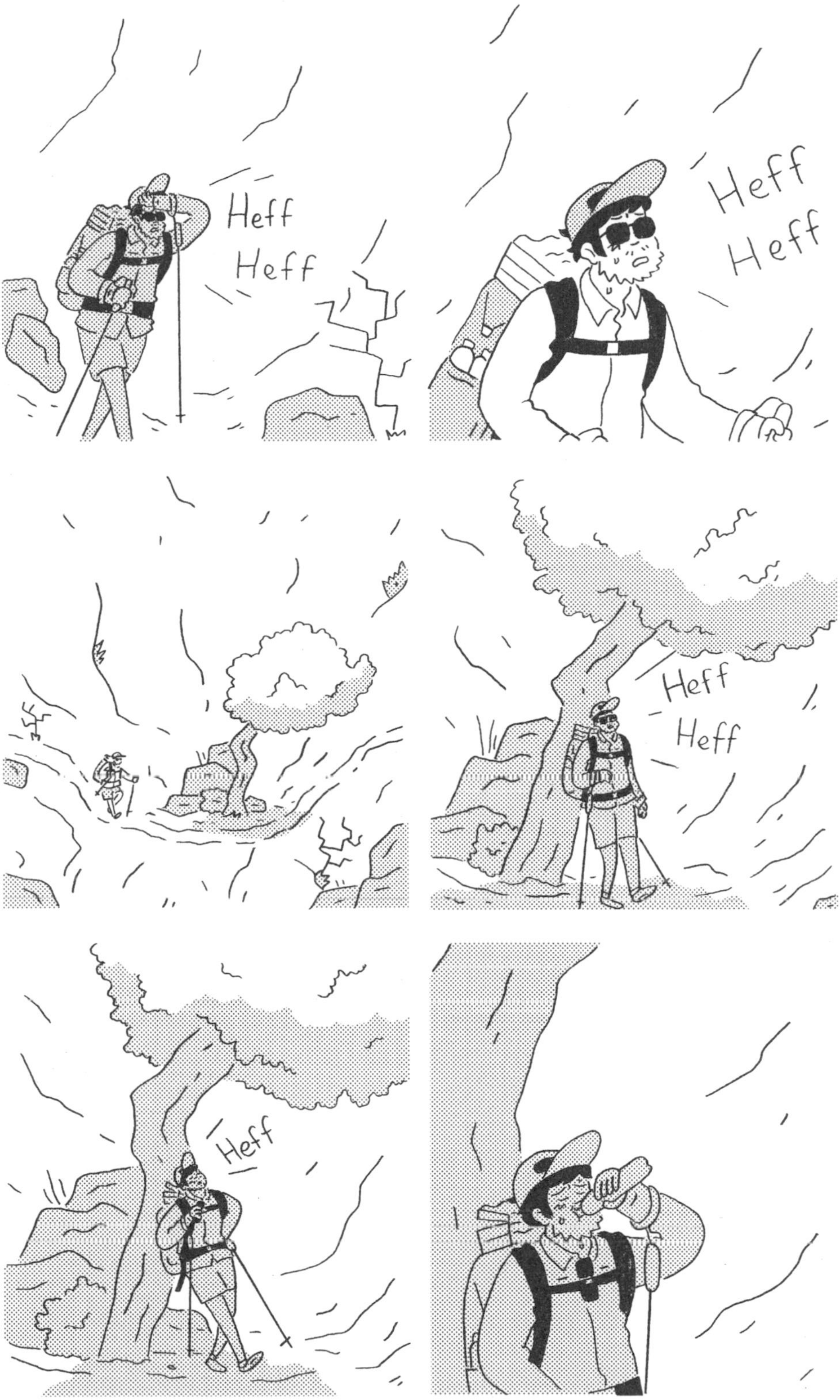
Heff
Heff
Heff
Heff
Heff
Heff
Heff

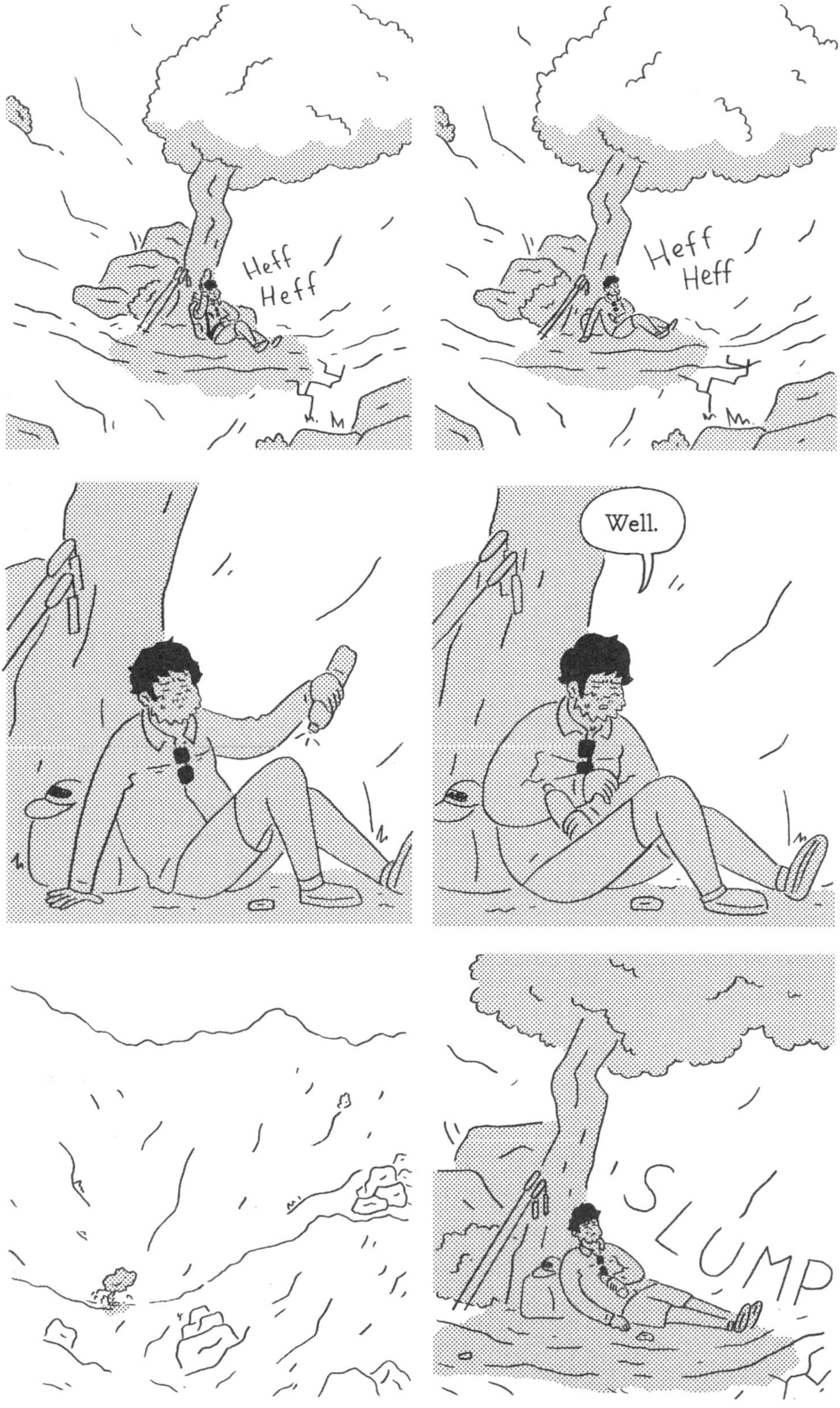
Heff Heff
Heff Heff
Well.
SLUMP

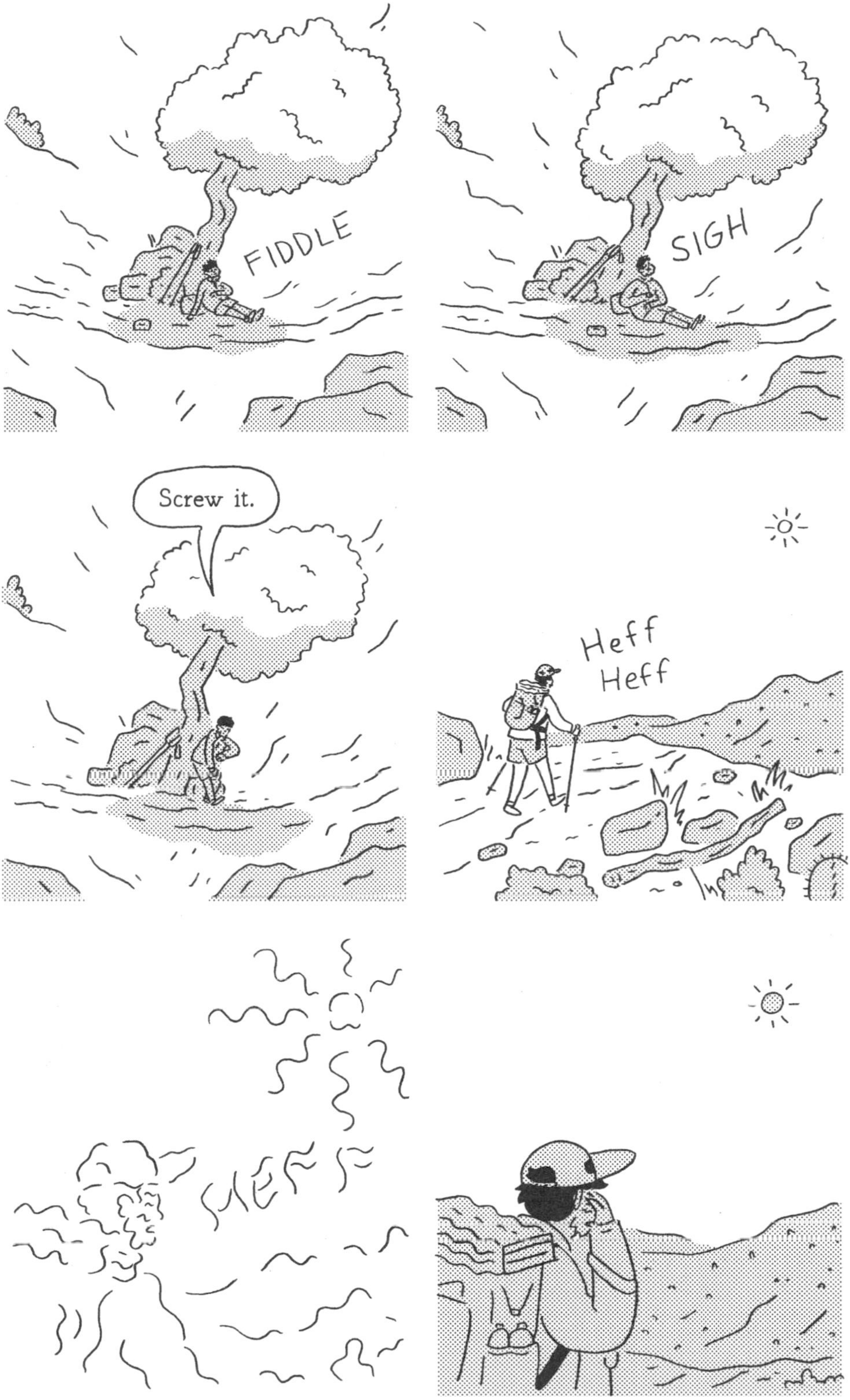
FIDDLE
SIGH
Screw it.
Heff
Heff

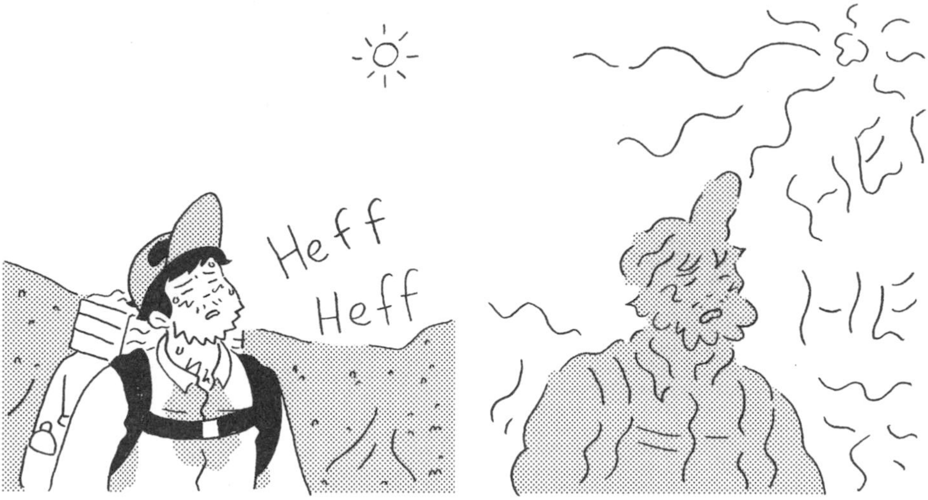
Heff
Heff

The next spring is an inch-deep puddle, full of mosquito eggs.

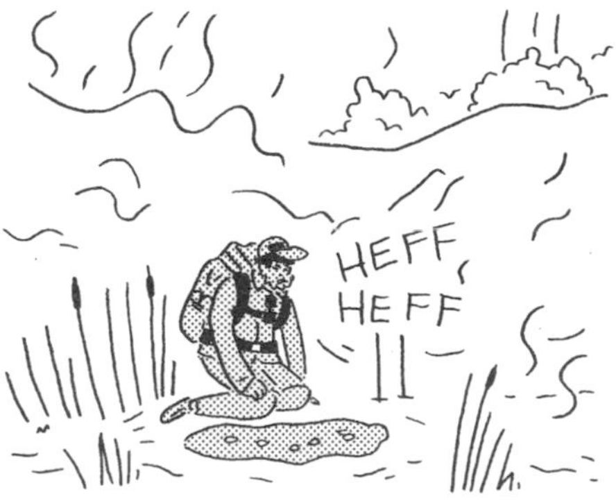
HEFF
HEFF

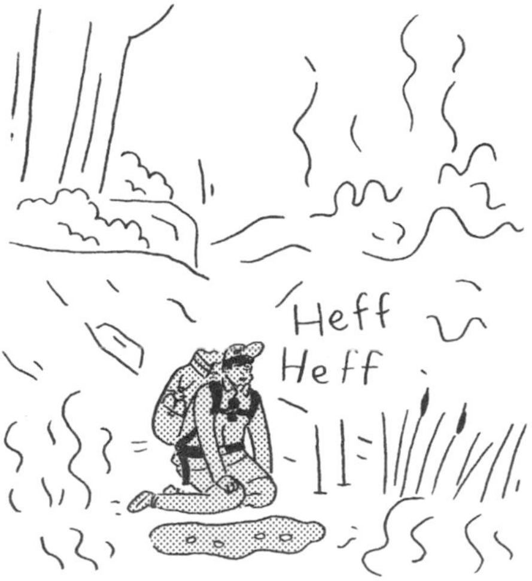
Heff
Heff

I consider it.

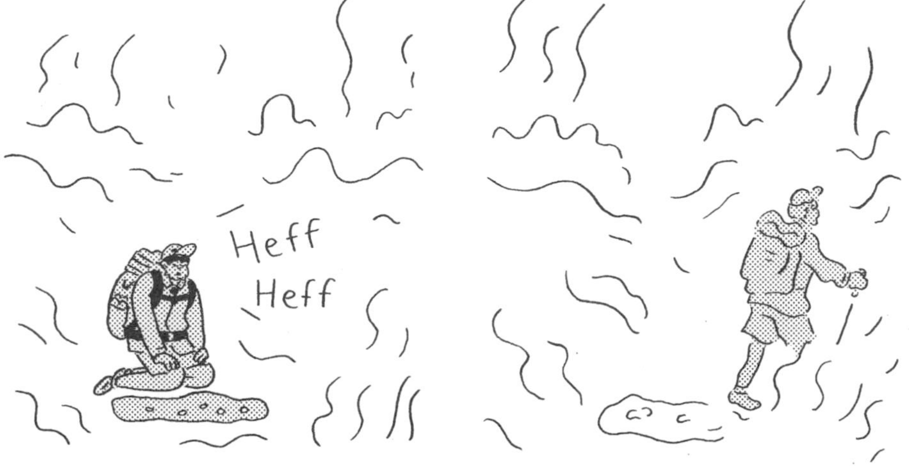
Heff
Heff

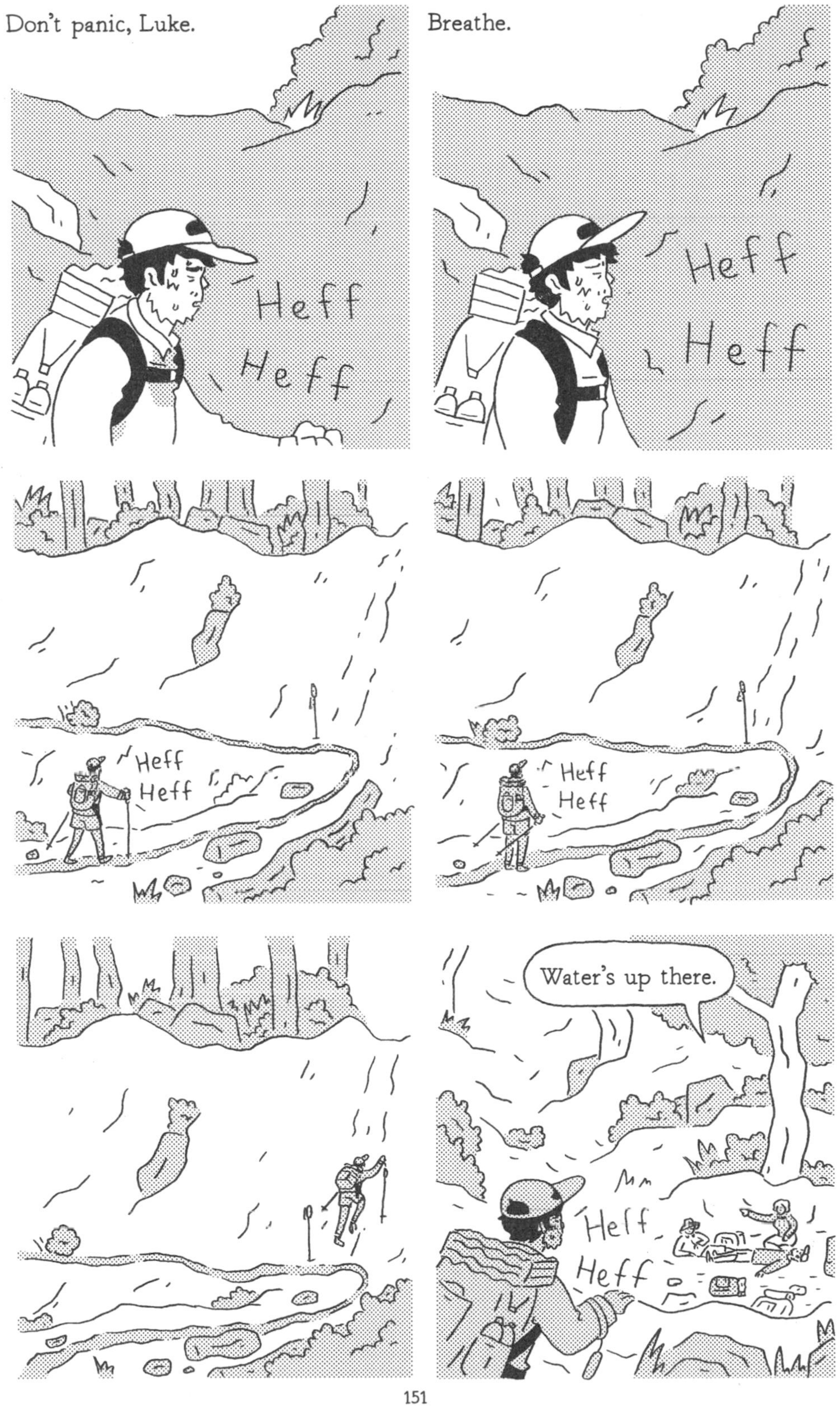
Don't panic, Luke.
Heff Heff
Breathe.
Heff Heff
Heff Heff
Heff Heff
Water's up there.
Heff Heff

The water is barely more than
a trickle.

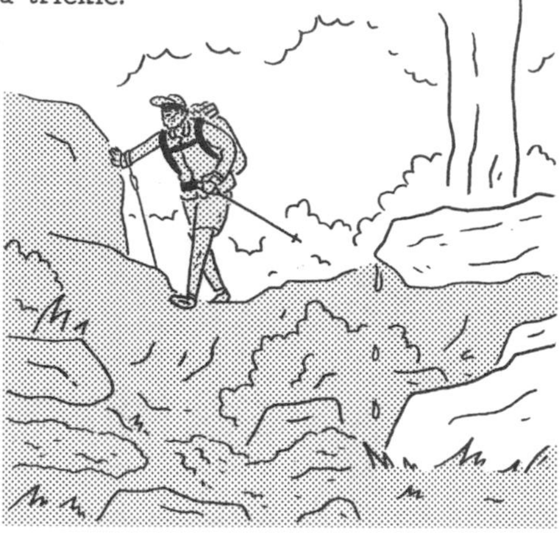

It takes ten minutes to fill a litre.

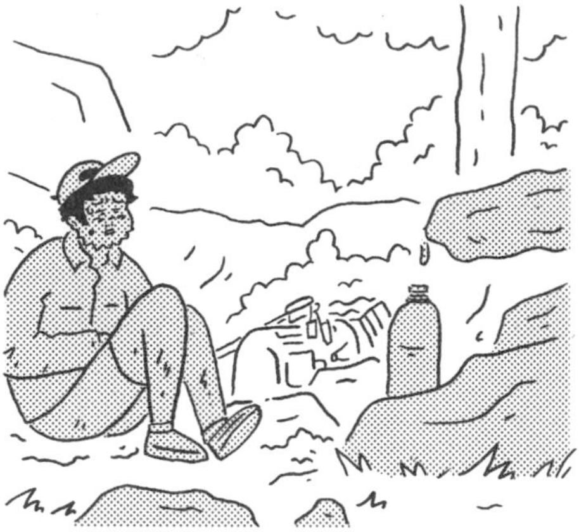

It feels like ten lifetimes.

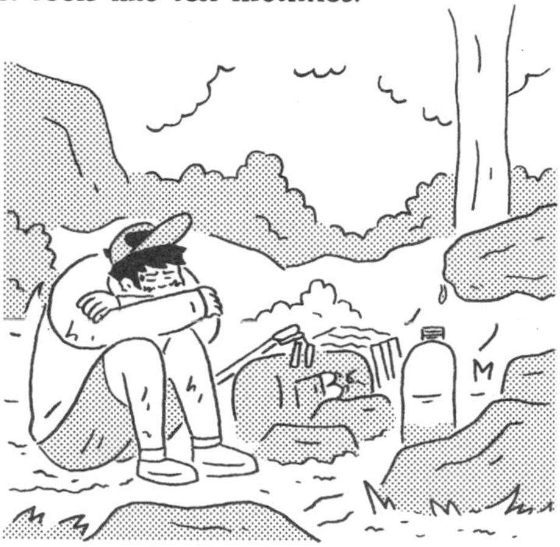

I drink. I collapse. Non-optional
shut down.

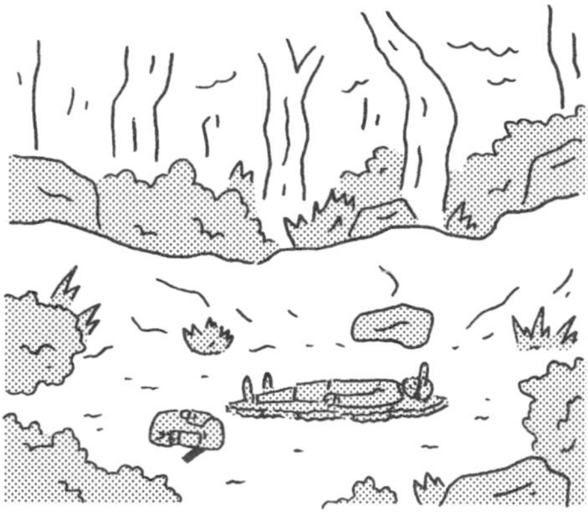

Heatstroke.

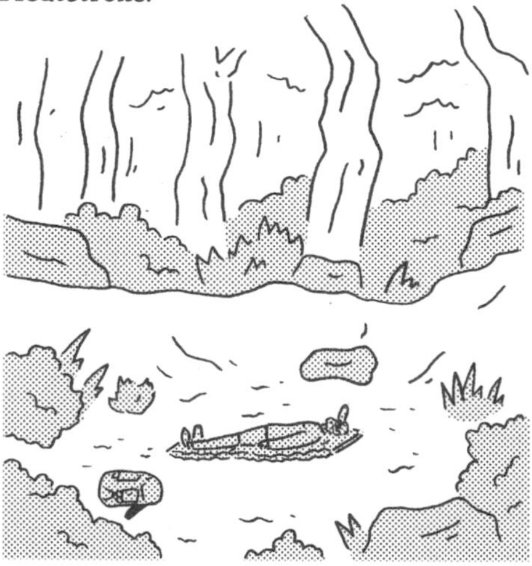

I never fucking learn.

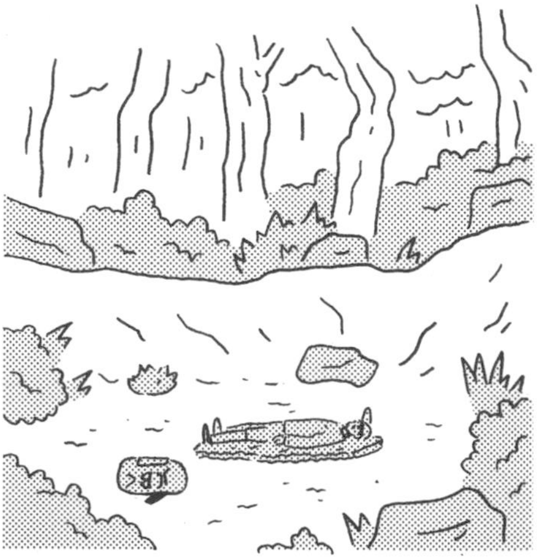

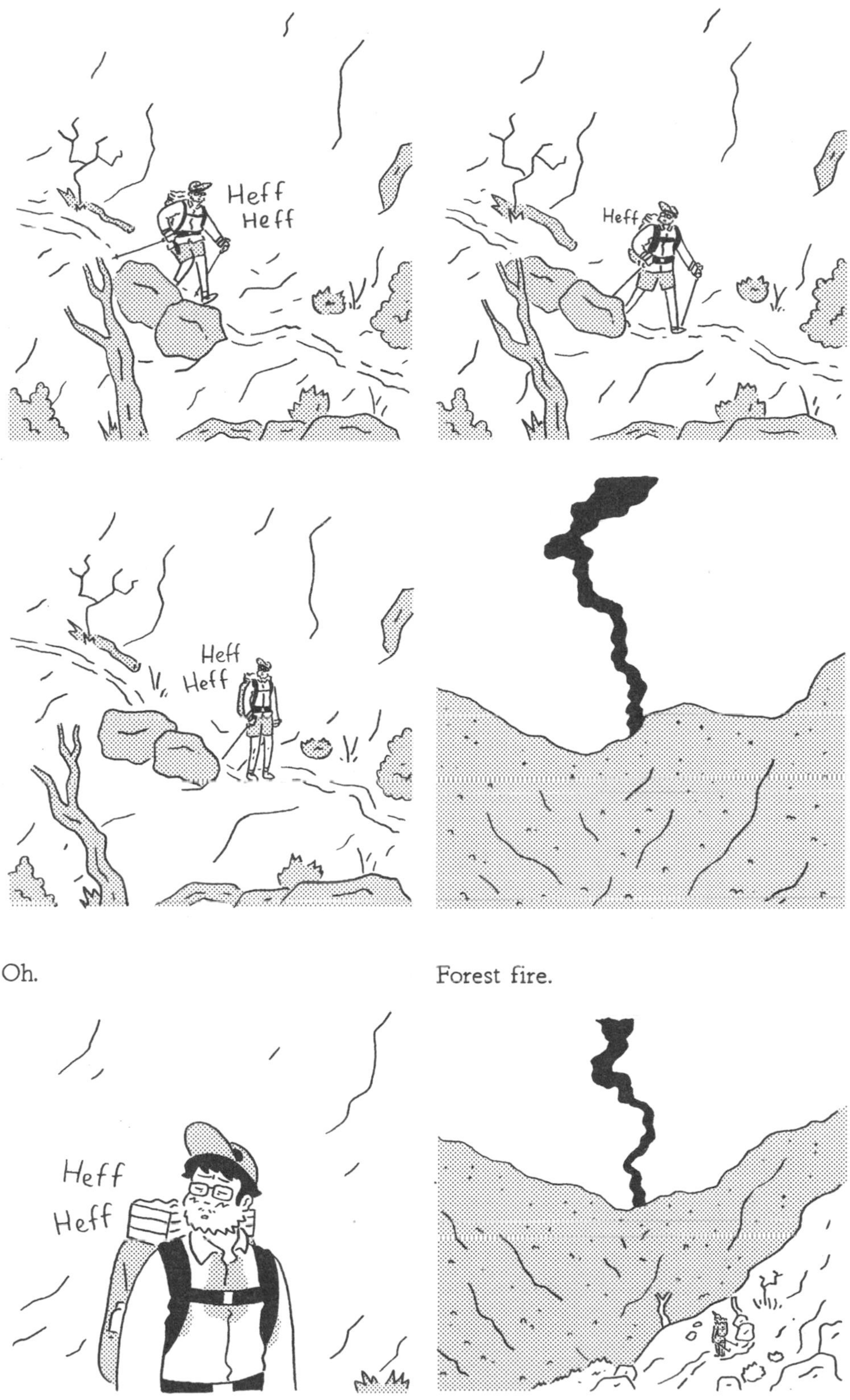
Heff
Heff
Heff
Heff
Heff
Oh.
Heff
Heff
Forest fire.

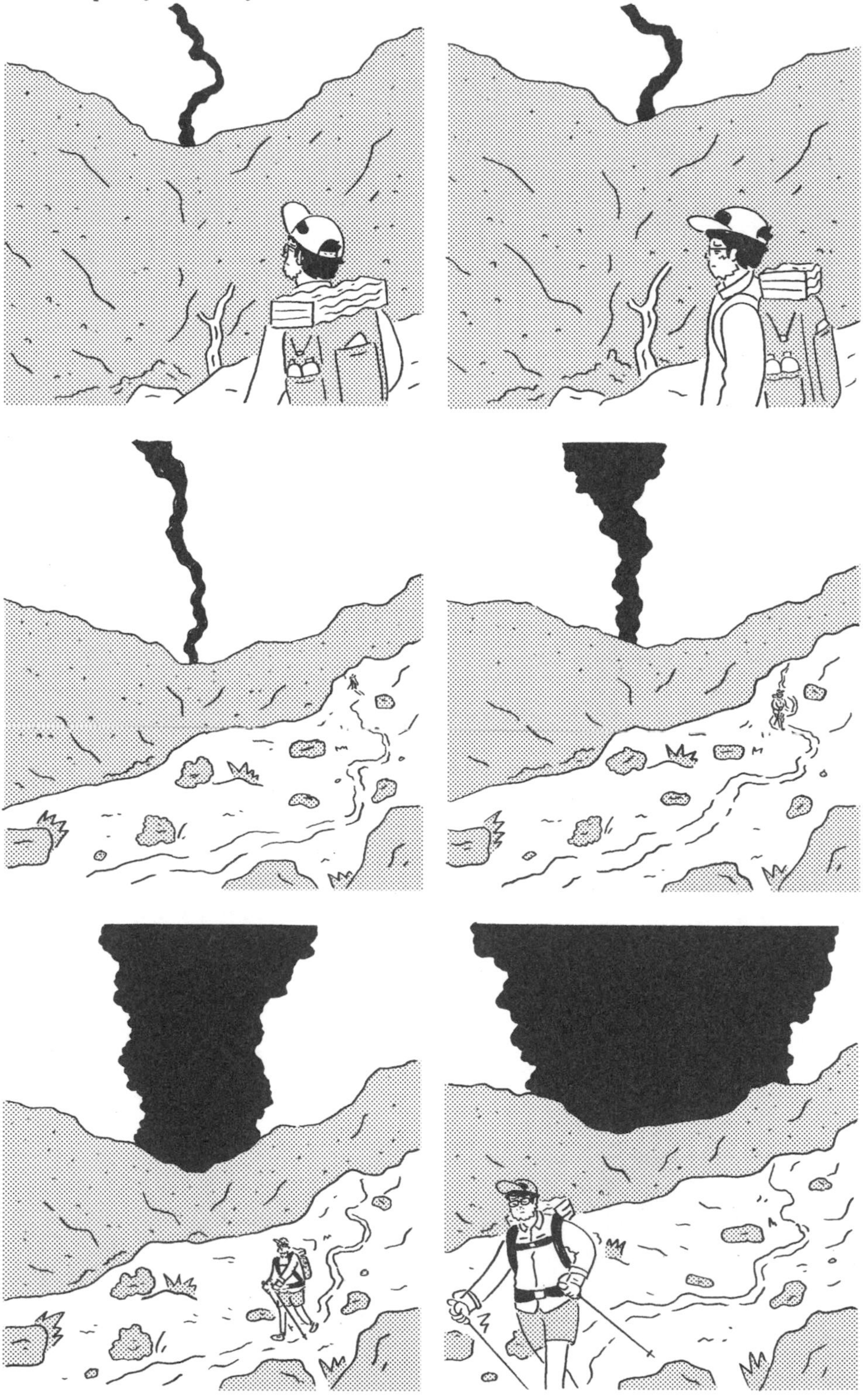
It looks pretty far away.
How fast do forest fires travel?

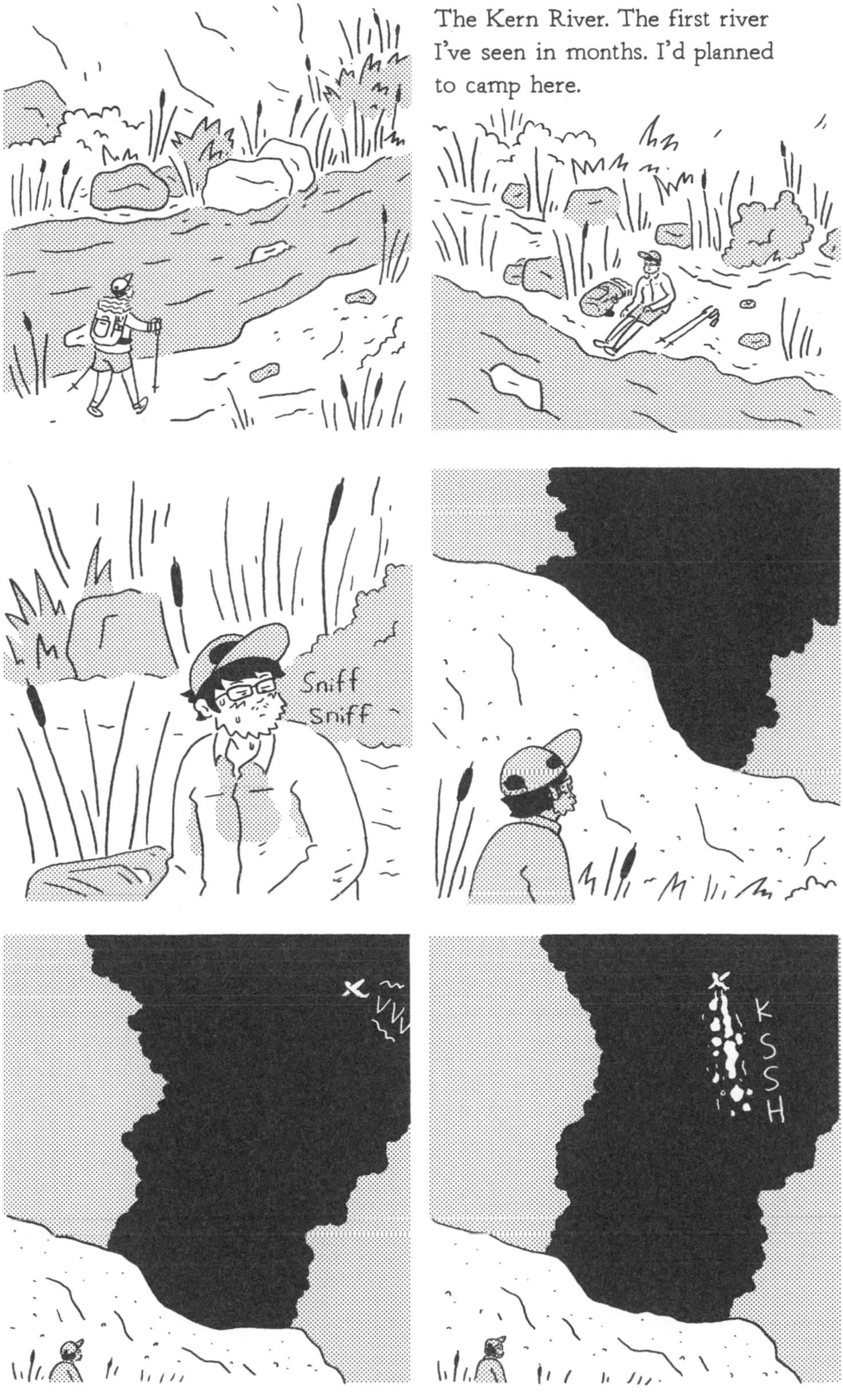
The Kern River. The first river I've seen in months. I'd planned to camp here.
Sniff
Sniff
KSSH

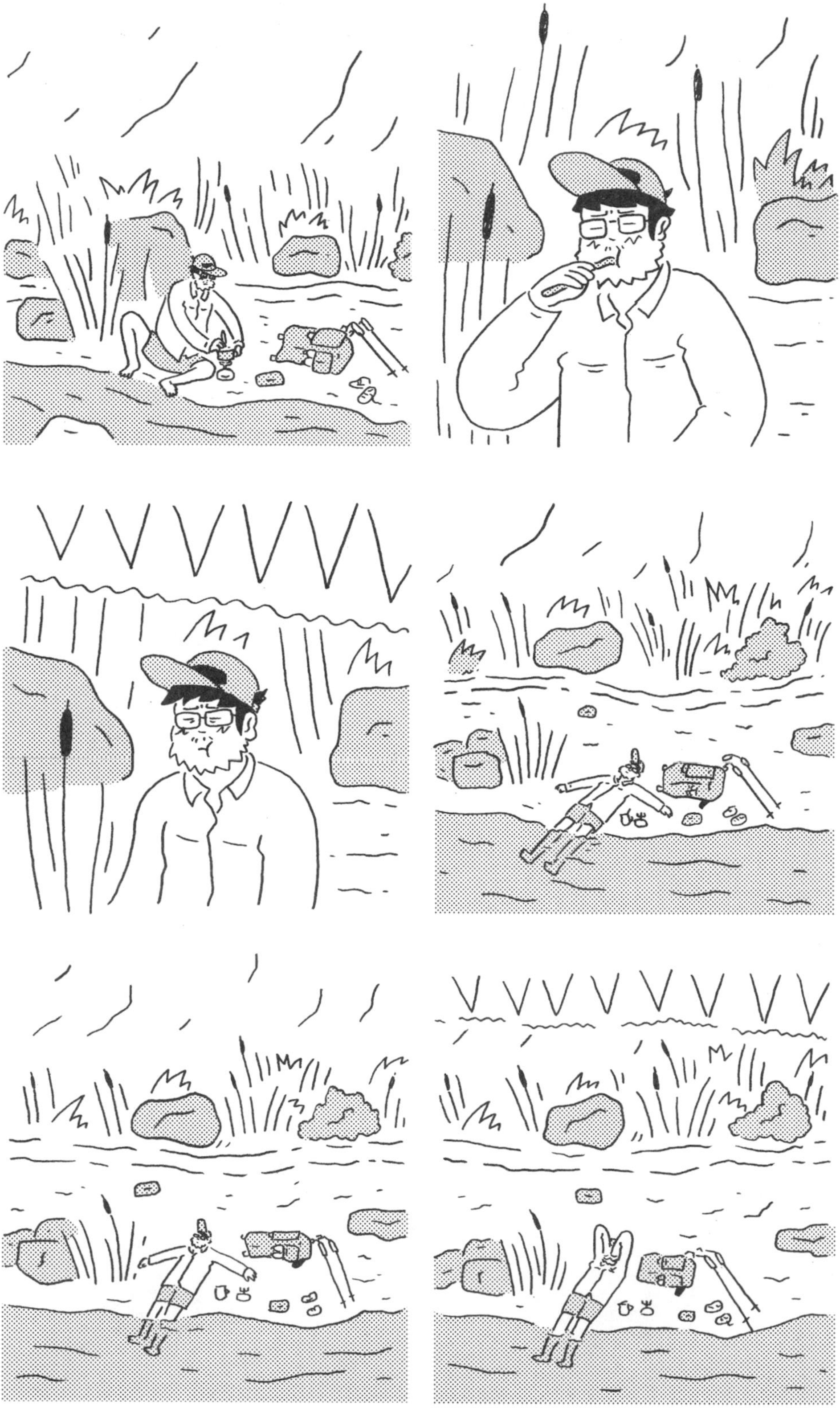

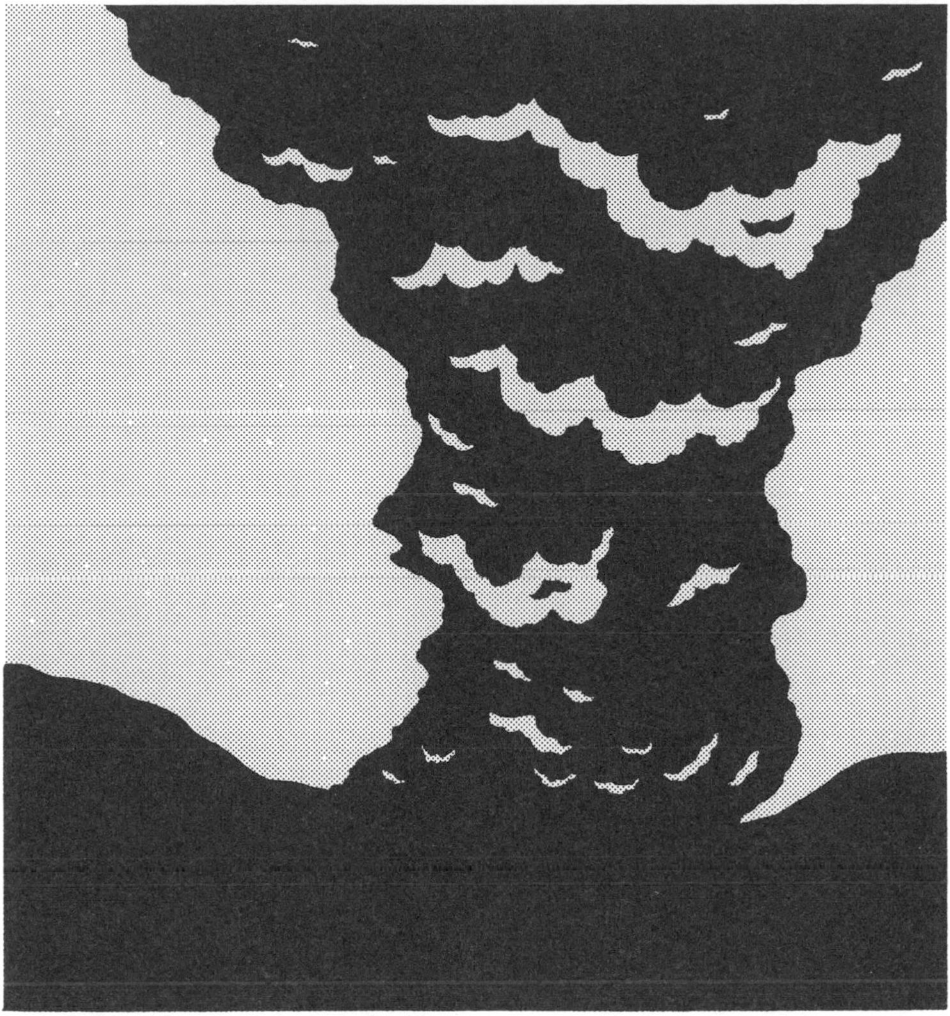

The sky is orange. Like the lights over L.A.

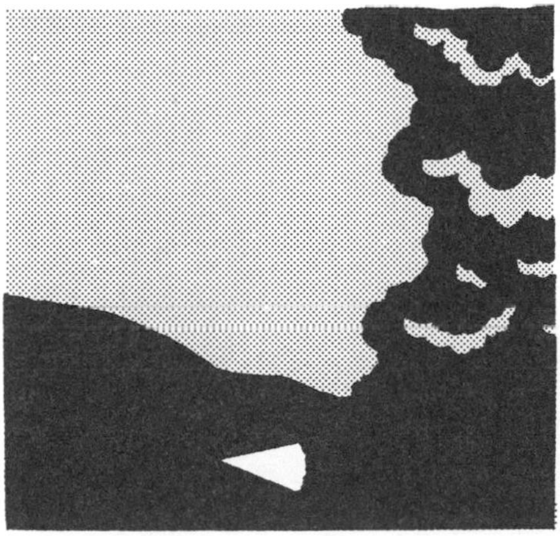

My headlamp bobs alone.

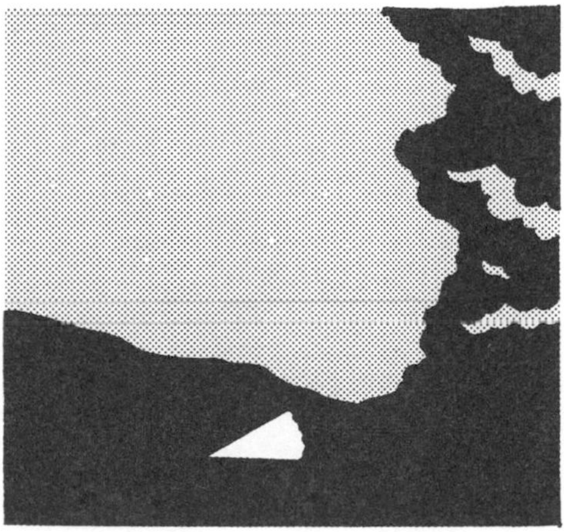

Heff
Heff
CLAP
Heff
Heff
CLAP
CLAP
CLA
CLAP
CLAP
CLA
CLAP
CLAP
CLAP
AP
CLAP
LAP
CLAP
CLAP
CL
CLAP
CLAP
CLAP
CLAP
CLAP

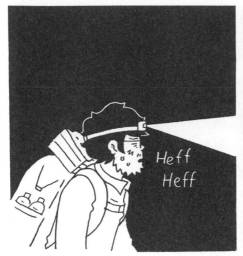

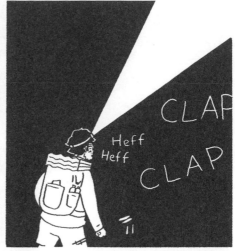

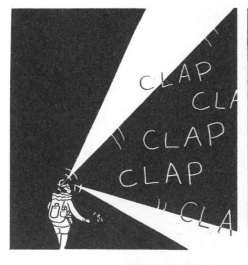

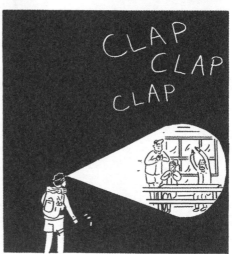

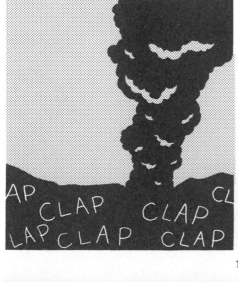

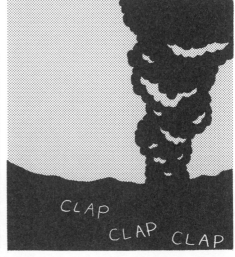

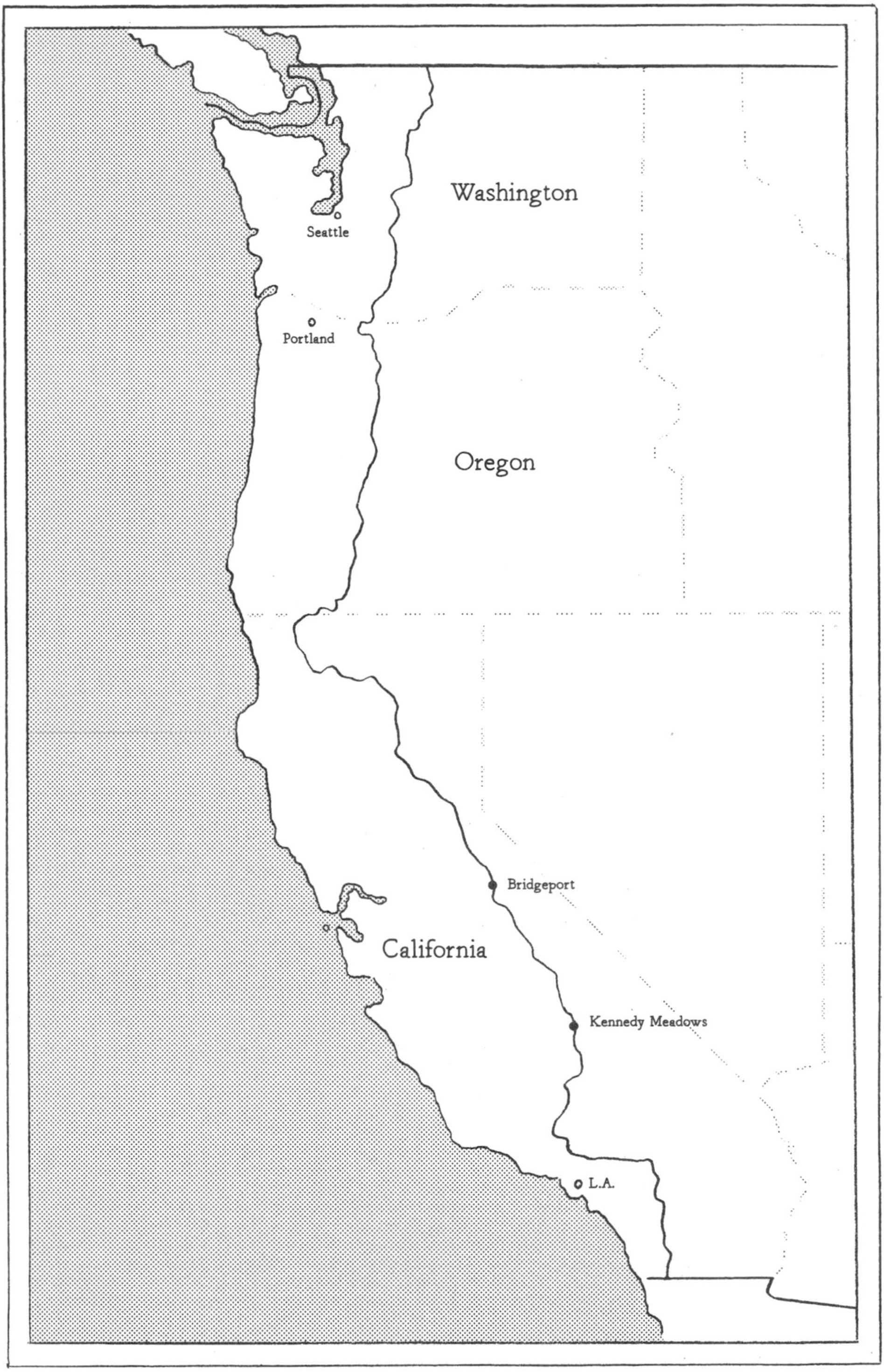
Washington
Seattle
Portland
Oregon
Bridgeport
California
Kennedy Meadows
L.A.

Chapter 3: The High Sierras

"America is not anything if it consists of each of us.
It is something only if it consists of all of us."
–Woodrow Wilson

After my first ejection in the summer of 2013, I focused all my energy
on returning to the USA as quickly as possible. My time in Ireland
was divided firmly between telecommuting for classes, working on my
thesis in isolation and filling out dozens of visa application forms. It was
a tense time, full of teases and disappointments. When I walked out of
the US embassy in Dublin with the knowledge that my new visa had
been granted, I was more relieved than elated.

I'd missed the first semester of my second year. This time, upon
stepping off the train in White River Junction, I was met not by
rapidly browning maple leaves but midwinter snow.

In my first year, I'd done my best to ignore my looming eviction.
Now, I was hyper-aware of how fleeting my time in the USA would
be. My new visa would terminate immediately after graduation, leaving
only a week to pack my things and leave.

I tried to savour my time there, but with countless hours of work
to complete, I spent most of my days squirreled away in the school
studio with Eleri for company.

I spent my nights online, long after Eleri had left the studio,
searching for a way to attain permanent residency. I researched obscure
visa categories and weighed my near-empty bank account against the
costs of hiring an immigration lawyer.

My only viable route to permanent residence was to get a job at a company large enough to satisfy the visa requirements, and I applied for many. I applied to jobs all over the country, in any major city that might have me. I especially applied to animation jobs in Los Angeles, where years later I would fly to begin my hike.

Nothing worked. My exit from the USA was inevitable.

We took one last road trip after graduation. Five of us, to a comics festival in Chicago. I both anticipated and dreaded that trip, excited to spend one last week with my friends, but knowing that the only thing that awaited me there was a one-way flight to Ireland.

I cheered with the others when we drove out of Vermont.

We crossed through small towns as we journeyed from roadside oddity to roadside oddity. The four days we spent moving through this lesser-seen America only compounded my hunger for more. This was my truest preparation for the PCT. We saw the world's largest can of soup, outside of a Campbell's factory, in rural Indiana. We drove through the birthplace of L. Frank Baum, the author of the Wizard of Oz books, where a big sign proclaimed: "There's no place like home!"

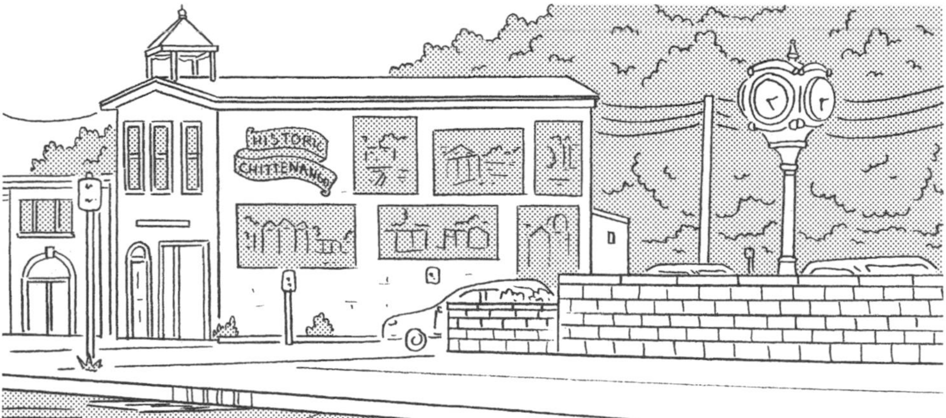
HISTORIC
CHITTENANGO

Still, my idealised America was cracked and this short road trip delivered the shattering blow. What started as a join-the-dots route of attractions between White River Junction and Chicago became a whistle-stop tour of suburban decay.

In Le Roy, New York, we stopped to visit a museum dedicated to Jell-O, only to discover that the town's economy had once relied almost entirely on the Jell-O factory and was devastated when it relocated.

In Buffalo, we drove through the suburbs to find an enormous art deco train station that had been built and never opened, simply left to rot, fenced off from the surrounding houses.

I slept in a tent, for only the second time in my life, at a small campsite in Indiana.

In Cleveland, Ohio, the final stop on our road trip to Chicago, we visited the house where Superman was created. We drove into a side of town where every second house seemed to be falling apart. Only the "Superman house" itself was in good condition. Outside on the fence, we found a large plastic Superman symbol, conspicuously mounted, shiny and bright amongst the otherwise dilapidated houses. An old man sat on the porch. We waved hello, and apologised for intruding.

"You all seem pretty normal compared to the people who usually stop by to see the house," he called out to us.

"We hope so."

"You want to see inside? I can take you to the Superman room."

Inside, his TV played a daytime chat show at high volume.

"Are you a Superman fan?"

"Oh, no. I mean, I used to watch the TV show back in the '50s when I was a kid, but I never read the comic books or anything. One day I just got a letter in the mail, saying that the house was some kind of historical monument, with some money to keep the place up. It was fans who put in that symbol thing, not me."

The Superman room was in his attic. It was covered in memorabilia. Superman wallpaper served as the backdrop for countless dolls, commemorative plates, action figures and other, more obscure merchandise. Like the symbol outside, the room was shiny and well maintained. Packed with stuff. A little bomb of Americana.

"People just keep sending me stuff," he offered, shrugging.

Superman beamed out at us from in front of American flags.

I said goodbye to my friends on a Chicago street, late at night. I hugged Eleri last. I tried my best not to cry.

I was jealous. Jealous of the people I was already pining for. Jealous that they didn't have to leave. After school, they would scatter too, but slowly, over the course of a whole year and under their own volition. My exit was swift and mandatory.

I wake, lying at an odd angle, halfway down a slope in the small campsite behind the Kennedy Meadows general store. After hiking twenty-eight miles to escape the fire, my legs feel like they're wrapped in barbed wire. Climbing the five steps to the door makes me grimace.

Inside the store, a heavily pregnant woman sits behind the counter. Her face is flushed, and she picks up her ringing landline for what I assume must be the hundredth time this morning to answer questions about the fire. "Yes, it's out. No, no houses were burned. Nobody is missing." We got off lucky.

I pick up my mail. The bear can and ice axe Luanne mailed here a month ago still look shiny and new. My food package, divided into a few dozen ziplock bags, looks beaten up and crumbly. I pack my resupply into my new bear can, a big plastic tube where anything edible or fragrant will have to live as I pass through bear territory.

For the next month at least, I'll be hiking through the High Sierra Mountains, a more remote section of trail that hovers above ten thousand feet. No roads, no towns, no trail angels. I'll see nobody but other thruhikers for five or six days at a time.

I say a quick prayer to the Universe; "No bears".

I find Mile 55, piece-by-piece, around the campsite behind the store. It's not quite the reunion I'd hoped for. They're all friendly, but this reunion is clearly a bigger deal for me than it is for them. I talk about hiking on with them but I fear that I'm now imposing myself.

I catch Little Spoon as he opens a resupply box, only to exclaim, "There's another one!". The rest of Mile 55 gather around as he pulls a grey T-shirt from the box. On the front, there is a silk screened photograph of Screech from *Saved by the Bell*.

"Another one?" I ask, as the rest of Mile 55 bursts into laughter.

"Someone's been mailing us mystery T-shirts," Chuckles explains, showing me her own, which reads: "Every Brunette Needs a Blonde Best Friend".

Centerfold's has the logo for Cactus Cooler, a local SoCal soda.

"Looks like you're up next, Toe Touch," says Little Spoon, as he pulls on his new shirt.

They are now only four strong. Camel, having taken a short break from trail to visit L.A., is stuck somewhere behind the new burn, though the rest of Mile 55 don't seem too concerned.

"He'll catch up soon," Little Spoon tells me as he loads and weighs his pack. "He's really fast".

Centerfold, the stoic member of the group, weighs his own pack, playfully jabbing Little Spoon when it comes in lighter on the scale. Toe Touch weighs in next, and her pack is by far the heaviest.

"I've got twelve days of food in here," she says, grinning, while hoisting her pack up on to her back with carefree ease. "I'm gonna go straight through all the passes. No town stops."

"Toe Touch has decided that town stops, zero days and resupplies are for mere humans, and therefore beneath her," adds Chuckles as she weighs in her own pack.

I weigh my pack last, smiling and shrugging with false humility when it comes in lightest of all.

"Bivvy's gone ultralight," Little Spoon teases.

"Supplies are for mere humans," I say in response.

I stand on the general store's deck in the cooler evening sun, watching the new hikers arrive and joining in the applause. I haven't taken a zero since Tehachapi and after a week hiking through the Mojave in a heatwave, my body is crying out for one. But Mile 55 is ready to depart, and despite my better sense, I decide to join them. I pushed to catch them, and even doubting that decision now, I know I should at least follow through with it.

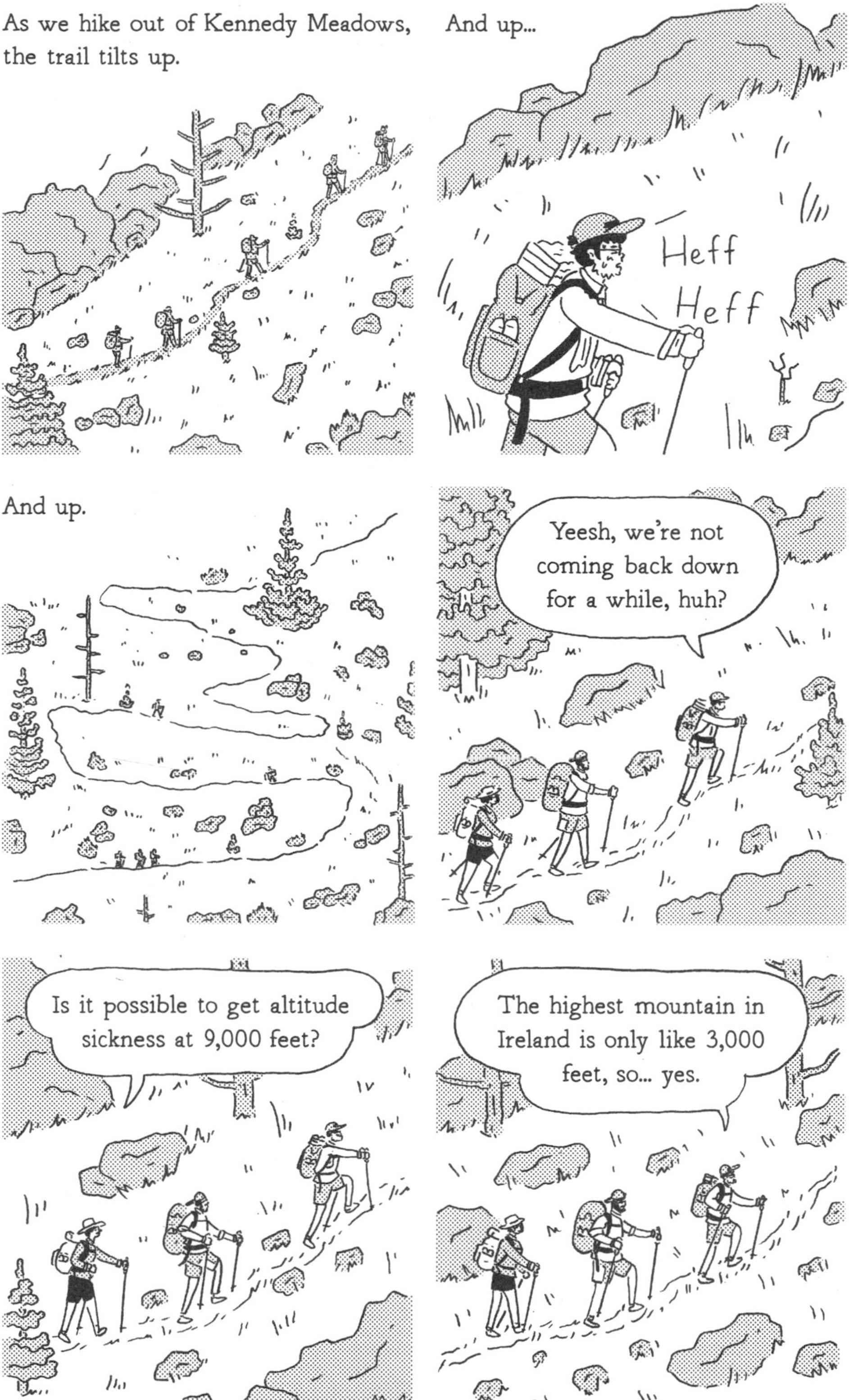
As we hike out of Kennedy Meadows, the trail tilts up.
And up...
Heff
Heff
And up.
Yeesh, we're not coming back down for a while, huh?
Is it possible to get altitude sickness at 9,000 feet?
The highest mountain in Ireland is only like 3,000 feet, so... yes.

We climb above 10,000 feet.

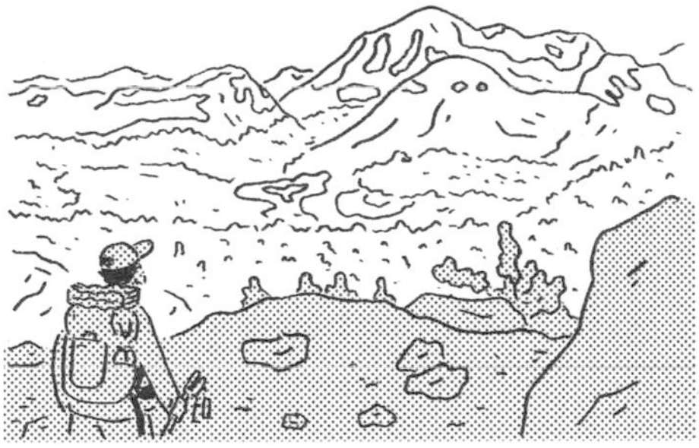

The views are insane.

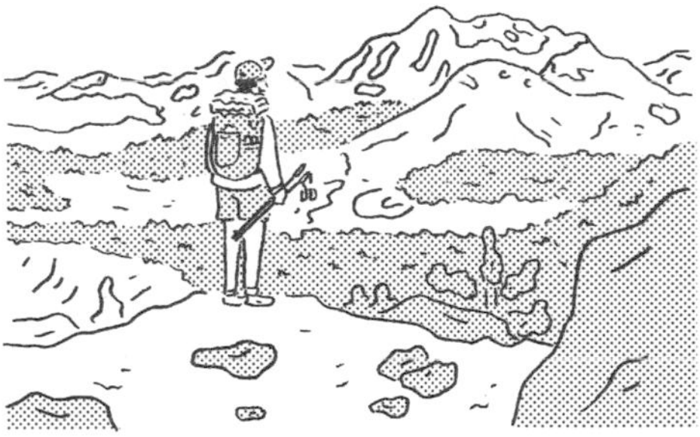

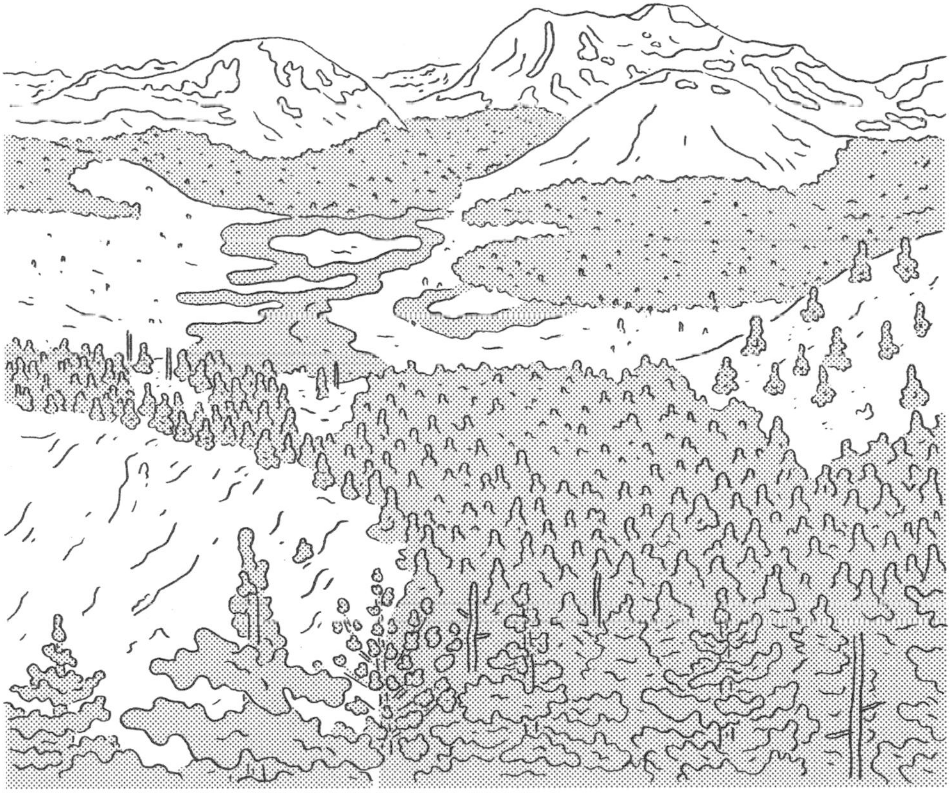

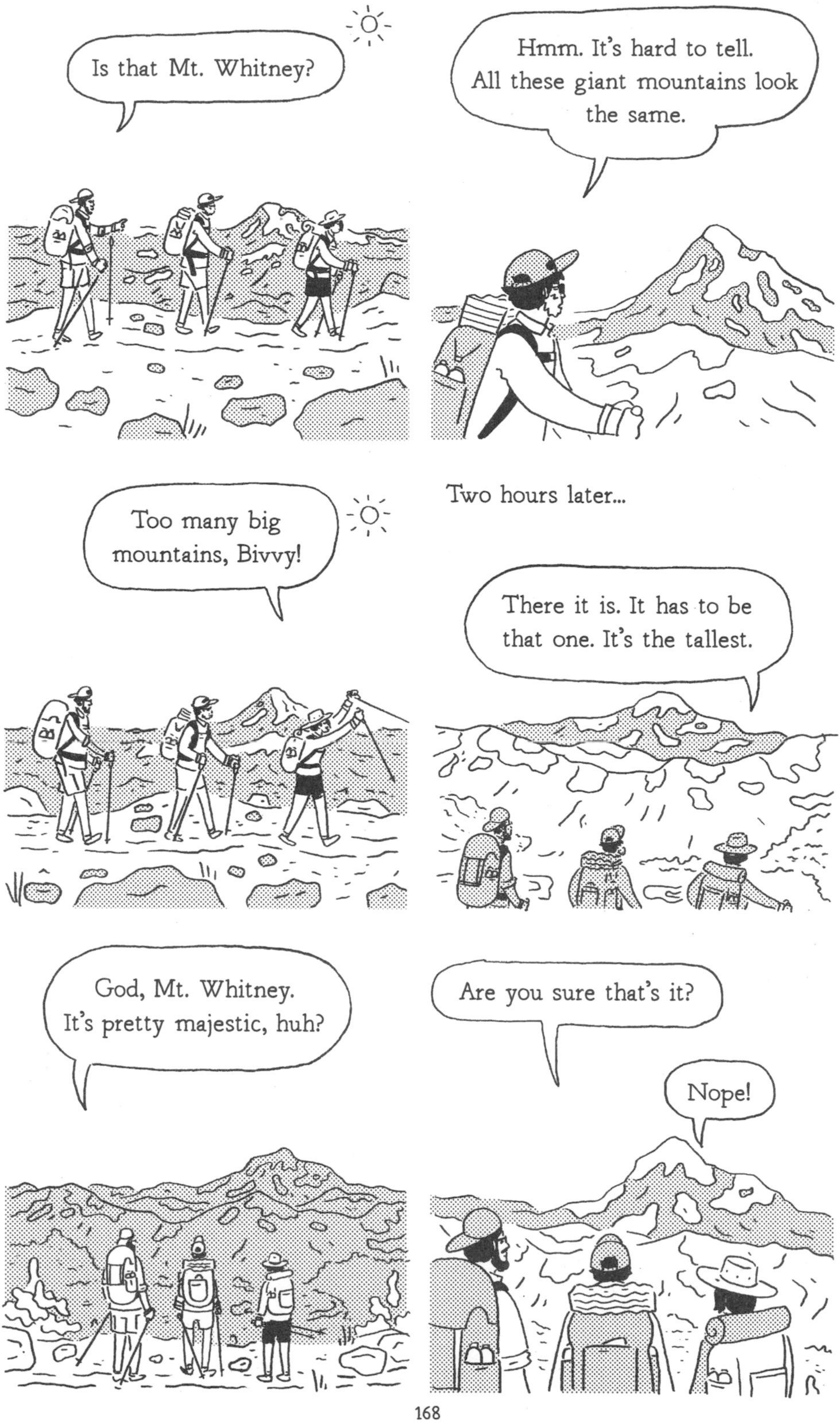
Is that Mt. Whitney?
Hmm. It's hard to tell. All these giant mountains look the same.
Too many big mountains, Bivvy!
Two hours later...
There it is. It has to be that one. It's the tallest.
God, Mt. Whitney. It's pretty majestic, huh?
Are you sure that's it?
Nope!

I ping-pong back and forth between the members of Mile 55.

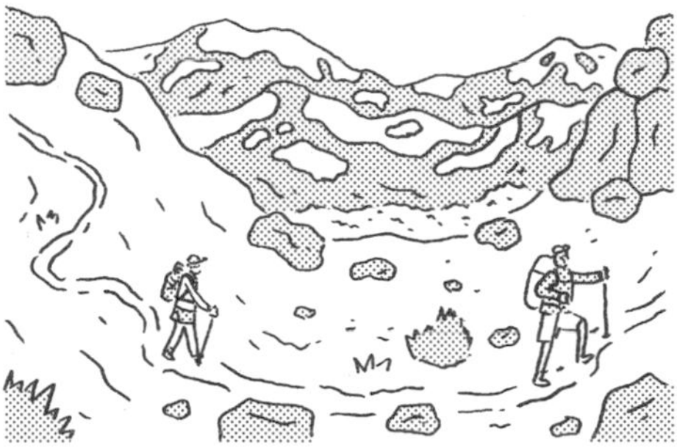

A few hours with Centerfold.

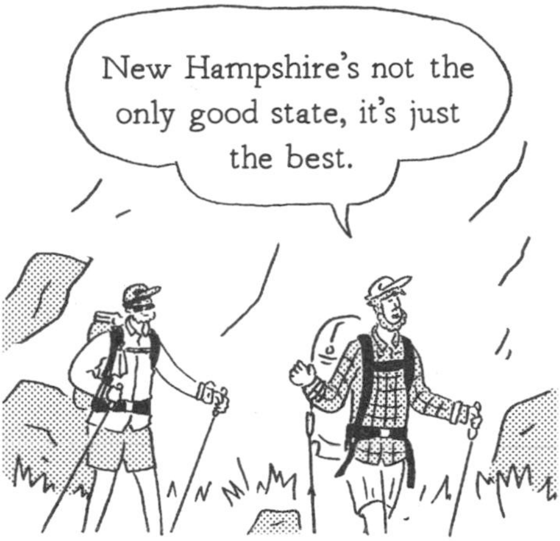
New Hampshire's not the only good state, it's just the best.

A few hours with Little Spoon and Chuckles.

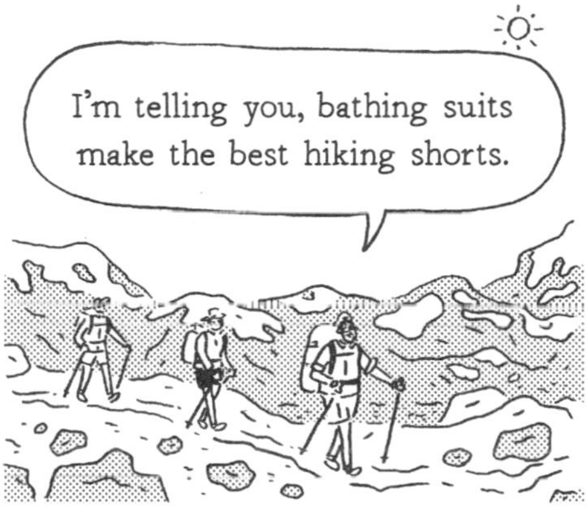
I'm telling you, bathing suits make the best hiking shorts.

A few hours with Toe Touch.

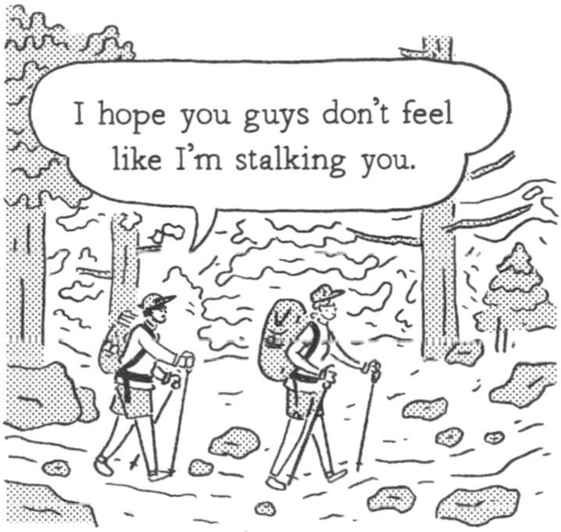
I hope you guys don't feel like I'm stalking you.

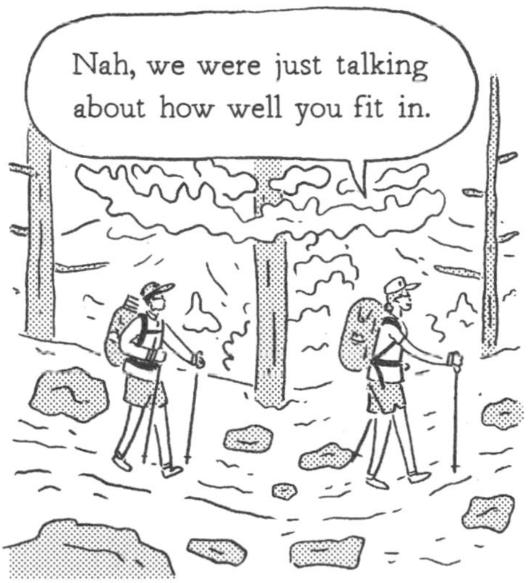
Nah, we were just talking about how well you fit in.

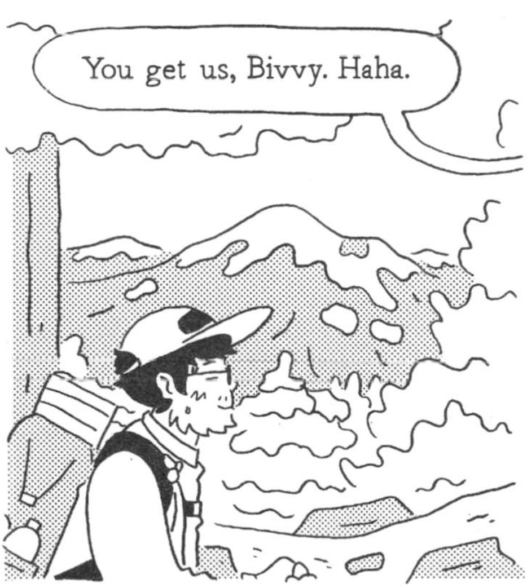
You get us, Bivvy. Haha.

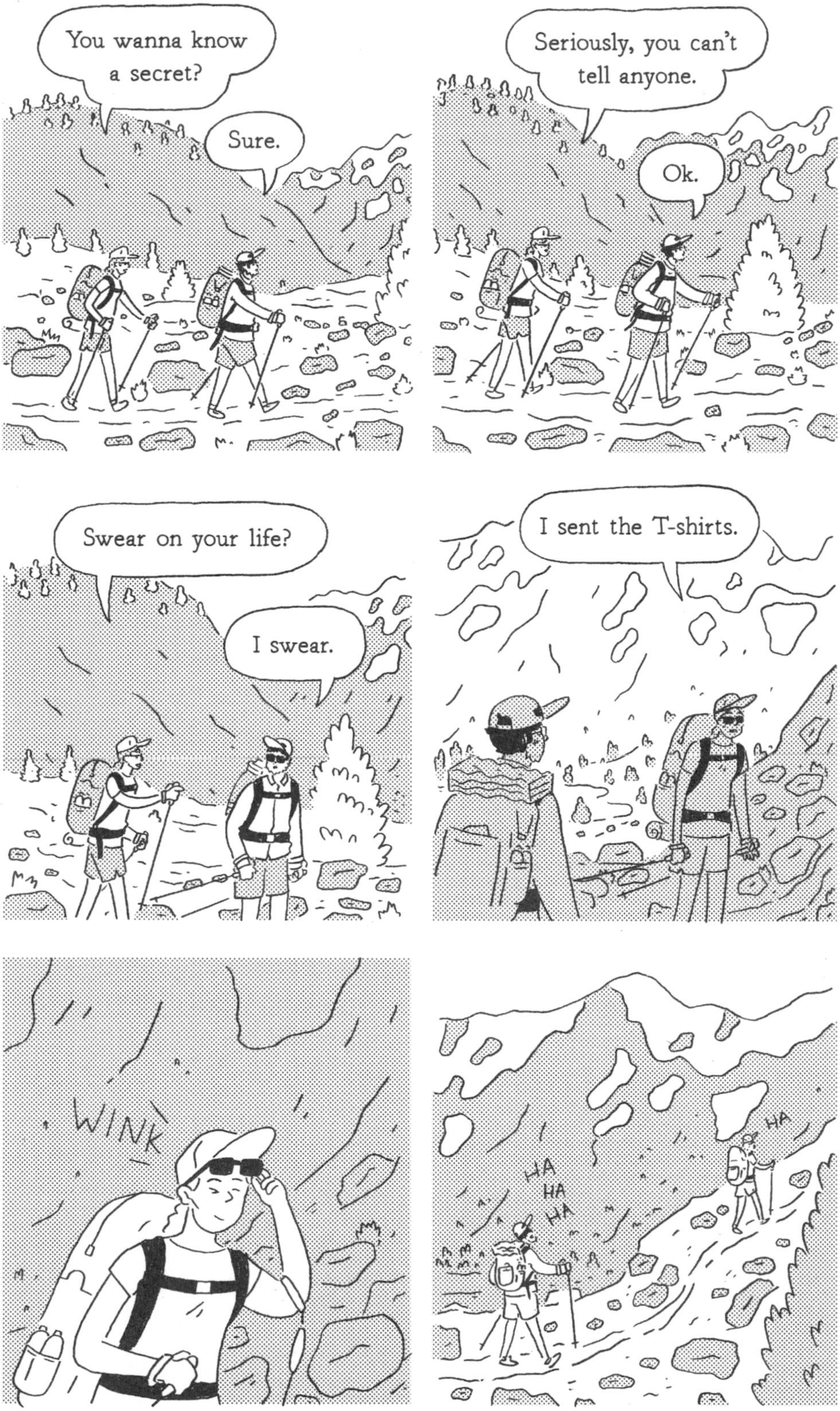
You wanna know a secret?
Sure.
Seriously, you can't tell anyone.
Ok.
Swear on your life?
I swear.
I sent the T-shirts.
WINK
HA
HA
HA
HA

After seven hundred miles of desert, the Sierras feel like a different dimension. We have entered a world of water. The water reports don't even cover this section, it's so plentiful here. Streams and rivers flow in every direction, and we scarcely need to hike five miles between sources. I carry most of my water bottles empty, and make a mental note to ditch a few in the next town.

I push on, eyes scanning for Mt. Whitney, the tallest mountain in the Sierras and in the "lower 48" states. A 14,500 foot giant.

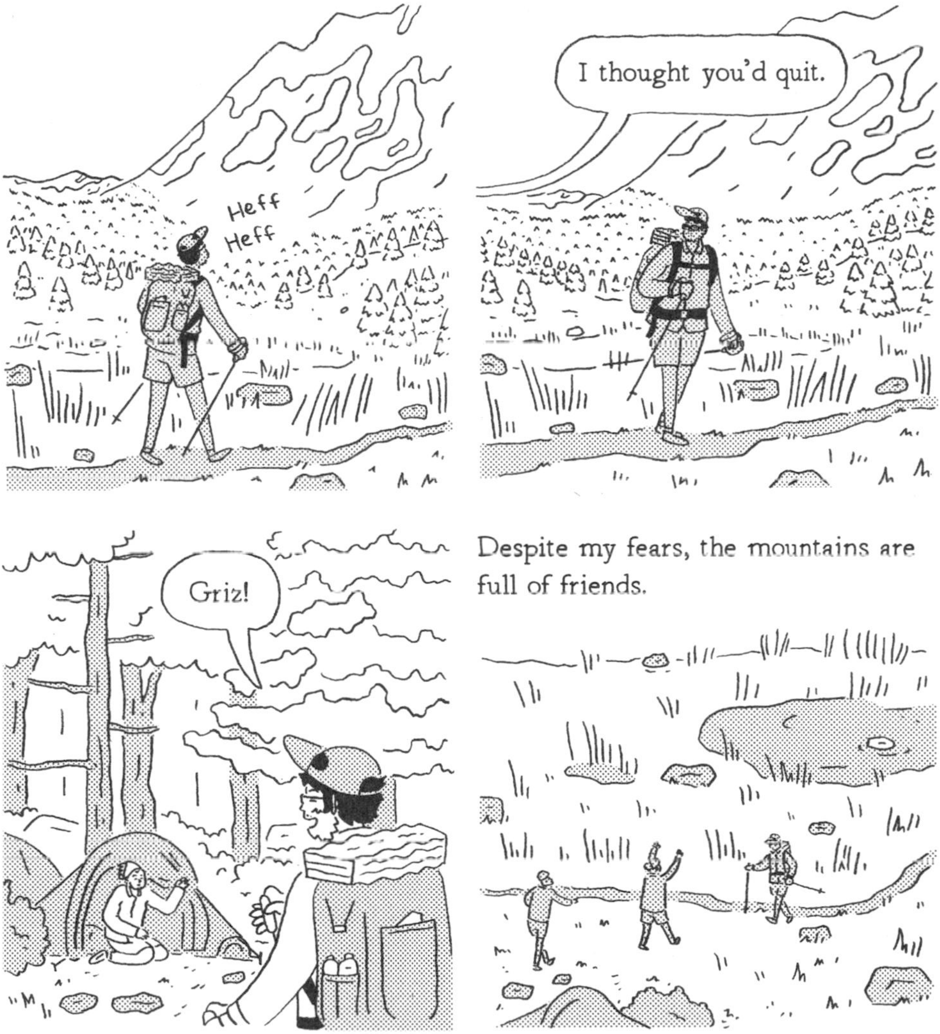
Heff
Heff
I thought you'd quit.
Griz!
Despite my fears, the mountains are full of friends.

Mt. Whitney 06/06/16. Day 52.

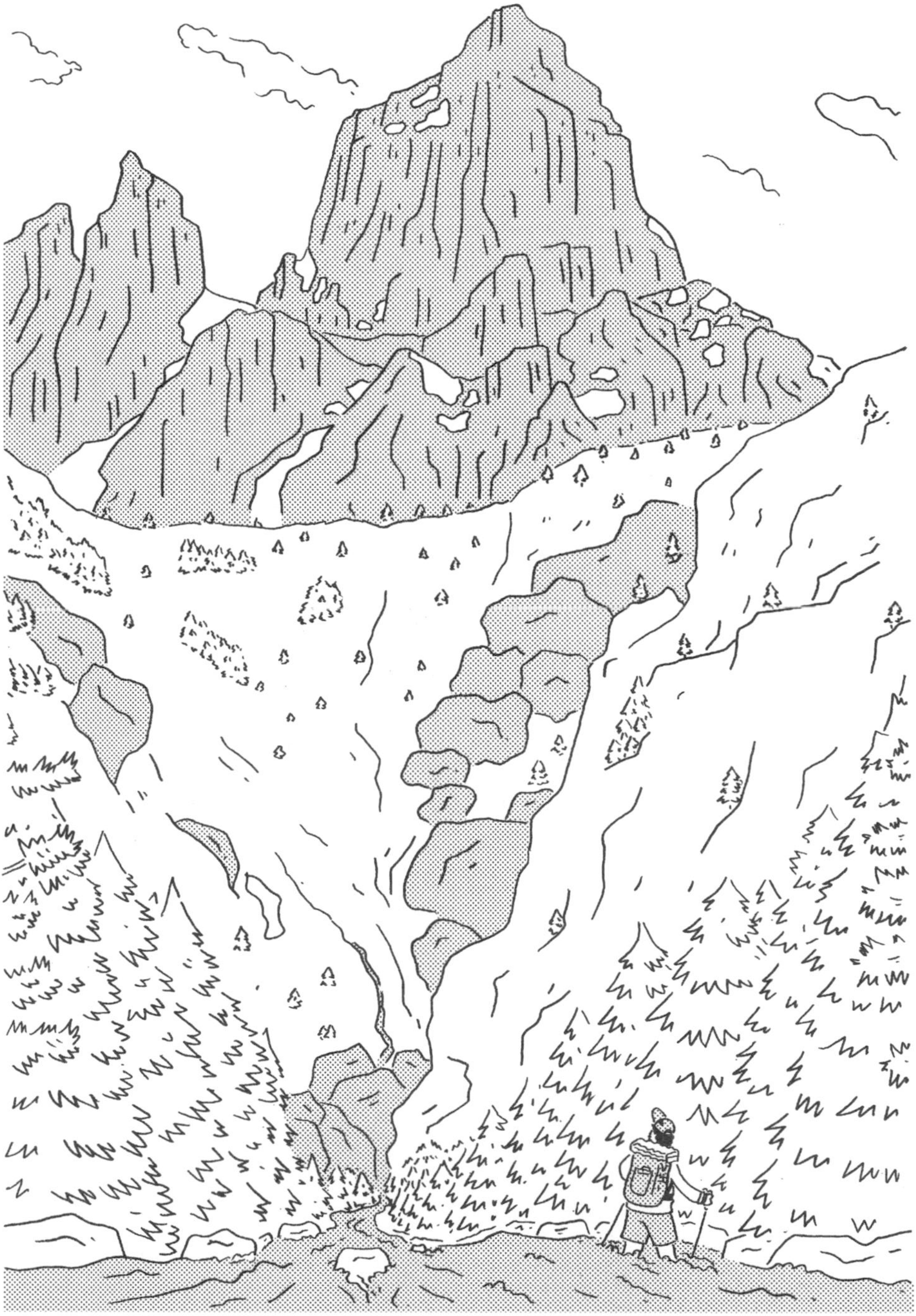

I wake late, and climb the first half of Whitney in a daze.

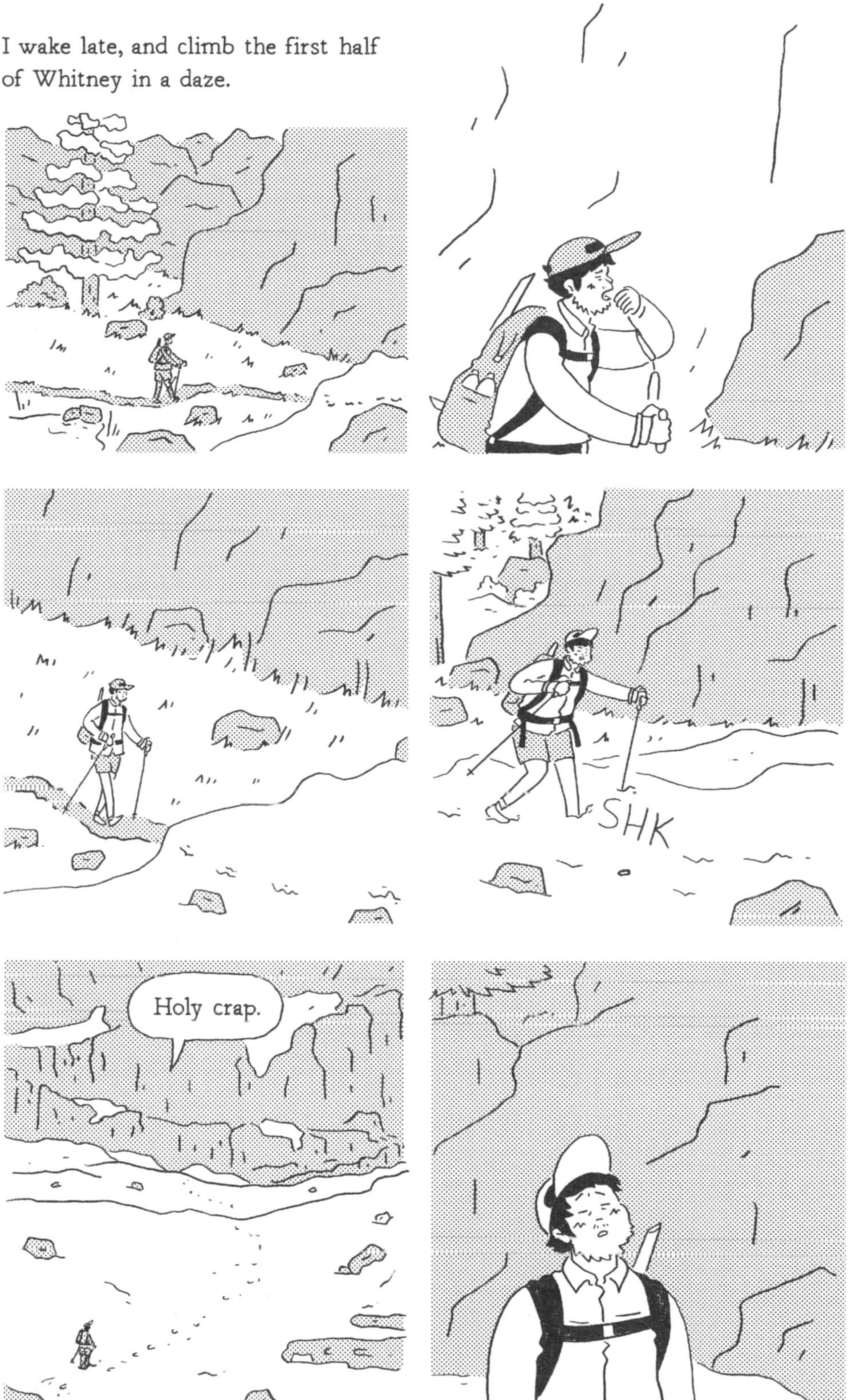
SHK
Holy crap.

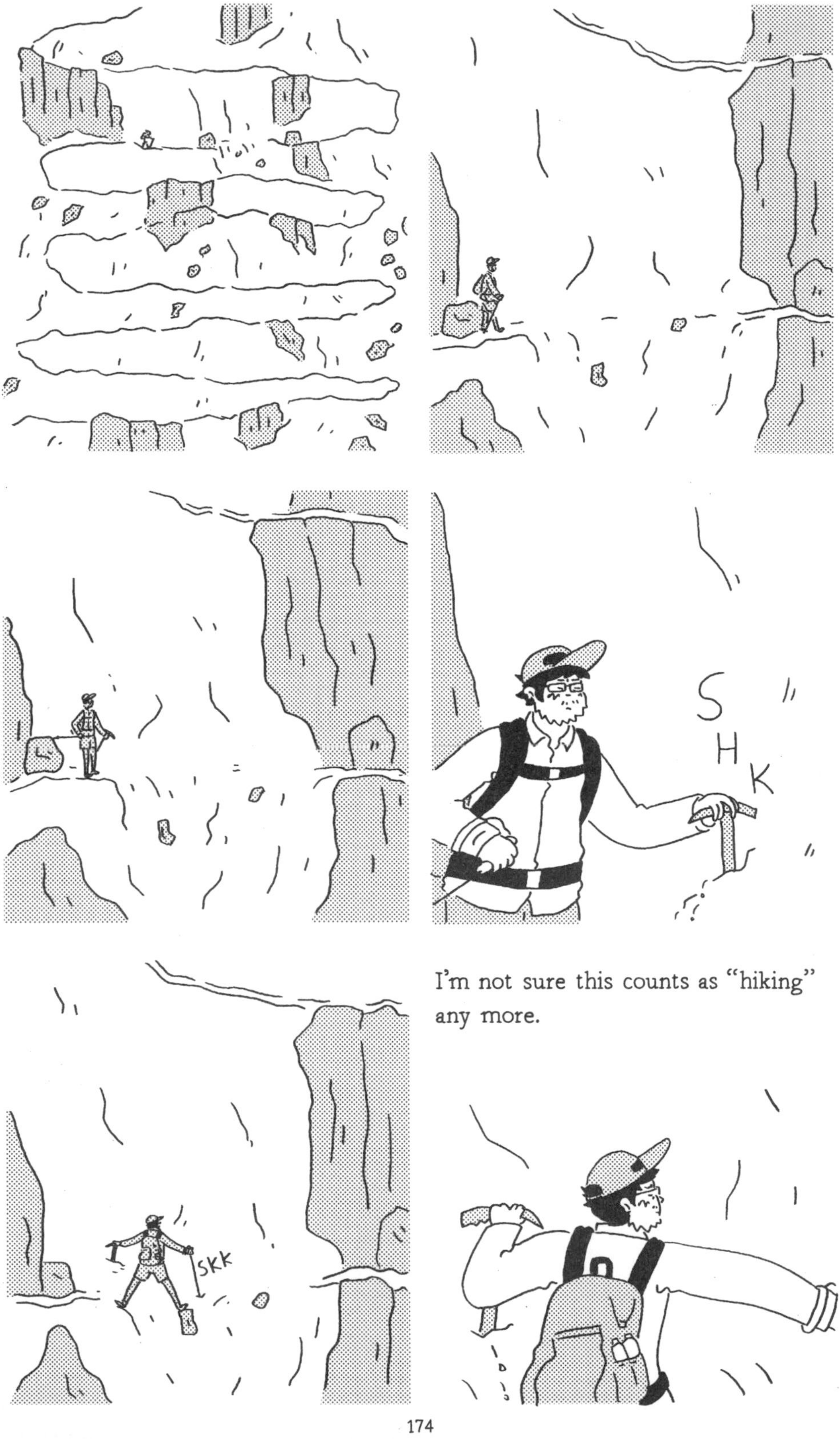
SHK
SKK
I'm not sure this counts as "hiking" any more.

Heff Hi. Heff

Heff
Heff

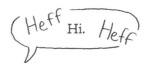

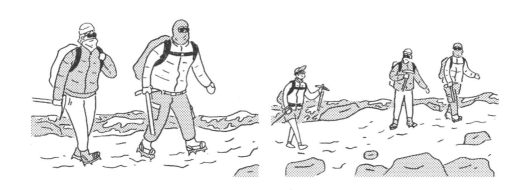

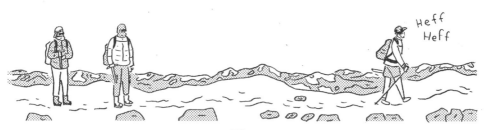

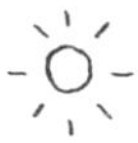

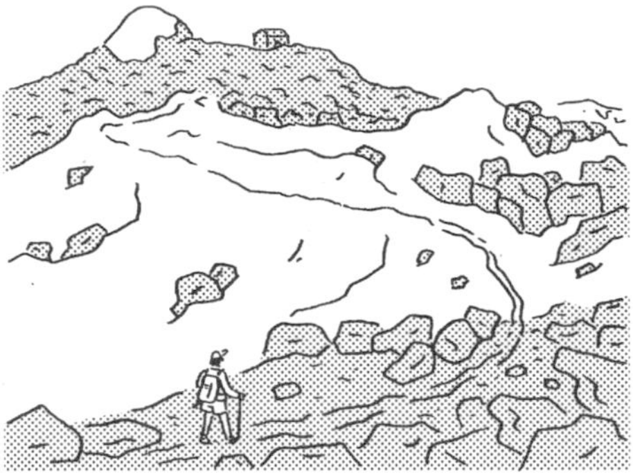

I catch Mile 55 at the summit.

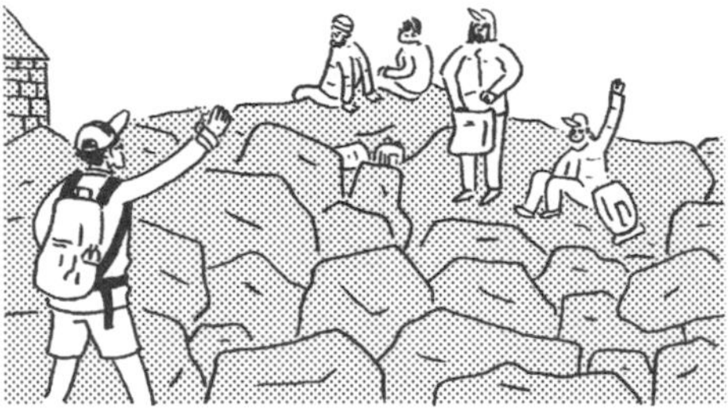

The views are extraordinary. Indescribable.

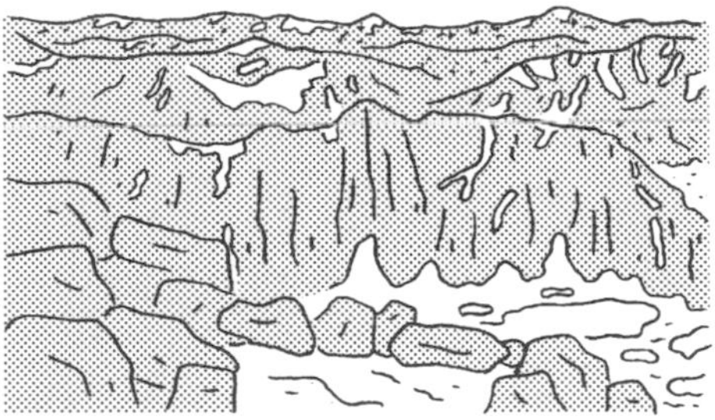

I take their picture.

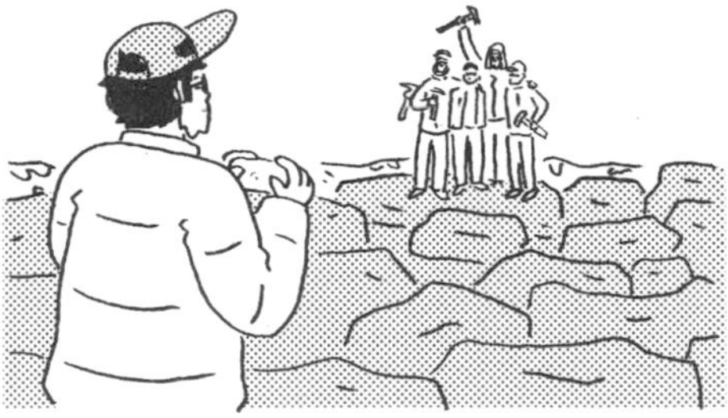

Toe Touch takes a picture of me, by myself.

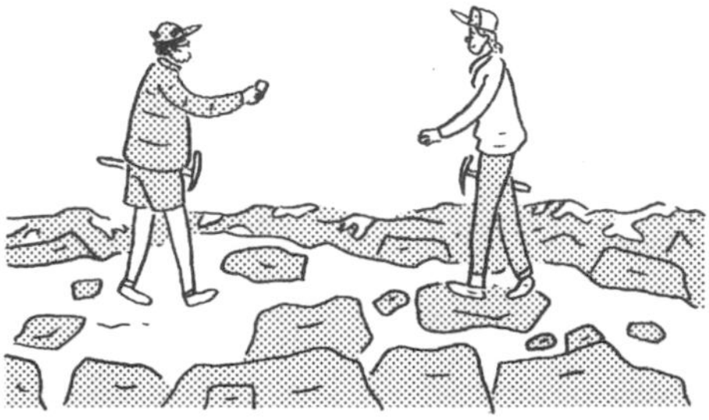

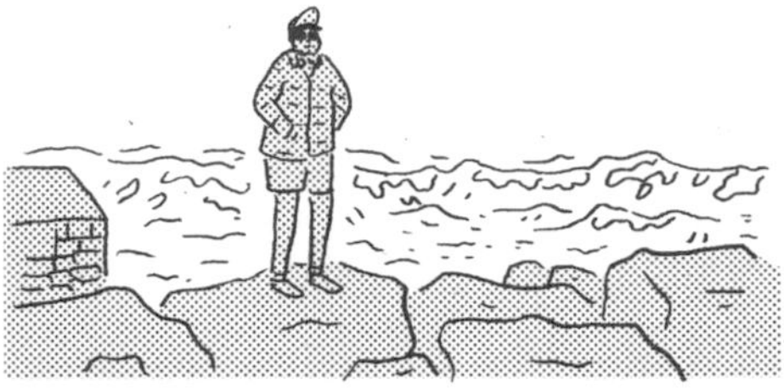

Most hikers slow down when they enter the High Sierras.
The landscape is punishing, and you need to adapt to a litany of
new factors. The weight of water is replaced by the bulk of a bear
can and the awkward sharp edges of an ice axe. Sun and sand are
replaced with water and snow. The desert, though not without its
own ascents, pales in comparison to the Sierra regime.

Our mileage has actually increased since entering the Sierra,
and we leave Griz and Craftsman behind at the base of Whitney,
pushing twenty-five-mile days. I'd resist, but on paper it all makes
sense. Bizarrely, pushing hard each evening and setting ourselves
up well for the next morning's pass makes the hike easier, since
we can avoid hours of struggling through soft snow.

Still, hiking with Mile 55 lifts my spirits.

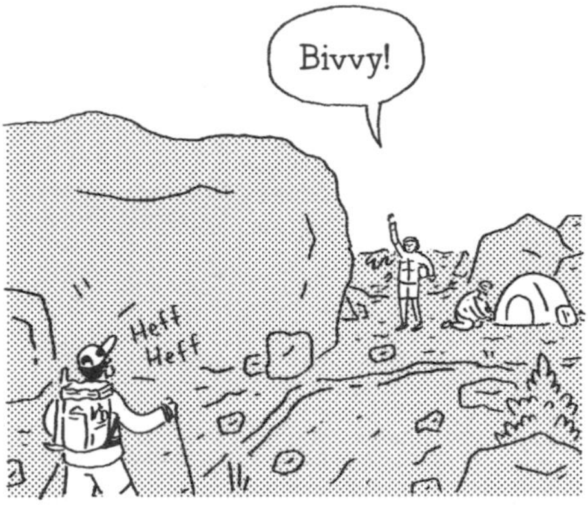
Bivvy!
Heff Heff

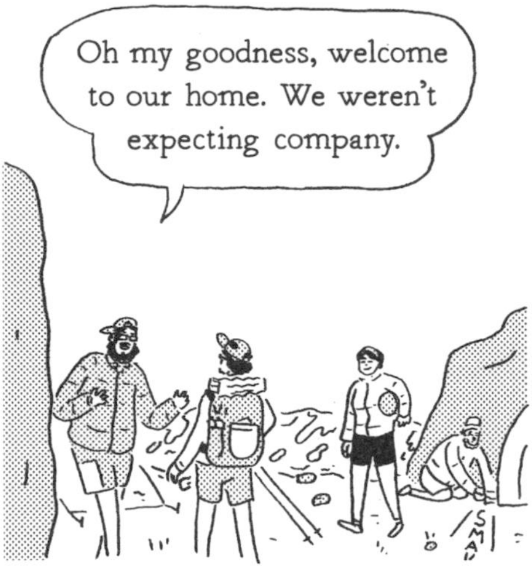
Oh my goodness, welcome to our home. We weren't expecting company.

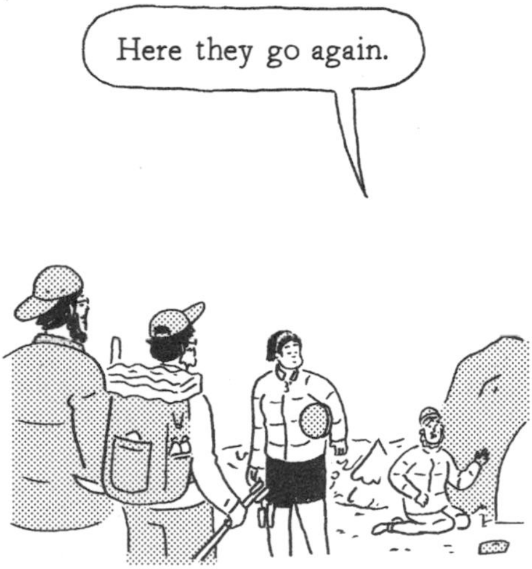
Here they go again.

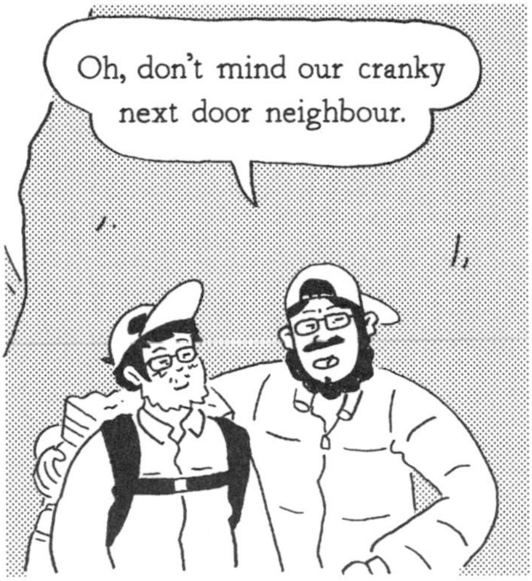
Oh, don't mind our cranky next door neighbour.

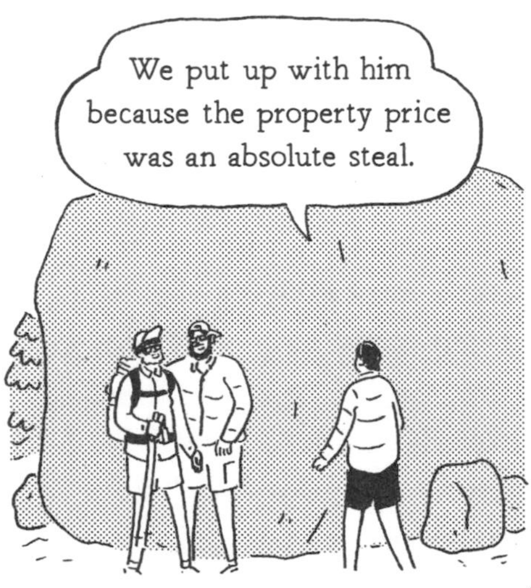
We put up with him because the property price was an absolute steal.

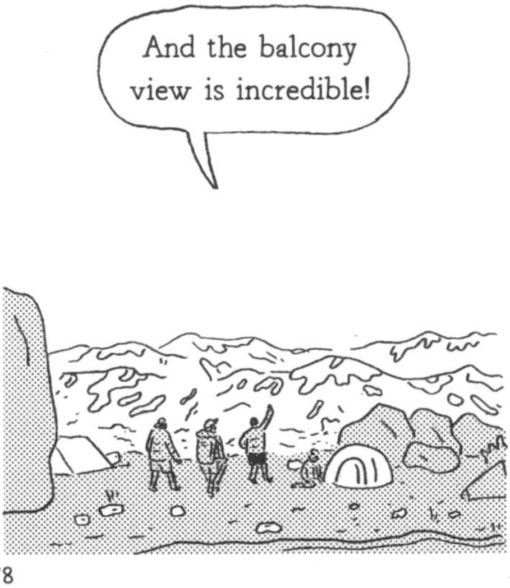
And the balcony view is incredible!

I hike with Centerfold, whose pace most closely matches my own.

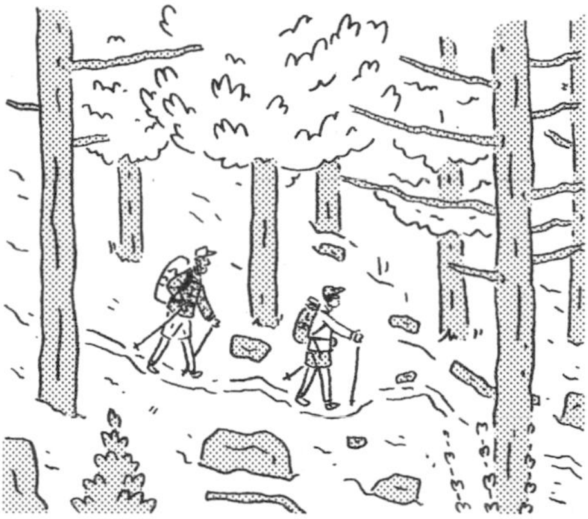

Centerfold is stoic, though I feel him warming up to me as we spend more time together.

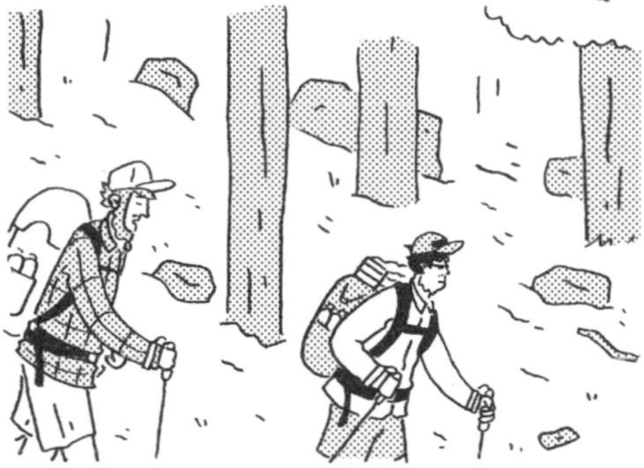

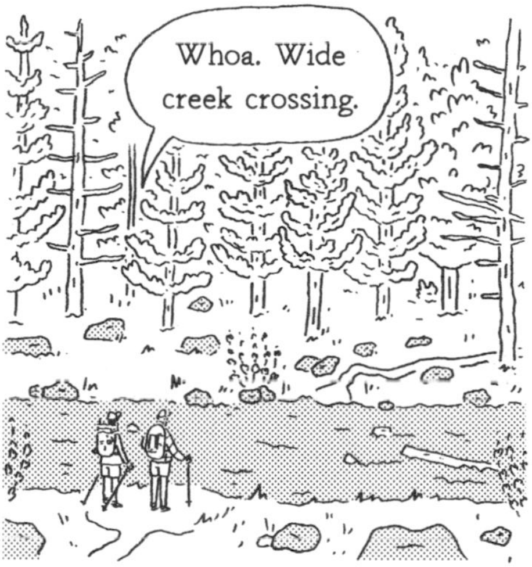
Whoa. Wide creek crossing.

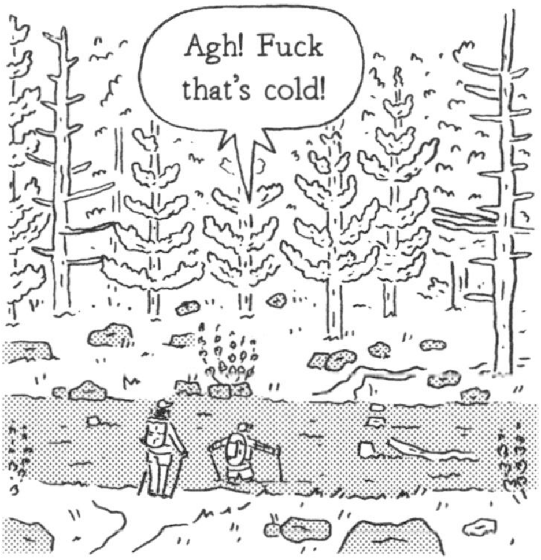
Agh! Fuck that's cold!

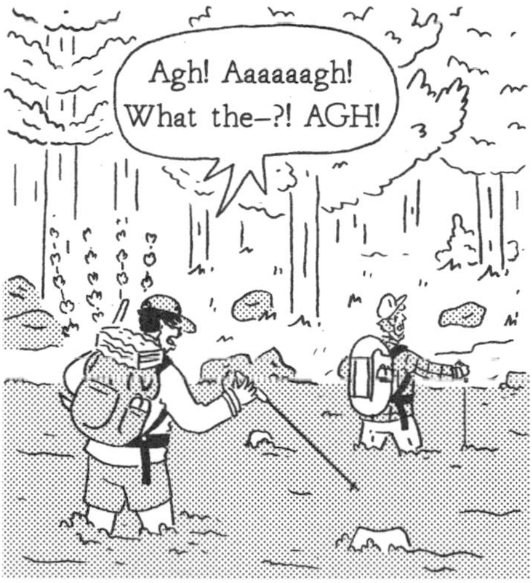
Agh! Aaaaaagh! What the–?! AGH!

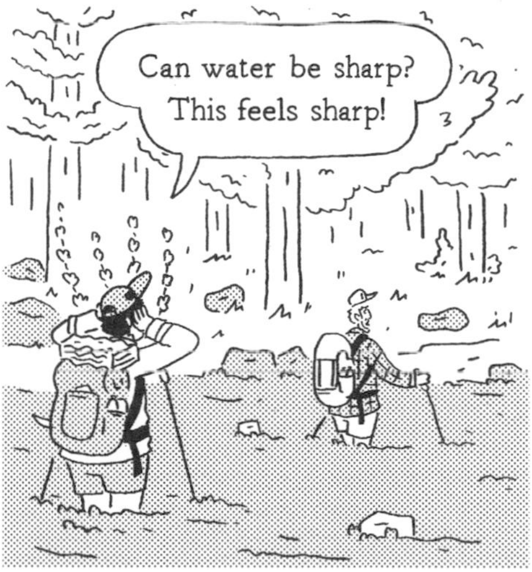
Can water be sharp? This feels sharp!

Still, I mostly hike alone, losing Centerfold part way through the day when I fail to match his confident, consistent pace.

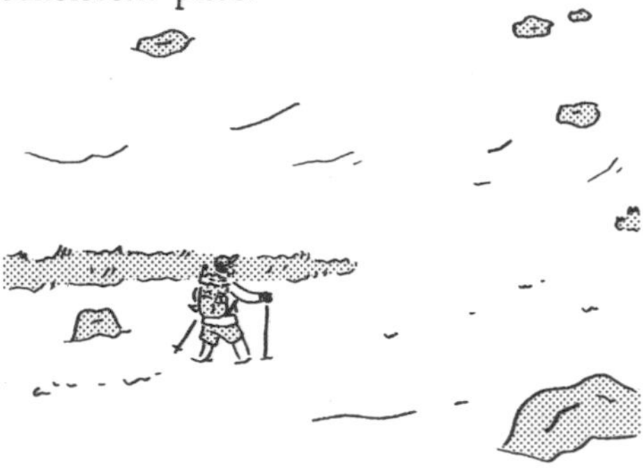

Like Mt. Whitney, I crest most of the passes unaccompanied.

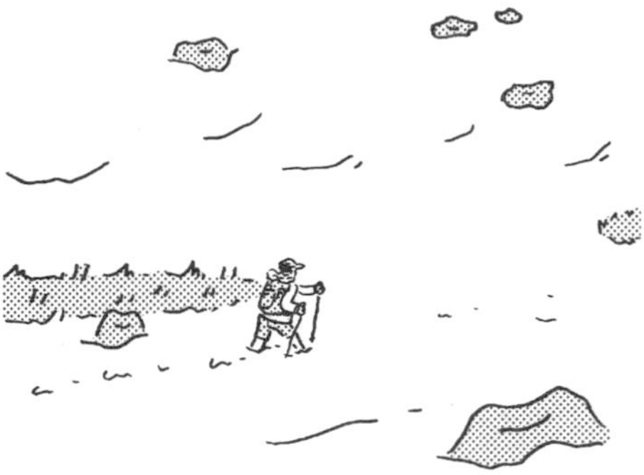

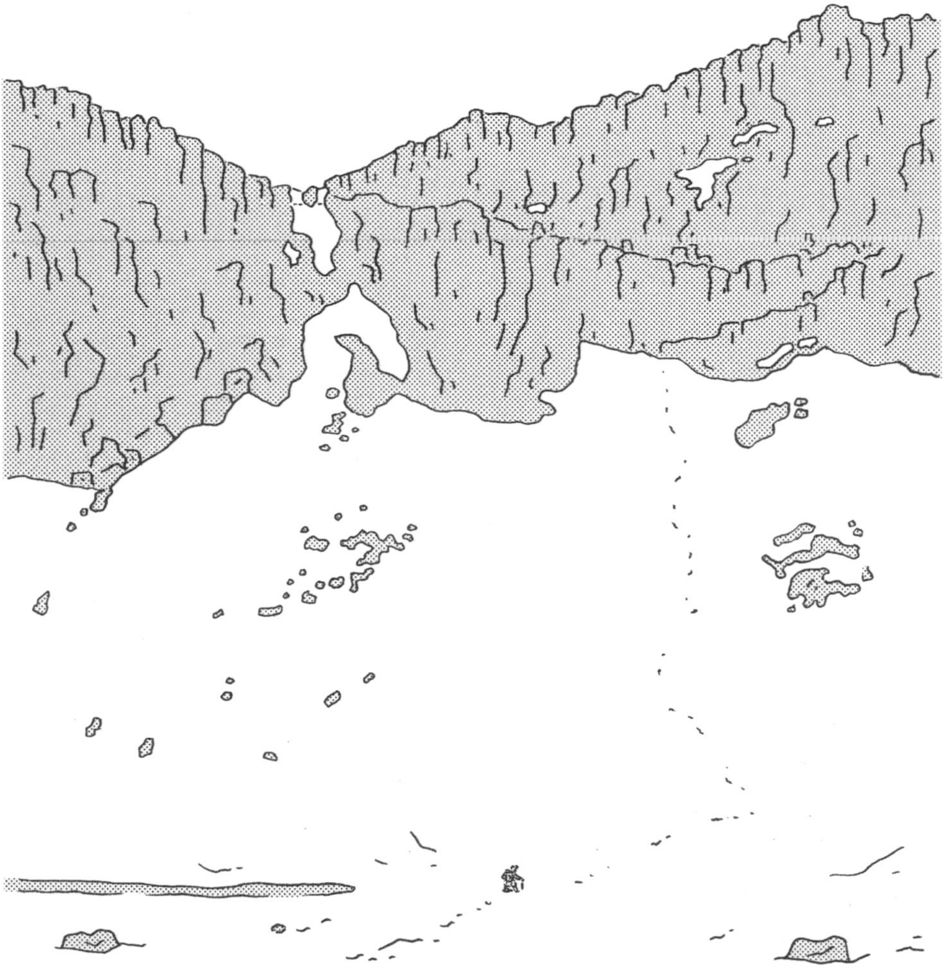

A narrow, six-inch-wide ledge crosses the notorious Forrester Pass ice chute. Six slippery inches between safety and a likely death.

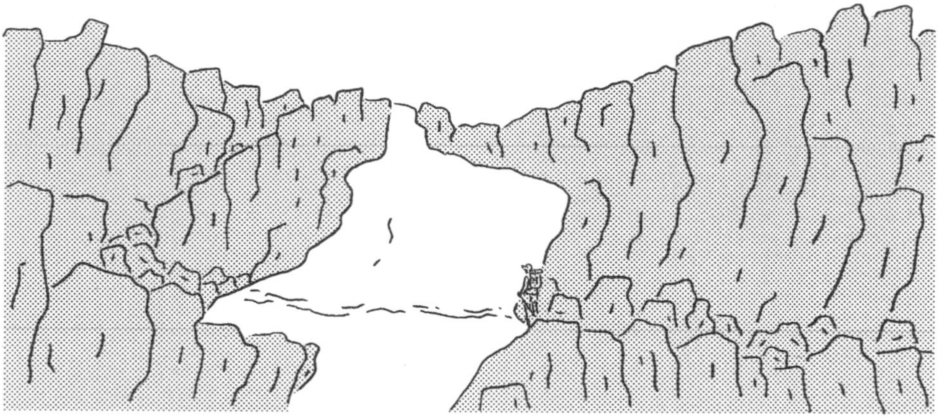

No big deal. No big deal.

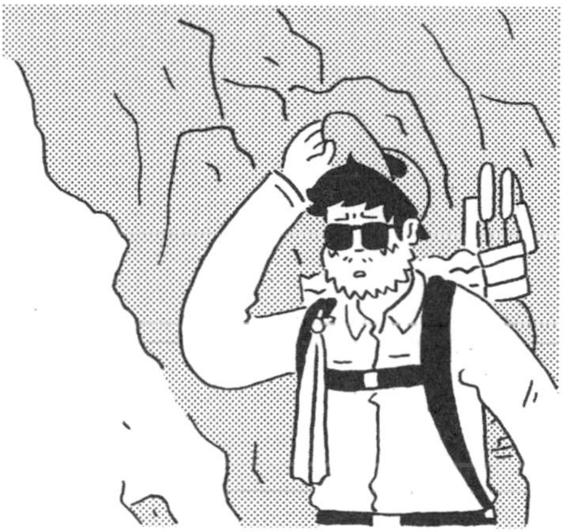

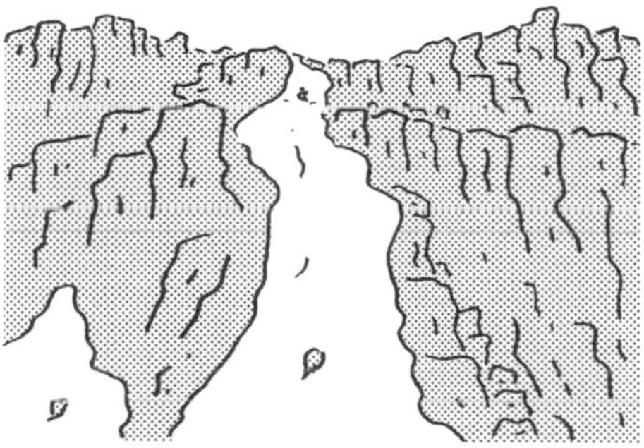

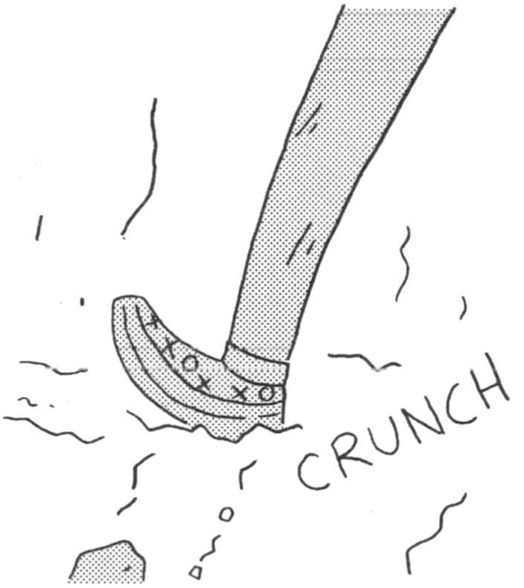
CRUNCH

Phew, phew. No big deal.

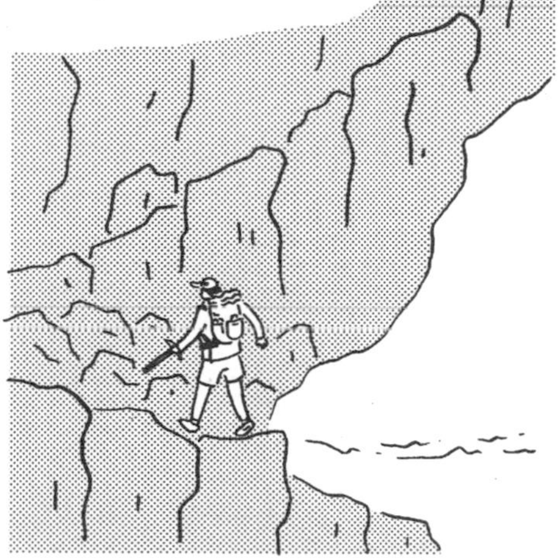

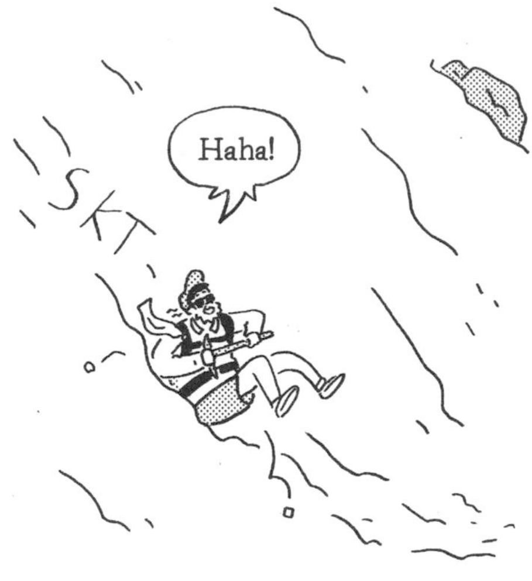
Haha!
SKT

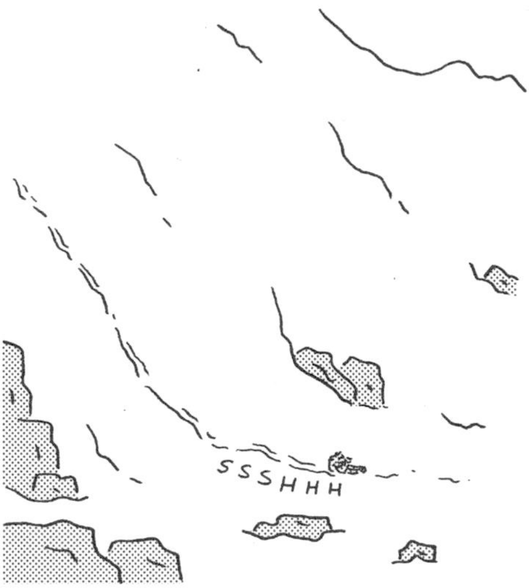
SSSHHH

I get lost in the snowfields and check my GPS constantly.

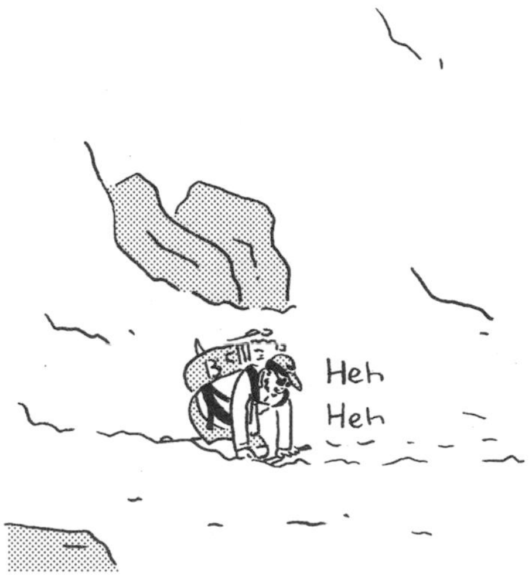
Heh
Heh

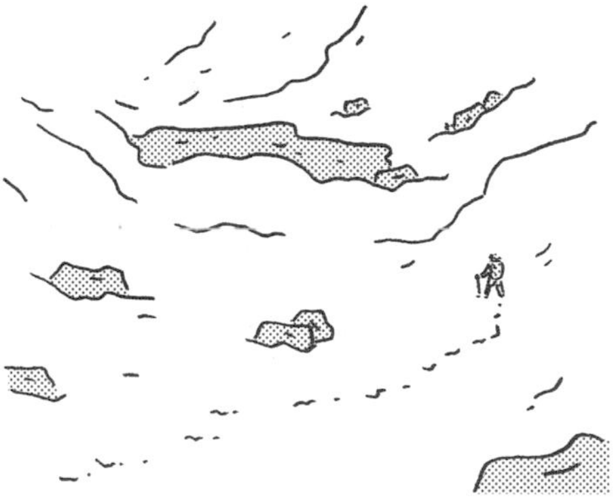

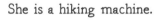

Deeper in the valley, I see Toe Touch pass me by, on the correct trail.

She is a hiking machine.

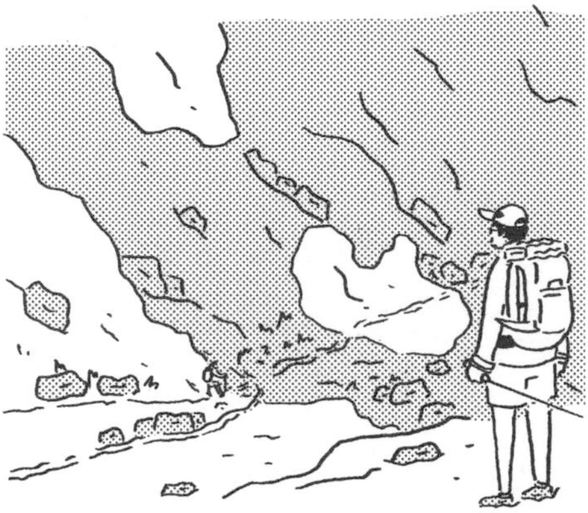

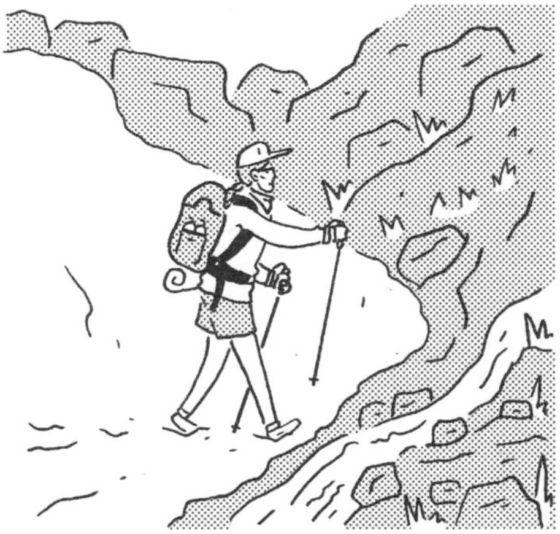

Kings Canyon 07/06/16. Day 53.

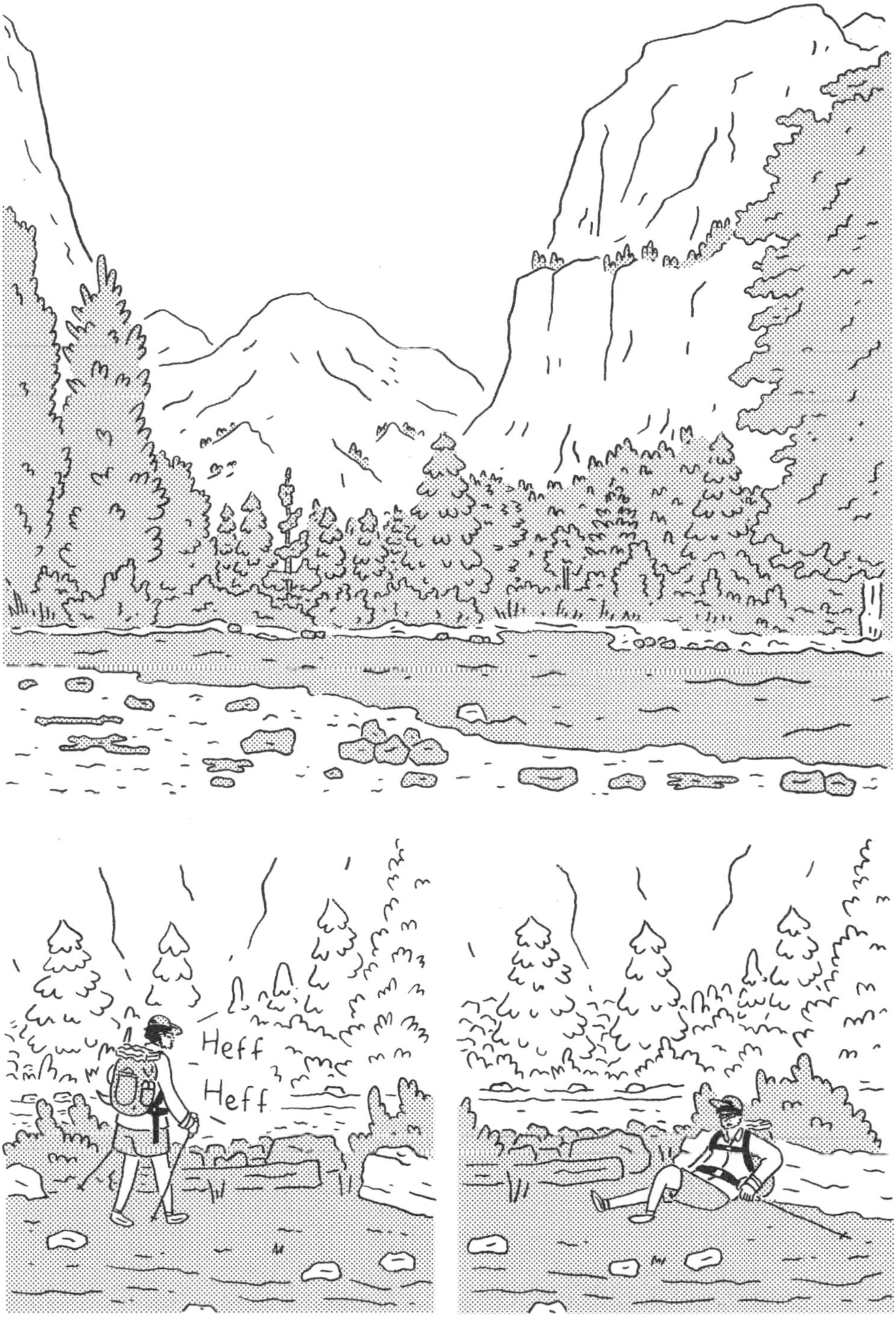

Heff
Heff

I am bone-tired. But unlike in the desert, I am hungry for more. The same hunger that brought me to America. To White River Junction. To the PCT.

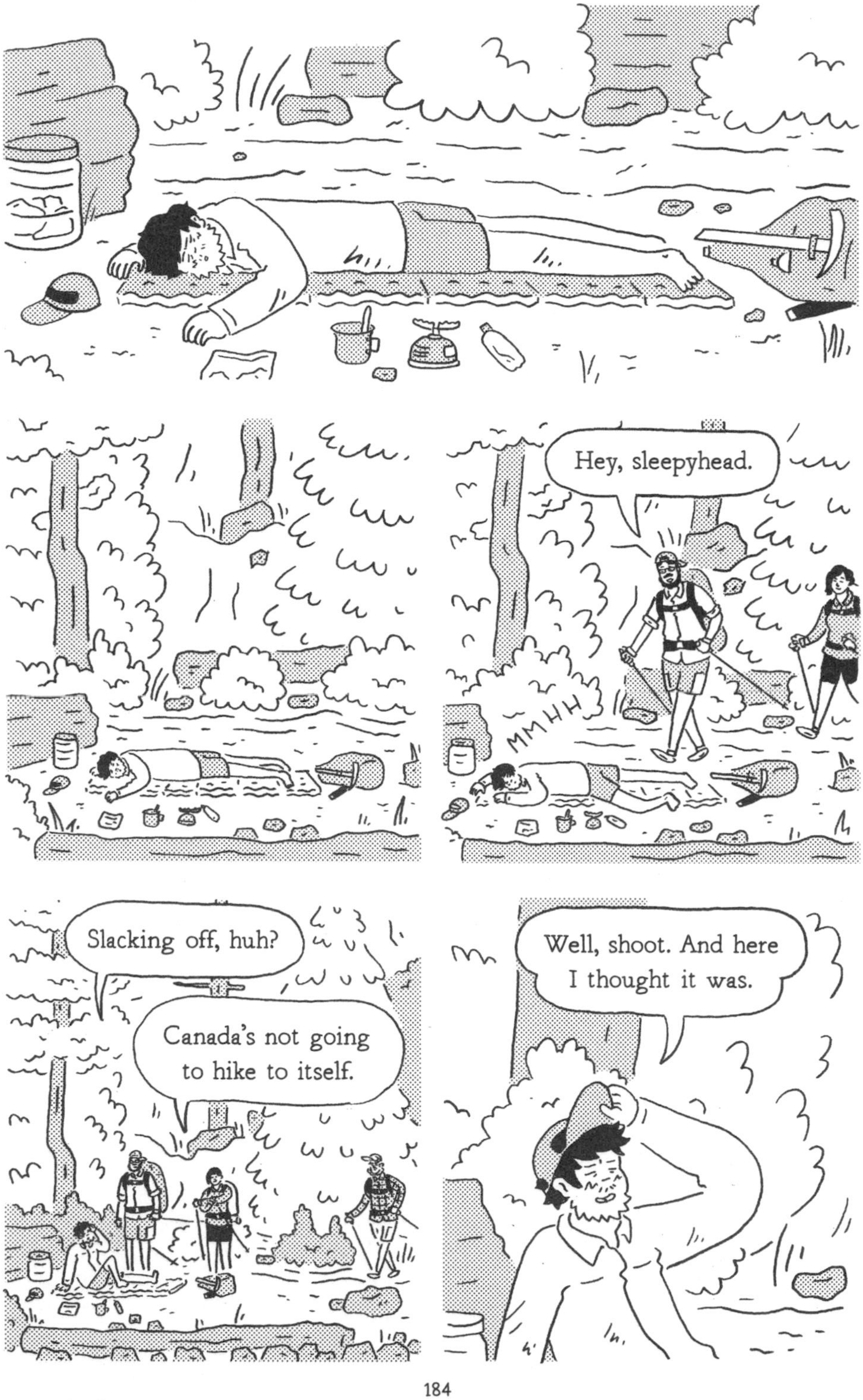
Hey, sleepyhead.
MMHH
Slacking off, huh?
Canada's not going to hike to itself.
Well, shoot. And here I thought it was.

The four of us form a hiker train, and try our best to catch Toe Touch.

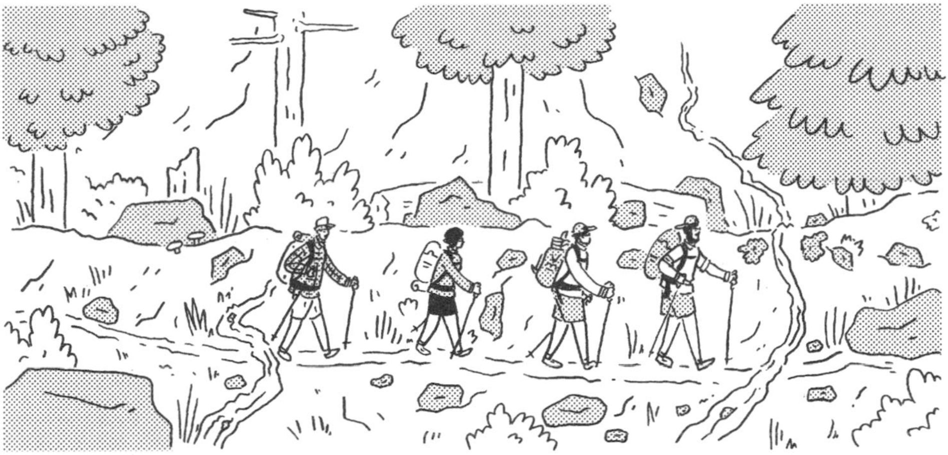

Each of us pushing and pulling the others through the sun-dappled forest.

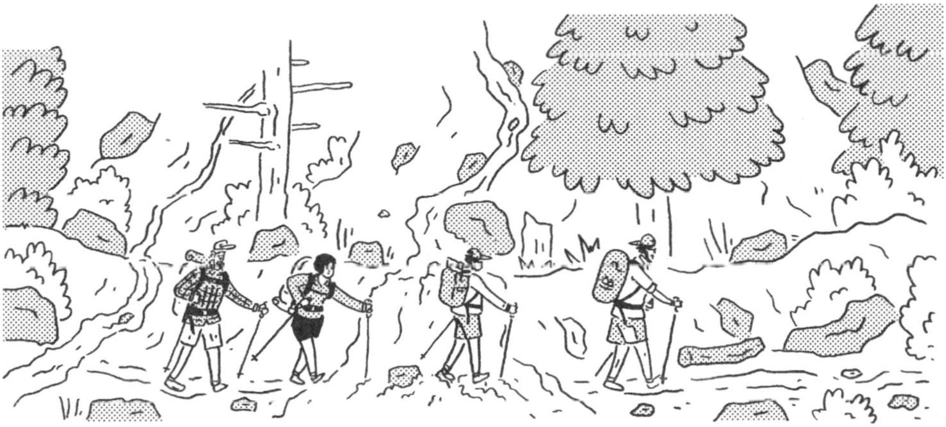

Little Spoon's powerful legs chew up the trail in front of me.

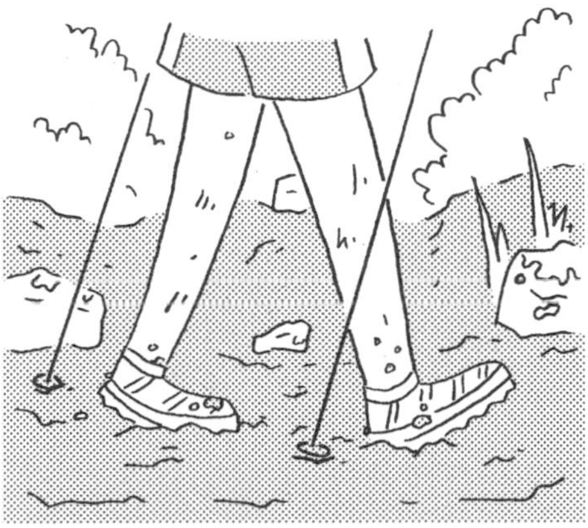

Chuckles' pound it back into shape behind.

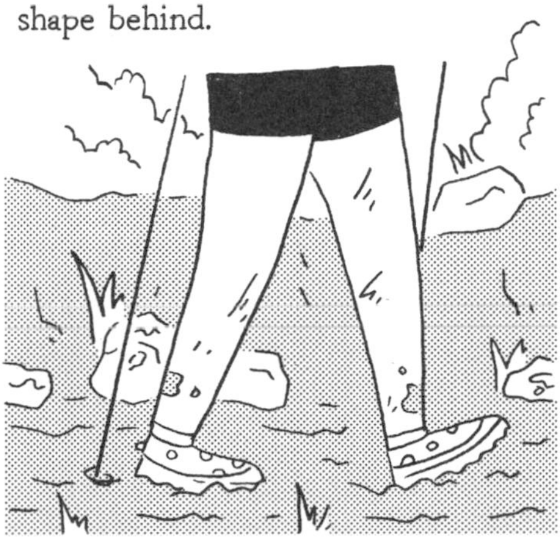

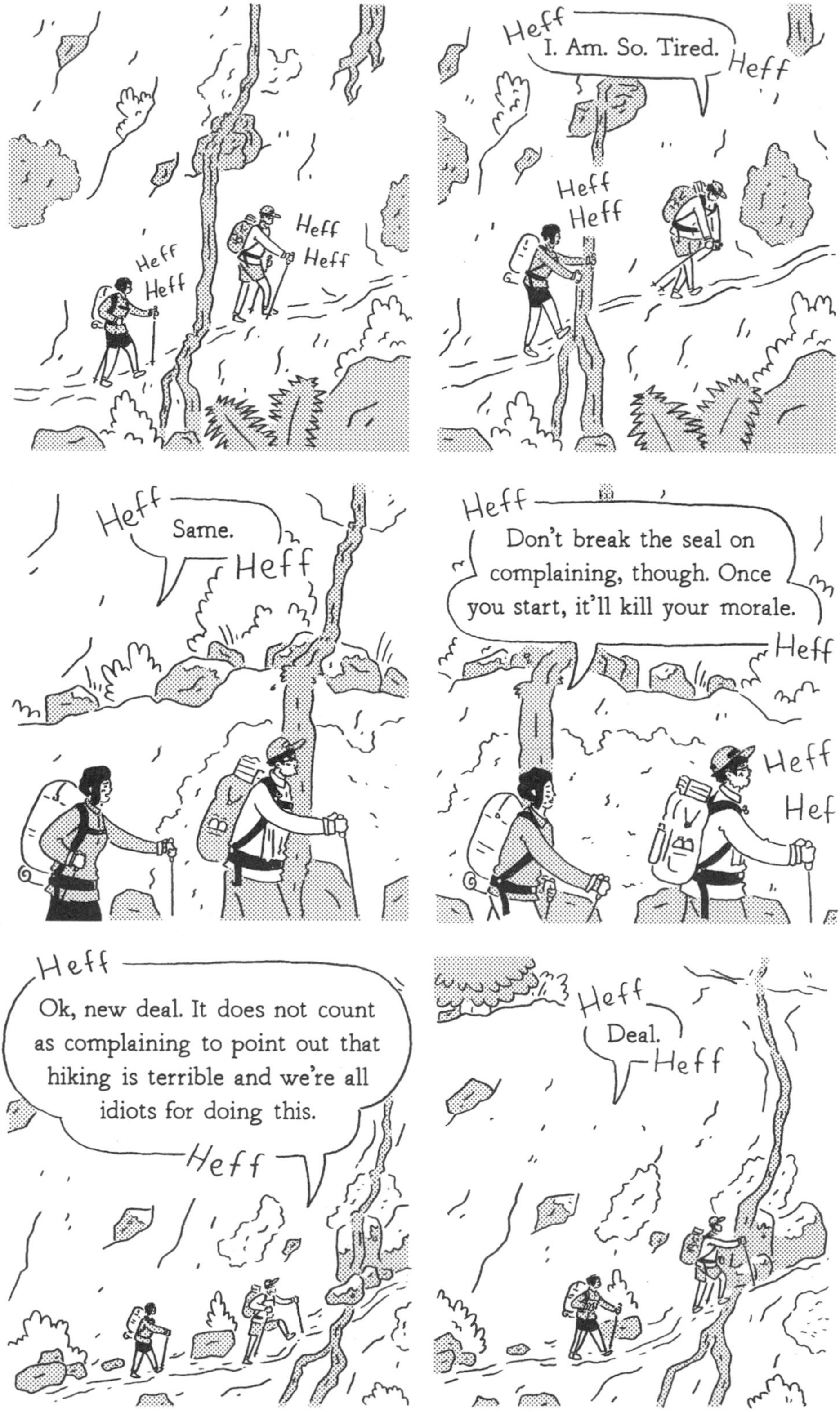
Heff
Heff
Heff
Heff
Heff
I. Am. So. Tired.
Heff
Heff
Heff
Heff
Same.
Heff
Heff
Don't break the seal on complaining, though. Once you start, it'll kill your morale.
Heff
Heff
Hef
Heff
Ok, new deal. It does not count as complaining to point out that hiking is terrible and we're all idiots for doing this.
Heff
Heff
Deal.
Heff

We catch Toe Touch and share a last meal together.

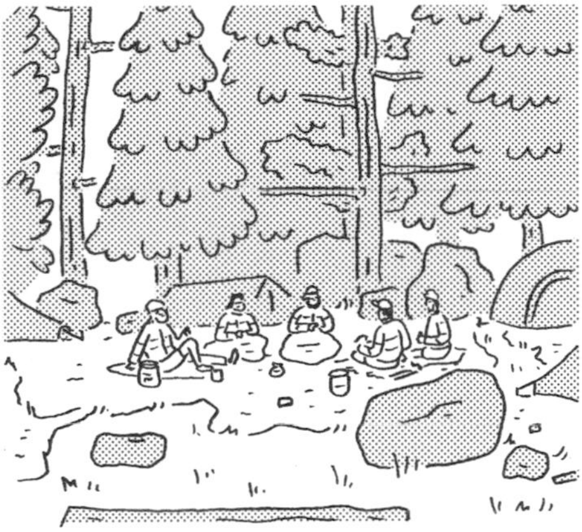

We leave for town tomorrow, while Toe Touch will continue on her twelve-day resupply-less quest.

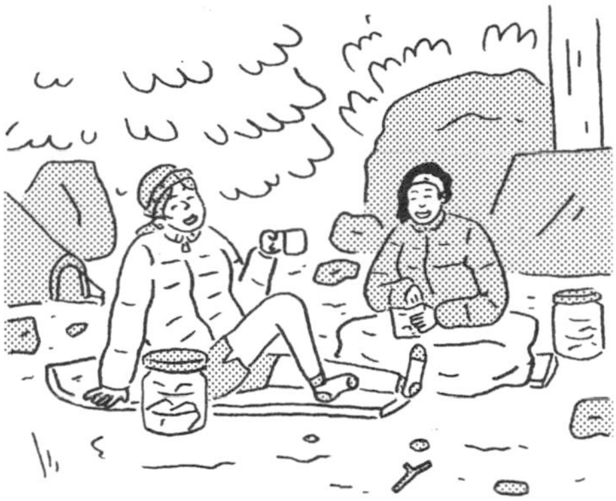

She and Chuckles hug goodbye as the sun begins to set.

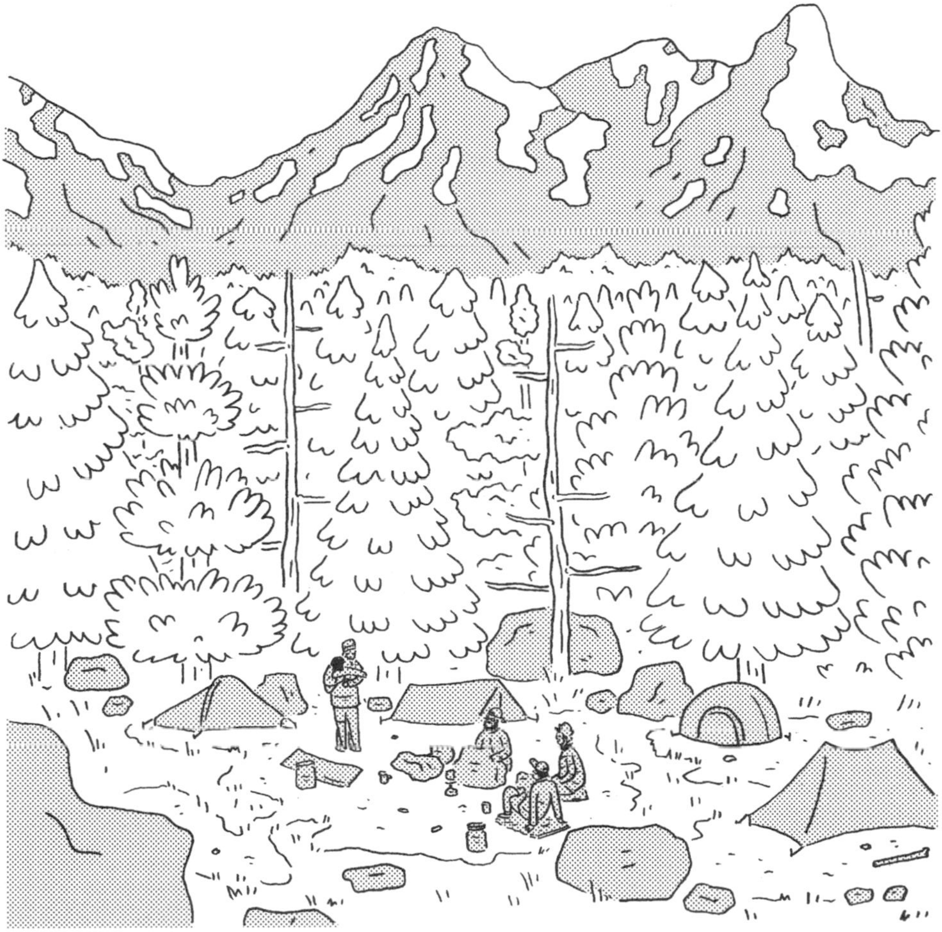

The drop from Kearsarge Pass is dramatic. From my snowy perch,
I stare down at the familiar desert, 10,000 feet below me.

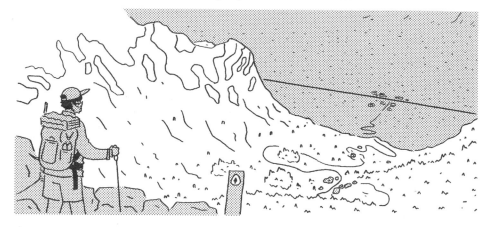

I pick my way down. Ten other hikers mill around by the road.

"Nobody wants to pick up a hiker," one grumbles. It's obvious
they've been waiting here for hours already.

I join them, and cover myself with sunscreen to shield against
the death rays. It isn't long before a big RV pulls up and offers to take
as many hikers as can fit into town. We pile in.

A Californian hiker tells me about the area as we stare out the
windows. We're only miles from Death Valley here, the hottest place
on Earth.

"This all used to be farm land, y'know. Before they built the
aqueduct to divert water to L.A.," he says as we cross the baking plain.

I can't help but think of the green lawns in Malibu.

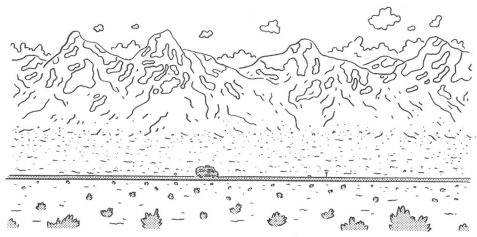

We spend three days in Bishop, eating tubs of ice cream.

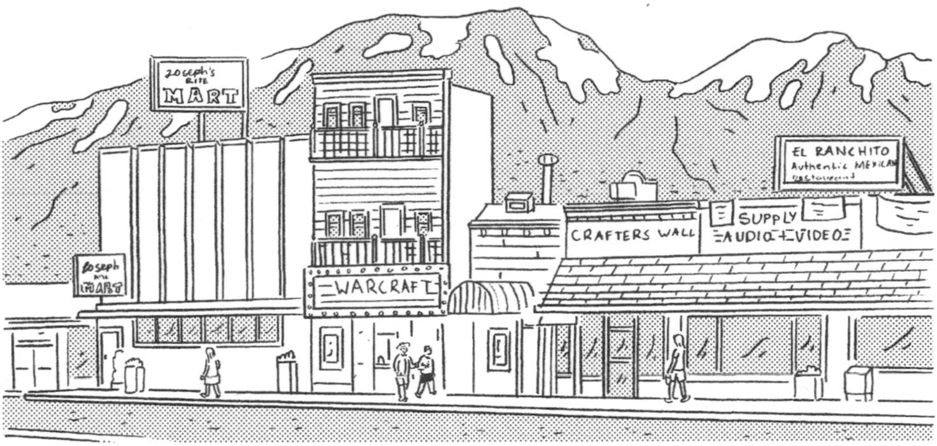
MART
WARCRAFT
CRAFTERS WALL
SUPPLY
AUDIO + VIDEO
EL RANCHITO

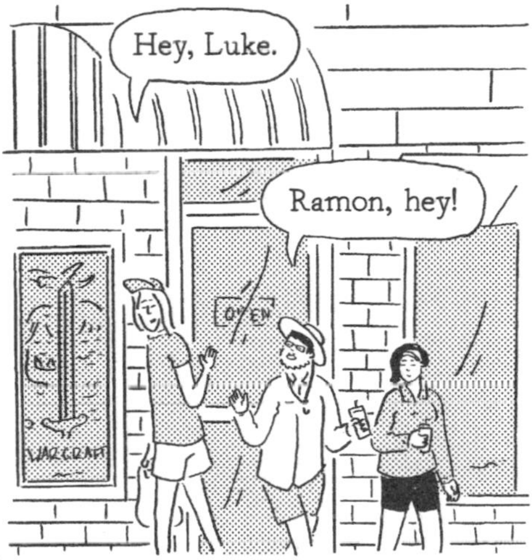
Hey, Luke.
Ramon, hey!

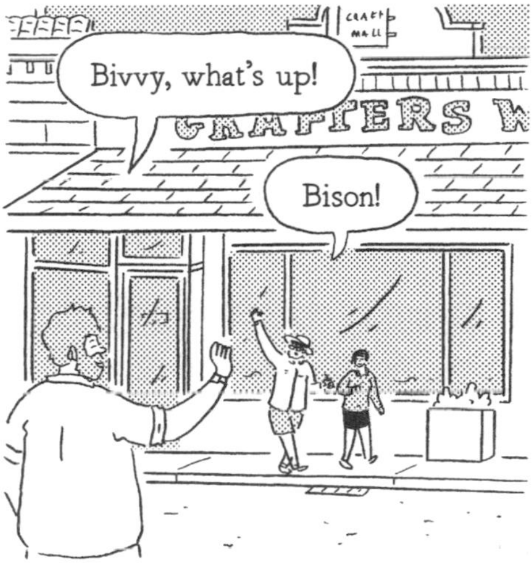
Bivvy, what's up!
Bison!

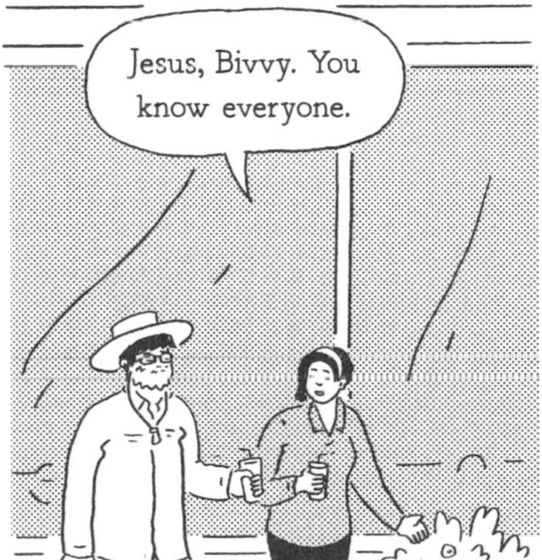
Jesus, Bivvy. You know everyone.

And for a moment, I see the benefits of hiking "alone".

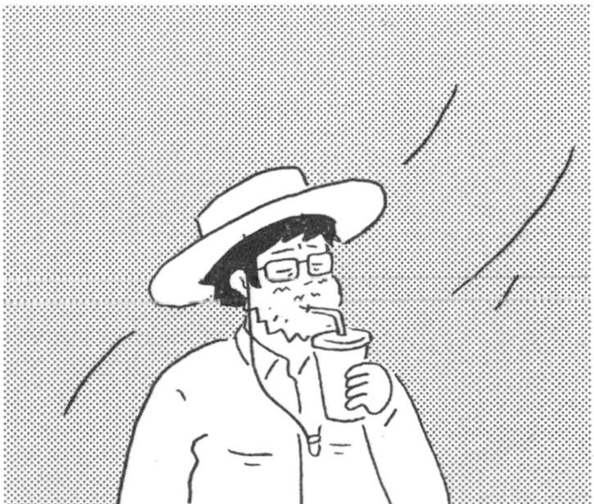

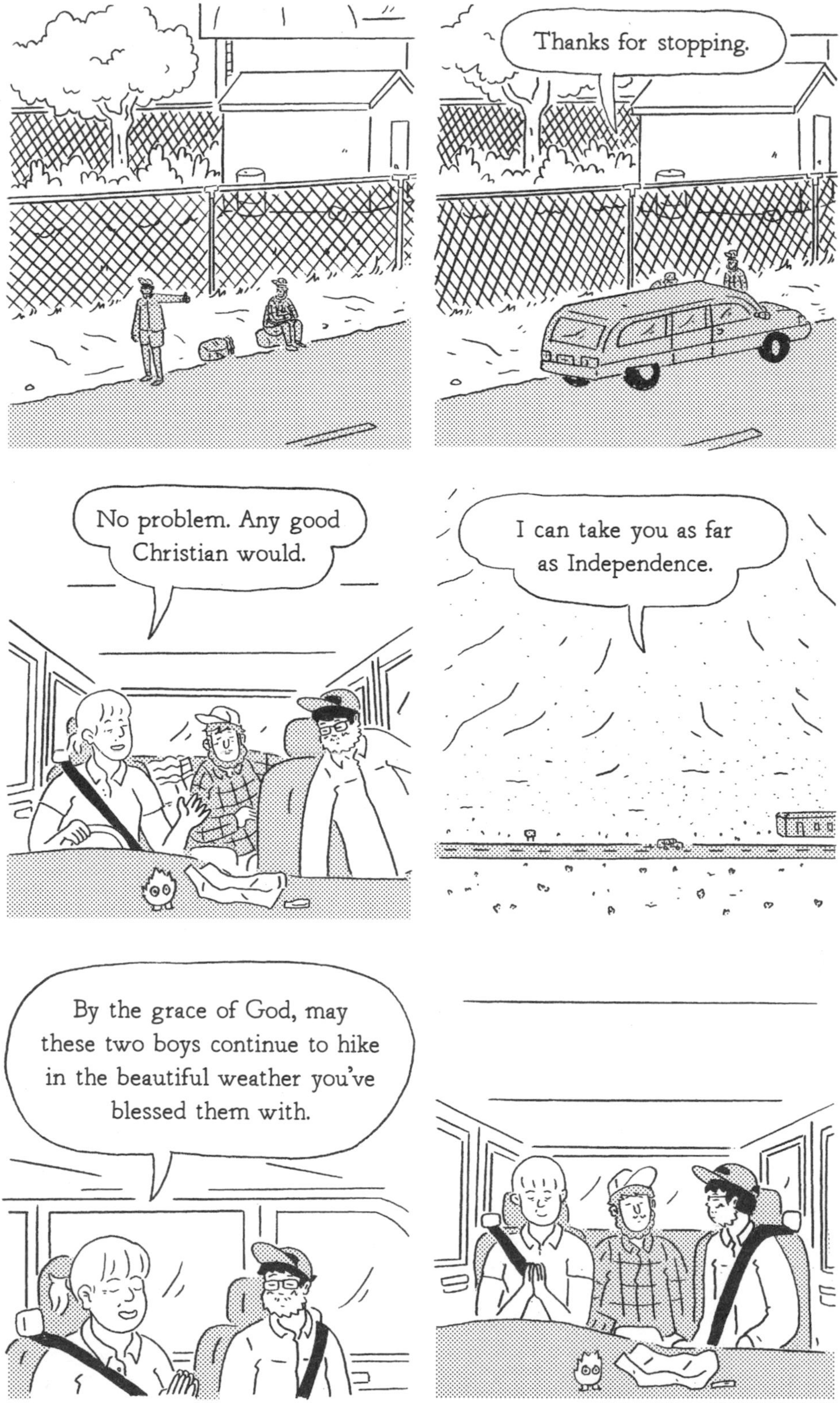
Thanks for stopping.
No problem. Any good Christian would.
I can take you as far as Independence.
By the grace of God, may these two boys continue to hike in the beautiful weather you've blessed them with.

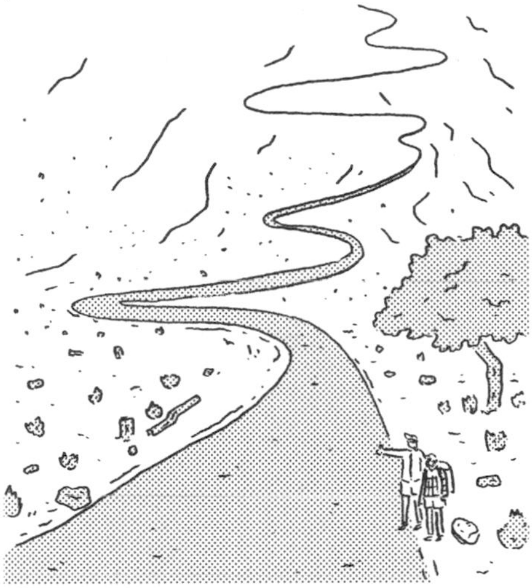

Tucked away from the main street in Independence, we find a museum commemorating the town's history.

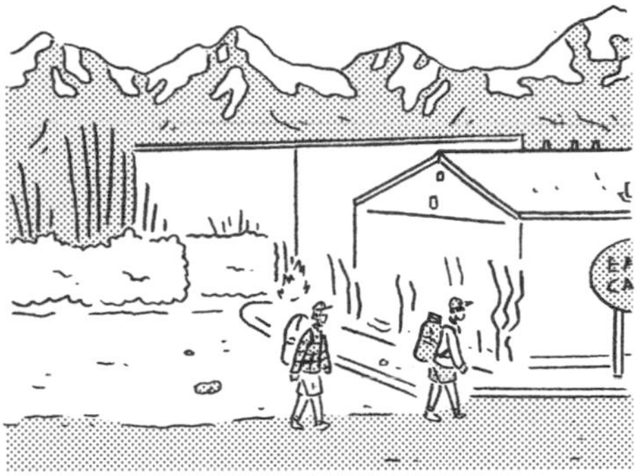

Complicated-looking vintage tractors.

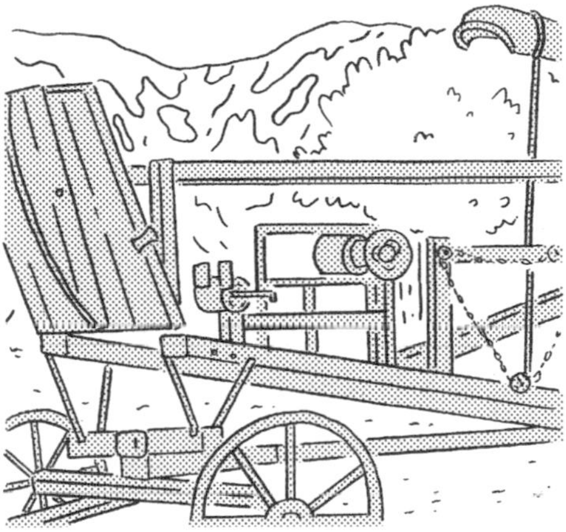

The Los Angeles Aqueduct.

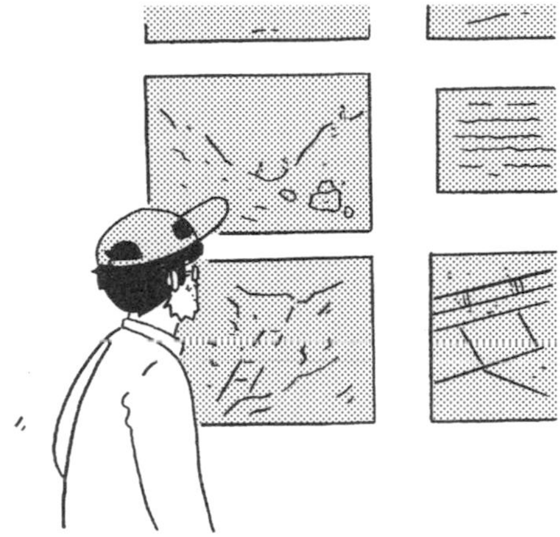

And the Japanese-American internment.

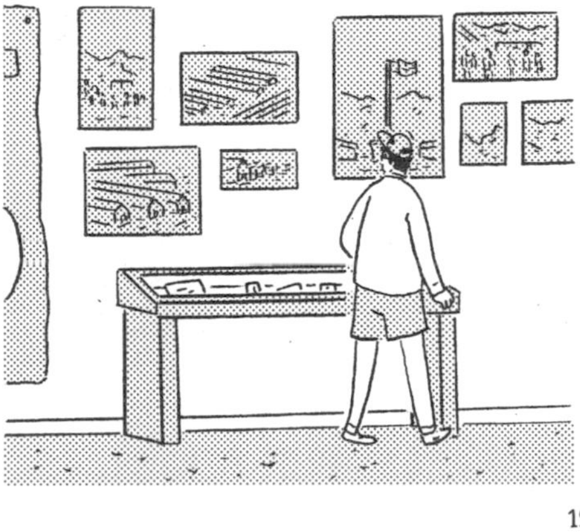

Ironically, one of the largest camps was here, in Independence.

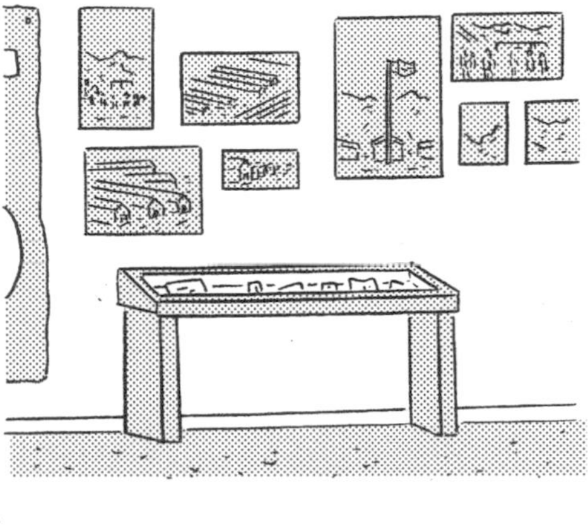

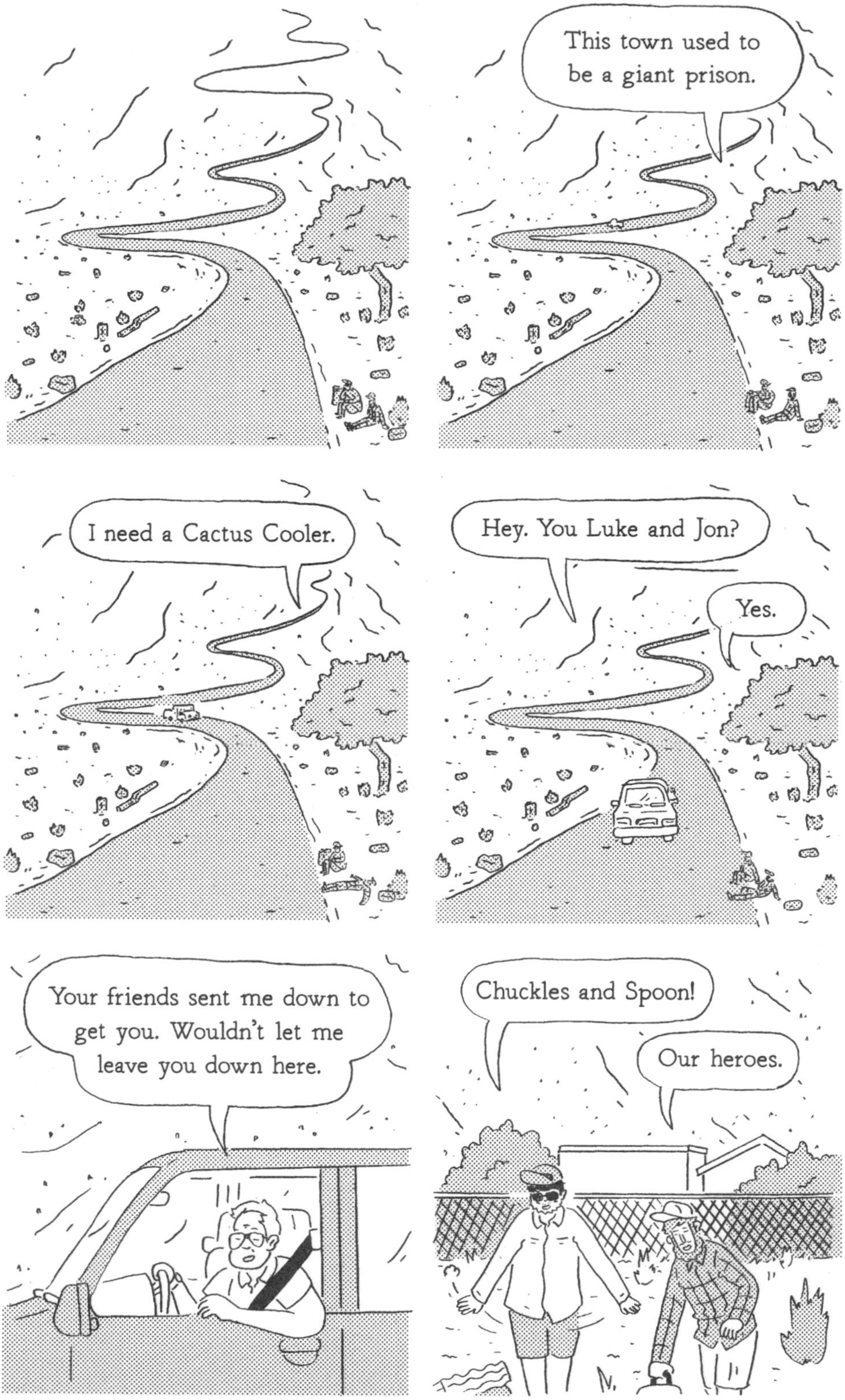
This town used to be a giant prison.
I need a Cactus Cooler.
Hey. You Luke and Jon?
Yes.
Your friends sent me down to get you. Wouldn't let me leave you down here.
Chuckles and Spoon!
Our heroes.

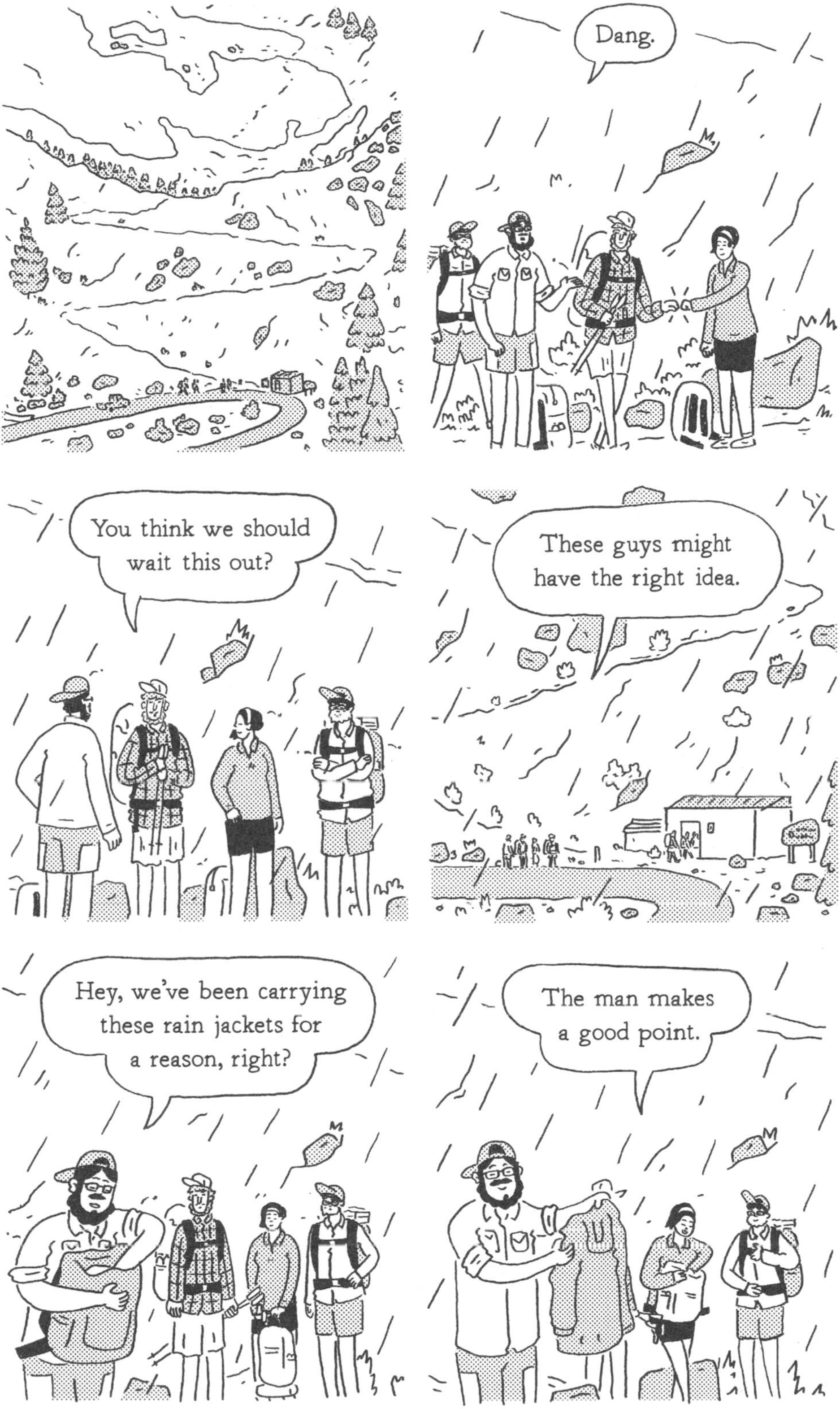
Dang.
You think we should wait this out?
These guys might have the right idea.
Hey, we've been carrying these rain jackets for a reason, right?
The man makes a good point.

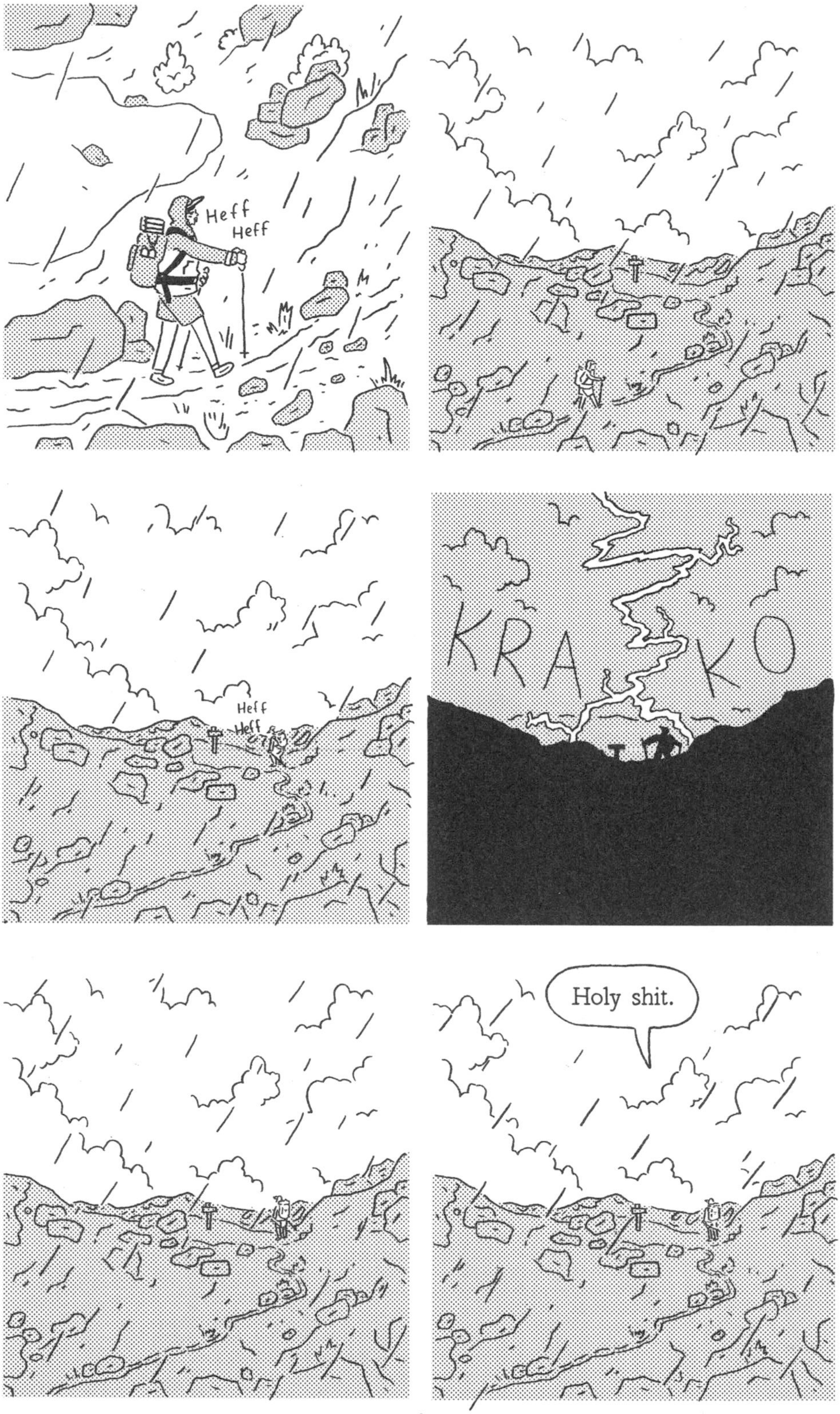
Heff
Heff
Heff
Heff
KRA
KO
Holy shit.

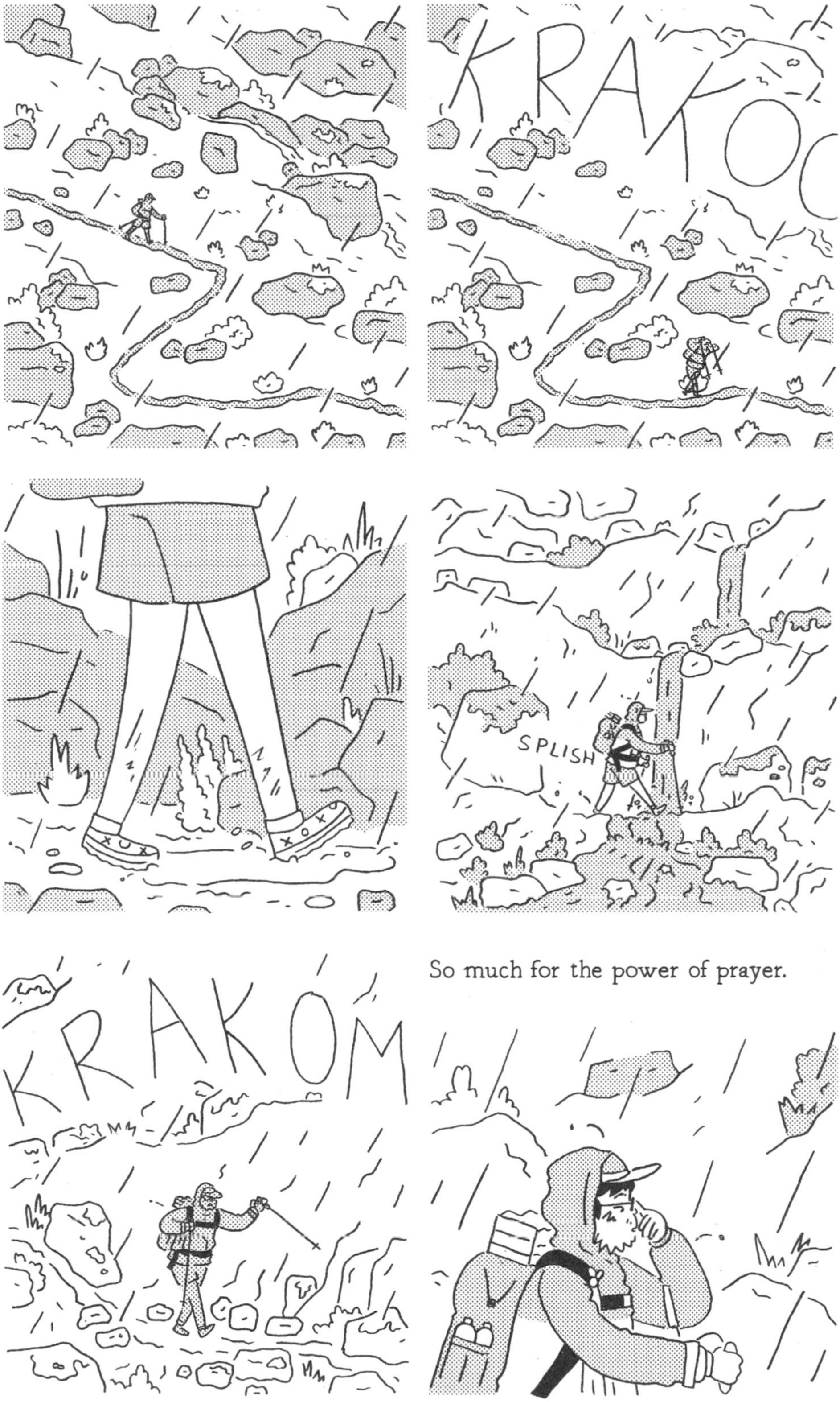
KRAKOO
SPLISH
KRAKOM
So much for the power of prayer.

I post up at some tree cover.

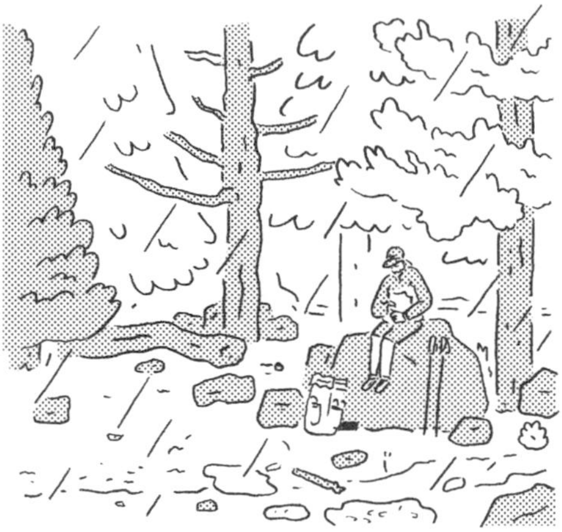

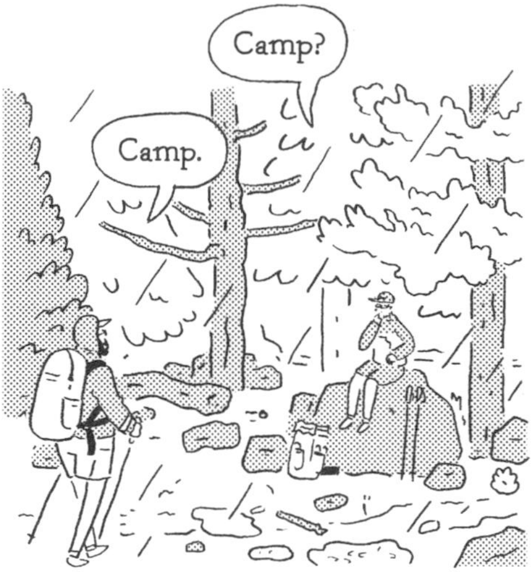
Camp.
Camp?

I try to count the seconds between the flash and the boom.

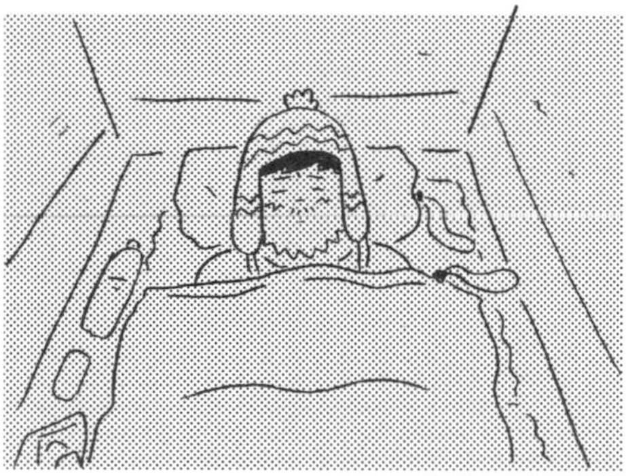

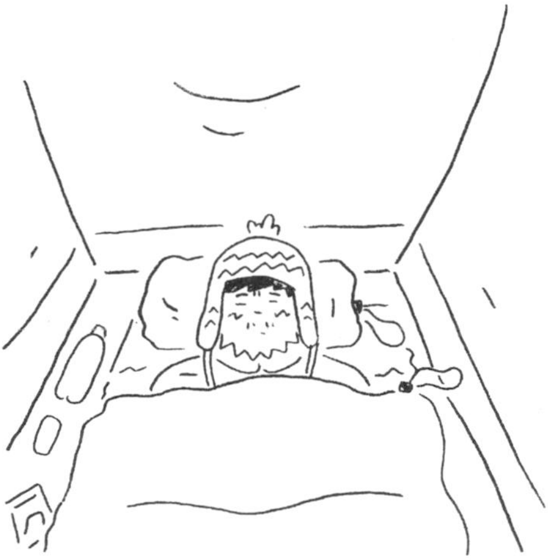

One.

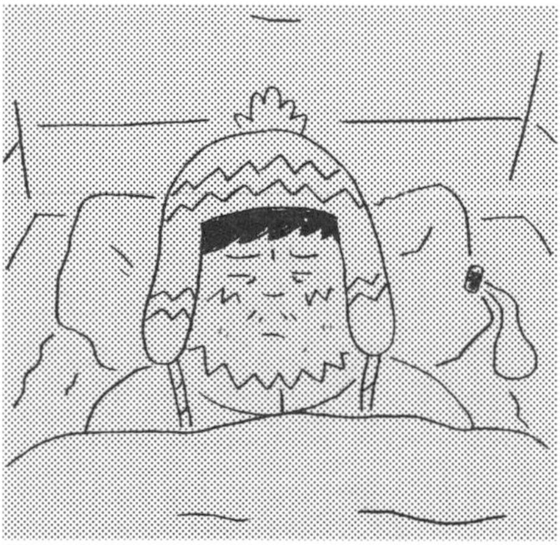

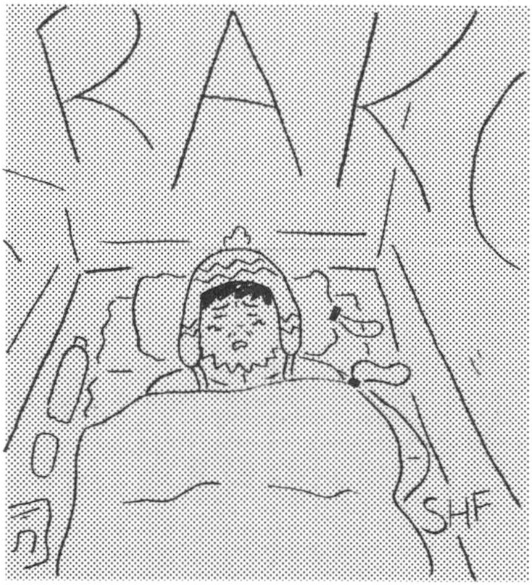
SHF

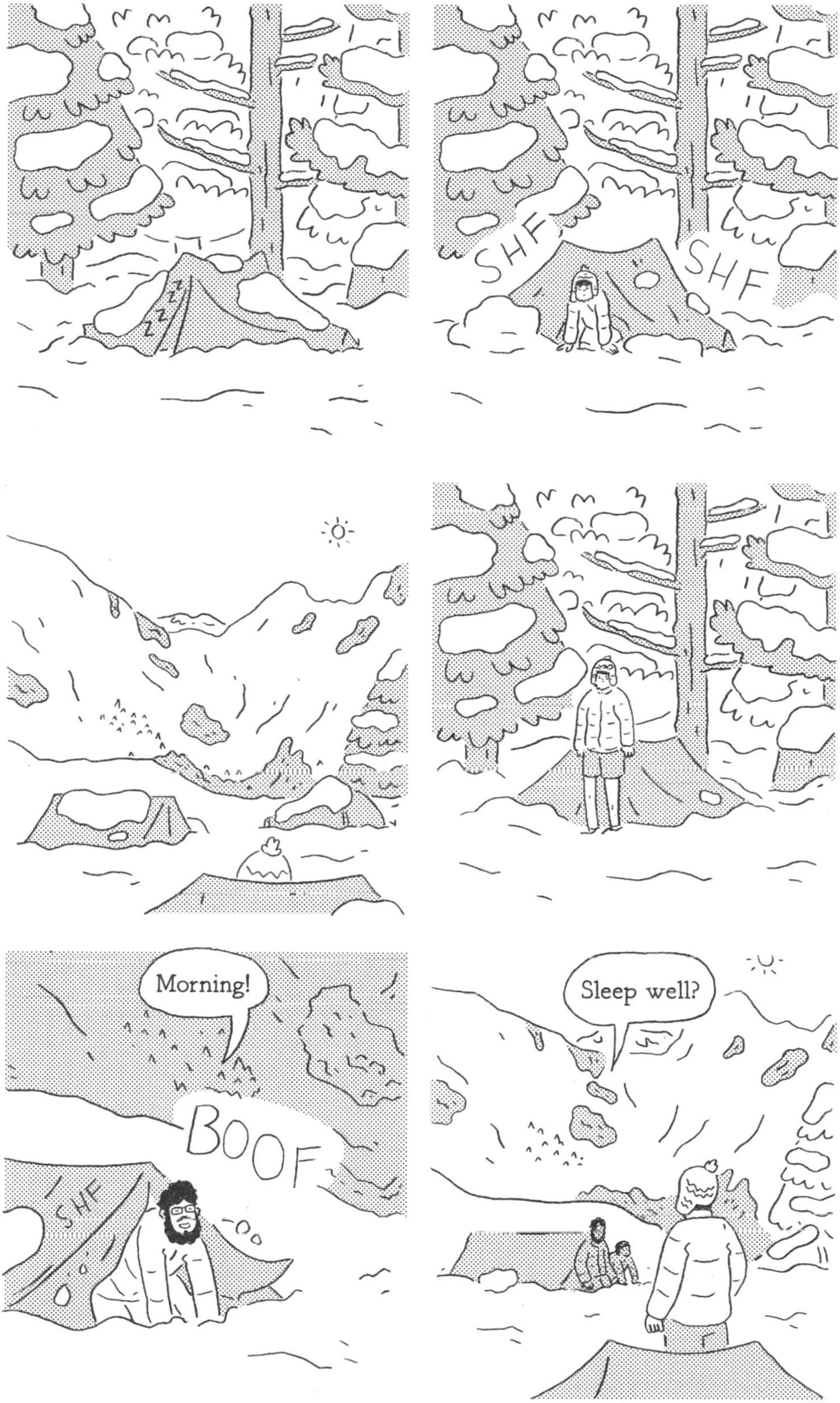
SHF
SHF
Morning!
BOOF
SHF
Sleep well?

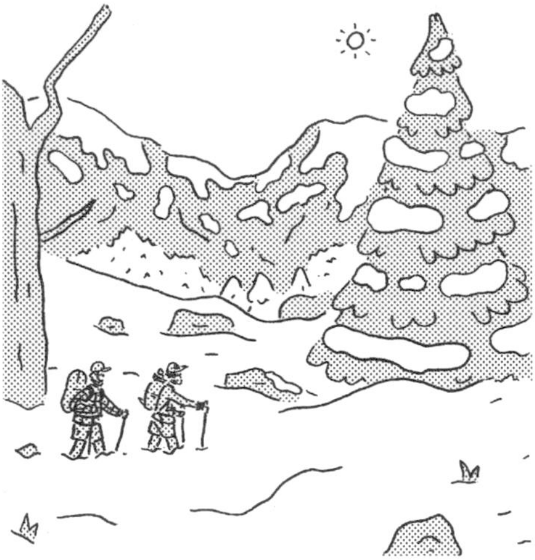

Without footsteps to follow in the snow, we forge our own meandering path.

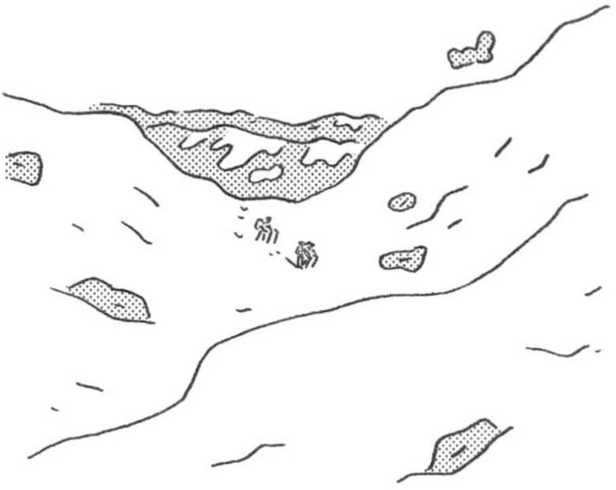

Weekend hikers pass by, heading in the other direction.

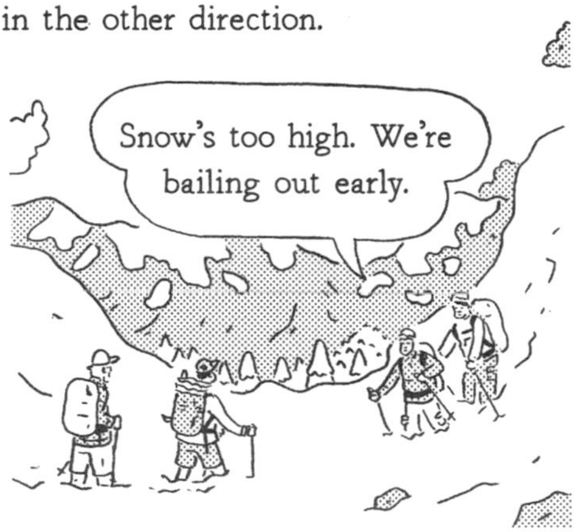
Snow's too high. We're bailing out early.

They give us spare food and matches.

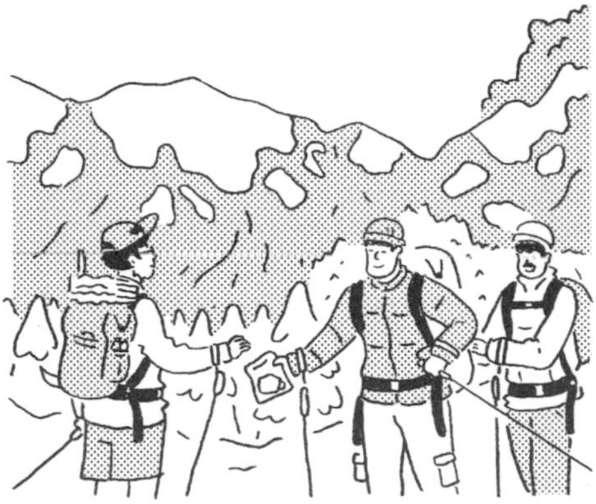

At the next pass, we chart our own course up the snowy face.

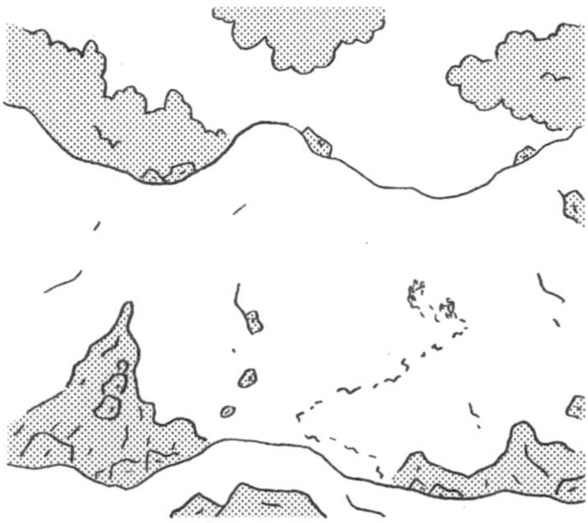

Progress is slow in the clinging, freezing powder.

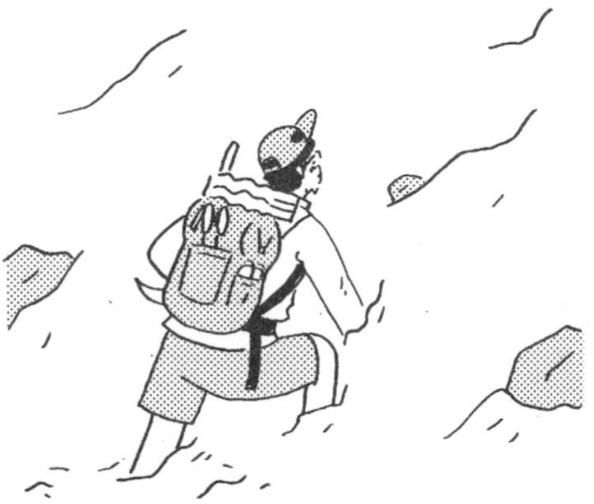

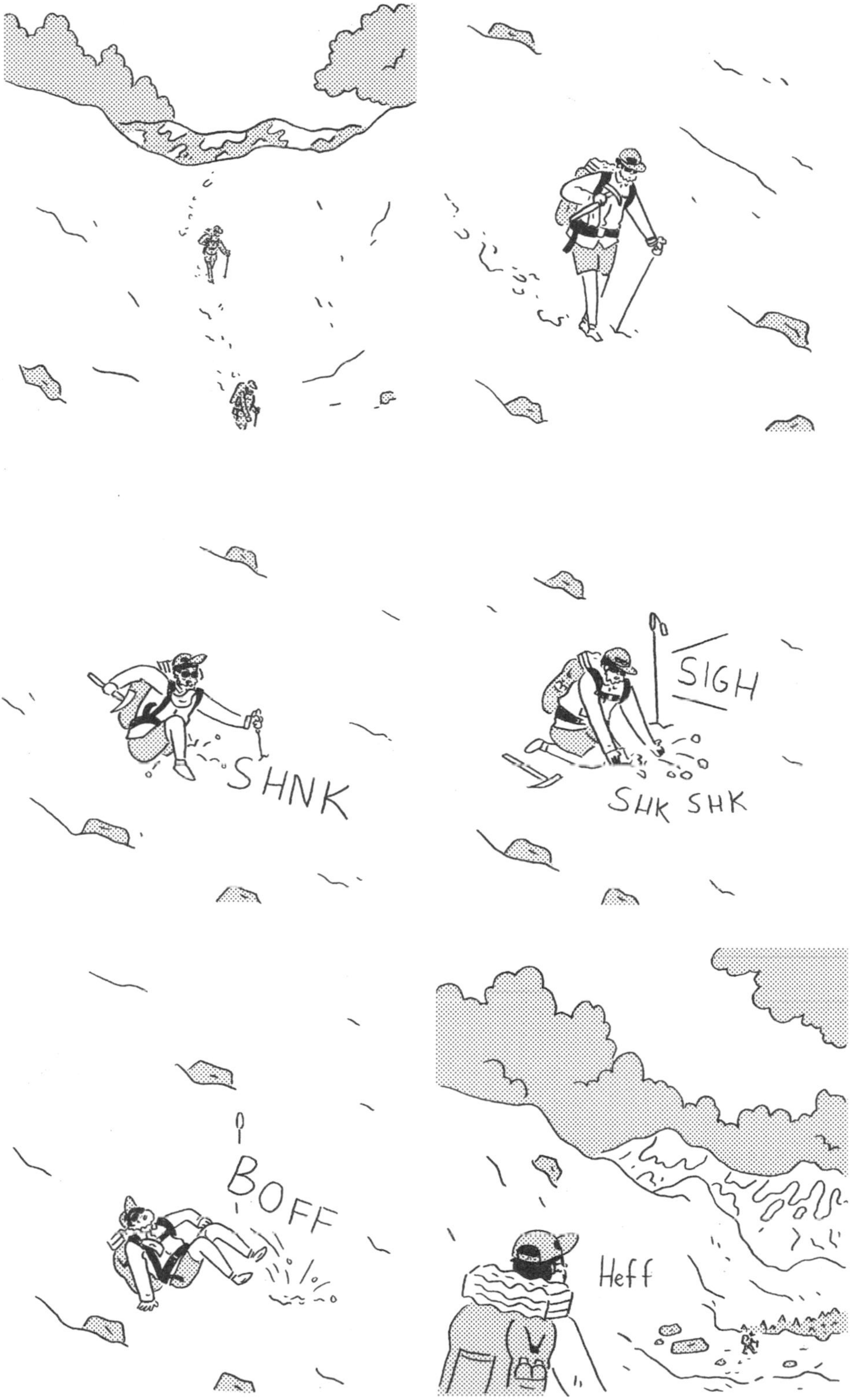
SHNK
SIGH
SHK SHK
BOFF
Heff

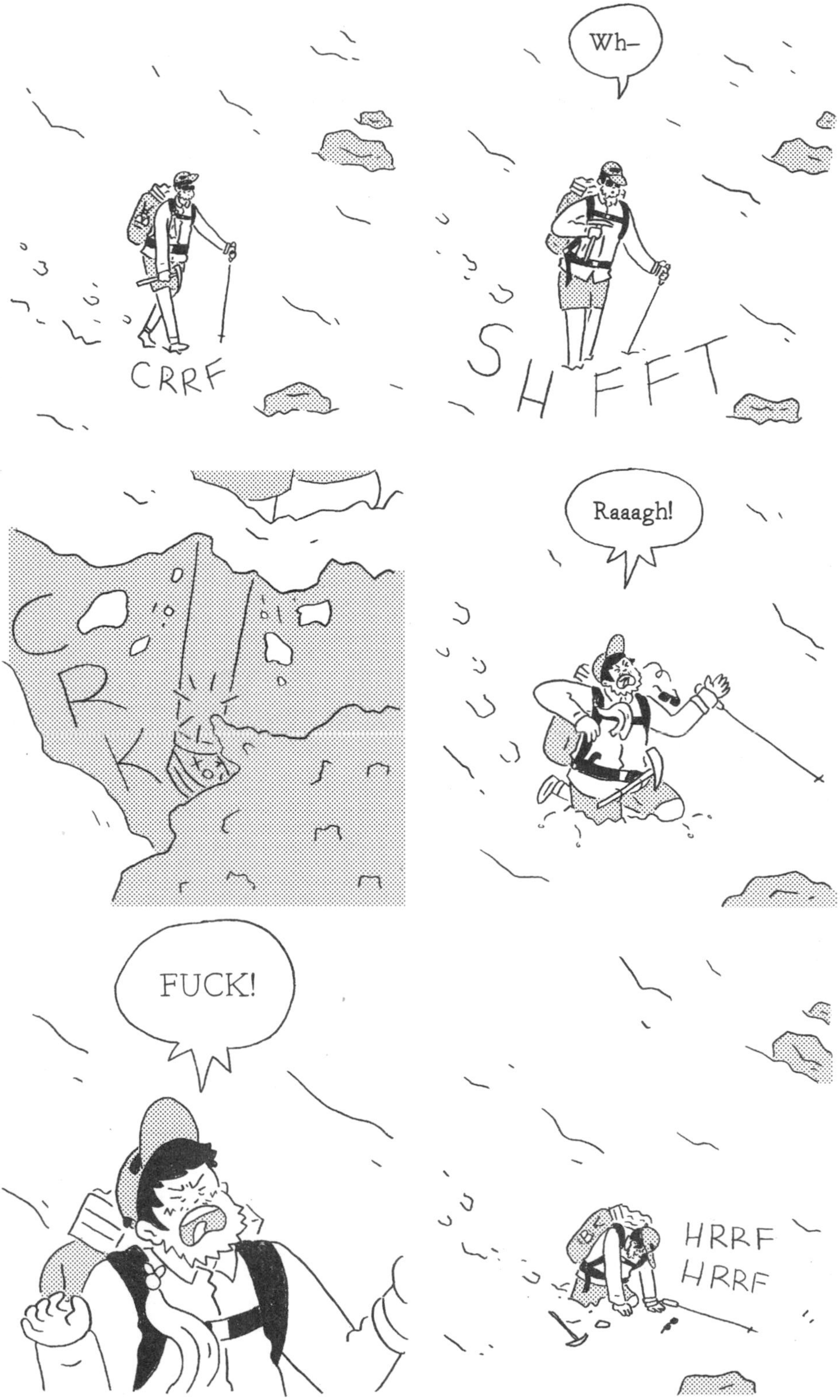
CRRF
Wh-
SHFFT
CRK
Raaagh!
FUCK!
HRRF
HRRF

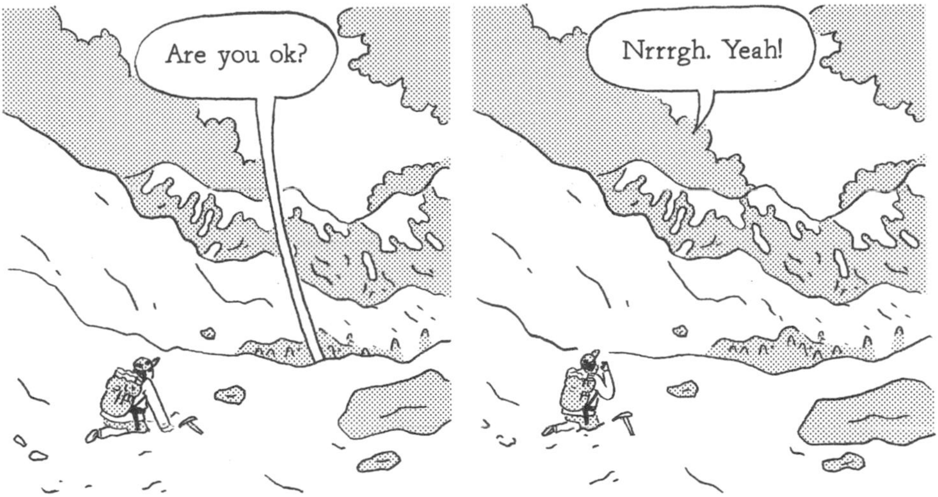
Are you ok?
Nrrrgh. Yeah!

Why the fuck did I say that?

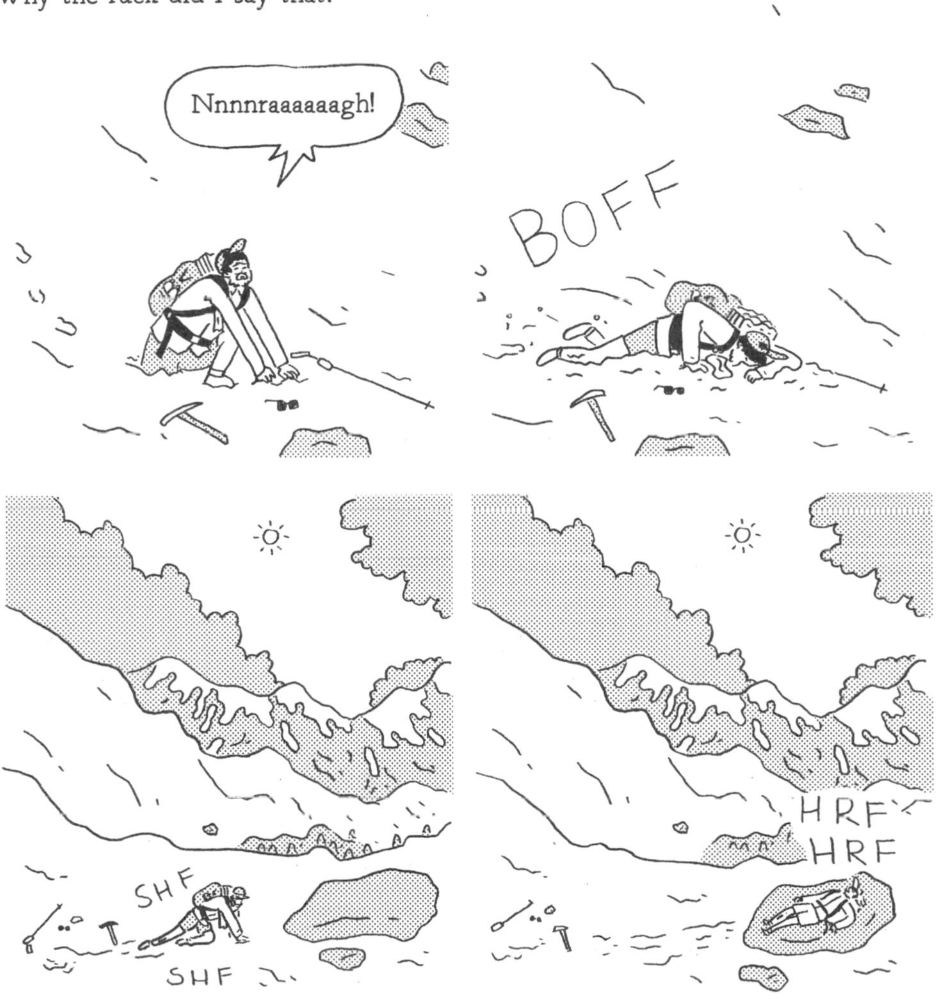
Nnnnraaaaaaagh!
BOFF
SHF
SHF
HRF
HRF

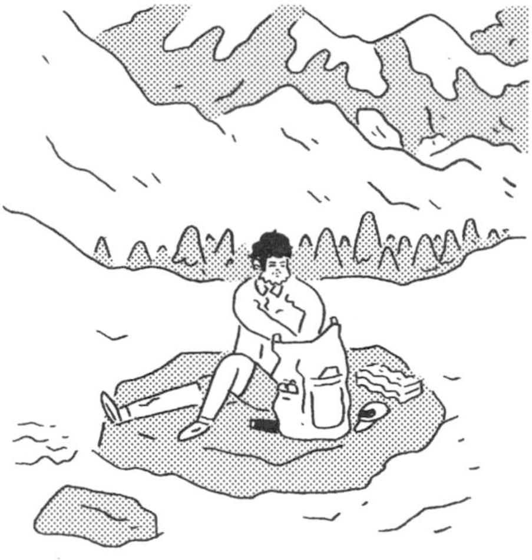

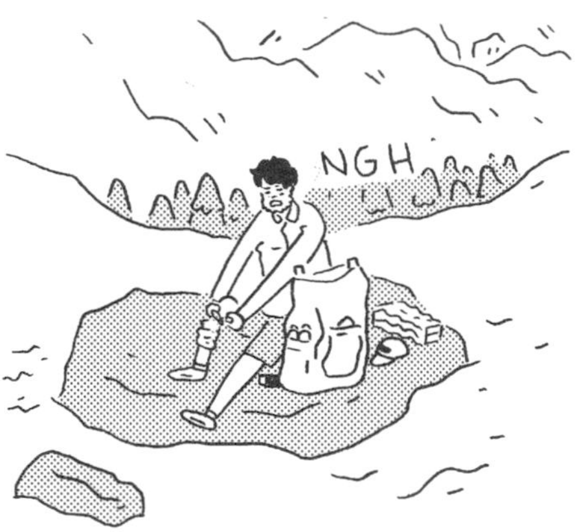
NGH

I pop some ibuprofen.

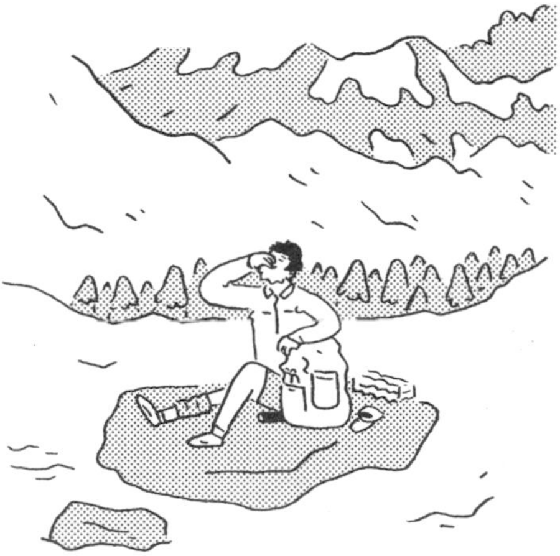

And, without a choice, I hike on, limping.

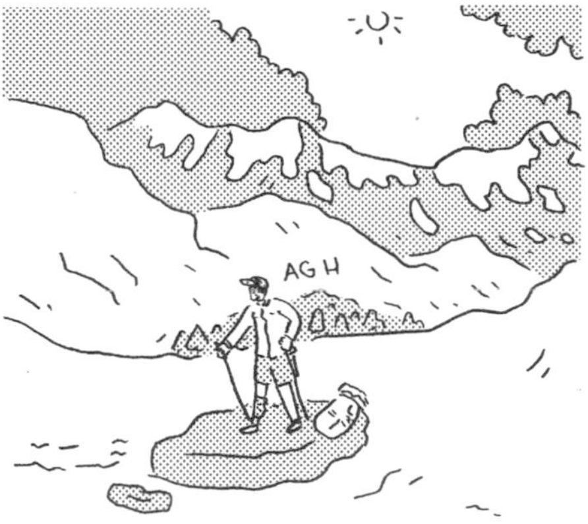
AGH

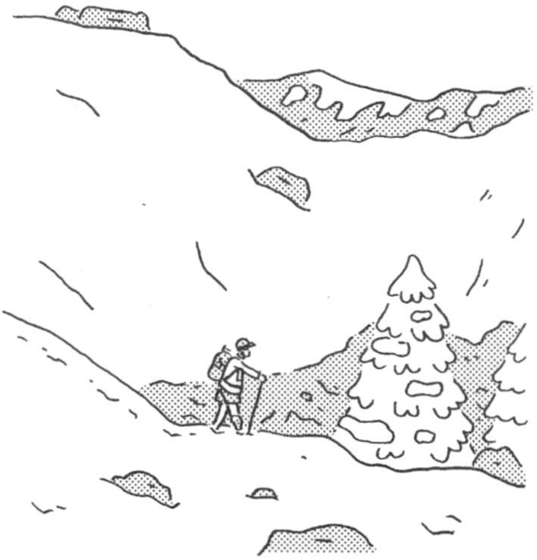

I feel, for the first time in my life, that I am tough.

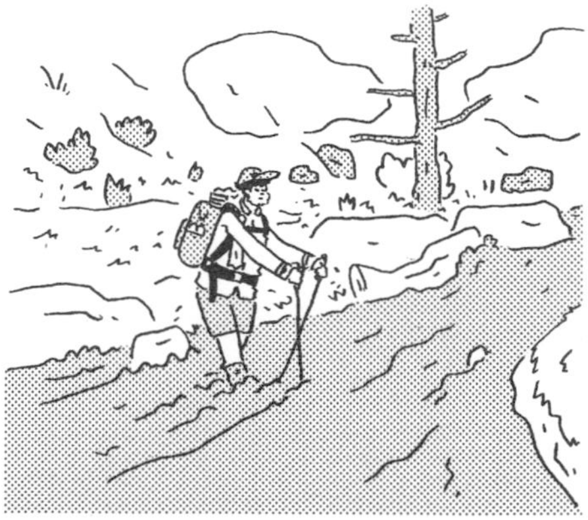

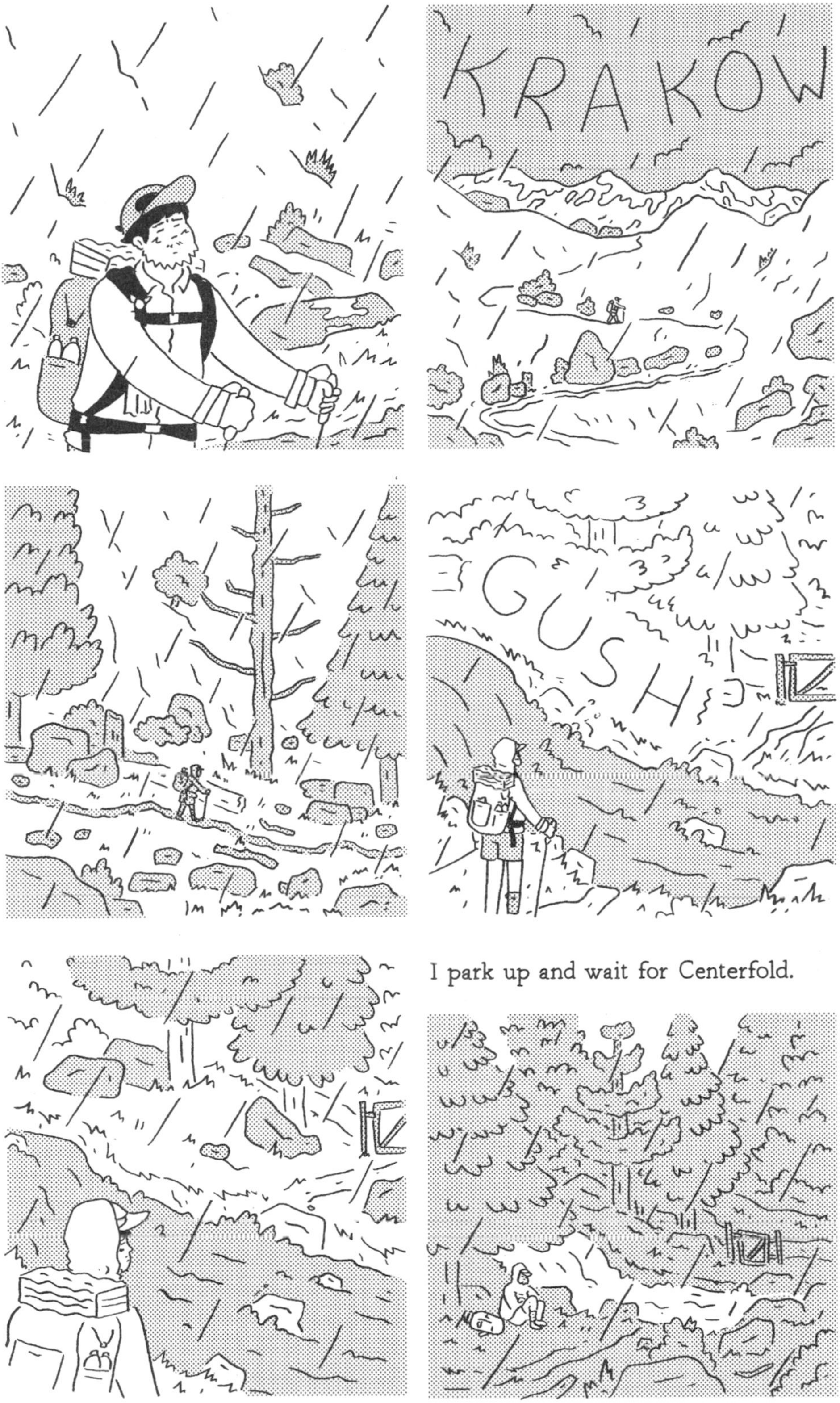
KRAKOW
GUSH
I park up and wait for Centerfold.

We cross together, tentatively.

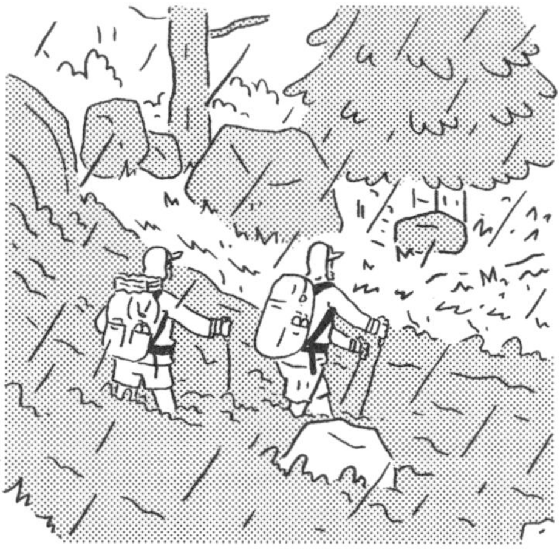

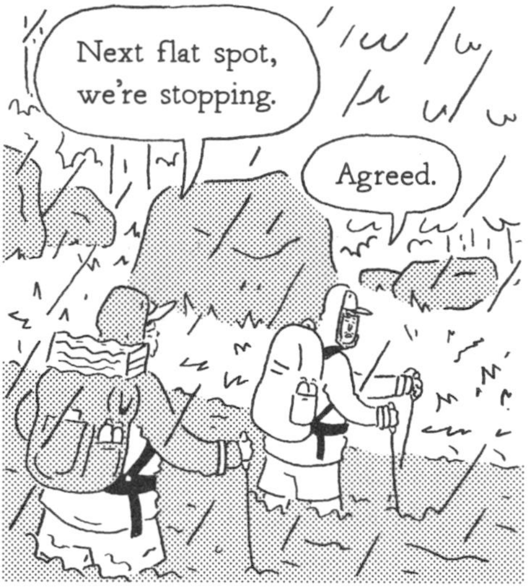

Next flat spot, we're stopping.
Agreed.

We camp in a little hollow, waiting for Chuckles and Spoon, but they never arrive.

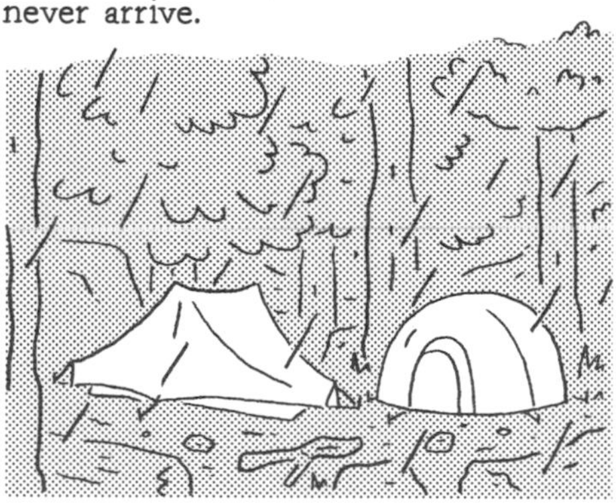

We are soaked. By the rain, the hail, the creek crossings and the melting snow. And we're freezing. We don't talk. I curl into a ball and try to keep warm as best I can. My sleeping quilt lies flaccid on top of me, the damp, deflated down inside doing nothing to protect me from the mountain cold. My leg throbs. A deep, red line cuts across my shin, though the skin isn't broken.

The lightning stops, as does the rain eventually, but I don't notice. I have fallen into a deep, death-like sleep.

In the morning, the sky has cleared, and I hike on, pausing in little patches of light to warm up my frigid hands.

I find Chuckles and Little Spoon down the trail, drying their gear in a patch of sun beside a bridge.

"We broke into a ranger cabin last night. Through a window. Started a fire," Spoon informs me.

"It was a survival situation, so I'm pretty sure that's not technically a crime."

"What jury would convict us!" Chuckles adds, smiling.

We return to our now familiar High Sierras pattern.

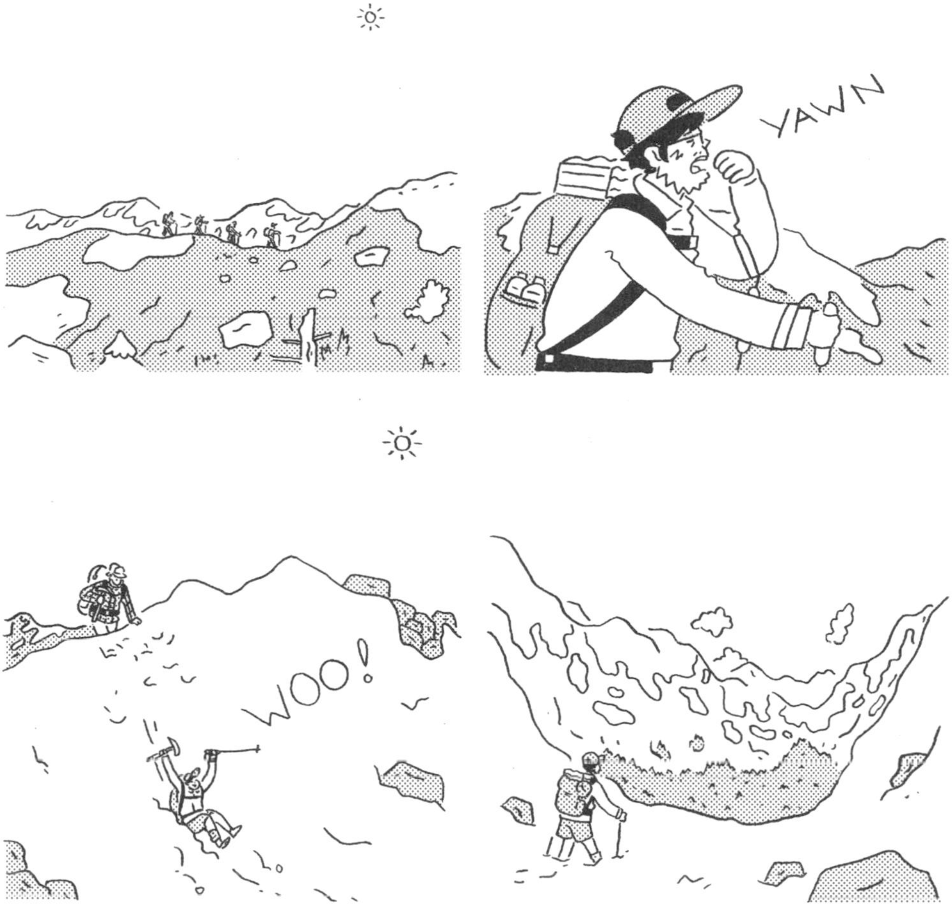
YAWN
WOO!

We have adapted to our new world.

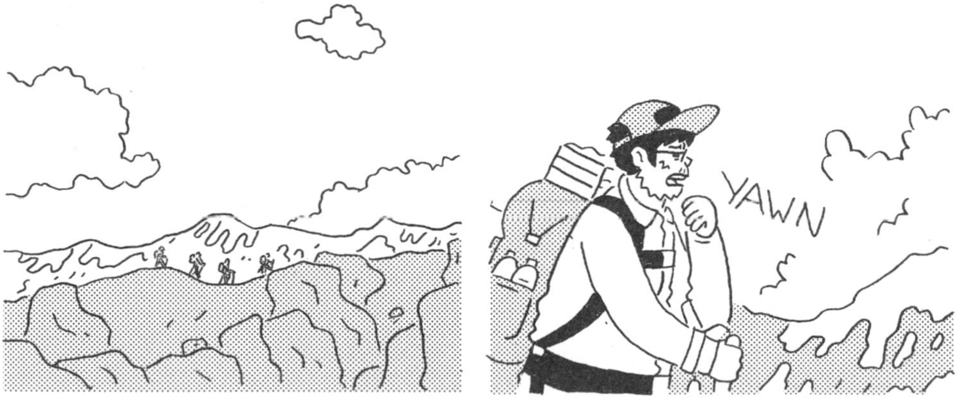
YAWN

My leg gives me pain as I hike, but I stay on a steady diet of vitamin I. I am becoming a stronger hiker, no longer passed by everyone else on trail, but actually passing hikers myself.

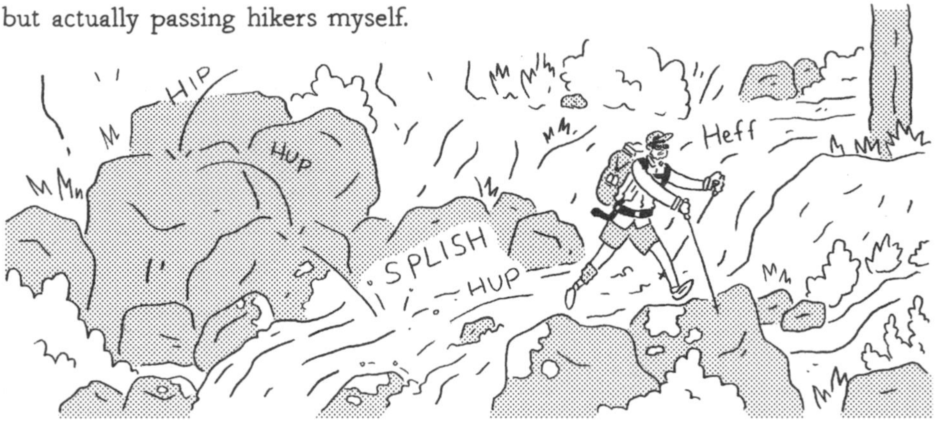
HIP
HUP
SPLISH
HUP
Heff

One night at camp, Camel appears, smiling.

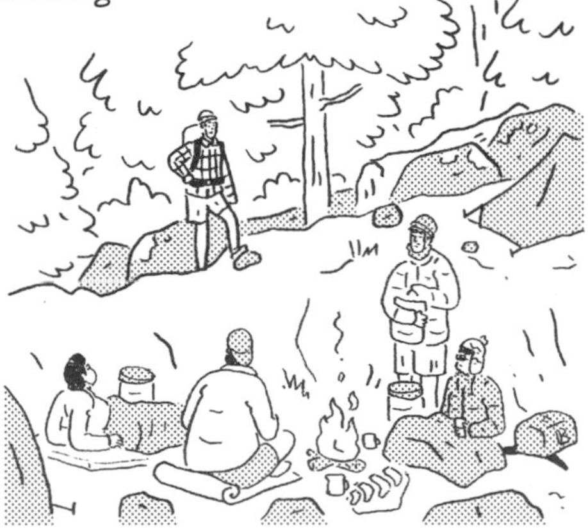

After some celebration, he pushes on ahead, taking Centerfold with him.

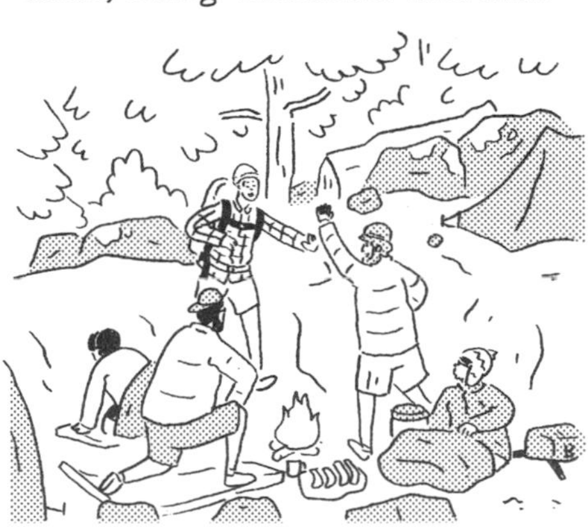

Chuckles, Spoon and I are left as a trio.

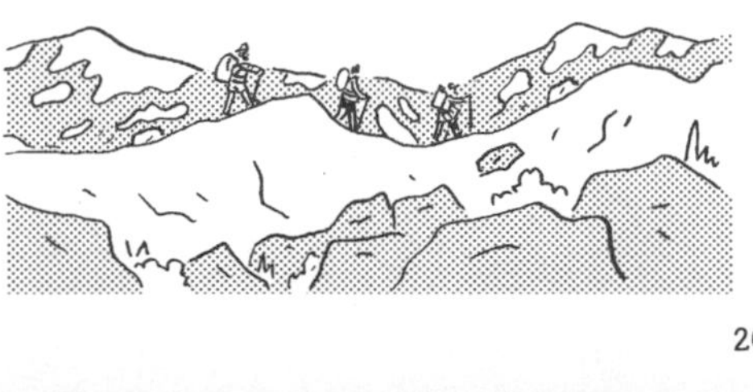

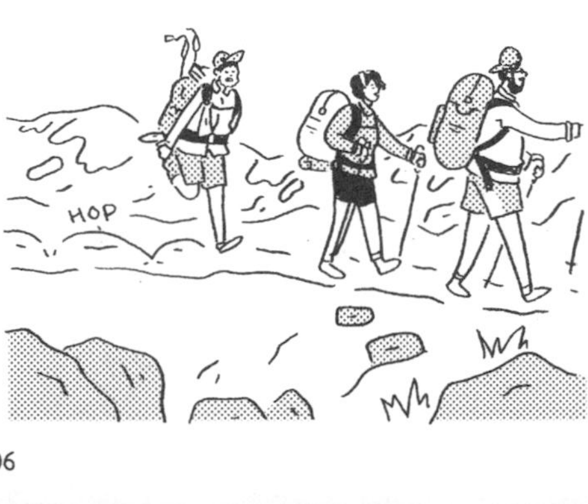
HOP

I hike alone. Chuckles and Spoon catch me when I stop to eat.

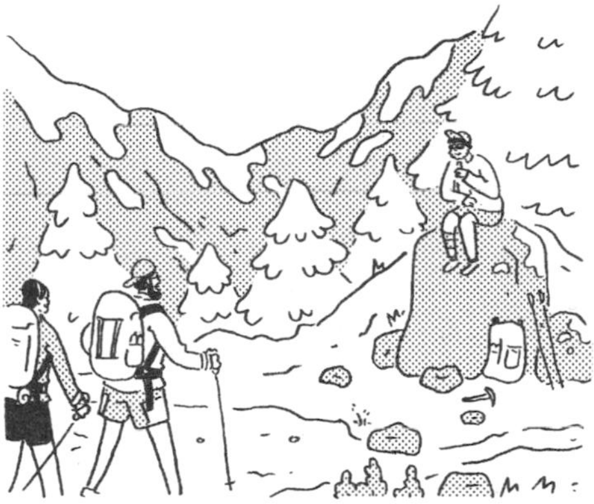

I make sure to pick campsites with space for two tents.

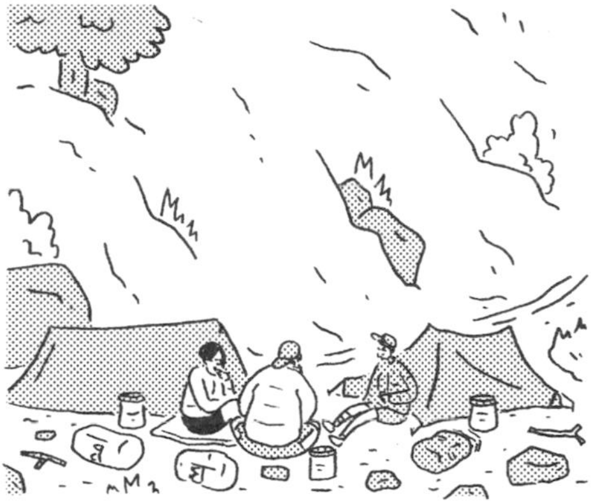

We reconvene at the big obstacles.

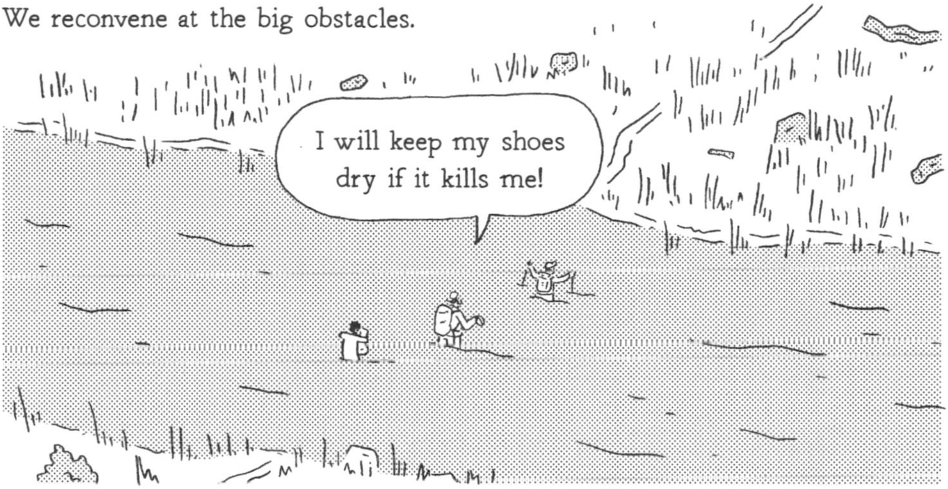
I will keep my shoes dry if it kills me!

Until eventually I lose them too.

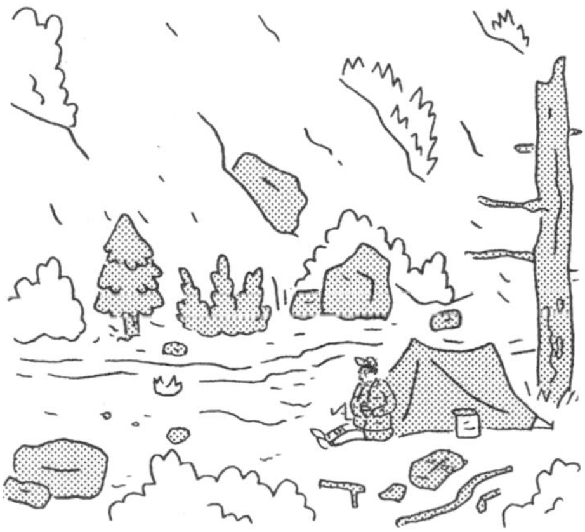

And once again, I hike alone.

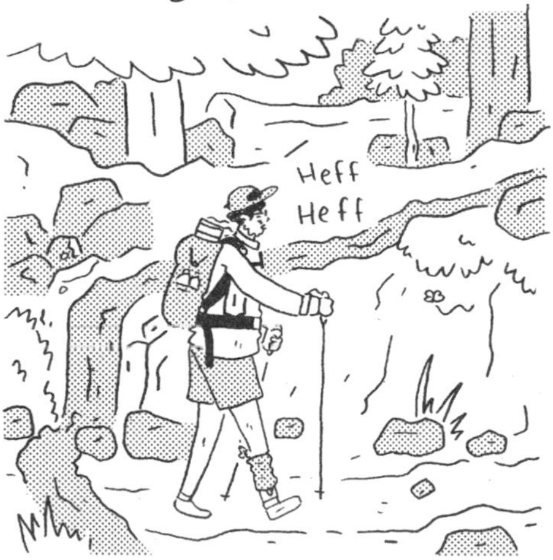
Heff
Heff

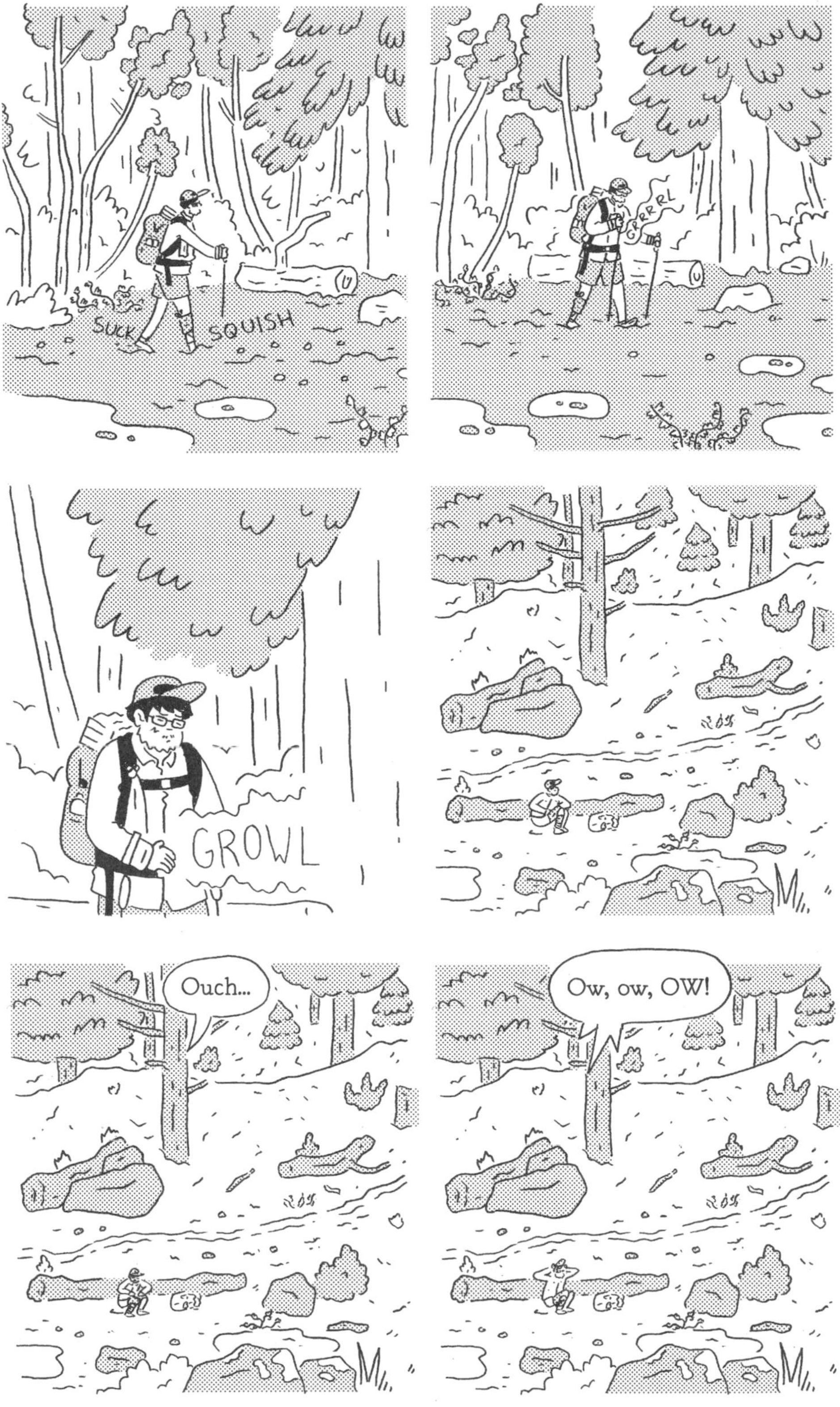
SUCK
SQUISH
GRRRRL
GROWL
Ouch...
Ow, ow, OW!

A terrible burning pain radiates from my asshole.

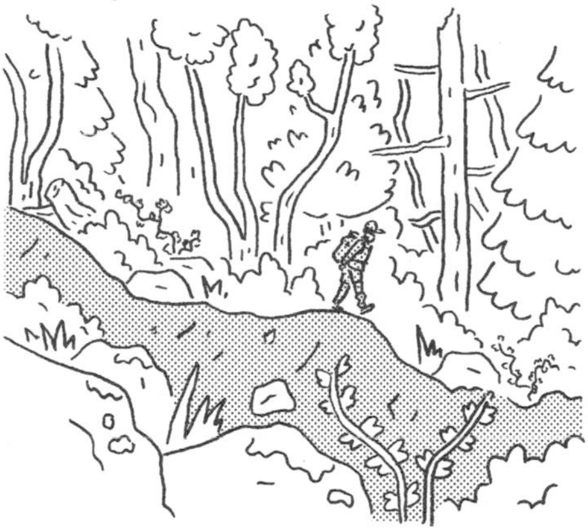

I employ my now time-tested solution. Ibuprofen and ignore.

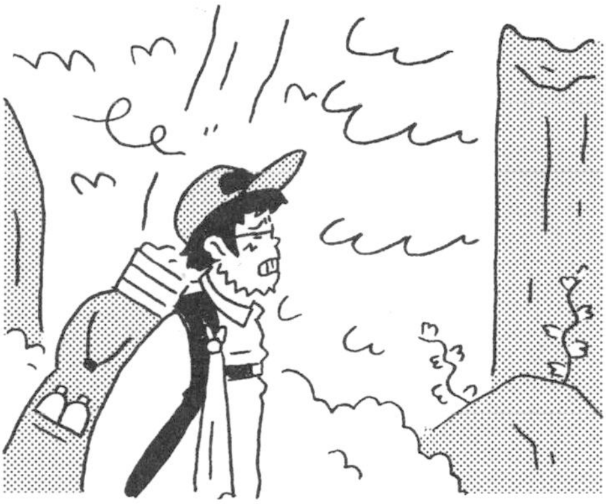

I detour to the remote Vermillion Valley Resort. The walk is excrutiating.

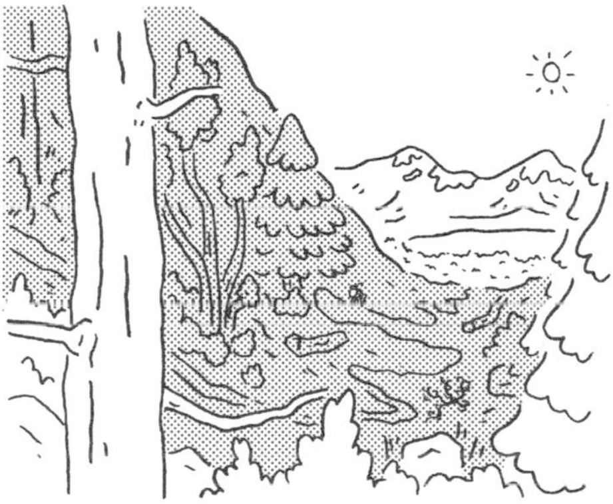

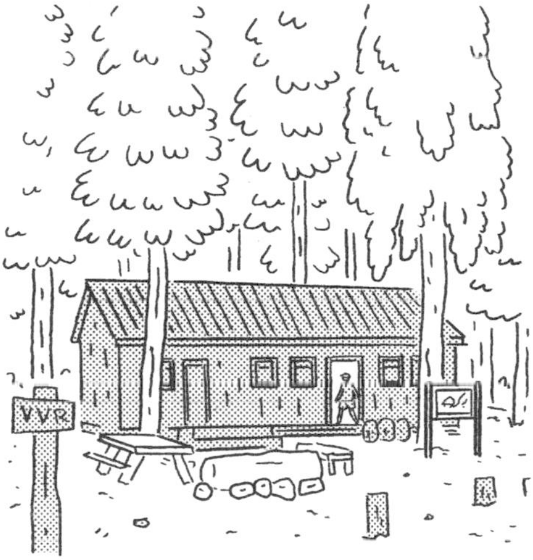
VVR

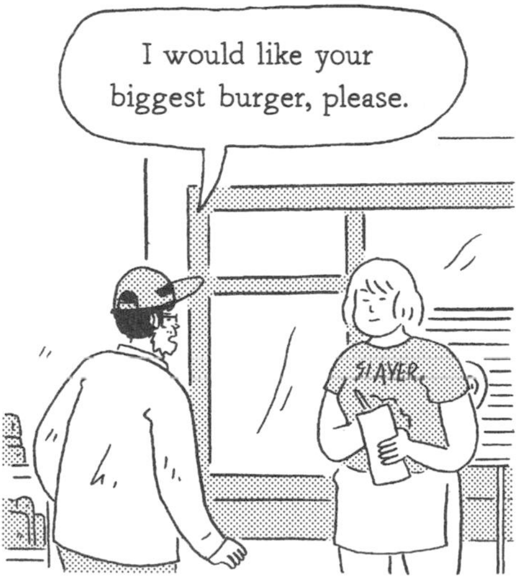
I would like your biggest burger, please.
SLAYER

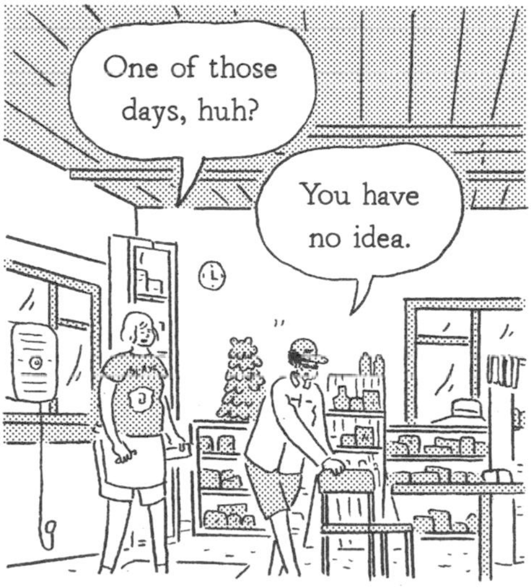
One of those days, huh?
You have no idea.

I pay to join a few other hikers on a boat back across the lake.

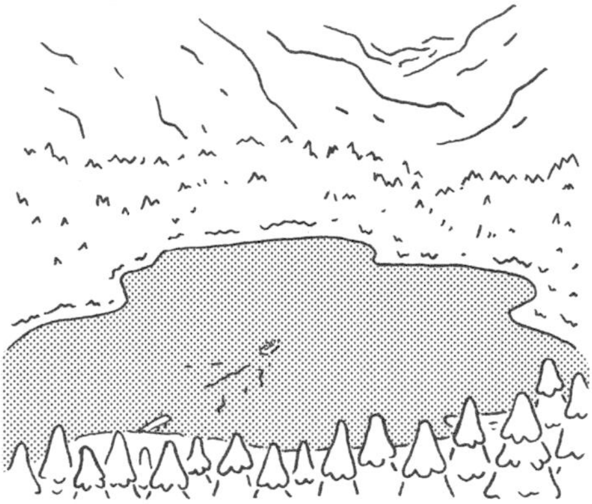

I just want to get to Mammoth, so I can take a shower and tend to my myriad wounds.

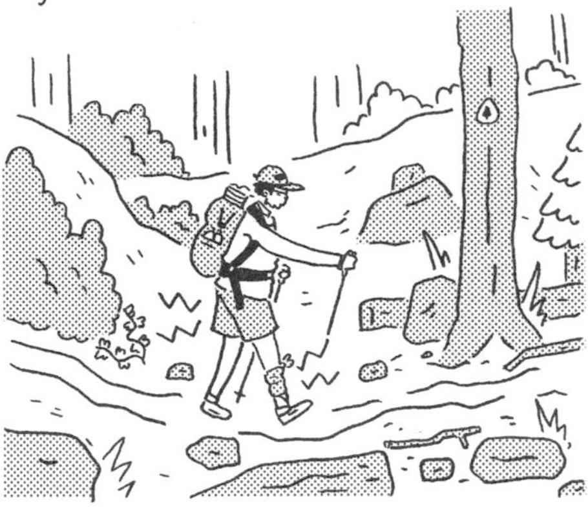

But the trail doesn't let up.

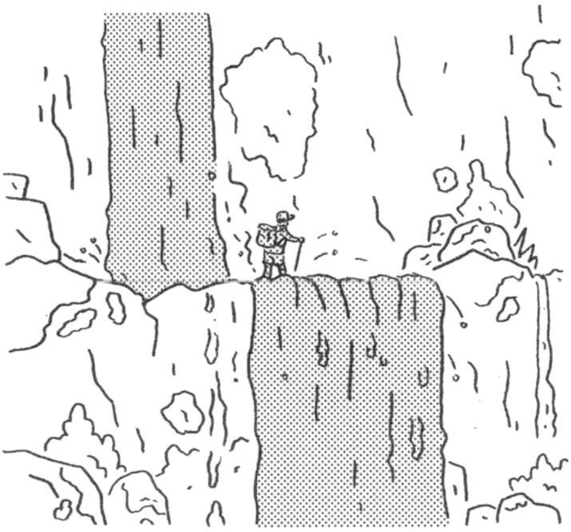

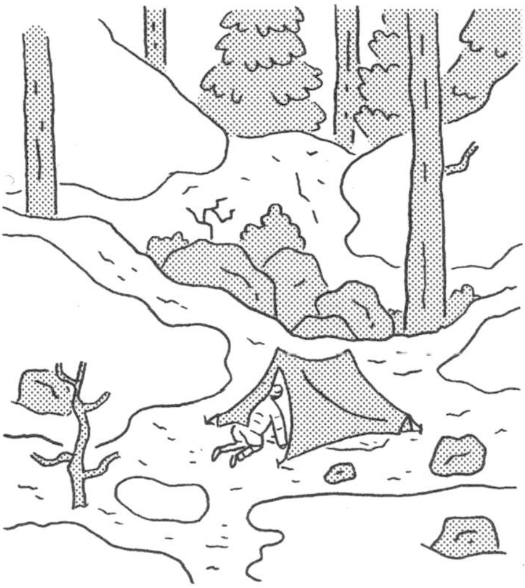

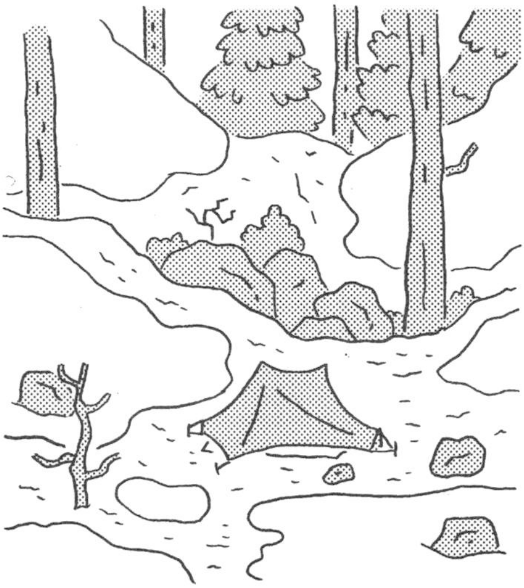

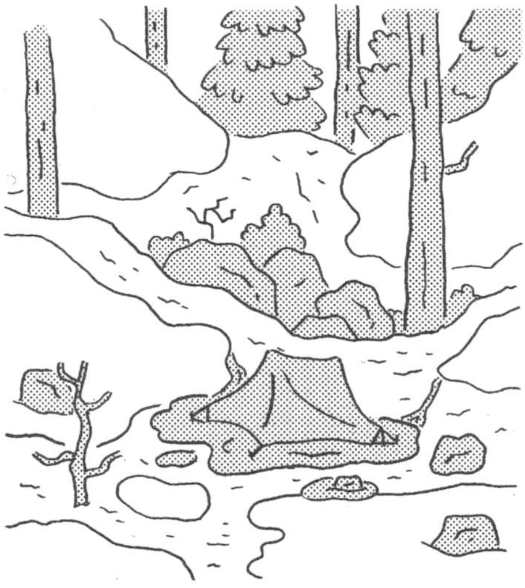

Mammoth 19/06/16. Day 65.

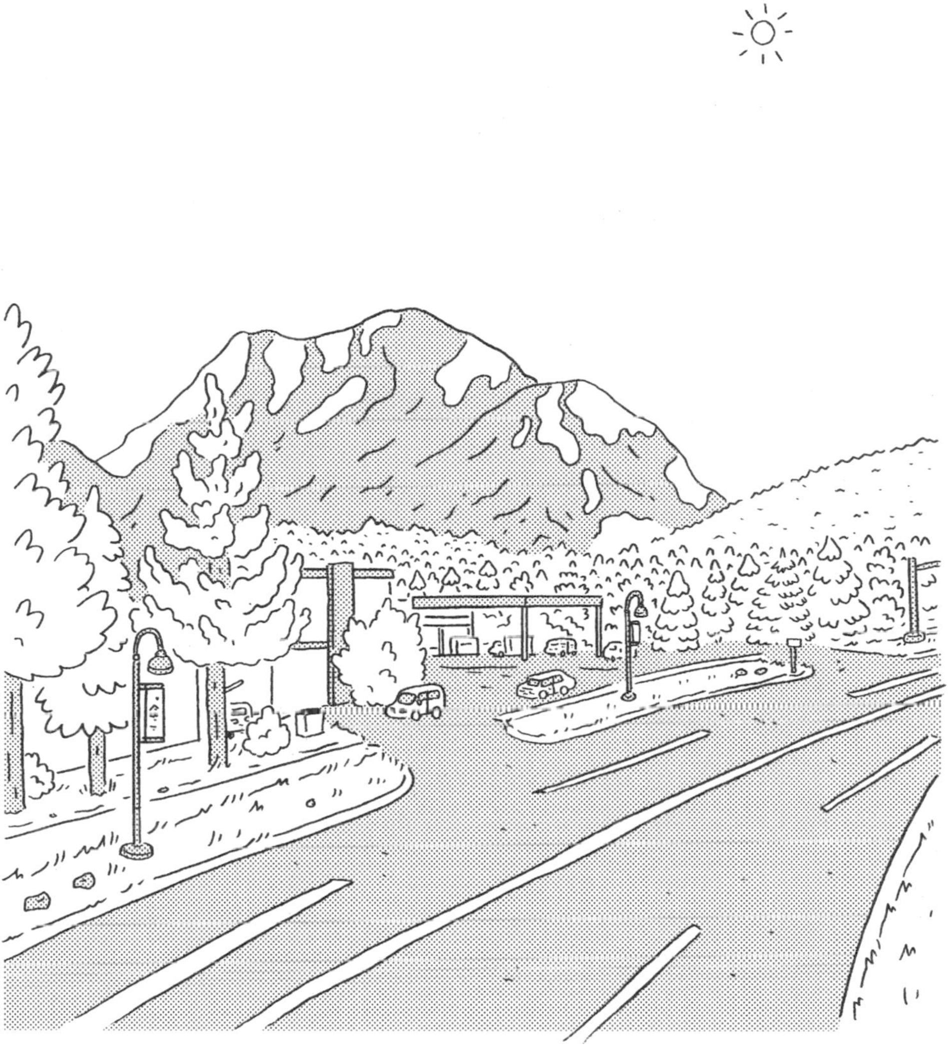

When I arrive, Mile 55 are having a reunion. It's the first time they've all been together since entering the Sierra.

We explore the town, and come across a finish line set up for a half-marathon. We get there just in time. There is only one more racer left, an older woman who hobbles down the road, looking embarrassed and breathing heavily. We cheer loudly, and applaud when she approaches.

"Just like the trail," Little Spoon says. "Last one to Canada, wins."

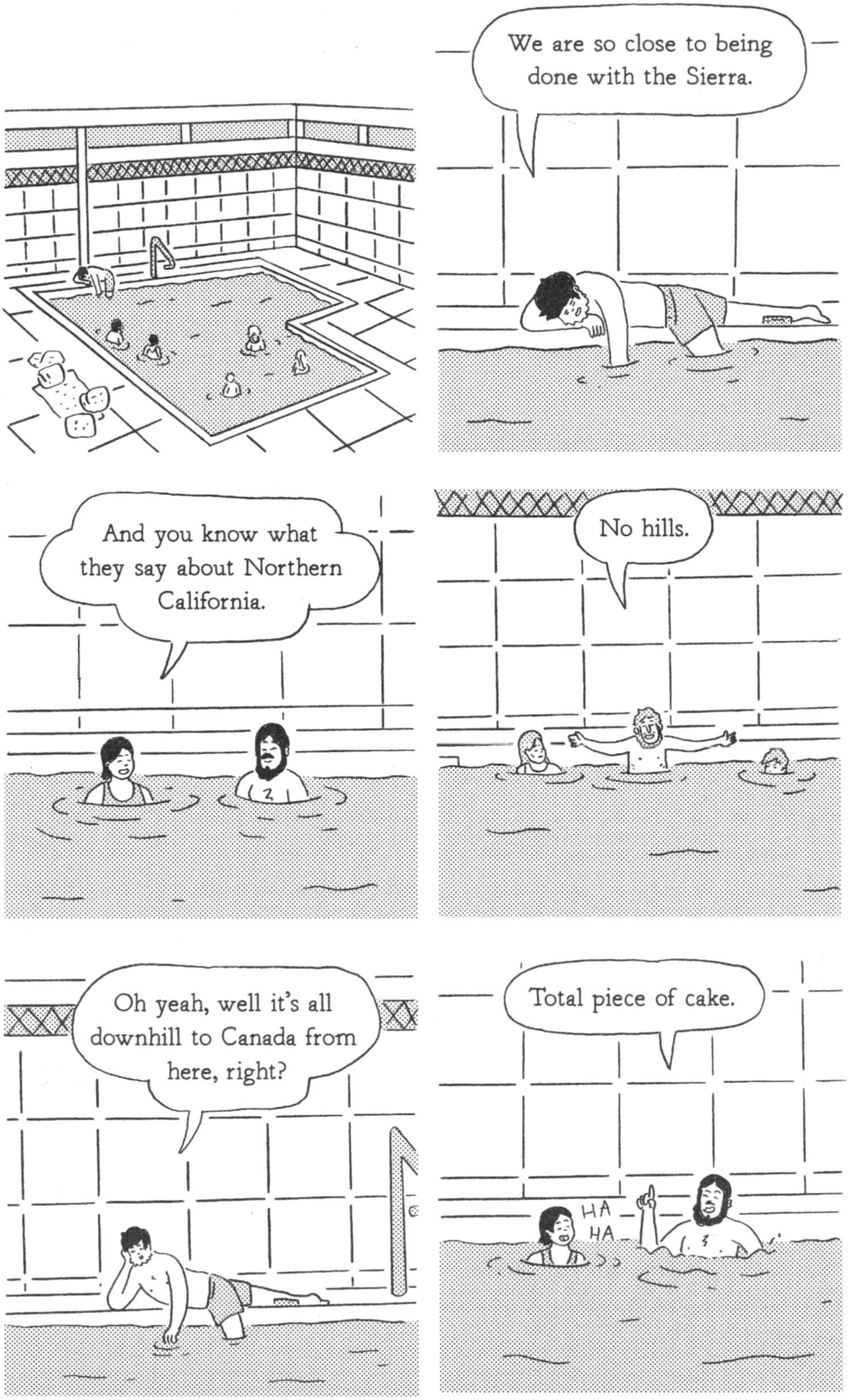

We are so close to being done with the Sierra.
And you know what they say about Northern California.
No hills.
Oh yeah, well it's all downhill to Canada from here, right?
Total piece of cake.
HA HA

I wake up and feel like trash. Both my leg and my asshole throb, the latter so painful that I resort to lying on one of the hotel room's beds belly-down while Centerfold and Camel watch a grizzly and absurd History Channel documentary about the discovery of electricity.

Everyone is ready to return to trail, except me, and I weigh the pull of their companionship against the drag of my injuries.

Outside a grocery store I find Griz, Craftsman and crew. I sit with them for a while, doing my best to pay attention while they deep dive on political history. I say my goodbyes once they get to the US Civil War — their knowledge greatly exceeding my ability to keep up.

I've finally nailed the art of the resupply, which basically means that I've discovered a rotation of foods that won't make me gag, even though I've been eating them all day, every day, for months now. Cheesy crackers, dried mango, cookies, tortilla chips — basically any junk food that won't spoil or be crushed too badly on trail.

Magazine covers stare out at me while I line up at the checkout counter. They all show the faces of forty-nine people, the victims of a homophobic mass shooting in Orlando. I start to tear up as the cashier rings up my things. The pull of companionship wins.

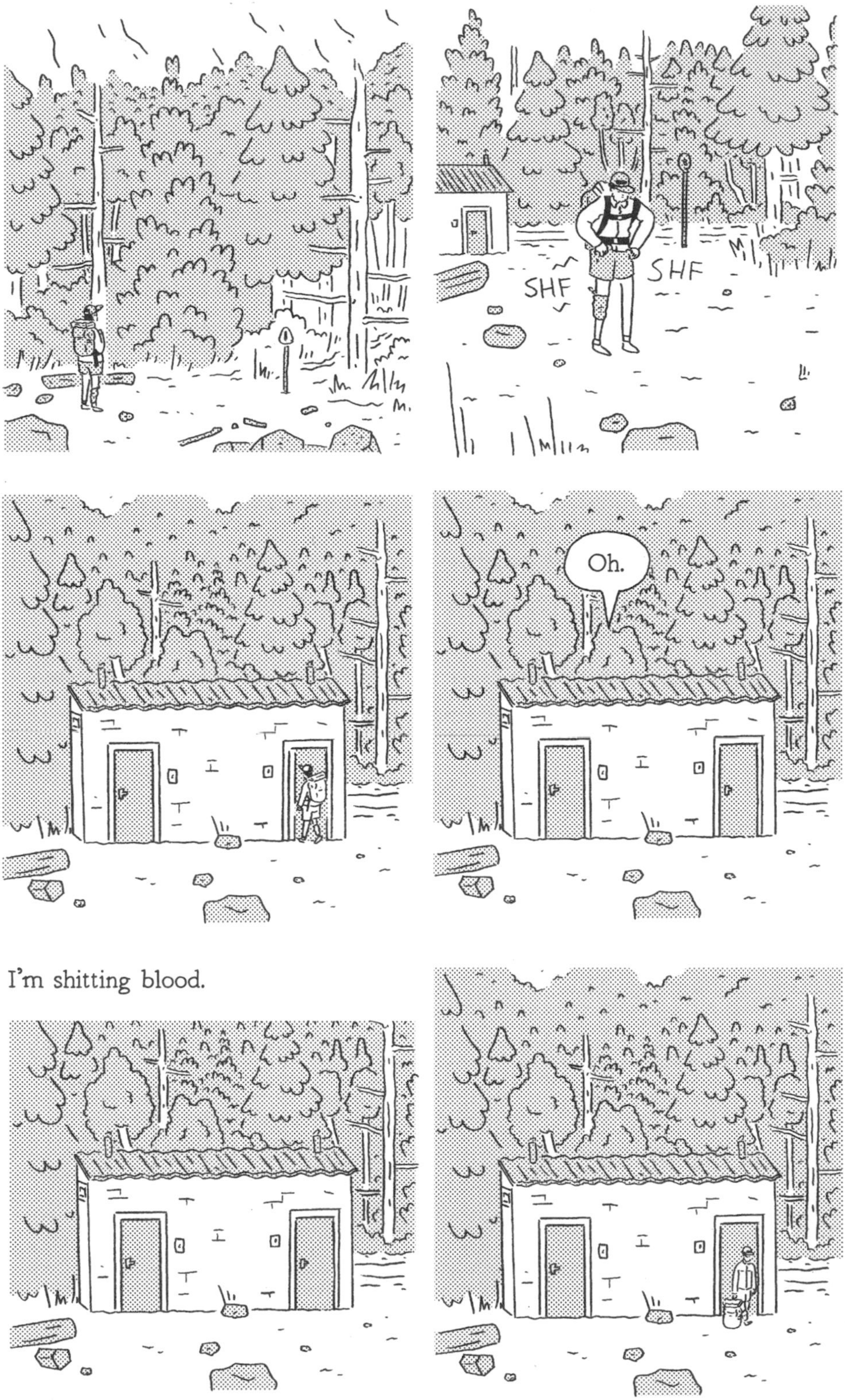
SHF
SHF
Oh.
I'm shitting blood.

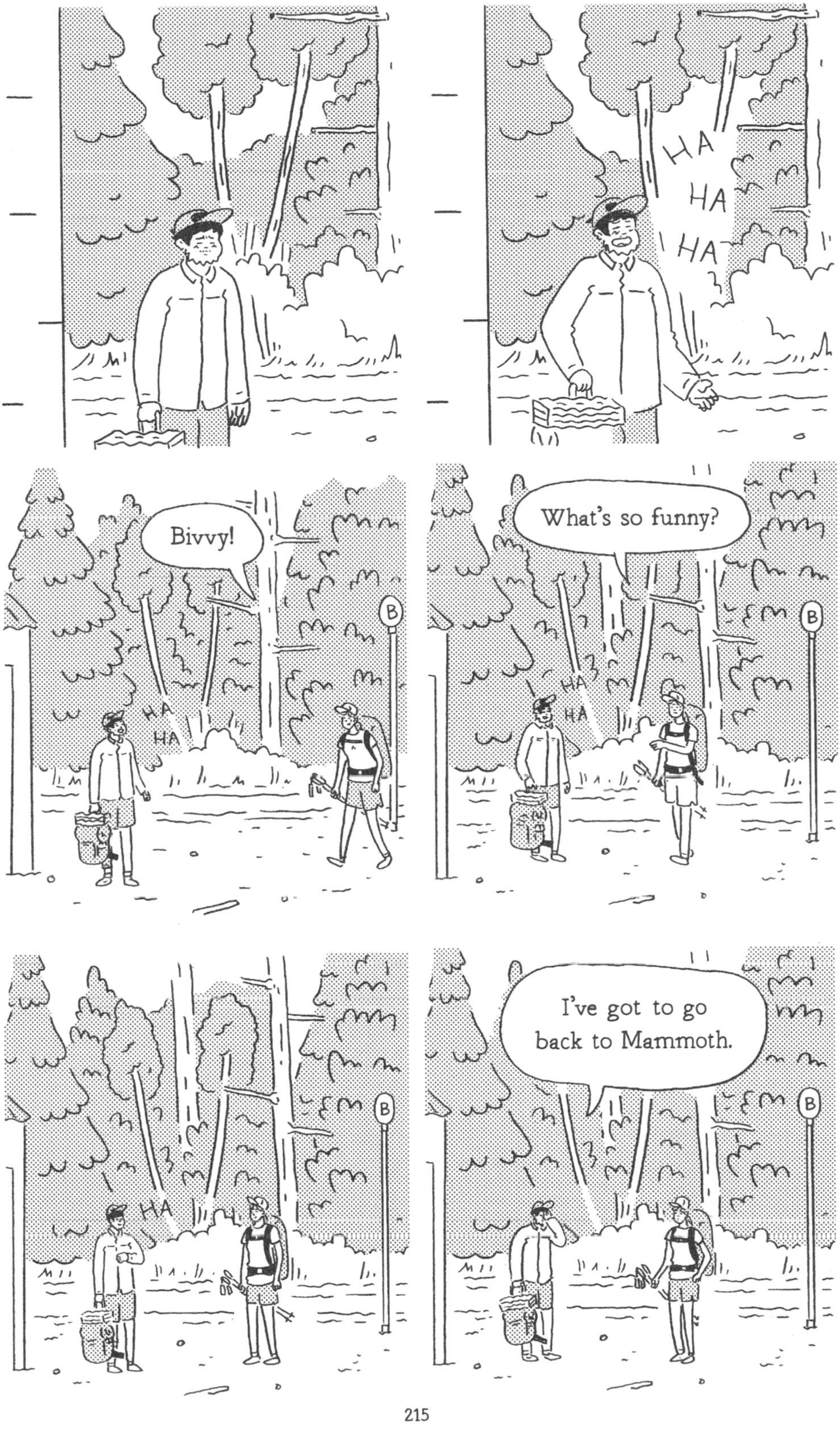
HA
HA
HA
Bivvy!
HA
HA
What's so funny?
HA
HA
HA
I've got to go back to Mammoth.

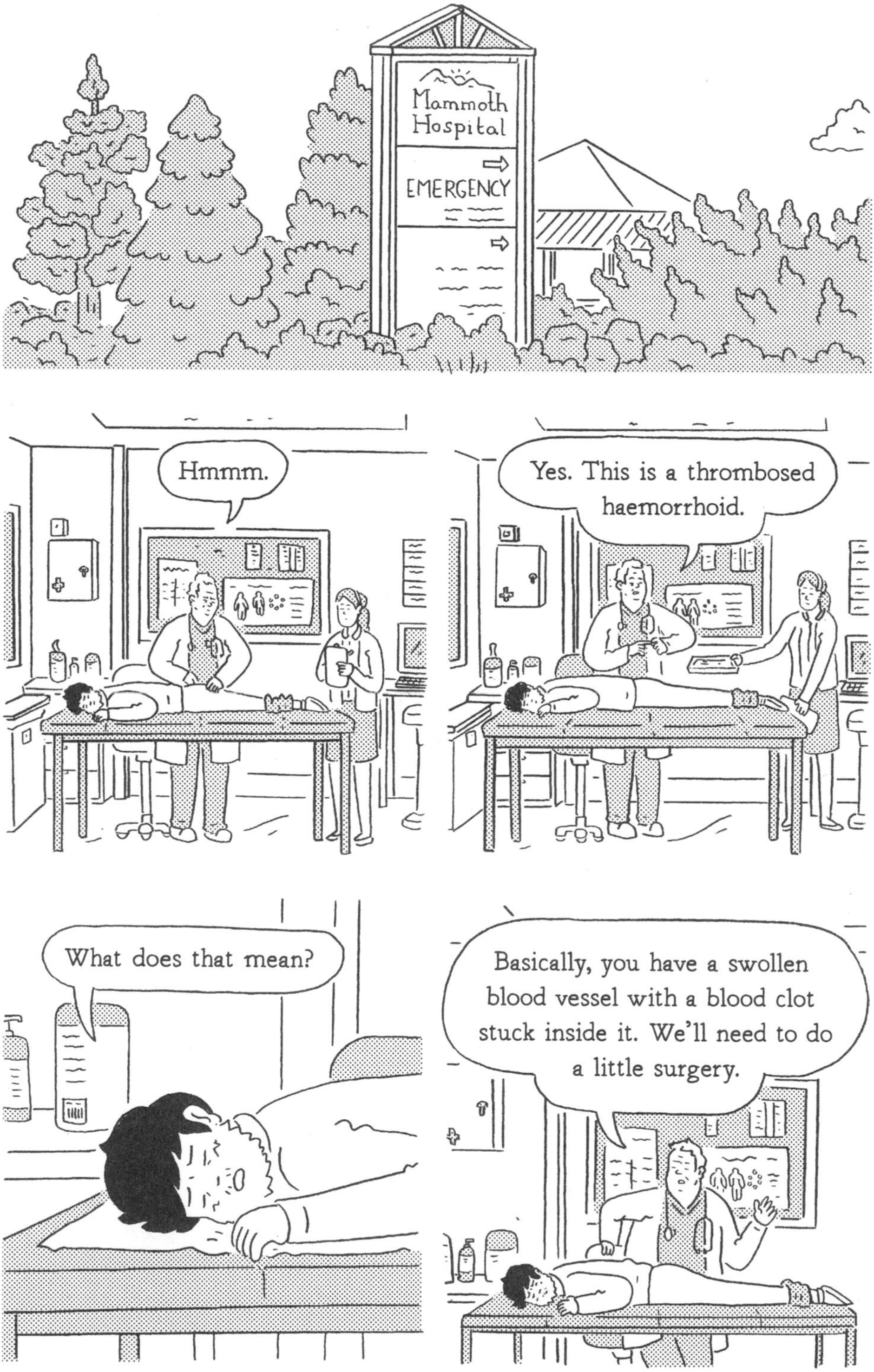
Mammoth Hospital
EMERGENCY
Hmmm.
Yes. This is a thrombosed haemorrhoid.
What does that mean?
Basically, you have a swollen blood vessel with a blood clot stuck inside it. We'll need to do a little surgery.

First comes the syringe to "numb" me. Then the scalpel.

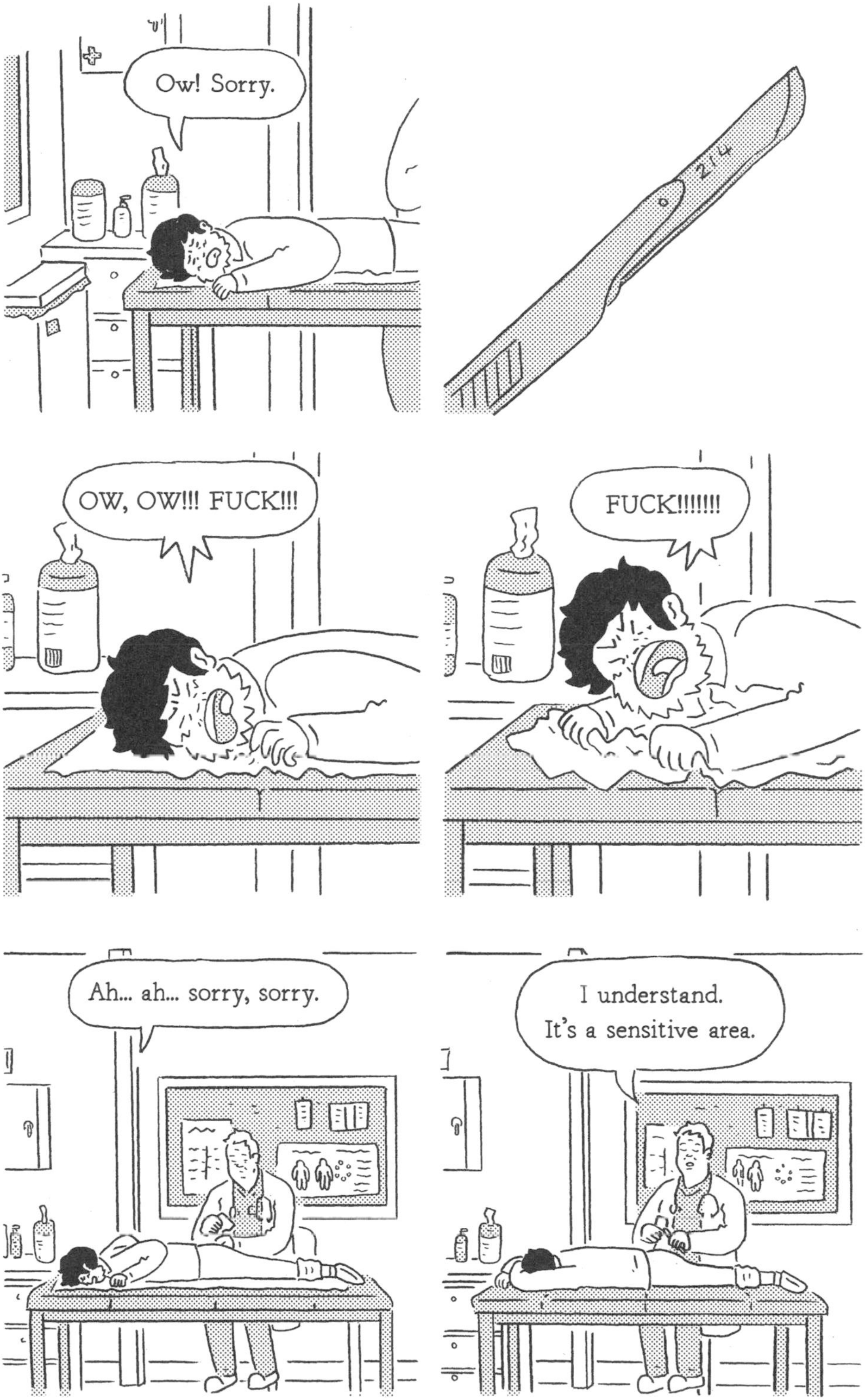
Ow! Sorry.
2 4
OW, OW!!! FUCK!!!
FUCK!!!!!!!
Ah... ah... sorry, sorry.
I understand.
It's a sensitive area.

I call my parents as I limp slowly back up Mammoth main street.

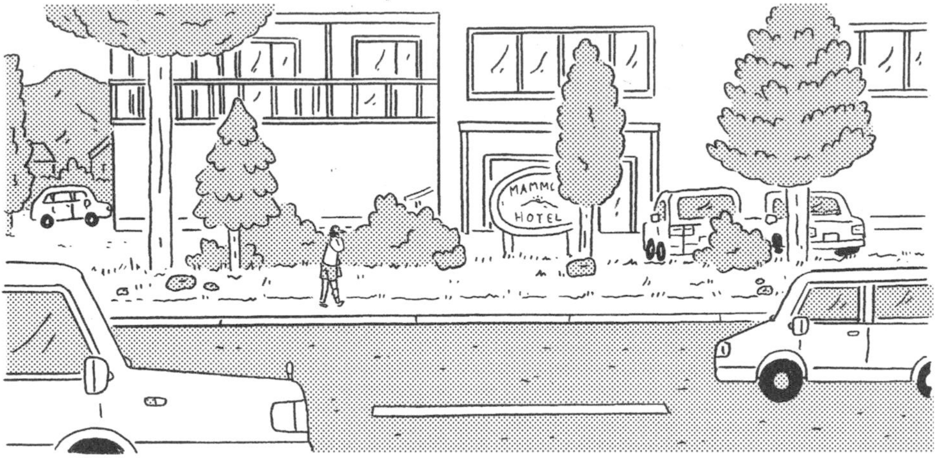
HOTEL

I try to sound strong and calm and competent.

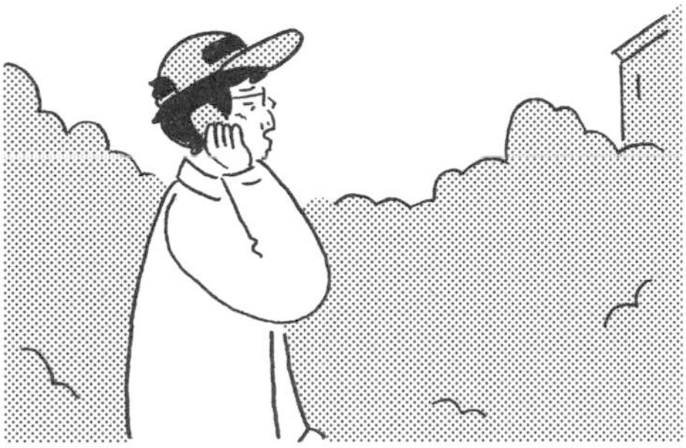

They express love and concern and support.

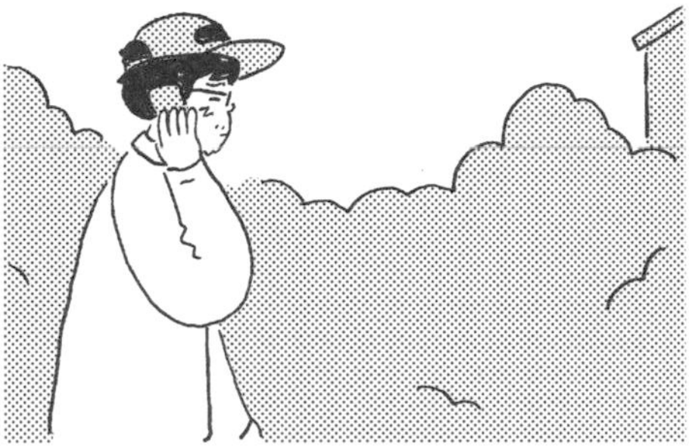

And for a moment, despite my best efforts...

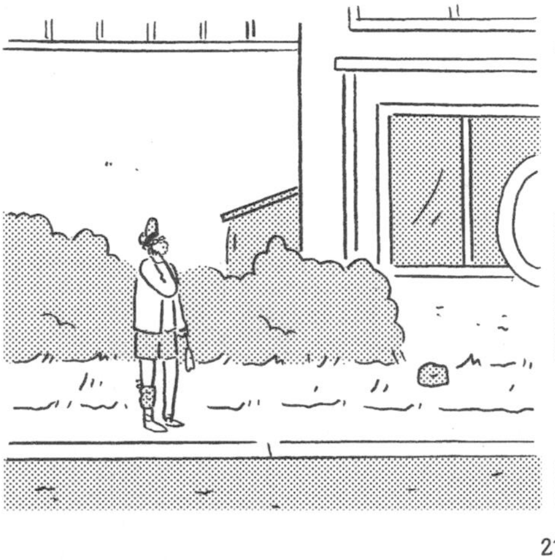

...I am weak and incompetent.

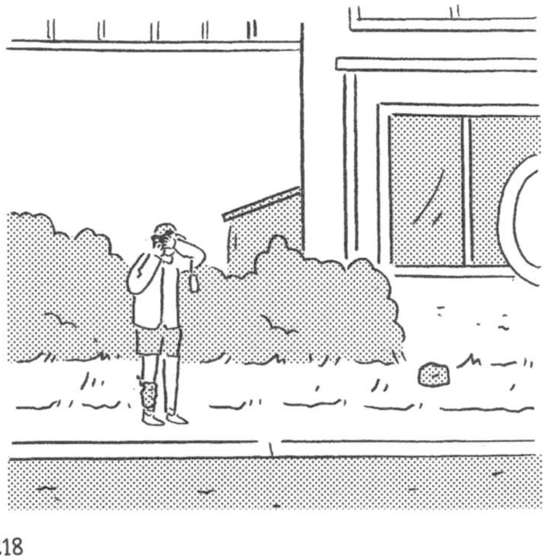

I spend eleven days in Mammoth, under doctor's orders.

I manage to keep a bed at a hostel. I can't really walk around for the first couple of days, but I don't really mind being cooped up in bed. My leg thanks me for it too, and feels a little less painful each day.

I eat at least one tub of ice cream every single day in Mammoth, in an attempt to gain back some weight.

I shave for the first time since beginning the hike, and buy some clothes in a charity shop to blend in a little better with the Mammoth locals. I am taken aback by how different I look.

I run into lots of other hikers I know. Hikers I'd left behind weeks ago in the desert. I meet up with Flashdance and Secret Squirrel, who continued to hike together after I left them in Lake Isabella. We get crappy burgers from a fast food joint.

Chuckles writes a blog, and I discover that the inevitable has finally happened – Mile 55's different hiking paces have drawn them apart, for good it seems. They'd managed to stick together from Campo, all the way up to the one-thousand-mile mark, but now they've scattered apart. I mourn that, a little. I consider skipping a section of trail to catch up with the group but now there isn't a group to catch up with. Besides, skipping now would break the continuous footpath I've been building from Mexico and would leave too much doubt in my mind that I'd experienced the PCT. Another American book, left open.

But my schedule is tight. On September 12th, I need to be in Washington, D.C. for work, so my end date is non-negotiable.

"That's why these eleven days are so frustrating," I tell Flashdance.

"What do you mean?"

"I know if I have to skip, I'll be skipping an eleven-day section."

But not now. There's still a possibility of finishing without missing any section. If I really focus, and increase my mileage, I can maintain my unbroken footpath.

I buy new shoes. They're shiny and unblemished. It feels like putting on a new pair of feet.

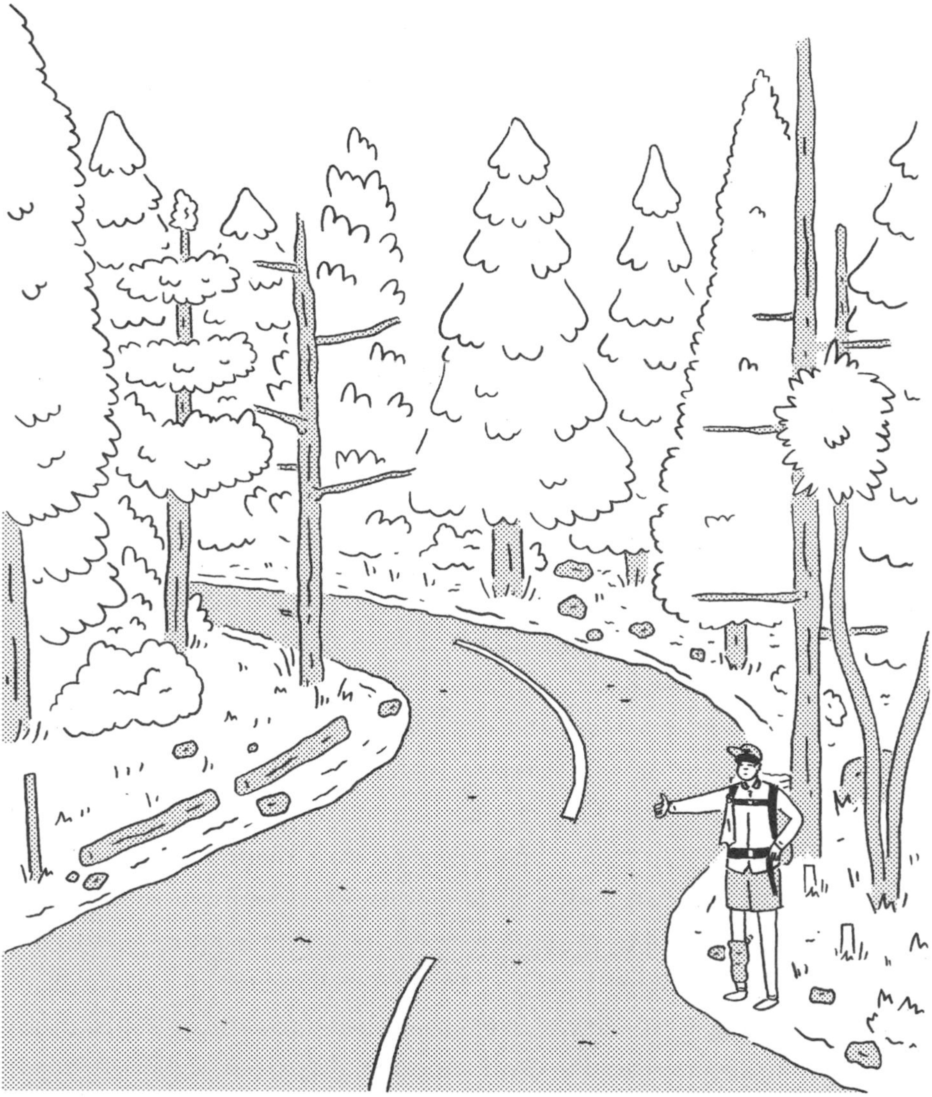

I return to trail alone.

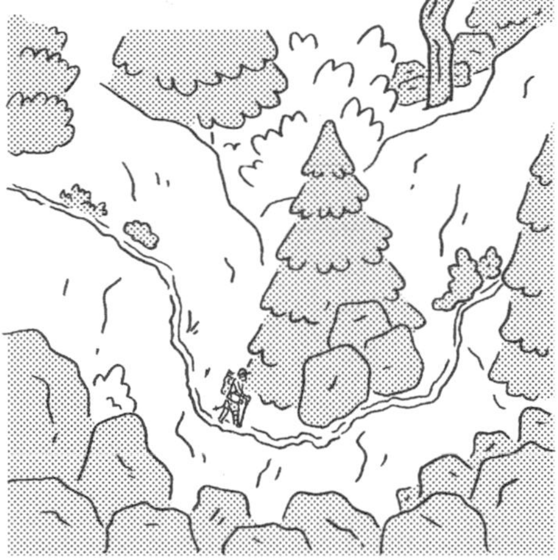

It's odd.

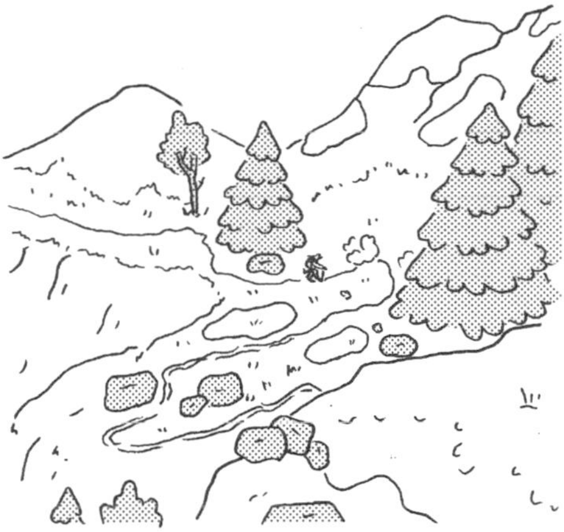

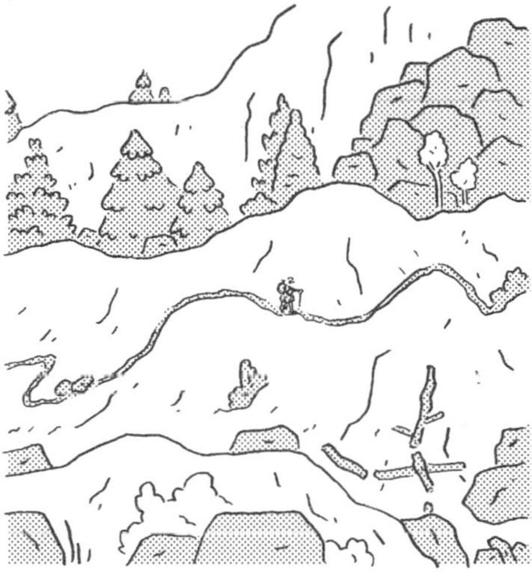

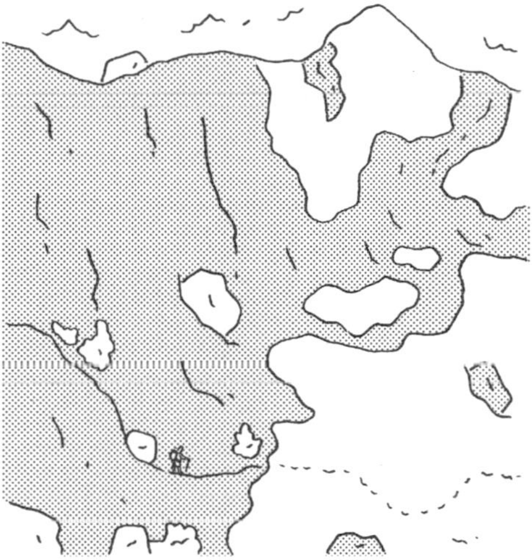

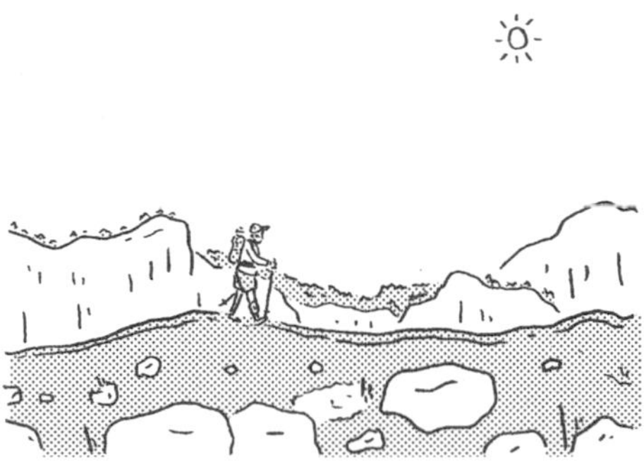

Quiet.

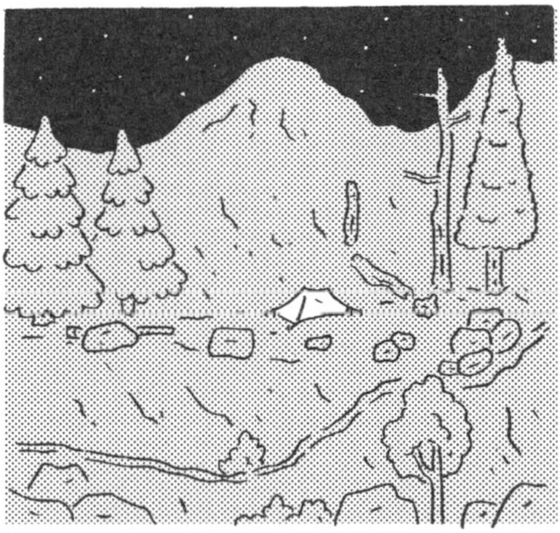

My last few days in the High Sierras are idyllic.

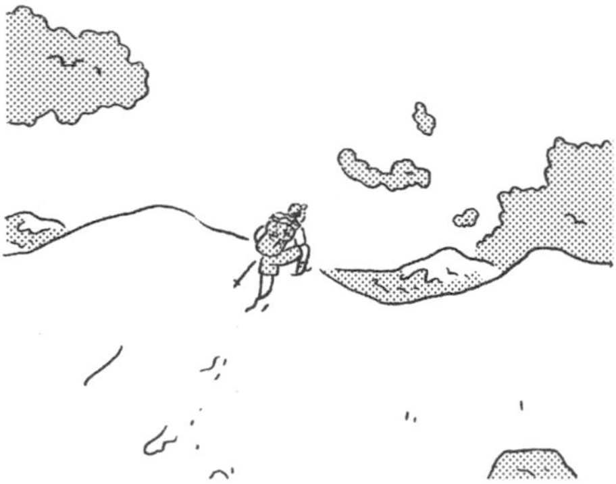

The passes get lower and the creeks, shallower.

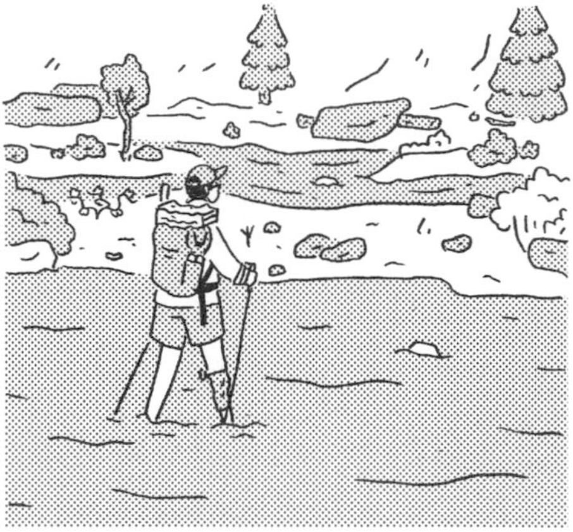

The milestones get bigger.

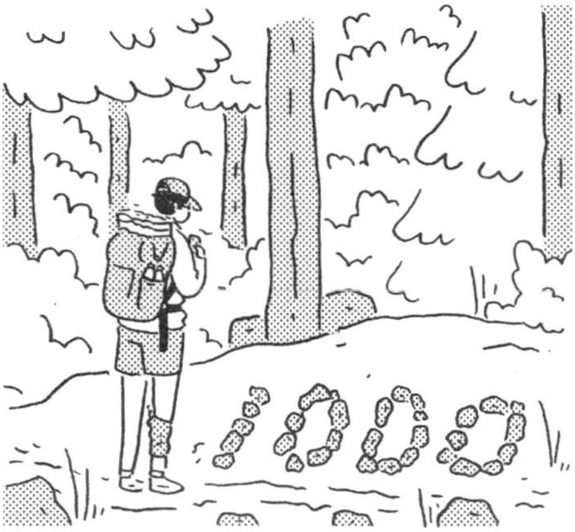
1000

I cross Sonora Pass on the 4th of July.

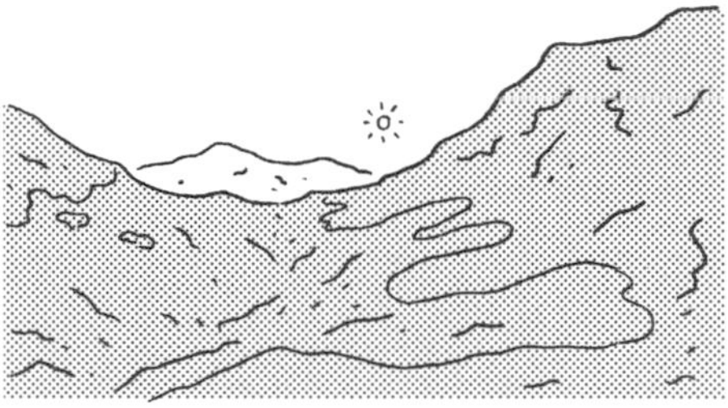

A trail angel gives me a soda. I sell my huge bear can to another.

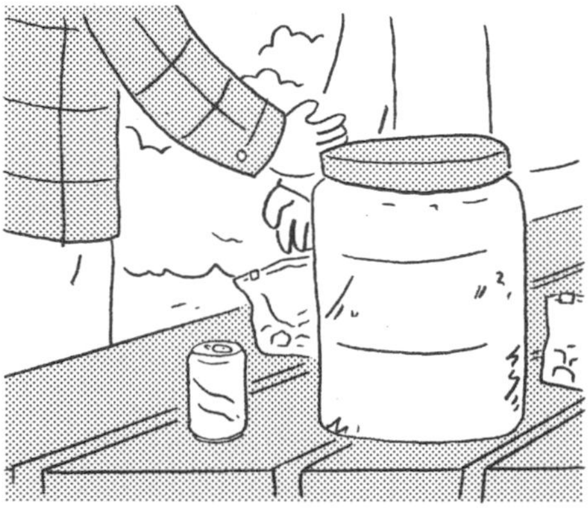

And I'm in the promised land.

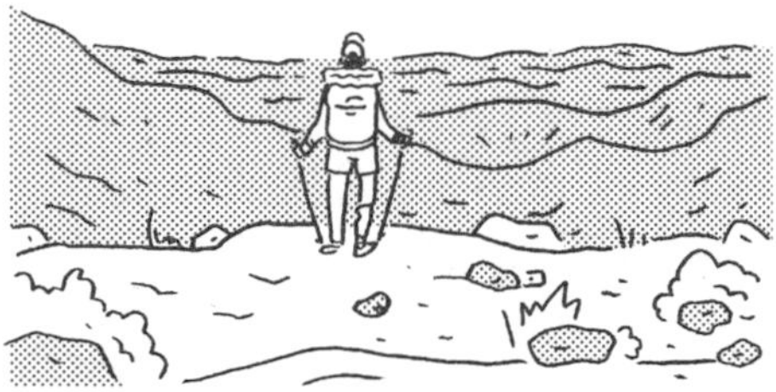

Bridgeport 04/07/16. Day 80.

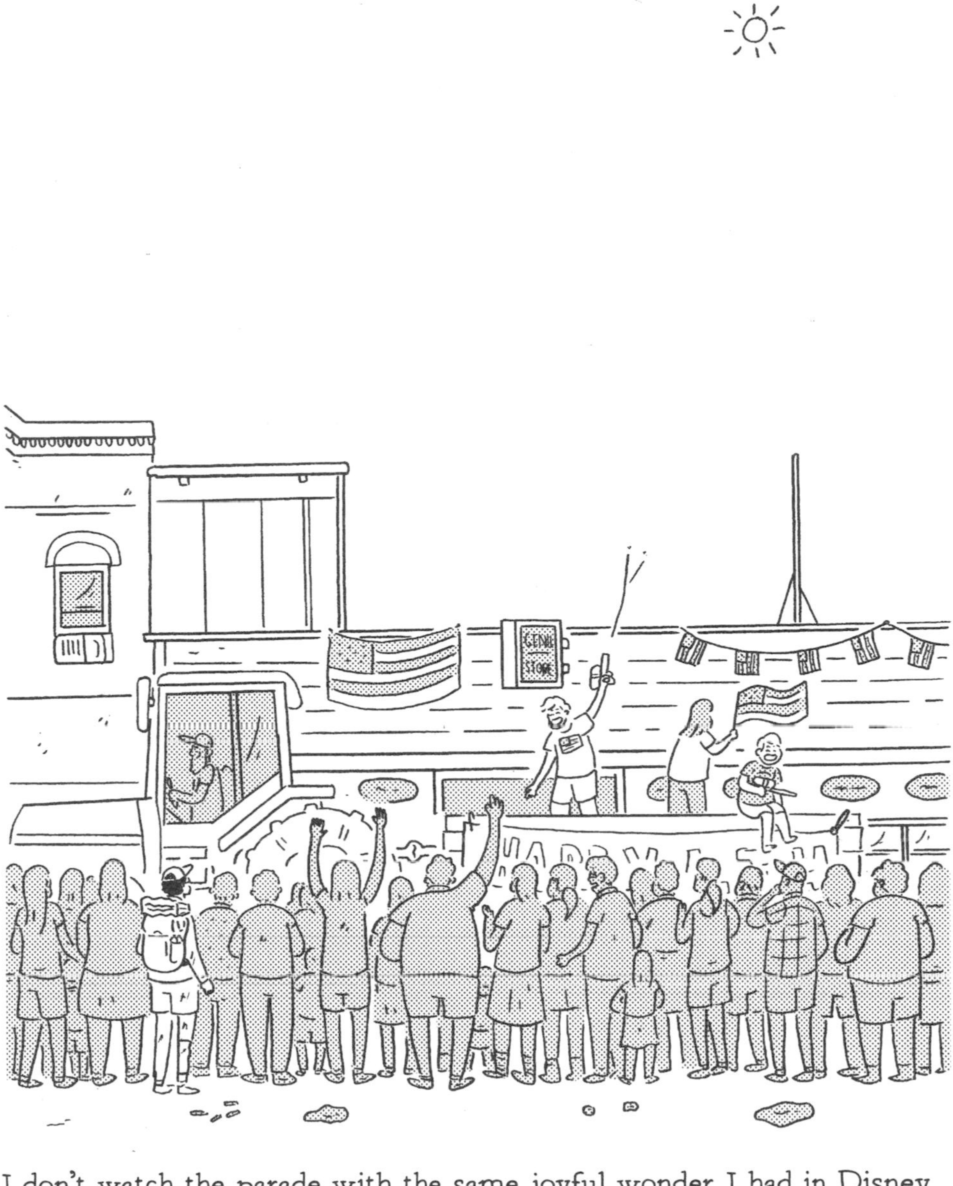

I don't watch the parade with the same joyful wonder I had in Disney World as a child. I feel like an abberation, standing filthy in my dull, brown hiking gear amongst the clean glamour of the red, white and blue. I feel separate; strange to everyone.

I think about the shooting in Orlando. I wonder if any people here would like to shoot me.

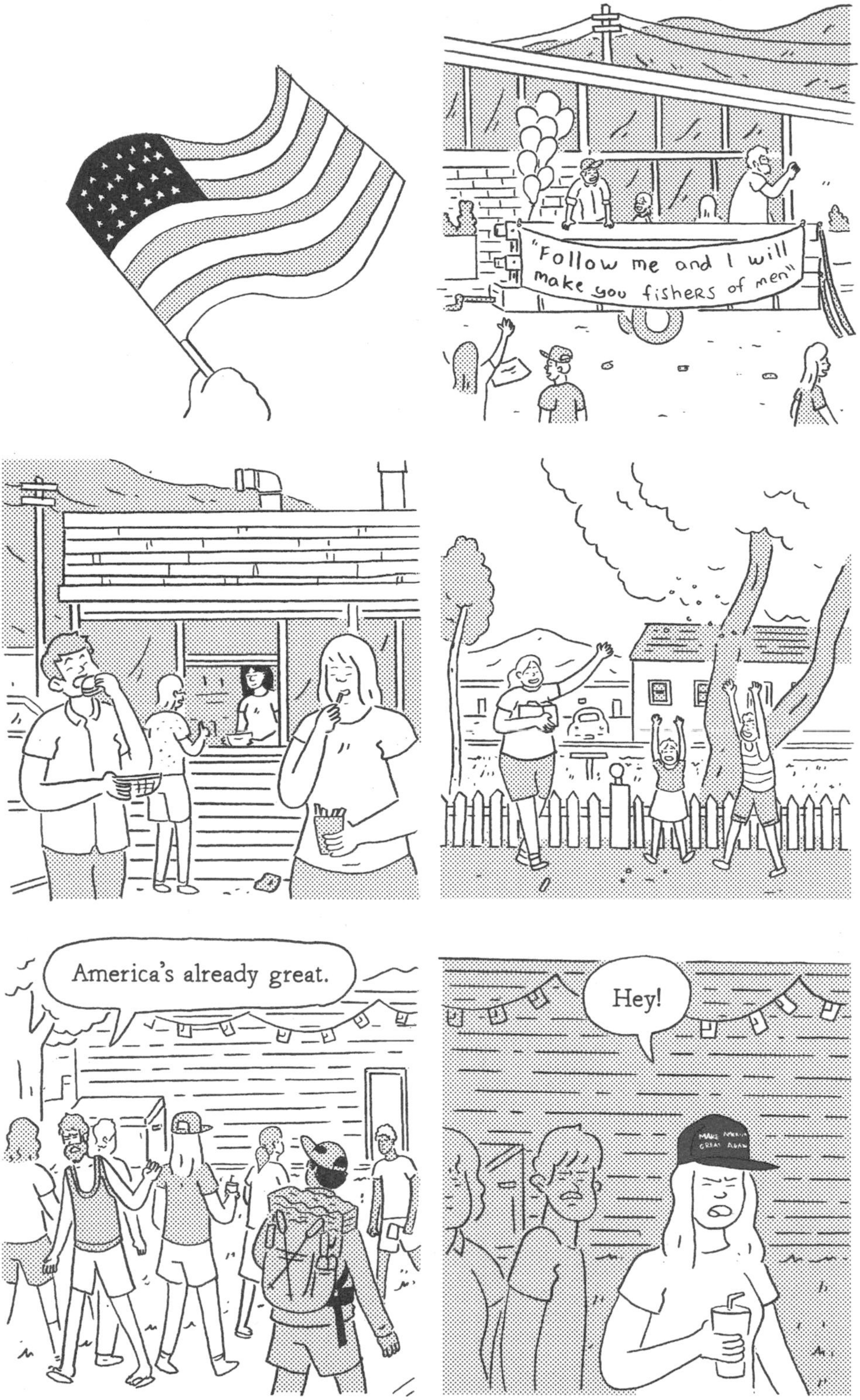
"Follow me and I will make you fishers of men"
America's already great.
Hey!

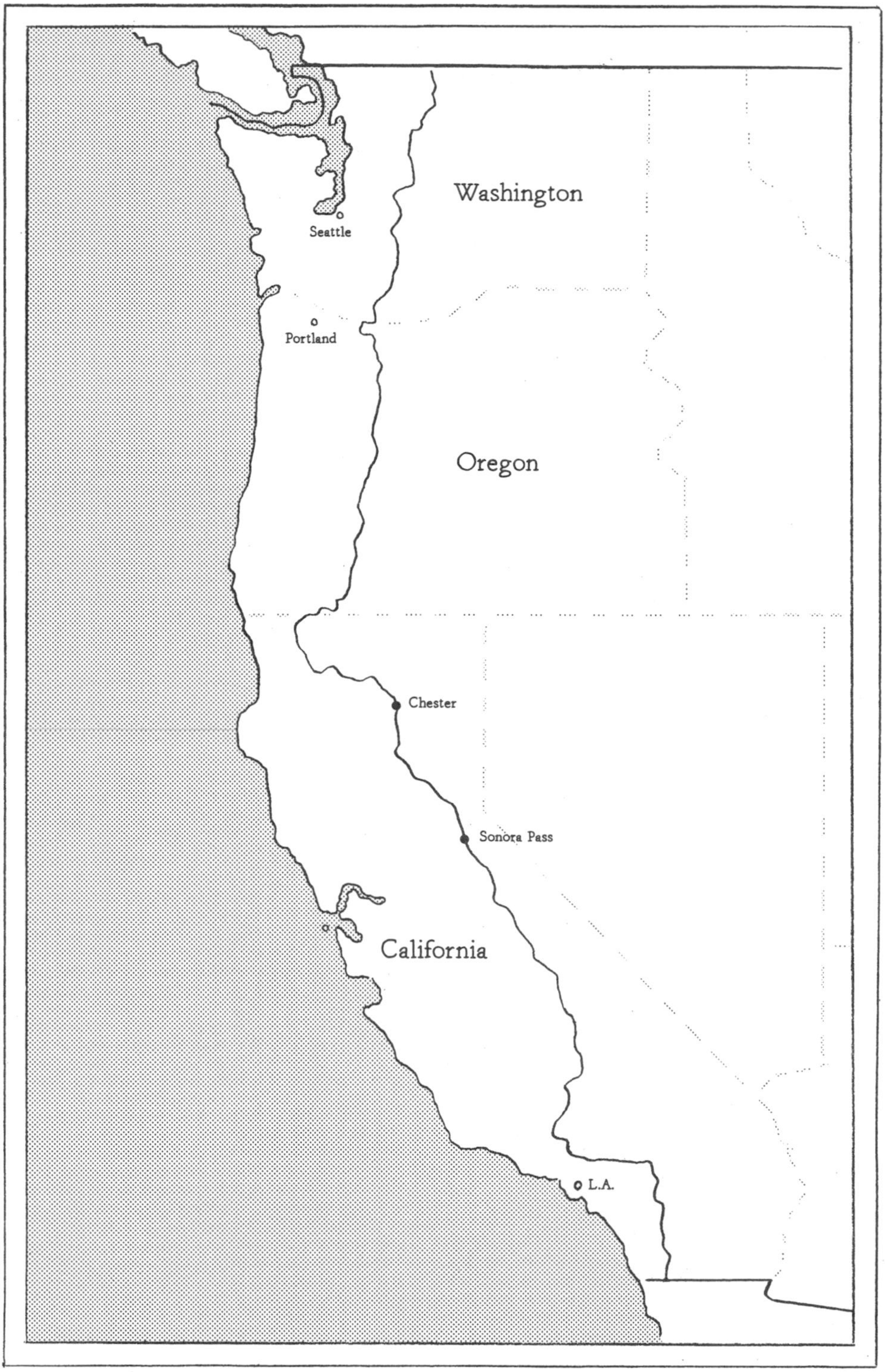
Washington
Seattle
Portland
Oregon
Chester
Sonora Pass
California
L.A.

Chapter 4: Northern California (Part I)

"I wanted real adventures to happen to
myself. But real adventures, I reflected,
do not happen to people who remain at
home: they must be sought abroad."
–James Joyce, *Dubliners*

Moving back to Ireland after my time in White River Junction was
challenging. I took it badly, more than I had any justification to. I was
depressed, and angry, and resentful.

More so, though, I felt lost. I'd invested myself so fully in moving
to America and studying comics, that now I'd finished, I had no
direction left. The needle of my compass was left spinning.

And Ireland provided no immediate answers. That summer,
I loafed in a cloud that wouldn't lift. Reading books and half-heartedly
making plans from the privileged comfort of my parents' suburban
home. That summer, too, I attended my first funeral, my great aunt's.
My family gathered in her home for her wake, an Irish funeral tradition
where the deceased's body is laid out to be visited. Dressed in black,
my family mourned. My grandfather sat strong in the living room,
presiding over her body. Everyone stood and prayed in unison; the Our
Father prayer I'd recited thousands of times as a child. I didn't join in.
I couldn't remember the words.

Later in the evening, boxes of photos emerged, yellowed with age. They were passed around and anecdotes were told – stories new to me. Many photos were of New York City, where my grandfather and his sister had lived earlier in life. I sat beside my mother as we looked through the photos, while she said things like, "Oh, remember him, Luke? We visited him in Boston when you were little."

I'd always just considered my American family to be "distantly related". Not truly part of our lives. When I met them as a child, I couldn't really understand how we were connected. We were "cousins" or "second cousins" or "first cousins, twice removed" depending on the household. It was only then, looking through that box of photographs, that I began to understand the threads of our relationship.

My grandfather's sister moved to the United States in the 1950s, the first of her family to emigrate. While working as a nurse in London, she met and married a G.I., following him to New York then bringing her family over after her. First, her sister, then her mother, then my grandfather and his brother. A full scale Irish exodus.

1950s New York is a much mythologised time and place for the Irish. It was a time of massive emigration, when young people from all over rural Ireland were forced to travel abroad in search of employment. The volume of plays, books and films about mid-century Irish travels to New York is basically innumerable.

The wake was the first time I saw pictures of my grandfather there. It was easy to understand the romance of the place in those little monochrome squares, capturing Central Park in the snow. My grandfather wore a long grey trench coat and brimmed hat. He smiled wide. A young man, my age.

My grandfather's family put down roots in the USA. His sisters and brother got married to Americans. They worked service jobs in restaurants and hotels. They had kids, joined unions, bought houses. Made lives. My grandfather worked for Canada Dry – the soda company whose ginger ale I'd drink on my lunch breaks in White River Junction.

My grandfather was the first of his family to return to Ireland.

"He didn't understand it there," my father once told me. "He didn't want to work just so he could survive. He wanted a life."

He moved back to Ireland the same year he'd left and his mother followed. He worked for the national Irish railway as a train conductor, met my grandmother and they married. My father was their first child, to be followed by six more.

They bought a house, and paid their mortgage with cheques sent home every Christmas by his two sisters.

"That's the reason we got to have Christmas as kids," my dad told me. "Because of the money from America."

My grandfather never really talked about living in America. Even while we were looking through the photos. Even when I told him I was moving there. I don't think it occurred to him to.

At the wake, he sat beside his sister, until he and she were the only ones left in the living room.

Every section of the PCT has its own reputation.

Thruhikers say two things about Northern California – that it is easy, and that it is boring. After the desert, Northern California is the section that inspires the most thruhikers to throw in the towel. Not because it is punishing but because the trail becomes dull there, a stark contrast to the awe-inspiring majesty of the High Sierras.

I could honestly use some boring.

I wake early on July 5th, excited to be in the promised land of easy hiking. I blast punk music in my headphones and power down the trail. I stop for nothing. I feel amazing. I wear the burning in my muscles like a merit badge.

The trail transitions into softer, forested hills with surprising speed. I eat miles for breakfast, half aided by the easier trail, half pushing to confirm its reputation.

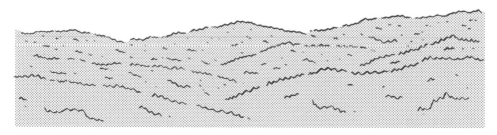

A barely-visible mobile phone tower sits off in the distance.

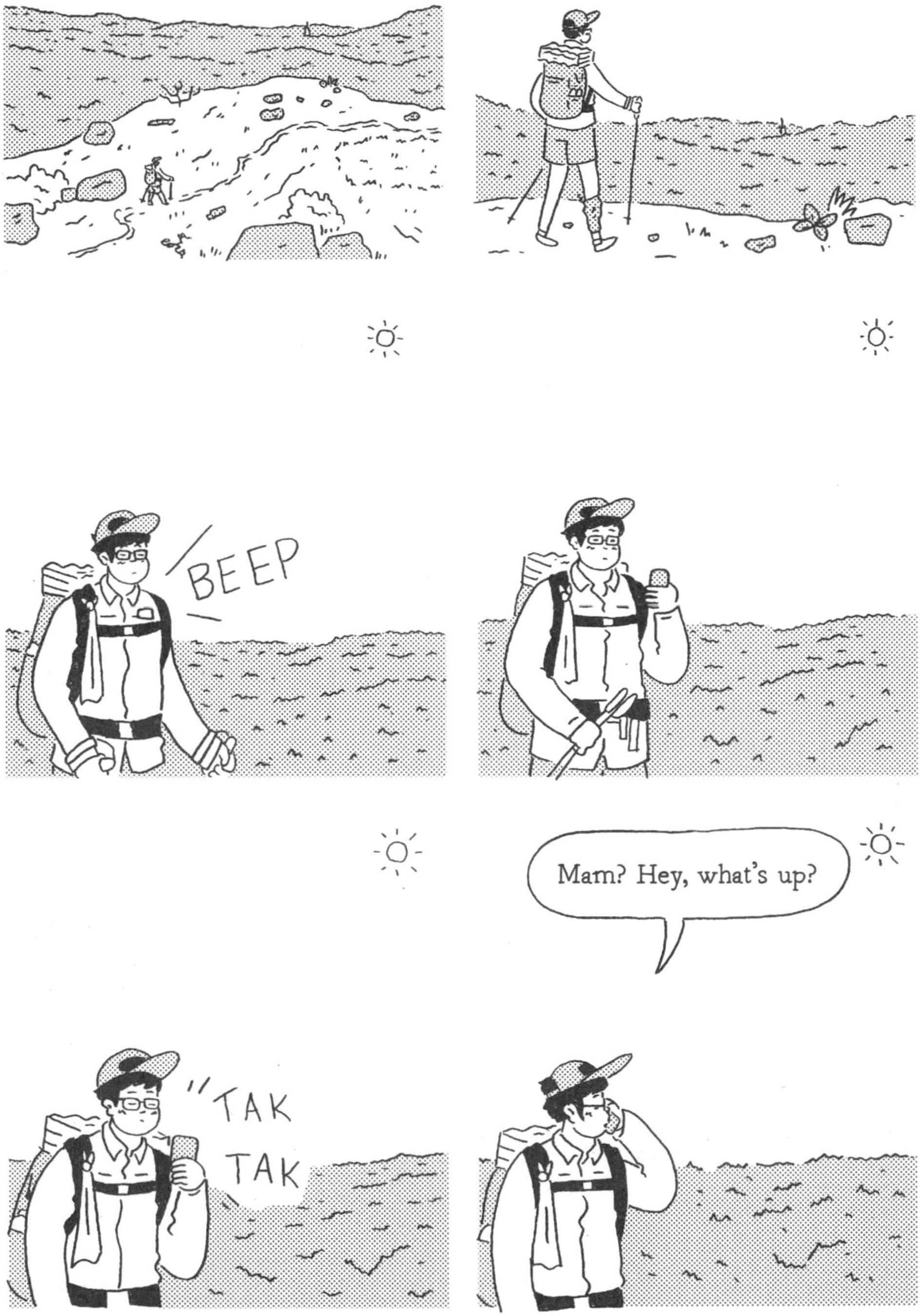
BEEP
TAK
TAK
Mam? Hey, what's up?

Luke... I have some bad news.
MAM
Your grandad. Your dad's dad... is in the hospital.
MAM
Well... It looks like he is going to die.
MAM
MAM
I... *ahem* I'll get to town. I'll call you back. Soon.

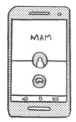

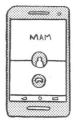

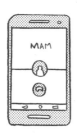

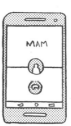

Tak
Tak

Tak
Tak

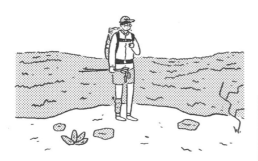

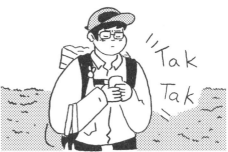

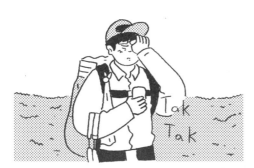

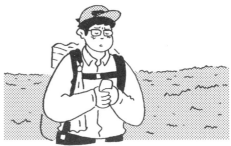

Hike, Luke.

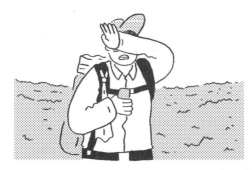

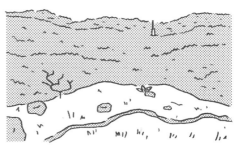

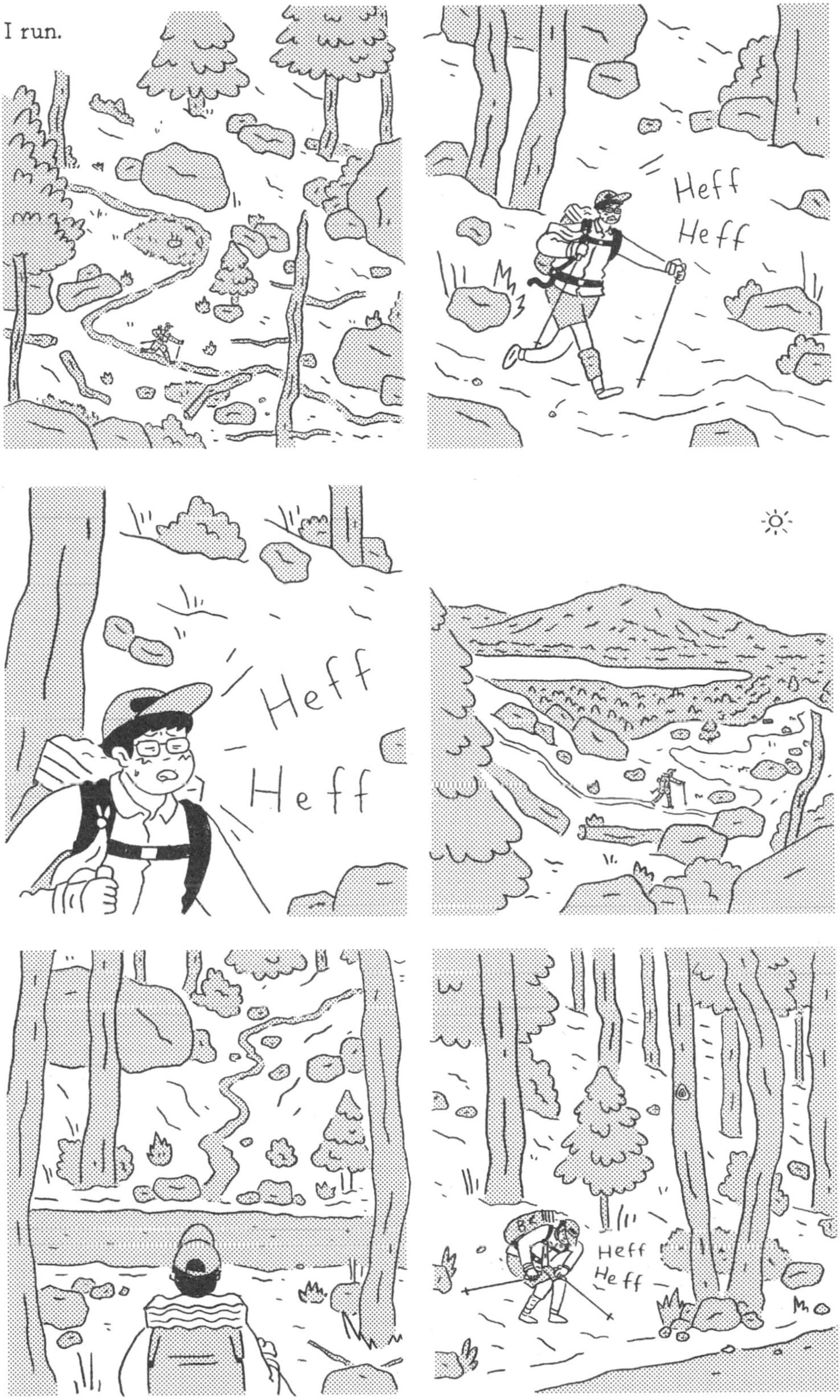

I run.
Heff
Heff
Heff
Heff
Heff
Heff

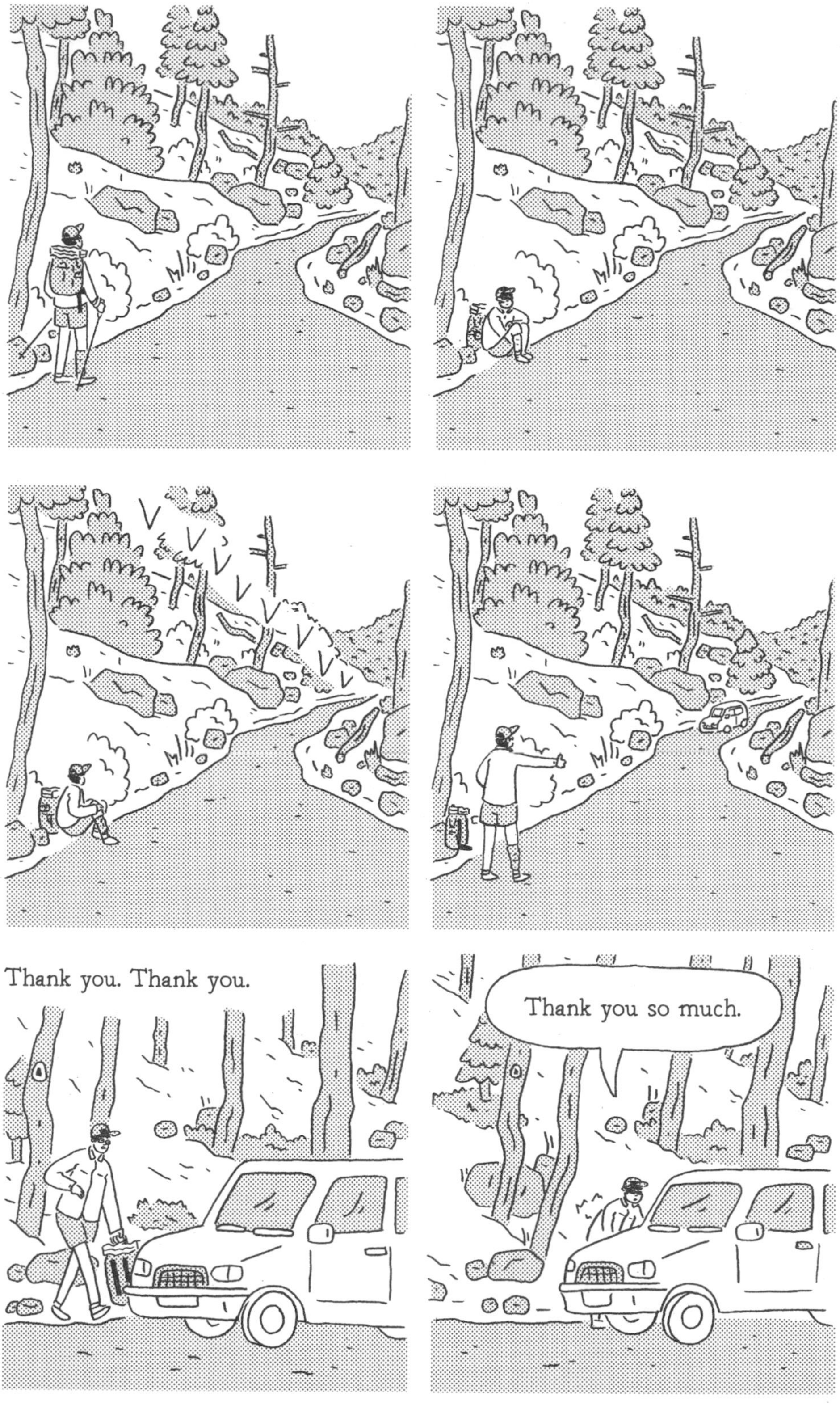
Thank you. Thank you.
Thank you so much.

I ride anxiously to South Lake Tahoe. Within an hour, I'm left by the intersection of two busy roads on the edge of town. I try to stay calm.

I try my luck at a shitty chain motel which is within walking distance. The owner practically flinches when I enter. Bad experiences with hikers, maybe.

"Excuse me. Do you have any rooms available for tonight?"

"Hmmm, I'm not sure. Not sure. We are very full. If you come back after we service the rooms, I can let you know."

It's already 3 pm. The rooms have obviously been serviced by now. Their parking lot is practically empty. I hold my tongue, and decide to call him on his bluff.

"Ok. Thank you."

When I return to the motel hours later, the owner looks disappointed, and when it becomes obvious to him that I am severely low on patience, he rents me a room.

I shower, then take a bath. I walk to the grocery store and buy way more food than I can eat. I sit on the lawn outside of the motel, and connect to their wifi. And I call home.

"We're just not sure right now, but it doesn't look good."

I'm not sure what to do. I feel cruel even thinking that I have options. Wouldn't a good person immediately rush home? Wouldn't they stop at nothing to see their grandfather again, one last time?

I could try to find a bus from here. Check all the airlines. Do my best. Even if I left now, it would take at least four days to get there.

"We really don't know anything, Luke. He could die tonight. You could miss him. You could miss the funeral, even. He's not eating. They won't let him eat."

I'm quiet. I'm not sure what to say, or do. "Maybe I should just... sleep on it. Wait until tomorrow. Stay in town. Stay in touch."

"He's happy. I should say that. He sang me Happy Birthday today."

I stay for a day without making any decisions, despite the ticking clock. I see three movies. I resupply. I ask myself if resupplying means I've made my decision. I don't know.

My brother flies home to Ireland from London. And my cousins.

I am the only one not there.

On the third morning, I call home.
My dad answers.

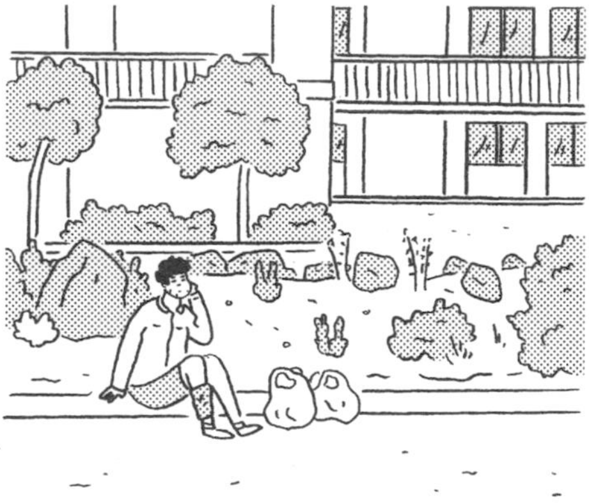

"He's taken a turn for the better.
It looks like he's going to be ok."

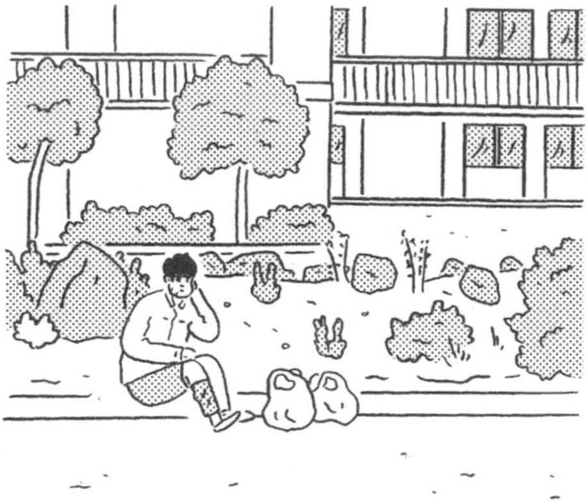

I wonder if he's lying to me.

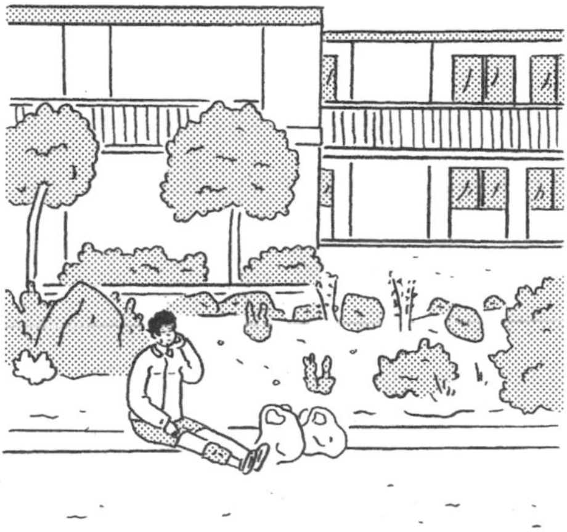

Giving me an out.

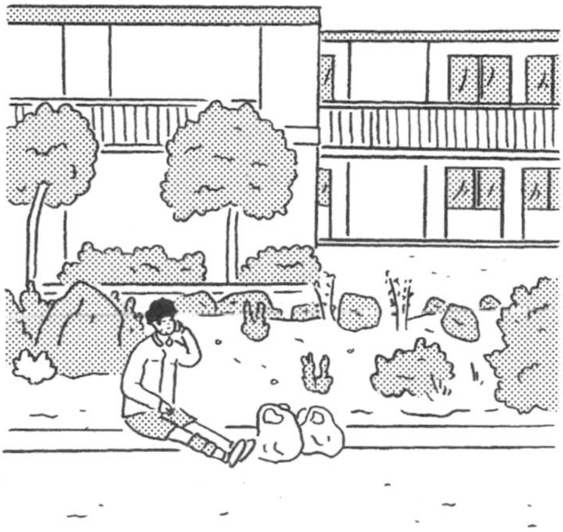

"You should keep hiking,"
he tells me.

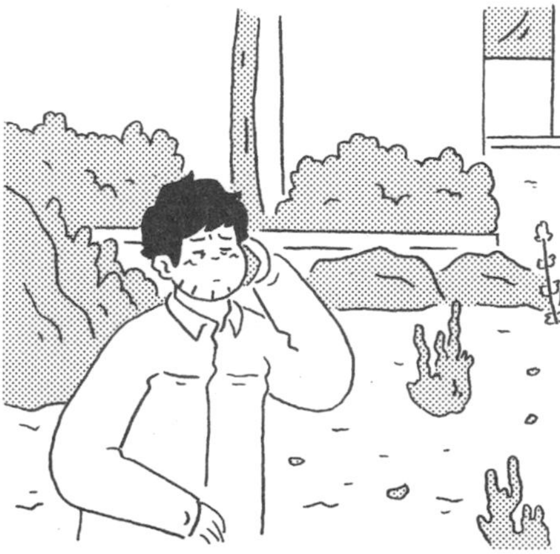

And I do.

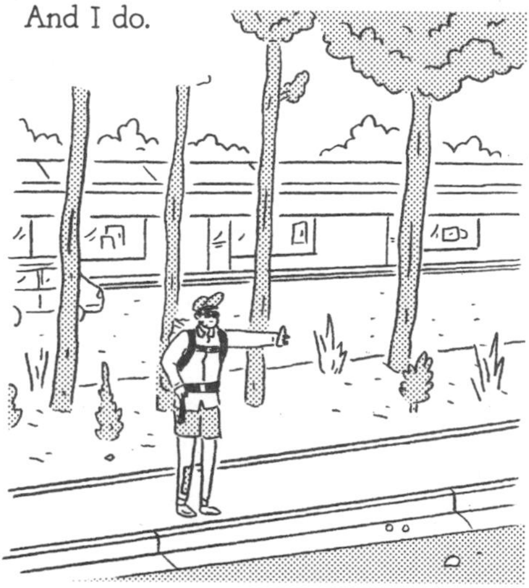

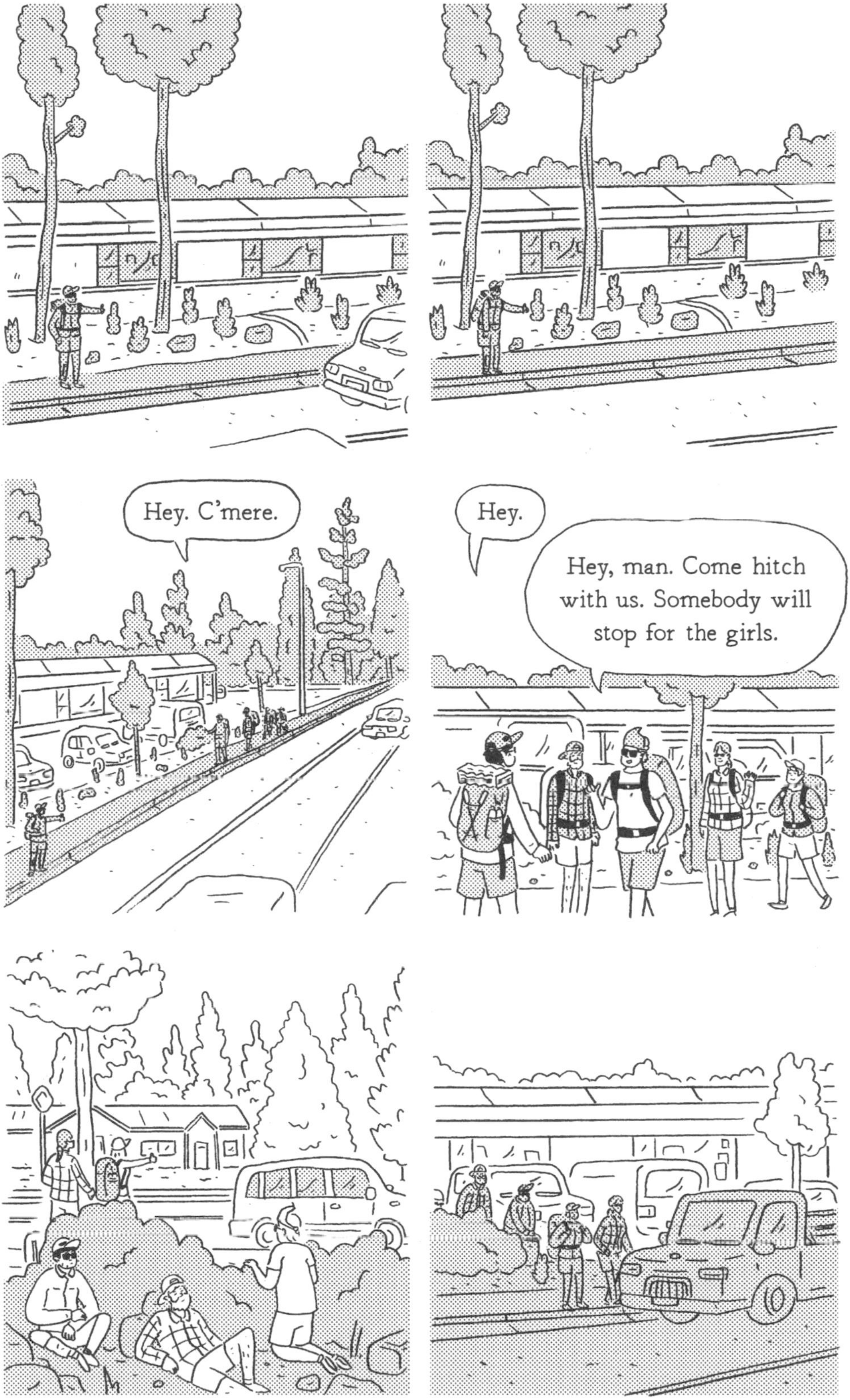
Hey. C'mere.
Hey.
Hey, man. Come hitch with us. Somebody will stop for the girls.

I expect to be distracted by thoughts of home, but my mind goes back into trail mode with surprising ease.

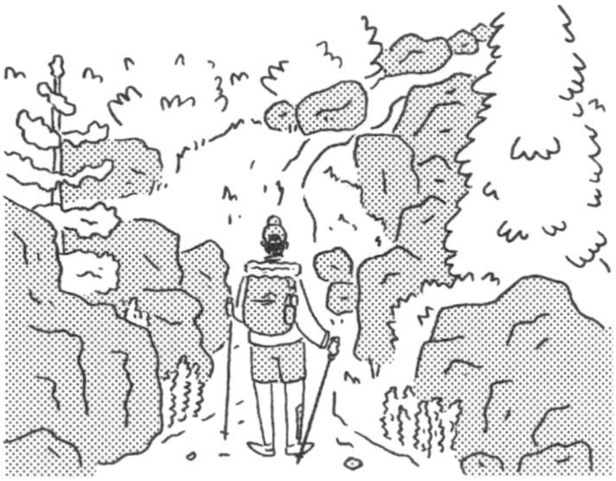

We follow the Tahoe Rim Trail.

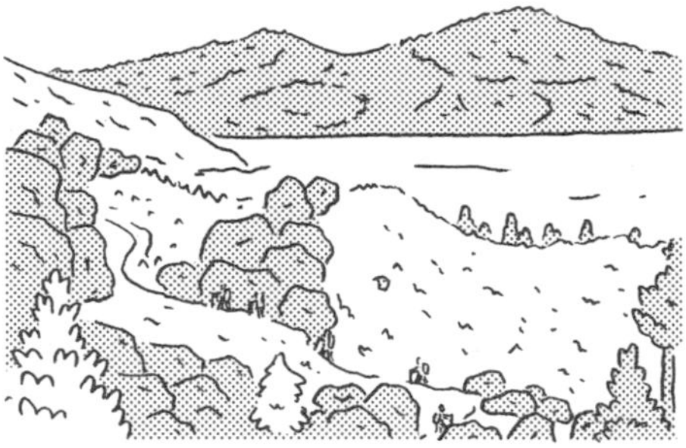

I stick with the hitch-hikers for a little while.

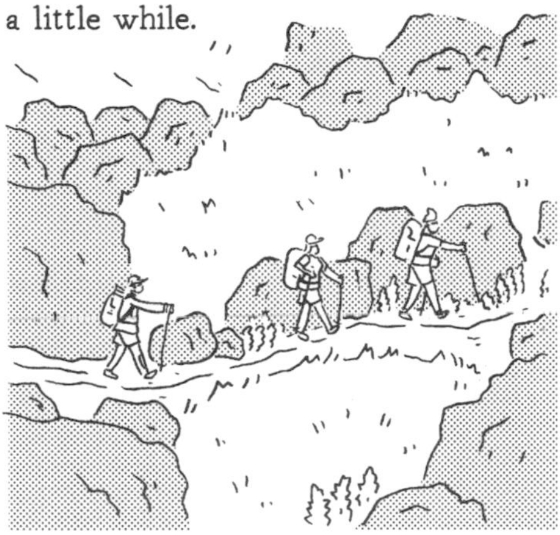

We hike, and chat, and talk about our favourite movies.

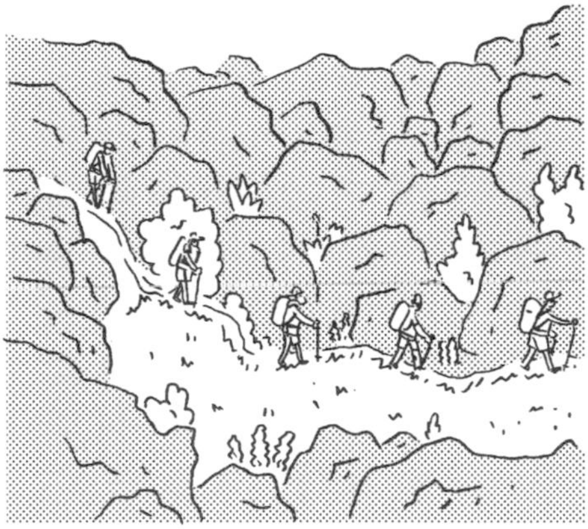

It's easy. I feel good.

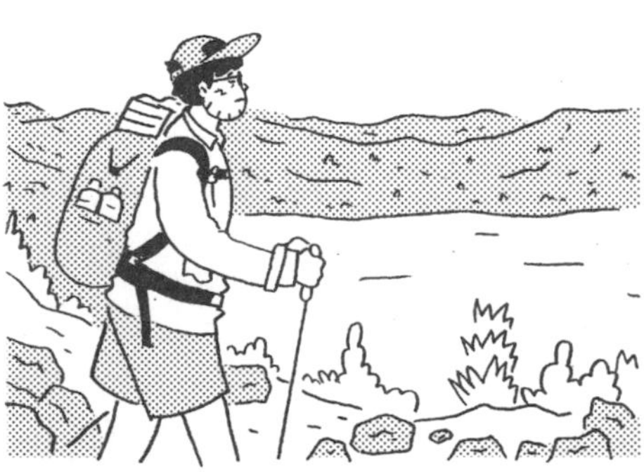

I'm in the promised land.

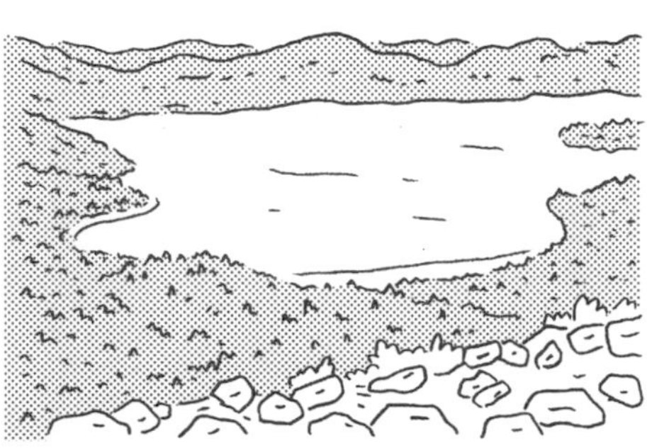

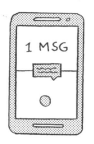

Hi, mam.

How's things?

"We just got some bad news."

My grandfather is going to die, she tells me. For sure this time.

When I'd left Ireland in April, I'd completed the by now familiar ritual of visiting each of my grandparents.

Just like every time I'd moved away, my parents had asked, "Would you like us to tell you if someone dies?"

I'd always scoffed at the idea. Of course they should tell me.

Well, now they've told me.

How's Dad?

She hands the phone over. I can hear
they're in a hospital.

"Ah, now. I'm ok, y'know."

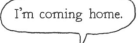

I'm coming home.

I try to plan as I walk, but I am so hungry.

I ran out of food last night.

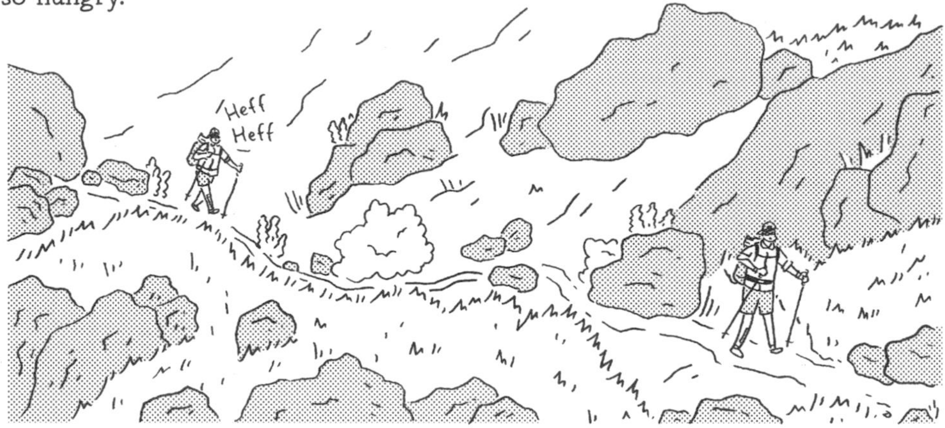
Heff
Heff

In Ireland, the doctors are making my grandfather fast, in case they need to operate.

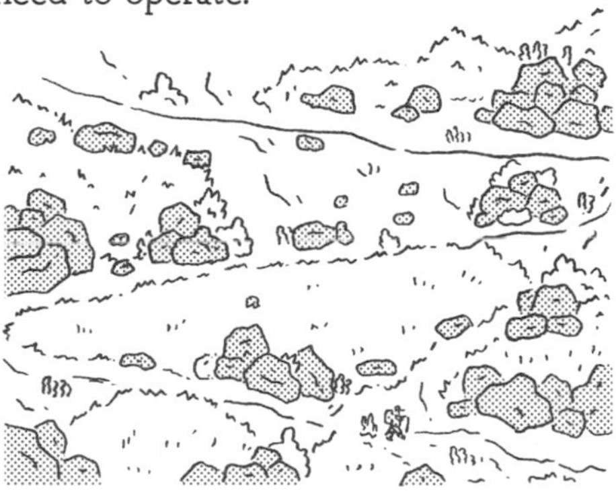

"Listen, Luke. You can do what you want. But I think you shouldn't come home. You should hear him talking about you."

"My grandson is in the middle of the Mojave Desert, and even he has more water than me."

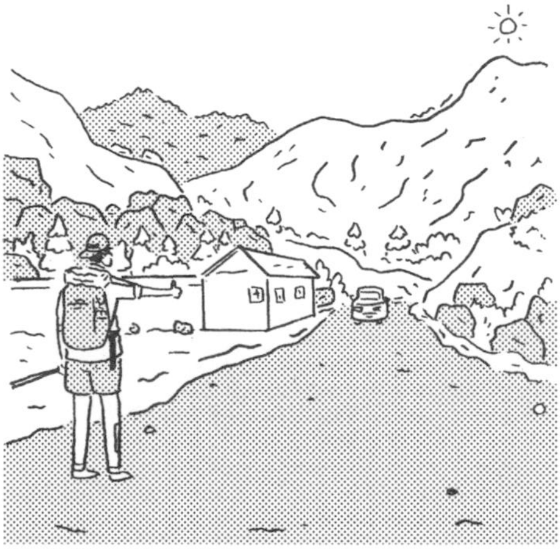

Truckee 11/07/16. Day 87.

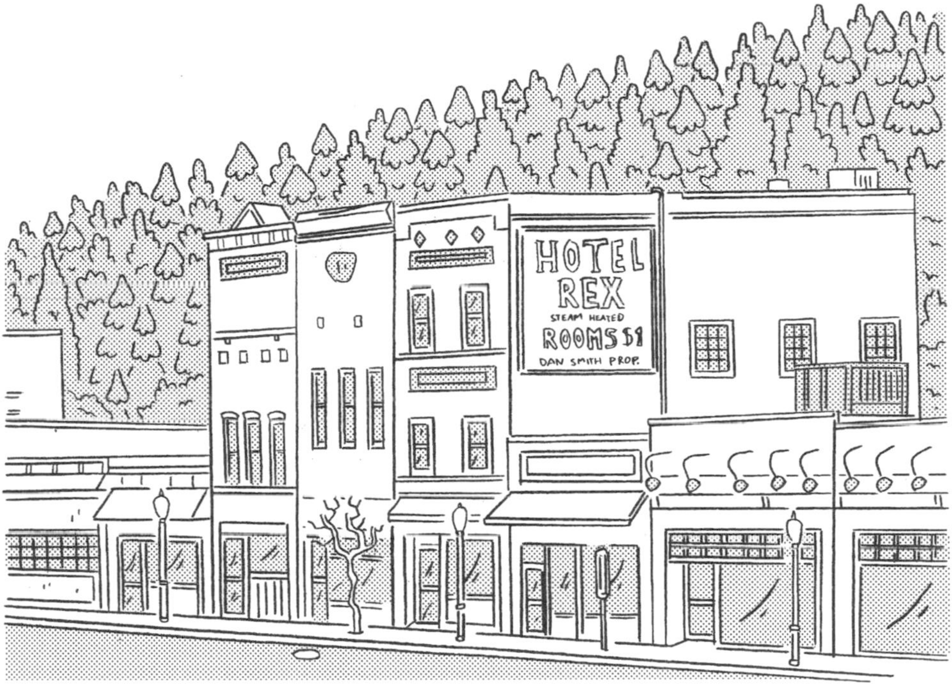
HOTEL
REX
STEAM HEATED
ROOMS $1
DAN SMITH PROP.

I call home, but their phones are busy, so I message some friends. Eleri responds first.

"I just arrived in Portland this morning. Phone call?"

Eleri's back in the USA. I'd forgotten. We'd planned to meet up when I crossed close to Portland, at the end of the Oregon section of the PCT. We talk. I talk, in circles.

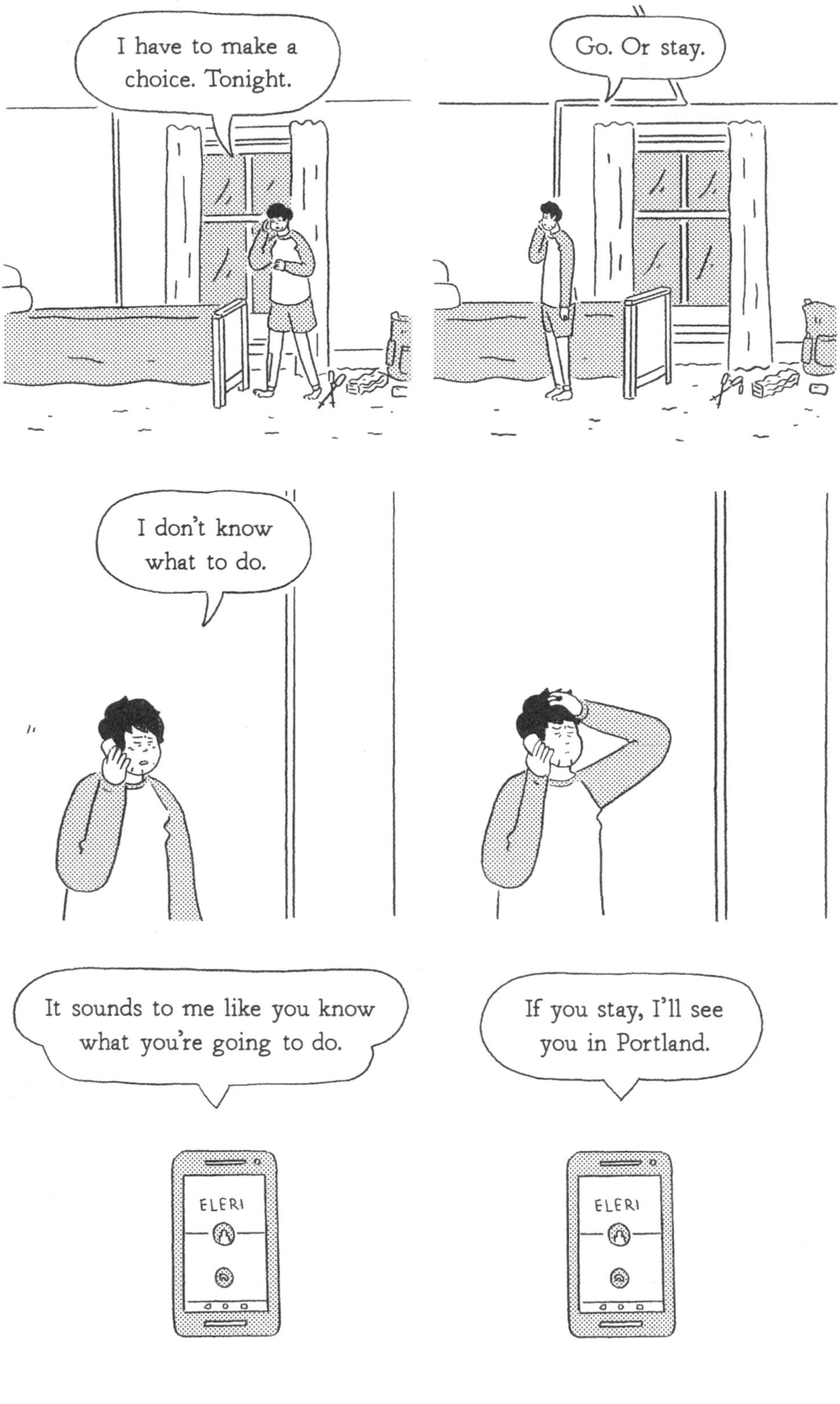
I have to make a choice. Tonight.
Go. Or stay.
I don't know what to do.
It sounds to me like you know what you're going to do.
ELERI
If you stay, I'll see you in Portland.
ELERI

By midnight, it's morning in Ireland. I talk with my mother and brother on the phone.

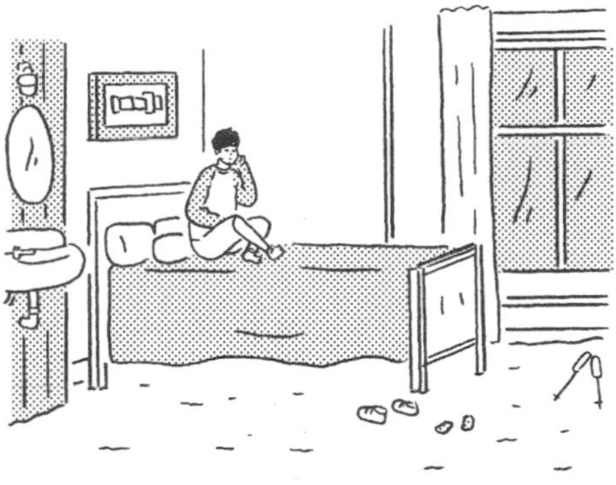

I imagine being there.

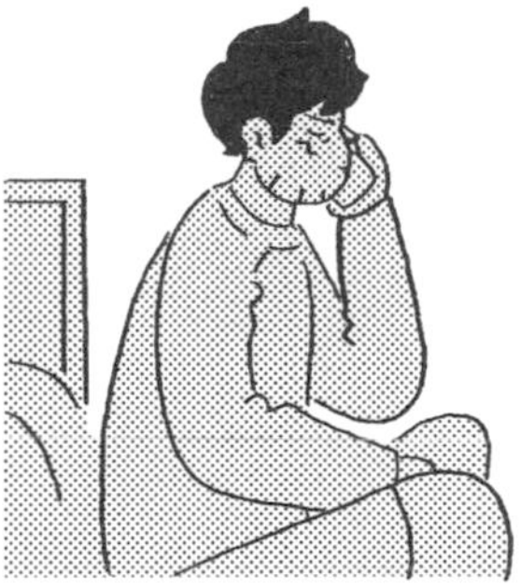

But the hospital I picture in my head must look nothing like where they actually are.

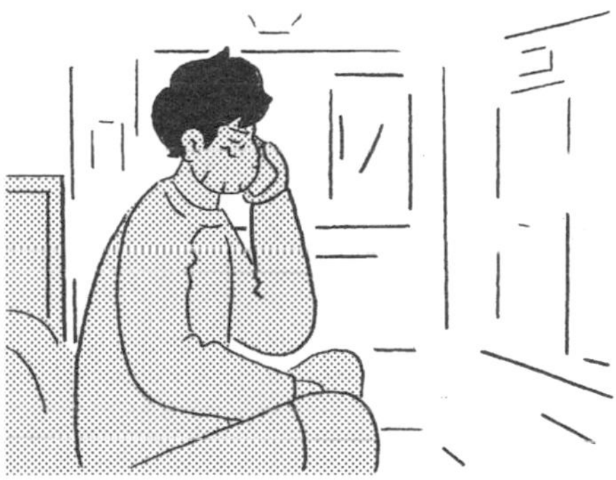

I see them in a waiting room, and the sounds I hear behind their voices add details to the scene.

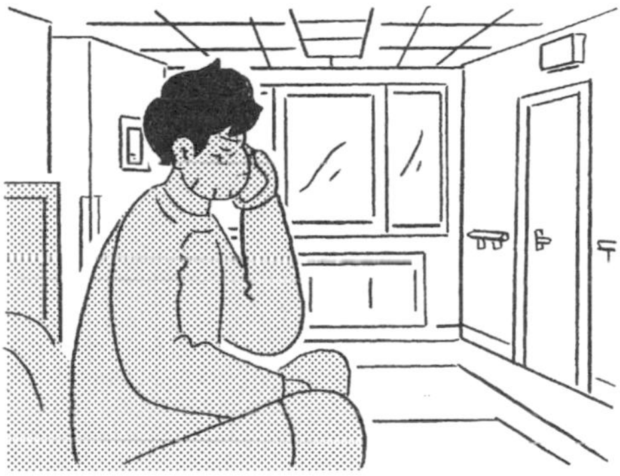

Squeaks become door hinges, echoing footsteps, long corridors. Snatches of conversation from aunts and uncles.

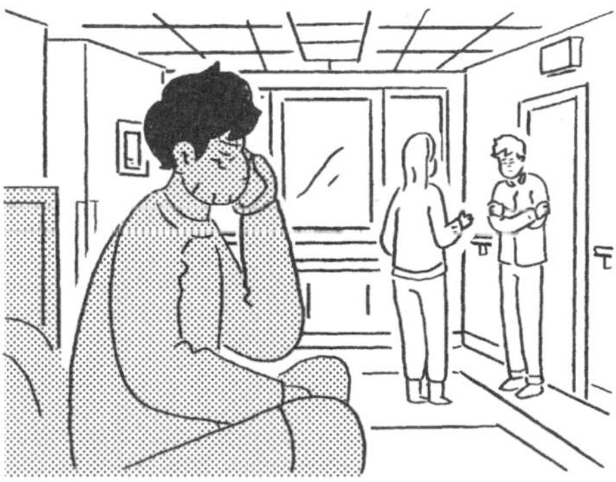

They ask me if I'd like to video chat my grandfather.

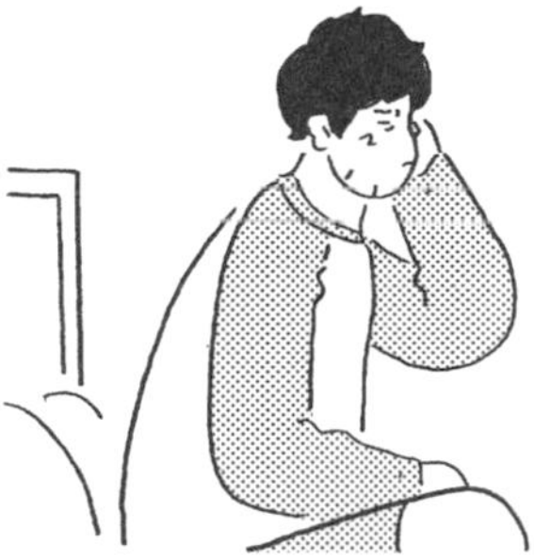

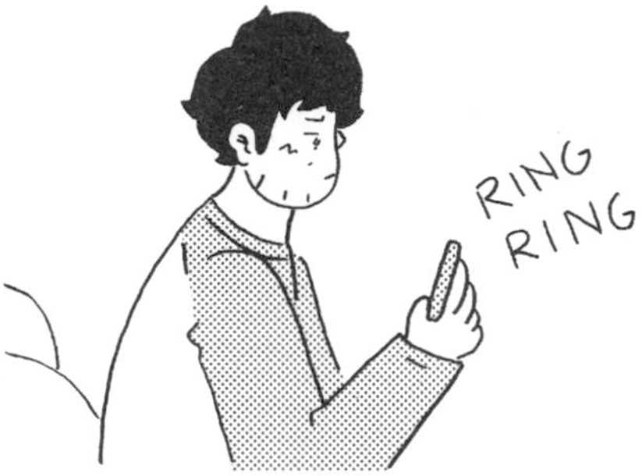
RING
RING

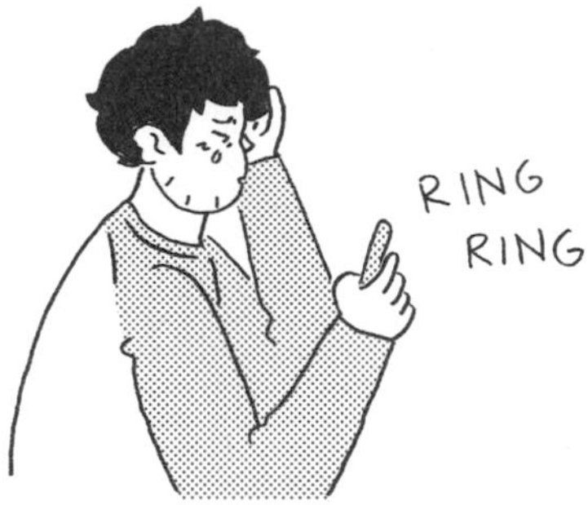
RING
RING

My dad holds his phone at a weird angle. I can only see the corner of my grandfather's head.

"Ah, Mr Luke."

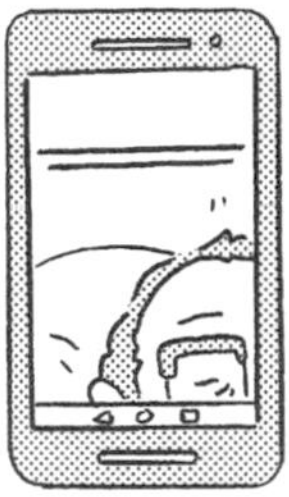

"Would you believe that I can't get a drop of water. Here I am in the wettest country on Earth and you in the middle of the Mojave Desert, with more water than me."

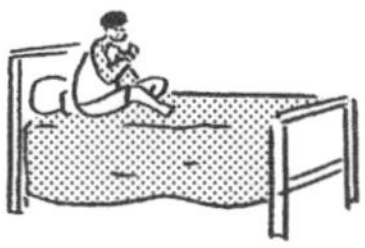

I hike hard, hoping to get between towns quickly, so I can keep up to date with news of my grandfather's health. I know that I am waiting for news of his death.

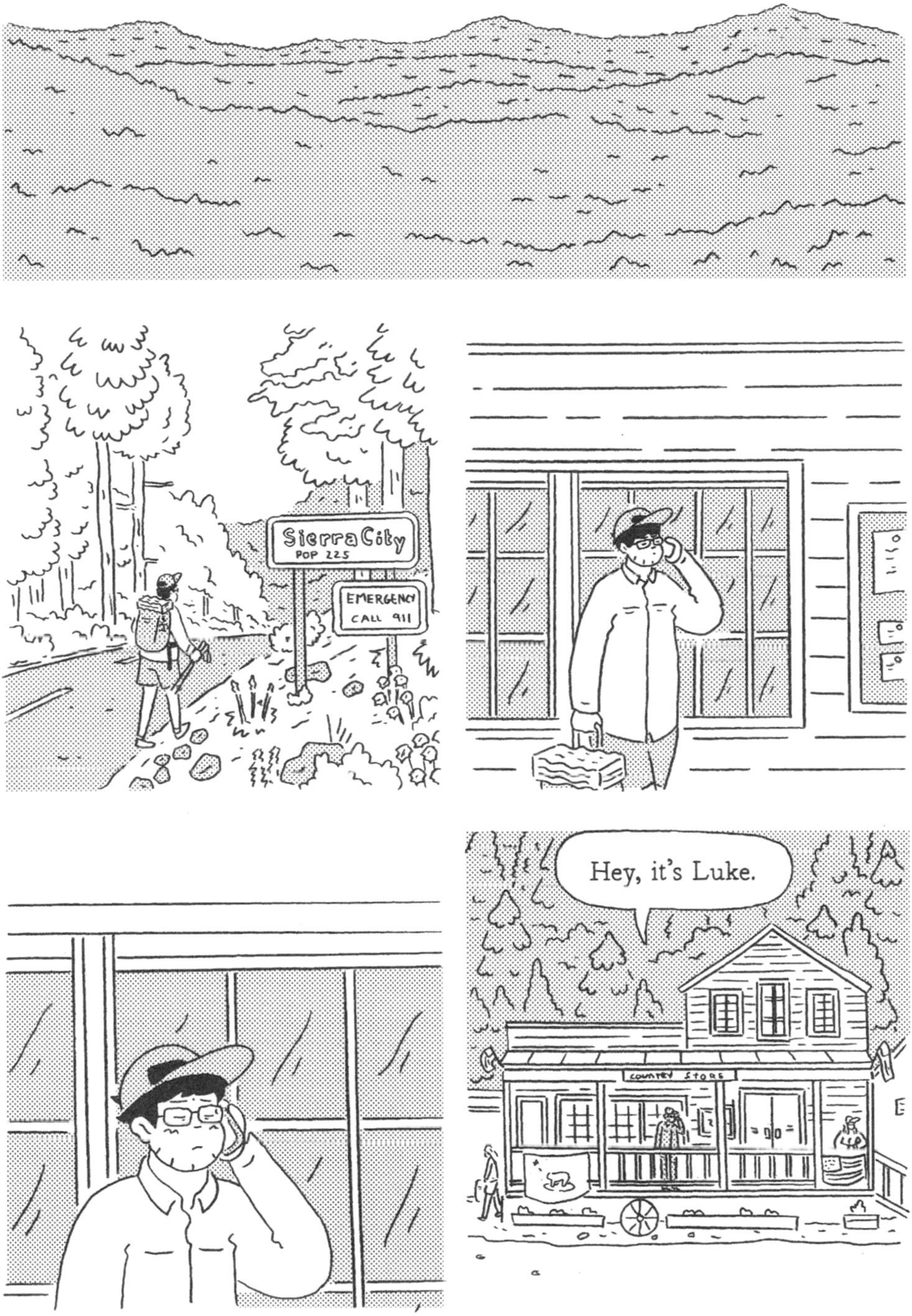
Sierra City
POP 225
EMERGENCY
CALL 911
Hey, it's Luke.
COUNTRY STORE

He's still alive.

They're at the hospital.

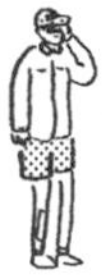

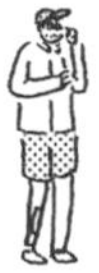

I talk to him.

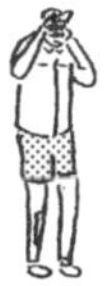

"Would you believe I can't get a drop of water..."

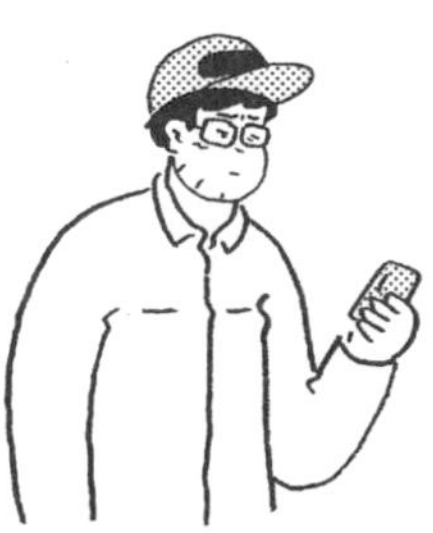

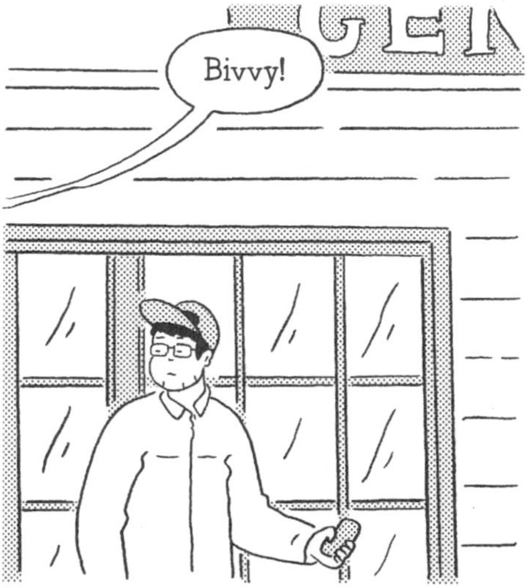
Bivvy!

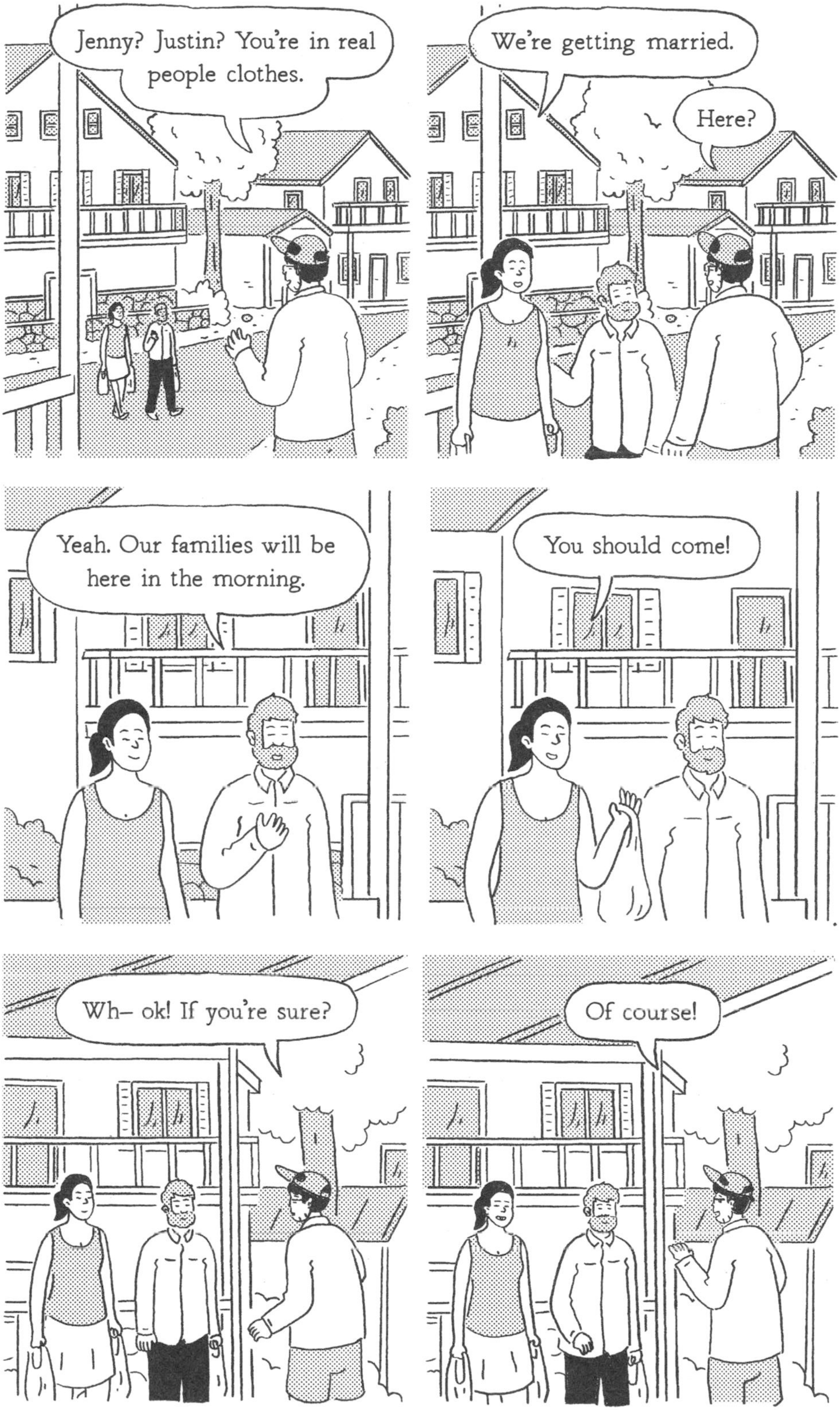
Jenny? Justin? You're in real people clothes.
We're getting married.
Here?
Yeah. Our families will be here in the morning.
You should come!
Wh– ok! If you're sure?
Of course!

I find a wedding card in the town's cramped little general store, and do my best to clean up before walking to the rehearsal dinner. I wear my sleep clothes, a thermal top and my spare pair of shorts, and feel extremely self-conscious when we arrive and see all of Jenny and Justin's family standing around, chatting in fancy suits and dresses.

The toasts are long but sweet. Jenny's college friends recite a poem about cheese, and their siblings each deliver a heartfelt speech. I feel guilty for being there, surrounded by somebody else's family while my own gathers around without me for a very different reason.

Jenny's brother, who is emceeing the toasts, cracks a joke about the thruhikers in attendance. We grin sheepishly and wave.

"And none of you are going to give a speech?" he jokes.

Three glasses of wine encourage me to stand up and prove him wrong.

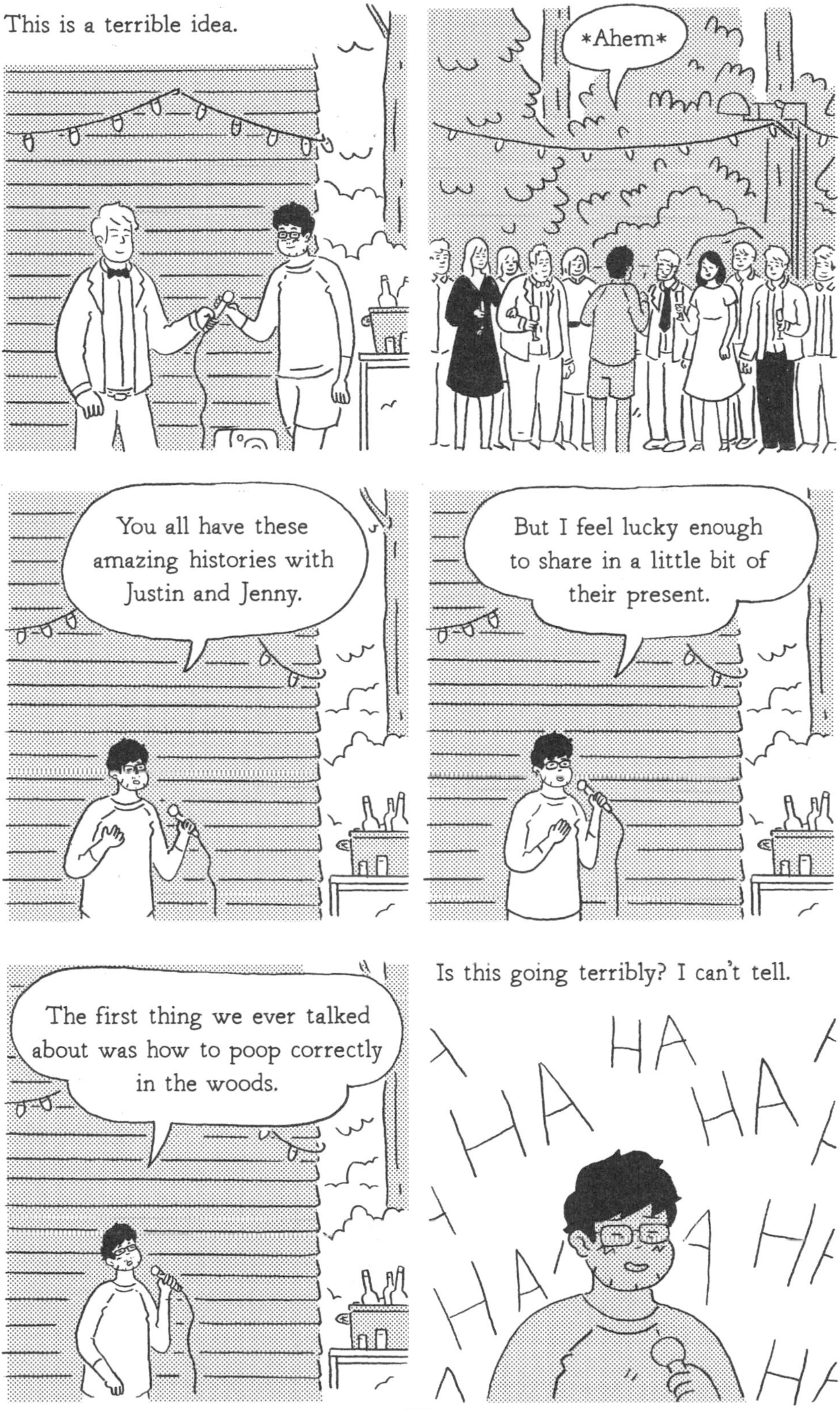
This is a terrible idea.
Ahem
You all have these amazing histories with Justin and Jenny.
But I feel lucky enough to share in a little bit of their present.
The first thing we ever talked about was how to poop correctly in the woods.
Is this going terribly? I can't tell.
HA HA HA HA HA

I sleep behind a picnic table, at the little public toilets in Sierra City.

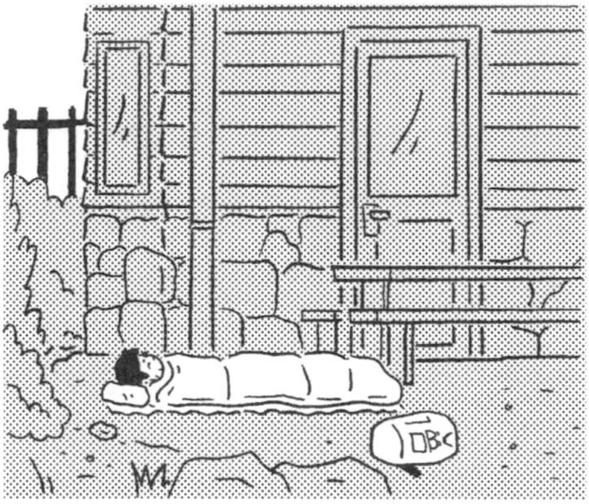

Another hiker snores somewhere nearby.

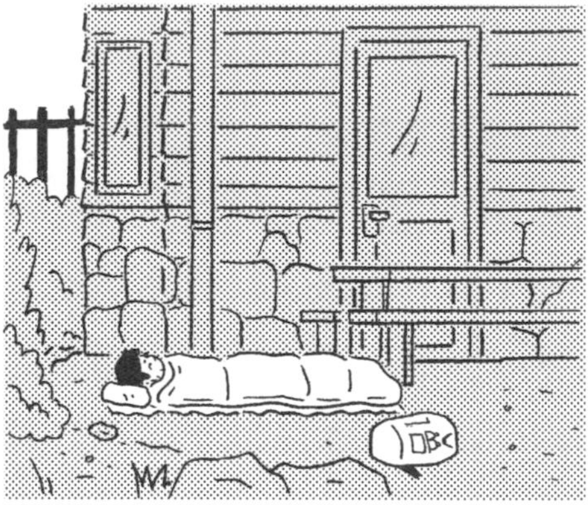

I can't see the stars here quite like I could in the desert.

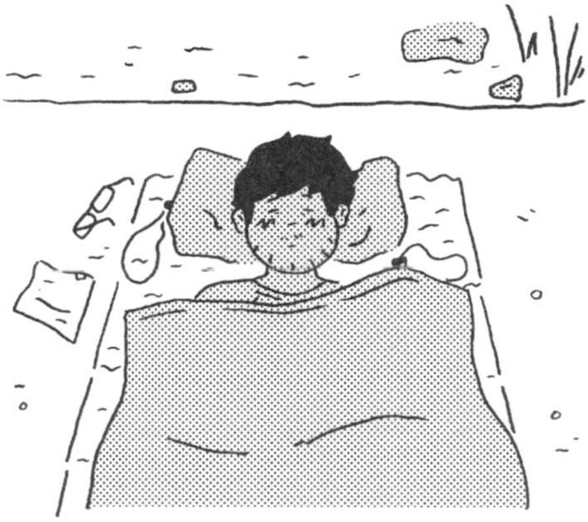

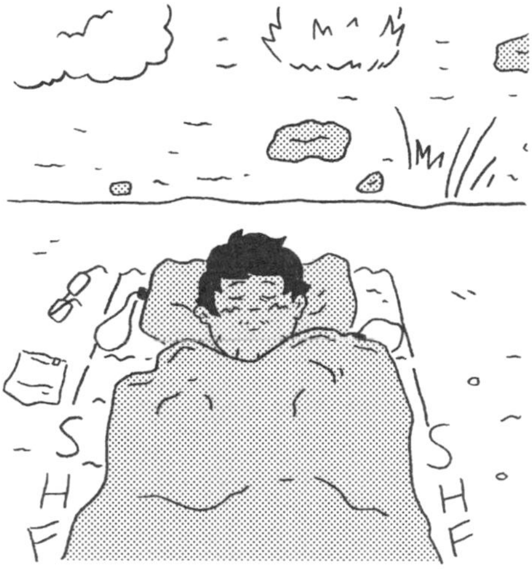
SHF
SHF

I leave town early, before the wedding.

I'm not sure why.

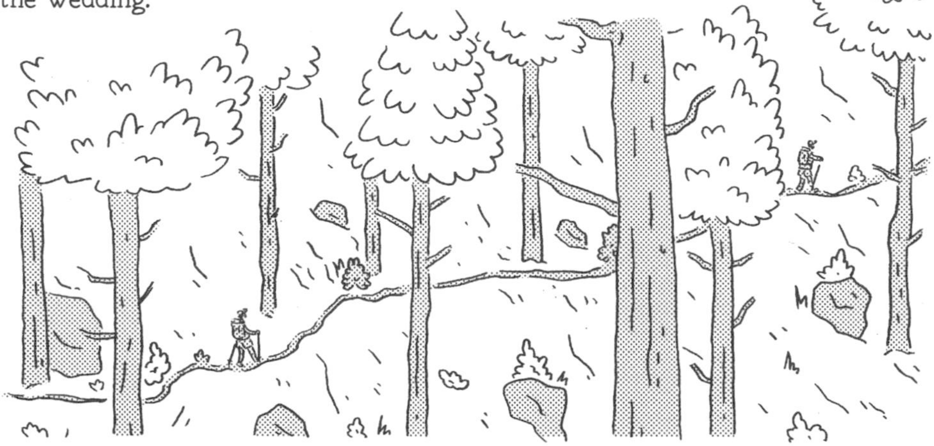

The promised land continues to flow beneath my feet. I fall in and out with crews of hikers, and enjoy their company. Mile 55 is still fractured, though I check on their progress online whenever I reach a town. I thought maybe if I hiked hard, I'd eventually catch up to them, but now everyone is hiking hard. We can feel the winter season lurking in the distance, promising to close the hiking window in just a couple of months. They maintain a steady distance.

The wait for news about my grandfather continues, too. He holds on, though the news I hear is never good, really.

The landscape in this part of California is lush and gorgeous. For the first time, I hike through real, dense forest. I pull twenty-five-mile days consistently now and feel a little less tired every day doing it.

I cowboy camp, somewhat confidently, until one night I'm woken by a fellow hiker's shouts of terror when he's nudged awake by a deer trying to lick the salt from his trekking poles.

I get texts from Stacy and tall, wise Ramon, who both tell me they've quit. They each got homesick and decided to call it. I, homesick, stubbornly stay on my path, despite the obvious consequences.

And I wait. And the miles fall away. And I wait.

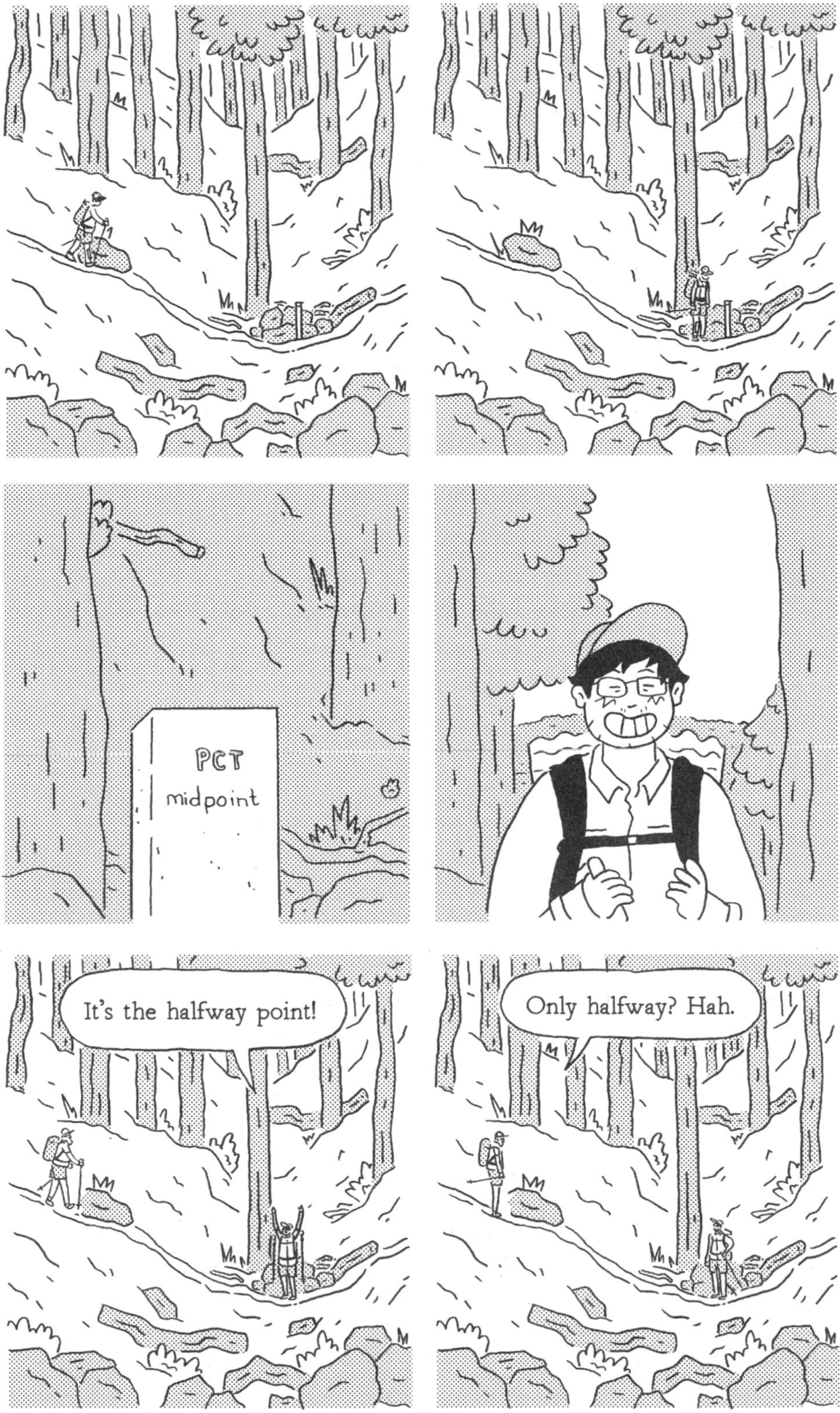
PCT
midpoint
It's the halfway point!
Only halfway? Hah.

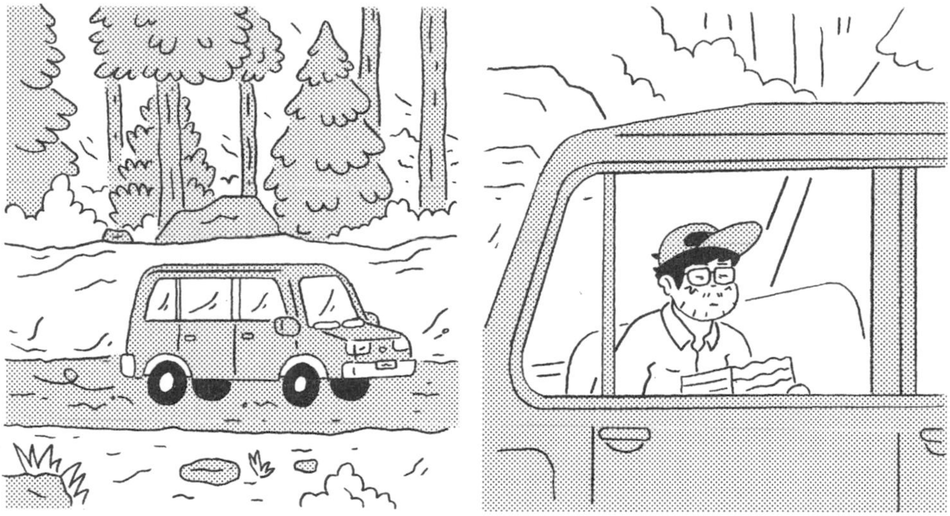

Chester 23/07/16. Day 99.

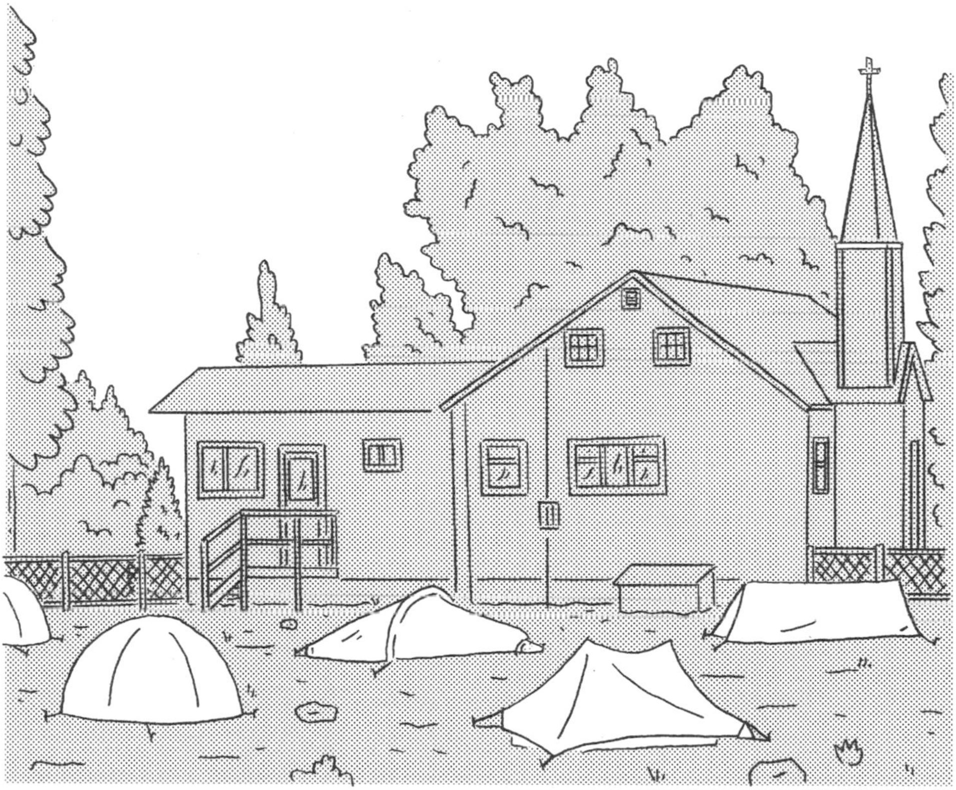

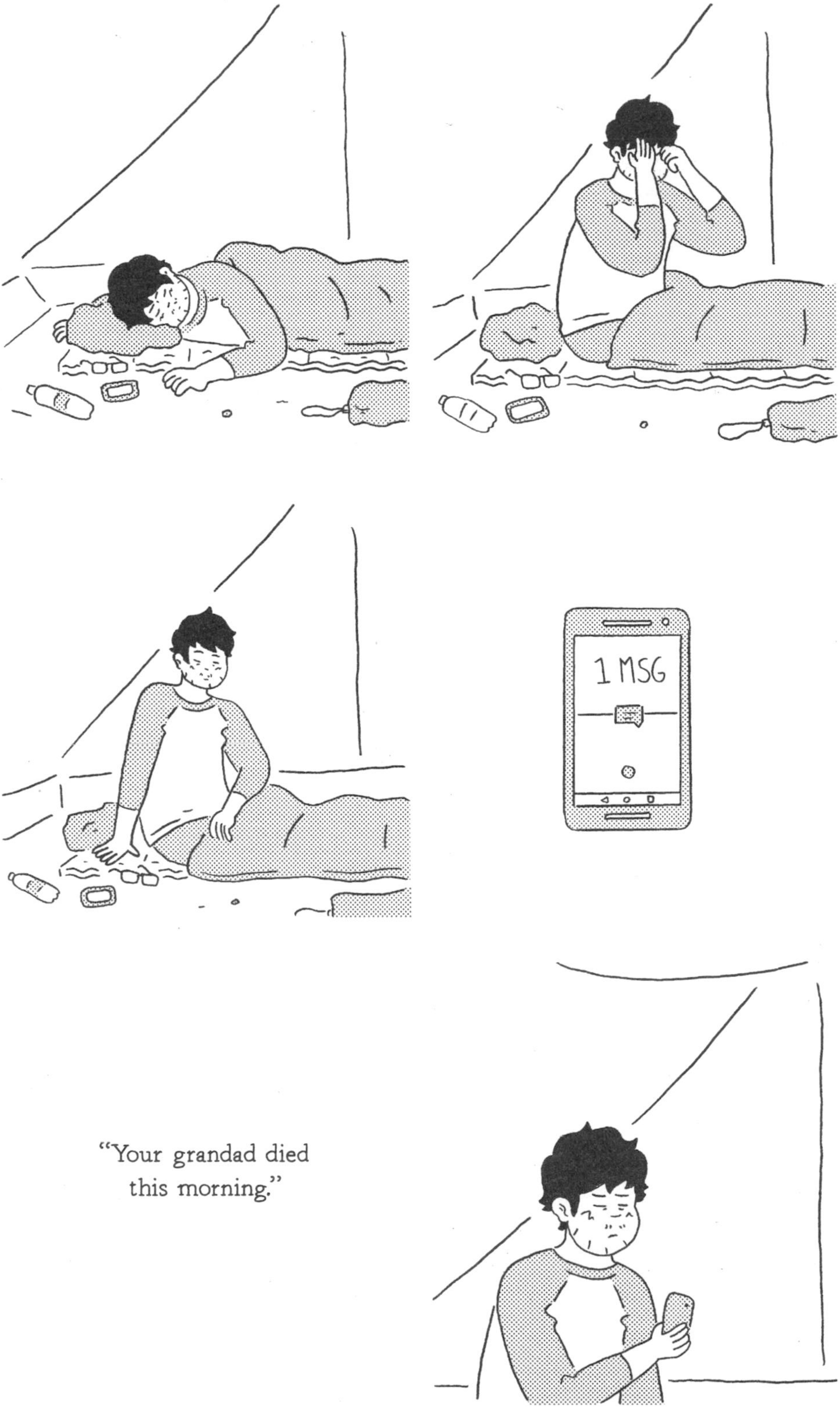
1 MSG
"Your grandad died this morning."

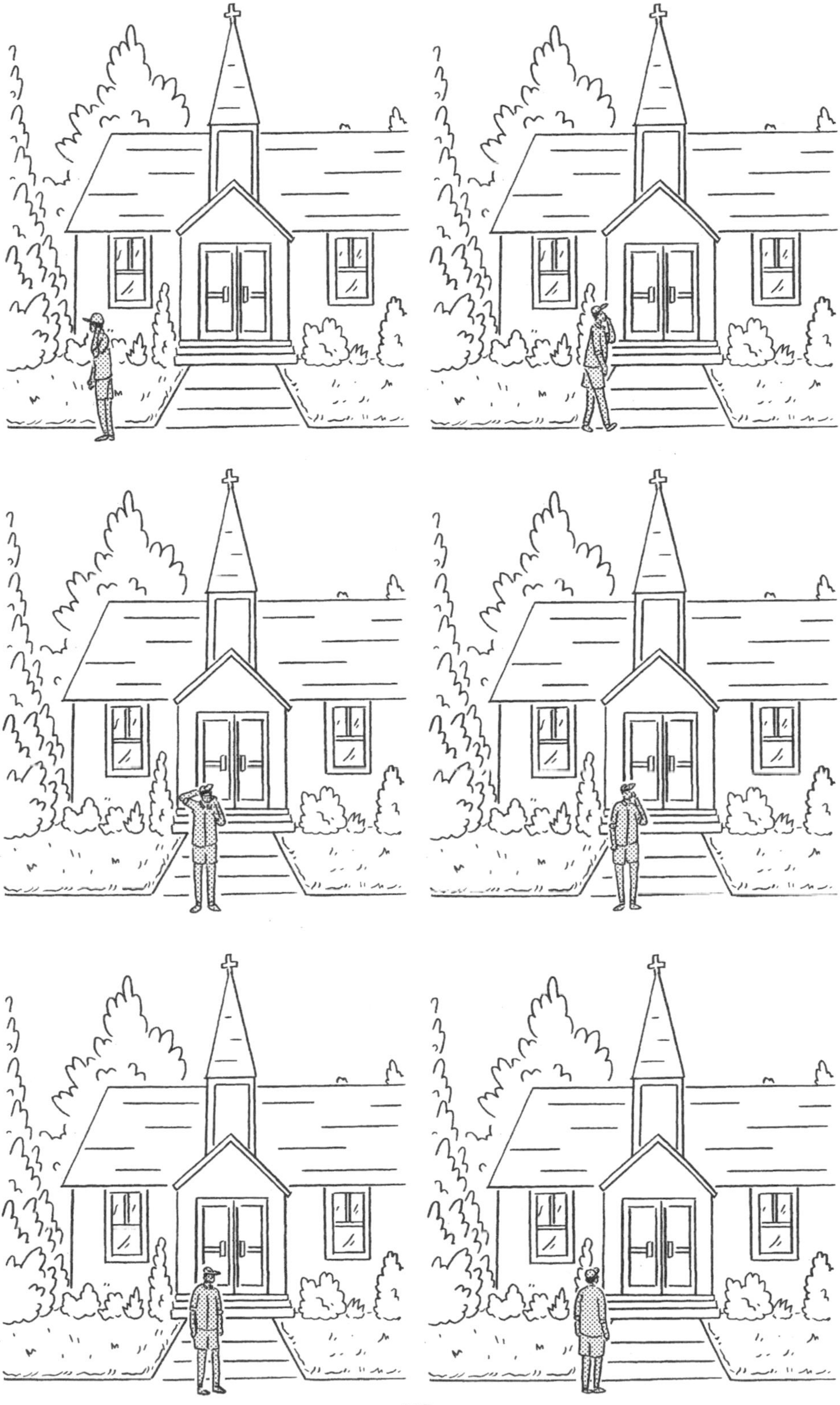

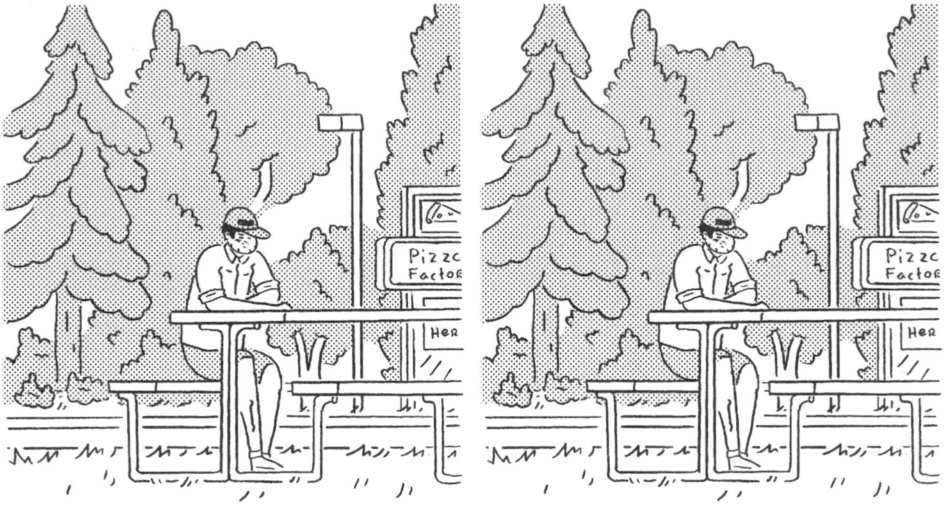

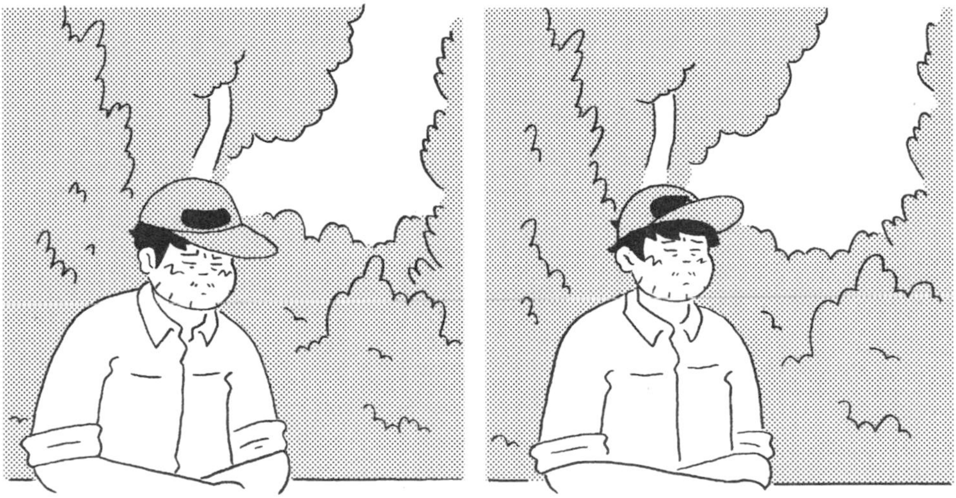

I'm skipping. Fuck it. Forget the unbroken footpath. Forget Mexico to Canada. Forget closure. Forget sentimentality. I'm skipping. I don't want to be alone.

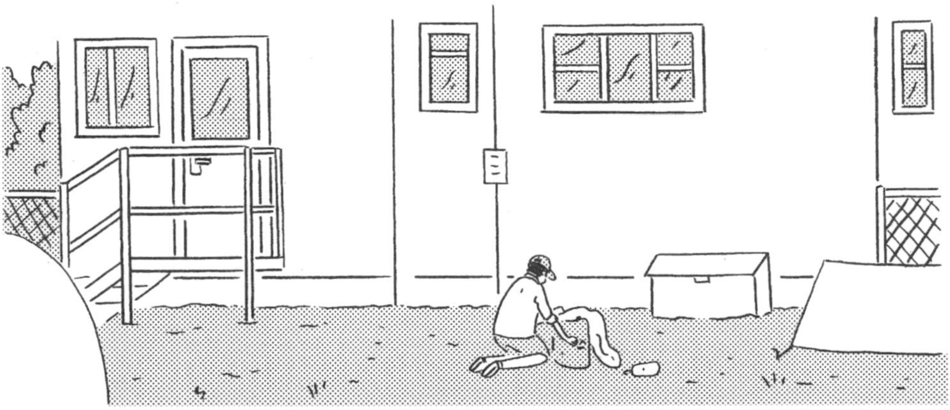

Griz and Craftsman's crew appear and, by sheer providence, are skipping ahead to Mt. Shasta, where the now-piecemeal Mile 55 will arrive in a couple of days. The trail provides, and I follow in their wake.

I feel grateful for their company. They have been the most consistent thing on the trail for me.

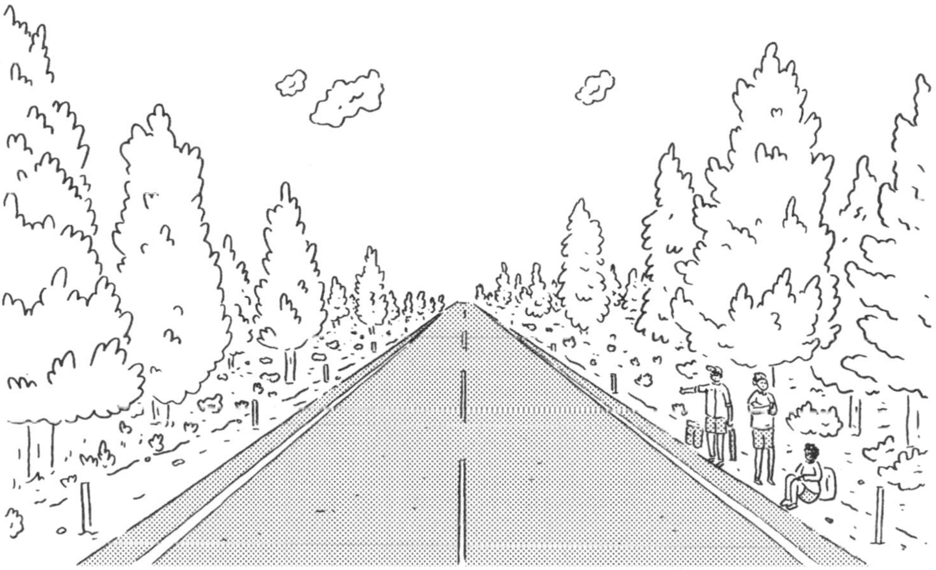

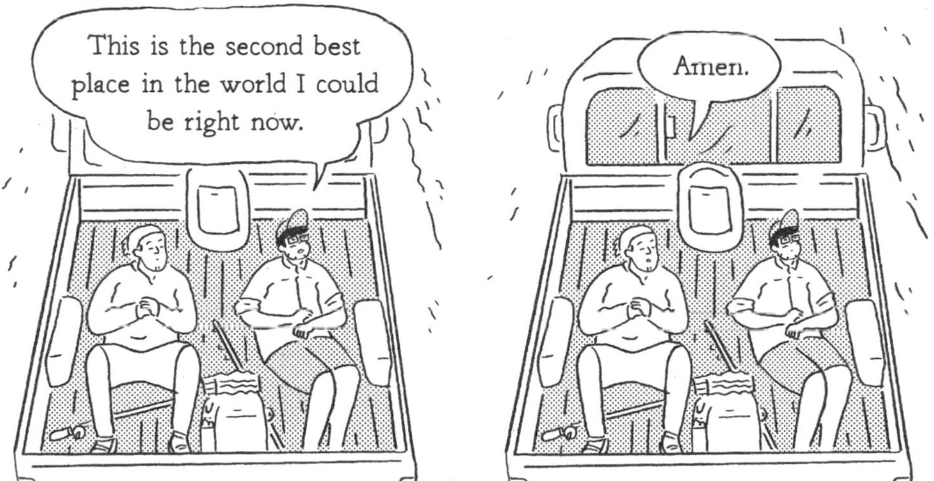
This is the second best place in the world I could be right now.
Amen.

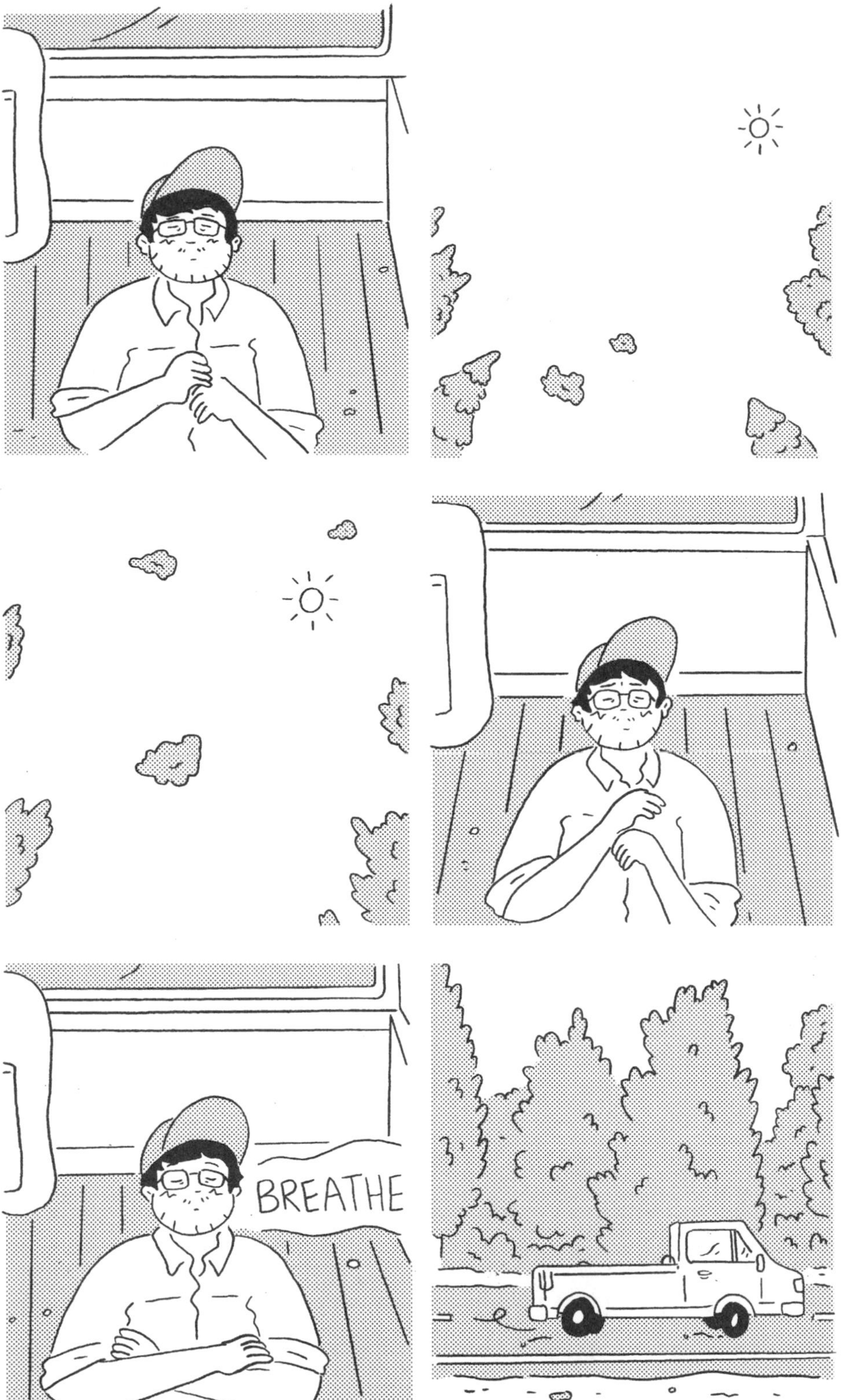
BREATHE

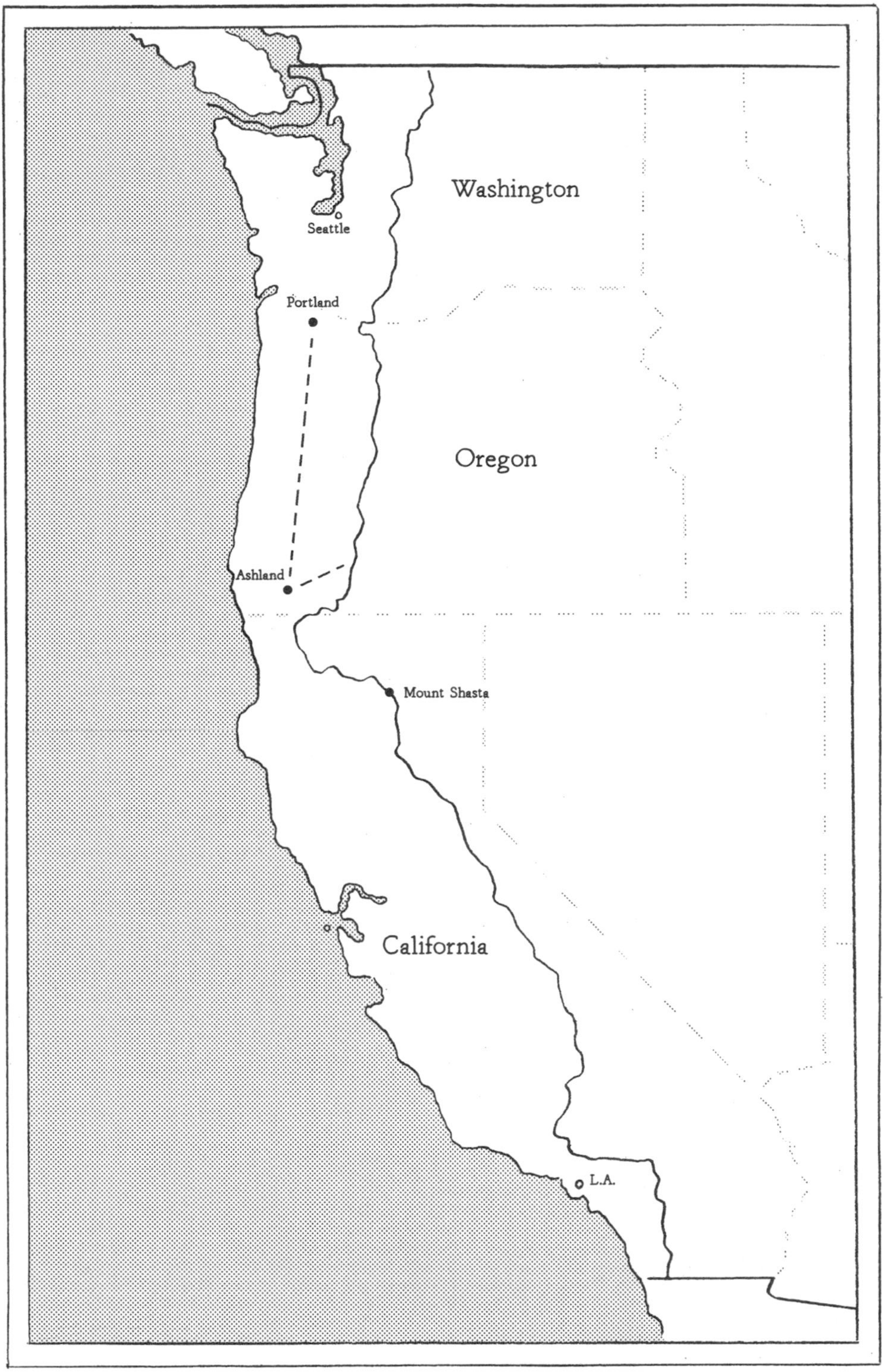
Washington
Seattle
Portland
Oregon
Ashland
Mount Shasta
California
L.A.

Chapter 5: Northern California (Part II) and Oregon

"The American dream is a crock.
Stop wanting everything. Everyone
should wear jeans and have three
T-shirts, eat rice and beans."
–Bill Hicks

It didn't help that I knew almost nobody my own age in Ireland by the time I'd moved back from the USA. They'd all left for other countries. Some were in the USA, some in the UK, Australia, France, Japan... "Generation Emigration" the newspapers called us.

Ireland, hit hard by the 2008 global financial crisis, had acquired its very own lost generation. People mostly left to find work, which was difficult to come by in Dublin. Youth unemployment soared above twenty per cent. Most, simply had no choice but to leave.

I applied for over one hundred jobs between my move back to Ireland and my departure for the PCT. I got one interview. They went with someone else. Employers were overrun with qualified applicants. One cinema told me that I was underqualified to sell tickets and fill buckets of popcorn – compared to the competition at least.

Every single one of my school friends now lived outside of Ireland. I couldn't blame anyone for leaving. I'd made the same choice myself two years earlier, when I'd moved to the US for school.

Still, my sense of feeling unmoored only grew more powerful the longer I remained in Ireland.

I lived with my parents in suburban Dublin. I took freelance jobs from American employers, and managed to scrape by financially. This presented its own challenges, but I tried not to complain. I was privileged enough to have parents who could afford to let their child live with them through his practical unemployment. Privately, I despaired. I started to resent my attitudes about Ireland. Why couldn't I just be happy there? Was it so different to White River Junction?

"There are more Irish living outside of Ireland than there are living inside of it," my dad repeated often while I was growing up.

We learned about emigration in history class from the time we were children. It's no coincidence that one of the only historical Irish events that Americans know about is the Irish potato famine, the butt of many jokes. It was the Great Famine that drove so many to leave, starved from their homeland. A million died, a million left. The population still hasn't recovered, over a century later.

In the books and plays we studied, this preoccupation with emigration was ever present. Despite what the posters for the Dublin literary festival would have you believe; James Joyce, Oscar Wilde and Elizabeth Bowen were not great lovers of the city, and left in turn for London or Paris.

In the '50s, when my grandfather and his family left, it was common for emigrants to never see their families again. They would have their own "American Wakes" on the night before their departure. A big party; a funeral for their Irish life. A chance to see everyone they love, and mourn for all of the funerals they'd miss.

We had our own ritual, when I, or my brother, or my cousins left Ireland to live abroad. A weekend of visiting everyone, in their own homes, as close to your departure as possible. It was a process with which I became quite familiar.

The legacy of mass emigration still lives on in modern day Ireland. The sad tradition of American Wakes was revived in the years following the 2008 global financial crisis. Despite the ease of air travel, funerals are still missed, and weddings, and new babies. And often, those that leave know that they will never live in Ireland again.

Mt. Shasta is a bizarre place, rammed with New Age, holistic, spiritualist shops. They dot every street, selling crystals and wands and other arcane paraphernalia.

The mountain itself soars high above the town, prominent amongst the lower, non-mountainous landscape. Even though Mt. Whitney is taller, Mt. Shasta looks much bigger, not surrounded by the hulking majesty of the High Sierras.

After a little while, I break away from Griz, Craftsman and crew, going to find the local campsite. We bump fists, like hikers do.

My unbroken footpath is now broken. Purists would scoff. I can't now say that I've walked from Mexico to Canada, unless I include a disclaimer about a hundred-mile hole somewhere in Northern California.

I hadn't wanted to skip. When I'd been stuck in Mammoth, I'd considered skipping, to catch back up with the remainder of Mile 55, but the desire to hike every inch of the trail had kept me on track.

Now, I don't care. Not even a little. I say it defiantly to myself, as though affirming my own point of view. I'm walking from Mexico to Canada. If somebody wants to take issue with that, let them walk thirteen hundred miles through snow and desert to tell me.

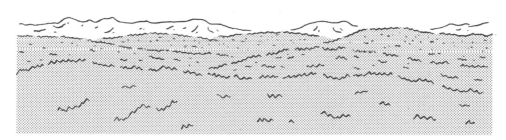

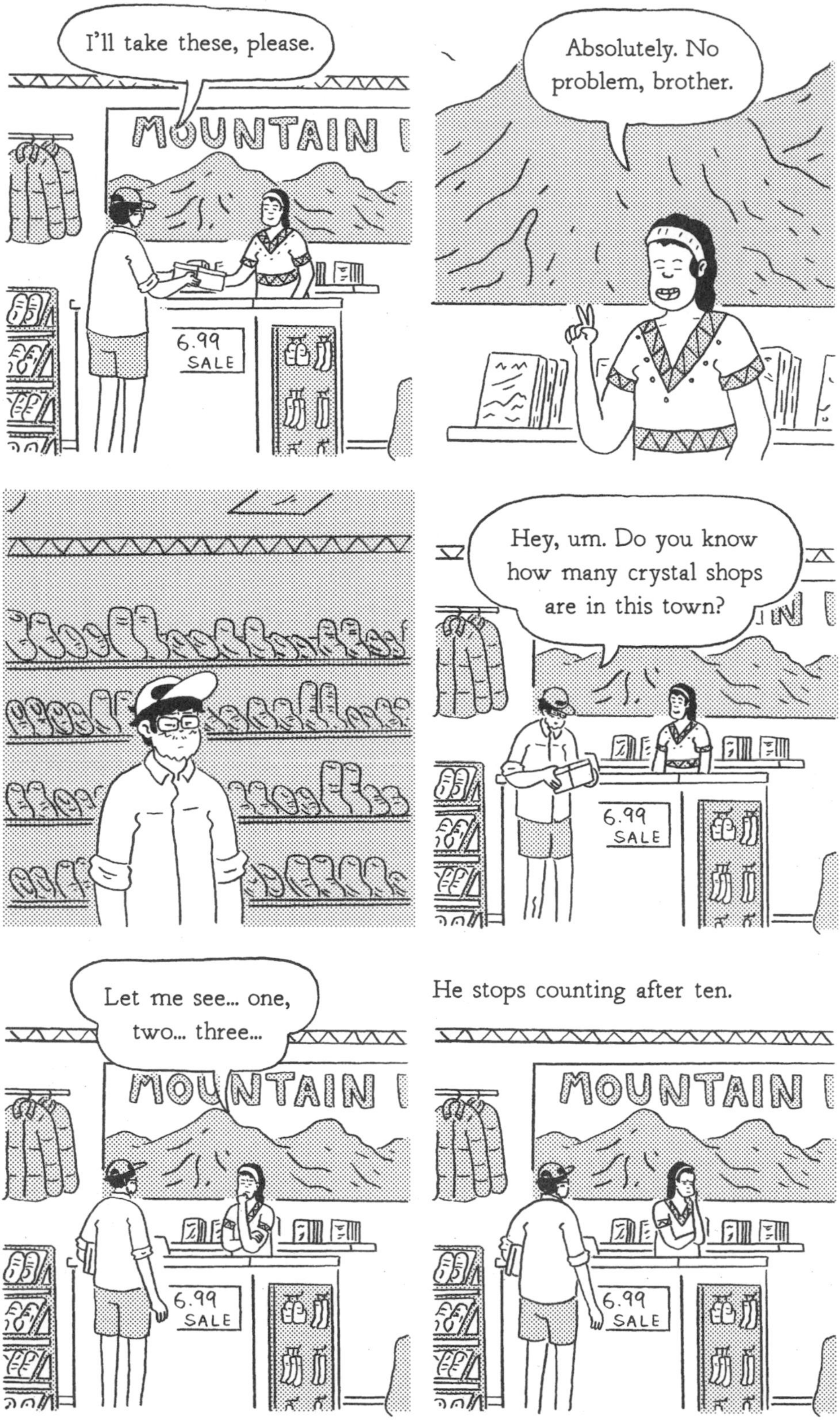
I'll take these, please.
MOUNTAIN
6.99 SALE
Absolutely. No problem, brother.
Hey, um. Do you know how many crystal shops are in this town?
6.99 SALE
Let me see... one, two... three...
MOUNTAIN
6.99 SALE
He stops counting after ten.
MOUNTAIN
6.99 SALE

My mother answers her phone. She sounds tired. I apologise for waking her, but she tells me that she wasn't asleep. My dad and brother are also awake. They just got back from my grandmother's house. I'd almost forgotten. It stabs at me that I'm not there. I should be there.

I apologise again, feebly, for calling late.

She asks me if I have seen a red butterfly. That a red butterfly had landed on my aunt's hand right after my grandfather had died. I roll my eyes from the safe distance of eight thousand kilometres.

"I see butterflies on trail every day," I say, hoping not to dismiss her sentimentality too rudely.

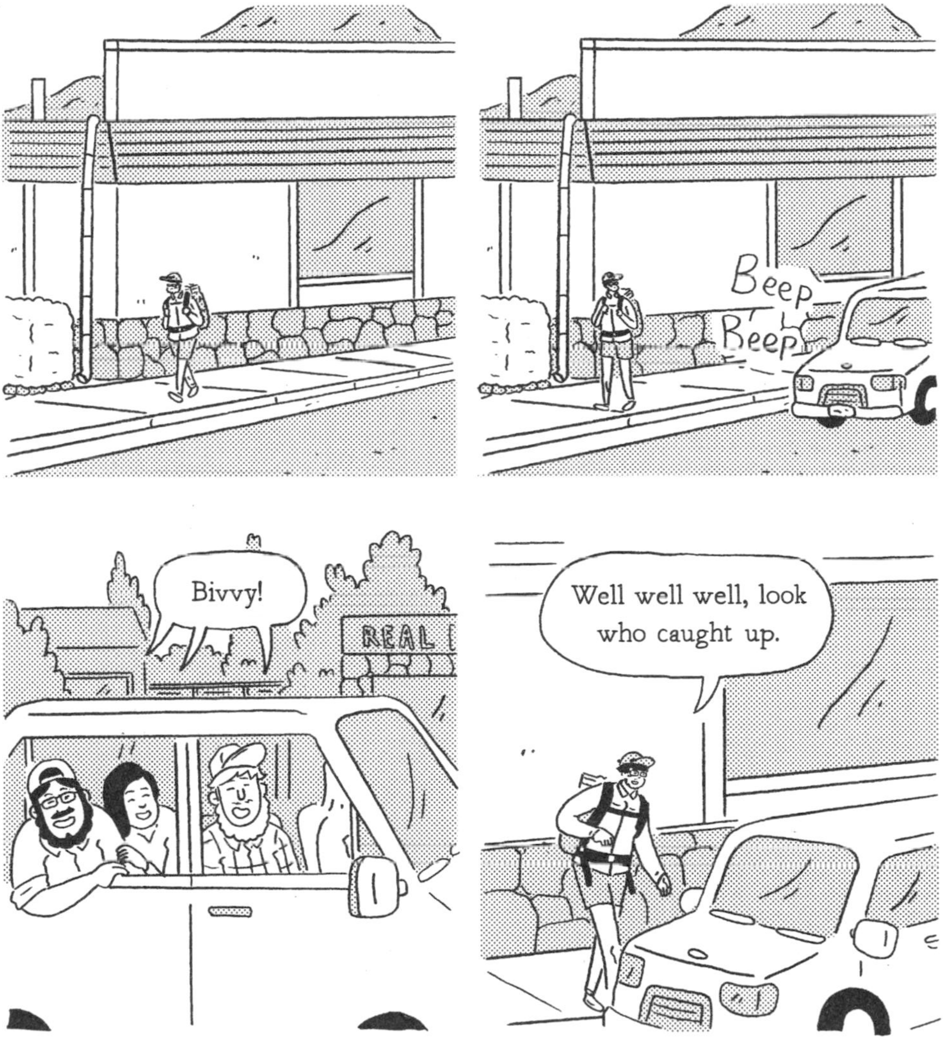
Beep
Beep
Bivvy!
REAL
Well well well, look who caught up.

We eat together for the first time since Mammoth.

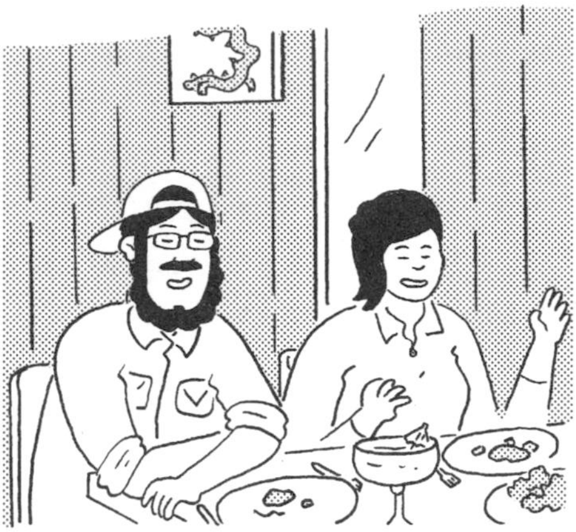

I feel my self uncoil.

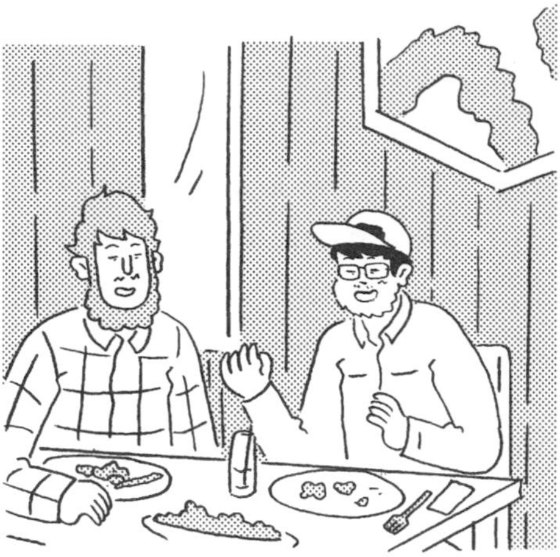

We raise a glass.

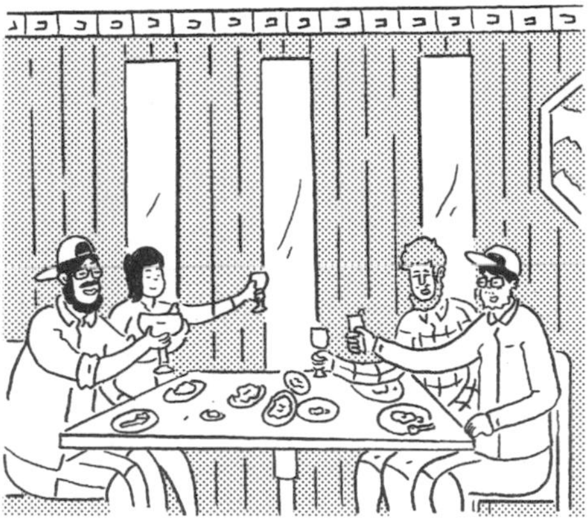

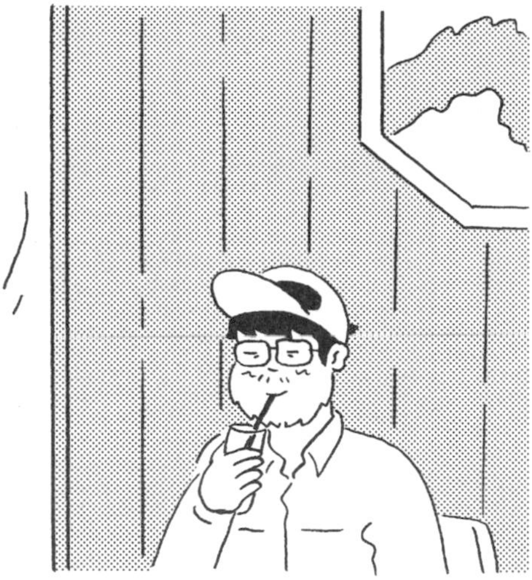

I leave town with Centerfold.

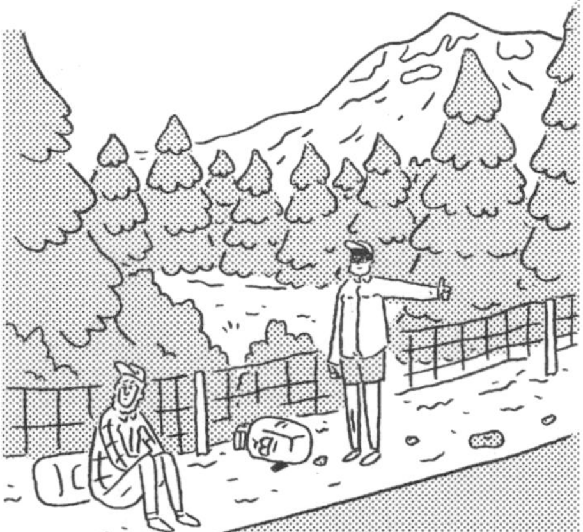

And Mile 55 drifts apart again.

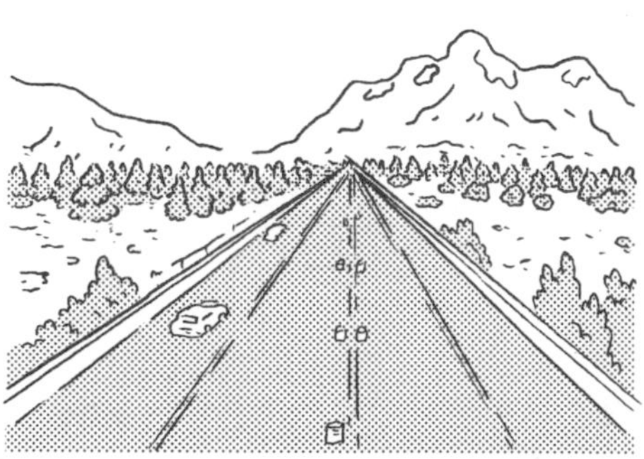

I lose Centerfold on the first day.

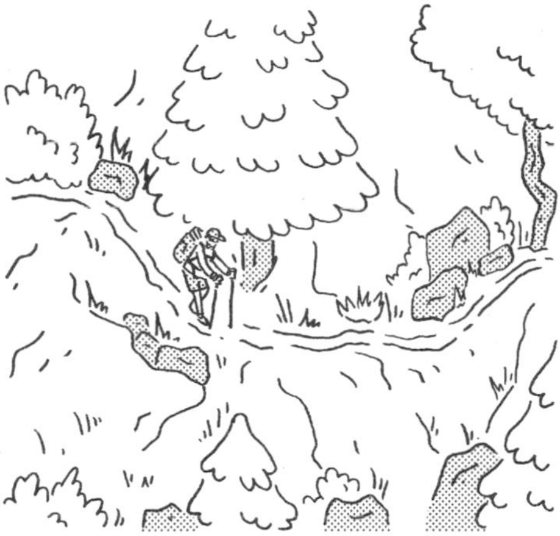

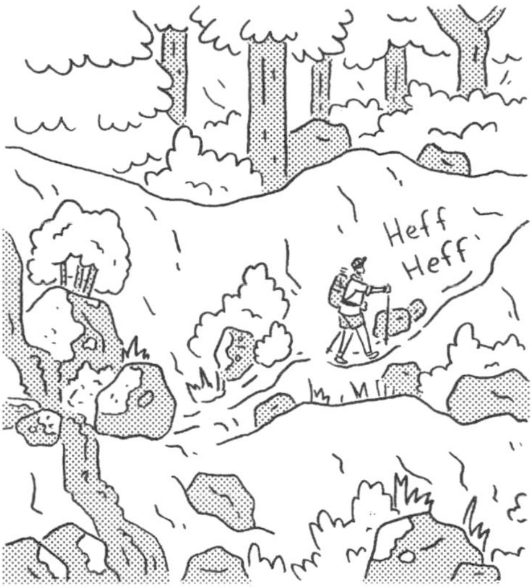
Heff
Heff

The next morning, I catch him.

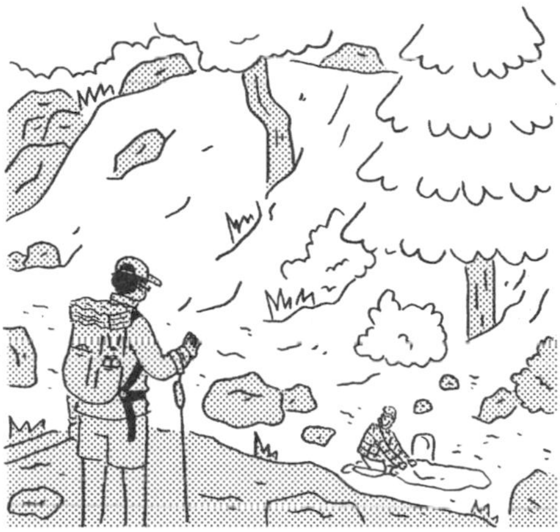

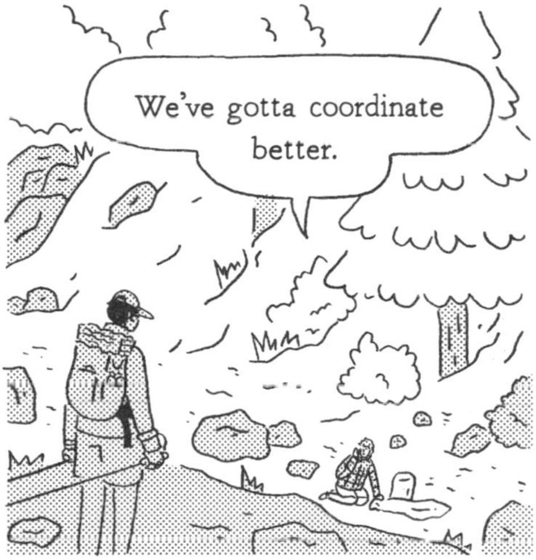
We've gotta coordinate better.

He passes me out again, and soon I'm left hiking my own hike, once more.

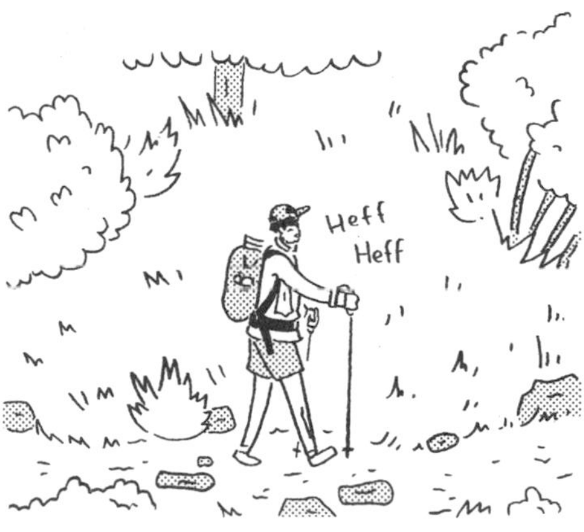
Heff
Heff

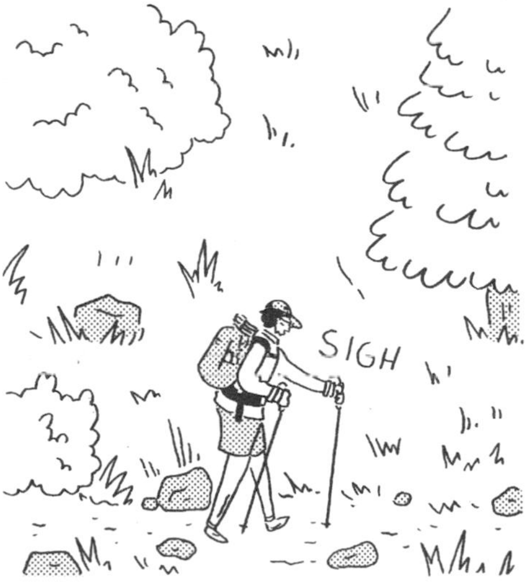
SIGH

The trail runs in a big loop around Mt. Shasta itself, which looms over me as I hike. For all my complaints, the trail is much easier than anything I've seen up until now.

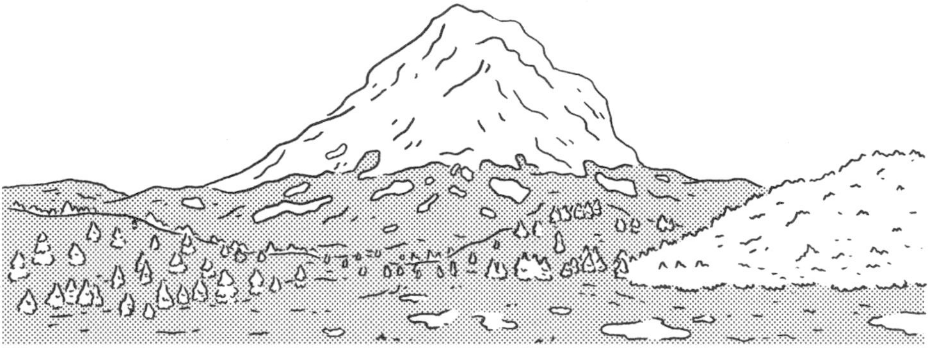

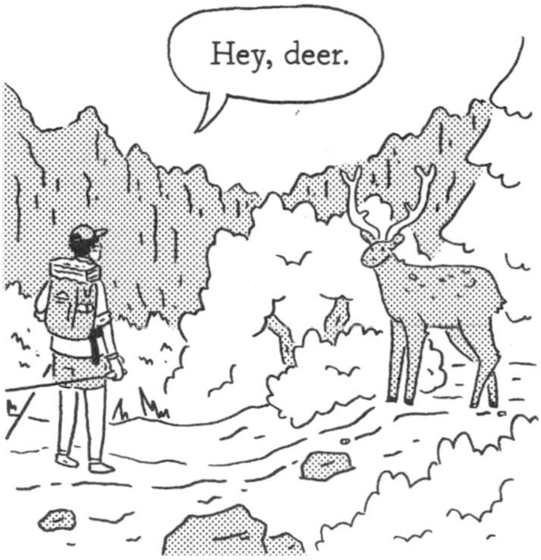
Hey, deer.

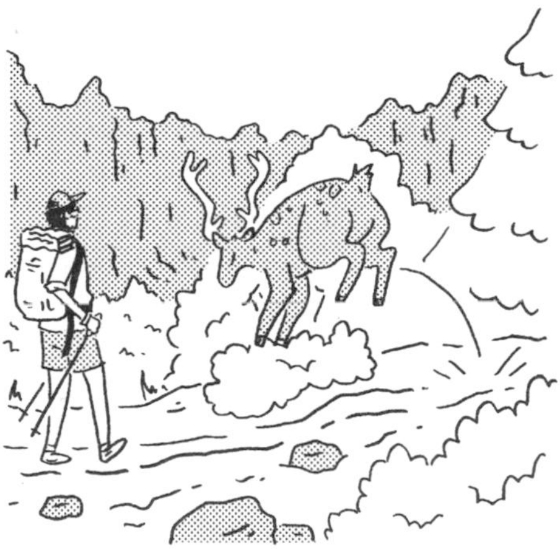

I am hiking through a Disney movie.

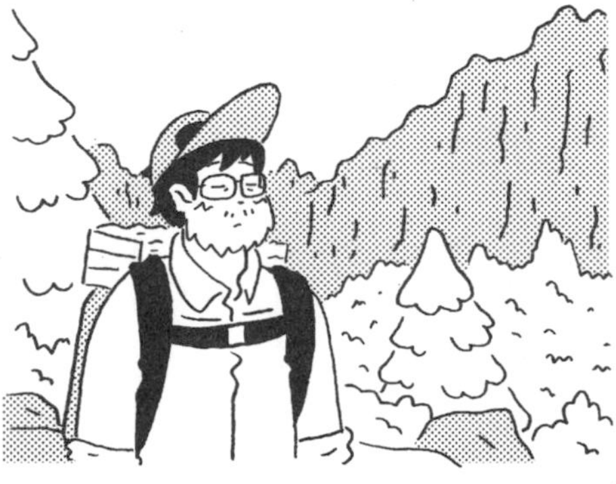

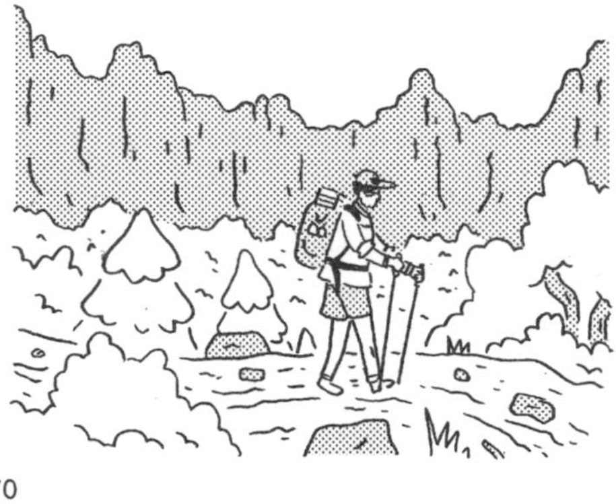

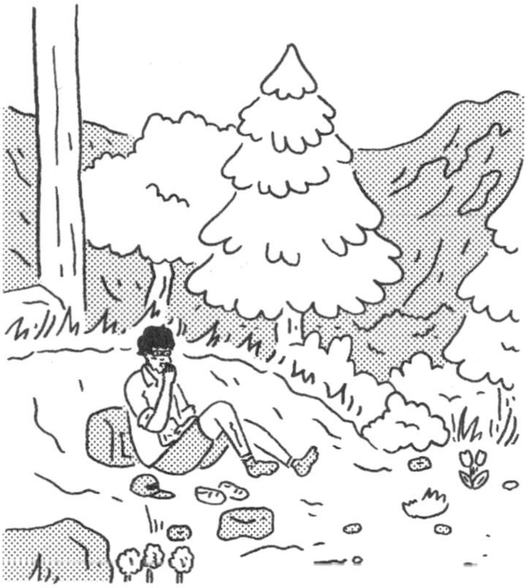

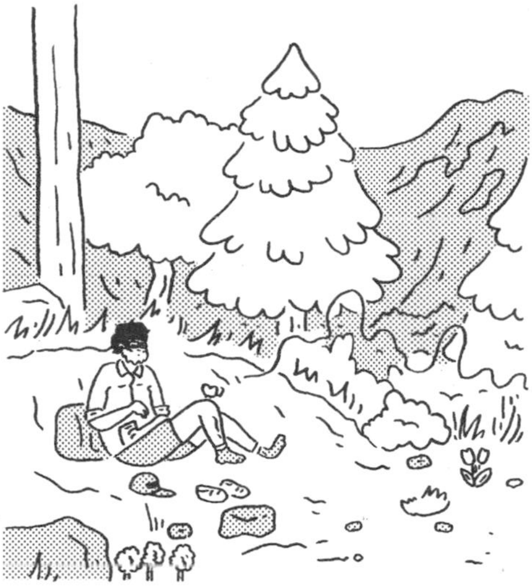

I breathe slowly, and take a moment to regard the butterfly before shooing it away. It flits off a little, before returning, settling on my knee again and again.

"You're just eating the salt on my skin," I say to it, like a dope, before falling back into silence and stillness.

I shoo it away again, but it returns, standing delicately, flexing its wings as it licks the salt from my knee. And all I can think of is that stupid phrase. The one you find on pillows and plates in cheesy gift shops. "If you love something, let it go. If it returns, it will be yours forever."

I never let go. I clutch and cling so tight as to crush. No butterfly would stand a chance. I hold on tight to people, and ideas, and identity, without any faith that they'd return if I let go. I'd chased Mile 55 across hundreds of miles of California desert. I'd spent night after night applying for jobs and visas. I'd cried over the USA and returned again and again, and what had it got me?

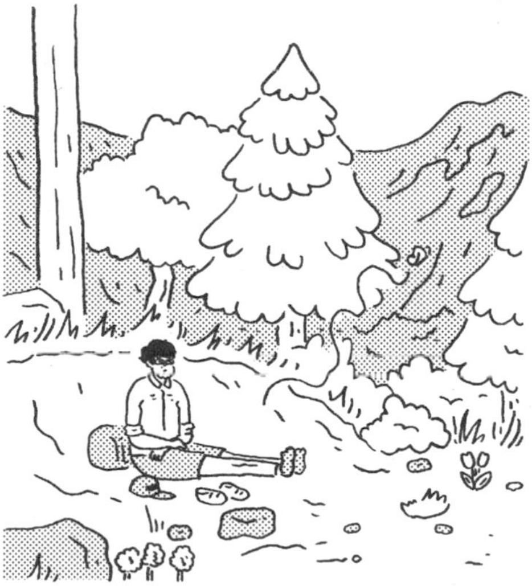

I stay still and let the butterfly eat its fill.

I think about my grandad as I hike.

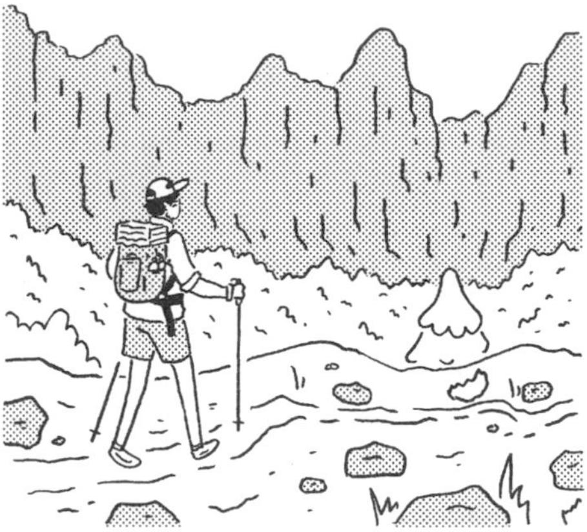

I'd cried on the phone but now, out here, I feel so removed.

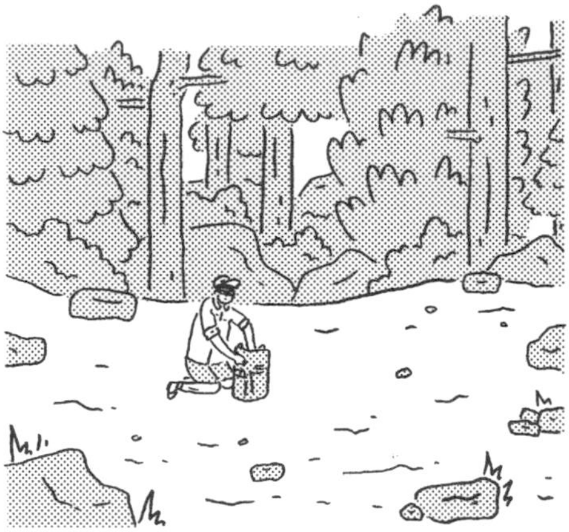

There is no evidence of his death here.

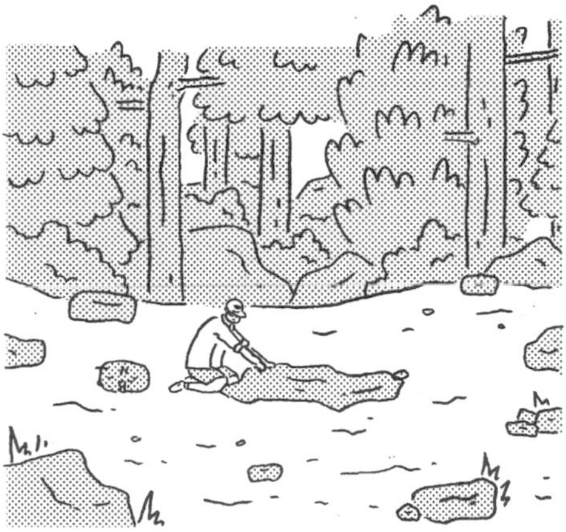

No sign anything has changed.

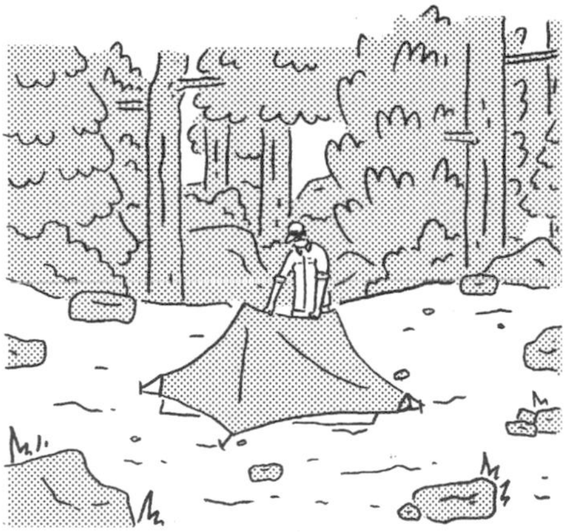

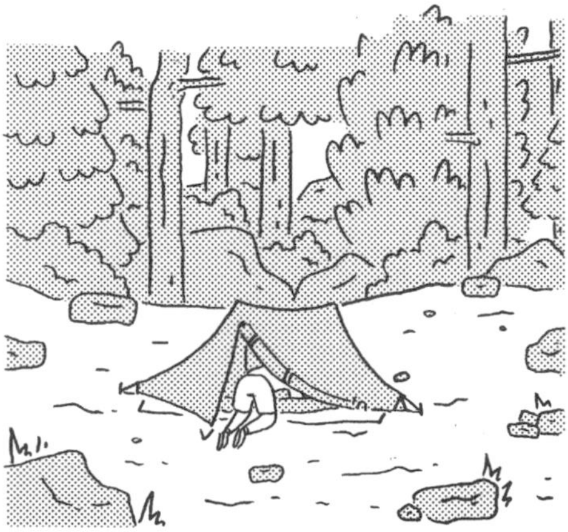

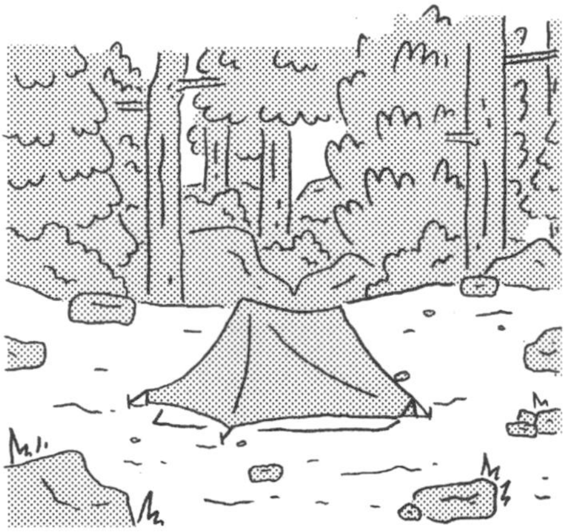

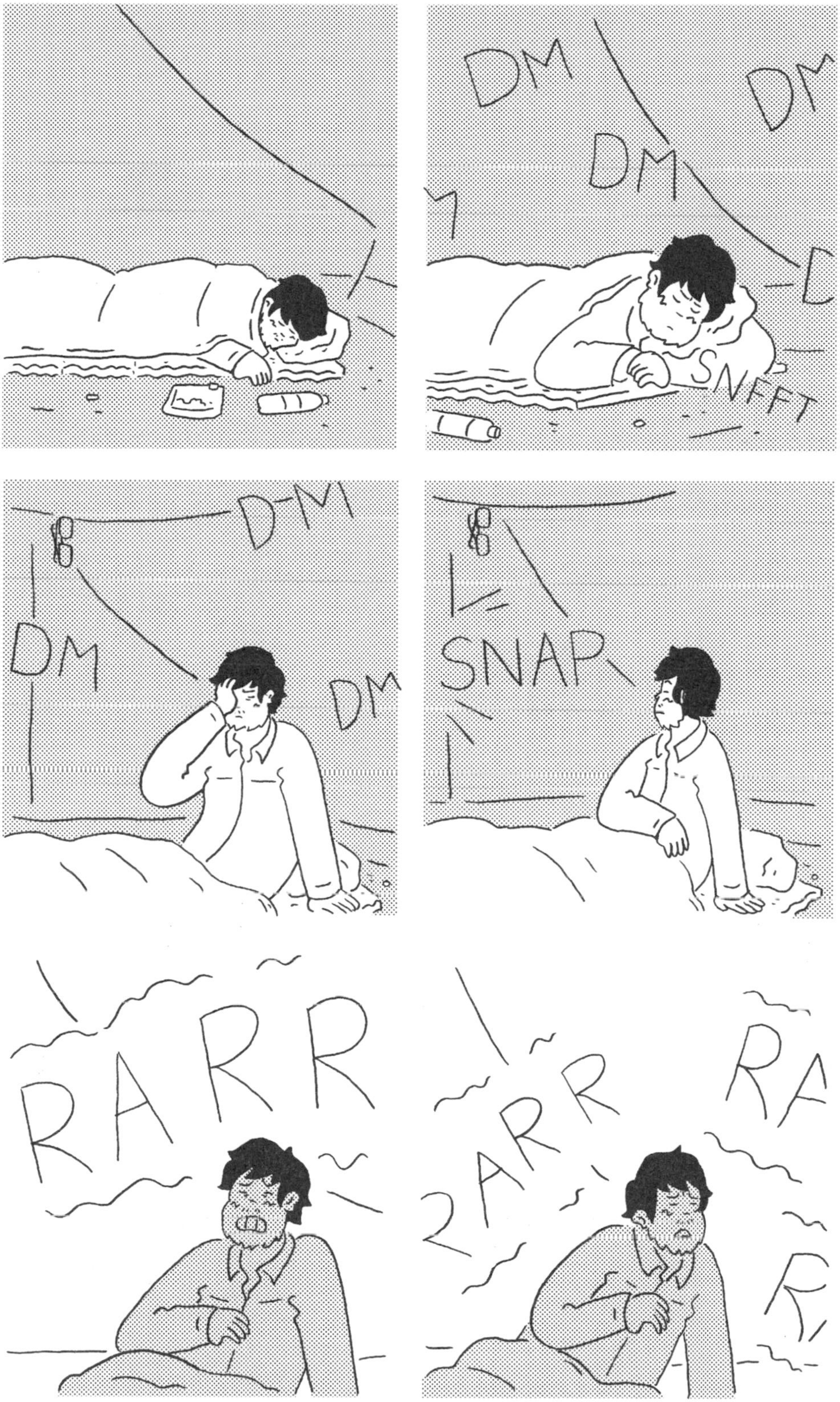
DM
DM
DM
D
SNFFT
D-M
DM
DM
SNAP
RARR
RARR
RA
R

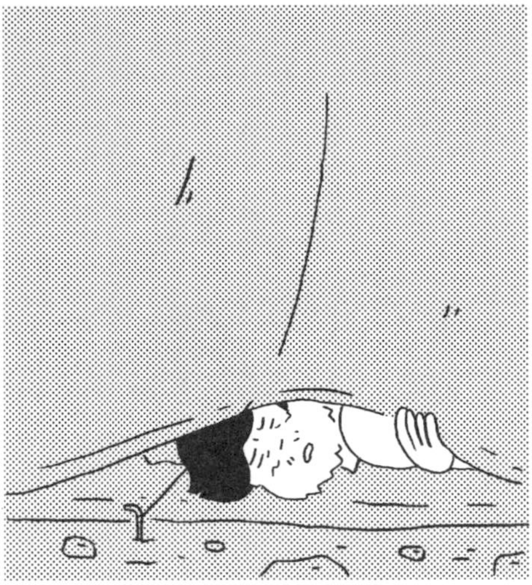

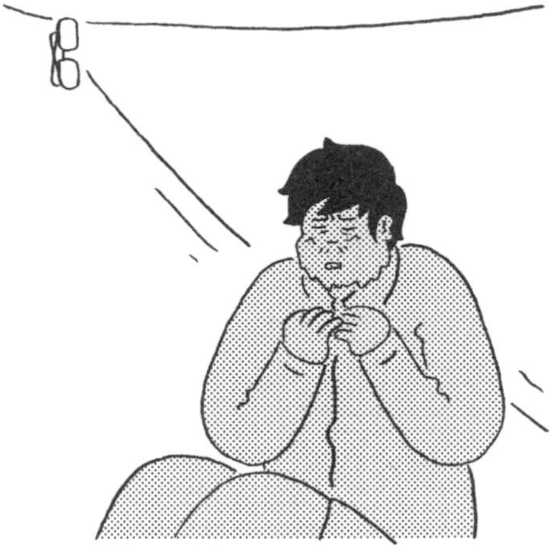

It's a mountain lion. Fuck. Fuck.

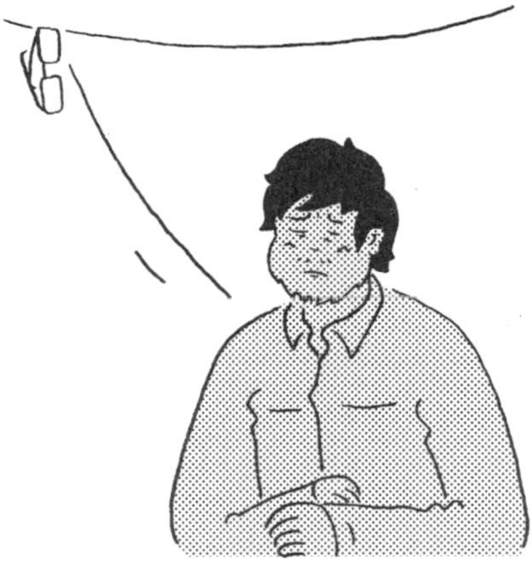

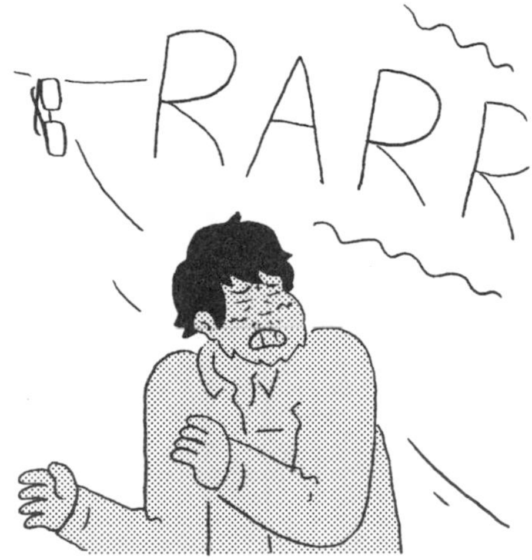
RARR

No signal, obviously.

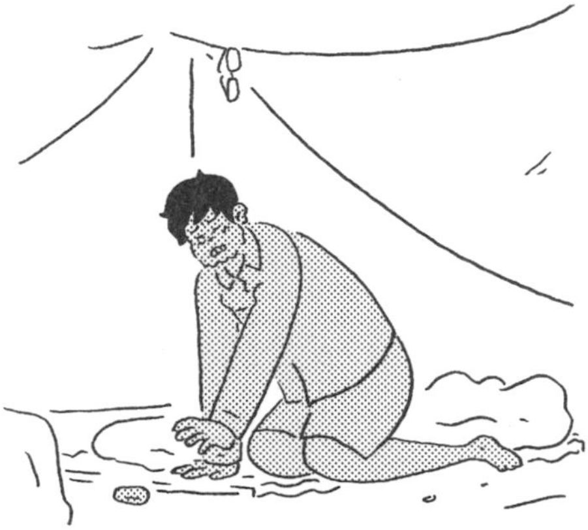

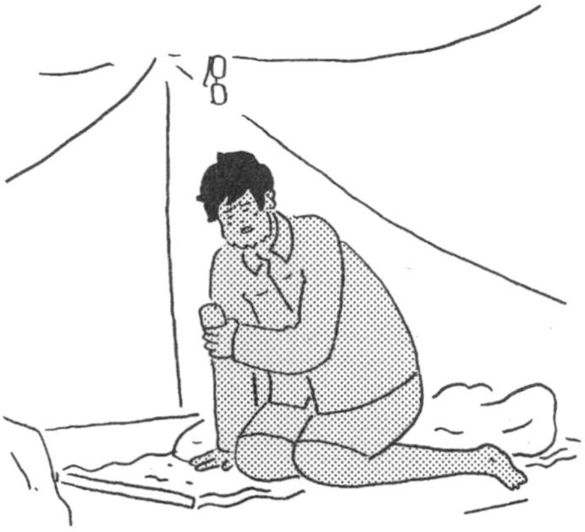

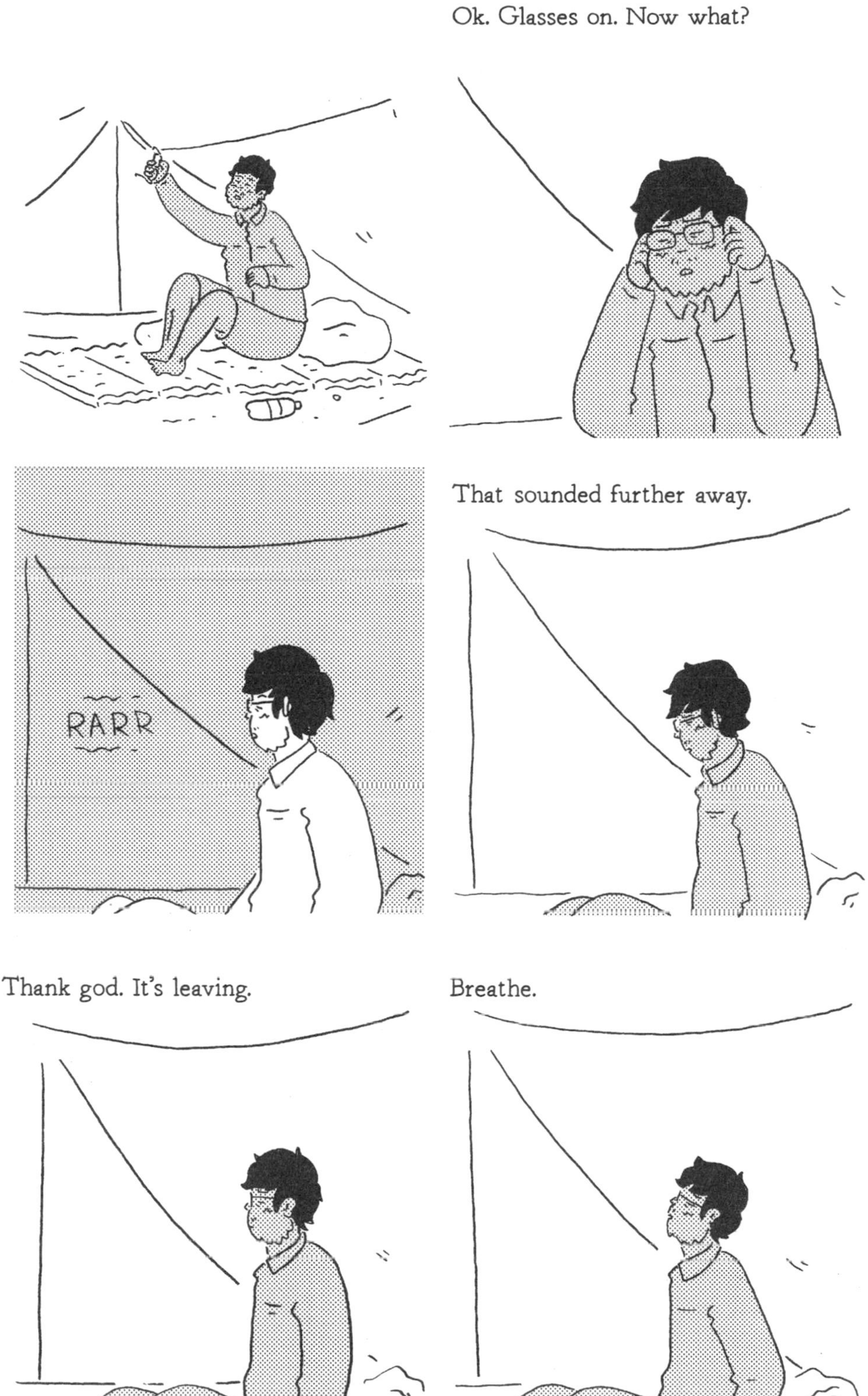
Ok. Glasses on. Now what?
RARR
That sounded further away.
Thank god. It's leaving.
Breathe.

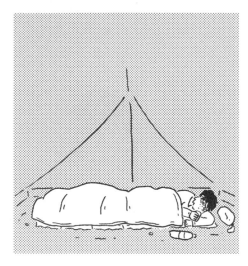

This is somehow my fault, I'm sure.

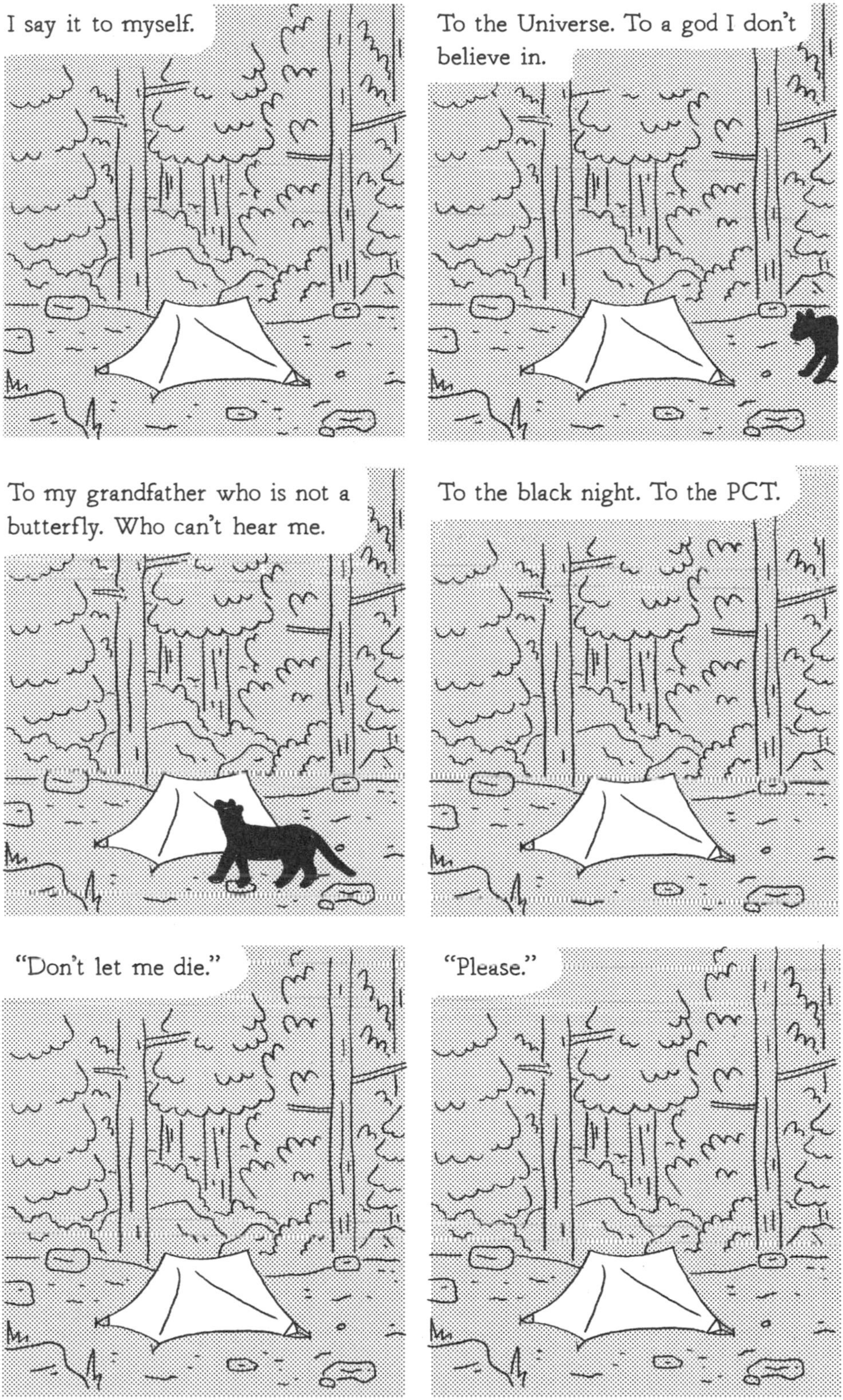
I say it to myself.
To the Universe. To a god I don't believe in.
To my grandfather who is not a butterfly. Who can't hear me.
To the black night. To the PCT.
"Don't let me die."
"Please."

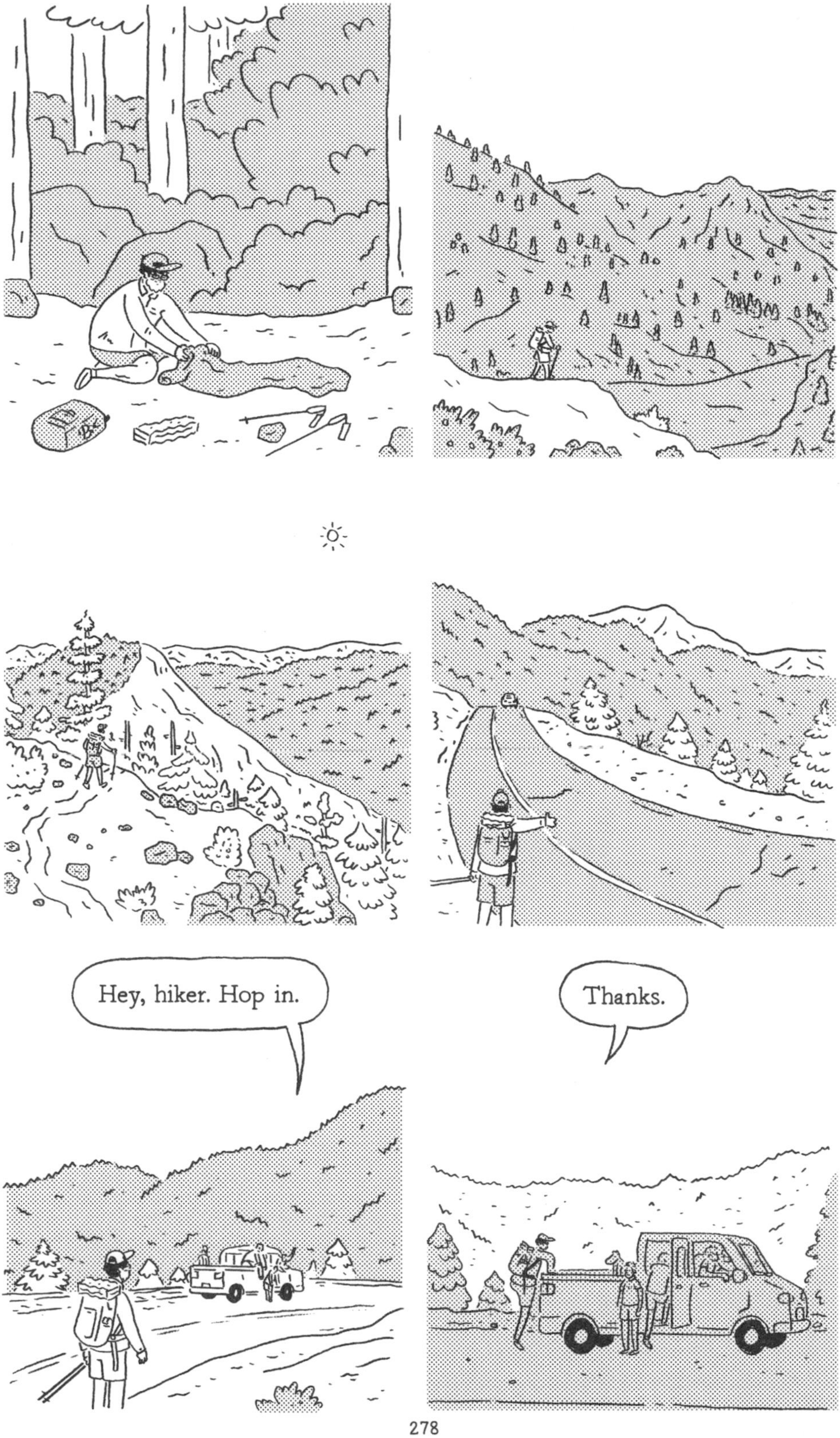
Hey, hiker. Hop in.
Thanks.

The driver looks about fourteen years old.

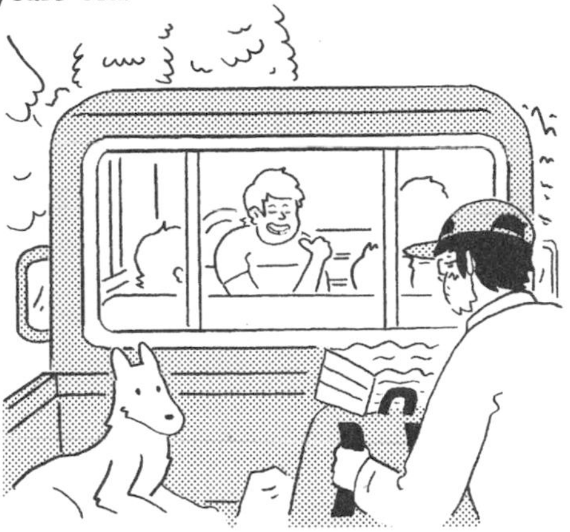

I'm left alone in the truck's bed with their dog, who seems eager to leap from the moving vehicle.

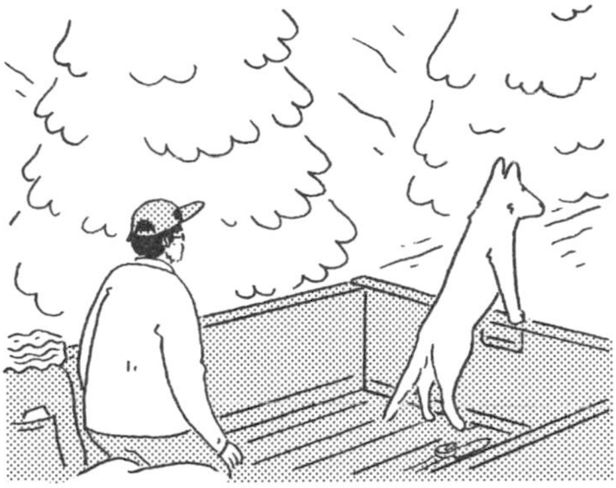

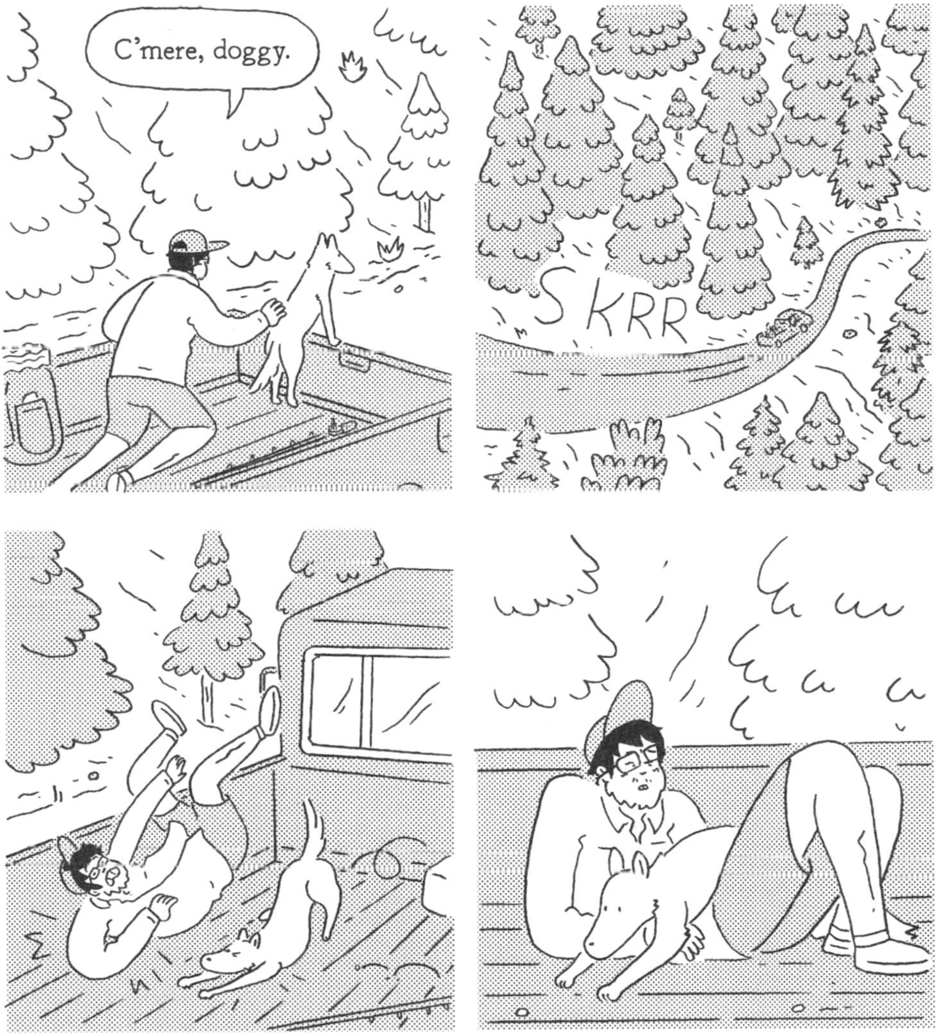
C'mere, doggy.
SKRR

I take an unplanned zero in Etna, waiting for Chuckles and Spoon to catch up.

I sleep in the "Etna Hiker Hut," a many-walled paradise, and swim at the local pool until they arrive.

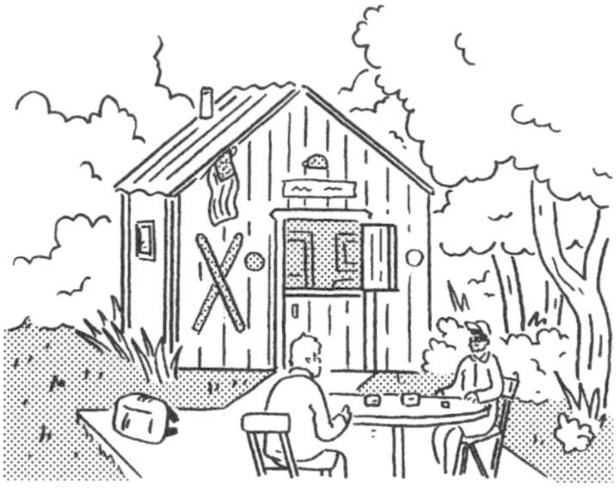

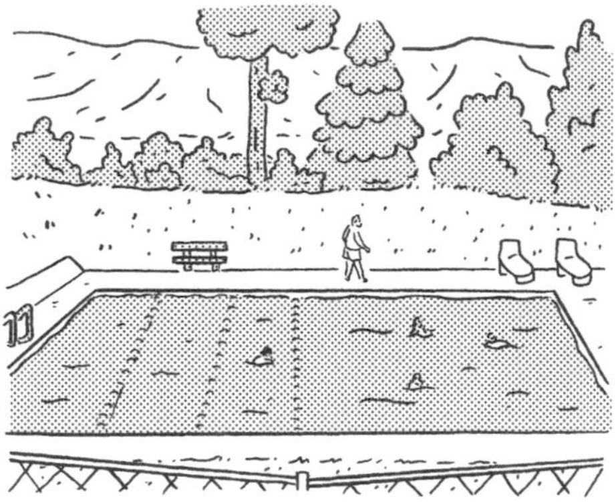

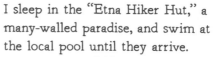

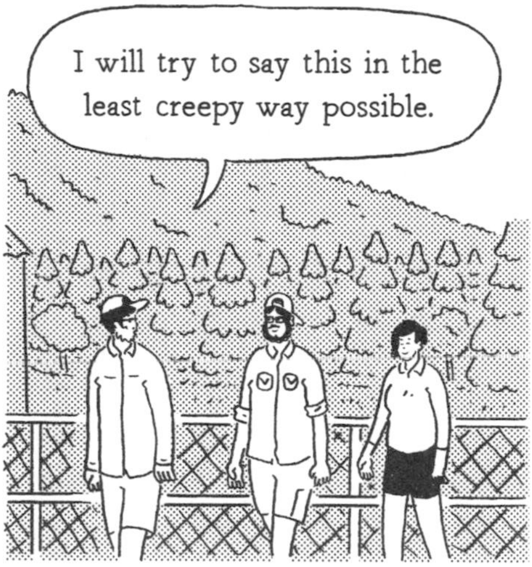
I will try to say this in the least creepy way possible.

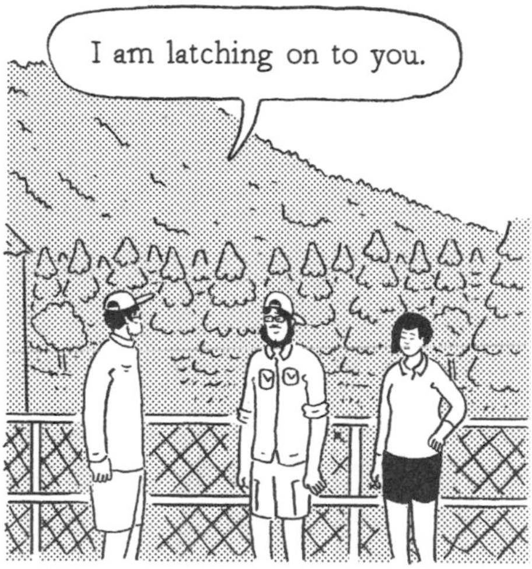
I am latching on to you.

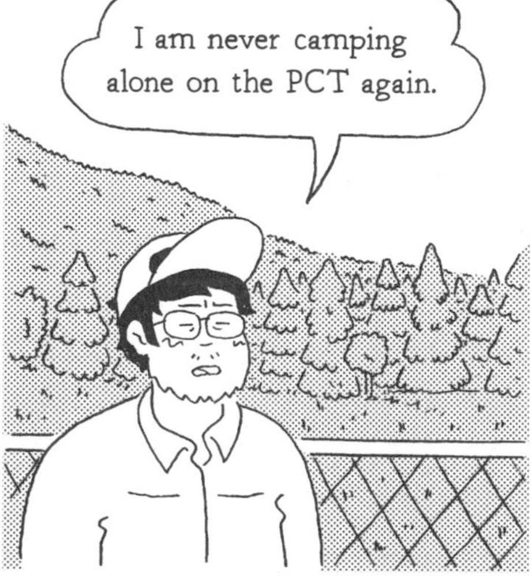
I am never camping alone on the PCT again.

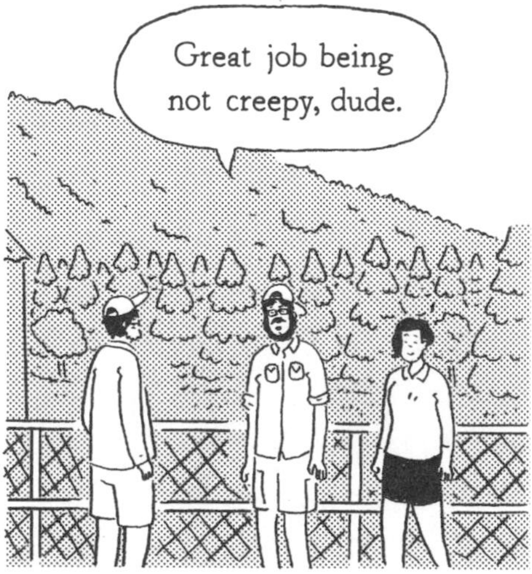
Great job being not creepy, dude.

I hike faster than Chuckles and Spoon.

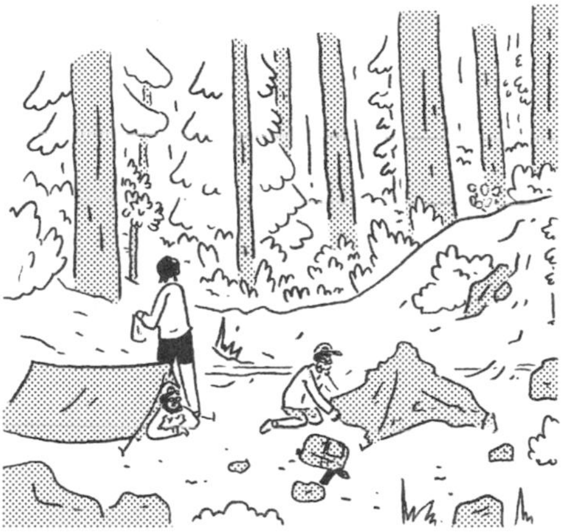

We establish a pattern. I take off early and hike a full day.

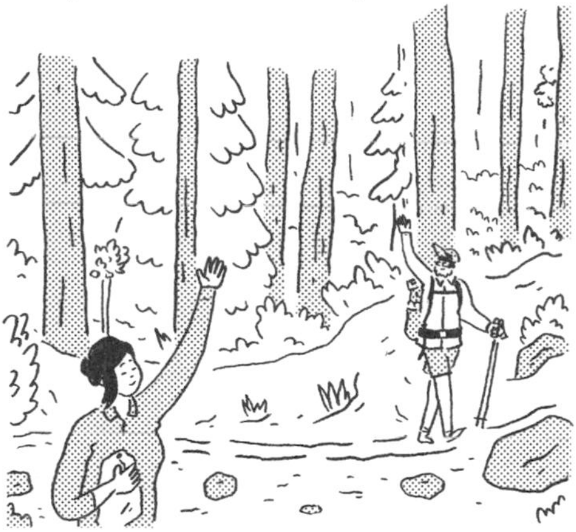

I set up camp and get some sleep.

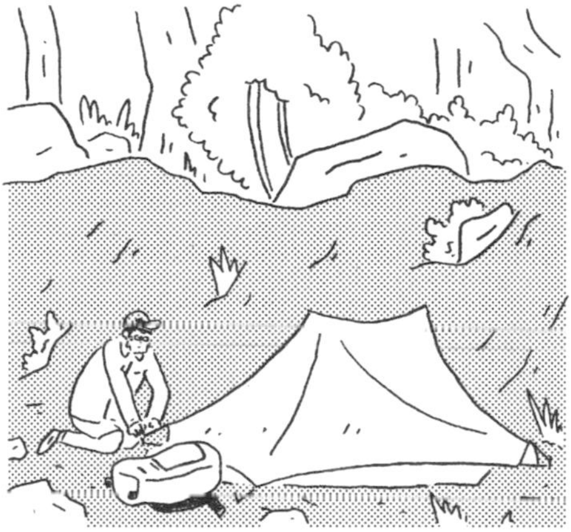

Some time around hiker midnight they arrive, waking me from sleep with creepy whispers.

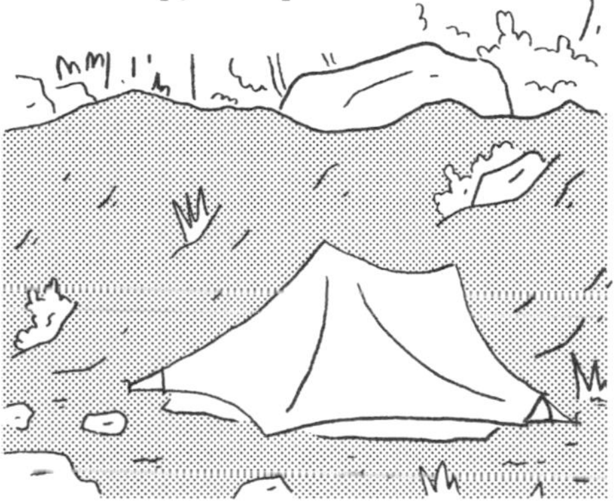

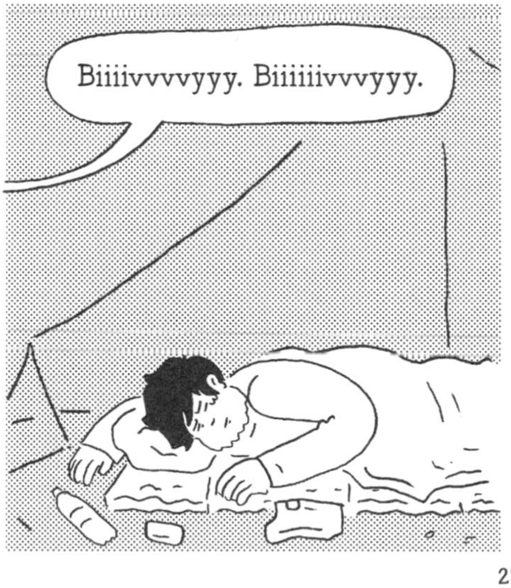
Biiiivvvvyyy. Biiiiiivvvyyy.

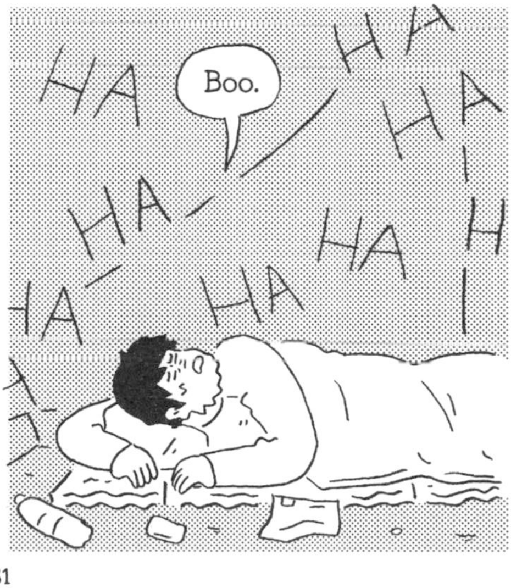
HA
Boo.
HA HA HA HA HA HA HA

The energy on trail is odd, as we continue to trek through Northern California. The hiking continues to be easy, but people are tired. The long term wear and tear of pushing our bodies to the limit over and over again is starting to show on people's faces. Still, as we approach the Oregon border, there is a certain electricity building.

I keep a close eye on my calendar as I hike. Though it's possible for me to finish on time if I don't skip again, it's extremely unlikely. And despite wanting to hike with Chuckles, Spoon and Centerfold, my resistance to skipping has simply eroded. I understand that fairly soon, I'll need to pull the trigger and skip ahead to Portland, where I can see Eleri and launch into the final stretch of Washington.

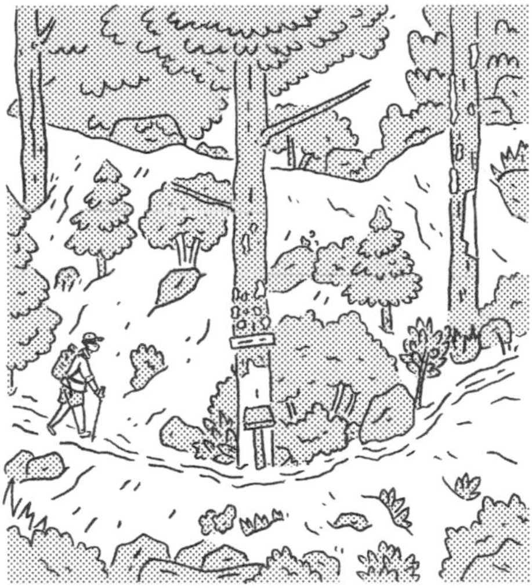

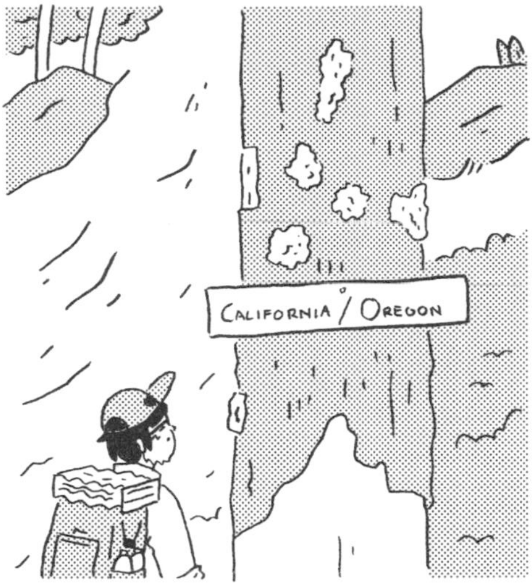
CALIFORNIA / OREGON

Holy crap.

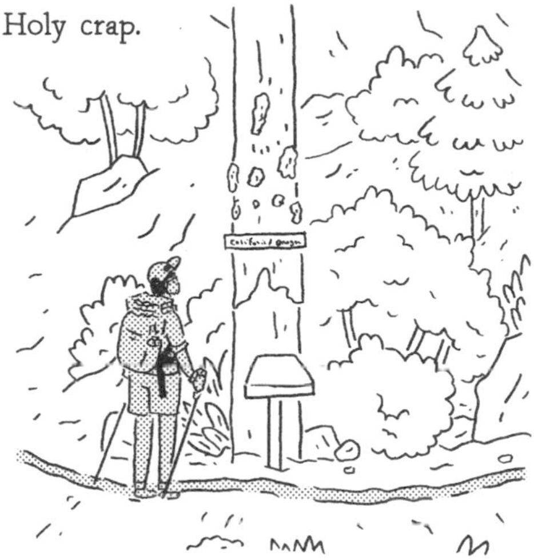

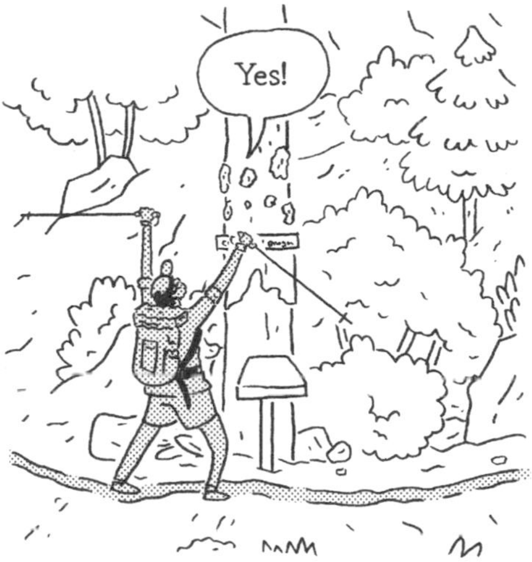
Yes!

One state down.

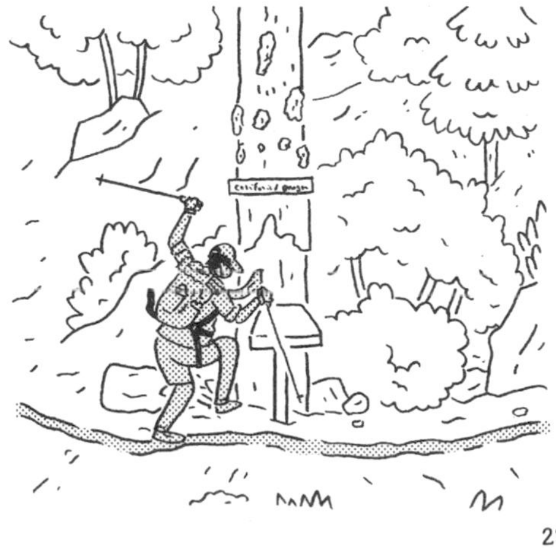

One state down!!!

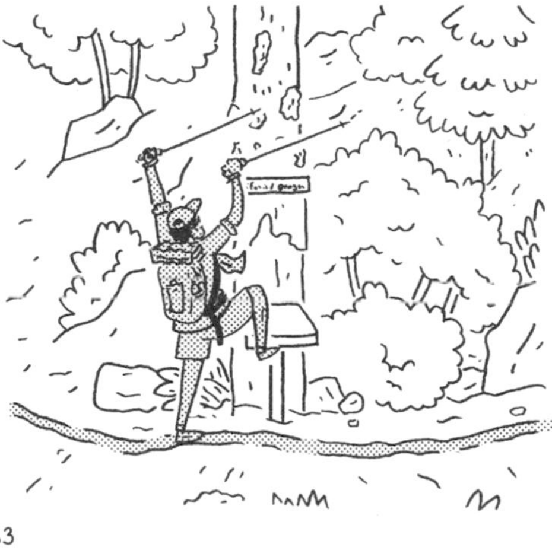

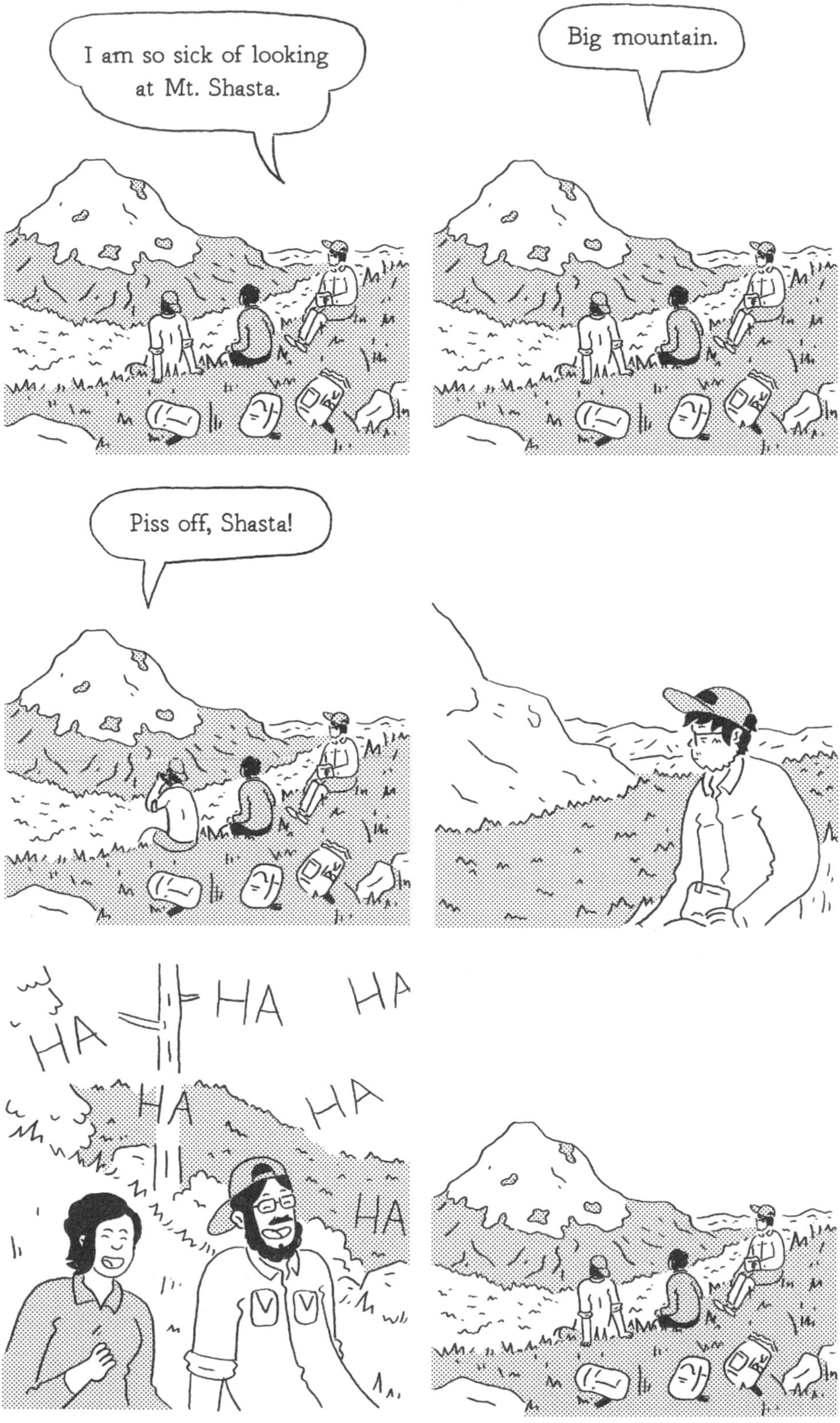
I am so sick of looking at Mt. Shasta.
Big mountain.
Piss off, Shasta!
HA
HA
HA
HA
HA
HA

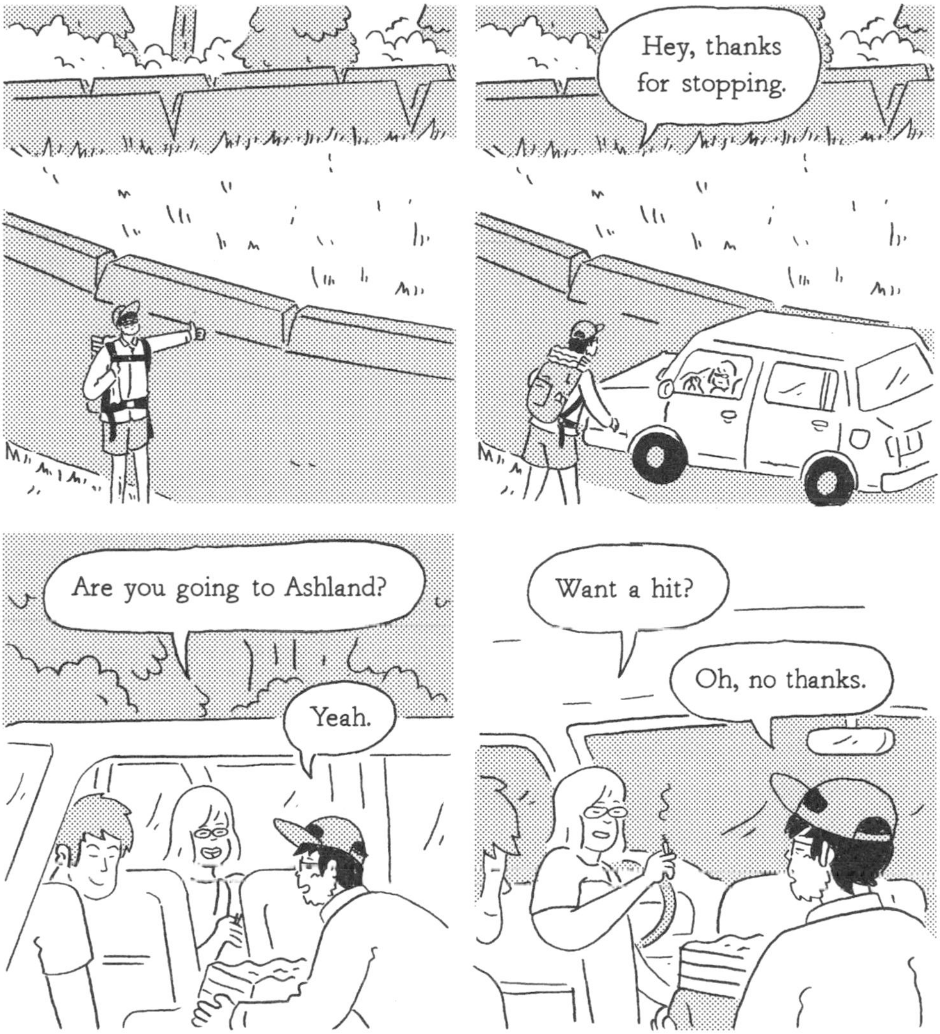
Hey, thanks for stopping.
Are you going to Ashland?
Yeah.
Want a hit?
Oh, no thanks.

I remember reading about Ashland being a centre for homeless LGBT youth, drawing kids in from across the country who have been kicked out by their parents. With nowhere to go, they follow the mild weather and artsy university town atmosphere.

I thank them for the ride, and offer them some cash, but they refuse. One of the men gets out and walks over to an underpass, where he retrieves a backpack stashed behind a cement column and returns to the car. Before getting in, he calls back to me.

"The church on Smith does free meals and laundry on Thursdays."

I thank him, and the three of them leave. The familiar feeling of guilt rises in my guts. I think of the stamp on my visa – "tourist" – and I feel like a tourist. In more ways than one.

We spend three days in Ashland, celebrating, watching movies, and making up resupply packages for Washington. We can't keep the smiles off our faces as we wander through the town, eating too much food and laughing at stupid jokes.

We finished California. The place we've lived for the last four months. Done! Oregon floats ahead, kind and gentle, with the craggy, tough Washington beyond.

On our last night in town, a notion takes root in my brain. Lighter. I need my pack to be lighter. I need to move! And so I root through my pack, pulling out everything non-essential and laying it out on the motel bedspread. I stare at the things I've carried for 1700 miles. Things intimately familiar to me in every way.

I leave my stove and pot. I dump my books.

My Bivvy, my namesake.

I weigh my pack. 9 lbs. Ultralight.

I'm ready to move.

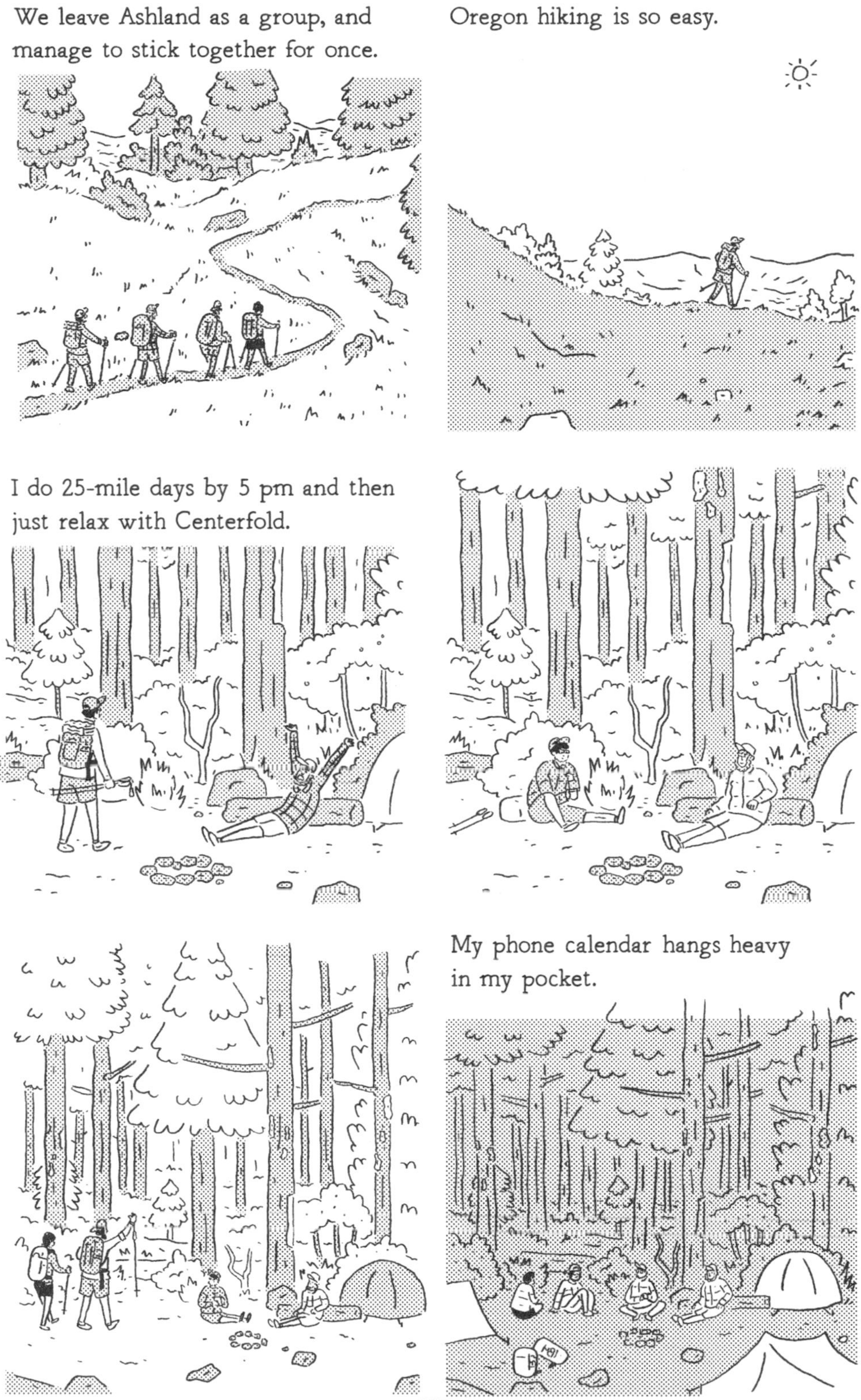
We leave Ashland as a group, and manage to stick together for once.
Oregon hiking is so easy.
I do 25-mile days by 5 pm and then just relax with Centerfold.
My phone calendar hangs heavy in my pocket.

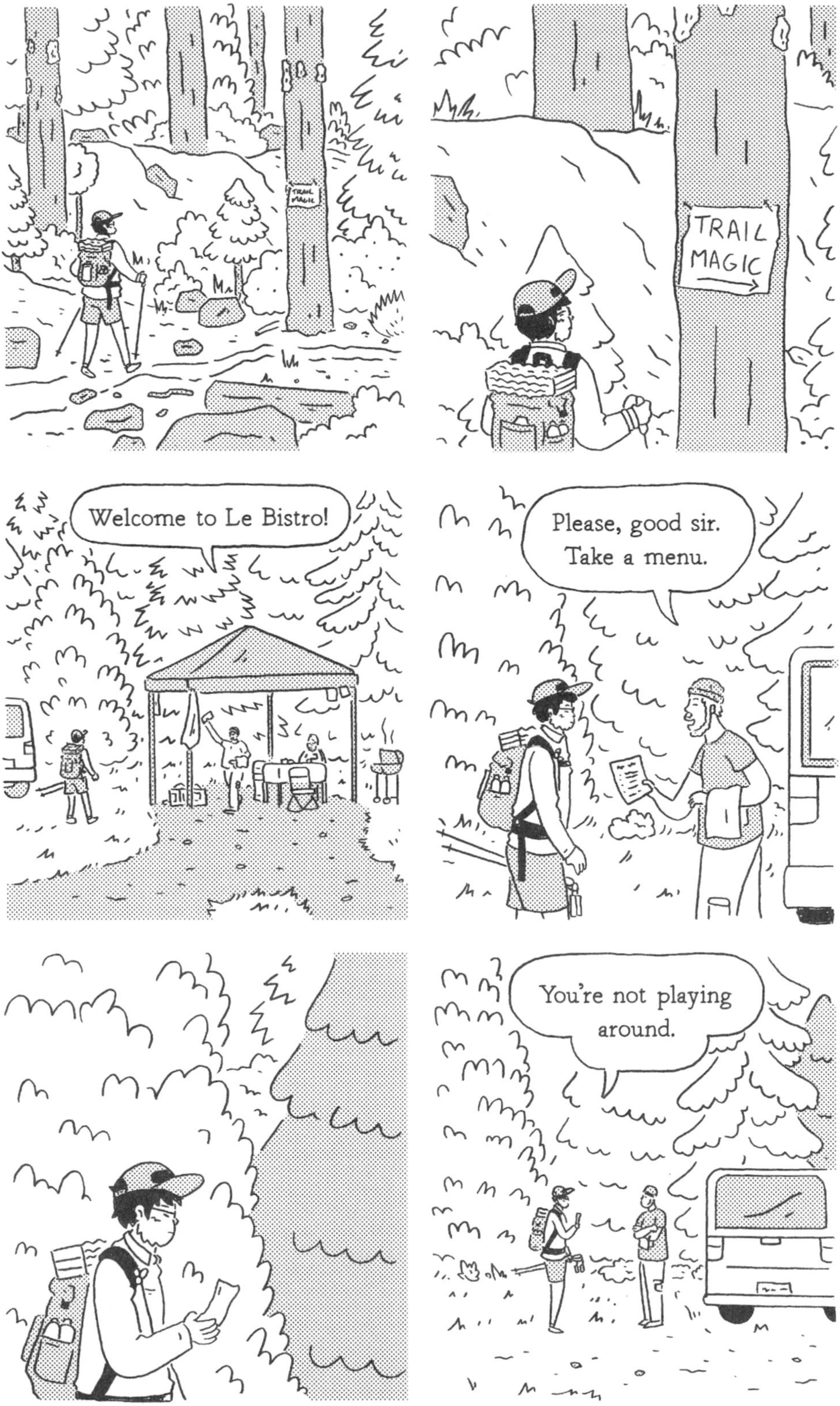
TRAIL
MAGIC
Welcome to Le Bistro!
Please, good sir. Take a menu.
You're not playing around.

We sleep at Le Bistro, after stuffing ourselves with delicious sandwiches.

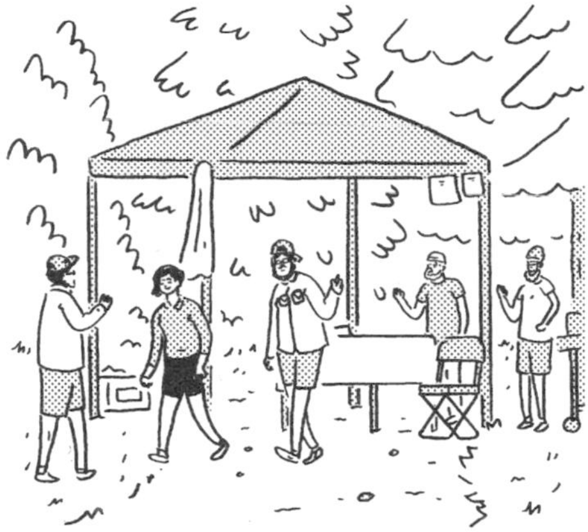

The trail angels take Molly and laugh and whoop at a meteor shower.

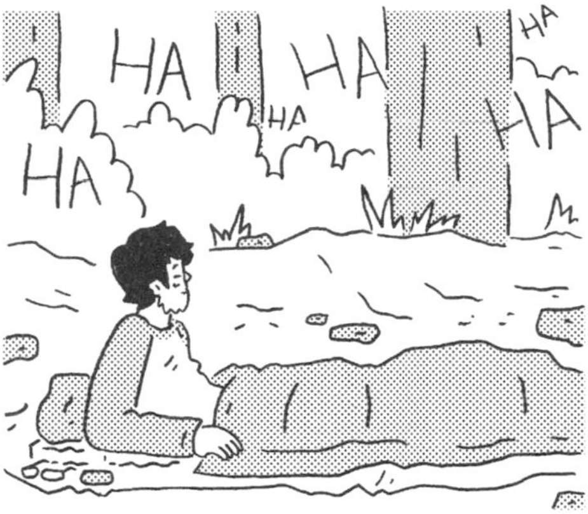
HA
HA
HA
HA
HA
HA
HA

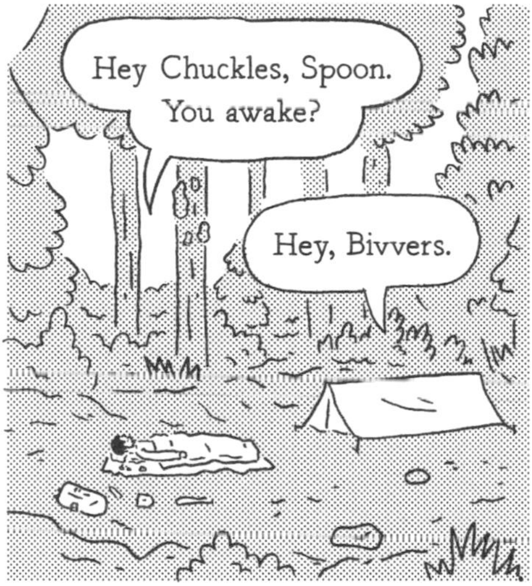
Hey Chuckles, Spoon. You awake?
Hey, Bivvers.

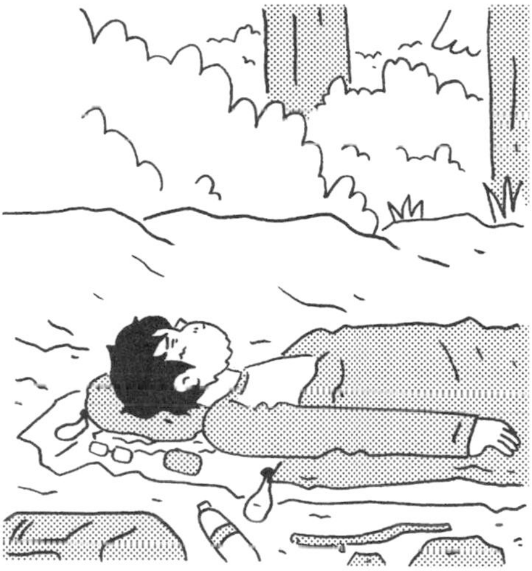

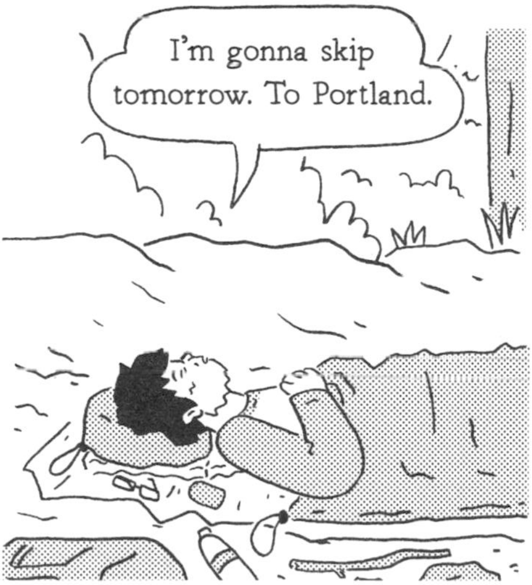
I'm gonna skip tomorrow. To Portland.

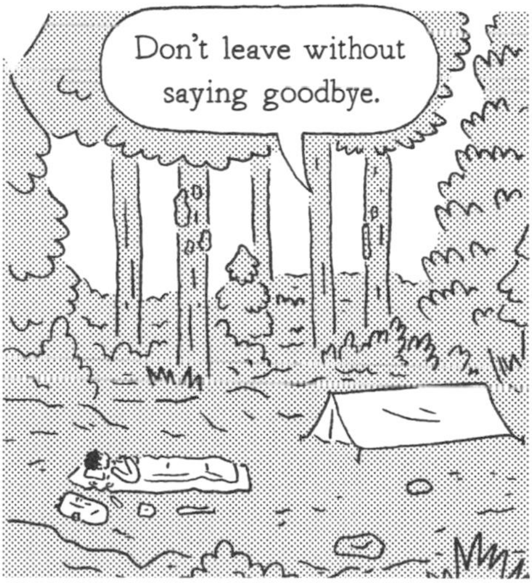
Don't leave without saying goodbye.

I wake in the cool morning before everyone else, and wander through the trees.

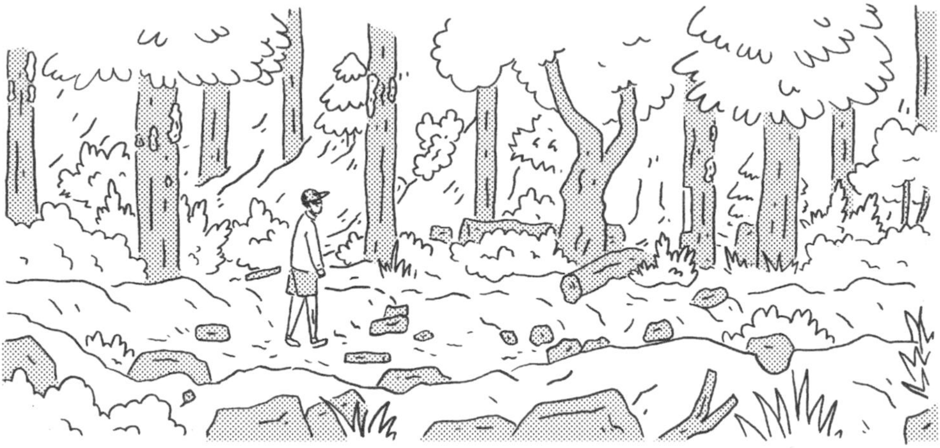

I say goodbye to Chuckles and Little Spoon.

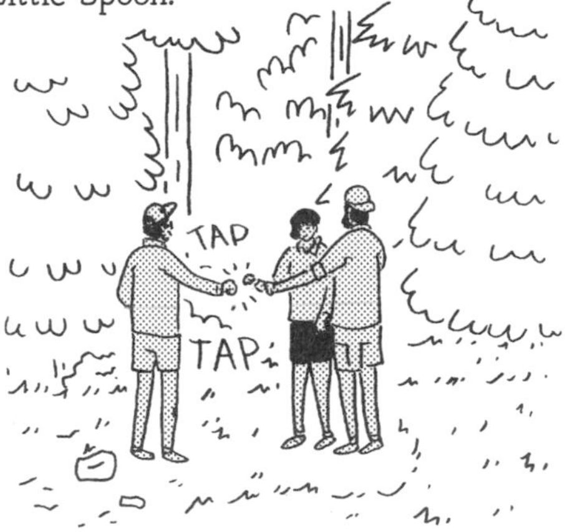
TAP
TAP

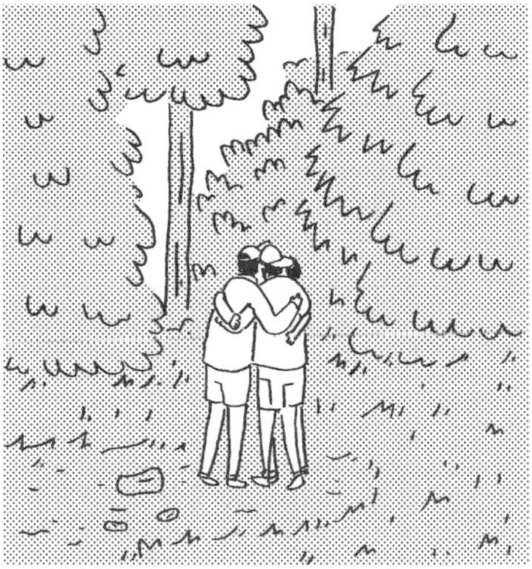

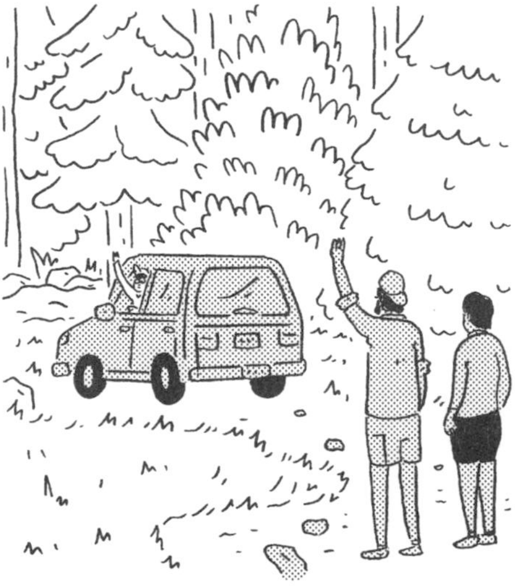

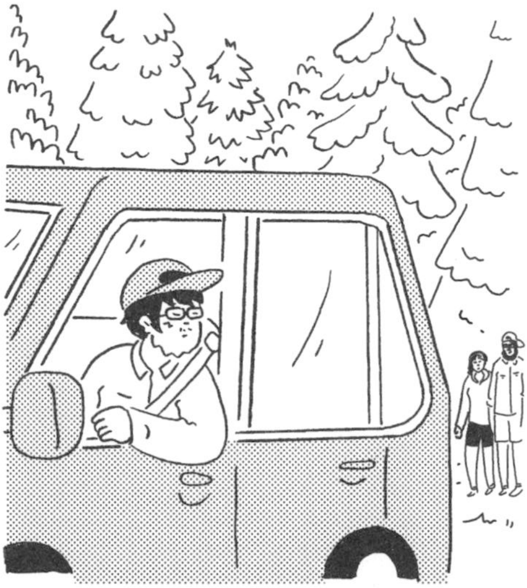

In four hours, I move two weeks' hiking miles.

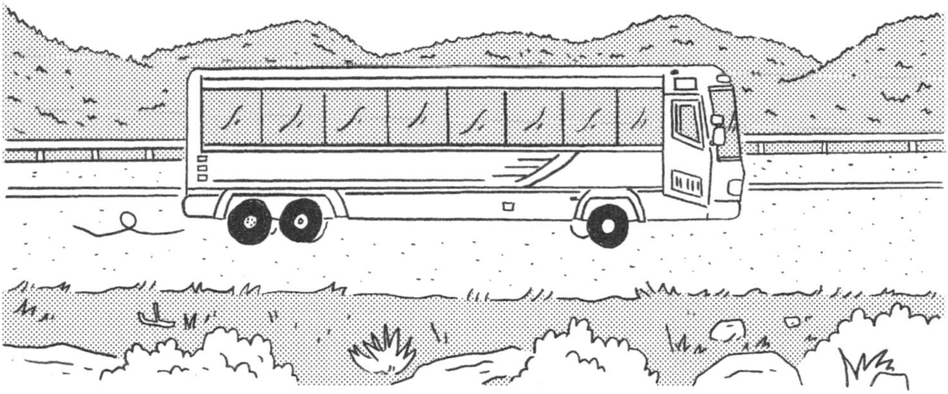

I meet Eleri at a sunny Portland cafe.

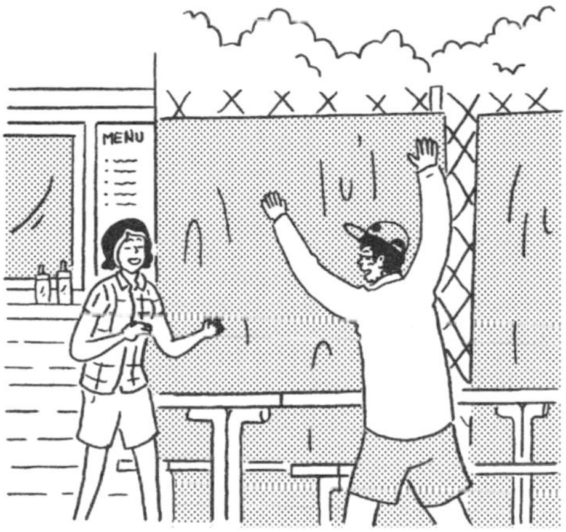
MENU

We hug, and it's like no time has passed.

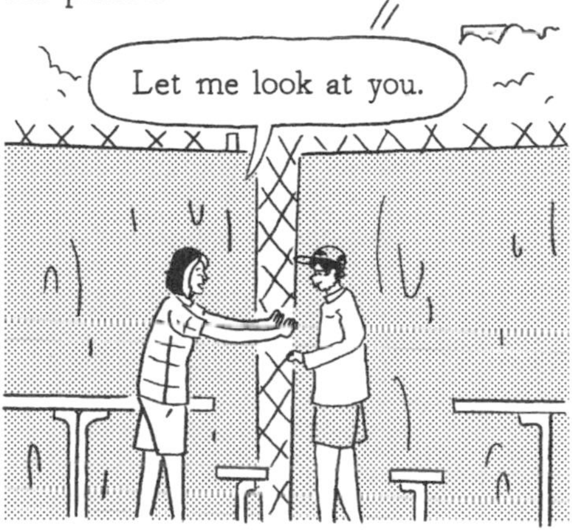
Let me look at you.

I realise that I have seen her twice a year since our graduation, across three different continents.

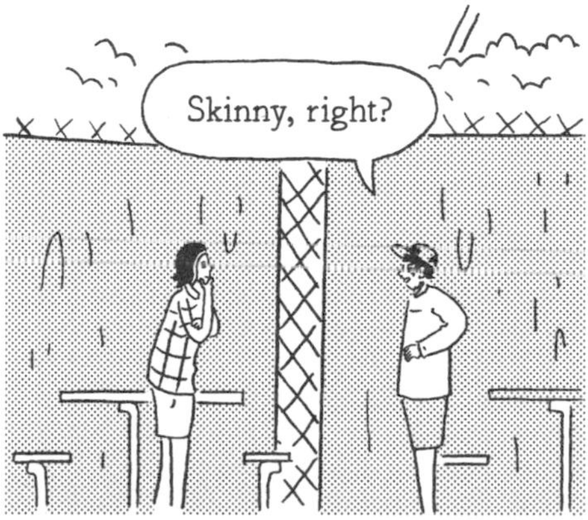
Skinny, right?

I realise I was an idiot to worry.

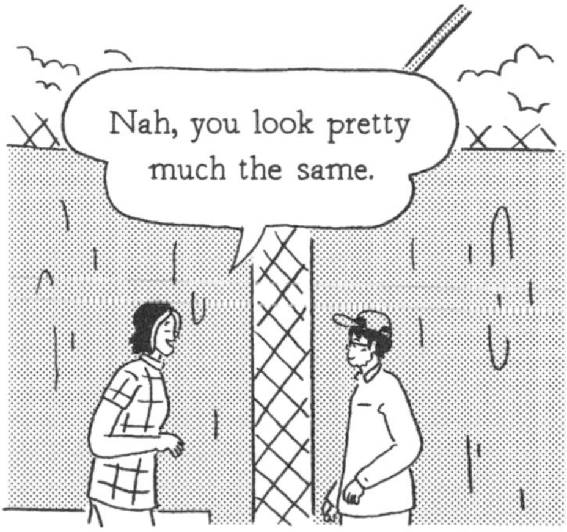
Nah, you look pretty much the same.

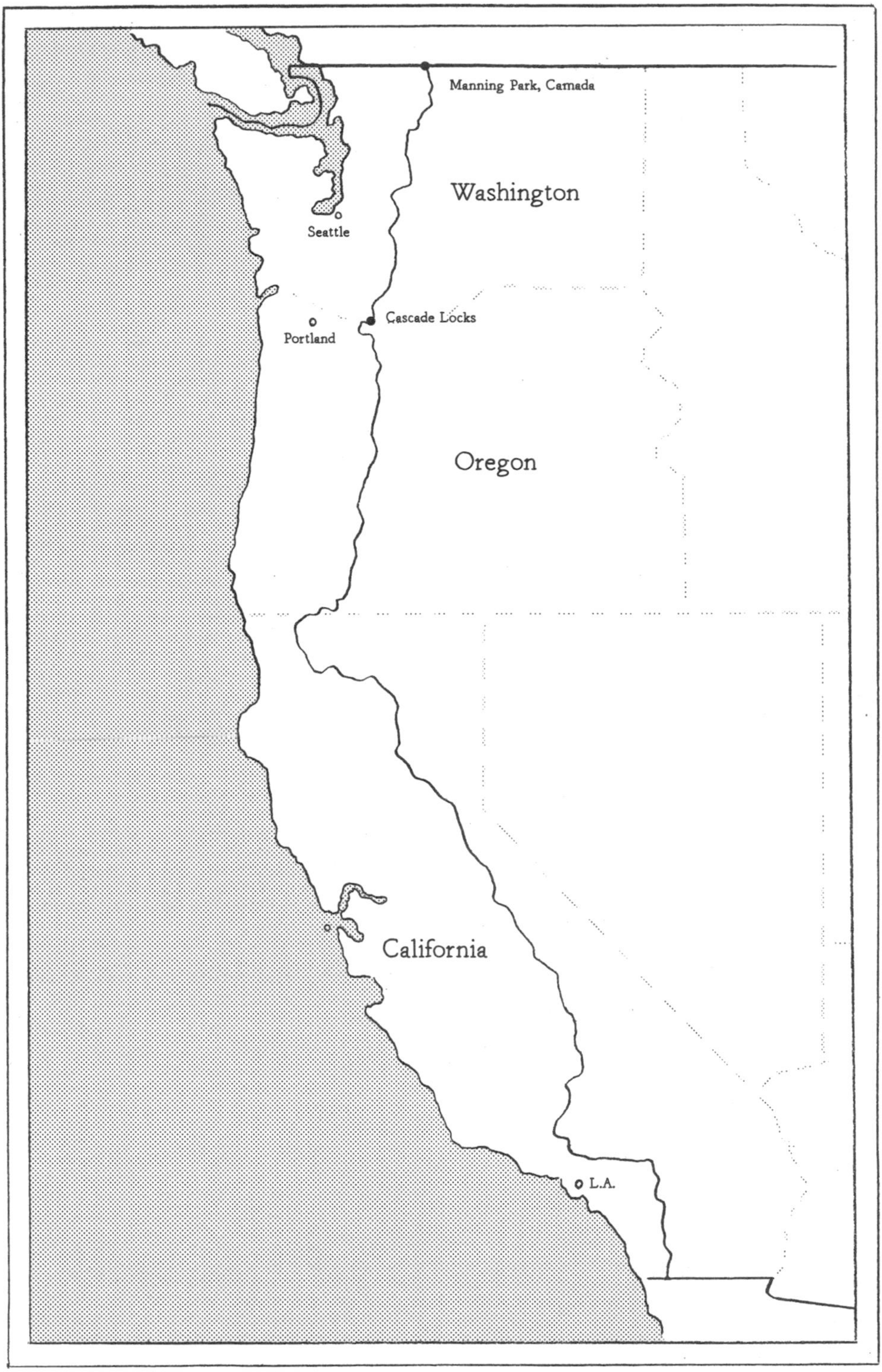
Manning Park, Camada
Washington
Seattle
Portland
Cascade Locks
Oregon
California
L.A.

Chapter 6: Washington

"America is a nation that conceives many odd
inventions for getting somewhere but it can
think of nothing to do once it gets there."
–Will Rogers

It feels appropriate that I learned about the PCT from a film trailer, the same way I'd heard about the cartoon school. The same way I'd learned about America as a child. It was *Wild*, the story of a woman who hiked 1100 miles of the PCT in 1997.

It captured my imagination immediately and refused to leave my brain in the weeks and months that followed. I entertained fantasies of taking off into the wilderness as I sat at my desk. I worked on comics full time, though I was basically unemployed, for all of the income it generated. The notion of moving out, finding somewhere to live and managing to pay rent and bills was nothing more than that, a notion. Despite my best efforts, and my many, many applications, I couldn't find regular employment in the post-crisis economy. But the PCT was out there, waiting. No bills, no landlords. Free to live on.

And it was something. Some new thing to use as the metre of my life's progress. I read the book *Wild*, the basis for the film, then saw the film when it was eventually released in Ireland, months after its US debut.

Then I read another book; and more books, and blogs, and watched online videos and listened to interviews, and special ordered documentaries. All in secret, at first. It gave me something to do in between emailing CVs and grinding out comics pages.

That winter, when I was offered my first book advance, I already knew how I would spend it.

I told my parents about the PCT not long after I'd knuckled down to work on that book. The advance was small, and to keep myself financially solvent, I needed to continue to live with them. It was impossible to keep it a secret, the books were starting to pile up on my shelves. Besides, it was really all I wanted to talk about.

I told them about it at a dinner celebrating my mother's birthday. We ate in a pub, tucked away on a back road not too far from our home. The pub burned turf in the fire, which made the whole place smell rich and earthy, like the Irish countryside.

My parents scoffed, at first – as did a lot of people – when I told them about my plan. I can't blame them, really. I'd never done anything remotely athletic in my life, no camping or backpacking. And while I felt positive that the hike was an excellent plan, I understood why people were so sceptical.

Eleri was the next person I told. I told her on the bus to Toronto, eight hours into our journey, once we'd run out of other things to talk about. She, more than anyone, expressed extreme scepticism.

"Well, have you ever gone camping before?"

"No."

"And why exactly do you think you'll enjoy it at all? What makes you think that you won't get out there for two days and then realise you hate it?"

The setting sun dyed everything orange. We sat at the very front of the bus, with a perfect view out of the front windows.

"I just know that I'll like it. I feel it."

I knew vagueness would push her buttons, but there was an unstated acknowledgement between us. She might be right. Hiking the PCT was a weird, out of character thing to do. But I wasn't lying either. Deep down, I did just feel it. I knew that hiking the PCT was the right decision. I needed something. Some direction.

I prepped for the PCT for almost two full years. I saved, and studied, and calculated in almost every free moment I could get. I started taking practice hikes. Ten miles every day. I thought that I could get myself trail ready by walking ten-mile loops down the level-smooth canal pathway near my parents' house.

Even in those ideal conditions, I knew that I was in disastrously bad shape. I'd gained a lot in White River Junction, including a small gut. "Comics will make you fat," a visiting artist once told me. And even after I'd returned to Ireland, hiking ten miles per day, I spent the other ninety per cent of my time glued to a desk, drawing pages, which took its own physical toll.

I did have moments of doubt in that time. I waited as long as possible before I began to purchase gear because part of me wouldn't believe that I was going to go and try this. Part of me urged the rest to stop, to put down roots. Work harder to find a job. Make some new friends. Stop spending every weekend locked away in my parents' house, working on comics and scrimping together every penny.

Only ten days before my flight to the USA, I slipped a disc in my back, laying me in bed for a week. I had an MRI scan, which my doctor scrutinised, as I told her I was planning on taking a hike soon.

"Exercise is good for a back injury," she told me. I neglected to mention the duration of the hike, nor the weight of the water-filled pack I'd soon be hauling through the California desert.

It felt like the perfect excuse to quit while I was ahead.

I did the rounds with my parents, visiting my grandparents, and hugging them, and telling them I'd see them soon.

I flew from Dublin, saying goodbye to my parents at departures, acting more confident than I was. I met Rachel and Mike in Los Angeles, and ate food that was way too spicy for me. I drove to San Diego with Rachel. I stayed with the trail angels there who told me never to quit on a bad day.

In the cool morning light, I rode in a car to the Southern Terminus. I took a picture beside the border wall.

And I hiked.

Marina, a trail angel, drops me off in Cascade Locks. The town is small and dominated by the hulking Bridge of the Gods, which hangs above it like a twisted sculpture.

Several hikers mill around the town's ale house, eating and drinking, and I'm immediately pulled back into trail world. I eat and drink too. I chat to some of the hikers. They're different than the hikers I left in Oregon. The middle-of-the-pack casualness of Spoon, Chuckles and Centerfold is absent here. They're not unfriendly, but they exude intensity. These are the people who have been forging the path for us all summer, pulling thirties since Northern California at least. And now I'm one of them, or a pretender in their ranks, at least.

I half expect everybody at the head of the pack to look like the ultralighter who passed me near Agua Dulce; lean and tall with long beards and tiny packs. And while there are plenty of scruffy trail beards, the hikers don't look lean. They look starved and exhausted. Their packs are huge. I wonder how the hell they walked five hundred more miles than me with those enormous things on their backs.

After we finish eating, I join a few head-of-the-packers as they walk further up the town's main street, and buy comically tall cones of soft-serve ice cream. They lighten up a little, and goof off as they try to shove the foot-tall towers of ice cream into their mouths before they begin to melt. Even at this they're competitive, egging each other on with bizarrely macho language as they gag and wince from brain freeze.

You've got to be tough to get to the head of the pack.

I get a small cone.

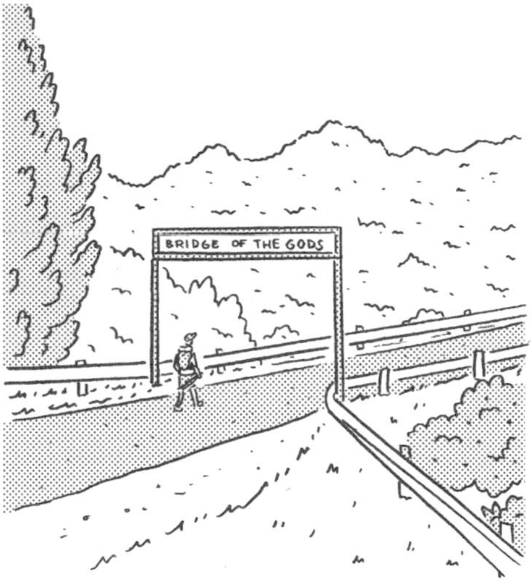
BRIDGE OF THE GODS

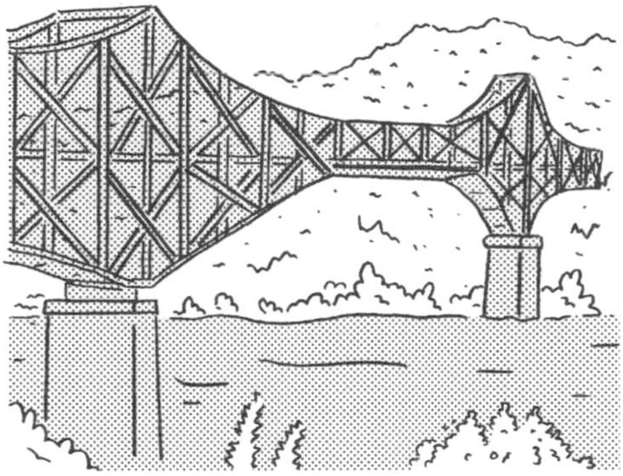

I spiral up, out of Cascade Locks into the Washington forest.

Another new world.

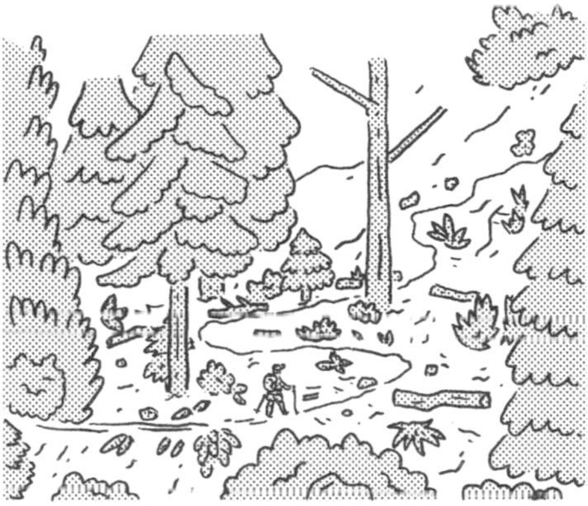

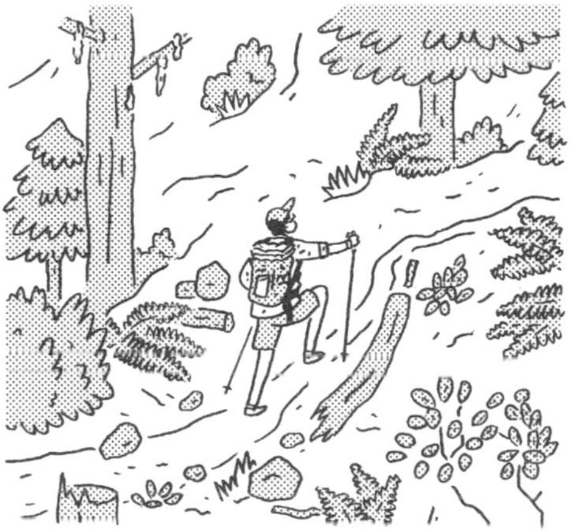

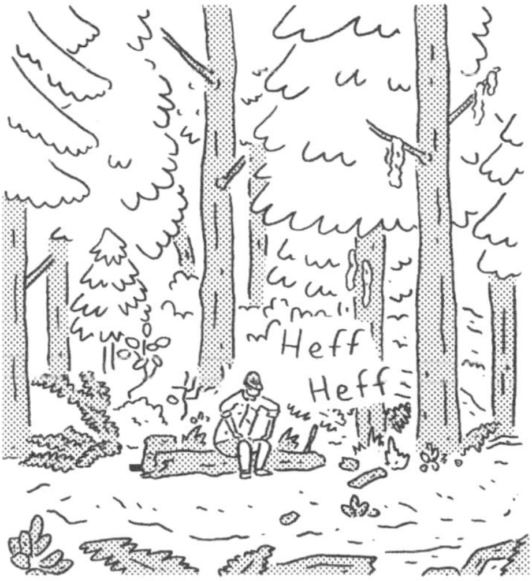
Heff
Heff

I'm glad to be back.

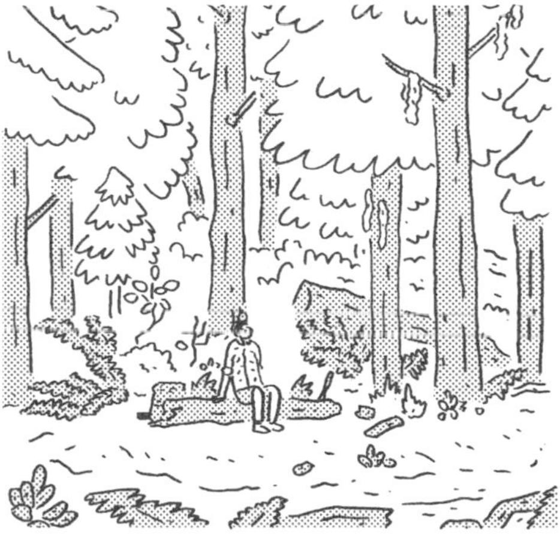

The hiking in Washington isn't easy. I'd heard it called the "Second Sierra" on trail before, alluding to its familiar pattern of pass-valley-pass hiking. Checking the elevation charts on my phone, I can tell it's going to be a challenge. The climbs are tall, though mercifully cut with switchbacks most of the way.

Even below the rainforest canopy, the late summer sun keeps me warm, just as the trees keep me sheltered from the breeze. I feel good. Though my body is fatigued, it's also strong. As strong as it has ever been. I have been exercising all day, every day, for months.

But as the sunlight begins to fade, and the trail is submerged in twilight, I do not feel very strong at all.

I am filled with terror.

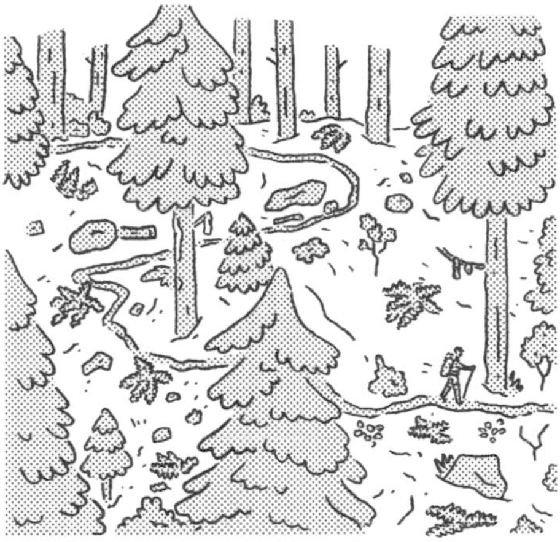

I can't sleep alone again. I can't.

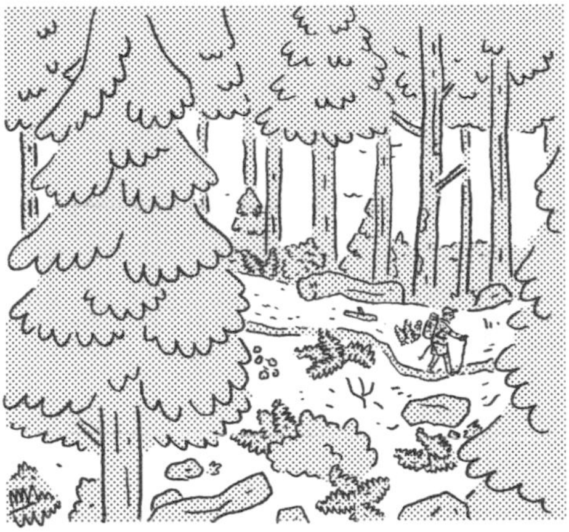

Not in the forest.

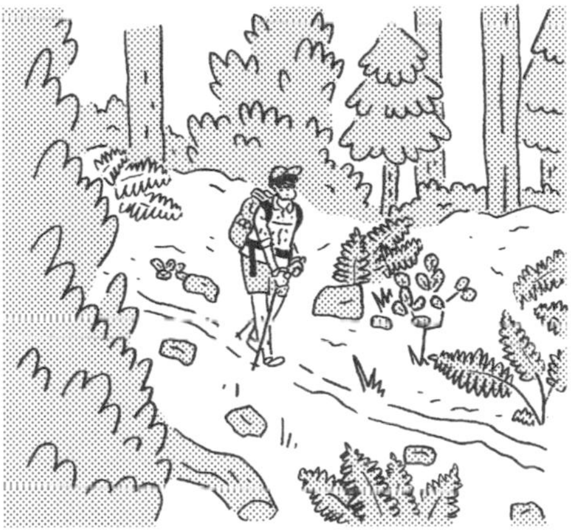

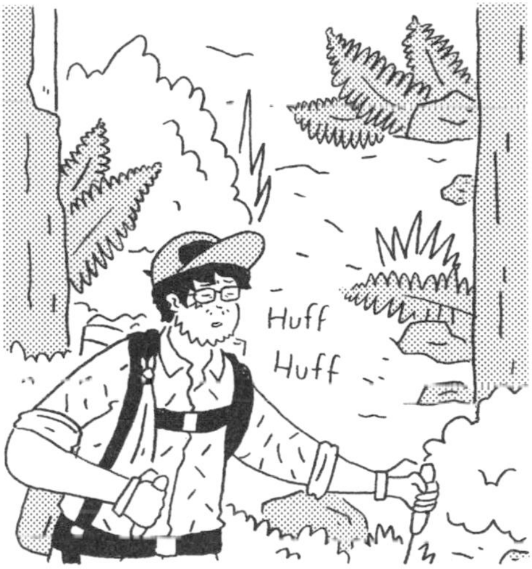
Huff
Huff

Stay calm, Luke.

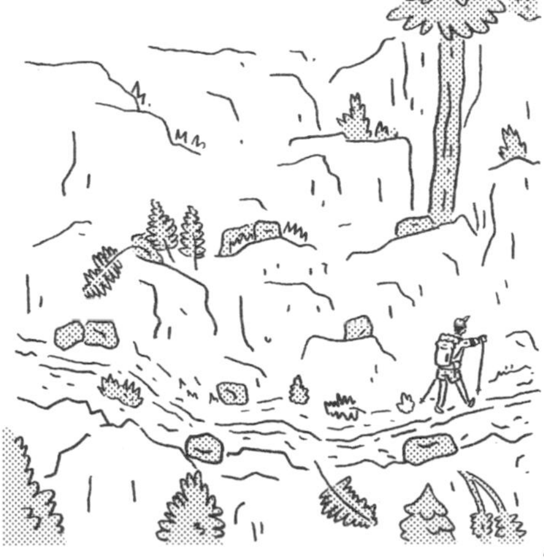

Just keep hiking.

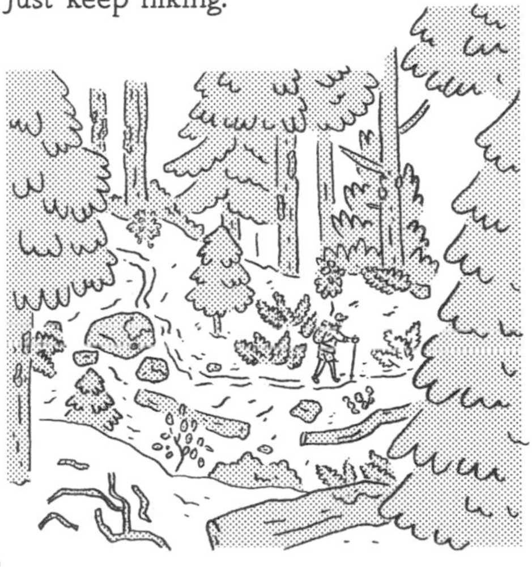

Twenty miles.

Twenty-five.

Twenty-eight. The furthest I have ever hiked in a day. But this time there's no fire to run from.

Only shadows.

Huff
Huff

Heff
Heff

"You happen to have room for one more?" I ask, approaching their campsite, trying to act casual, like I hadn't just been rushing through the twilight for hours, trying to find someone to camp with.

"We can make room," says a smiling hiker with short curly hair. She extends her fist. "I'm Pretzel."

"Bivvy," I respond, and bump her fist, before settling down to dig out my own food, which has been rehydrating in a plastic jar.

"You're going stoveless?" asks the other female hiker, who introduces herself as Jukebox. "You're gonna miss hot food when the weather turns."

"I needed to lighten my pack if I wanted to keep up with all you fast hikers."

"You're not a fast hiker?"

"No, just a cheater."

Pretzel and Jukebox remind me of Mile 55 a little. They're as competitive as the rest of the head-of-the-packers for sure, but they're a little lighter about it. They don't seem to take themselves too seriously.

Bankshot, the other hiker in camp, skipped a section like me. He's taking the opposite approach in attempting to blend with the faster hikers. Where I choose self-effacement, cracking jokes about being a cheater, Bankshot acts macho – and a little taciturn. Still, he's friendly enough, and I'm glad to be surrounded by people as my first day in Washington turns to night.

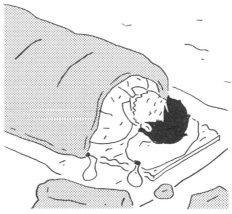

Head of the pack.

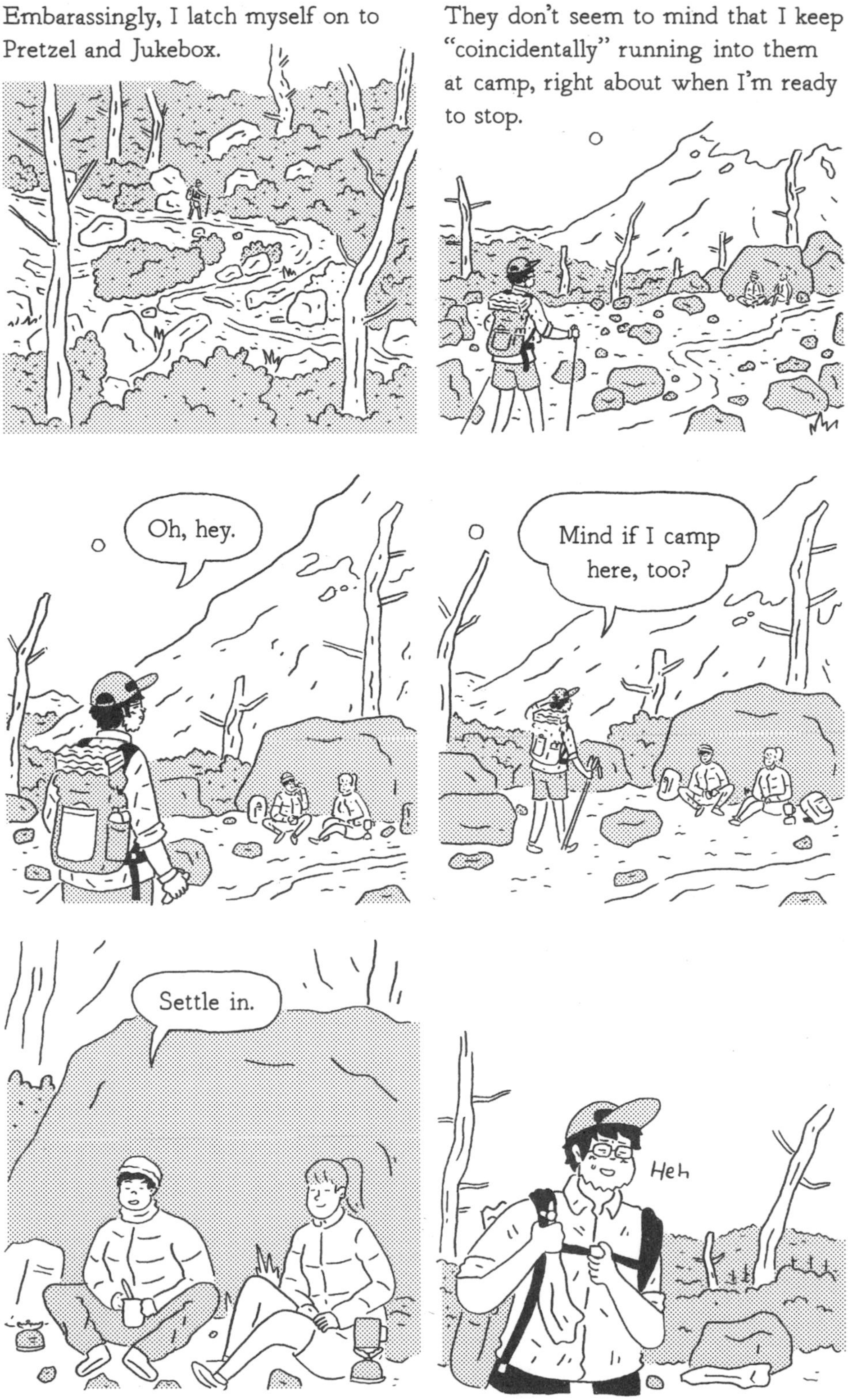
Embarassingly, I latch myself on to Pretzel and Jukebox.
They don't seem to mind that I keep "coincidentally" running into them at camp, right about when I'm ready to stop.
Oh, hey.
Mind if I camp here, too?
Settle in.
Heh

The three of us trip together through the passes and small towns of the state.

On the way out of Trout Lake, I hitch-hike with a kombucha-maker, who teaches me how to forage for berries along the trail, and from then on, I move a little slower, stopping every once in a while to pick the huckleberries, wild blueberries, salmonberries and my favourite of all, thimbleberries, to supplement my cracker-filled food bag.

We do our best to enjoy the last of the summer's good weather, cowboy camping every night under the pale, blue sky, falling asleep before it even gets a chance to turn black. We hike through dry stretches, and an enormous burn, reminding us that not even rainy Washington is safe from forest fires.

We all know that "the carwash" is coming.

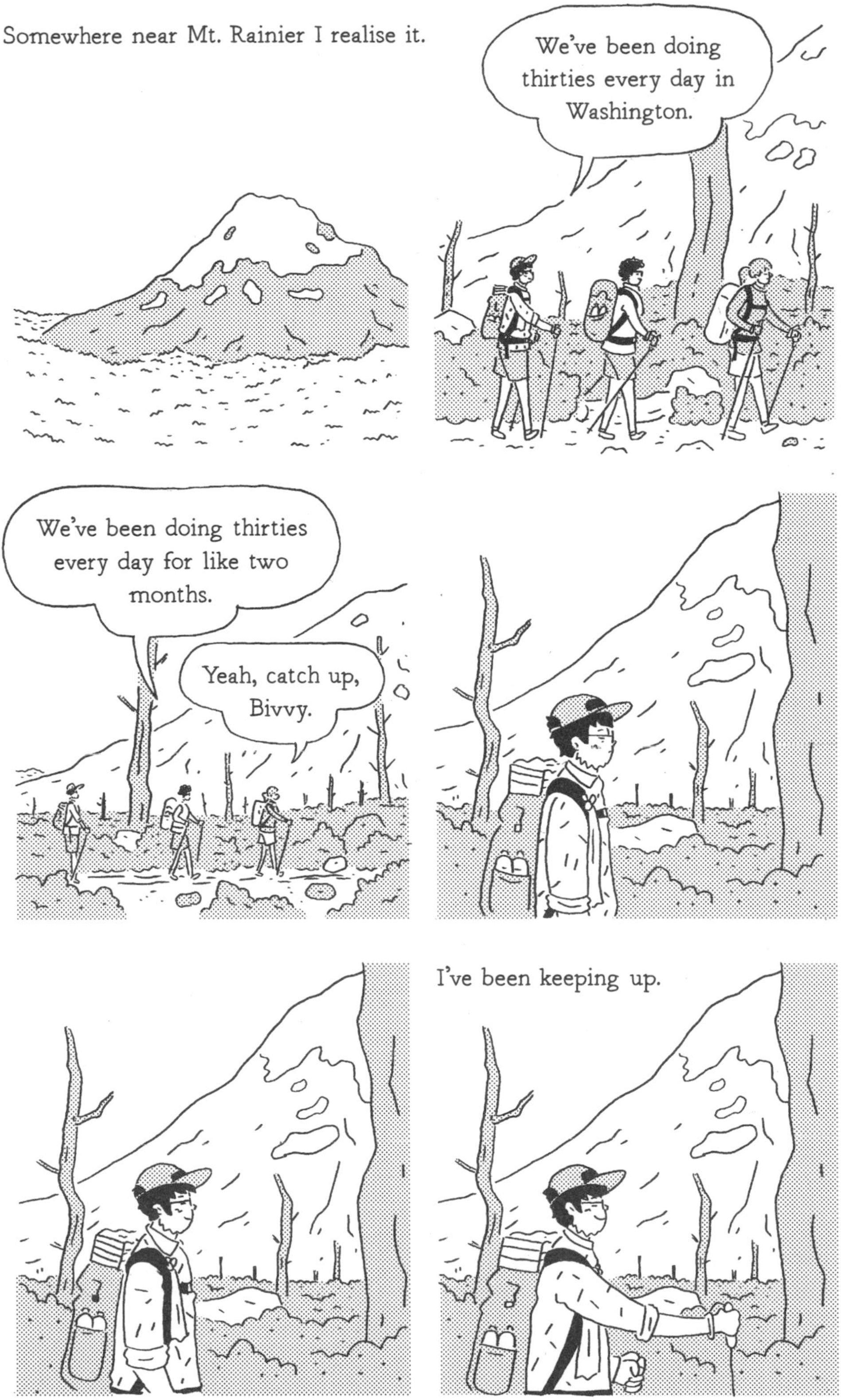
Somewhere near Mt. Rainier I realise it.
We've been doing thirties every day in Washington.
We've been doing thirties every day for like two months.
Yeah, catch up, Bivvy.
I've been keeping up.

Soon, it's more than keeping up.
I'm actually faster than them.

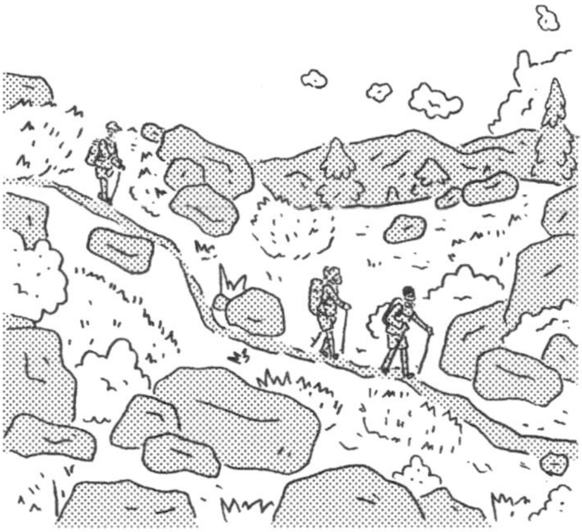

I pass them every day.

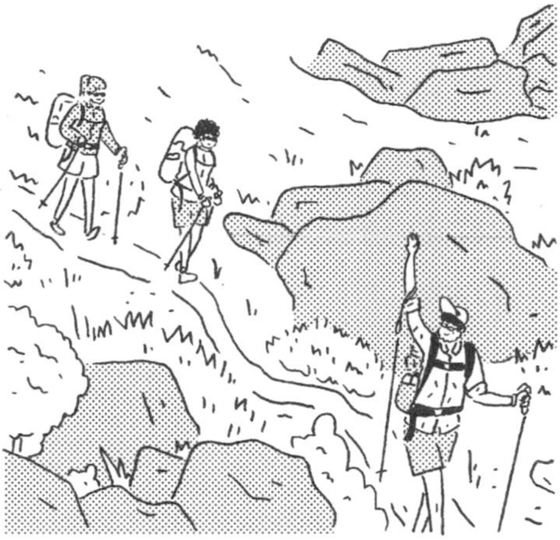

It makes sense. They've been running on empty for longer than I have.

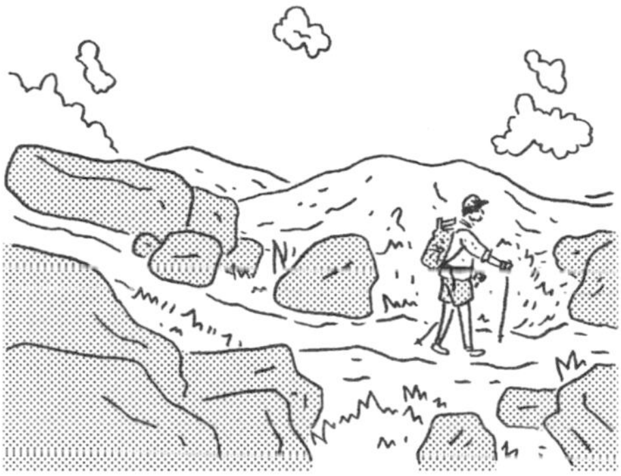

Still, it doesn't fail to hit home.
I am a strong hiker. Finally.

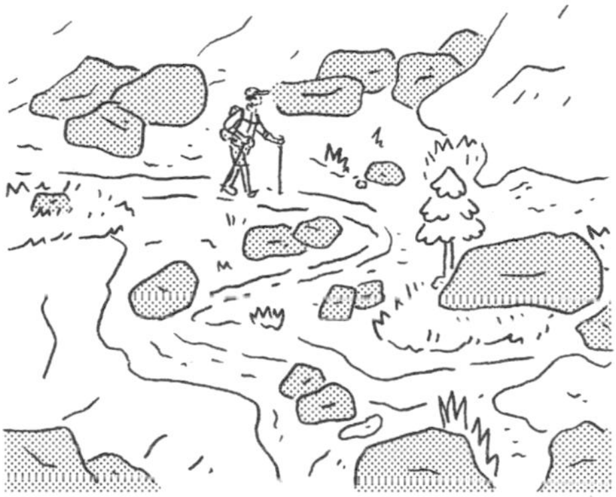

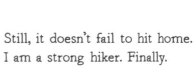

Turns out all I needed was to be traumatised by some mountain lions.

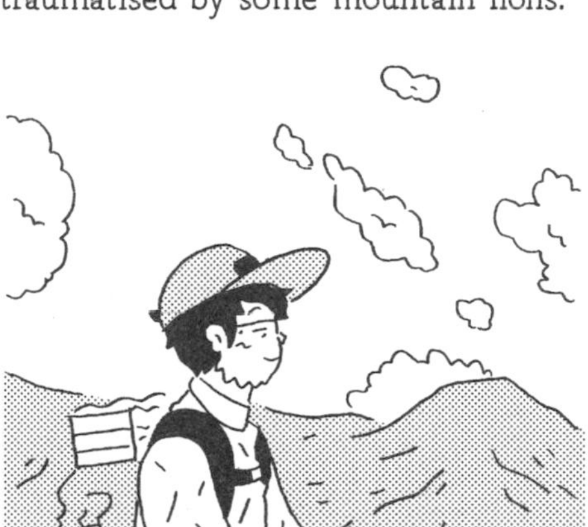

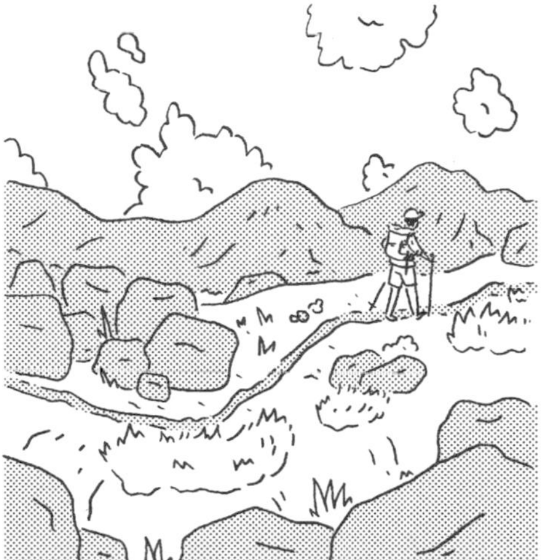

In every endeavour, there is a point of no return. It's hard to say where mine was. Was it the moment I discovered the PCT to begin with? When I didn't quit at Cajon Pass? Or maybe when I returned to trail from L.A. with Luanne? Was it when I didn't go home to see my grandfather? Was it when he died?

I can't say. I don't know. But I know that it has passed. There is no going back from here. In a matter of weeks, no matter what, I will stand at the border between the USA and Canada.

That is what I tell myself as I finish circling Mt. Rainier with Pretzel and Jukebox. They're leaving trail at White's Pass for a few days, so I'll have to continue on alone.

I think back on what Griz told me when I'd decided to quit in Southern California.

"If you feel like you've gotten everything you wanted out of the trail, it's ok to stop. And good for you, man. You made it really far."

Now, four months later, I've gotten everything I wanted out of the trail, save for one thing. I want an America with no "what ifs".

I want closure.

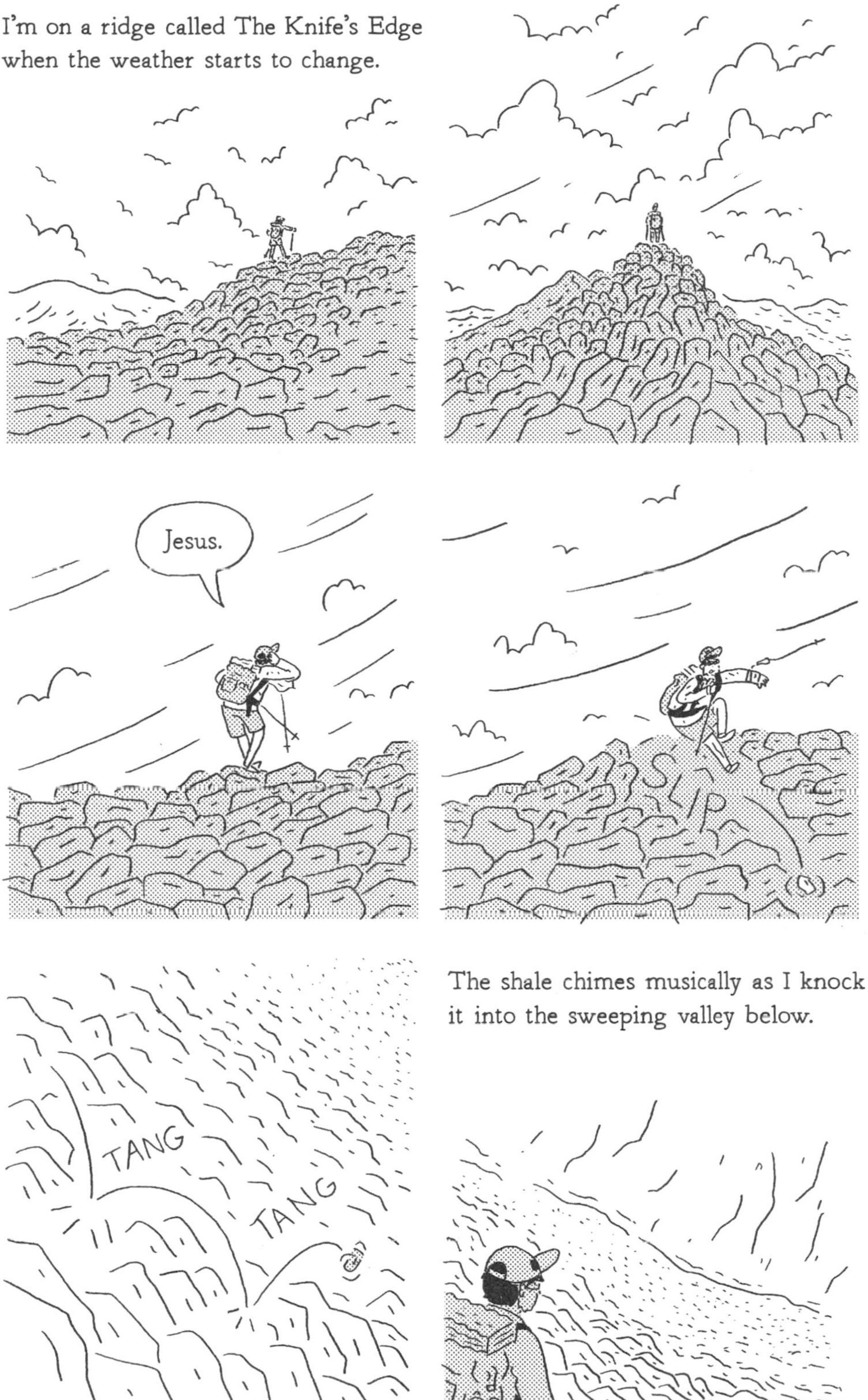
I'm on a ridge called The Knife's Edge when the weather starts to change.
Jesus.
SLIP
TANG
TANG
The shale chimes musically as I knock it into the sweeping valley below.

We just miss the start of the rain. As I descend The Knife's Edge, the clouds begin to drip. I convince Pretzel and Jukebox to split a hostel room with me at the off-season ski lodge nearby.

We crank the heat, and I tear apart my resupply box, eating bits and pieces of my trail food. Pretzel and Jukebox watch the Olympics on TV. I watch the rain and wind blow outside.

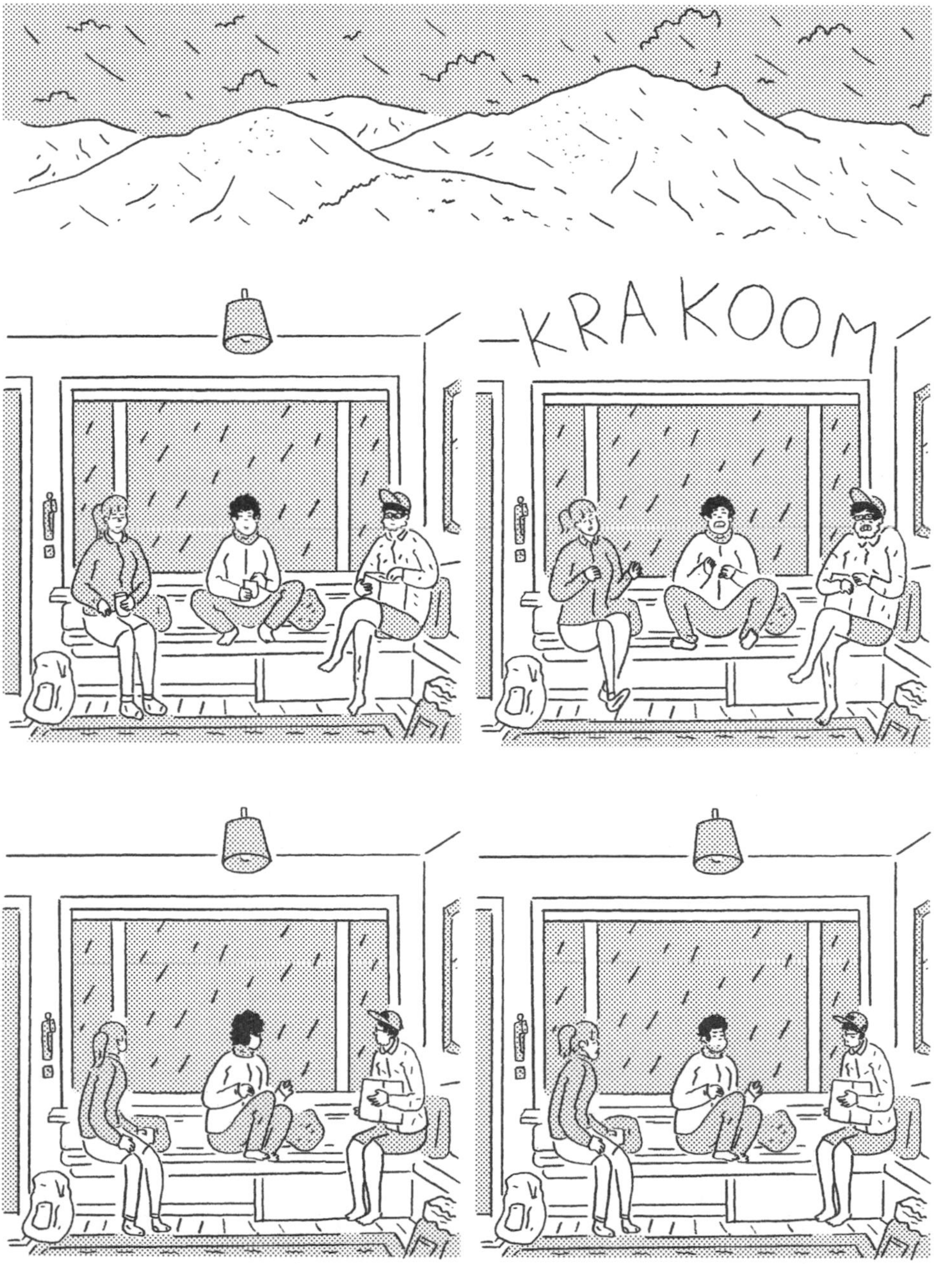
KRAKOOM

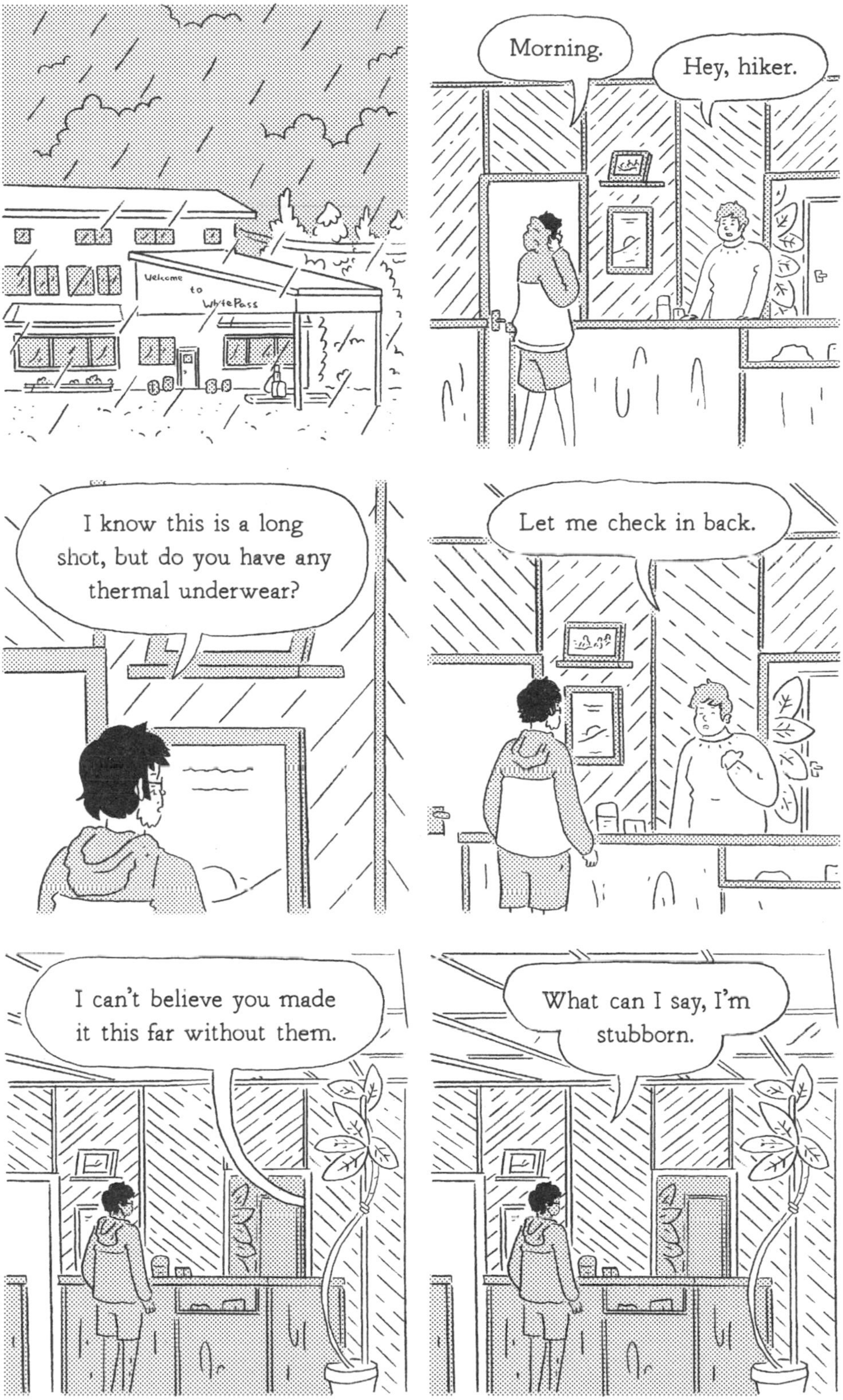
Welcome to WhytePass
Morning.
Hey, hiker.
I know this is a long shot, but do you have any thermal underwear?
Let me check in back.
I can't believe you made it this far without them.
What can I say, I'm stubborn.

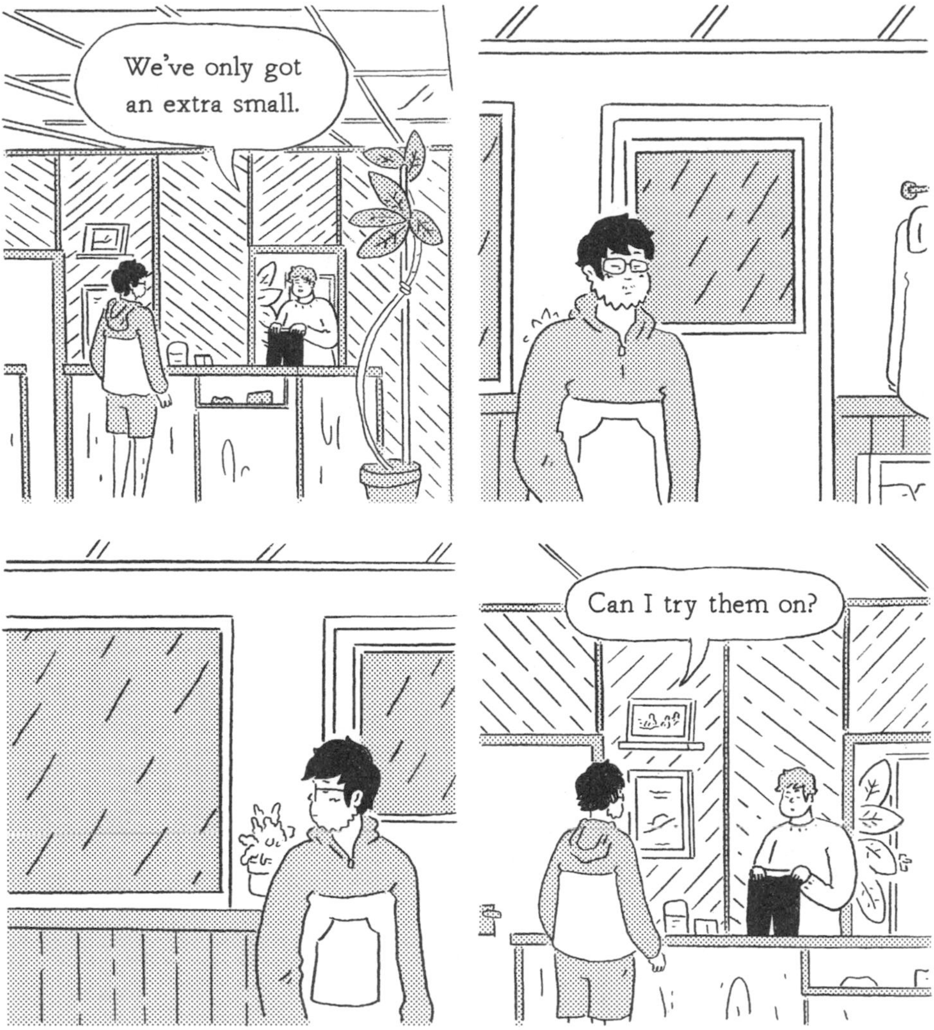
We've only got an extra small.
Can I try them on?

They fit, with a little room to spare. I've never worn anything smaller than a medium before in my life.

I shouldn't be surprised, really. I feel tiny. I'm wasting away. I must have lost at least a quarter of my body weight since beginning the trail almost five months ago. I know that my dwindling weight is a ticking clock, maybe even more so than the encroaching bad weather. I'm becoming calorie deficient, I can feel it. Feel myself slowing down. I don't have the stores of body fat to support this kind of physical abuse for much longer. I buy the extra small underwear and I hike.

Washington transforms in the rain.

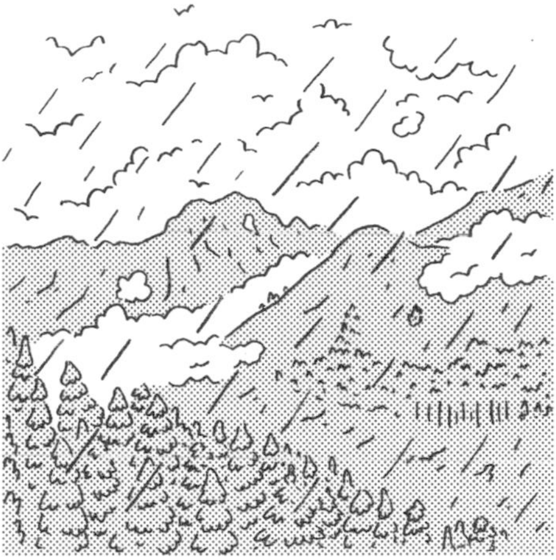

The loamy forest is dank with mist and animated to the soundtrack of pattering drops.

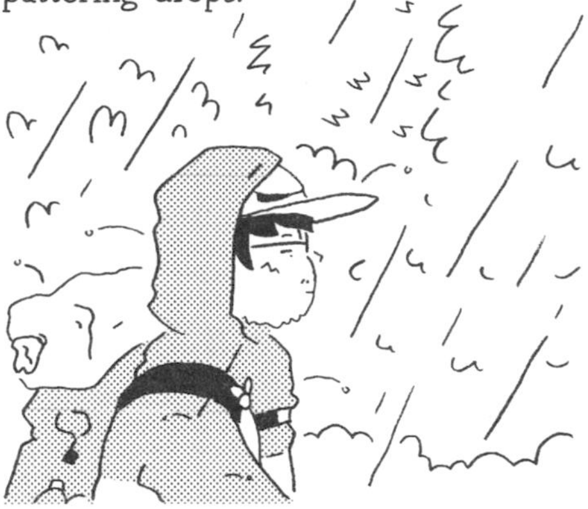

Big flat salmonberry leaves slap my legs as I hike.

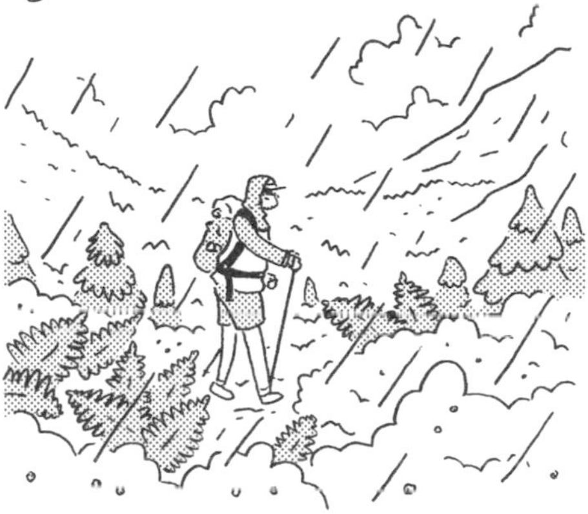

"The carwash".

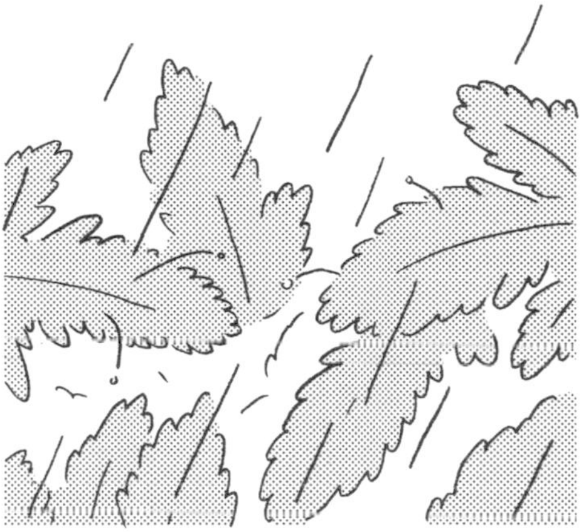

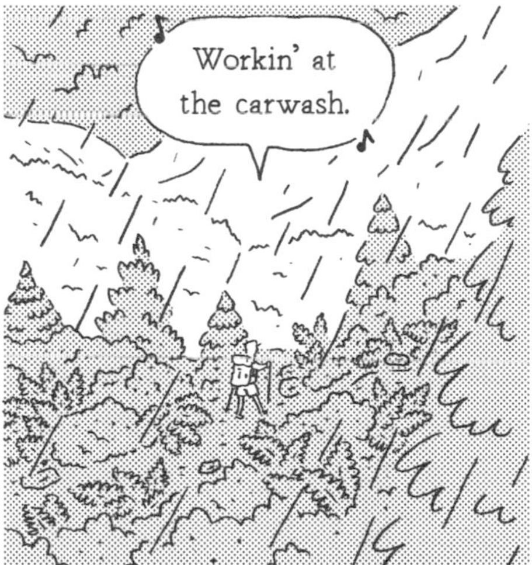
Workin' at the carwash.

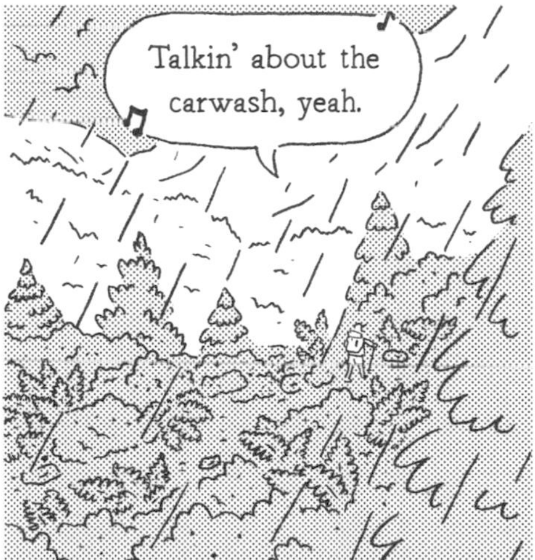
Talkin' about the carwash, yeah.

Bankshot catches up to me, and we become hiking partners, mostly by accident.

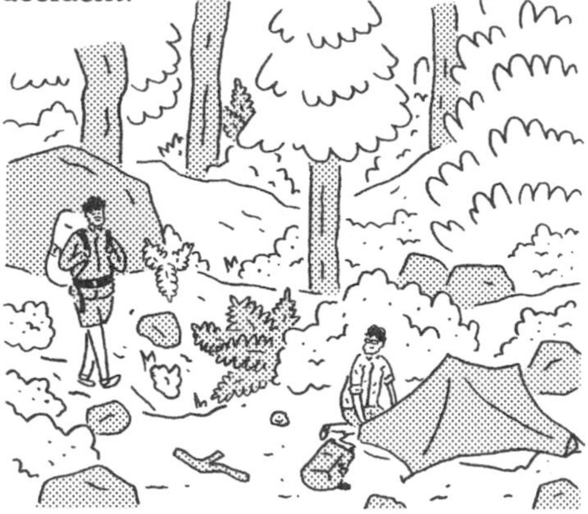

Our paces are similar, and he seems to dislike camping alone, too.

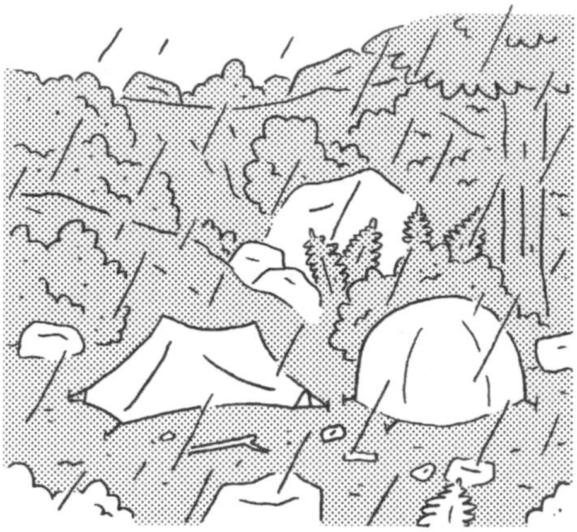

The Washington miles continue to fall away.

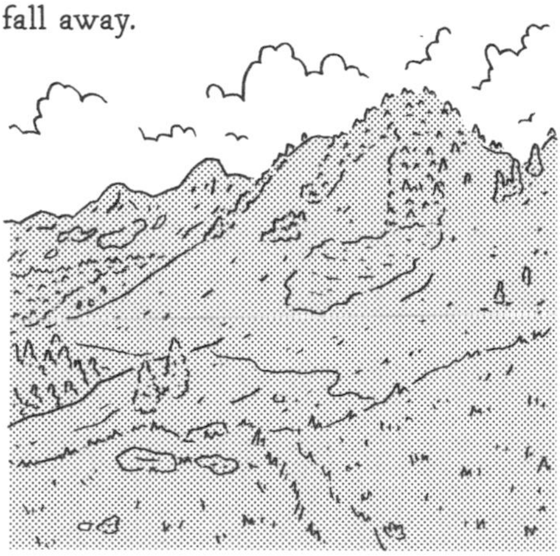

We trip through the now rare small towns, grateful for any chance to sleep indoors, away from the rain.

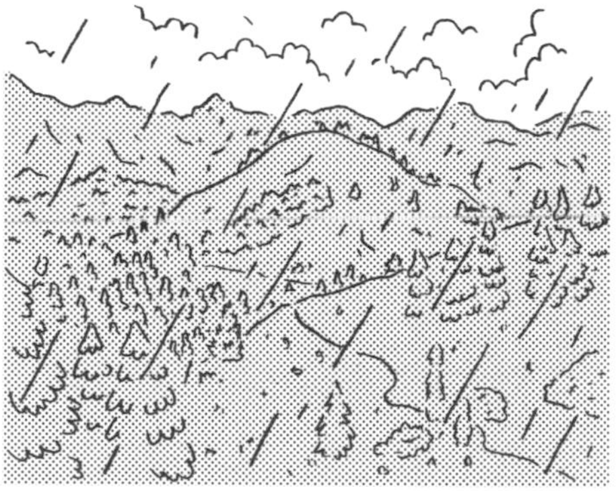

We hike with focus.

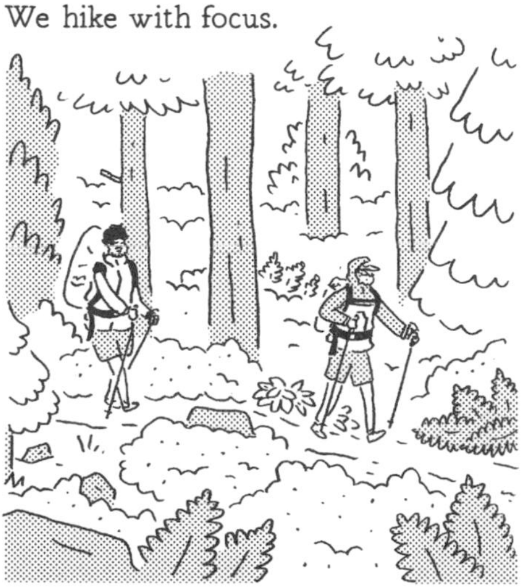

Canada lives in our brains.

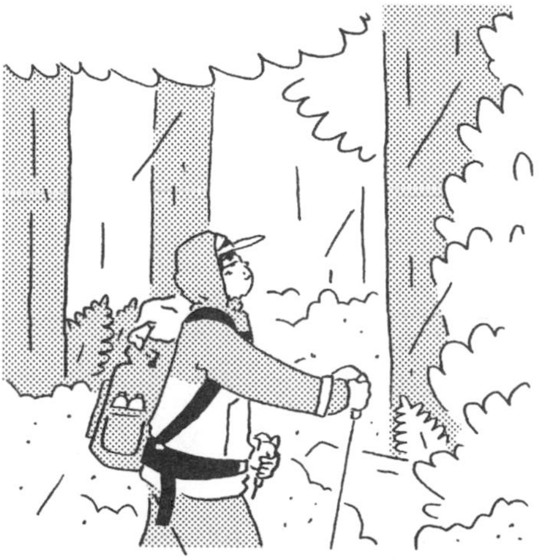

I hike out of Baring Town. Bankshot and I fall in with the head-of-the-packers who ate the giant ice creams in Cascade Locks and we camp with them most nights. There is something about a rainy trail that pushes hikers together. I'm glad to have the company. I'm really glad to have my new thermal underwear, but even with them I shiver all night.

Waiting in town for good weather isn't an option any more. We won't get any good weather windows large enough to complete the remaining sections, which in the Washington Cascades are long. Most take five days at least, and even then the stops are remote.

We push on through the rain.

And are in the storm before we know it.

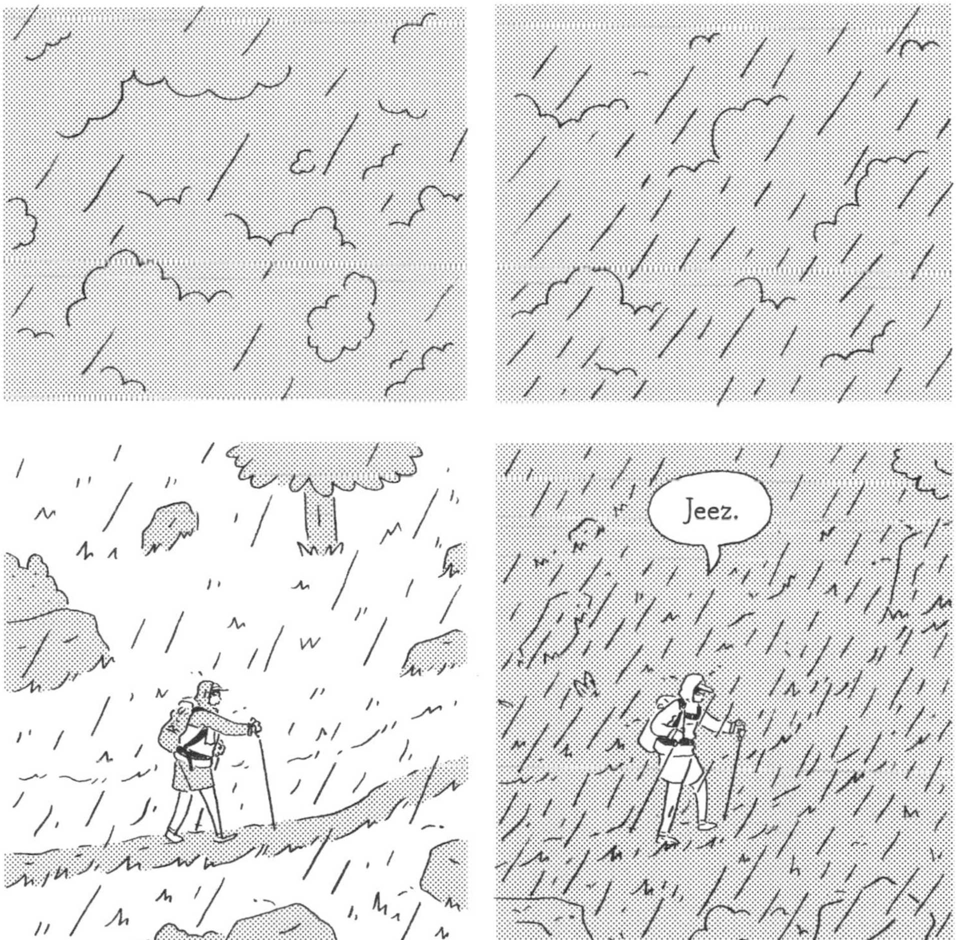
Jeez.

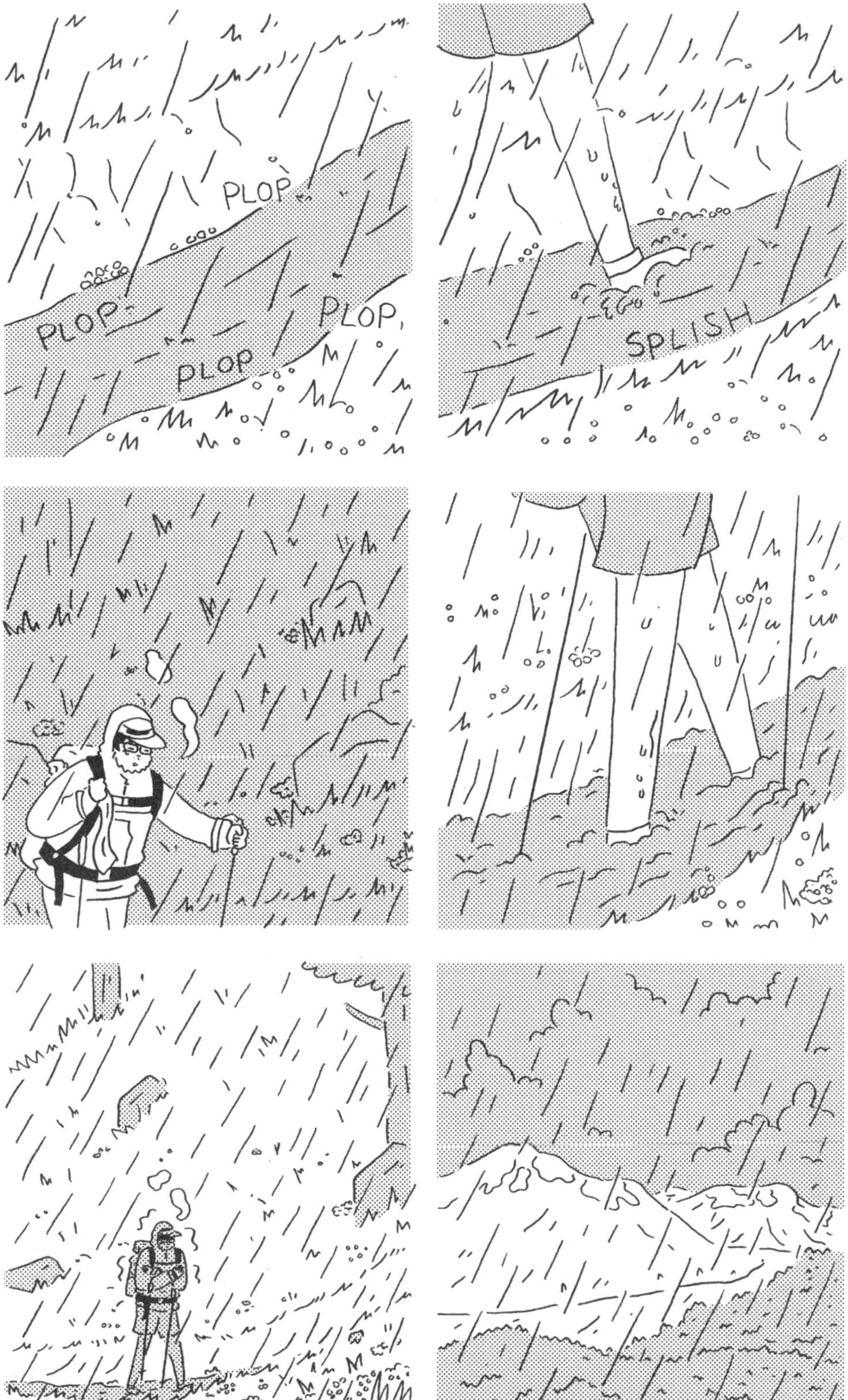
PLOP
PLOP
PLOP,
PLOP
SPLISH

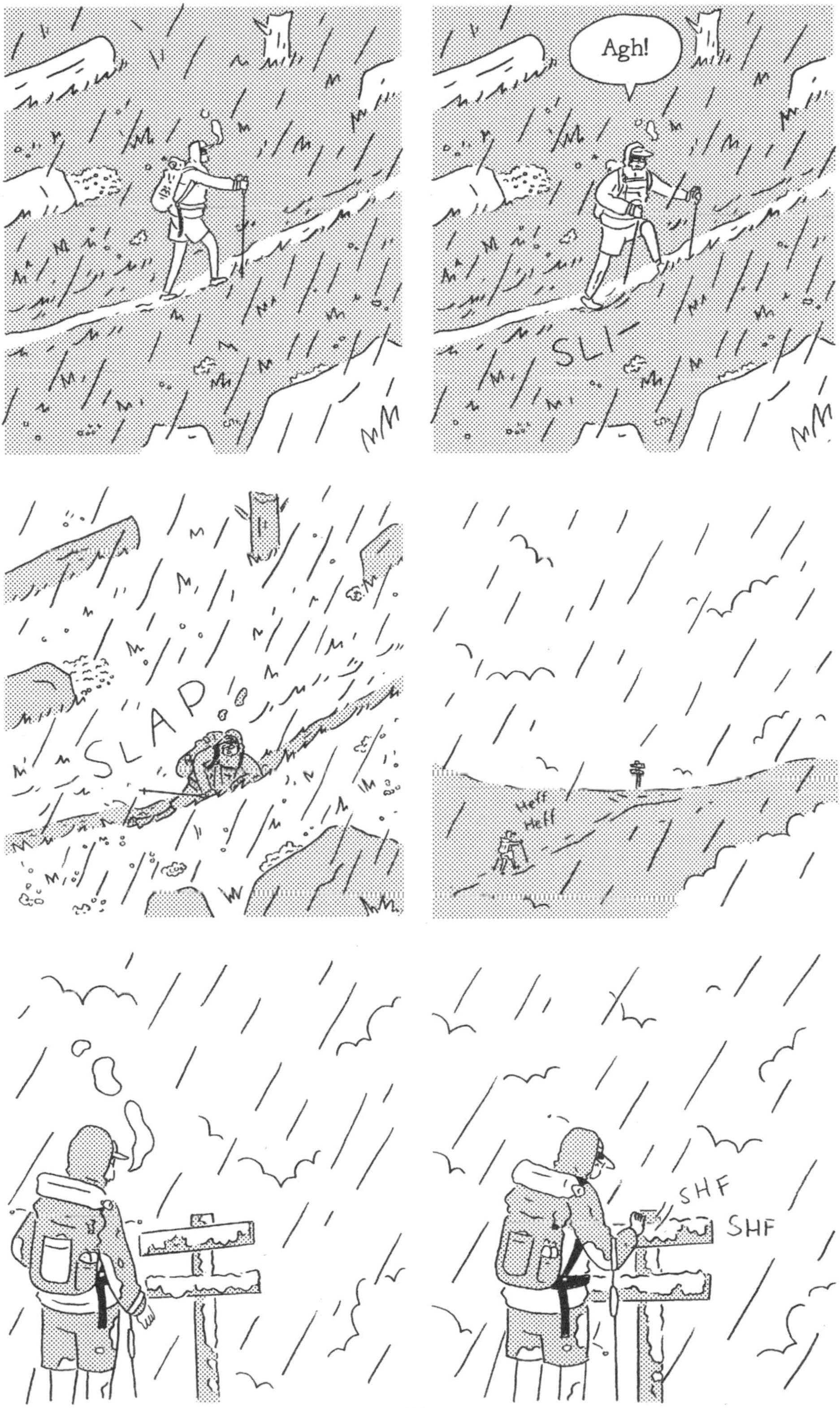
Agh!
SLI
SLAP
Heff
Heff
SHF
SHF

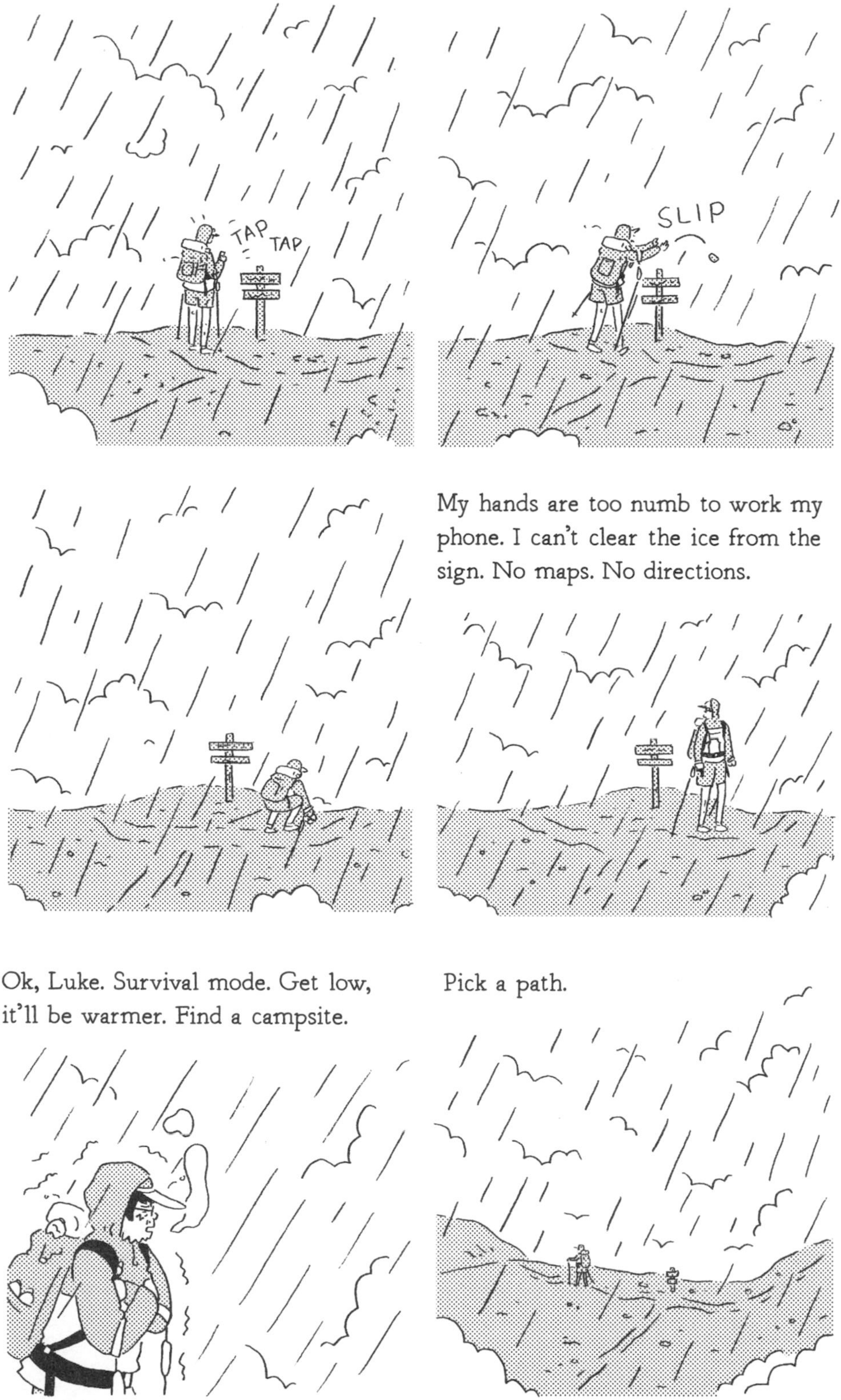
TAP TAP
SLIP
My hands are too numb to work my phone. I can't clear the ice from the sign. No maps. No directions.
Ok, Luke. Survival mode. Get low, it'll be warmer. Find a campsite.
Pick a path.

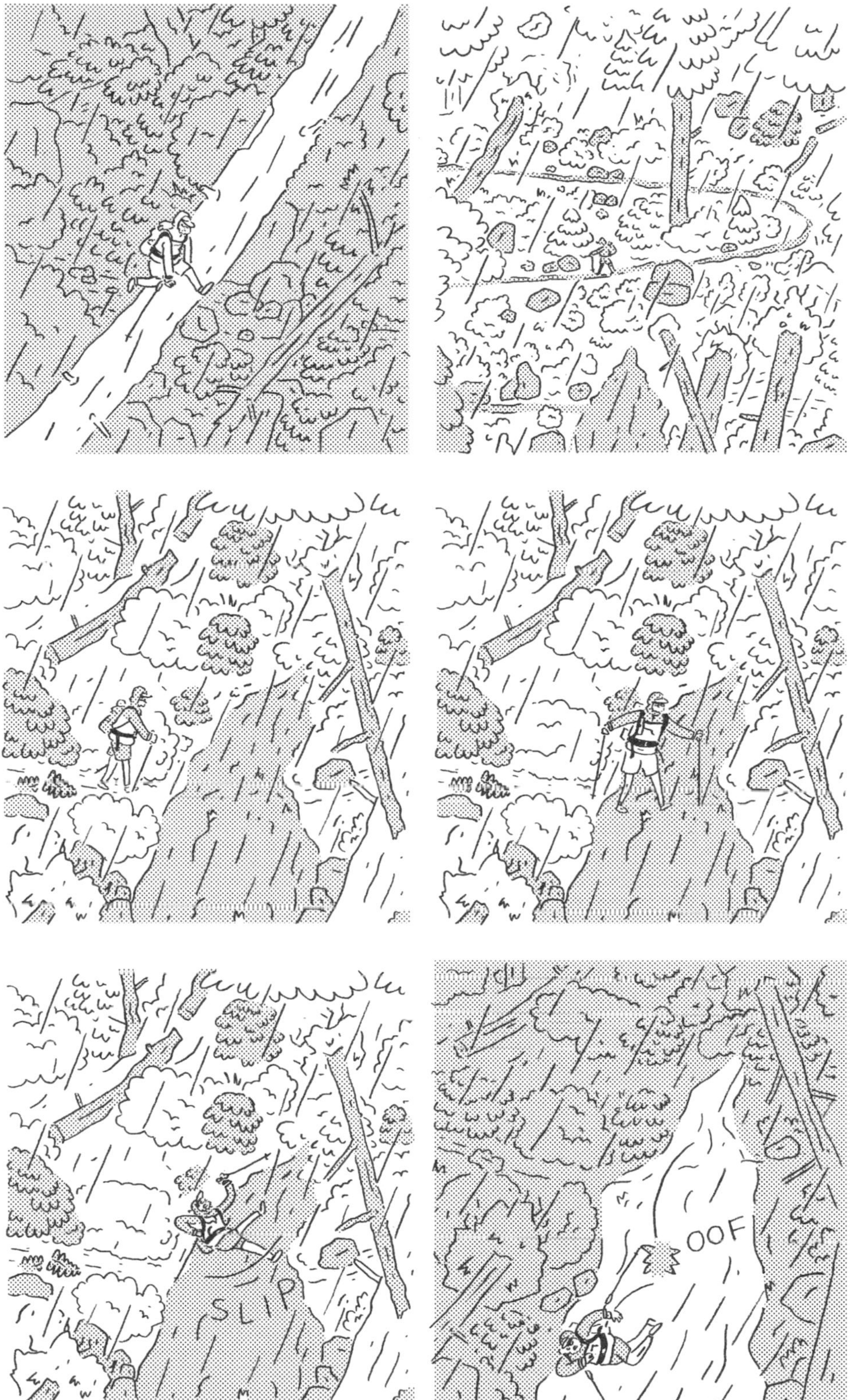
SLIP
OOF

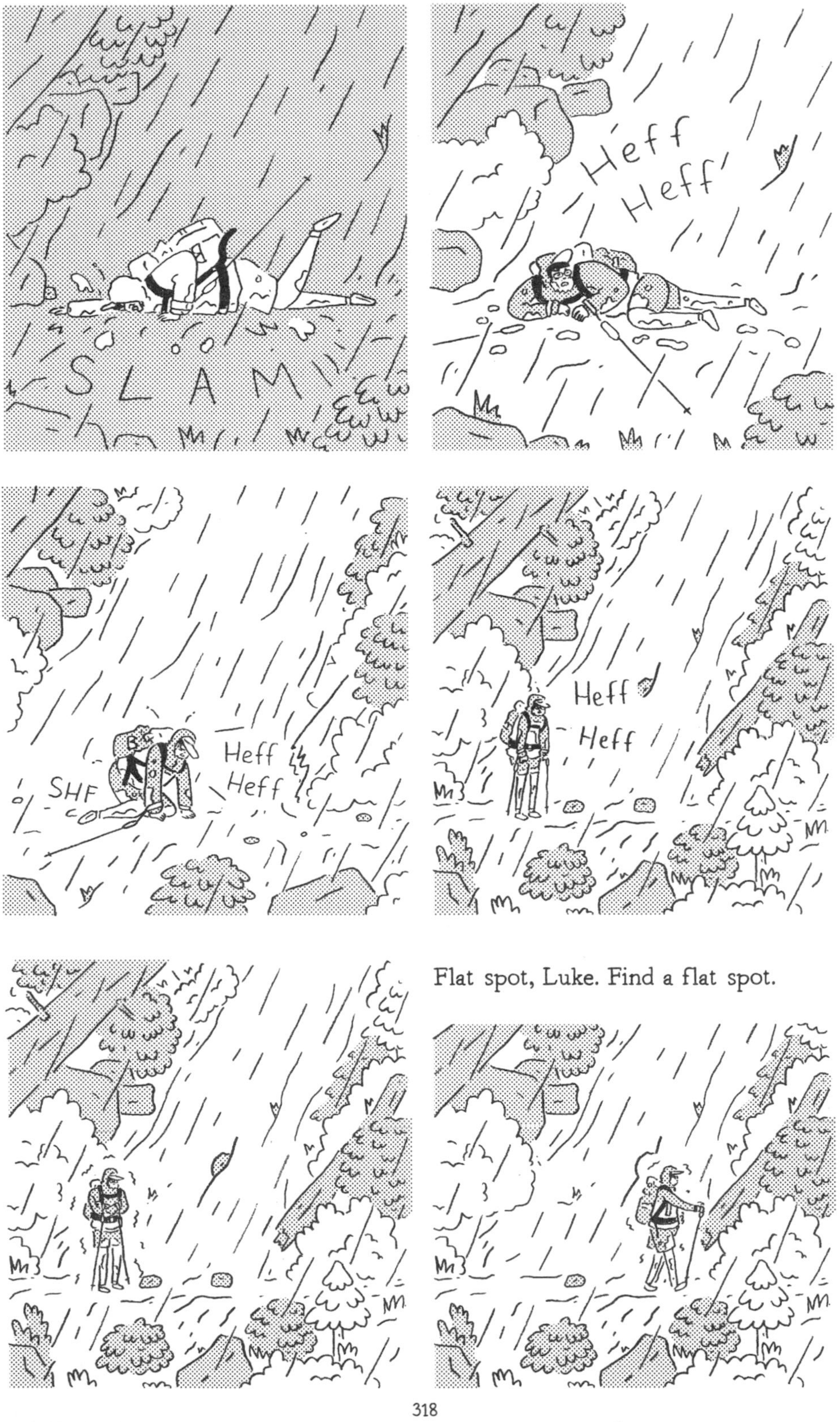
SLAM
Heff
Heff
SHF
Heff
Heff
Heff
Heff
Flat spot, Luke. Find a flat spot.

Bankshot is still behind me, up the ridge.

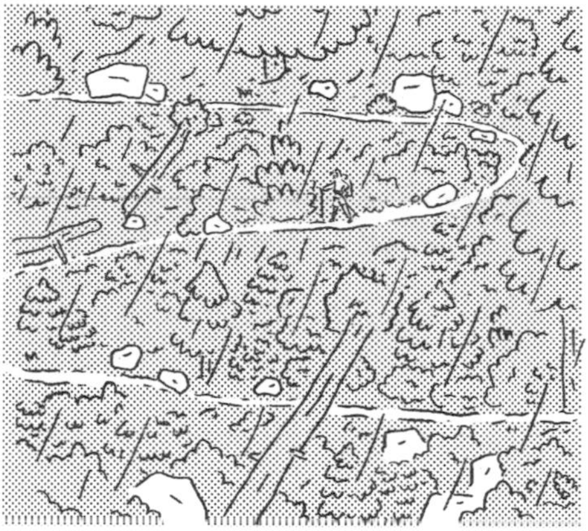

The front-of-the-packers are ahead. I won't catch them.

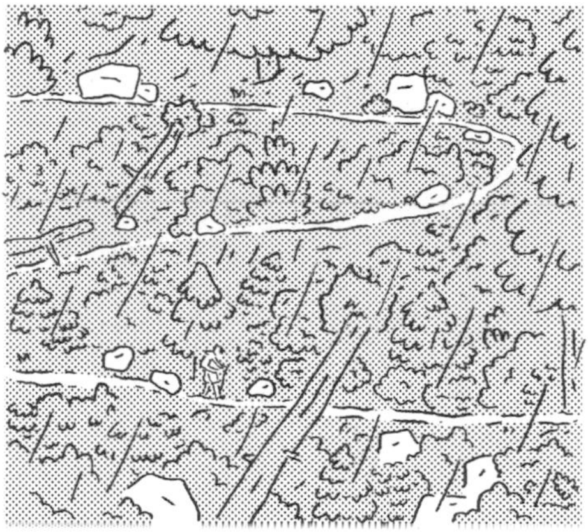

The choice is clear. Camp alone, or die.

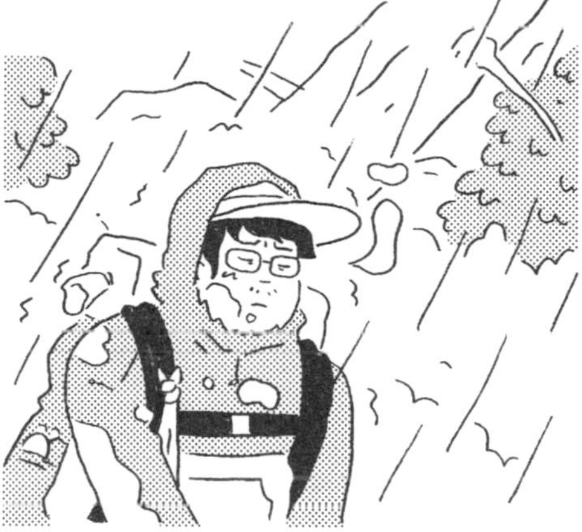

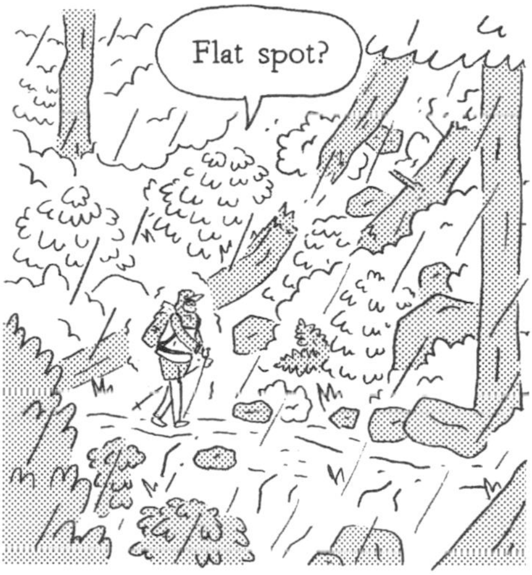
Flat spot?

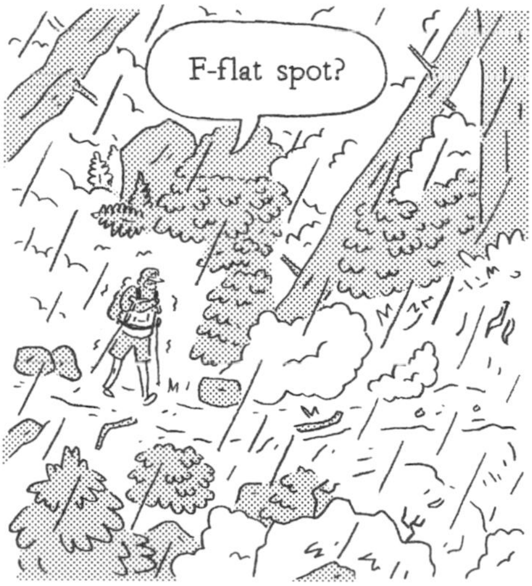
F-flat spot?

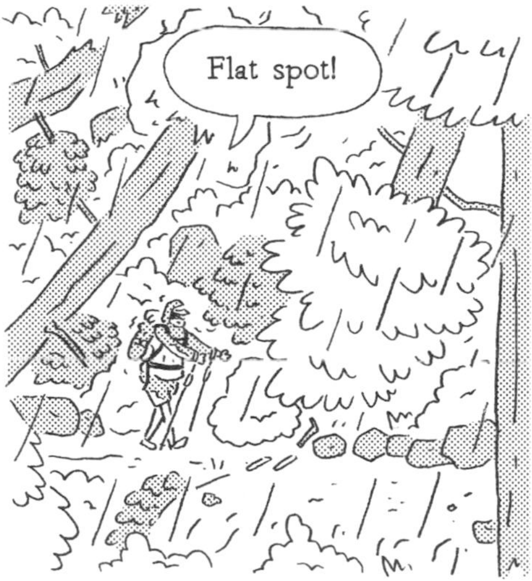
Flat spot!

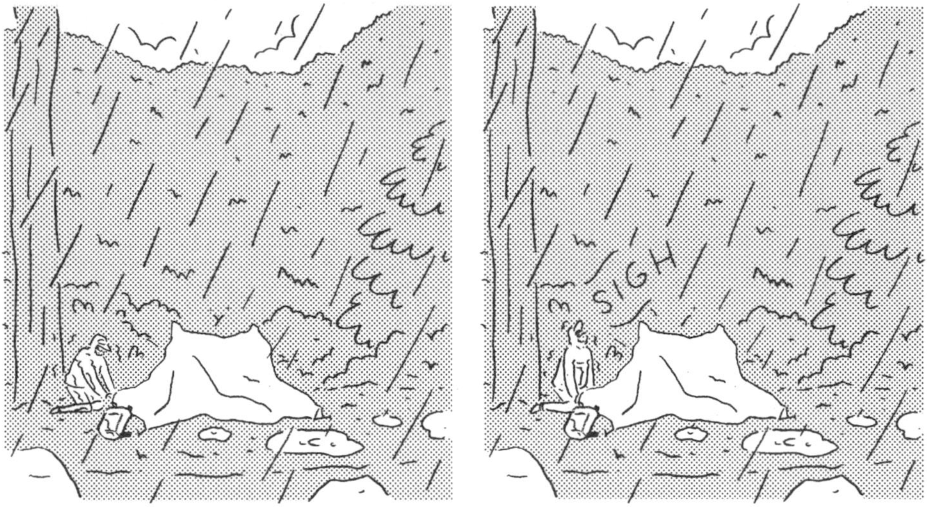
SIGH

"Just get in your tent," I mutter, as I struggle to tie knots with my big useless claws.

When the tent is standing in a just-substantive-enough fashion, I crawl inside and strip off my wet clothes inside the tiny vestibule. My body does not want to reassume a human temperature.

I dig through my already shrunken-looking food bag. I eat almost everything in there. My body needs calories to reheat and I can't resist, partially out of hunger and partially out of boredom.

It takes three hours for me to stop shivering.

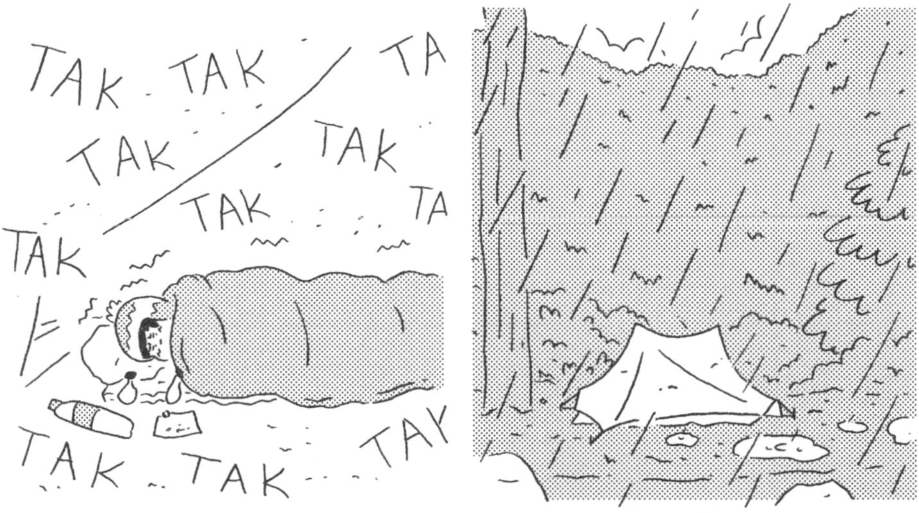
TAK TAK
TA
TAK
TAK
TAK
TA
TAK
TAK TAK
TAY

I wake in a sorry state and pull back on my wet gear.

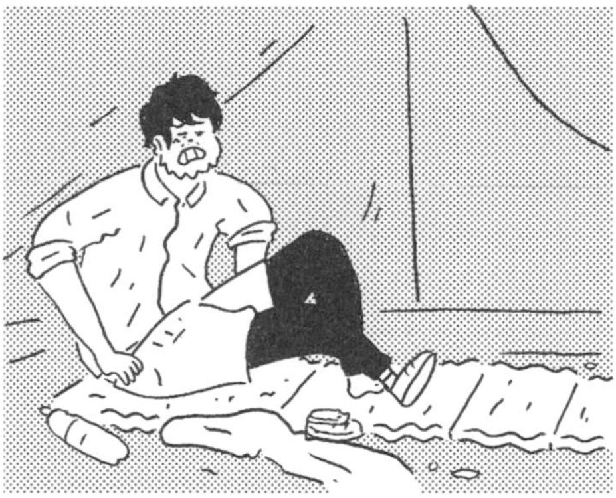

My shoes are destroyed, shredded as I slipped down the switchbacks.

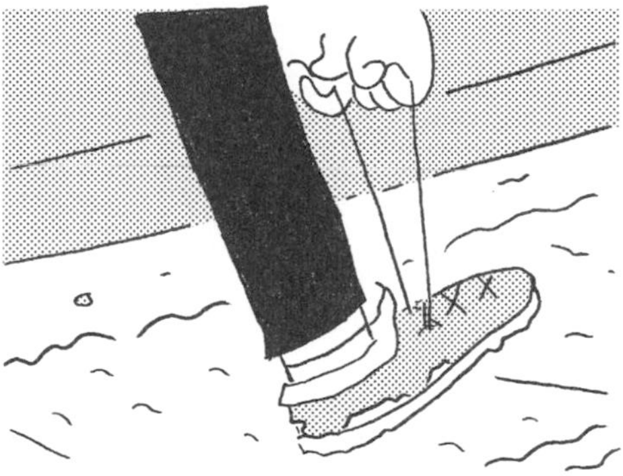

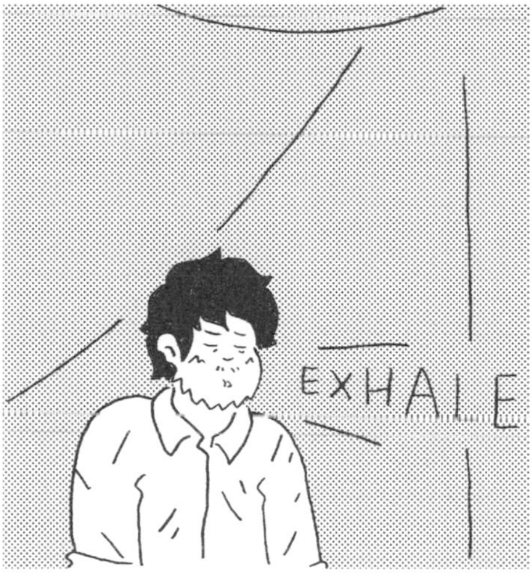
EXHALE

Sharp plastic stabs into my feet as I hike.

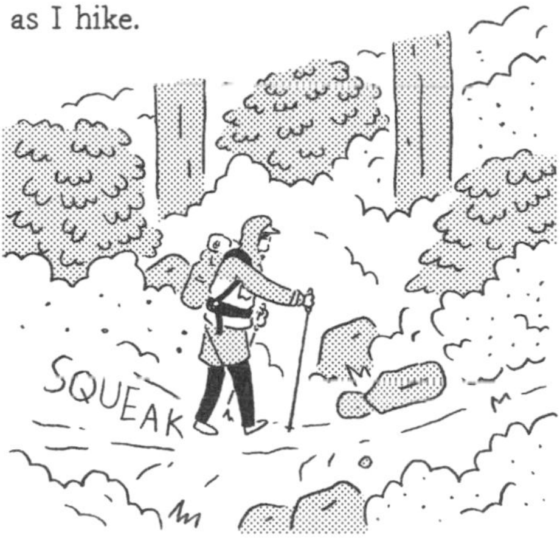
SQUEAK

Stehekin, one of the more talked about stops in Washington, is still two days ahead. My food bag is basically empty.

There are no roads into Stehekin; you can only enter via boat, pontoon plane, or by hiking in. The isolated town is famous for its bakery. I've been hearing about that bakery for two thousand miles. I suspect I will be thinking about it solidly for the next two days.

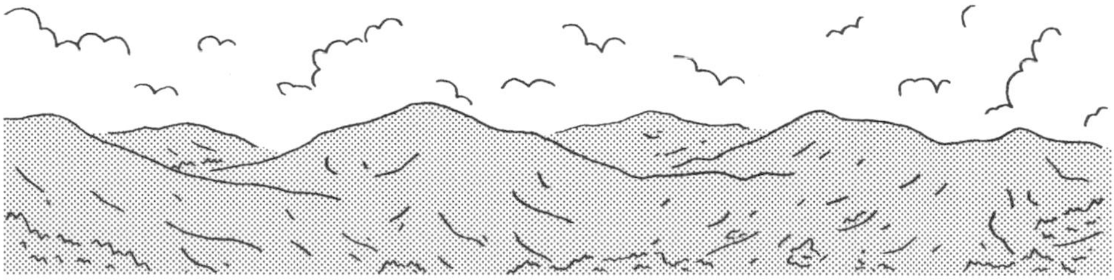

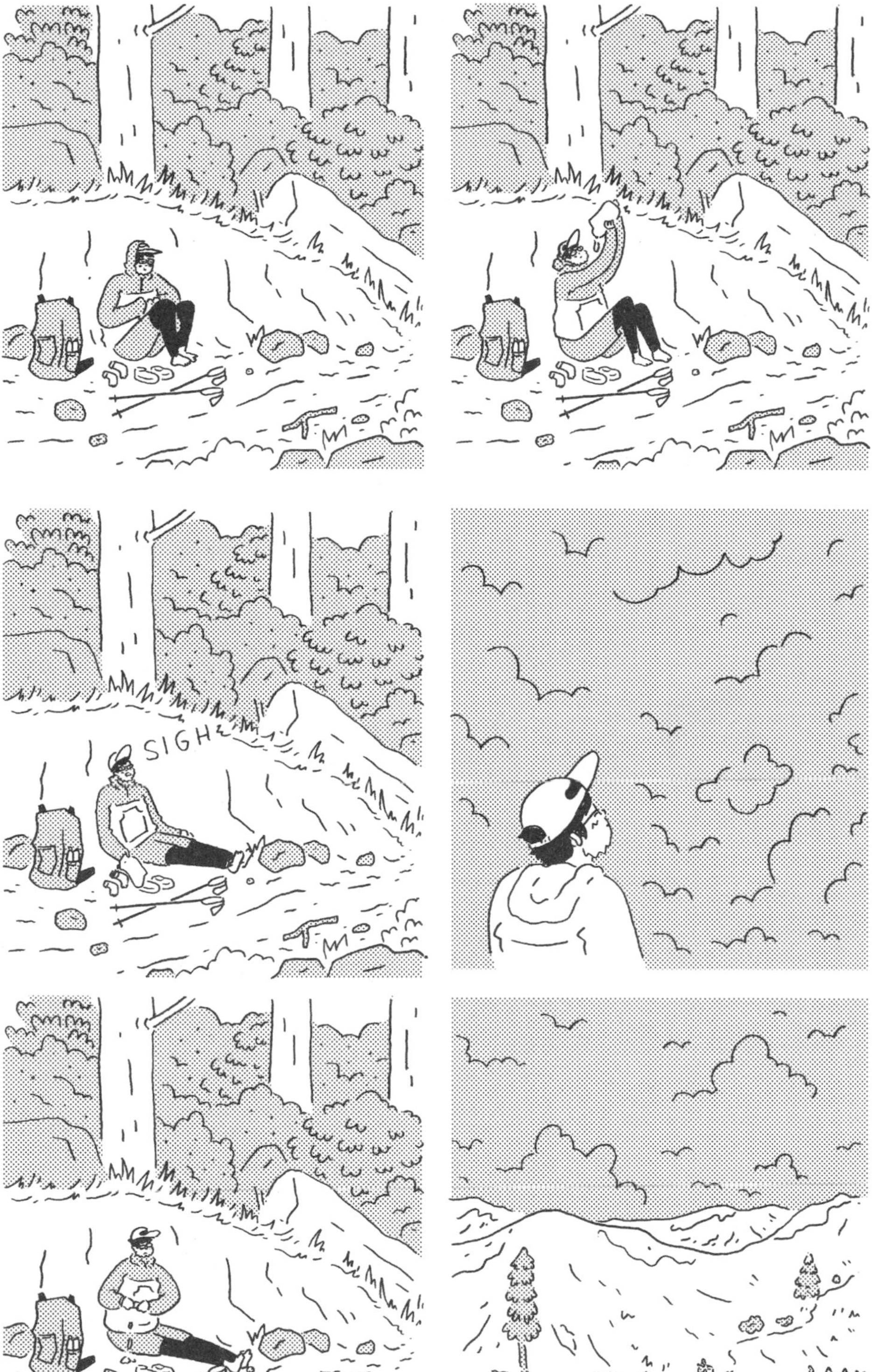
SIGH

I eat berries from the side of the trail as I hike.

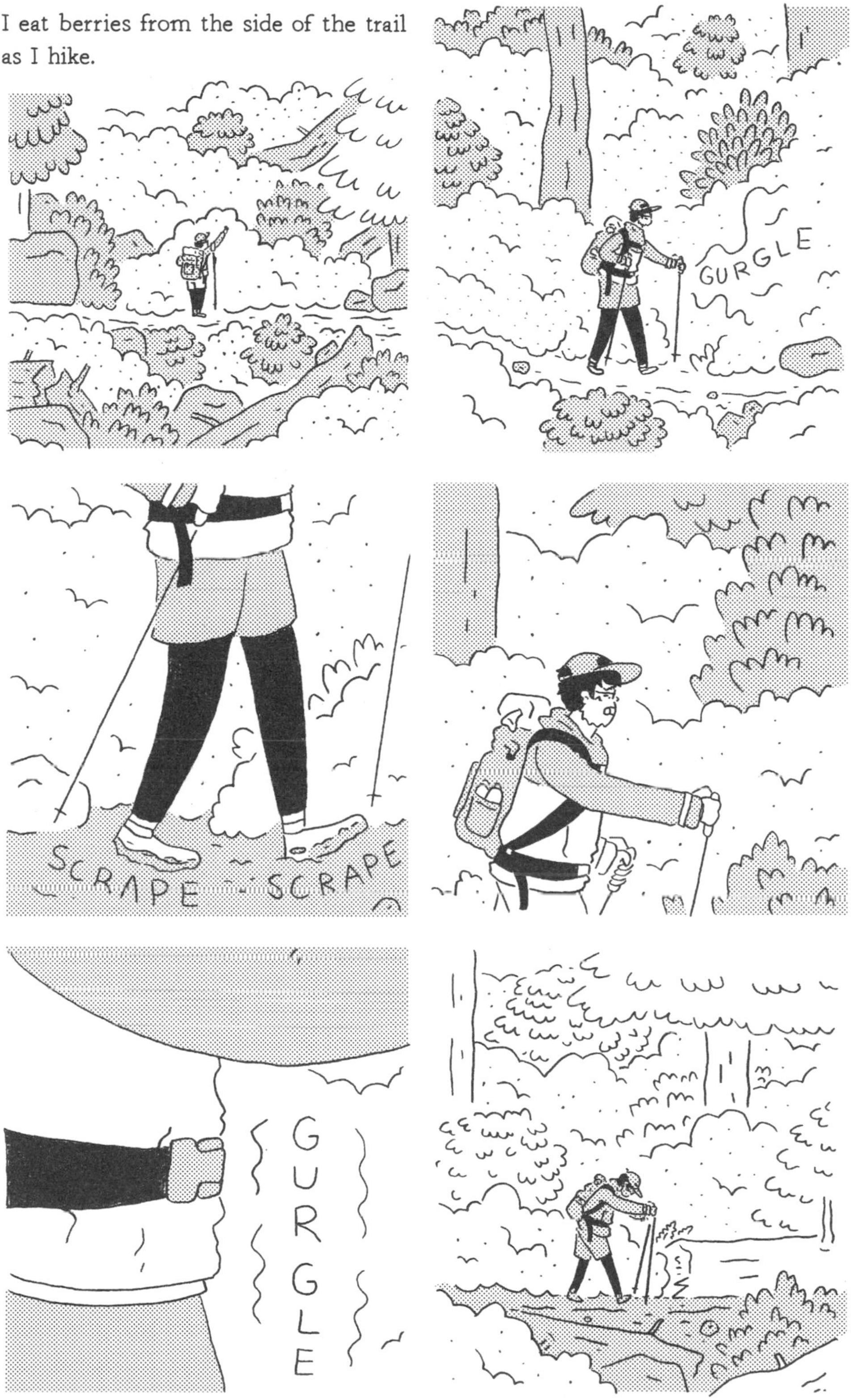
GURGLE
SCRAPE SCRAPE
GURGLE

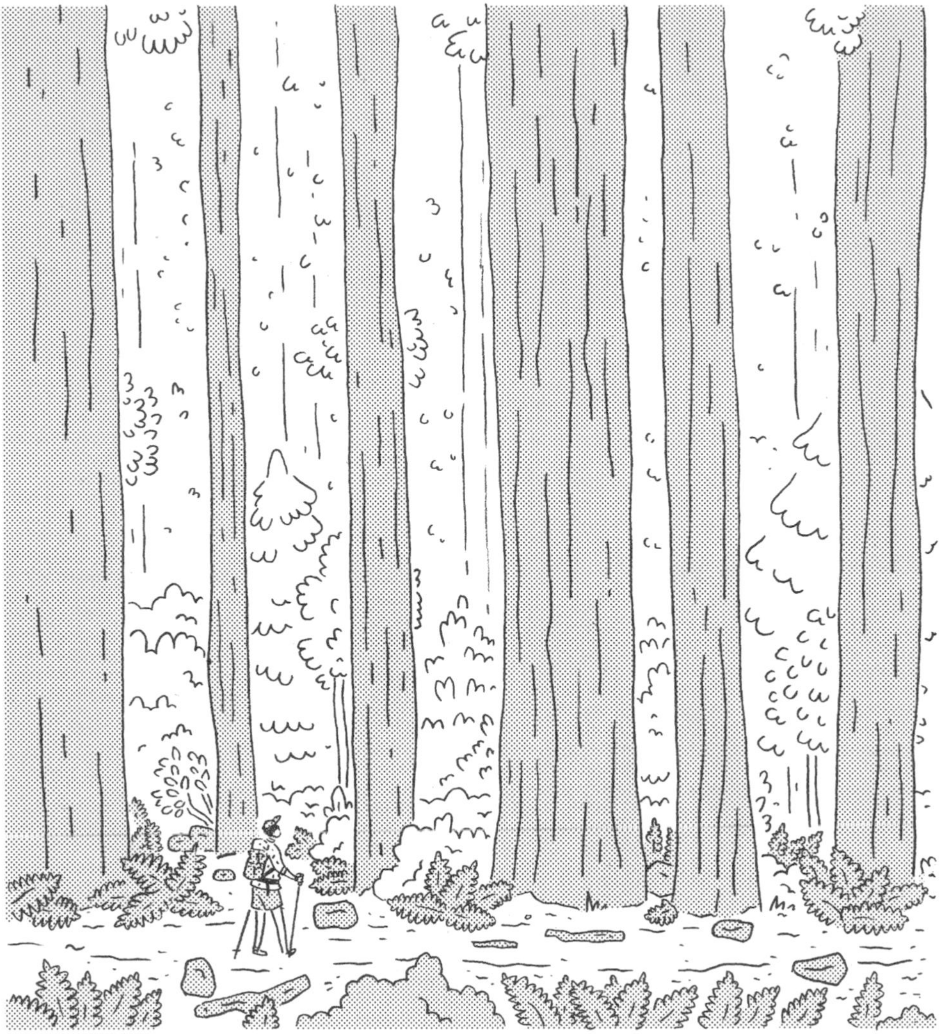

I'm hungry. Not just for food, but to finish the trail. I'm close. Stehekin is the final town stop on the PCT. I am ready to be done. I'm ready to shower every day, and to change my clothes, and to cook real food. I'm ready to see my friends, and my family, and get back to work.

I am a wreck. But a strong wreck, in spite of everything. And my wrecked, strong, stupid body will carry me on, for one week more at least. Despite its current protestations, it hasn't let me down yet.

I imagine standing at the monument. I'll probably cry when I see it. Or laugh. Cackle, more likely.

At night, rats chew through my pack to eat the crumbs from my garbage. I'm almost mad I didn't think of that first.

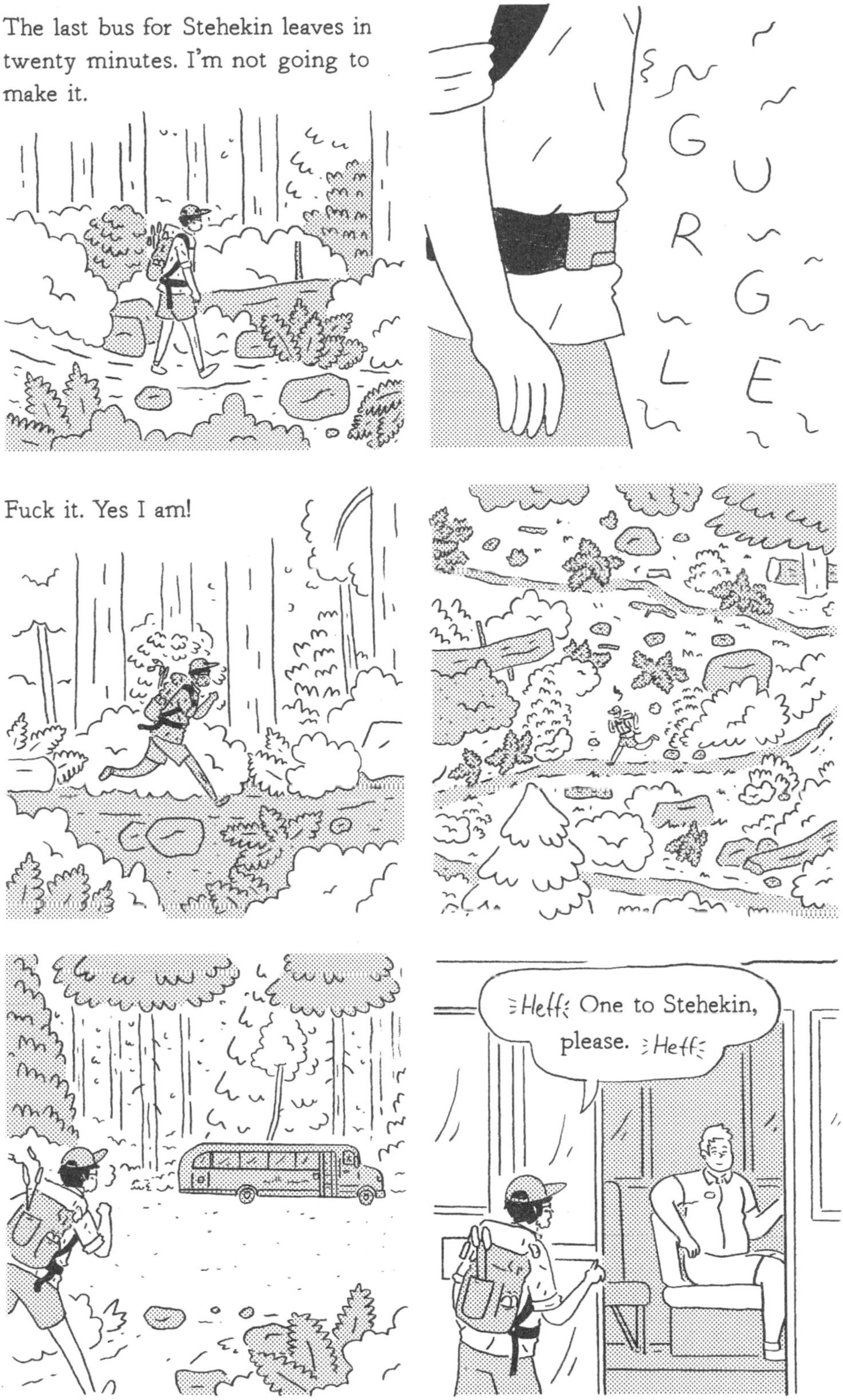
The last bus for Stehekin leaves in twenty minutes. I'm not going to make it.
GURGLE
Fuck it. Yes I am!
Heff One to Stehekin, please. Heff

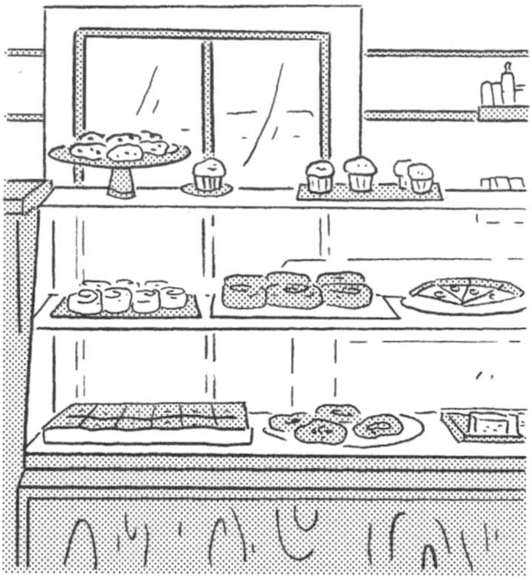

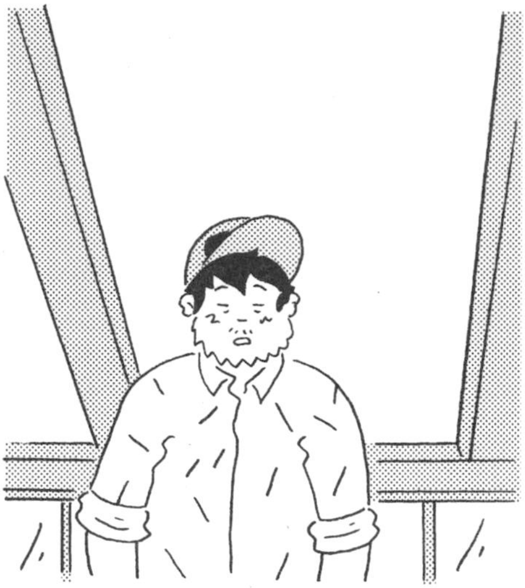

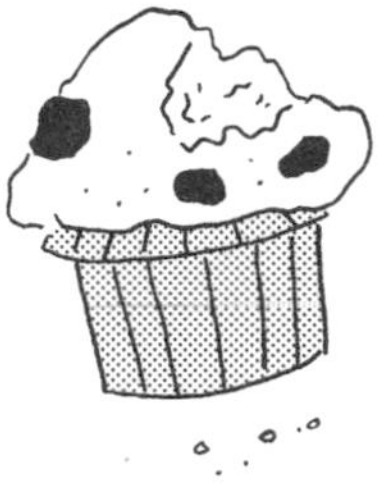

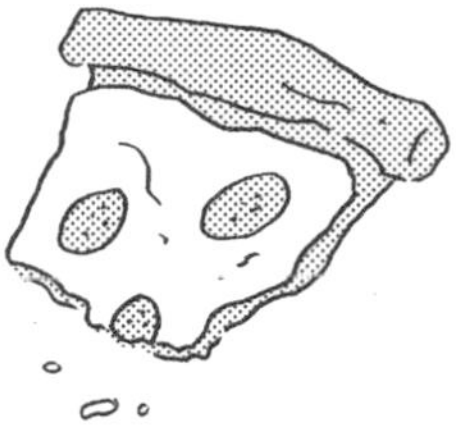

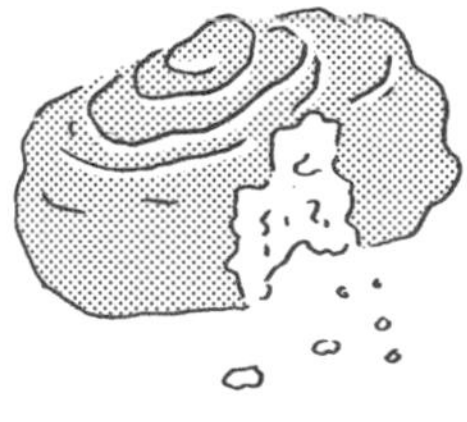

I eat my fill.

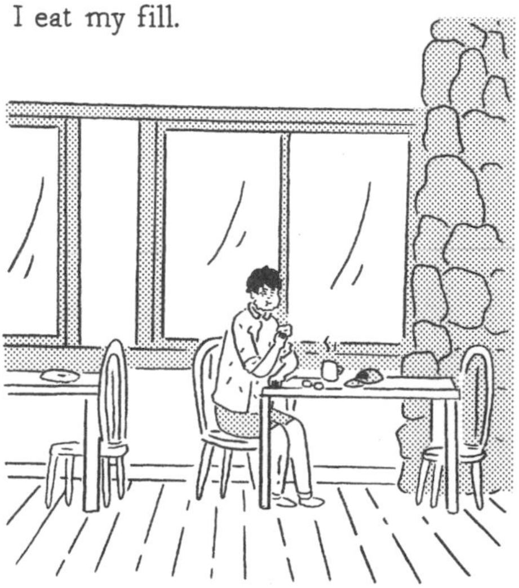

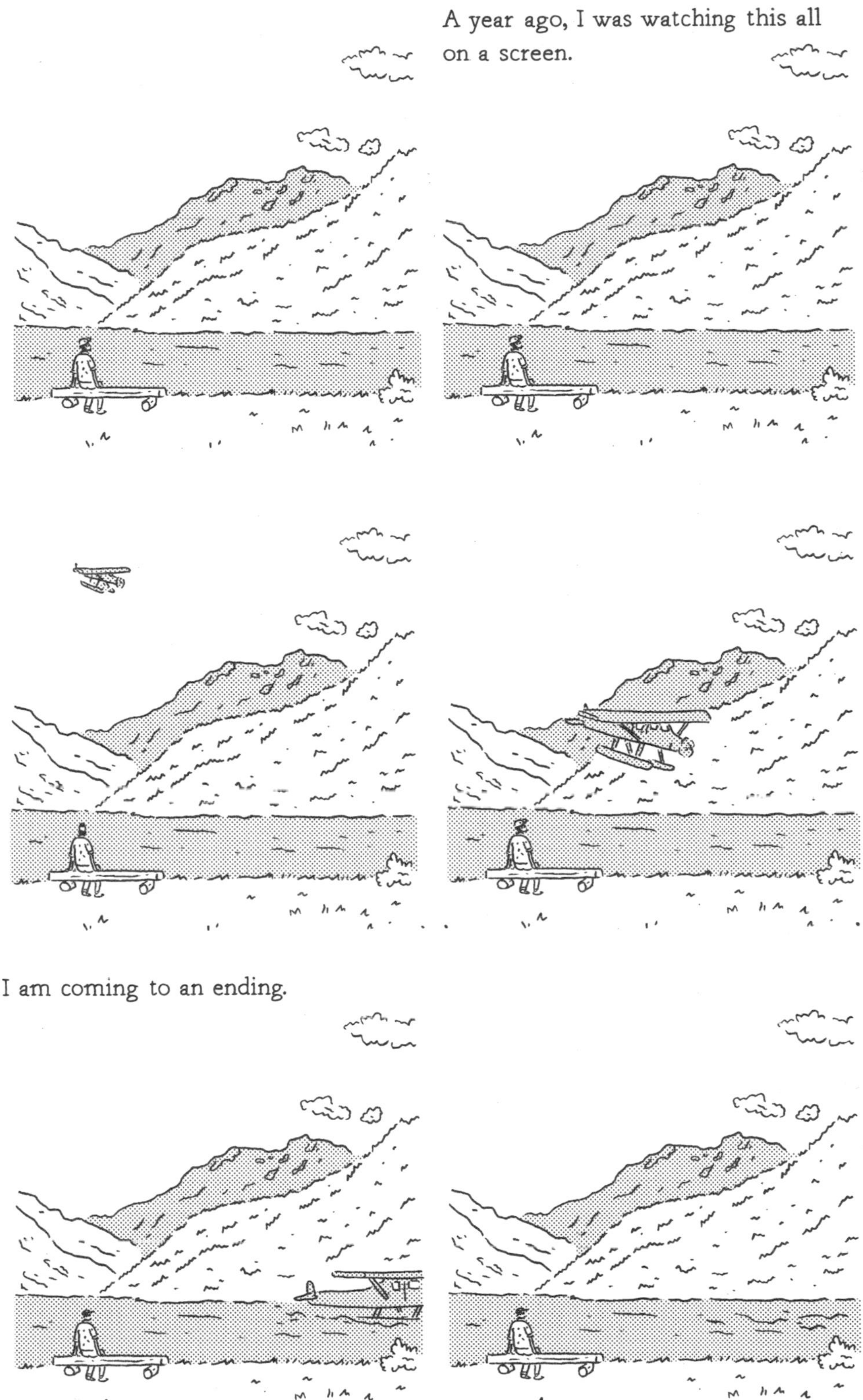
A year ago, I was watching this all on a screen.
I am coming to an ending.

Bankshot and I hike the last few days on trail, surrounded by other hikers.

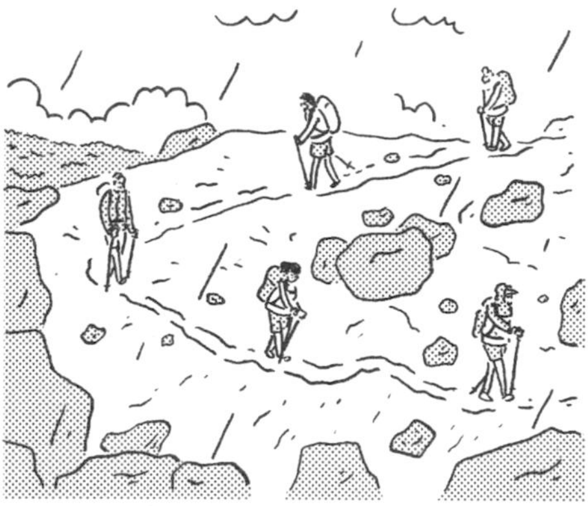

We make for a surprisingly international group.

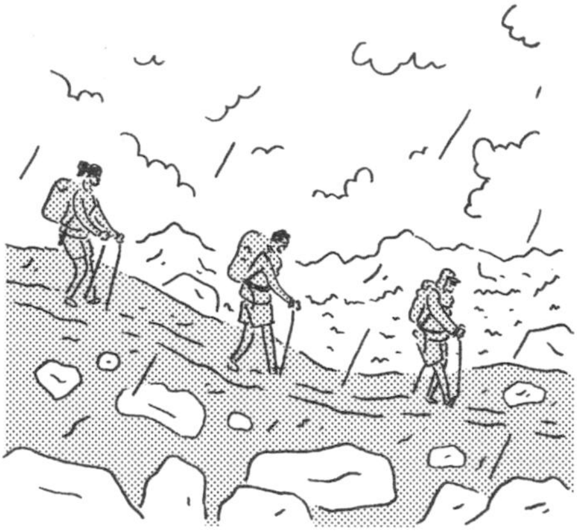

Swiss, Swedish, English, Canadian...

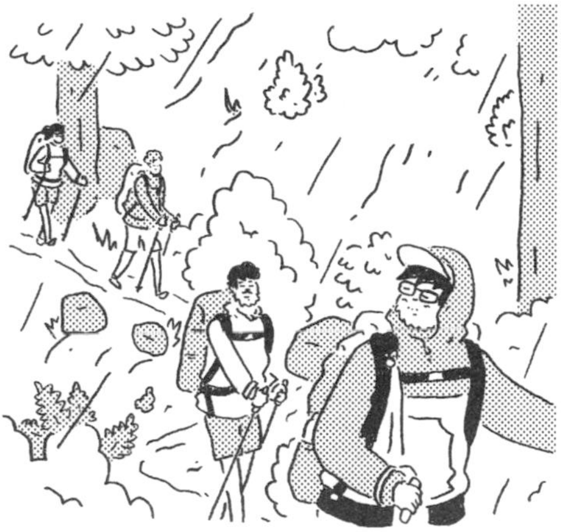

And me.

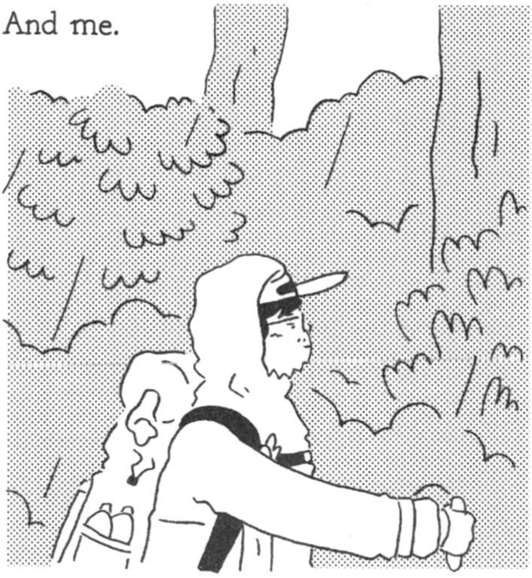

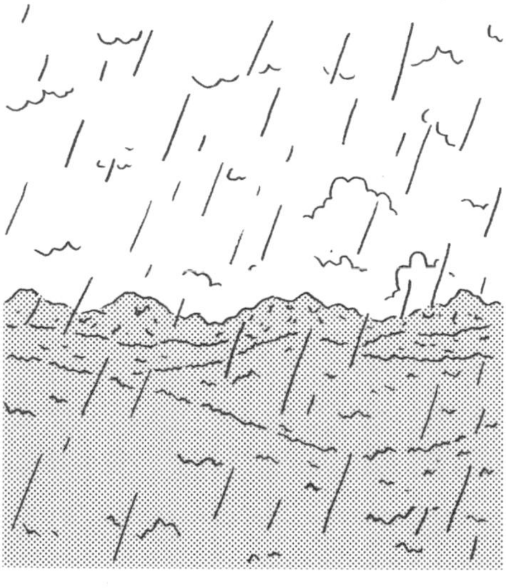

Rain has a way of bringing hikers together on trail.

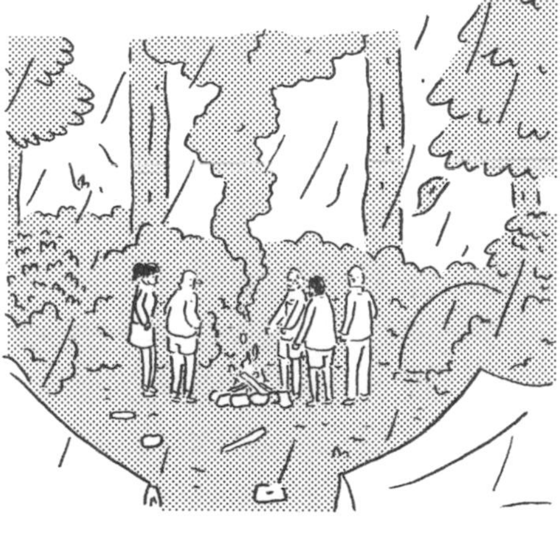

09/09/16. Day 147.

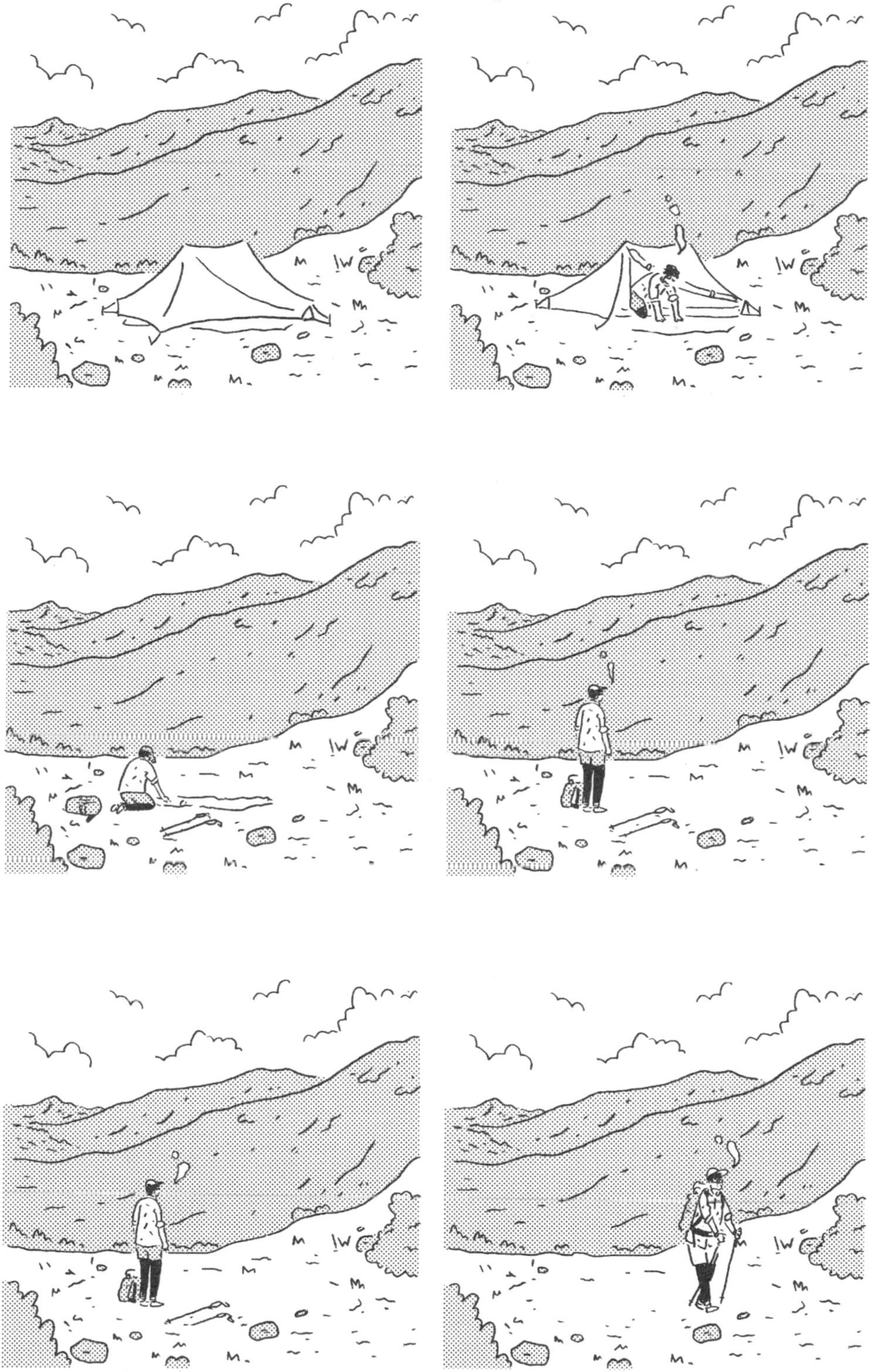

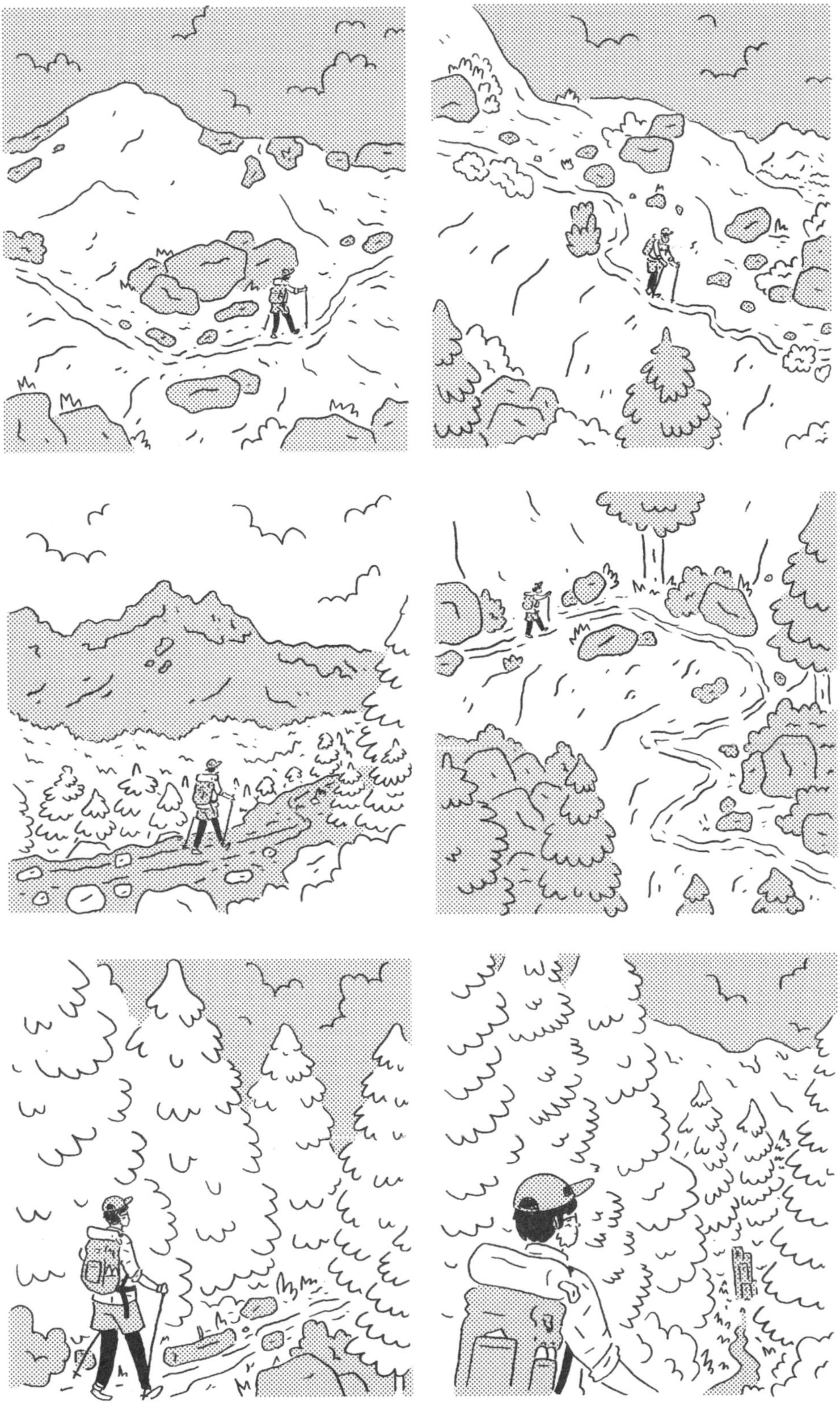

I don't cry. I don't cheer. I'm not sad, or overwhelmed. In this moment, I am two things – tired and relieved. More tired and more relieved than I have ever been before.

I am happy, and I exhale. There is no Walt Disney ending. I don't feel changed. Not yet.

I get to stop now. Stop hiking, and maybe with time, stop other things too. Stop knocking at a door that doesn't want to let me in.

I'll walk to Manning Park Lodge, and I'll get a room in their staff quarters, the last room they have. I'll step into a sauna, and feel warm for the first time since the storm above Milky Creek. I'll sleep under four blankets.

And I'll get a bus to Vancouver, and a plane to Philadelphia, and a bus to D.C. And I'll see my American friends at the Small Press Expo, the same place we'd road-tripped that first week in White River Junction. And I'll fly back to Ireland. And Donald Trump will win the election. Fires will rage in California. And I'll wake from nightmares of lions at my tent. And I'll feel like a crazy person when I talk to people about the trail. And I'll ache to come back.

I'll apply for more jobs in Los Angeles, despite myself. This time around I'll feel guilty about doing it. And then, for a while at least, I'll let it go. I'll lay a compass on my grandfather's grave. The compass I'd carried for 2660 miles, but never once needed to use.

I sign the register "For Gus," my father's and grandfather's name. And I hike on.

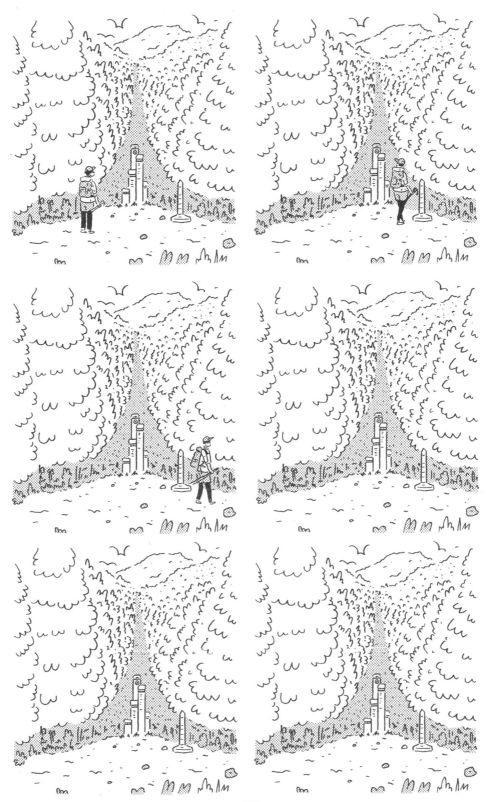

Luke Healy is a cartoonist from Dublin, Ireland. For a
little while, he lived in the USA, studying at The Center for
Cartoon Studies. Then a little while longer, going on a hike.
At the time of writing, he lives in London, UK. And he hopes
that won't change for a little while, at least.